ACTING
An International Encyclopedia

ACTING

An International Encyclopedia

Beth Osnes

Sam Gill
Consulting Editor

ABC-CLIO

Santa Barbara, California   Denver, Colorado   Oxford, England

Copyright 2001 by Beth Osnes

Library of Congress Cataloging-in-Publication Data
Osnes, Beth.
   Acting : an international encyclopedia / Beth Osnes ; Sam
Gill, consulting editor.
      p. cm.
   Includes bibliographical references and index.
   ISBN 0-87436-795-6 (alk. paper); 1-57607-804-3 (e-book)
   1. Performing arts—Encyclopedias.   I. Gill, Sam.   II. Title.
PN2035 .O84 2001
791'.03—dc21
                                           2001005744

06   05   04   03   02   01   10 9   8   7   6   5   4   3   2   1

This book is also available on the World Wide Web as an e-book. Visit abc-clio.com for details.

ABC-CLIO, Inc.
130 Cremona Drive, P.O. Box 1911
Santa Barbara, California 93116-1911

This book is printed on acid-free paper ∞.

Manufactured in the United States of America

Contents

ACTING
An International Encyclopedia

ACTING
An International Encyclopedia

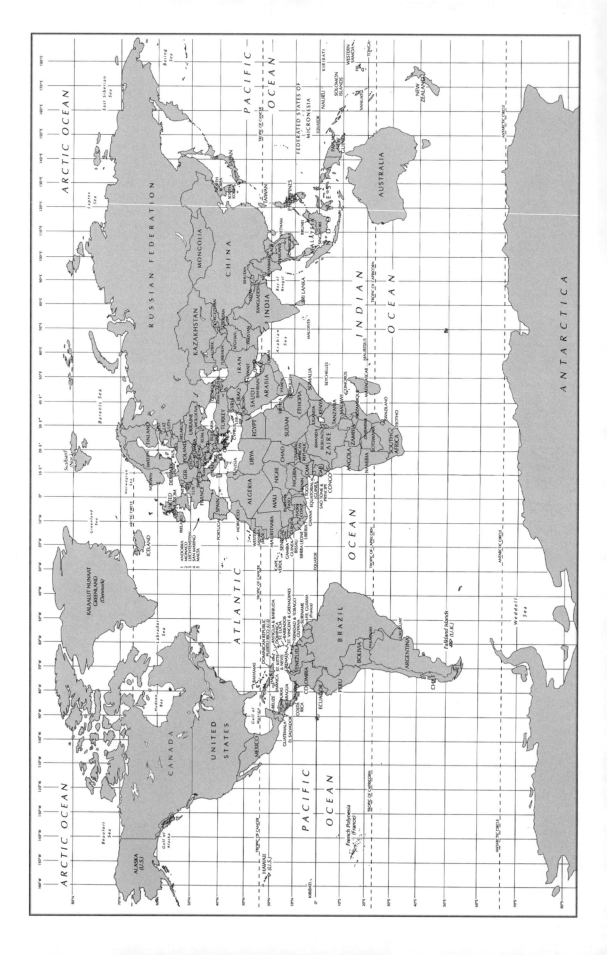

A

Abbey Theatre
Ireland

An Irish repertory company founded in 1904 in a building donated by a wealthy theater enthusiast, Miss A. E. F. Hornimann. Inspired by nationalism amongst the Irish, playwrights William Butler Yeats (1865–1939), Augusta Gregory (1852–1932), and John Millington Synge (1871–1909) created the Abbey Theatre. These poetic writers who wanted to give voice to the native spirit of Ireland, free from any political group both ideologically and financially, free from the need for popular consensus and free from European influence. In their plays they utilized the language of the common people, realistic yet naturally poetic. Their actors were amateurs, with a very natural acting style derived from a cultural propensity toward dramatics, unspoiled by outside influence. **William Fay** and his brother Frank were among the finest of the actors in these early years. Other excellent actors during this time were Dudley Digges (1879–1947), Barry Fitzgerald (1888–1961), J. A. O'Rourke, Marie NicShuibhlaigh (died in 1958), and two sisters, Marie O'Neill (1887–1952) and Sara Allgood (1883–1950). From the late 1920s to the 1950s the Abbey Theatre became more conservative in its content, style, and form but remained popular with audiences.

In 1951 the theater building was destroyed by a fire, and the Abbey moved into the Queen's Theatre. With government financial assistance a new theater was built on the original site in 1966. The Abbey Theatre remains an excellent venue for new Irish playwrights, such as Hugh Leonard with his comedy-drama *Love in the Title*, 1999.

References: Fraizier, Adrian. *Behind the Scenes at the Abbey.* Berkeley: University of California Press, 1990; Hunt, Hugh. *The Abbey: Ireland's National Theatre, 1904–1978.* Dublin: Gill & Macmillan, 1979; Mikhail, E. H. *The Abbey Theatre: Interviews and Recollections.* Totowa, NJ: Barnes & Noble, 1988.

Abhinaya
India

Term used in Indian theater and dance to describe a gesture or action that expresses a particular emotion.

References: Menon, Narayana, and Saryu Doshi. *The Performing Arts.* Bombay: Marg, 1982.

Absurdism
France

A post–World War II artistic movement that expressed the belief that truth is unknowable and the world irrational. The term was first applied to the work of dramatist Albert Camus (1913–1960) whose plays, such as *Caligula* written in 1938, dramatize the absurd condition of humankind. Primary writers of the absurdist viewpoint are Samuel Beckett (1906–1989), Eugène Ionesco (1912–1994), and Jean Genet (1910–

1986). This movement was labeled by Martin Esslin's book *The Theatre of the Absurd* in 1961.

Actors in these dramas are challenged to accept new paradigms of reality and progress logically from there in their building of a character. They are challenged to reach for their desires while maintaining or creating meaning around them. Absurd plays are not merely ridiculous or random, nor do the actors within them act as though they were. They are purposeful attempts to demonstrate absurdity in life as the playwright sees it.

In plays by Ionesco, actors spout clichéd lines that espouse values received from the machine of society, lines that are ultimately meaningless. In his plays actors must reach for meaning for their characters given absurd limitations, as when a deaf-mute tells the audience the meaning of life in *The Chairs*, 1952. Through the actor's effort the playwright's purpose is realized, to demonstrate the theme of nothingness pervasive in the world. In Beckett's play *Happy Days*, 1961, the female protagonist rambles on optimistically about petty details of her life while buried in sand to her waist. As the sand gradually increases she still refuses to be dismayed by her predicament. In all absurdist dramas actors are bringing to life the human struggle for meaning in a world seemingly void of it.

See also Existentialism
References: Coe, Richard. *The Vision of Jean Genet.* New York: Grove, 1968; Gaensbauer, Deborah. *The French Theater of the Absurd.* Boston: Twayne Publishers, 1991; Genet, Jean. *The Selected Writing of Jean Genet.* Hopewell, NJ: Ecco, 1993; Gordon, Lois. *The World of Samuel Beckett.* New Haven, CT: Yale University Press, 1996; Hayman, Ronald. *Samuel Beckett.* New York: Ungar, 1973; Lamont, Rosette. *Ionesco: A Collection of Critical Essays.* Englewood Cliffs, NJ: Prentice-Hall, 1973.

Abua Masquerade

Nigeria

A masked dance with dramatic elements performed by the Abua, a fishing and agricultural people. The most important Abua masquerade is the *Onwuema*, with much spiritual significance, followed in importance by the *Egbukele*, which is more for entertainment. Each Abua village has its own Onwuema cap mask, representing a water

spirit. The performances rid the village of the evil that accumulates over the year in preparation for the beginning of the next year.

Both performances occur outside among a gathering of observers. The audience takes an active role in performances, with young and old singing, dancing, and drumming. Performers wear carved headpieces that cover the entire head. Cloth is sewn to the underside of the cap mask that drapes over the body of the performer. A loop of young palm fronds is hung around the neck and locust beans are tied round the ankles to supply rhythm.

References: Ekwuema, Lazarus E. N. "Nigerian Performing Arts, Past, Present and Future, with Particular Reference to Igbo Practice." *Presence Africaine* 92, 2 (1975): 195–213; Eyo, Ekpo. "Abua Masquerades." *African Arts* 7, 2 (Winter 1974): 52–55.

Acropolis

Greece

The citadel of Athens. This fortress, which enjoys a commanding position overlooking the city, was the location for the annual festival of the **City Dionysia,** performed each year in late March. The Theater of Dionysus was built, probably in the middle of the sixth century B.C., on the hillside sloping down from the southern side of the Acropolis.

References: Bieber, Margarete. *The History of the Greek and Roman Theater.* Princeton, NJ: Princeton University Press, 1961; D'Ooge, Martin Luther. *The Acropolis of Athens.* New York: Macmillan, 1908; Pausanias. *The Acropolis of Athens: As Described by Pausanias, Other Writers, Inscriptions and Archaeological Evidence.* Chicago: Ares, 1976; Taplin, Oliver. *Greek Tragedy in Action.* Berkeley: University of California Press, 1978.

Action Song

New Zealand

A modern dance performed by male and female **Maori** of New Zealand. Combining the poetry of words and movements, performers relate their hand and body movements to the words of the accompanying songs. European tunes have been adapted to fit the style of words and movements that is distinctively Maori. A harmonious blending of old traditions with new influences, the Action Song is a living art form that accurately displays contemporary Maori culture.

References: Barlow, Cleve. *Tikanga Whakaaro: Key Concepts in Maori Culture*. New York: Oxford University Press, 1991; Dansey, Harry. *The Maori in Colour*. London: Reed, 1973.

Actors Studio
United States

Workshop for actors in New York, founded in 1947 by Elia Kazan, Cheryl Crawford (1902–1986), and Robert Lewis. Actors had to audition for a lifelong membership in this training group, organized to avoid the financial pressure of commercial theater. At the Studio there developed a new distinctly American form of the Method, based on the teaching of the Russian **Stanislavsky**, an approach that arguably still remains the quintessential style of acting in America.

Lee Strasberg, who had been one of the founding members of the **Group Theater,** began teaching at the Studio in 1949 and served as its director from 1951 until his death in 1982. He trained the best of American actors through the years, including **Marlon Brando**, Paul Newman, Kim Stanley, James Dean, Anne Bancroft, **Marilyn Monroe**, Dustin Hoffman, Robert de Niro, Al Pacino, Shelley Winters, and Geraldine Page. Strasberg was a master at unleashing the expressiveness of actors. Some say the Method as he taught it was psychologically damaging for the actors themselves, since the work relied heavily upon the actor's past experiences and dredging up old pain, but no one can argue with the results he got out of his actors. He nurtured a lot of talent for both stage and film and created apt actors for the psychological dramas of the time, such as those by **Tennessee Williams**. Some praise the Actors Studio for its psychological realism, achieved through inward introspection, while others criticize it for being self-indulgent, characterized by actors so inwardly focused that all that results is slouching shoulders and inarticulate speech.

Elia Kazan directed some outstanding films, such as *A Streetcar Named Desire*, 1951, *On the Waterfront*, 1954, and *East of Eden*, 1955, showcasing the Method acting of the Actors Studio's members. The Studio continues its tradition of training many of the best actors in America. Since the late 1980s the Actors Studio has produced a television series featuring interviews with the leading actors of our time.

References: Garfield, David. *The Actors Studio: A Player's Place*. New York: Collier, 1984; Hirsch, Foster. *A Method to Their Madness: The History of the Actors Studio*. New York: Norton, 1984.

Actual Death in the Theater
Italy, Mexico, Turkey

Actual death on the stage has been a sanctioned occurrence throughout history in some places around the world. In Roman ancient drama, near the third century blood thirst had reached a peak such that gory death scenes were enacted in which a slave or condemned criminal was actually killed. Until the 1940s in **Turkey** Shiite Muslims enacted a Persian **passion play** that sometimes became so frenzied that performers would commit suicide. In **Mexico** the Aztec would costume a slave to represent the god **Quetzalcoátl** and actually sacrifice him on the final day of the festival.

See also Roman Theater, Ancient; Slave Actors

Adavus
India

A basic rhythmic unit of dance with a specific tempo and set movements in **Bharata Natyam,** classical female temple dance. *Adavus* were originally called *Karanas* in the **Natya Sastra,** ancient sacred Hindu text on dramaturgy, which describes 108 dance units, giving directions for body positions, movements of feet and legs, and hand gestures. There are approximately 15 groups of *Adavus*, which are further broken down into types.

References: Massey, Reginald, and Jamie Massey. *Dances of India*. London: Tricolour, 1989.

Adler, Stella (1903–1992)
United States

Actress and teacher from a long line of actors; worked with the **Group Theater** and was a primary person in bringing the **Stanislavsky** System of acting to the **United States**. Her father, Jacob Adler, active in the **Yiddish Theater,** was known as the Jewish **Henry Irving,** and her mother, Sarah Adler, was also a great actress. Stella began acting as a child with her parents and toured **England** and the United States, even appearing on Broadway.

Adler, a tall blonde with an attractive regal air, was one of the strongest performers at the **Group Theater**. Her best role was in Clifford Odet's *Awake and Sing!* in 1935, as a downtrodden Depression-era housewife. In the same year she traveled with her husband, Harold Clurman, to Paris to meet with Stanislavsky. They studied with him for over a month and specifically discussed how the Method was being used in the United States and what problems the Group Theatre were facing. Adler differed with Lee Strasberg, who was very internal in his approach to the Method. Adler stressed the use of the imagination and transcending the actor's limited life experience. She stressed thorough investigation into the play's circumstances to find guidance for the actor creating a role.

In 1949 she created and directed the Stella Adler Conservatory in New York. In 1966 she began teaching at the Yale Drama School.

> **References:** Adler, Stella. *Stella Adler on Ibsen, Strindberg, and Chekhov.* New York: Knopf, 1999.

Aeschylus (525–456 B.C.)
Greece

The first ancient Greek playwright whose work survives. The efforts and developments of earlier ancient playwrights were brought to near perfection in the dramatic works of Aeschylus. Focusing on cosmic conflicts, Aeschylus was representative of the world of early fifth-century Greece, in which the primary concern of the society was the relationship of human beings with the gods. Since the characters of Aeschylus were types rather than full-fledged individuals, they had only a limited number of salient traits.

Aeschylus is credited with many important innovations that have influenced the development of Western theater. **Thespis** is believed to be the first actor to separate himself from the chorus, thus creating dramatic confrontation. Aeschylus heightened the dramatic intensity even farther by introducing the second actor. He also gave more depth to minor characters, such as watchmen or slaves, than had been done before. Aeschylus in-

troduced definite costumes for the actors by making improvements on costume elements that were used by participants in Dionysian rituals.

Aeschylus wrote both tragedy and satyr plays, which are burlesque comedies; only seven of at least seventy plays he wrote are extant. These are *The Persians,* 472, *Seven against Thebes,* 467, *The Oresteia,* 458—a trilogy consisting of *Agamemnon, The Libation Bearers,* and *The Eumenides—The Suppliants,* date unknown, and *Prometheus Bound,* date unknown.

> **See also** Dionysus; Euripides; Greek Tragedy; Sophocles
> **References:** Bieber, Margarete. *The History of the Greek and Roman Theater.* Princeton, NJ: Princeton University Press, 1961; Capps, Edward. "The Stage in the Greek Theatre According to the Extant Dramas." Ph.D. diss., Yale University, 1891; Ireland, S. *Aeschylus.* Oxford: Oxford University Press, 1986; Ley, Graham. *A Short Introduction to the Ancient Greek Theater.* Chicago: University of Chicago Press, 1991; Scott, William Clyde. *Musical Design in Aeschylean Theater.* Hanover: Published for Dartmouth College by University Press of New England, 1984; Sheppard, John Tresidder. *Aeschylus & Sophocles: Their Work and Influence.* New York: Longmans, Green, 1927; Taplin, Oliver. *Greek Tragedy in Action.* Berkeley: University of California Press, 1978; Thomson, George Derwent. *Aeschylus and Athens: A Study in the Social Origins of Drama.* London: Lawrence and Wishart, 1946.

Aesop
Italy

Popular tragic actor of the first century B.C. in Rome, born in Greece. Known for his powerful tragic acting and his emotional fire, he reportedly got so carried away while performing the role of Atreus that he killed a slave-actor performing opposite him.

> **See also** Roscius
> **References:** Bieber, Margarete. *The History of the Greek and Roman Theater.* Princeton, NJ: Princeton University Press, 1961; Chinoy, Helen Krich, and Toby Cole. *Actors on Acting.* New York: Crown, 1970.

Africa

The African continent is home to a variety of cultural traditions and thereby to a variety of cultural expressions through the performing arts. The northern part of Africa is much more Middle

Eastern, as it was a part of the Ottoman Empire, and accordingly it is primarily discussed under the heading **Arab Theater**; it is also much more European, because of its geographic proximity to Europe. Sub-Saharan Africa is home to innumerable African tribes and peoples and languages, evident from the fact that there are over a hundred distinct languages in **Nigeria** alone. By the late nineteenth century, this area was divided into spheres of influence by various European countries, primarily France, Great Britain, Portugal, Belgium, Germany, Spain, and Italy. In most of Africa independence movements had brought an end to European colonial rule by the 1960s. In South Africa, however, domination by the minority of European descent continued until 1994.

Theatrical activity in Africa can be divided into three categories, precolonial indigenous performances, colonial performances, and postcolonial (often anticolonial) theater. These categories often overlap, since, for example, many indigenous performances continued to be performed even after colonization. Each period did however greatly affect mostly all theater during its time, whether that theater was a product of a previous period or a recent creation.

Little is known of the theatrical performances of Black Africa prior to European influence, especially when one considers what richness must have existed, based on the scanty reports of early European missionaries and traders. African people did not record their scripts, as almost all theater was improvised, nor did they document their cultural history. What is known of this period is based primarily on reports by European missionaries and traders, or on the work of scholars who, either during or after colonial times, researched the ancient forms that were still intact (though most likely evolved to some degree). Though a homogeneous view of black African theater would be simplistic and inaccurate, some common trends do emerge from an overview of dramatic expression in Africa.

African theater, the theater of Black Africans, has always served a higher purpose than mere entertainment or diversion. From its ritual roots through to its recent anticolonial expression of protest, African theater has accomplished an essential function in sustaining the community. In precolonial times this function took such shapes as ridding the village of evil for the new year, praising a mighty chief or hunter, or preparing warriors for battle.

Theatrical conventions that prevailed during the precolonial period involved such an active relationship between audience and performer that the audience was an equal participant. The performing area was most often a clearing in the center of the village, or a clearing just outside the village if the preparations for a performance required secrecy. Customarily no setting was constructed to place the action of a performance in a different locale. Trance and spirit possession, usually involving masks, were often elements of performances. Performances were rooted in the community's supernatural beliefs and were most often associated with festivals, rituals, and ceremonies. Performers were almost exclusively men, who were often part of a secret society that kept the details and mechanics of performances hidden from women and uninitiated males. Males performed all female roles, male roles, and the parts of animals and spirits. Female impersonation was a talent highly regarded by audiences, who delighted in witnessing a male imitate the stylized movements of a woman. One exception to the male-only rule is found in the **Sande Masks** of **Sierra Leone,** in which female initiates performed masked dances as part of their training to become adult women of the community.

Indigenous African religion holds that the spirits can enter the human world through masks. The human masked performer, who is often in a trance or possessed, embodies the spirit, lending his human body for supernatural expression. Masked performances occurred and still occur throughout sub-Saharan Africa. Praisesinging, another common performance form, features one male who heaps praise upon a chief or hunter through poetry, song, and gestures. The **Mai Komo** of **Nigeria** and **Niger,** and the **Imbongi** of South Africa are two traditions of praisesingers. Numerous traditions of traveling performers thrive throughout Africa, from single performers, such as the **'dan Kama,** a juggler, dancer, and comic performer solely dedicated to praising food, to groups of traveling minstrels such as **'yankama,** who sometimes perform vulgar satires.

Colonial theater consisted primarily of European colonizers performing classic texts from their own cultural heritages. Since colonizers took control over schools for Black Africans, sometimes these productions were staged in schools by black students. The most famous school for theater was the Ecole William Ponty in Senegal. Many clubs and organizations, such as the **Amicale** in Niger, were organized by European administrators and a small African elite to present plays and even engage in competitions with neighboring colonies.

Postcolonial theater in Africa began as a theater of protest, usually against the colonizing power from which the people sought independence. Once independence was gained for each country, political theater generally continued as a critical watchdog over emerging African governments. The prominent Nigerian playwright, **Wole Soyinka**, is probably the most eloquent of the individual political and social reformers who have spoken through their plays. Because the restrictive regime of apartheid continued for so long, oppressing the black Africans in South Africa until 1994, the theater of protest in that country is arguably the most vibrant and artistically elevated in all of Africa, perhaps in the world.

As black Africans continue to search for their own theatrical traditions, apart from European colonial models, it seems that what thrive are improvised performances focused on some local concern that integrate comedy with seriousness and often music and dance with theatrical expression. This tendency is evident in the success of *Wasan Kwaikwayo,* Hausa plays from **Niger,** the **Worker Plays** of South Africa, and the **Trios,** concert parties including improvised comic skits of **Ghana.** Much of contemporary African theater is enriched by incorporating elements of traditional village theater such as masking and audience involvement.

In general, theatrical scholarship on Africa disproportionately focuses on colonial theater and recent African literary forms that adhere to the Western model, in other words, on plays that are scripted and performed to a largely inert audience. The richness and variety of the interactive live performing arts of Africa created by black Africans is a treasure yet to be discovered by those outside the immediate communities that give birth to them. The absence of written texts in the

African languages certainly diminishes the influence of African theater, but it does not subtract anything from its true value. The indigenous theater of Africa stands as an excellent example of how theater can contribute to sustaining harmony, well-being, and vitality in a community.

See also Egypt; Algeria; Morocco; Madagascar; South Africa; Benin; Ethiopia; Ghana; Mali; Niger; Nigeria; Sierra Leone

References: Asante, Molefi K. *African Culture: The Rhythms of Unity.* Westport, CT: Greenwood, 1985; Banham, Martin. *African Theatre Today.* London: Pitman, 1976; East, N. B. *African Theatre: A Checklist of Critical Materials.* New York: Africana, 1970; Fabian, Johannes. "Popular Culture in Africa: Findings and Conjectures." *Africa* 48, 4 (1978): 315–334; Murdock, George. *Africa: Its Peoples and Their Culture History.* New York: McGraw-Hill, 1959; Nwoko, Demas. "The Aesthetics of African Art and Culture." *New Culture* 1, 1 (1978): 3–6; Ottenberg, Simon. "Afikpo Masquerades: Audience and Performers." *African Arts* 6, 4 (1973): 32–36; Sofola, J. A. *African Culture and the African Personality: What Makes an African Person African.* Ibadan, Nigeria: African Resources, 1973.

African American Theater
United States

The spirit of African performance, brought into America by violently displaced black Africans who had been made into slaves, has had a powerful influence on the performing arts in America, easily apparent in music and dance, though less so in theater. There were some early attempts to perform theater in the Western format by African Americans such as William Henry Brown, who established the African Grove Theater in 1821. Mister Brown, as he is most commonly known, also wrote the play *The Drama of King Shotaway* (1823), which is credited with being the first black-authored drama in America. His African Company, which presented programs of classical and popular plays, music, ballet and opera through the early 1920s, was constantly harassed by white hoodlums and was eventually forced to close by the police, ostensibly for disturbance of the peace. After the Civil War (1861–1865) the highly trained Anna (1856–1930) and Emma (1858–1899) Hyers toured the country. Bob Cole (1868–1911) organized a stock company of African Americans and a school for acting in 1887 in New York. After 1920 more opportunities to act in serious dramas arose, such as those enjoyed by Charles Gilpin (1878–1930), who in 1920 gained great acclaim for his performance in *The Emperor Jones* by **Eugene O'Neill** (1920) with the Provincetown Players. In 1943, Paul Robeson (1898–1976) played the title role in **Shakespeare**'s *Othello,* a role most often played by a white actor in blackface, in a record-breaking run in New York. Other great African American actors to emerge were Richard Harrison (1864–1935), Ethel Waters (1900–1977), and Canada Lee (1907–1952).

A more indigenous style of African American performing was copied and exaggerated by whites in blackface in the **minstrel,** a kind of show popular in the nineteenth century, and then copied again by African American minstrels, who began to imitate a white stereotype of themselves. Some leading black minstrels were Earnest Hogan (1865–1909) and Sam Lucas (1840–1916). African Americans also created many popular **vaudeville** troupes, including Sissieretta Jones's Black Patti Troubadours and Gus Hill's Smart Set (1902–1903). Seating was segregated at most of these events, and sometimes blacks were not allowed at all. Another popular form of theater that was relatively early to introduce African American performers into the mainstream was the musical. The first black musical *A Trip to Coontown,* hit Broadway in 1898.

A true African American theater, with African American actors performing scripts by African Americans for a majority African American audience began to materialize with successes such as the **American Negro Theatre** in the 1940s and 1950s and with successful individual actors, writers, and directors such as **Alice Childress**. Lorraine Hansberry's (1930–1965) *A Raisin in the Sun* appeared on Broadway in 1956 with a nearly all-black cast. The play deals seriously with issues of identity, dreams and maintaining dignity for African Americans in a predominantly white society. Other important African American writers include James Baldwin (1924–1987), who wrote *Blues for Mister Charlie,* 1964, and *Les Blancs* (The Whites), which was first produced in 1970, and Le Roi Jones, later Amiri Baraka, who wrote the revolutionary *Dutchman,* 1964, about a white woman seducing and killing an intellectual black man. Maya Angelou began her show business career as a nightclub singer and worked her way up to performing in *Porgy and Bess* (1954–1955) throughout Europe on a tour. On Broadway she portrayed a black dressmaker in *Look Away* (1973). For the theater she has written *And Still I Rise* (1979) and *On a Southern Journey* (1983). Ntozake Shange wrote the choreopoem, a poetic piece set to movement, for *colored girls who have considered suicide / when the rainbow is enuf,* 1976, in which she created a musical language and style of presentation true to the African American experience by breaking down the language of her oppressors and adding more movement, poetry, and rhythm. In 1963 Hazel Bryant (1939–1983) established the Afro American Total Theater in New York, later changed to the Richard Allen Center, where she produced a wide variety of productions, from gospel-style musicals to an all-black version of O'Neill's *Long Day's Journey into Night* (1981). She also served on the Black Theater Alliance (1969–1982), an umbrella group for struggling black theaters. Another important African American playwright is August Wilson, who wrote *Fences,* 1985, *The Piano Lesson,* 1987, and *Two Trains Running,* 1990. Suzan-Lori Parks's play *Venus* (1996), directed by Richard Forman, at the Public Theater in New York focuses on how choice does not exist for those suffering sexism, racism, economic strife or physical threats. Actress Adina Porter excelled in her portrayal of Venus.

See also Africa

References: Fraden, Rena. *Blueprints for a Black Federal Theatre, 1935–1939.* New York: Cambridge University Press, 1994; Hatch, James, ed. *Black Theatre U.S.A.: Plays by African Americans, 1847-Today.* New York: Free Press, 1996; Hay, Samuel. *African American Theatre: An Historical and Critical Analysis.* New York: Cambridge University Press, 1994; Malloy, James. *Black Theatre: The Making of a Movement, California Newsreel.* San Francisco: California Newsreel, 1992; Mitchell, Loften. *Black Drama: The Story of the American Negro in the Theatre.* New York: Hawthorn, 1967; Peterson, Bernard. *The African American Theatre Directory, 1816–1960: A Comprehensive Guide to Early Black Theatre Organizations.* Westport, CT: Greenwood, 1997.

African Ballets

Theatrical performances that are a synthesis of drama, music, song, and dance. These performances, which are not, as the name implies, Western ballets, were popularized by students from secondary schools and by clubs such as **Amicales.** Ballets are inspired by indigenous cultural traditions, but are truly original creations, often choreographed with great care and attention to detail. Most ballets contain some dialogue, and many enact a story. Song and dance are the essential elements of ballet, which distinguishes them from *Wasan Kwaikwayo,* a popular form of improvised theater, in which song and dance may be present but are not necessary ingredients. Ballets preserve the cultural and artistic heritage of the black African people while allowing it to evolve.

References: Beik, Janet. *Hausa Theatre in Niger: A Contemporary Oral Art.* New York: Garland, 1987; Chaibou, Dan-Inna. "La Theatralite en Pays Hawsa." Université Nationale de Côte d'Ivoire, 1978–1979.

African Cinema

Algeria, Burkina Faso, Egypt, Guinea, Kenya, Mali, Mauritania, Morocco, Senegal, South Africa, Tanzania, Tunisia, Zimbabwe

Cinema on the African continent began with **Arab Cinema,** first in **Egypt** in the late 1920s, later in other North African countries, including **Algeria, Morocco,** and **Tunisia.** The first work by a sub-Saharan African filmmaker occurred in Guinea in 1953 with the film *Mourani.* The work of **Ousmane Sembene** of Senegal, the leading filmmaker of sub-Saharan Africa, had an international vision of his own country's complexities. His films bring out the ironies and difficulties of being a country in transition with sensitivity and humor. Most of the cinema outside of North Africa has emerged in France's former colonies in West Africa, including Senegal, Burkina Faso, Mauritania, and **Mali.** Films are also being produced in East Africa, notably in Kenya and Tanzania.

In southern Africa the British were not as active in supporting and encouraging film during colonial times as was France in West Africa. Thus, the history of film in the south has mostly been instances of Western directors using southern Africa for a location but bringing in their own actors and crews, doing little to develop the local talent. More recently, however, some local filmmakers have produced quality works to establish names for themselves, notably Michael Hammon of **South Africa** and Godwin Mawuru of Zimbabwe.

References: Katz, Ephraim. *The Film Encyclopedia. A Short History of the Movies.* 4th ed. New York: Macmillan, 1986; Ukadike, Nwachukwu Frank. *Black African Cinema.* Berkeley: University of California Press, 1994.

Agin
Bali, Java, Malaysia

Literally, "wind." When one says that a person has the Agin, it means that one is deeply moved by a performance. To be a *dalang,* puppet master, for the *Wayang Kulit,* traditional shadow puppet theater, it is highly preferable to have the *Agin.* As one great puppet master from Malaysia, Dalang Hamzah, said, "You can drink tea without sugar, just as you can perform technically without the *Agin.* However, tea is so much better with sugar, just as a performer is so much better with the *Agin.*"

References: Osnes, Mary Beth. "A Survey of Shadow Play in the Malaysian Traditional Shadow Puppet Theatre." Ann Arbor, MI: Proquest, 1992; Sweeney, P. L. *The Ramayana and the Malay Shadow-Play.* Kuala Lumpur: National University of Malaysia Press, 1972.

Albania

The area that is now Albania was conquered by the Romans, the Slavs, and finally the Turks, who in the fourteenth century converted the population to Islam. Albania was declared a republic in 1920. After 1944 Albania was allied with the USSR, but broke with them in 1960 to form an alliance with China. In 1992 Albania became a non-Communist country. It is believed that a rich folk theater tradition that developed in the fourth century still flavors performance styles today. Near the end of the nineteenth century the first Albanian play was written and performed, *The Wedding of Lunxheria* (1874) by Koto Hoxhi (1824–1895). At this time many amateur theater clubs were formed. Through popular support, the theater flourished after independence was achieved in 1912. The conservative government began to censor the theater by the 1930s. The first professional theater was founded in Tirana in 1945. In 1989 this theater company finally became the National Theater. Major dramatic works from Europe were the most popular plays being produced in the 1940s and 1950s. Native scripts were encouraged by the state, which subsidized theater, in the 1960s and 1970s. By the early 1990s over twenty professional theater groups existed, all receiving funding from the state. The National Theater continues to be the most important theater institution in Albania.

References: Hassiotis, Natasha. "On Stage: Euripides in Albania: 'The Women of Troy' in Athens." *Ballet International-Tanz Aktuell* (January 1999): 58.

Algeria

Prior to World War I, Algeria had two forms of theater, **Karagoz**, the Turkish form of shadow puppet theater, which often ridiculed French authorities and was outlawed in 1843, and **Fasl Mudhik**, Egyptian farces. Following the war, audiences who had been exposed to high-quality French theater troupes grew tired of native forms. Western-style comedy created by two men became the mainstay of modern Algerian theater. Rashid Ksentini (1887–1944) wrote delightful comedies such as *My Cousin from Istanbul*, and a singer, Bashtarzi Muhi'l-Din, who turned actor and playwright in 1930, was the creator of Algerian musical theater. His career began by performing simple plays that featured popular Algerian songs. His later work developed far beyond that into comedy of manners, such as *A Marriage by Telephone*. He was head of the Arab theater performing in the Opera House at Algiers.

In the 1950s Algerian theater was openly revolutionary in declaring the evils of the French colonists in plays such as *Nahu an-Nour* (Toward the Light) (1958). In 1958 the National Liberation Front Arts Company was started in exile in Tunisia, becoming the National Theater Company of Algeria upon its return in 1963. In 1987 a quarter-century of Algerian independence was celebrated with many new performances and visiting theater companies. In the 1990s a wide range of theater, from the National Theater to experimental groups, thrived.

The Algerian National Institute of Cinema allowed for the production of many high-quality feature films in the 1970s. Themes included liberation struggles, treatment of women, and the pressure of urban living. Two movies by filmmaker Muhammad Lakhdar Hamina, *The Oracle Winds,* 1966, and *Chronicle of the Hot Years,* 1975, were prize winners at the Cannes Film Festival in France.

References: Landau, Jacob. *Studies in the Arab Theater and Cinema.* Philadelphia: University of Pennsylvania Press, 1958; Moreh, S. "The Arabic Theatre in Egypt in the Eighteenth and Nineteenth Centuries." *Etudes Arabes et Islamiques* 3 (1975): 109–113; Moreh, Shmuel. *Live Theatre and Dramatic Literature in the Medieval Arab World.* New York: New York University Press, 1992; Mostyn, Trevor, and Albert Hourani, eds. *The Cambridge Encyclopedia of the Middle East and North Africa.* New York: Cambridge University Press, 1988; Rosenthal, Franz. *Humor in Early Islam.* Westport, CT: Greenwood, 1976; Salmane, Hala, Simon Hartog, and David Wilson, eds. *Algerian Cinema.* London: British Film Institute, 1976.

Alienation Effect
Germany

A term introduced by **Bertolt Brecht** for purposeful alienation of an audience from the emotional and sentimental aspects of a drama. This effect is desired in order to keep the audience objective and aware of the larger social issues being presented by the work. To realize this desired alienation effect, Brecht had actors step out of character during a performance to directly address the audience. Other devices include the use of placards that announce the outcome of the scene to follow so that the audience does not get carried away by the suspense of the drama, characters speaking about themselves in the past-tense, and characters verbally explaining their stage directions.

See also Piscator, Erwin

References: Rouse, John. *Brecht and the West German Theatre: The Practice and Politics of Interpretation.* Ann Arbor: University of Michigan Press, 1989; Speirs, Ronald. *Bertolt Brecht.* New York: St. Martin's, 1987; Weideli, Walter. *The Art of Bertolt Brecht.* New York: New york University Press, 1963; Willett, John. *The Theatre of Erwin Piscator: Half a Century of Politics in the Theatre.* London: Eyre Methuen, 1978.

Allen, Woody (1935–)
United States

American film actor, director, and writer, who is one of America's most inventive, idiosyncratic,

Woody Allen in Annie Hall (1977). For this film, Allen was awarded Academy Awards for Best Director, Best Original Screenplay, and Best Picture. (Kobol Collection/United Artists)

and prolific filmmakers. His character, seemingly on and off screen, is that of a nervous neurotic Jew obsessed with his mother and sexuality. His glasses and befuddled expression, his relentless examination of relationships with therapists, his thick New York accent, all contribute to make him a one-of-a-kind, irreplaceable icon of American culture.

Writing comedy since his adolescence, Allen started performing his work in cafes in New York. His first film was *What's New, Pussycat?* in 1965. By the 1970s Allen was most commonly writing, directing, and starring in all of his movies, including *Sleeper*, 1973. He gained acclaim with *Annie Hall*, 1977, co-starring Diane Keaton. Just as Allen's character seemed the same in life as in his films, so too, his romantic life most often included his present favorite female co-star. After Keaton came Mia Farrow, with whom he made the critically acclaimed *Hannah and Her Sisters*, 1986. Allen continued to grow and mature as a filmmaker with *Crimes and*

Misdemeanors, 1989. *Sweet and Lowdown*, 2000, starred Sean Penn and centered on a fictional jazz guitarist and his mute girlfriend. Allen is also an accomplished jazz clarinetist and performs regularly on Monday nights in a New York club.

References: Jacobs, Diane. *But We Need the Eggs: The Magic of Woody Allen.* New York: St. Martin's, 1982; Wernblad, Annette. *Brooklyn Is Not Expanding: Woody Allen's Comic Universe.* Rutherford, NJ: Fairleigh Dickinson University Press, 1992.

American Negro Theater
United States

African American theater founded in Harlem, New York, by Abram Hill (1942–1995) and Fredrick O'Neal in 1940 to portray the lives of African Americans honestly, leaving behind the stereotypical versions. In their plays they tried to discover an acting style based in the character and rhythms of

African Americans. Hiring both black and white actors, their first production, in 1941, was *Natural Man*. Other successful shows were *On Striver's Row* by Abram Hill and Philip Yordan's *Anna Lucasta*, 1944, which transferred to Broadway, where it enjoyed over 957 performances. Outstanding actors to receive training and emerge from this company were Ruby Dee, Harry Belafonte, **Alice Childress**, and Sidney Poitier.

The group toured the **United States** and Europe until it disbanded in 1953. It was not able to achieve all of its goals, but is still important historically as an influential model and the most successful sustained attempt of its time to create an African American theater.

See also African American Theater
References: Hay, Samuel. *African American Theatre: An Historical and Critical Analysis.* New York: Cambridge University Press, 1994; Malloy, James. *Black Theatre: The Making of a Movement, California Newsreel.* San Francisco: California Newsreel, 1992; Peterson, Bernard. *The African American Theatre Directory, 1816–1960: A Comprehensive Guide to Early Black Theatre Organizations.* Westport, CT: Greenwood, 1997.

Amicales
Niger

A shortened version of the name of a club, Amicale des Fonctionnaires de Niamey, established around 1940 for the creation of plays in French based on the French theatrical model. The purpose of the club was to present plays as a form of diversion for the actors and spectators, both groups who were mainly French administrators and a very small local African elite. There were other such clubs, which competed against each other in dramatic competitions held throughout French-speaking African countries. These clubs of colonial times have disappeared and have been succeeded mostly by popular improvisational theater.

References: Beik, Janet. *Hausa Theatre in Niger: A Contemporary Oral Art.* New York: Garland, 1987; Chaibou, Dan-Inna. "La Theatralite en Pays Hawsa." Université Nationale de Côte d'Ivoire, 1978–1979.

Anagnorisis
Greece

The moment of recognition, during which a character discovers the truth about himself or herself in an ancient **Greek tragedy,** a moment that is usually the climax of the play.

References: Bieber, Margarete. *The History of the Greek and Roman Theater.* Princeton, NJ: Princeton University Press, 1961; Taplin, Oliver. *Greek Tragedy in Action.* Berkeley: University of California Press, 1978.

Ancient Greek Theater

The artistic and cultural achievements of the Greek classical age, from approximately 500 to 336 B.C., have inspired and influenced Western culture profoundly. Models for democracy, architecture, and drama from ancient Greece, especially Athens, still influence the world in the twenty-first century. What we know of ancient Greek theater leads us to believe that the collaborative efforts of playwrights, musicians, actors, dancers, and costumers must have made for a spectacular experience. Witnessed from the enormous open-air stone amphitheaters, the Greek myths were brought to life by masked actors who could both utter eloquent speech and fly into a furious rage.

Neither the exact date of origin nor the influences and motivations are known for the Greek theater. Early influences could be ceremonies and major festivals from Egyptian civilization in the first millennium B.C., such as those surrounding the Osiris myth. **Homer** created the *Iliad* and the *Odyssey,* the first records of Greek mythology still extant today, and it is on these epics and others believed to be by Homer that the stories of ancient Greek theater, especially tragedy, are based. Dramatic impersonation developed from the **dithyramb**—a kind of hymn honoring the Greek god of wine, **Dionysus**—and was an act of worship performed at festivals for Dionysus, known as **Dionysia.** The most lavish of these festivals, the Athenian **City Dionysia,** hosted the first dramatic competition, of which **Thespis** was the winner in 534 B.C.

The highest level of playwriting was achieved in fifth-century Athens, with works that are still considered to be among the greatest of Western dramatic literature. Greek theater continued to thrive through the fourth and third centuries, but the focus shifted from the playwrights to the actors. In 336 B.C. Alexander the Great came to

VIII.

Corniola

Agata

Terra Cotta

Masks used in classical Greek drama, from a seventeenth-century work by Francesco de Ficoroni, Le Maschere Sceniche e figure comiche d'antichi romani. (The Art Archive/Casa Goldoni Museum Venice/Dagli Orti)

power, the spread of Greek culture created by his conquests marked the beginning of **Hellenistic theater**; comedy was favored over tragedy, and actors, instead of playwrights, became the highlight of all theatrical events. In 146 B.C. the Romans took over mainland Greece, thus marking the final decline of Greek theater and the renewed emergence of Roman theater.

Ancient Greek theater was written in three distinguishable forms. **Greek tragedy,** in its most famous examples, centers around a protagonist engaged in a moral struggle of high consequence that leads to his or her ruin or extreme unhappiness. The great tragedians **Aeschylus, Sophocles,** and **Euripides** were all often winners of the dramatic contest at the City Dionysia. At the end of each day of competition at the City Dionysia, each playwright also performed one **satyr play,** which is an often obscene play of comic relief. These plays featured a chorus of men dressed as **satyrs,**

followers of Dionysus who were half man and half beast. **Greek comedy,** the third dramatic form, originated perhaps from the **padded dancers** of the early sixth century B.C. According to Aristotle, in his dramatic treatise the *Poetics,* comedy featured men as worse than they are. Thus, the folly of human action is exposed, and human weakness is indulged for comic effect. The most acclaimed playwright from the period of Greek comedy known as Old Comedy is **Aristophanes,** whose political satire was as biting as it was clever. **Menander** was the best-known playwright of New Comedy, and he focused more on comical domestic situations.

Greek dramas were performed by male actors exclusively. One of the most famed performers was **Polus,** who lived in the fourth century B.C. Aside from the actors who performed the main roles, other performers were the members of the **Greek Chorus,** which numbered from fifteen to fifty. Their chief function was to sing and dance the choral odes that divided the acts of a drama.

Greek theaters were widely dispersed; they were built any place the Greeks colonized and developed a city-state—in present-day Turkey, Sicily, and even in the south of France. The audience, numbering up to 15,000, sat in rising rows forming a half circle around the performing area. Greek theaters were most often set in a natural amphitheater that was set into the steep sides of a hill. The acoustics were so remarkable in these outdoor theaters that the unamplified human voice could be heard from the stage anywhere in the audience. Such theaters remain in **Epidaurus** and on the side of the **Acropolis** in Athens, though both are somewhat eroded and have been altered through the centuries. The orchestra is the circular playing area closest to the audience. This centerpiece was the main acting area and the area in which the chorus sang and danced. There were *eisodoi* or broad ramps leading to the orchestra from either side that were used by most of the audience when arriving and by the actors for most of their entrances and exits. On the far side of the orchestra was the **skene,** or scene house, which functioned as a background for the action of the play and a changing room for the actors. Various stage properties may have been used, such as chariots, altars, or statues. Two stage machines were utilized to great dramatic effect. The first was a low platform, the **ekkyklema,** upon which tableaus were exposed to reveal the results of the often violent acts that were committed offstage. The second was the crane used to fly actors impersonating the Greek gods, making it possible to bring in a god to bring about a happy ending, whence the term *deus ex machina*, or "god from a machine."

See also Egypt

References: Arnott, Peter D. *The Ancient Greek and Roman Theatre*. New York: Random House, 1971; Bieber, Margarete. *The History of the Greek and Roman Theater*. Princeton, NJ: Princeton University Press, 1961; Butler, James. *The Theatre and Drama of Greece and Rome*. San Francisco: Chandler, 1972; Cornford, F. M. *The Origins of Attic Comedy*. London: Edward Arnold, 1914; Ley, Graham. *A Short Introduction to the Ancient Greek Theater*. Chicago: University of Chicago Press, 1991; Webster, Thomas Bertram Lonsdale. *Greek Theatre Production*. London: Methuen, 1970.

Ancient Mime

Italy

Early form of Roman dramatic entertainment, usually performed by a solo unmasked performer who used only gestures, movement, and exaggerated facial expressions to dramatize a story. Originally from Sicily, mime developed as early as the fifth or fourth century B.C. Plots for mime performances were short and often indecent stories or humorous burlesques taken from lower-class and urban life. Adultery was a popular subject. Mime was given its first literary form by Decimus Laberius (106–43 B.C.); it was often performed during the intermission of more serious dramas. By the first century B.C. mime was much more popular than masked dramas because Roman audiences liked to see the facial expressions of the performer and because it sketched ordinary life using current themes. In the later centuries of the Roman Empire, which lasted from 27 B.C to A.D. 476, mime reigned almost exclusively over the stage, and often it mocked the gods to the point of absurdity. With its overriding popularity, mime replaced the **Atellana,** a form of masked farce.

The costume for mime performers was a motley dress of patched fabric with either no shoes or light sandals. Women found a rare opportunity to perform in mime, even though in the beginning it was confined to male performers. Female mime artists who became famous include Cytheris, mistress of Mark Antony, who was known for her craft and artistry; and **Theodora,** first mistress and then wife of the Byzantine emperor Justinian in the sixth century A.D. She was known for her sharp wit and shamelessness.

On the day Caligula was murdered, the robber Laureolus was nailed to a cross in a mime performance and died before the eyes of the spectators. Also at this time female mime performers appeared topless on stage. Mime was the primary target of Christian teachers who were against what they considered degenerate forms of theater, because of the activities listed above and because Christian ceremonies and rites were sometimes ridiculed. Near the final decline of the Empire, mime attempted to compete with the games in the amphitheater by appealing to the audience's thirst for gore.

References: Arnott, Peter D. *The Ancient Greek and Roman Theatre*. New York: Random House, 1971; Bieber, Margarete. *The History of the Greek and Roman Theater*. Princeton, NJ: Princeton University Press, 1961; Chinoy, Helen Krich, and Toby Cole. *Actors on Acting*, New York: Crown, 1970; Taylor, David. *Acting and the Stage*. Boston: George Allen & Unwin, 1978.

Ancient Pantomime

Italy

Scenes performed by masked actors using only movement and gestures for expression during the Roman Empire, 27 B.C.–A.D. 476. Pantomime developed partly from **Mime,** in which performers without masks dramatized short, usually humorous, skits, using only facial expressions, movement, and gestures. In pantomime solo actors performed a monologue or scene featuring Greek mythology from a **Roman comedy** or **Roman tragedy.** One actor performed many roles by changing masks while a chorus or one singer sang or spoke the story.

Roman audiences grew tired of the endlessly repeated subjects of tragedy, but they still craved the art of acting, and pantomime was the form to satisfy that hunger. The form had great popular appeal in Rome, and the performers of it were nearly worshipped by their fans. Actors were handsome, well-built men whose movements were expressive and flowing. They used refined gestures and were versatile enough to evoke a wide variety of moods and emotions. A good education and a knowledge of mythology were a must for performers.

Graceful silk costumes that accented movement served as costumes for performers. The masks that were worn were similar to those worn in tragedy, except that those for pantomime had closed mouths. Pylades, who came to Rome from Greece in 20 B.C., introduced the tragic pantomime with stories taken from Greek mythology, and this type lived on through the rest of antiquity. In 22 B.C. Bathyllus introduced the comic pantomime, featuring such characters as Pan and Echo, or Satyr and Amor. This type did not last long. A chorus or solo performer in the background sang lyrics written by contemporary poets. These songs were usually a revamping of the words of the popular tragic scene that was being performed

See also Livius Andronicus

References: Beacham, Richard. *The Roman Theatre and Its Audience.* Cambridge, MA: Harvard University Press, 1992; Bieber, Margarete. *The History of the Greek and Roman Theater.* Princeton, NJ: Princeton University Press, 1961; Gentili, Bruno. *Theatrical Performance in the Ancient World: Hellenistic and Early Roman Theatre.* Amsterdam: Gieben, 1979; Taylor, David. *Acting and the Stage.* Boston: George Allen & Unwin, 1978.

Andreini, Isabella
Italy

Famous actress of **commedia dell'arte,** improvised sixteenth- and seventeenth-century Italian comedy, who played the *Innamorata,* or young female lover. Celebrated actress of the Gelosi company, she was considered to be the first great professional actress of Western theater. As playwright, poet, and actress, she was honored in Italy and France by all social classes, including royalty. Her first name became a stock character in the *Innamorata* category, since she created her own specific variation on the role.

Isabella was highly regarded because of her talent and loveliness, even though before her eminence it was thought to be immoral and shameless for a woman to be in the theater. It was in the commedia that women assumed an important

position for the first time in Western theater. When she died giving birth, the city of Lyon went into public mourning in her honor.

References: Chinoy, Helen Krich, and Toby Cole. *Actors on Acting,* New York: Crown, 1970; Rudlin, John. *Commedia Dell'Arte: An Actor's Handbook.* London and New York: Routledge, 1994.

Ankai Nat
India

Operatic dance-drama enacting the legend of **Krishna,** the eighth and most important incarnation of the Hindu god **Vishnu;** originated in the sixteenth century in Assam, a state in northeastern India. *Ankai Nat* is a beautiful synthesis of classical and folk theater traditions of the region. Lyrical plays, which describe the greatness of Krishna through episodes of his life, are written in the vernacular. Religious, social, and cultural community centers act as patrons for this form. They care for and train the performers. Each performance is viewed as an offering to Krishna.

A performance begins with the **Sutradhara,** the narrator, entering wearing a white skirt and turban. He sings invocations while dancing. Then he introduces the story and the characters for the specific story being performed. Actors make dramatic entrances from behind a white curtain held by two people. When Krishna finally enters, the other performers shower him with flowers. The Sutradhara stays on the stage commenting on the action throughout the show. Dancing and singing are stressed more than dialogue, and even the dialogue is delivered in a lyrical manner. Most action, including battle scenes, is choreographed as dance.

The setting for performances is a rectangular prayer hall called a *Namghar,* which is attached to the area where images of the deities are kept in a temple. Actors perform facing a high pedestal, upon which are sacred Hindu texts. The outer walls of the hall are usually painted with different scenes of Krishna's life.

Krishna's costume is a gold-embroidered velvet jacket. The actor portraying Krishna also wears a necklace of fragrant flowers and carries a flute in his hands. Some of the other characters are masked. Natural dyes from the area are used for makeup color. Color choice is symbolic of the inner nature of the dramatic character. For example, a demonic nature is indicated by black, brutality by red, and saintliness by white; light blue always indicates Krishna.

References: Varadpande, Manohar Laxman. *Krishna Theatre in India.* New Delhi: Abhinav, 1982; Vatsyayan, Kapila. *Traditional Indian Theatre: Multiple Streams.* New Delhi: National Book Trust, 1980.

Antistrophe
See Greek Chorus

Antoine, André (1858–1943)
France

Actor, theatrical innovator of naturalism on the stage, and pioneer of modern theater. Antoine founded Théâtre Libre (Free Theater) in 1887, in opposition to what he saw as the shallowness of the **Comédie Française** and other respectable theaters of the time. He wrote a pamphlet, "The Théâtre Libre," in 1890 that severely criticized the training of actors taught at the Conservatoire, the most prestigious training academy for actors in France, for the exaggerated enunciation and stock gestures they used. He wanted conversational tones in acting and genuine movements of the body in accord with the character's desires and personality. He wanted his actors "to live" rather than "to act." The core company of his Théâtre Libre consisted of amateur performers who by day worked as chemists, merchants, dressmakers, and so on. Still, these actors impressed the critics of their day with their arrestingly truthful acting, as brought out by Antoine.

In 1906 he was appointed director of the Odéon Theatre. He produced the work of naturalist writers Emile Zola (1840–1902), Leo Tolstoy (1828–1910), **August Strindberg** (1849–1912), and **Henrik Ibsen** (1828–1906). He developed a natural style of acting with his company, he and his actors drawing their inspiration from the essence of the play and real-life actions and reactions.

References: Chinoy, Helen Krich, and Toby Cole. *Actors on Acting.* New York: Crown, 1970; Chothia, Jean. *Andre Antoine.* New York: Cambridge University Press, 1991; Waxman, Samuel Montefiore. *Antoine and the Theatre-libre.* Cambridge, MA: Harvard University Press, 1926.

Anyein Pwe
Myanmar

Variety show, consisting of dancing, comedy routines, and both Western and traditional music. The word *pwe* is the generic term for any kind of performance in Burma.

References: Brandon, James R. *Brandon's Guide to Theatre in Asia.* Honolulu: University Press of Hawaii, 1976.

Apache Mountain Spirit Dance
United States

Also called Mountain Spirit Dance; Indian dance done to invoke the *gaan*, spiritual beings who manifest their great power in the wind; done by the White Mountain Apache in Arizona. It is performed by four male dancers, dressed in elaborate headdresses and masks, and one clown. Headdresses extend over three feet high, fanning out in elaborate designs. The medicine man decides

U Lu Maw, one of the famous Moustache Brothers, readies his traditional costume for an Anyein Pwe performance in Mandalay, Myanmar (formerly Burma). (Photo by Beth Osnes)

what design of body paint should be painted on the performer's torso, arms, and legs. Faces are covered with black translucent cloth. The purpose of the dance is to bring blessings or healing.

Singers, drummers, and a presiding medicine man stand to one side of the designated dance area. A clown enters from the east, does funny bits, and then blesses each of the four cardinal directions while whirling a piece of wood on a thong to create the sound of the wind, which heralds the coming of the *gaan*. From the east again enter each of the four dancers, and they move around the central fire in a snake-like formation. Their movements include lunges and twists that tip the headdresses back and forth. Then they suddenly stop and strike dramatic poses. During the dance the performers touch the person for whom the ceremony is being done, thereby throwing off that person's sickness.

References: Ganteaume, Cecile. "White Mountain Apache Dance: Expressions of Spirituality." In *Native American Dance: Ceremonies and Social Traditions*, ed. Charlotte Heth, 65–81. Washington, DC: Starwood, 1992.

Apuodaw
Myanmar
Character in the Burmese marionette theater.

See also *Yokthe Pwe*

Arab Cinema
Algeria, Egypt, Iran, Iraq, Lebanon, Morocco, Tunisia, Turkey
Though Egypt is the center of the Arab film industry, other countries, such as **Iran, Turkey, Lebanon, Tunisia, Morocco, Algeria,** and **Iraq,** also host film industries of their own. Still, the most famous Arab film actors are Egyptian, and stars of other Middle Eastern countries are often Egyptian. Many youths of these countries are attracted to film acting because it is accessible to the lower classes and compensated amply enough to make for luxurious living.

Islamic extremists have long wanted censorship or a total ban on cinema because of what they deem to be illicit love scenes and other morally corrupting content. Some Islamic groups have campaigned to prohibit women attending the cinema. In the 1980s the quantity of films being made in the Middle East was on the decrease, but the quality seemed to be improving. This is evident in the success gained by many Arab films at European film festivals. Also, the Arab Film Week in Paris is an excellent showcase for Arab films. The Egyptian Film Institute has trained promising filmmakers such as Asma El Bakri, who created *Proud and Beggars* (1991–92). Egypt is also home to the Cairo International Film Festival.

References: Landau, Jacob. *Studies in the Arab Theater and Cinema.* Philadelphia: University of Pennsylvania Press, 1958; Mostyn, Trevor, and Albert Hourani, eds. *The Cambridge Encyclopedia of the Middle East and North Africa.* New York: Cambridge University Press, 1988.

Arab Theater
The theater of the Middle East and North Africa, where Arabic has been spoken for hundreds of years. Arab theater also exists in non-Arab countries in which there is a sizable Arab minority, such as the Americas. The idea that there should be some indigenous style of theater that is uniquely expressive of the Arab people is only about a hundred years old.

The birth of modern Arab theater was in 1848 in **Syria,** but it soon shifted to **Egypt,** where the best playwrights and actors immigrated in search of better conditions and a more tolerant political climate. Actors were amateurs, freely moving from one troupe to another. The most valued actors were those who could sing well, because the musical element in theater was predominant. Actresses began to appear on stage at the turn of the century where they were once restricted, but these women were, as a rule, Jews or Christians. It was not until World War I that Muslim women, some of whom came from good families, began appearing on stage to promote the emancipation of Muslim women.

Egyptian theater troupes began touring throughout other Arabic-speaking lands in the nineteenth century, which did much to encourage and influence Arab Theater in those countries. Theater is almost non-existent in the Arabian Peninsula, partly because of the limited scope of European influence in the region and because of strong Islamic feelings. Though there is some optimism that the elusive new Arab theater may continue to grow and flourish, there is also the fear of decline in the face of governmental censorship and Islamic backlash. Theater is almost nonexistent in Libya, partly because of the limited scope of European influence, partly because of strong Islamic religious sentiment.

See also Algeria; Iran; Iraq; Israel; Jordan; Lebanon; Morocco; Saudi Arabia; Tunisia; Turkey; Yemen

References: Cachia, P. "The Dramatic Monologues of Al-Ma'arri'." *Journal of Arabic Literature* 1 (1970): 129–136; al-Khozai, Mohamed. *The Development of Early Arabic Drama.* London, New York: Longman, 1984; Landau, Jacob. *Studies in the Arab Theater and Cinema.* Philadelphia: University of Pennsylvania Press, 1958; Moreh, S. "The Arabic Theatre in Egypt in the Eighteenth and Nineteenth Centuries." *Etudes Arabes et Islamiques* 3 (1975): 109–113; Moreh, Shmuel. *Live Theatre and Dramatic Literature in the Medieval Arab World.* New York: New York University Press, 1992; Mostyn, Trevor, and Albert Hourani, eds. *The Cambridge Encyclopedia of the Middle East and North Africa.* New York: Cambridge University Press, 1988; Rosenthal, Franz. *Humor in Early Islam.* Westport, CT: Greenwood, 1976.

Arabic Shadow Puppet Theater
Egypt

An indigenous Egyptian style of shadow puppet theater dating from the thirteenth century which describes society and life in Islamic Egypt. It is significantly different from the Turkish **Karagoz,** another form of shadow puppet theater, in that in the Egyptian form there are no permanent characters and the plays and puppets are different. Performing in rowdy coffeehouses to uneducated villagers and children, the *Muqaddam,* or puppet master, performs written scripts using rawhide puppets to project shadows on a white screen so that only the shadows are visible to the audience. The dominant comedy in these plays is created by puns and obscenity. As the Muqaddam cannot move all the puppets himself, he often hires his students to be his assistants and even gives them scripts so that they can perform the lines for some of the lesser characters.

On a simple stage white linen is hung up and a strong light set behind. Puppets are made of brightly painted transparent rawhide. They are 20–28 inches high with articulated limbs manipulated by long sticks attached to the ends. Extra

holes are punched into the chest and stomach of puppets to bypass Islam's opposition to representations of the human form. Puppet masters argue that these holes ensure the puppet's lifelessness. Muhammad ibn Daniyal (1248–1311) wrote the first plays known for this form; many playwrights followed him. The plays are often written in verse, so students generally adhere to the script when performing, since it is very difficult to improvise in verse. Only the experienced masters can improvise more into written texts. Texts performed in a crude sort of spoken Arabic are sung or spoken quite loudly to compete with the talking in the cafe. Three or four musicians playing tambourines, oboe, and drum, accompany the performance.

Traditionally novices develop their skills under the supervision of a trained master. Novices not only learn how to manipulate puppets, recite, and sing from teachers, but also write down their versions of stories. In the twentieth century shadow puppet theaters were closed, but some performances in Cairo and Alexandria continue.

References: Kahle, P. "The Arabic Shadow Play in Egypt." *Journal of the Royal Asiatic Society of Great Britain and Ireland (J. R. A. S.)* (1940): 21–34; Landau, Jacob. *Studies in the Arab Theater and Cinema.* Philadelphia: University of Pennsylvania Press, 1958; Moreh, S. "The Arabic Theatre in Egypt in the Eighteenth and Nineteenth Centuries." *Etudes Arabes et Islamiques* 3 (1975): 109–113.

Aragoto
Japan

"Rough business" male character type in **Kabuki,** popular dramatic form of the seventeenth century.

Arangetram
India

Debut performance for a young dancer of **Bharata Natyam,** classical female solo temple dance.

See also Balasaraswati

References: Menon, Narayana, and Saryu Doshi. *The Performing Arts.* Bombay: Marg, 1982.

Ardhanarishwara
India

Form of **Shiva,** Hindu god, as half woman and half man. Parvati, Shiva's wife, is the female side, and Shiva is the male side. This form of Shiva depicts two opposing forces, masculine and feminine, as one body. Each constituting one side, the male and female biological forms meet in a glory of aesthetic beauty and union.

> References: Gargi, Balawanta. *Folk Theater of India.* Seattle: University of Washington Press, 1966.

Ardja
Bali, Java

Romantic dance-opera performed for temple festivals and private events by professional troupes. Attractive young women portray most roles. In Java the communication of the stories occurs through song and dance. The actors almost never speak. The stories have quickly moving plots that are drawn from romantic stories about lovers in Javanese legends from the twelfth and fourteenth centuries. Stories are also drawn from the **Panji tales,** the *Mahabharata,* and the *Ramayana.* In Bali this is the only form of theater in which a front curtain is used. Performances do not begin until midnight and continue into the early morning hours. Highly refined characters speak and sing in *Kawi,* the ancient Javanese language, which is translated into common Balinese by the clown characters, not without the clowns adding their own criticism and puns. There is an abundance of physical humor and verbal word play.

> References: Bandem, I Made. "Notes on the Development of the Arja Dance Drama." *Indonesia Circle* 3 (March 1983): 28–32; Brandon, James. *Theatre in Southeast Asia.* Cambridge, MA: Harvard University Press, 1974; Brandon, James R. *Brandon's Guide to Theatre in Asia.* Honolulu: University Press of Hawaii, 1976; Covarrubias, Miguel. *Bali.* New York: Oxford University Press, 1972; Hood, Mantle. "The Enduring Tradition: Music and Theatre in Java and Bali." In *Indonesia,* ed. Ruth McVey. New Haven, CT: Yale University Press, 1963.

Arena Theatre of the Philippines

Community theater based in Manila, founded in the 1960s, with sixty branch theater groups on the Philippine islands. This link between the cosmopolitan urban theater artists and the rural folk theater performers benefits both groups. The productions are written by Philippine authors about Philippine concerns. Shows use Western theatrical conventions almost completely instead of indigenous performance forms.

> References: Brandon, James. *Theatre in Southeast Asia.* Cambridge, MA: Harvard University Press, 1974; Mahores, Resil B. "Folk Drama & Social Organisation." *Philippine Studies* 29 (1981): 230.

Argentina

Before the Spanish invasion in the 1530s, indigenous nomads resided around the river La Plata in present-day Argentina. In fact there was a great variety of peoples and tribes occupying the territory of present Argentina. Some of the main groups are the Diaguitas, Timbúes, Caingúas, Mocoretas, Charrúas and Agaces, many of which have now completely disappeared. Immigration from Europe starting in the mid-nineteenth century increased the population of Argentina dramatically, also causing the culture to be highly Eurocentric. The Argentine theater was for years the most hospitable and fruitful in South America, marred for a time by the oppressive dictatorship of Juan Domingo Perón, 1944–1955.

Since Argentina came under Spanish rule in 1536, Spanish colonial theater of many forms was present, both secular elite forms and religious dramas. One of the first known theatrical traditions native to Argentina and Uruguay was the **Teatro Gaucho,** highly popular at the end of the nineteenth century. Staged in circus arenas, complete with stampeding horses and elaborate fight scenes, these plays brought to life the popular cowboy of South America, the **gaucho.**

In 1910 a law was passed that gave a large portion of all royalties to playwrights. As a result many gifted writers were attracted to the theater, and often they doubled as managers. Leonidas Barletta, an author-manager of the early twentieth century, began the Teatro del Pueblo, a theater dedicated to offering quality entertainment to the working class at an affordable price. Also of the early and mid-twentieth century, the famous actress Lola Membrives reigned as Argentina's leading star. **Argentinean Jewish theater** also flourished from 1900 to the 1940s. When the spark in Argentina's theater began to dim in the 1940s, the baton was handed on to

Chile, which was just beginning to foster a vigorous theater life.

Decades of military regimes since Perón were hard on the arts, since any "leftist" expression was sternly censored. The remnants of the highly developed professional theater artists turned to producing highly metaphorical or allegorical scripted works that were critical of the government but adequately veiled to escape censorship. As political and social stability continues to increase in Argentina, the forecast for theater is improving.

References: Barnard, Tim. *Argentine Cinema*. Toronto: Nightwood Editions, 1986; Glickman, Nora, and Gloria F. Waldman. *Argentine Jewish Theatre: A Critical Anthology*. Cranbury, NJ: Associated University Presses, 1996; Medrano, Hugo. "Argentine 'Theater of the Grotesque.'" *Americas* 37, 2 (March–April 1985): 56–57; Versènyi, Adam. *Theatre in Latin America: Religion, Politics, and Culture from Cortés to the 1980's*. New York: Cambridge University Press, 1993; Weiss, Judith A. *Latin American Popular Theatre: The First Five Centuries*. Albuquerque: University of New Mexico Press, 1993; Williams, A. R. "Eighty Years of Elegance and Excellence." *Americas* 39, 5 (September–October 1987): 14–19.

Argentinean Jewish Theater

Argentina has the largest Jewish population in Latin America and has produced a rich dramatic repertory. One of the earliest flowerings of Jewish culture in Argentina was the **Yiddish theater,** most popular 1900–1930, first presented by foreign companies. Ironically, these tours were financed by pimps trafficking Jewish women from Eastern Europe to Argentina for prostitution, strengthening the age-old association between prostitution and the theater. Foreign visits of prestigious European actors during this time fueled the excitement for local Yiddish theater to be produced by amateur actors and directors in the Jewish community.

Popular Jewish theater began in Argentina in 1932 with a group initially named *Prolet Bine* (Proletarian Stage), who later changed their name to Idisches Folks Theater. Famous actors of this time include Berta and Pauline Singerman, Cipe Lincovsky, and Fanny Brener, many of whom moved from the theater to the cinema. By the 1930s Jewish dramatists began writing in Spanish instead of Yiddish. After the 1940s Argentinean Jewish theater artists became part of their country's mainstream, in their attempt to represent Jewish culture with eloquence to a largely anti-Semitic society.

References: Glickman, Nora, and Gloria F. Waldman. *Argentine Jewish Theatre: A Critical Anthology*. Cranbury, NJ: Associated University Presses, 1996.

Aristophanes (448–380 B.C.)
Greece

Popular ancient Greek comic playwright; only creator of Old Comedy whose works survive. Aristophanes was a master at mixing sophisticated wordplay with unsophisticated physical comedy. Highly satirical regarding political matters, he often focused his plays on an antiwar theme, ridiculing the pettiness of those who waged war. For most of his writing career Athens was at war with Sparta, its rival city-state. As a champion of the peace party, he tried to influence Athens to make peace, but the peace he so yearned for came too late; democracy had already fallen by the time the war was over.

Aristophanes' work was very influential in the development of Western comedy. In his last surviving play he almost completely does away with the **Greek chorus,** giving the play a distinctively modern feel. Many of the indecent jokes centered on the large phallus attached to the padded costumes worn by male characters. It is believed that in Aristophanes' plays actors parodied famous characters wearing masks that were recognizable to the audience. Socrates, the great Greek philosopher satirized in *The Clouds*, is said to have stood up in the audience at a performance to allow the rest of the audience to see his resemblance to the masked actor portraying him.

Aristophanes is believed to have written thirty plays, but only eleven survive, of which *Lysistrata*, written in 411, is the most famous. In *Lysistrata* the women go on a sex–strike, refusing to have sex with their husbands until peace is made with Sparta. His plays often took their name from the chorus, as in *The Knights*, *The Wasps*, and *The Frogs*. The public found his work amusing, but the leading people in society, whom he lampooned, never granted him the honorary status in society they bestowed upon the tragic poets. Indeed, comic poets in general did not enjoy a high status in society.

See also Greek Comedy

References: Arnott, Peter D. *The Ancient Greek and Roman Theatre.* New York: Random House, 1971; Bieber, Margarete. *The History of the Greek and Roman Theater.* Princeton, NJ: Princeton University Press, 1961; Ehrenberg, Victor. *The People of Aristophanes: A Sociology of Old Attic Comedy.* New York: Barnes & Noble, 1974; Hubbard, Thomas K. *The Mask of Comedy: Aristophanes and the Intertextual Parabasis.* Ithaca, NY: Cornell University Press, 1991; Lord, L. E. *Aristophanes: His Plays and His Influence.* London: Harrap, 1925; Murray, Gilbert. *Aristophanes: A Study.* New York: Russell & Russell, 1964; Sandbach, F. *The Comic Theatre of Greece and Rome.* New York: Norton, 1977; Solomos, A. *The Living Aristophanes.* Ann Arbor: University of Michigan Press, 1974; Strauss, Leo. *Socrates and Aristophanes.* New York: Basic, 1966; Webster, Thomas Bertram Lonsdale. "The Costume of the Actors in Aristophanic Comedy." *Classical Quarterly* 5 (1955): 94.

Aristotle
See Poetics

Arlecchino
Italy

Type of **Zanni,** comic servant stock character in **commedia dell'arte,** improvised Italian comedy of the sixteenth and seventeenth centuries. Partnered with **Brighella,** Arlecchino and his mental shortcomings usually complicated the clever scheming of Brighella. Originally the role of Arlecchino was a peasant boy. He was usually the servant to **Pantalone,** the duped father or husband, **Capitano,** the Spanish braggart, or **Dottore,** the pedantic old scholar. Constantly in his hand, even when he was turning a somersault, was his **Batocchino,** known in English as a slapstick, made of two thin pieces of wood kept apart at the handle that when slapped together create a loud sound, whence the term slapstick comedy.

Arlecchino had a slow mind but a quick and agile body. Plots were often complicated because of his misunderstandings in carrying out an order. His vocal delivery was coarse and guttural. His costume was made of colorful diamond-shaped patchwork with a small black hat and a half mask made of black leather. The actors Tris-tano Martinelli (1557–1630) and Evaristo Gherardi (1663–1701) were largely responsible for creating this role.

References: Craig, Edward Gordon. "The Characters of the Commedia Dell'Arte." *The Mask* (January 1912); Rudlin, John. *Commedia Dell'Arte: An Actor's Handbook.* London and New York: Routledge, 1994.

Armenia
See Soviet Cinema; Soviet Union

Artaud, Antonin (1896–1948)
France

Theorist, actor, director, visionary, and poet. Artaud was an idealist and an extremist who created a dissatisfaction with artifice, mediocrity, and complacency in the theatrical experience. His many revolutionary essays on theater were collected in *Le Théâtre et son Double* (The Theatre and its Double) (1938). He began as an actor of the stage and screen, appearing in the film *Passion de Jeanne d' Arc* (The Passion of Joan of Arc) in 1922.

In 1927 he founded the Théâtre Alfred Jarry to achieve the liberty he witnessed in other artistic mediums such as music and painting. For the most part, he chose surrealist dramas to produce there. Artaud was hugely inspired by the playwright, Alfred Jarry (1873–1907), especially his blasphemous comedy *Ubu Roi.* That play represented for Artaud the culmination of the forces that he hoped would bring about the end of the theater as it existed in France at that time.

In 1931 Artaud witnessed a performance of dance from **Bali,** which greatly expanded his idea of what theater was capable of; he saw it as providing a trance-inducing initiation into an experience in which the elemental and essential nature of humankind could be explored. He often used terms of violence to describe these states, words such as crime, rape, cannibalism, and savage, but he seemed to be aiming at a sort of utopia of a theater in which primal urges were satisfied and fed. In this "theater of cruelty" he described the actor as an athlete of the heart who metaphorically raped the audience out of their apathy.

Many prominent theater artists have been influenced by and have experimented with Artaud's theories, individuals such as **Jerzy Grotowski**, **Peter Brook**, and **Richard Schechner**, and groups such as the **Living Theater** and the **Open Theater.**

References: Artaud, Antonin. *Le Theatre et son Double.* Paris: Gallimard, 1938; Artaud, Antonin. *The Theatre and Its Double.* Trans. Mary Caroline Richard. New York: Grove, 1958; Esslin, Martin, *The Encyclopedia of World Theater,* New York: Charles Scribner's Sons, 1977; Sellin, Eric, *Dramatic Concepts of Antonin Artaud,* Chicago: University of Chicago Press, 1968.

Artists of Dionysus
See Dionysian Artists

Ashtapadi Attam
India
Name for **Gita Govinda,** operatic dance-drama, as it exists in Kerala State.

Atellan Farce
See Atellana

Atellana
Italy
Farcical style of play, named after the town in southern Italy from which it originated; performed by masked actors. *Atellanae* were originally improvised, but as these plays grew in popularity scripts were written. In 89 B.C. the genre was given literary form in Latin. The speech, style of humor, and costumes were all rustic, since scenes were set in small farm towns or villages. After the demise of the Roman Republic, during the empire that followed (27 B.C.–A.D. 476), Atellanae became more popular than full-length tragedies and comedies based on the Greek model.

A predecessor to the later Italian **commedia dell' arte,** the Atellana was based on stock characters— Pappus the grandfather, Maccus and Bucco the fools, and Manducus the greedy ogre. Since the actors wore masks, they sometimes dared to criticize those who took part in public affairs and even the emperor, which proved to be dangerous, since an actor who criticized Nero was banished for life. Another actor who attacked Caligula, a Roman emperor who lived from 12 to 41 A.D., was burned to death in an amphitheater.

References: Bieber, Margarete. *The History of the Greek and Roman Theater.* Princeton, NJ: Princeton University Press, 1961; Taylor, David. *Acting and the Stage.* Boston: George Allen & Unwin, 1978.

Australia
A country that includes a whole continent, Australia enjoys an isolation that has led to unique flora, animal species, and culture. The original inhabitants, now known as the aborigines, are believed to have arrived from Southeast Asia as much as 40,000 years ago. Aside from possible interaction with the people of New Guinea, the aborigine culture evolved in complete isolation until the first European explorers were sighted in the seventeenth century. In the eighteenth century the Dutch named this mammoth "discovery" New Holland, and in 1770 Captain James Cook explored Australia and later clamed it for Great Britain. Great Britain used Australia primarily as a penal colony until the first half of the nineteenth century. As British colonists settled in new areas, the aboriginal populations were displaced and sometimes exterminated. Since 1901 Australia has been a Commonwealth country of Great Britain.

Other than the Australian aboriginal dance-dramas, theater did not exist in Australia until European-style theater began in Sydney in 1833; it was a welcome diversion from horse racing, cockfights, and other forms of gambling. Other colonial towns followed suit, presenting commercially viable popular entertainment. Theater managers would try a variety of combinations for an evening's bill to please an audience. Often a program included one play in its entirety and the best-loved scenes of another. Local theater companies and an occasional touring company from Britain performed in the many theaters started by entrepreneurs, who built theater chains.

The star system was in full force in Australia in the nineteenth century. Leading male and female actors were promoted more than the plays, and they dominated the company, choosing plays that would best show off their talents. These stars even commissioned the writing of plays to highlight themselves. In a specially tailored melodrama, *All* for *Gold*, Alfred Dampier and his two daughters, Lily and Rose, performed to tearful audiences until the girls were too old to carry off the parts.

It was hardly a privileged minority that attended the theater. In 1874, when the population of Melbourne was about 110,000, it was reported that 93,000 saw the play *Struck Oil* by J. C. Williamson. Audiences demanded constant change in the repertory, such that plays were rewritten again and again to provide variety.

Material for dramas came from many sources, from European plays to actual incidents. Popular scenes from existing plays were fitted into story lines from some other source. A popular scene from George Darrell's *Sunny South* featured a female star giving a horsewhipping to a villain. This scene was such a hit that it was written again into another play. By the end of the nineteenth century the rage was for plays about Australian subjects set in Australia. Stock situations and characters like those used in Wild West dramas popular in North America were extremely successful.

The introduction of the motion pictures to Australia largely replaced live theater as the popular choice for entertainment. Twelve of the first twenty films made in Australia, starting in 1906, were naturally bushranging stories. Attempts in the theater, such as the Pioneer Players, 1922–1926, started by Louis Esson, were unsuccessful at dragging Australian audiences away from movies, vaudeville, and successful touring American melodramas. The U.S. film industry dominated the Australian movie scene, with British films as a faraway second. One compensation for the demise of big commercial theaters due to film was that small amateur theater groups performing serious plays began to spring up.

Governmental support for the performing arts began in the twentieth century, with, for example, the founding of the Australian Elizabethan Theatre Trust in 1953. The building of large performing halls, such as the Sydney Opera House, in the 1950s was proof of serious government commitment to developing culture in Australia. Also, a younger and more intellectual audience was developing to support dramatic productions of a serious nature. In successful plays such as *The Summer of the Seventeenth Doll*, Australian audiences heard Australian characters speaking the Australian idiom of the streets. A true Australian na-

tional theater was beginning, which continues to develop and blossom today. In film Australia has a long history of collaborating with American and British filmmakers who enjoy the inexpensive local crews in Australia but keep creative control to themselves. The film *The Sundowners* (1960) is an example of that. The worldwide success of *Crocodile Dundee* (1986) brought fame to its producer, director, writer and actor, Paul Hogan. Baz Luhrmann is one Australian director who has consistently been admired throughout the world with his higly stylized movies such as *Strictly Ballroom* (1993), *Romeo and Juliet* (1996) and *Moulin Rouge* (2000–2001).

References: Allen, Elphine. "Australian Aboriginal Dance." In *The Australian Aboriginal Heritage: An Introduction through the Arts*, ed. R. M. Berndt and E. S. Phillips. Sydney: Australian Society for Education through the Arts in Association with Ure Smith, 1973; Brisbane, Katherine, ed. *Australia Plays*. London: Nick Hern, 1989; Chisholm, A. H. "Aborigines: Dancing." In *The Australian Encyclopedia*, ed. Ronald M. Berndt and Catherine H. Berndt. East Lansing: Michigan State University Press, 1958; Fotheringham, Richard. *Sport in Australian Drama*. Cambridge: Cambridge University Press, 1992; Horne, Donald. *The Australian People*. London: Angus & Robertson, 1972; Kimber, Robert. *Performance Space As Sacred Space in Aranda Corroboree: An Interpretation of the Organization and Use of Space As a Dramatic Element in the Performance of Selected Aboriginal Rituals in Central Australia*. Ph.D. diss., University of Colorado, 1988; Kingston, Beverley. *The Oxford History of Australia*. Vol. 3. New York: Oxford University Press, 1988; McGuire, Paul. *Australian Theatre: An Abstact and Brief Chronicle in Twelve Parts*. London: Oxford University Press, 1948;

Australian Aboriginal Theater

The indigenous people of Australia, known as the aborigines, have a belief system based on events believed to have occurred in what is called the Dream Time, in which mystic ancestors gave shape to the landscape. The events that occurred are considered to be sacred. A form of communal ceremony, sometimes referred to as a *Corroboree*, involves dramatic ritual based upon this magico-religious tradition. It involves song cycles, dancing, and mime. The belief is that performers are born with a gift for performing and have special performance skill. All present

A group of Australian aborigines paint their bodies in preparation for a corroboree. (E.O. Hoppé/Corbis)

are involved with different tasks such as dancing or chanting. The setting is created in a cleared performance space, in which beaters create a powerful rhythm and singers repeatedly chant traditional verses.

Theater in the Western sense, scripted plays performed for an audience, involving aborigines was slow to develop. There are records of white settlers enjoying the spectacle of the Corroboree in the nineteenth century as a sort of novelty. Aborigine stock characters, portrayed by white actors, appeared in many plays by white settlers such as *The Adventures of a Settler*, 1845, by J. R. McLachlan. The aborigine was most often portrayed as the "noble savage," or as the comic quick-thinking and resourceful native who invariably saves the day, as in *The Duchess of Coolgardie*, 1896.

A more realistic and sympathetic portrayal of aborigines occurred in 1927, with Katherine Susannah Prichard's play *Brumby Innes*, which showed the horrific treatment the aborigines received in the outback. In the 1940s black-white (or aboriginal-white settler) relations became the subject of the New Theatre movement in Melbourne, where aborigines actors collaborated and performed in productions. In the 1970s aboriginal actors also performed in *A Refined Look at Existence*. Out of political protest for land rights in 1972 grew many indigenous theaters, such as National Black Theatre in Sydney, Nindethana Theatre in Melbourne, and Noongar Theatre in Perth. Finally, aboriginal actors began enacting the works of aboriginal playwrights.

Contemporary aboriginal theater has been especially prolific in Western Australia, where theater artists draw upon the strands of the mystic acts of their ancestors, ceremonies, and oral traditions that lend themselves to dramatic enactment. Jack Davis wrote and performed in *The Dreamers*, 1982, for the Western Australian Theatre Company. Another performance in which the native culture dramatized by aborigine actors was *My Spiritual Dreaming*, 1993 at the Festival of Perth at the University of Western Australia, in which a central storyteller controlled the unfolding drama.

> **References:** Kimber, Robert. "Performance Space as Sacred Space in Aranda Corroboree." Ph.D. diss., University of Colorado, 1988; Parsons, Philip, and Victoria Chance, eds. *Companion to Theatre in Australia*. Sydney: Currency Press, 1995.

Austria

The earliest theater known in Austria consisted of **passion plays** performed by theatrical troupes as early as 1455, which dramatized German epics of heroic feats. These passion plays can be traced to the small town of Sterzing in the Tyrol. Troupes were formed under the direction of Stoffl Schopfer and Vigil Raber. Some of the earliest farces, or Viennese *Posse*, were recorded from 1514. In the mid-sixteenth century Jesuit schools used the rustic farcical form already in secular practice to attract the unconverted and educate them in the Christian faith. Wandering players from **England** arrived in Austria in the late sixteenth century, bringing with them a popular form of theater that featured coarse humor. They erected their stage wherever the authorities allowed, in a courtyard or the market place. A practitioner of this form, **Joseph Anton Stranitzky**, was the first actor using the German language to gain a permanent company for his comedies.

The house of Habsburg in Vienna was the center for the creation of the Austrian theater. The house of Habsburg was one of the principal sovereign dynasties of Europe from the fifteenth to the twentieth centuries. There is a long tradition of dramatic spectacle designed to symbolically demonstrate the righteousness of what they believed to be their divinely appointed rule. The two major forces in the seventeenth century were Jesuit theater, which by then used classical themes to convey a religious message, and opera, both of which were richly ornate and utilized complex stage design and machinery. Early exposure to **Italian opera** influenced Viennese theater toward love of spectacle and musical expression. In 1776 the ruler of Austria, Joseph II, established a national literary theater at the Burgtheater and banished the popular theater to the suburbs of the city where, against all odds, it continued to flourish. In the nineteenth century popular theater met with more extreme censorship but continued nevertheless, mainly because of the delightful comedies written by Joseph Alois Gleich (1772–1841), Karl Meisl (1775–1853), and Adolf Bauerle (1786–1859). Two great comic actors from this era were **Ferdinand Raimund** and his successor, Johann Nestroy (1801–1862).

Austrian theater was affected by the spread of realism throughout Europe, but resisted it as well, since the movement was in opposition to the opulent Baroque style created in Austria. Theater reached a high point in the early twentieth century with expression of a true Austrian spirit in the operas of Hugo von Hofmannsthal (1874–1929) and Richard Strauss (1864–1949). In 1919 Hofmannsthal created an annual theater festival in Salzburg. Leading actors from this time include Joseph Kainz (1858–1910) and Renate Muller (1907–1937). The Burgtheater continued as a strong force for quality German-speaking theater, with such strong actors in the 1930s as Raoul Aslan and Paula Wessely.

Experimental theater in Austria prospered in the 1960s with the work of playwright Peter Handke (born in 1942), who wrote *Offending the Audience*, 1966, in which four actors directly confront the audience and their expectations of a theatrical event. In his play *The Ward Wants to Be the Warden*, 1969, there is no spoken language, only mimed action. Currently Austria's theater is highly subsidized, with many permanent acting companies throughout Innsbruck, Salzburg, and Bregenz.

References: Brockett, Oscar. *Century of Innovation: A History of European and American Theatre and Drama since 1870.* Englewood Cliffs, N.J.: Prentice–Hall, 1973; Brown, Bruce Alan. *Gluck and the French Theatre in Vienna.* New York: Oxford University, 1991; Griffin, Robert. *High Baroque Culture and Theatre in Vienna.* New York: Humanities Press, 1972; Hartnoll, Phyllis. *The Oxford Companion to the Theatre.* New York: Oxford University Press, 1967; Robertson, Ritchie, and Edward Timms, eds. *Theatre and Performance in Austria: From Mozart to Jelinek.* Edinburgh: Edinburgh University Press, 1993.

Auto Sacramental
Spain

A one-act drama bringing to life personified abstractions of tenets related to the Eucharist, the holy bread sacramentally eaten by Christians, and various other Biblical themes. Actors portray characters such as Holiness, Sin, and the Devil. During the sixteenth century *Autos* were performed outdoors to celebrate the church festival **Corpus Christi,** in order to affirm the power of the church, its sacraments and dogma. During the mid-sixteenth century the development of the Autos coincided with the rise of the professional actor and the proliferation of acting companies. The same companies performed public secular dramas and religious dramas. In fact, the council members of each Spanish city carefully eyed the public performances known as *Corrales,* named for the type of space in which they were performed, to discern the best acting company to hire for the Autos for the Corpus Christi.

The master dramatist of the Auto was Calderón de la Barca (1600–1681). These dramas were originally performed on a scaffold before the church, but later on two-storied wagons that included an acting platform and elaborate machinery to hoist actors or scenery. The Auto combined characteristics from the English **morality play** and the **mystery play.** Professional acting companies were hired by the city's council organizing the Corpus Christi procession. Along with the performances of the Autos, the actors performed short farces and dances as interludes to the drama. These became increas-

ingly popular, until secular elements began to dominate performances.

In 1765 a royal decree prohibited performances of the Autos because it was deemed offensive to mix the sacred with the profane by putting religion on the stage in the manner of the Auto. The twentieth century has seen some resurgence of this form in revivals of seventeenth century Autos and some modern secularized versions in traditional form.

References: McKendrick, Melveena. *Theatre in Spain: 1490–1700.* New York: Cambridge University Press, 1989; Polito, Antonio. *Spanish Theatre: A Survey from the Middle Ages to the Twentieth-Century.* Salt Lake City: Department of Languages, University of Utah, 1967.

Ayang
Cambodia

Another name for *Nang Sbek Touch,* shadow puppet theater. The name *Ayang* comes from the term *Wayang* (show) in the *Wayang Kulit,* shadow puppet theater of Indonesia and Malaysia. The term Ayang also refers to the clown character in this shadow play, who has a protruding fat belly and resembles the god-clown **Semar** of Java and **Pak Dogol** of Malaysia.

References: Brunet, Jacques. "The Comic Element in the Khmer Shadow Theatre." In *Traditional Drama and Music of Southeast Asia,* ed. Mohd. Taib Osman, 27–29. Kuala Lumpur, Malaysia: Dewan Bahasa Dan Pustaka Kementerian Pelajaran Malaysia, 1974.

Azerbaijan

See Soviet Cinema; Soviet Union

Aztec Theater
Mexico

The indigenous Aztec civilization that once inhabited present-day Mexico was defeated by the Spanish in 1519, when the Spanish explorer Hernán Cortés led his soldiers to present-day Mexico City and, after a two-year campaign against the Aztec, captured the city and beyond. Pre-Columbian indigenous theater for the Aztec was centered mainly around rituals and ceremonies of a religio-theatrical kind, with an emphasis on nature. Part of the Aztec religion includes a highly evolved calendrical system. Aztec narratives tell of how the gods created the world out of their own blood, thus making them dependent on human sacrifices for their own survival. Many ceremonial performances culminate in a human sacrifice, such as the festival for the Aztec god **Quetzalcoátl.**

There is also a record of a ritual representation with many theatrical elements done for the Aztec god Huitzilopochtli. It was a ritual dance of a theatrical nature, in which boys portrayed birds and butterflies while the adults portrayed the individual gods. The actors were costumed in clothing with insignias to identify their characters, and elaborate sets were built. There was no division between spectator and actor in pre-Columbian theater, as all shared the communal goal of worshipping and appeasing the gods.

When the Christian missionaries spread throughout Mexico to convert the Aztec, they utilized many of the ritual aspects of the indigenous Aztec theater.

References: León-Portilla, Miguel. *Aztec Thought and Culture: A Study of the Ancient Nahuatl Mind.* Trans. Jack Emory Davis. Norman: University of Oklahoma Press, 1963; Phelan, John Leddy. *The Millennial Kingdom of the Franciscans in the New World: A Study of the Writings of Gerónimo de Mendieta (1525–1604).* Berkeley: University of California Press, 1956; Versènyi, Adam. *Theatre in Latin America: Religion, Politics, and Culture from Cortés to the 1980's.* New York: Cambridge University Press, 1993.

B

Baga Bundo

Mali

Rite performed by masked dancers on the second day after the death of an important person, performed as part of **Dama,** death anniversary ceremonies. The performance is meant to appease the soul of the deceased. In a public square, over a blanket that is placed on the ground, five male performers enact the *Baga Bundo*. Four performers wear the *Bede*, or young girl mask, which is made of black fibers and cowrie shells. The remaining performer wears the *Sirige*, or house mask, which towers to a height of 20 feet. The four dancers impersonating young girls dance around the elder of the *Awa* society, a secret society made up of circumcised males of the village, around a sister of the person who died, and around the Sirige performer. Then each Bede performer takes a place at a corner of the blanket. Each kneels to the accompaniment of heavy drumming and commences beating the ground with millet stalks. Once the elder of the Awa society recites a formula, the Sirige faces the blanket, which represents the deceased, from a few feet away and touches the top of his mask to the ground on both sides of the blanket by bending forward, a gesture that asks pardon of the deceased. Once the Sirige retreats, the crowd continues to dance and chant.

In recent decades versions of the Baga Bundo have been developed for tourist shows. In this theatrical setting the final act of bowing to the deceased loses all symbolic meaning and becomes a spectacular act of acrobatics.

> **References:** Griaule, M. *Masques Dogons*. Paris: Institut d'Ethnologie, 1938; Imperato, Pascal James. "Contemporary Adapted Dances of the Dogon." *African Arts* 5, 1 (1971): 28–33, 68–71.

Balasaraswati

India

Srinivasan Balasaraswati Varadan (1918–1984), known simply by her middle name, was a famous dancer of **Bharata Natyam,** classical female solo temple dance, in the first half of the twentieth century. She was born of a family that had excelled in music and dance for many generations. At the age of four she began training with a famous teacher, Kandappan (1899–1941), a stern disciplinarian from whom she received grueling training and an understanding of music. She had her **Arangetram,** or debut performance, at the age of seven, after which she entered the ranks of professional dancers. At this first public recital she showed composure, advanced technique, and rhythmic accuracy. She was a supreme artist, with an uncanny sensitivity to music. In the early twentieth century, professional dancers were looked down upon, even though they were in demand for performances. Balasaraswati raised the status of dancers in society simply by her undeniable elegance and mastery.

References: Menon, Narayana, and Saryu Doshi. *The Performing Arts*. Bombay: Marg, 1982.

Bali

Indonesia

A tiny island in the Indonesian archipelago, Bali is host to some the most exquisite dance-drama forms known to the world. Highly refined styles are executed with dignity and confidence by village people in honor of the Hindu gods. There is no star system, nor personal gain to be gotten by performers; all is created as a pure form of worship. In a young dancer's face one can see the wisdom of many incarnations as she makes herself a pure medium for the gods to express themselves. Bali is possibly the most fertile culture for artistic expression in the world.

The powerful influence of Indian culture, Indian dance styles, and the Hindu epic tales, the **Mahabharata** and the **Ramayana,** cannot be underestimated when examining Balinese performing arts. When the Islamic conversion of Southeast Asia occurred, roughly between 1300 and 1750, the people of the western part of Java fled to the island of Bali rather than convert to Islam. Being isolated on this self-contained island for so long, the form of Hinduism practiced in Bali evolved to incorporate local geographic forces, it is now a form of Hinduism found nowhere else in the world.

For female performers, **Legong** dance-drama is the highest expression of grace and femininity. It is usually performed by young girls under the age of thirteen; the dancers enact brisk controlled sequences of pure dance and pantomime dramatic scenes narrated by storytellers seated to the side of the dance floor. For male performers, the male war-dance **Baris** epitomizes ideal masculine energy. Stylized duels by middle-aged men who strike dramatic poses while holding spears culminate in the enacted death of one of the opponents. A recent development by a young Balinese man, Mario, is **Kebyar,** a solo male dance that combines the styles of Baris and Legong to visually interpret musical moods.

Trance is a dominant feature of many performance forms in Bali that ritually cleanse the spirits of the performers and, vicariously, the audience. **Barong** is the dominant trance-dance on the island of Bali; it enacts the conflict between good and evil that is central to their Hindu beliefs. The personification of evil, Rangda, casts a spell, forcing men to turn their daggers to their own chests. They wrestle with her magical hold over them, never actually piercing their skin. A Brahman priest restores order, and the village is ritually balanced once again. A less complex trance-dance, performed by children to contact the spirits for advice and good fortune, is known as **Sangyang.** In the 1930s a type of trance-dance, **Ketjak,** evolved from *Sangyang.* The *Ketjak,* or monkey dance, is performed by a huge chorus of men sitting in concentric cirlces chanting monkey sounds, while in the center young girls enact scenes from the *Ramayana.*

There are other less prominent dance-drama forms in Bali as well. **Wayang Topeng** is a masked dance-drama that blends Indian-style dance with Javanese masked dance styles. Styled after the shadow puppet theater, **Wayang Wong** (or **Wayang Orang**) is a dance-drama that started in the eighteenth century in Java. More often performed in Java than in Bali, **Ardja** is a romantic dance-opera performed by attractive young women for temple festivals. Since the tourist market in Bali and Java has increased so much in the last thirty years, **Sendratari,** a form of dance-drama without words, has been developed to entertain tourists.

The shadow puppet theater, the **Wayang Kulit,** enjoys great popularity in Bali and is a treat at any celebration or festival. One puppet master, known as a **dalang,** manipulates all of the flat rawhide puppets from a seated position behind the white muslin screen. Only the shadows are visible to the audience as they swoop in and out of view, enacting the Hindu epic tales. The music of the **gamelan,** the traditional orchestra, gives accent and drama to the movement of the shadows. A local god-clown character of Javanese origin, **Semar,** translates the ancient language used by the refined god characters while adding humorous comments all his own.

Drama Gong is a new form of spoken realistic drama in Bali that is based on traditional stories. It is accompanied by a live gamelan, but includes no dance.

References: Bandem, I Made. "Notes on the Development of the Arja Dance Drama." *Indonesia Circle* 3 (March 1983): 28–32; Belo, J. *Bali:*

Rangda and Barang. 2d ed. Seattle: Monographs of the American Ethnological Society, 1966; Brandon, James. *Theatre in Southeast Asia.* Cambridge, MA: Harvard University Press, 1974; Covarrubias, Miguel. *Bali.* New York: Oxford University Press, 1972; Eiseman, Fred B. *Bali Sekala & Niskala: Essays on Religion, Ritual, and Art.* Berkeley, CA: Periplus Editions, 1989; Emigh, John. "Playing with the Past: Visitation and Illusion in the Mask Theatre of Bali." *Drama Review* 20, 2 (June 1979): 11–36; Hood, Mantle. "The Enduring Tradition: Music and Theatre in Java and Bali." In *Indonesia,* ed. Ruth McVey. New Haven, CT: Yale University Press, 1963; Jenkins, Ron. "Becoming a Clown in Bali." *Drama Review* 2 (June 1979): 49–56; McKean, Philip F. "From Purity to Pollution? The Balinese Ketjak (Monkey Dance) as Symbolic Form in Transition." In *Imagination of Reality: Essays in Southeast Asian Coherence Systems,* ed. A. L. Becker and Aram A. Yengoyan, 293–302. Norwood, NJ: Ablex, 1979; Neuhaus, Hans. "Barong." *Djawa* 18 (1937): 203–239; Reed, C. L. "Bina Suarga: A Balinese Shadow Play As Performed by Ida Bagus Ngurah." *Asian Theatre Journal* 3, 1 (1986): 1–33; Yousof, Ghulam-Sarwar. "Traditional Theatre in South East Asia." *Performing Arts* 2 (July 1985): 37–49; de Zoete, Beryl, and Walter Spies. *Dance and Drama in Bali.* London: Faber & Faber, 1938.

Ball, Lucille (1911–1989)
United States
America's leading female comedian in both film and television from the 1940s to the 1960s, best remembered for her popular television show *I Love Lucy* (1951–1957), in which she starred with her husband, Desi Arnez. She began training for a career in acting at the age of fifteen and began to get some bit parts in movies in 1933. Slowly her movie parts grew larger and often served the purpose of comic relief. In *Dance Girl Dance,* 1940, Ball portrays the delightful Bubbles in a supporting role. Ball's final feature film was *Mame,* 1974. Ball is lovingly remembered for her exaggerated facial responses, her swaggering airs, and her ability to throw herself completely into even the silliest of comic situations.

> **References:** Ball, Lucille. *Love, Lucy.* New York: G. P. Putnam's Sons, 1996; Horowitz, Susan. *Queens of Comedy: Lucille Ball, Phyllis Diller, Carol Burnett, Joan Rivers, and the New Generation of Funny Women.* Amsterdam: Gordon and Breach, 1997.

Ballet de Cour
Denmark, France
A lavish dramatic spectacle that included dance, which grew out of the Italian **Intermezzo** popular in Europe during the sixteenth century. The original *Ballet de Cour* was performed in 1581 at the Petit-Bourbon Palace in Paris. The structure of a typical production began with exposition communicated through a song or lively speech, followed by five loosely related episodes and ending with a grand ballet, a closing dance in which the audience at court joined. Actors in these performances often played allegorical characters that in some way glorified their royal sponsor. For example, in Scandinavia in 1634, King Christian IV was portrayed as Neptune.

> **References:** Marker, Frederick. *A History of Scandinavian Theatre.* Cambridge: Cambridge University Press, 1996.

Baltic Theater
See Estonia; Lithuania; Latvia

Bangladesh
Theater in Bangladesh is Bengali theater and thus is the same as theater in West Bengal in India. Though the predominant religion in Bangladesh is Islam, **Jatra,** or popular opera, performers pass freely between Bengali-speaking regions in mostly Hindu India and Bangladesh.

In 1947 India and Pakistan were partitioned, Pakistan being made up of present-day Pakistan as West Pakistan and present-day Bangladesh as East Pakistan. Spoken modern drama had modest beginnings around this time, mainly centered in Dacca. The yearning for independence from Pakistan inspired many Bengali playwrights to create dramas that exposed the repression of their people. Bangladesh has been independent from Pakistan since 1971, and now the present generation of theater artists struggle to define their unique cultural identity.

> **References:** Brandon, James. *The Cambridge Guide to Asian Theatre.* New York: Cambridge University Press, 1993; Hyder, A. R. Z. "'A Small House beside a Highway': A Play for Television with an Essay, Development of Drama and Theatre in East Pakistan." Master's thesis, University of Hawaii, 1968.

Bangsawan

Malaysia

Improvised drama performed by traveling troupes in temporary structures. Shows are interspersed with popular songs and dances to please the mostly rural audiences. It was developed by Malays in the twentieth century, and it is popular rather than classical in nature. It was influenced by the Javanese **Ketoprak** and the Sundanese **Sandi-wara,** both forms of dance-drama. In the 1920s troupes performed wherever the Malay language was understood: Singapore, Sumatra, Borneo, and Java. Material for the dramas is drawn from Malaysian history, movie story lines, Arabian love stories, and Islamic literature. *Bangsawan* reached its peak in the 1920s and is almost extinct today, probably because of the accessibility of movies and television throughout even rural areas.

> **References:** Brandon, James R. *Brandon's Guide to Theatre in Asia.* Honolulu: University Press of Hawaii, 1976; Yousof, Ghulam-Sarwar. "Traditional Theatre in South East Asia." *Performing Arts* 2 (July 1985): 37–49.

Barba, Eugenio (1936–)

Denmark, Norway

Theatrical reformer and innovator, dedicated to a cross-cultural exploration of performance and theater as an expression of life's vitality. He is a tireless explorer of the art of acting and the specific styles and techniques of cultures throughout the world.

Born in Italy, in 1954 Barba moved to Norway to work and attend the University in Oslo. From 1960 to 1964 he studied in **Poland** with **Jerzy Grotowski** and was heavily influenced by his "poor theater." He started the Odin Teatret (Odin Theater) in 1964 and two years later was invited to work in Denmark where his NORDISK TEATER-LABORATORIUM (Nordic Theater Laboratory) was supported by the Danish government. His theater was a revolt against the "rich theater," with its psychological realism and expensively derived illusions. When Barba worked with the Odin Teatret, he insisted on a rigorous daily training that contributed to the group's development of excellence, tight ensemble, and longevity (the company lasted twenty years). The group took one to two years to prepare for a performance

and insisted on performing to an audience of no more than seventy people even when on tour.

After the Odin Teatret, Barba founded the International School of Theatre Anthropology (ISTA), as an active comparative study of acting techniques from around the world, taking into account each culture's perspectives on acting. ISTA is a laboratory for international research that brings together specialists in theater, anthropology, sociology, science, and specific masters of cultural traditions. Cultural performance traditions from around the world are used to train actors. Masters from India, Bali, Japan, and China are invited to become students to introduce them to experiences beyond their own respective cultural traditions. In his laboratory, Barba analyzes the act of performing worldwide by examining minute details such as balance and the way performers use eyes, feet, and hands. Barba has public sessions all over Europe to teach.

> **References:** Barba, Eugenio. *Beyond the Floating Islands.* New York: PAJ Publishers, 1986; Barba, Eugenio and Nicola Savarese. *The Secret Art of the Performer: A Dictionary of Theatre Anthropology.* New York: Routledge, 1991; Marker, Frederick. *A History of Scandinavian Theatre.* Cambridge: Cambridge University Press, 1996.

Barbados

A small easterly island of the Caribbean island chain, Barbados enjoys an interesting history of theater from its settlers. Although the Spanish removed virtually all the indigenous Arawaks of Barbados by the mid-1500s, the island was not claimed until the British arrived in 1625 and, with them, twice as many African slaves. During colonial rule the white masters suppressed remnants of the black African's native culture, so that the only visible theater consisted of sporadic performances given by traveling players from America or England and the work of local white amateur groups.

One of the earliest exceptions to the white-only rule for public performing was a production of John Home's tragedy *Douglas,* put on by the free black population of Bridgetown in 1805. The show received a good review, but that same review stated that such theatrical activities were not appropriate for nonwhites. Throughout the nineteenth century, many traveling groups from the

Americas and from overseas performed in the several permanent theaters, groups such as the Italian Opera Company in 1882 and McDowell Vaudeville Company in 1886. These foreign visits inspired no less than six different amateur groups in Barbados to create their own productions. The predominant form of theater, other than direct importations from Europe or the United States, was the popular revue. One such show, which developed into a musical comedy, was *Passport to Heaven*, 1950, by a black woman, Joyce Stuart. This show introduced Joe Tudor, 1922–1970, a comedian and one of the leading actors of Barbados, who did much during his career to improve the image of local entertainers.

Once Barbados gained independence in 1966, the government promoted theater through festivals, educational programs, and community programs that used theater as a tool for solving group problems. The population of Barbados is now over 90 percent people of African descent. Some aspects of African culture that survived the period of enslavement emerge in popular forms of entertainment such as the annual Crop Over festival and the Kadooment carnival.

See also Caribbean Theater

References: Banham, Martin. *African Theatre Today.* London: Pitman, 1976; Hewitt-Myring, Philip. "The Open-Air Theatre in Barbados." Bim 7, 25 (July–December 1957): 56–57.

Baris

Bali

Male war–dance. *Baris* literally means "in line" or "in military formation." This dance, apparently created in Bali, epitomizes the ideal masculine energy. It is performed at ritual feasts in villages. Middle-aged men dance with long spears in a double line, striking dramatic poses and making aggressive noises. Intense emotions create extreme passion in facial expressions and tension in the entire body. The music grows in intensity until a battle scene is enacted. The dance is over when one character slays another after a long stylized dual. This form has evolved to what is now called *Baris Pendet*, in which individual dancers portray military heroes, delivering dialogue while dancing. A good Baris dancer must be able to sit on his heels with his body straight and his knees spread out to the side. He must have an expressive face and voice to fit the type of character he portrays: a deep voice for strong characters and a high voice for young heroes. The costume consists of a white cloth headdress with a high triangle in the back and fresh flowers all along the front. Performers wear tight pants with a short coat and layered scarves over their breasts. The musical accompaniment is provided by a Balinese **gamelan**, the traditional orchestra, that plays standard melodies and interludes that lead the dancers to specific types of movement.

References: Brandon, James. *Theatre in Southeast Asia.* Cambridge, MA: Harvard University Press, 1974; Brandon, James R. *Brandon's Guide to Theatre in Asia.* Honolulu: University Press of Hawaii, 1976; Covarrubias, Miguel. *Bali.* New York: Oxford University Press, 1972; de Zoete, Beryl, and Walter Spies. *Dance and Drama in Bali.* London: Faber & Faber, 1938.

Barong

Bali

Trance-dance enacting the conflict between good and evil forces. This ritual performance is done whenever bad occurrences seem to be outweighing the good occurrences in a specific area. *Barong* is the name of the good lion figure, and Rangda is queen of the evil spirits. She is portrayed by a masked actor with long sagging breasts and long, sharp fingernails. Her movements are jerky and frighteningly erratic. Each performance starts with scenes from the **Ramayana** or the **Mahabharata** in dance and dialogue. Then performers from the village go into trance and try to kill Rangda. However, her evil powers force the men to turn their daggers against their own chests. Men wrestle with this magic hold over them, not ever really piercing their skin. The men wear only a black and white checkered sarong, so that their upper torsos are exposed. Then a Brahman priest sprinkles holy water over the men, and they return to their normal state. The ritual is concluded for the time being. This enactment of the struggle between good and evil is central to the belief system of the Balinese, which is based on the balance between these two forces.

References: Belo, J. *Bali: Rangda and Barong.* 2d ed. Seattle: Monographs of the American Ethnological Society, 1966; Brandon, James. *Theatre in Southeast Asia.* Cambridge, MA: Harvard University Press, 1974; Brandon, James R. *Brandon's Guide to Theatre in Asia.* Honolulu: University Press of Hawaii, 1976; Hood, Mantle. "The Enduring Tradition: Music and Theatre in Java and Bali." In *Indonesia*, ed. Ruth McVey. New Haven, CT: Yale University Press, 1963; Neuhaus, Hans. "Barong." *Djawa* 18 (1937): 203–239; de Zoete, Beryl, and Walter Spies. *Dance and Drama in Bali*. London: Faber & Faber, 1938.

Barrault, Jean-Louis (1910–1994)

France

Actor, director, and theatrical innovator; known as a highly experimental theater artist who was and remains an inspiration to many innovators. From 1931 to 1935 Barrault acted at the Théâtre de l'Atelier, during which time he trained with French mime artist **Etienne Decroux.** In 1935 Barrault directed and performed in an adaptation of William Faulkner's novel *As I Lay Dying* in mime. He was part of the **Comédie Française** from 1942 to 1946, where he performed lead roles in *Le Cid* by Pierre Corneille and *Hamlet* by **William Shakespeare.**

From 1946 to 1956 Barrault and his wife, noted actress Madeleine Renaud, ran the Renaud-Barrault Company. In 1959 he became director of Théâtre de l'Odéon and continued there until 1968, when he was dismissed for aiding antigovernment student rioters. He then returned to independent theater creations and went on to produce many more experimental works in alternative settings, such as a wrestling ring.

In his work he employed an exaggerated use of gesture to draw out stylized comedy and integrated mime even into his productions of tragedies (see **Mime**). Barrault himself appeared in many films, most notably in *Les Enfants du Paradis* (1944) as the great mime artist Jean-Gaspard Deburau (1796–1846).

References: Andre, Frank. *Jean-Louis Barrault*. Hamburg: Johannes Maria Hoeppner, 1957; Barrault, Jean-Louis. *The Theatre of Jean-Louis Barrault*. New York: Hill and Wang, 1961; Chinoy, Helen Krich, and Toby Cole. *Actors on Acting*. New York: Crown, 1970; Leiter, Samuel. *From Stanislavsky to Barrault: Representative Directors of the European Stage*. New York: Greenwood, 1991.

Barrymore Family

United States

An American acting family spanning over 150 years; intermarried with the Drew family. Louisa

Lane Drew (1820–1897), leading actress-manager of her time, acted among and established a fine company of actors in Philadelphia in the 1860s. Her children, John Drew (1853–1927) and Georgiana Drew (1856–1893), both became actors as well; Georgiana married the well-established English actor Maurice Barrymore (1847–1905). Their children adorned both Broadway and Hollywood with three of their brightest stars. Lionel (1878–1954) begrudgingly entered the theater and ended up making over 200 films in Hollywood. Ethel (1879–1959) was a great beauty and a fine wit, who played opposite **Henry Irving** in *The Bells* in 1901.

John (1882–1942) began acting in 1903 in New York as a comedian, but by 1916 had turned to more serious drama. Under the direction of Arthur Hopkins he matured into an accomplished actor of classics. He rehearsed rigorously and completely researched his roles, such as the title role in **Shakespeare**'s *Richard III*. In playing *Hamlet* in 1922, he explored the intricacy of every aspect of the character. He acted in some Hollywood films and returned to the stage in his old age a lesser actor, weakened by excessive drinking. *The Royal Family*, 1927, was a play written by Edna Ferber (1887–1968) and George S. Kaufman (1889–1961) about the Barrymore family.

John's children, Diana Barrymore (1921–1960) and John Barrymore Jr. (born in 1932), were both actors whose careers were destroyed by addictions. The origins of this great American legacy are reflected in the name of the actress Drew Barrymore (born in 1975), granddaughter to John Senior, who gained fame early with E.T. in 1982, fell into addiction, overcame it, and enjoys a thriving career in Hollywood, starring in many dramas and comedies.

References: Alpert, Hollis. *The Barrymores*. New York: Dial Press, 1964; Kobler, John. *Damned in Paradise: The Life of John Barrymore*. New York: Atheneum, 1977; Kotsilibas-Davis, James. *The Barrymores: The Royal Family in Hollywood*. New York: Crown, 1981.

Batocchino

Italy

A slapstick; used as a comic device in **commedia dell'arte,** improvised comedy of the sixteenth and seventeenth centuries. The comic servant charac-

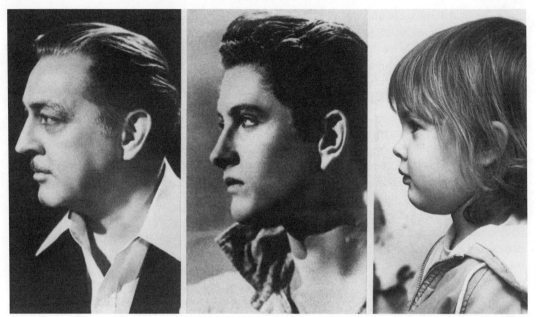

Three of the Barrymore clan, (left to right) John Barrymore, his son, John Drew, and the latter's daughter, Drew Barrymore. (Bettmann/Corbis)

ter, **Arlecchino,** was in constant possession of a *Batocchino* and was often trying to hit others with it or was himself being struck with it by his master. It was made of two thin pieces of wood kept apart at the handle. When someone was his by it, it created a loud noise, comically exaggerating the impact of the blow whence the term slapstick comedy.

> **References:** Rudlin, John. *Commedia Dell'Arte: An Actor's Handbook.* London and New York: Routledge, 1994.

Beckett, Samuel
See Absurdism; Existentialism

Bedu
Ghana, Ivory Coast
Masked dance-drama performed by the Nafana people of the far west and central region of **Ghana,** extending into the Ivory Coast. *Bedu* masks appear one lunar month of the Nafana year, known as the dance moon. During this month the masks appear nearly every night but are never seen in the daytime. Bedu rites are purification rituals, which can also be understood as part of a winter solstice festival. By visiting all the dwellings, the *Bedu* performers absorb all that is bad so the new year may commence fresh and clean.

The term *Bedu* comes from the name of the kind of spirit who lives in the mask. By wearing the mask the performer becomes one with the spirit for the duration of the dance. The *Bedu* speaks its own language, which no human can understand. If these masked figures want to greet you, feed you, or even beat you, they communicate their reasons for their actions quite explicitly through movement and gesture. The privilege of performing is inherited, so only certain families know the secrets. The community never knows who the dancer is, so they can more readily believe it is a true spirit in their midst.

Of the two types of masks, one represents masculinity and the other femininity. The female Bedu mask can be up to 11 feet high. The movements of this female character, performed by a man, include turning side to side, floating along the ground with tiny steps, and kneeling to honored guests. The male *Bedu* mask is smaller, and the entire figure is only 9 feet tall. His movements are stronger and more varied with leaps, turns, quick looks in all directions, and fast knee falls.

Another aspect of this event is socially sanctioned ritual abuse, which is not actual abuse but, rather, enacted insults. Members of the opposite sex can imitate abuse of each other, employing lewd gestures and crude insults. Though these assaults appear humorous, there is a serious intention underlying the laughter. Participants are purged of negative feelings and can start the new year with a clear heart.

The *Bedu* masks are carved whole from a large section of a tree. Natural dyes such as red clay, charcoal, and white clay, are used to decorate the masks. Performers are costumed entirely with raffia made from tree bark in long strips. The female Bedu style of dress is two pieces of cloth worn in traditional West African style. Performances occur in a cleared circle in a public outdoor area. Drummers control the dances through their beating rhythms. Singers police the dance circle, keeping it clear using sticks and whips so that the masked figures do not collide with an observer.

For unknown reasons this form has ceased to be performed in Ghana, but it can still be found in the Ivory Coast.

References: Kennedy, Scott. *In Search of African Theatre.* New York: Scribner, 1973; McHardy, Cecile. "The Performing Arts in Ghana." *Africa Forum* 1, 1 (Summer 1965): 113–117; Opoku, A. A. *Festivals of Ghana.* Accra: Ghana Publishing, 1970; Williams, Drid. "The Dance of the Bedu Moon." *African Arts* 2, 1 (1968): 18–21.

Belarus
See Soviet Cinema; Soviet Union

Belasco, David (1859–1931)
United States
Actor, writer, and manager for the stage; pioneered realistic lighting and stage effects. Belasco's father was an actor who moved the family to California during the Gold Rush. In 1882 young David moved to New York where he worked at Madison Square Theater. He got his chance to create his vision of realistic stage settings at the Lyceum Theater in 1886. He became a producer with *The Heart of Maryland*, 1895, starring Leslie Carter (1862–1937). In 1907 he started the Belasco Theater, where he staged naturalistic productions with detailed stage settings and many lighting innovations. Belasco was the first to conceal the footlights to achieve greater naturalism.

He created richly subtle lighting effects, such as the setting of the sun in *Madame Butterfly* (1900), which lasted over ten minutes. Belasco is reputed to have been a tyrant with his actors and to have had a fierce temper. He is also known for having fought against the Theatrical Syndicate monopoly of theatrical productions, which disbanded by 1915.

References: Winter, William. *The Life of David Belasco.* New York: Moffat, Yard, 1918; Marker, Lise-Lone. *David Belasco: Naturalism in the American Theatre.* Princeton, NJ: Princeton University Press, 1975; Winter, William. *The Life of David Belasco.* New York: Moffat, Yard, 1918.

Belgian Cinema
Feature films have been produced in Belgium since the 1920s, but the industry has been slow to develop, since its neighbors **France** and the **Netherlands** have been more prolific and attracted much Belgian talent. Director Jaco von Dormael gained international recognition with his film *Toto le Heros* (Toto the Hero), 1991. The film *The Wall*, 1999, directed by Alain Berliner, focuses on the social tensions between Belgium's French- and Flemish-speaking sectors. The Flanders International Film Festival in Ghent was started in 1974 by a group of film lovers and is still going strong today as a nonprofit organization.

References: Katz, Ephraim. *The Film Encyclopedia.* New York: Harper Perennial, 1994; Lim, Dennis. "Film: 'The Wall'; 'The First Night of My Life.'" *Village Voice* 44, 10 (16 March 1999): 134; Swart, Sharon. "Benelux: Flanders Fest Marks 25th Anniversary." *Variety* 372, 8 (5 October 1998): 55; van Hoof, Paul. "25th Flanders International Film Festival–Ghent: Elmer Bernstein & Michael Kamen at the Flemish Opera." *Soundtrack* 17, 68 (Winter 1998–1999): 48–50; Young, Deborah. "Film Review: 'The Wall.'" *Variety* 371, 12 (3–9 August 1998): 40.

Belgium
Belgium is divided into three regions: Flanders, which is Dutch-speaking, Wallonia, which is French-speaking, and Brussels, which is the bilingual capital. The French-speaking part of the country has modeled its theater after the theater in Paris. In the Flemish region theater is modeled after theater in the **Netherlands.** Belgium was

made a part of the Netherlands in 1815, but in 1830 became an independent monarchy.

There is early evidence of Flemish theater. Secular plays performed for the nobility date back to the thirteenth century, which proves there was a court tradition of theater. There were religious **miracle play**s and **mystery play**s as well. One from the late fourteenth century was called *The Seven Joys of Mary*. In the fourteenth century, the bourgeoisie grew more interested in the theater, and it became more organized and was written by rhetoricians. This led to the early formation of an amateur secular theater. In the sixteenth and seventeenth centuries the Flemish amateur actors, the Rederykers, were closely tied to the guild system. It was the efforts of these actors and writers of the time who kept the indigenous culture alive during the subsequent rule of the Spanish, the Austrians, and the French.

In 1919 the Flemish People's Theater sought to increase its appeal to the common people. A remarkable director at FPT was Johan de Meester Jr. (1898–1986). One of the greatest and most influential Belgian dramatists was Maurice Maeterlinck (1862–1949), a symbolist, who wrote *Pelléas and Melisande* (1893) and won the Nobel Prize for literature in 1911.

After World War I Jules Delacre, at the Théâtre du Marais, trained a company of actors who produced quality work in French. In 1945, after World War II had ended, the Antwerp Theater Company became the National Theater and was given the task of training actors and promoting the social standing of actors in society. The Studio was created for experimental works and as an actor training facility. This group also had a touring troupe that performed in outlying areas. The theater in Ghent was dissolved after World War II and not reestablished until 1965, with the founding of NTG (Nederlands Toneel Gent/Dutch Theater Ghent).

The late 1960s and early 1970s were years of social upheaval, felt also in the theater. Young artists and actors opted for small experimental groups such as Trojan Horse and Dirty Mong and His Filthy Friends. By 1975 state subsidization of theater was firmly established, and the trend was away from urban theater groups touring the provinces toward local theater groups in outlying areas performing the plays they chose. The 1980s

were a time during which the traditional borders between artistic disciplines diminished. Jan Fabre (born in 1958) was a director of this style, who integrated sculpture, dance, and theater at his own company, Helena Troubleyn, in Antwerp, and internationally. The trend toward decentralization of theater from the urban centers continued into the 1990s.

See also **Symbolism**

References: Liebrecht, Henri. *Histoire du Théâtre Francais Bruxelles au XVIIe et au XVIIIe.* Geneva: Slatkine Reprints, 1977; McCann, John. "Opera around the World: Belgium: Antwerp." *Opera* 49, 11 (November 1998): 1355; Morckhoven, Paul Van. *The Contemporary Theatre in Belgium.* Brussels: Information and Documentation Institute, 1970; Olaerts, Ann. "Flemish Playwrights." *Articles* 7 (Summer 1991); Quaghebeur, Marc. "The Current Situation of the French-Language Theatre of Belgium." In *An Anthology of Contemporary Belgian Plays*, ed. David Willinger, 291–295. New York: Whitston, 1984; Quaghebeur, Marc. "Introduction to Belgian Theatre." *Gambit* 11, 42–43 (1986): 9–24; van Hoof, Paul. "25th Flanders International Film Festival-Ghent: Elmer Bernstein & Michael Kamen at the Flemish Opera." *Soundtrack* 17, 68 (Winter 1998–1999): 48–50; van Schoor, Jaak. "The Contemporary Flemish Scene." In *An Anthology of Contemporary Belgian Plays, 1970–1982,* ed. David Willinger, 6–10. New York: Whitston, 1984.

Benin

Benin, a former French colony, known as Dahomey until 1975, has had a rich history of indigenous performing arts. One spectacular example is the **Gelede,** a masked dance-drama in which male and female *Gelede* characters make visible the play of power between the sexes. There are also the *Adjogbo* dancers, whose purpose is to seek out evil spirits, and the *Zangbeto,* or watchmen. There was also a popular tradition of puppet theater in the Ouweme region of Benin up to the early twentieth century.

In recent decades, a few troupes such as the Troupe Théâtrale et Folklorique d'Ekpe (The Theatrical Folkloric Troupe of Ekpe), founded in 1956, and the Troupe Théâtrale Towakomou (Theatrical Troupe of Towakomou), founded in 1976, have presented performances of cultural dances and folklore. However, the development of a modern theater in Benin, beyond a handful of plays being written, has been minimal. The inactivity is generally blamed on a succession of governments that all failed to create a support structure for the development of the arts.

> **References:** Banham, Martin. *African Theatre Today.* London: Pitman, 1976.; Cornevin, Robert. *Le Theatre en Afrique Noire et a Madagascar.* Paris: Le Livre Africain, 1970; Drewal, Henry John. "Efe: Voiced Power and Pageantry." *African Arts* 7, 2 (1974): 26–29, 58–66, 82–83.

Benshi
Japan

Storyteller for Japanese silent films. The *Benshi* was a man who stood at the side of the screen telling the story on the screen in detail, commenting on the action, and improvising some of the actor's lines. Early films became so dependent on the Benshi that movies did not develop a visual language of their own. Often an audience attended a film merely to enjoy the commentary of a particularly clever or popular Benshi. This practice of having a narrator comment on the action was a convention borrowed from **Kabuki**, a highly stylized dramatic form from the seventeenth century. Sound films came to Japan a decade later than in the West. In 1932 the Benshi and theater musicians called a strike against the film industry for introducing sound films. Nevertheless, the Benshi was made obsolete by talking films and is now extinct.

Bergman, Ingmar (1918–)
Sweden

Director, prolific in both film and theater. He is innovative in his use of theatrical staging and design, but technical aspects are always subordinate to the living actor and the dynamics of the acting ensemble. In live performance Bergman is known for his refreshing interpretations of the European classics continually striving to expose their inner core of truth. Bergman is able to extract the best performance from actors by the power of his own intensity and enthusiasm. He is also a master at casting the best actor for a role and at deeply observing his actors to discover what roles they hold within them. Bergman has gathered a core of favorite actors—such as Andre Ek (1916–1979),

Gertrud Fridh, Bibi Andersson, Harriet Anderson, Ingrid Thulin, and Naima Wifstrand—who perform in both his films and theatrical works.

In 1944, at the age of twenty-six, Bergman became artistic director of the Halsingborg City Theater. In 1946 his first independent film, *Crisis*, was released, and that same year he became director of Gothenburg City Theater. A richly creative time in Bergman's life began in 1952 when he began a six-year residency as director of Malmo City Theater, where he created works that brought him to the attention of all of Scandinavia. In 1956 he gained international recognition for his filmmaking with *Smiles of a Summer Night* and *The Seventh Seal*.

In 1963 he became the head of Sweden's National Theater. Throughout the 1960s and 1970s he wrote and directed dramas for television, though he felt the medium more limited than film or theater. In the late 1960s, he began guest-directing engagements all over Europe. In 1976 Bergman moved to Germany and began directing at the Residenztheater in Munich. He is a continually inspired and striving director, who most often directs plays by the authors **Henrik Ibsen**, **Tennessee Williams**, **August Strindberg**, and **Shakespeare**.

In 1984 his film *Fanny and Alexander* won him four Academy Awards.

> **References:** Bergman, Ingmar. *Images: My Life in Film.* Trans. Marianne Ruuth. New York: Arcade, 1994; Marker, Frederick. *A History of Scandinavian Theatre.* Cambridge: Cambridge University Press, 1996; Marker, Lise-Lone, and Fredrerick Marker. *Ingmar Bergman: A Life in the Theater.* New York: Cambridge University Press, 1992; Tornqvist, Egil. *Between Stage and Screen: Ingmar Bergman Directs.* Amsterdam: Amsterdam University Press, 1995.

Berliner Ensemble
See Weigel, Helene; Brecht, Bertolt

Bernhardt, Sarah (1844–1923)
France

Born Henriette-Rosine Bernard, one of the most renowned and eccentric actresses in Western history. Her appeal is said to have resided in her natural grace, slender beauty, intelligence, and energy. She is credited with clear expressive acting and an exceptionally evocative speaking voice. In 1895

George Bernard Shaw wrote that her art lay not so much in making the audience think more highly or feel more deeply, but rather in making the audience feel admiration for her. The dramatic nature of her off-stage life included such antics as sleeping in a coffin and keeping wild animals as pets. As a stage actress she traveled the world giving visiting performances. At fifty-six she began acting in films and continued, even after the loss of one leg, until her death at seventy-nine.

Her first appearance was in a small role at the **Comédie Française** in 1862, the next at the Théâtre de l'Odéon in 1869. After the commotion of the Franco-Prussian war she returned to the Comé die-Française in 1872 to perform some of her greatest roles, the title roles in Jean Baptiste Racine's *Andromaque* and *Phèdre*, and Doña Sol in Victor Hugo's *Hernani*. Leaving France, she toured on her own in the **United States**, **Mexico**, most of Europe, **Egypt**, and **Australia**. In 1893 she took over the Théâtre de la Renaissance and renamed it Théâtre Sarah Bernhardt.

Bernhardt maintained a love-hate relationship with the medium of film and claimed she detested it after viewing herself in her film debut, *Hamlet's Duel*, in 1900. Yet she continued to appear in films. Her performance in *La Dame aux Camélias* (Camille) was critically acclaimed and a popular success. After losing her leg in 1915 she appeared in two more films. In 1923, when she was seventy-nine, her hotel room was used as a studio so that she could appear in the film *La Voyante* (The Clairvoyant), but unfortunately she died before the film was completed.

See also French Cinema

References: Aston, Elaine. *Sarah Berhardt: A French Actress on the English Stage.* New York: St. Martin's, 1989; Richardson, Joanna. *Sarah Bernhardt.* London: M. Reinhardt, 1959; Salmon, Eric, ed. *Bernhardt and the Theatre of Her Time.* Westport, CT: Greenwood, 1984.

Bharata Natya Sastra

See Natya Sastra

Bharata Natyam

India

Classical female solo dance; it evolved from women's temple dancing in Tamil Nadu State and flourished through the south of India. *Bharata Natyam* is one of the oldest classical dance forms of India, dating back to the eighth century a.d. It is primarily a devotional dance for the Hindu gods, which vibrantly celebrates pure rhythm and enacts the yearning for spiritual and physical love and union. Previously known as **Dasi Attam**, the dance of the **Devadasis** (female temple maids), the term **Bharata Natyam** came into general use perhaps to disassociate dance from disreputable practices associated with the Devadasis, namely prostitution. During British rule in India, roughly 1792–1947, **Bharata Natyam** was suppressed for its bold sensuality. The twentieth century has witnessed a great revival of this cultural treasure.

One female dancer performs an evening recital, which lasts 3–4 hours. Musicians and singers sit to the side and provide the musical accompaniment. The dancer coordinates the stamping rhythm of her feet with the expressive mixture of body positions, subtle neck and eye movements, and **mudras**, hand gestures that make up a symbolic language. Some of the dances are pure rhythmic dance, *Nritta*, and some are narrative, *Nritya*, in which a story is stylistically pantomimed. An evening's performance is structured like a holy temple. Although there are no actual doorways on stage, the dancer metaphorically enters through the outer hall, represented by the first dance, crosses into the halfway hall, represented by the next dance, and eventually enters the holy inner sanctum. This structure is seen as a perfect symbol for union with the divine, so no changes or innovations are allowed.

Much of the dance is performed with the knees and feet pointing outward with the body held as low as possible. The powerful stamping of a dancer's feet is executed in intricate rhythmic patterns, sometimes at a blinding speed. The dancer's hands form different mudras in quick succession. The hands must have great agility and strength to quickly strike these positions. For example, a mudra called *Stripatako* is formed by holding the first, second, and fourth fingers straight upward and the third finger bent at the second joint at a right angle from the hand, with the thumb tucked in. As a dancer turns, lunges, or stamps, she follows her hands with her gaze.

Followers of *Bharata Natyam* believe that where the hand moves the eye follows; where the eye goes the mind follows; where the mind goes contemplation occurs, and **rasa**, a joyous spiritual experience, is created. The face of the dancer communicates emotion. Her expressions suggest profound emotion, but they are fleeting, as the story continues and she must move onto the next mood.

The dancer tries to transcend her individual consciousness to express the universal essence of emotions and feelings described in the songs she is dramatizing. The dancer can experience freedom and beauty through mastery over the mechanical elements of her performance. Discipline makes her free, and the entire design of the art form leads the dancer to a yogic balance and cosmic union. By sacrificing her self-consciousness, the dancer allows the audience to experience rasa through her performance.

Before the twentieth century *Bharata Natyam* was always performed in temples. Now it is performed on secular stages, but it is still considered devotional. There are no properties used by the dancer, and there is no scenery. The costume is a silk sari with much gold embellishment. Arm bracelets, nose earring, gold ornamentation along the hairline, and ankle bracelets with bells are the jewelry worn by a dancer. Intricate designs are painted on the palms of the hands and around the soles of the feet in a natural red dye. The dancer outlines her eyes with black and wears a dot of makeup or a jewel low on her forehead between her eyes. The songs are based on episodes from the great Hindu epic tales, the **Mahabharata** and the **Ramayana,** and other stories about the Hindu gods. Often the story revolves around the young **Krishna,** the eighth and most important incarnation of the Hindu god **Vishnu,** with the dancer portraying a young woman desiring his love. The theme is almost always love, religious or erotic. The longing for union with a lover is seen as a near perfect symbol for the human yearning for spiritual union.

The dancer wears thick leather ankle wraps with bells sewn onto them to provide a part of the rhythmic accompaniment to her dance. Other music is provided by a variety of drums, cymbals, flute, vina (a stringed instrument played with the fingers), and violin. There are rhythmic interludes in the narrative sections of a recital, during which the dancer abandons the story for a time to burst into a purely rhythmic dance sequence. During these rhythmic dances the main drummer and the dancer are completely attuned, anticipating each other's next move as though of one mind.

Historically there have usually been male teachers who taught technique, actual dances, and an understanding of music to young dancers. *Bharata Natyam* was first performed by Devadasis and women of royal families (see **Shantala,** a queen from the eleventh century). There is evidence in temple carvings that men did perform *Bharata Natyam* early in its development, and, indeed, men still perform today. The **Natya Sastra,** and ancient Hindu text on dramaturgy, describes 108 dance units, originally called *Karanas.* These are body positions, movements of the feet, head, and legs, and hand gestures. Evolved from Karanas are **Adavus,** the dance units currently used by *Bharata Natyam* practitioners, of which there are approximately 15 groups, each further broken down into types. A dancer rarely reveals how many Adavus she knows, as it is a professional secret and a telling sign of how accomplished a dancer is. **Arangetram** is the name for the debut performance.

Recent innovations include having the dancer change costumes between dances and having explanatory announcements, both of which are seen by loyal followers as interrupting the flow and breaking the mood of a performance.

See also Balasaraswati; *Odissi; Kuchipudi*
References: Brandon, James R. *Brandon's Guide to Theatre in Asia.* Honolulu: University Press of Hawaii, 1976; Massey, Reginald, and Jamie Massey. *Dances of India.* London: Tricolour, 1989; Scott, A. C. *The Theatre in Asia.* New York: Macmillan, 1972; Varadpande, Manohar Laxman. *Krishna Theatre in India.* New Delhi: Abhinav, 1982.

Bhava
India
Feeling or emotion. According to the **Natya Sastra,** 2,000-year-old sacred book of Hindu dramaturgy, there are eight *Bhava:* love, laughter, sorrow, anger, energy, fear, disgust, and astonishment.

See also *Rasa*
References: Gargi, Balawanta. *Folk Theater of India.* Seattle: University of Washington Press, 1966.

Bhavai

India

Rural drama from western India, believed by practitioners to have been inspired by fourteenth-century devotional songs. Now *Bhavai* is entertainment in poor rural areas of Gujarat State, north of Bombay. Performances take place in a circle drawn in the earth and are made up of eight to ten skits linked together by a narrator. The skits are mostly original secular scenes, which are humorous or uplifting, in that they demonstrate a positive attitude toward life. Language is sometimes Sanskrit, but mostly Gujarati or Hindi.

At the beginning of a performance a circle 20 feet in diameter is drawn in the dirt with a sword. A goddess is invoked. Her presence makes the space within the circle sacred. Only performers are allowed inside the circle after that point. Performances take place in or near a temple in the open air. The audience sits around the designated acting circle, leaving a pathway open for actors to enter and exit. There are torches all around the circle to light the playing area. The night's program begins with two comic skits. The skits that follow include dances and songs, all relating to conflicts from normal life. Many stereotypes are portrayed such as the henpecked husband, the greedy merchant, and the disgruntled wife in an arranged marriage saddled with a bratty husband half her age. Kings or generals are preceded into the circle by guards and servants carrying torches. There is a lighting effects man, who sits to the side with an oil torch, ready to rush to light the face of an actor striking a pose or to hold it by a king in a procession.

Singers are seated along the inside of the performance circle who sing lyrics with the actors. Musical accompaniment is provided by long trumpets that create a blaring noise, robustly played drums, and a harmonium that plays the melody. There are only male performers, so female impersonators play female roles. Makeup is usually white, red, and black, with exaggerated mustaches and eyebrows. The braggart character wears white stripes with dots on his face.

Troupe members are expected to remain celibate for six months during performance time to keep up their energy.

References: Brandon, James R. *Brandon's Guide to Theatre in Asia.* Honolulu: University Press of Hawaii, 1976; Gargi, Balawanta. *Folk Theater of India.* Seattle: University of Washington Press, 1966; Vatsyayan, Kapila. *Traditional Indian Theatre: Multiple Streams.* New Delhi: National Book Trust, 1980.

Bhutan

With much of the population in this Himalayan enclave still living medieval lives, the ancient Tibetan-style Buddhist rituals thrive as an integral part of balanced living. Bhutan was established in the sixteenth century and came under British rule for nearly a century starting in 1865. Independence was declared in 1949.

High drama and the antics of clown characters compete at the religious festival *Tsechu* in the eastern city Tashigang. Performed in the inner courtyard, this three-day festival brings to life the ancient tales of the high Himalayas, which center on the triumph of good over evil. One part of the festival features a dignified dancer in a rainbow-colored robe with long full sleeves swirling to the rhythm of drums and cymbals. His dance recalls the story of King Langdarma, a courageous monk who concealed a bow and arrow in the sleeve of his gown, with which he killed an evil monarch when dancing close before him.

Throughout the festival there are six masked clown actors making fun of the pageantry and any symbolic act that strikes their fancy. Their obscene parodies and blatantly disrespectful jokes are tolerated by the abbots and heartily enjoyed by the townspeople. Along with their full wooden masks, clowns wear a costume of rags and usually short ragged pants that expose the legs.

References: Karan, Pradyumna Prasad. *The Himalayan Kingdoms: Bhutan, Sikkim, and Napal.* Princeton, NJ: Van Nostrand, 1963; Karan, Pradyumna Prasad. *Bhutan: A Physical and Cultural Geography.* Lexington: University of Kentucky Press, 1967; Rahul, Ram. *Modern Bhutan.* New York: Barnes & Noble, 1972; Scofield, John. "Life Slowly Changes in a Remote Himalayan Kingdom." *National Geographic* 150 (November 1976): 658–683.

Bio-Mechanics

Russia

A system based on the physical actions of the actor; developed by **Vsevolod Meyerhold** and used as his primary guide in directing. Rejecting a theater built on psychology and introspection, Meyerhold held that if the actor could execute the physical expression of an emotion, he or she could communicate that emotion to the audience in a profound and visceral way. Meyerhold wanted to provoke an effective response in the audience through sensory channels and kinaesthetics, not intellectually or psychologically. He admired the elegance and grace of a skilled worker and recognized the artfulness in the worker's movements. He sought to instill that same efficiency and physicality in his actors. Meyerhold also drew upon sports to discover a physicality that could be expressive for the actor.

To make actors aware of the essential movement, Meyerhold developed bio-mechanic exercises based on rhythm, stability and balance. He believed the whole body must participate in every movement. In the 1990s, Meyerhold's system of bio-mechanics enjoyed a resurgence, and many theater artists in Russia are experimenting with its principles.

References: Barba, Eugenio and Nicola Savarese. *The Secret Art of the Performer: A Dictionary of Theatre Anthropology*. New York: Routledge, 1991; Braun, Edward. *Meyerhold: A Revolution in Theatre*. Iowa City: University of Iowa Press, 1995; Gladkov, Aleksandr Konstantinovich. *Meyerhold Speaks, Meyerhold Rehearses*. Trans. Alma Law. Amsterdam: Harwood Academic, 1997; Hoover, Marjorie. *Meyerhold: The Art of Conscious Theater*. Amherst: University of Massachusetts Press, 1974; Schmidt, Paul. *Meyerhold at Work*. Trans. Paul Schmidt. Austin: University of Texas Press, 1980.

Boal, Augusto (1930–)
Brazil, France, Peru

Brazilian theater director, practitioner, theorist, and innovator associated with **Latin American liberation theater,** which started in the 1970s committed to giving the poor of Latin America a voice and dignity. Some of Boal's performances involve only trained actors, while others involve both trained actors and participants from the audience. Much of his theater is an internal community process, in which he promotes awareness of one's social situation and its limitations, of how even one's body is bound by tradition and class. He has created many acting exercises and techniques that foster awareness of the body as a means or recipient of oppression.

He was originally based at the Arena Stage in São Paolo, Brazil where he was in charge of the theater. In the 1970s he was hired by the Peruvian government in their campaign against illiteracy. Boal developed a theatrical language to be used for this purpose that, when applied, demanded that everyone involved be an actor and that subjects for performances concern everyone in a given society, regardless of class or social standing. He developed and employed techniques in which actors take on personas, physically, facially, and in their behavior taking on the attributes of a certain social role, such as a policeman or an overworked mother. He also developed "Forum Theatre" in which audience members are asked to propose solutions to a given problem and both the performers and audience enact some of them. In all his work the audience is challenged to be an active participant, so that the revolutionary spirit engendered in performances can emanate into the world through those who experience his works.

Beginning in 1976 he was based mostly in Europe, more specifically in Paris, where he headed the Center for Investigative and Popularization of the Boal Method of Active Techniques of Expression. He has traveled extensively throughout the Americas and Europe. He resumed working in Brazil in 1987.

See also **Bolt, Alan; Buenaventura, Enrique**

References: Boal, Augusto. *Theater of Oppression*. Paris: La Decouverte, 1985; Gutiérrez, Gustavo. *A Theology of Liberation*. Maryknoll, NY: Orbis, 1973; Quiles, Edgar. "The Theatre of Augusto Boal." Ph.D. diss., University Microfilms, 1981; Versènyi, Adam. *Theatre in Latin America: Religion, Politics, and Culture from Cortés to the 1980's*. New York: Cambridge University Press, 1993.

Bolt, Alan (1930–)
Nicaragua

Theater director and in many ways the most radical proponent of **Latin American liberation theater,** which was begun in the 1970s to give a voice and dignity to the poor of Latin America. The work of his company, *Nixtayolero* (meaning "new dawn"), grows directly out of recent Nicaraguan history. His method for creating theater is to go with his company to live with poor Nicaraguan communities of mostly Indians to discover their needs and how they experience oppression in their lives. Through the creative process the people clearly identify their needs and gain some empowerment and realization. He uses theater as a means to break through the colonial mentality, to allow Nicaraguans to see clearly and to express themselves, free from oppressive colonial models. When the actors go to these communities, they bring with them whatever practical skills they can, such as agricultural or veterinary techniques to help in farming. The theater production is not the goal, but is rather a useful tool in a process aimed at liberation. Bolt's home base is La Praga, a farm in Matagalpa province, where he and his company give workshops.

See also Boal, Augusto; Buenaventura, Enrique
References: Gutiérrez, Gustavo. A Theology of Liberation. Maryknoll, NY: Orbis, 1973; Versènyi, Adam. Theatre in Latin America: Religion, Politics, and Culture from Cortés to the 1980's. New York: Cambridge University Press, 1993; Weiss, Judith A. Latin American Popular Theatre: The First Five Centuries. Albuquerque: University of New Mexico Press, 1993.

Booger Dance
United States

A dance-drama of the Cherokee, a people indigenous to the Southwest of the **United States**; performed in the winter by boisterous masked characters known as Boogers in a public setting. Boogers are ghosts (the term comes from bogeymen) of foreign invaders who, in this dance, are symbolically satiated and sent on their way. Boogers are lewd, lustful, and ridiculous, always grabbing at the women in the assembly and strutting arrogantly. In this most overtly dramatic of the Cherokee dances, foreigners are mocked and shown as beasts.

Four to ten male performers impersonate various foreigners such as Chinese, Africans, and Europeans, and even pretend to speak in their foreign language. Performers wear wooden masks with exaggerated human features, such as a big round nose, rosy cheeks, and bushy eyebrows for a white man. Masks can also be made of gourds or even wasp nests. Boogers are costumed in a sheet of cloth or a quilt over their shoulders. Performers sometimes wear a phallus made of gourd and flash female onlookers. All masked performers are given names, usually obscene, such as Big

Testicles or Rusty Anus, or tamer, more descriptive names such as Spaniard or Black Man. Boogers also wear animal masks at times.

The night of a performance begins with some social dancing by the onlookers. At an assigned time, the masked Boogers enter boisterously and seat themselves on a log bench. The host asks them who they are, where they are going, and what they want. The host interprets their answers for the crowd, usually saying that the Boogers want riches and (mostly) women. A group of singers, one playing a drum, provide music while each Booger in turn does a solo dance, an exaggerated grotesque dance like a white man trying to imitate an Indian dance. Performers must express themselves through pantomime, since they never speak directly to the audience. Then all the Boogers dance a Bear or Eagle Dance together. Following that, the host and the singers each take a puff of a ceremonial pipe. Then an equal number of women in normal dress and Boogers perform a line dance. The Boogers are sexually exhibitionistic with the women, enacting the lustful nature of foreigners. The women's dancing with them is a symbol of submission to these invaders. At the end the Boogers exit through the crowd, grabbing at women, making girls scream and giggle in delight.

References: Broom, Leonard, and Frank Gouldsmith Speck. Cherokee Dance and Drama. Berkeley: University of California Press, 1951.

Booth, Edwin (1833–1893)
United States

Actor who introduced a more subtle approach to acting in America; son of the English actor Julius Brutus Booth (1796–1852). Edwin began acting as a young man, most often performing on tour with his father in Shakespearean productions. In 1851 an eighteen-year-old Edwin performed Richard III for his erratic father, who refused to go on stage, and met with great success. After his father's death he continued to perform many of his father's classic roles. Edwin was a quiet and intelligent actor who used a natural style that focused on the refined elements of expression rather than grand gestures. Booth's style formed a strong contrast to that of Edwin Forrest, who popularized a grand and oratorical style of delivery in the **United States** One of Edwin's greatest successes came with his touching portrayal of Hamlet.

In 1863 he became manager of Winter Garden Theater in New York, where he performed with his brothers, also actors, Junius Brutus Booth (1821–1882) and the notorious John Wilkes Booth (1838–1865) who assassinated President Lincoln in 1865 during a production at the Ford's Theater. From 1869 to 1873 Edwin ran the Booth's Theater in New York. There he played many Shakespearean roles, often opposite his wife, Mary McVicker. After the financial demise of his theater, he took to touring internationally, reaching a high point in London in 1882, when he and **Henry Irving** alternated playing the roles of Othello and Iago opposite each other.

See also **Shakespeare, William**

References: Booth, Edwin. *Between Actor and Critic: Selected Letters of Edwin Booth and William Winter.* Princeton, NJ: Princeton University Press, 1971; Goodale, Katherine. *Behind the Scenes with Edwin Booth.* New York: Houghton Mifflin, 1931.

Bosnia and Herzegovina

The area that is now the Republic of Bosnia and Herzegovina was conquered by the Turks in the fourteenth century, placed under the control of Austria-Hungary in 1878, became part of Yugoslavia in 1918, and then declared independence in 1991. The recent fierce conflict between Bosnia's Serbs, Muslims, and Croats has made the production of theater difficult. In the 1980s one-person scripts by leading actors such as Narodno Pozoriste Sarajevo and Zijah Sokolovic gained great popularity. In 1980 the Academy of Dramatic Arts was founded in Sarajevo. In the early 1990s a theater called the Open Stage Shore began, which started a trend in "new primitivism" in theater. See **Yugoslavia** for history of theater in this area.

References: Kuftinec, Sonja. "Playing with Borders: Dramaturging Ethnicity in Bosnia." *Journal of Dramatic Theory and Criticism* 13, 1 (Fall 1998): 143–156; Musafija, Mair. "Bosnia-Herzegovina." In *The World Encyclopedia of Contemporary Theatre*, ed. Don Rubin, 143–154. New York: Routledge, 1994; Yarovskaya, Marianna. "Reviews: 'Underground.'" *Film Quarterly* 51, 2 (Winter 1997–1998): 50–54.

Branagh, Kenneth (1961–)
England

English actor and director of both stage and film, born in Belfast from a working-class family; sometimes compared with **Laurence Olivier**. In 1979 Branagh won a scholarship to attend the Royal Academy of Dramatic Art. He began acting for television and then joined the **Royal Shakespeare Company** in 1984, where to rave reviews he performed the title role of **Shakespeare**'s *Henry V.* Throughout his career he has performed mainly Shakespeare, often playing opposite his former wife, **Emma Thompson**. In 1986 he started a theater, Kenneth Branagh's Renaissance Theatre Company, focusing on the creative artistry of the actor, preferring the freedom of his own company to the security of a larger company. He became an actor-director to unleash the creativity and imagination of the actor. He has directed and starred in many films, including *Henry V,* 1989, for which he was nominated for an Academy Award for both Best Actor and Best Director, *Dead Again,* 1991, and *Much Ado about Nothing,* 1993.

References: Branagh, Kenneth. *Beginning.* New York: Norton, 1990.

Brando, Marlon (1924–)
United States

American stage and film actor who made fashionable the Method style of acting, influenced by the Russian theorist and practitioner **Stanislavsky**. At the age of twenty he had his Broadway debut with *I Remember Mama* and by 1947 reached stardom on Broadway with his brutish portrayal of Stanley Kowalski in *A Streetcar Named Desire* by **Tennessee Williams** and later in a 1951 film version. Brando studied the Method at the **Actors Studio** and there honed his internally focused, naturalistic style of acting. The outward manifestation of this style often meant mumbled lines and a seeming indifference to the audience. This style of acting was unprecedented, but Brando was seized upon by the younger generation as a rebellious counterculture prototype.

His compelling personality and physical allure added to the appeal of his intense performances in the film *Julius Caesar,* 1953, and *On the Waterfront,* 1954, for which he won an Academy Award. The 1960s were less successful for Brando, in part because he could not obtain suitable roles to match his style of acting, in part because of his unwillingness to work with many directors. A second wave of popularity and opportunity arrived in the 1970s, when he portrayed the title role in *The Godfather*, 1972, for which he won his second Academy Award. That same year he made the controversial *Last Tango in Paris*, in which he gives a shockingly honest performance of an emotionally damaged middle-aged man entering a sexual liaison with a near stranger. He masterfully embodies both brutality and vulnerability in his relations with this young lover. Later in 1979 he appeared in *Apocalypse Now*. Since the 1980s he has made mostly only cameo appearances in a few films, such as *The Freshman* (1990) and *Free Money* (1999). He accepted a more sizable role in the film *The Score* (2001).

References: Grobel, Lawrence. *Conversations with Marlon Brando*. London: Bloomsbury, 1991; McCann, Graham. *Rebel Males: Clift, Brando and Dean*. New Brunswick, NJ: Rutgers University Press, 1993; Schickel, Richard. *Brando: A Life in Our Times*. New York: Atheneum, 1991.

Brazil

The Portuguese arrived on the coast of present-day Brazil in 1500 and found an indigenous population with whom they quickly formed economic relations. With increased interaction, due to the sugar export business, most of the indigenous people were wiped out by a smallpox and measles epidemic. This greatly increased the amount of African slaves brought in to work the plantations. Brazil gained independence from Portugal in 1822, though the rich whites of Portuguese descent continued to rule. Regardless, the popular culture is profoundly influenced by the African population, which was freed from slavery in 1888. "Legitimate" culture is modeled after European theater. However, the Portuguese language has undergone such changes in Brazil that Portuguese plays are not even produced for modern Brazilian audiences unless significantly modified.

The first genius of the Brazilian theater was António José da Silva (1705–1739) known as "the Jew." He was a comic satirist of the upper crust during the eighteenth century. His dramatically abrupt life ended when he was murdered by the Inquisition. The first dramatist to provide roles of Brazilian character in a Brazilian setting was Luíz Carlos Martins Penna (1815–1848), who provided comedies, tragedies, and one tragic farce for the Brazilian stage.

The Brazilian carnival is a major popular festival, almost always occurring in the month of February. This three-day celebration is rooted both in the tradition of celebrating before the beginning of Christian Lent on Ash Wednesday and in pagan festivals from Egypt, Greece, and Rome. However, the carnival is Brazilian in style and character and influenced heavily by the Afro-Brazilian freed slaves. Music, spectacular processions, dramatic skits, costuming, and the *Samba* dance all take to the street in a festival that is known worldwide.

In contemporary Brazilian theater of the last few decades, actor-producer Procopio Ferreira has contributed much to Western-style theater with productions of imported European dramas and Brazilian classics and comedies. The most lively centers for Western-style theater are Rio de Janeiro and São Paulo.

See also Boal, Augusto; Latin American Cinema
References: Johnson, Randal. *Cinema Novo X 5: Masters of Contemporary Brazilian Film*. Austin: University of Texas Press, 1984; Milleret, Margo. "Acting into Action: Teatro Arena's Zumbi." *Latin American Theatre Review* 21, 1 (Fall 1987): 19–27; Neves, David. "In Search of the Aesthetics of the Brazilian Cinema." *New Orleans Review* (1982): 63–68; Perrone, Charles A. "Dissonance and Dissent: The Musical Dramatics of Chico Buarque." *Latin American Theatre Review* 22, 2 (Spring 1989): 81–94; Quiles, Edgar. "The Theatre of Augusto Boal." Ph.D. diss., University Microfilms, 1981; Versènyi, Adam. *Theatre in Latin America: Religion, Politics, and Culture from Cortés to the 1980's*. New York: Cambridge University Press, 1993.

Bread and Puppet Theatre
United States

Street theater created by sculptor and choreographer Peter Schumann in New York in 1962; utilized often huge puppets. Schumann moved to the United States from Germany in 1961. He wanted a theater that would be as basic to people's lives as bread, whence the name of his theater. Schumann applied Brechtian techniques to achieve the **alienation effect** through his work

The Bread and Puppet Theatre performance in northeastern Vermont, 1996 (James P. Blair/Corbis)

with puppets. Rather than having puppets speak, the pieces often had a narrator, and untrained actors were used to manipulate the puppets, with the emphasis being on the movement of the puppets. These productions were raw and rough, yet somehow mythical, using archetypal puppets of the kind that convey types rather than individuals. Bread and Puppet figures began appearing at various public demonstrations in the late 1960s. One of their primary puppets was Uncle Fatso, a caricature of President Lyndon Johnson. The group did not charge admission to their open-air performances.

They created *A Man Says Goodbye to His Mother,* 1968, which was a pacifist play about the Vietnam War. The group moved to the Vermont countryside in 1970, and all lived on a farm together. In 1972 they performed *The Stations of the Cross,* in which Christ was played by a woman, a more creative force than man in their view. Since 1974 the group has not been a permanent company but still comes together to create some special projects.

References: Bigsby, C. W. E. *A Critical Introduction to Twentieth-Century American Drama.* New York: Cam-

bridge University Press, 1985; Brecht, Stefan. *Peter Schumann's Bread and Puppet Theatre.* New York: Routledge, 1988.

Brecht, Bertolt (1898–1956)
Germany
Playwright, director, and theorist, who had an enormous influence on the modern theater throughout the Western world. Brecht experimented with theatrical methods being put forth by others, such as non-naturalistic acting techniques, integration of music and dancing, and commentary styles of acting. He excelled and emerged as the most influential and innovative theater practitioner of his time. He brought to realization the **epic theater,** which was first formulated by **Erwin Piscator**, a form of political theater that challenges an audience to remain active and thinking throughout a performance.

Brecht's first play was *Drums in the Night,* 1922. When the play was successful and moved to Berlin, Brecht followed and became an assistant for **Max Reinhardt** at the Deutsches Theater (German Theater), where Brecht also collaborated with Piscator. In 1928 Brecht collaborated with the composer Kurt Weill to create the highly successful *Threepenny Opera. Man ist Man* was produced in 1931, starring his wife, **Helene Weigel,** and Peter Lorre (1904–1964).

When Hitler came to power in 1933, Brecht and his wife fled to Denmark and then to the **United States**. Some of Brecht's best known and appreciated works emerged during his time of exile, such as *Mother Courage and Her Children*, 1941, *Galileo*, 1943, *The Good Person of Setzuan*, 1943, and *The Caucasian Chalk Circle*, 1948. In 1949 Brecht returned from exile to live in East Germany and founded the Berliner Ensemble, a permanent company of actors with whom he worked intimately. It was during this time that his theories and the culmination of his vision were realized. He introduced the **alienation effect** to acting, which involved the actor "showing" a character to an audience rather than "becoming" the character. Another technique used to produce this effect is the announcement of the action of a scene before the scene begins, so that the content of the action is stressed over the emotional suspense of the scene. The imaginary fourth wall between the room on stage and the audience is also broken, and the actor often talks directly to the audience. The intent is to keep the audience alert, involved in the message, and thinking.

The influence of Brecht's work on contemporary theater cannot be overestimated. His plays continue to be regularly produced, and his theories about acting and production permanently changed the face of theater.

References: Mumford, Meg. "Brecht Studies Stanislavski: Just a Tactical Move?" *New Theatre Quarterly* 11 (August 1995): 241–258; Rouse, John. *Brecht and the West German Theatre: The Practice and Politics of Interpretation*. Ann Arbor: University of Michigan Press, 1989; Speirs, Ronald. *Bertolt Brecht*. New York: St. Martin's, 1987; Weideli, Walter. *The Art of Bertolt Brecht*. New York: New York University Press, 1963.

Breuer, Lee (1937–)
United States
Writer, performer, director; founded the Mabou Mines Company in the late 1960s. Breuer was a director at the San Francisco Actor's Workshop in the early 1960s and later worked in Germany with the Berliner Ensemble and then in Poland

with **Grotowski**. With his own group, the Mabou Mines, Breuer created a series of "animations," which were poetic fables creatively enacted by human actors. Performed at the Guggenheim Museum in New York in 1970, *The Red Horse Animation*, like many of his works, had an animal as its main character. This horse was portrayed by three actors on the floor enacting the movements of a horse. Next came *The B Beaver Animation*, in 1974, and then *The Shaggy Dog Animation* in 1978, which was a comic story of love between a dog and its master using puppets, singers, and live music. In 1979 he presented *A Prelude to Death in Venice* at the Mark Taper Forum, starring actor Bill Raymond, who performed with an almost life-size puppet in a dialogue that was extremely funny and poignant.

During the 1980s Breuer served as director of the Yale School of Drama, where he experimented with many Asian and African performing techniques. *Ma Ha Bhar ANT a*, in 1992, was Balinese-style *Wayang Kulit* shadow puppet theater piece, using ant puppets to satirize American culture.

References: Bigsby, C.W.E. *A Critical Introduction to Twentieth-Century American Drama*. New York: Cambridge University Press, 1985; King, Bruce, ed. *Contemporary American Theatre*. New York: St. Martin's, 1991.

Brighella
Italy
Comic servant character in **commedia dell'arte**, improvised sixteenth- and seventeenth-century Italian comedy. As a subtype of the **Zanni**, the comic servant character, Brighella was always the boss, lording it over **Arlecchino**, another comic servant character. He moved about slyly like a cat, stirring up the plots with his meddling and intrigues. His costume included a white jacket, trousers, and hat, all with green trim and accents. On his face he wore a half mask made of black leather.

References: Craig, Edward Gordon. "The Characters of the Commedia Dell'Arte." *The Mask* (January 1912); Rudlin, John. *Commedia Dell'Arte: An Actor's Handbook*. London and New York: Routledge, 1994.

Brook, Peter (1925–)
England
English director of theater and film, whose contribution to the unfolding of Western theater has

been outstanding. His first production was Dr. *Faustus,* at the age of eighteen. Sir Barry Jackson (1879–1961) hired Brook to direct for the Shakespeare Memorial Theatre at Stratford-upon-Avon when he was barely twenty. Brook went on to enjoy a wide range of directing opportunities with a variety of theaters and actors, such as **Shakespeare**'s *King John* in 1945 at the Birmingham Repertory Theatre, starring Paul Scofield. In 1962 Brook was appointed codirector of the **Royal Shakespeare Company,** and in 1963 he started a workshop session, along with American director Charles Marowitz, called Theatre of Cruelty, after the essays by French theorist **Antonin Artaud**, where they improvised on many avantgarde theories. The spectacular product of this work was their production of *Marat/Sade,* 1964, by **Peter Weiss** and *US,* 1965, about the Vietnam War. Both of these plays were a direct attack on British norms and the status quo.

Before leaving for France in 1970, Brook directed his inspired version of *A Midsummer Night's Dream* for the RSC, using an all-white set and circus elements, including low-flying trapeze for the fairies. Once in Paris, he established his International Center for Theatre Research with **Jean-Louis Barrault**, which attracted a number of international performers. Here productions experimented with a rich variety of cultural performance traditions, and they toured widely.

Brook directed a stunning nine-hour version of the Indian Hindu epic tale, *The Mahabharata,* 1985. In opera, he directed both a stage and a film version of *Carmen.* Brook has made many films, some seen as pretentious, which are largely extensions of his stage experiments, including *Lord of the Flies,* 1963, *Marat/Sade,* 1967, *The Tragedy of Carmen,* 1983, and *The Mahabharata,* 1990. In 1998 Brook directed Mozart's *Don Giovanni* in Italy. At London's Young Vic theater, Brook directed *Le Costume* (The Suit) (2001), a French adaptation by Marie-Hélène Estienne.

> **References:** Brook, Peter. *The Shifting Point.* New York: Harper & Row, 1987; Hunt, Albert, and Geoffrey Reeves. *Peter Brook.* New York: Cambridge University Press, 1995.

Budai Xi
See Po-the-hi

Buddha
China, India, Japan

A title applied to an enlightened person, literally meaning "enlightened"; almost always applied to Siddhartha Gautama (560–480 B.C.), from northern India. The son of a rich feudal lord, Siddhartha was brought up in luxury and at a young age married a princess, with whom he had a son. Discontentment haunted him during his years as a young man, leading him to make a complete break with his former life to seek out enlightenment through asceticism and meditation. One night, sitting beneath the Bodhi tree, he finally reached enlightenment and was transformed into the Buddha. He went forth to minister to all of those in ignorance and suffering, and gained many followers.

The Buddha believed that the cycle of reincarnation, as believed in **Hinduism,** could be broken if a person cultivates a state of detachment from worldly things and desires. This state the Buddha called Nirvana, and he taught that it could bring rest to the soul and end the cycle of reincarnation. *Jataka,* tales of former births of Guatama Buddha, are often dramatized in Thailand and Cambodia.

> **See also** Zen Buddhism
> **References:** Aherne, Consuelo Maria, Paul Kevin Meagher, and Thomas C. O'Brien, eds. *Encyclopedic Dictionary of Religion.* 3 vols. Washington, DC: Corpus Publishers, 1979; Eliade, Mircea, ed., *The Encyclopedia of Religion.* 16 vols. New York: Macmillan, 1987.

Buddhism
Asia

Religion based on the teaching of the **Buddha**; originated in the fifth century B.C. in India. A gathering of sayings and rules, called the *Tripitika* (Three Baskets), was collected by the Buddha's early followers. This writing serves as the primary scriptural base for Buddhism.

Like **Hinduism,** Buddhism includes a belief in reincarnation, holding that the soul is reborn into a lower or higher life form after death depending on how that person lived. However, the Buddha believed that the endless cycle of reincarnation could be broken if a person cultivated a state of detachment from worldly goods and desires. This state, known as *Nirvana,* could bring rest to the soul and end the cycle of reincarnation. To aid his followers in achieving this, the Buddha created guidelines for living that are summed up in the Eightfold Path as right view, right thought, right action, right livelihood, right effort, right mindfulness, right concentration, and right speech.

After the death of the Buddha, the monastic followers split into different schools. The most prominent division occurred between Theravada and Mahayana Buddhism. Theravada Buddhism focuses on the life and teachings of the Buddha in a traditional fashion. This form predominates in Sri Lanka, Burma, Thailand, and Cambodia. Mahayana Buddhism takes a more liberal view of Buddhist teaching and believes in seeking to become a bodhisattva. A bodhisattva is a being who compassionately refrains from entering nirvana in order to save others and who is worshiped as a deity in Mahayana Buddhism. This form predominates in China and Japan. Another movement arose in the seventh century A.D. in China and Japan known as **Zen Buddhism,** which focused heavily upon meditation as a means to enlightenment.

Buddhism spread all over the world, but, ironically, around A.D. 700 lost its influence in its birthplace, India, where Islam began to spread in A.D. 711 and a reawakening of Hindu beliefs took over. The **Jataka,** tales of the Buddha's former births, and other animal stories have been dramatized around Asia in such forms as **Lakon Bassak,** a Cambodian dance-drama, and **Yokthe Pwe,** a Burmese marionette play.

References: Aherne, Consuelo Maria, Paul Kevin Meagher, and Thomas C. O'Brien., eds. *Encyclopedic Dictionary of Religion.* 3 vols. Washington, DC: Corpus Publishers, 1979; Eliade, Mircea, ed., *The Encyclopedia of Religion.* 16 vols. New York: Macmillan, 1987.

Buenaventura, Enrique (1925–)
Colombia

Theatrical director, important in **Latin American liberation theater,** which began in the 1970s, with the purpose of giving a voice and dignity to the poor of Latin America. Through his work he created a unique collaborative dramaturgical style. For example, with his company, Teatro Experimental de Cali (Experimental Theater of Cali), he created a production entitled *Soldados* (The Soldiers) in 1966 about a strike on a Colombian banana plantation set in 1928. He performed his initial draft of the script to a variety of audiences, workers, intellectuals, and peasants, and culled their responses, continually modifying the script to accommodate their suggestions. The final product was a play created by the audience and the actors. Thus, the theatrical event did not impose a point of view on the audience, but, rather, gave them one based on their experience, their reality.

His works are heavily influenced by the theatrical space, more specifically, the space dynamics created between actor and audience. He calls for an active spectator so that the critical awareness of both the audience and the actors is raised by the shared performance experience. Often he uses Latin American stories, myths, and songs as a starting place for the actors' improvisation. Based on these initial ideas, a theater piece is created. Buenaventura's company disbanded in 1990, but his work and his methods continue to be extremely influential in Latin America and throughout the world.

References: Buenaventura, Enrique. *El Arte Nuevo de Hacer Comedias y el Nuevo Teatro.* 5. Cali, Colombia: TEC Publications, n.d.; Gutiérrez, Gustavo. *A Theology of Liberation.* Maryknoll, NY: Orbis, 1973; Versènyi, Adam. *Theatre in Latin America: Religion, Politics, and Culture from Cortés to the 1980's.* New York: Cambridge University Press, 1993; Weiss, Judith A. *Latin American Popular Theatre: The First Five Centuries.* Albuquerque: University of New Mexico Press, 1993.

Bufo
Cuba

Popular satirical theater form that came to Cuba from Paris, where it originated, via Spain during the Ten Years' War (1868–1878). The name comes from the Italian verb meaning "to puff out one's cheek in mockery." As a nationalistic satire, *Bufo* focused on the Cuban reality of the time rather than imitating European culture as theater had done before it. It is related to the Italian **commedia dell'arte,** the popular improvised comedy of the seventeenth century, but uses the Cuban character types of **Género Chico,** a popular operatic form. Chief character types were the unscrupulous Negro and his mulatto girlfriend who often outwits the simpleminded Spanish immigrant. The chief characters were from the lower classes, and situations in the plot allowed them to ridicule and criticize the Spanish upper class. After a period of inactivity, the form has been resurrected and is used in contemporary Cuba to satirize contemporary enemies of the common people.

Bufo is identified by the following characteristics: use of Cuban music (usually a parody), use of both prose and poetry, one-act structure, Cuban setting and Cuban characters, and a *Guaracha* at the end, a Cuban dance in which all actors harmoniously participate.

> **References:** Banham, Martin. *African Theatre Today.* London: Pitman, 1976; Palls, Terry Lee. "The Theatre in Revolutionary Cuba: 1959–1969." Ph.D. diss., University of Kansas, 1974.

Bugaku

Japan

Traditional temple dance brought to Japan from China and Korea in the seventh century A.D. This form of dance was popular with local audiences at shrines and temple festivals. *Bugaku* has many characteristics in common with **Noh,** Japan's classic masked dance-drama, such as wooden masks for performers, costumes rich in color and fabric, and a structure of dance following a set pattern: introduction (*jo*), development (*ha*), and climax (*kyu*). **Noh** drama developed from this form due to court patronage and court tastes for refinement. The dance was performed to a Chinese-inspired musical accompaniment of flutes, drums, lute, zither, and panpipe. It is still performed in Tokyo twice a year.

> **References:** Immoos, Thomas. *Japanese Theatre.* Trans. Hugh Young. Originally published as *Japanisches Theater.* New York: Rizzoli, 1977; Inoura, Yoshinobu, and Toshio Kawatake. *The Traditional Theater of Japan.* New York: Weatherhill in collaboration with Japan Foundation, 1981; Kawatake, Toshio. *Japan on Stage: Japanese Concepts of Beauty as Shown in the Traditional Theatre* (Butai no oku no Nihon). Trans. P. G. O'Neill. Originally published as *Butai No Oku No Nihon.* Tokyo: 3A, 1990; Scott, A. C. *The Theatre in Asia.* New York: Macmillan, 1972.

Bulandra, Lucia Sturdza (1873–1961)

Romania

Romanian actress, theater manager, and teacher, who directed the Bulandra Theater (originally the Municipal Theater) beginning in 1947, when it reopened after being closed during the war. Starting with only nine performers, she created a company of first-rate actors and greatly expanded the size of the company and the number of performances. As an actress she had vitality and charm. She helped many young aspiring playwrights by appearing in their plays. She also had a school for acting, where she taught and encouraged many prominent actors. Her husband, Tony Bulandra (1991–1943), was also a prominent actor.

> **References:** Lamb, Ruth Stanton. *The World of Romanian Theatre.* Claremont, CA: Ocelot, 1976.

Bulgaria

Turkish rule (under the Ottomans) prevailed from 1396–1878 in Bulgaria. Communist rule, with Soviet aid, took power in 1946 and held it until 1991, when a new constitution took effect that was no longer Communist. There is no evidence of either religious or secular theater in medieval Bulgaria. Dramatic activity began in the mid-nineteenth century with some staged dramatic dialogues. Many amateur societies formed and enacted Bulgarian translations of European classics. A schoolmaster, S. I. Dobroplodnij (1820–1894), wrote the first Bulgarian play, *Mikhail*, 1856, and performed it in a cafe using his students as actors. Two of his student actors later became important Bulgarian playwrights, Dobri Vojnikov (1833–1878) and Vasil Drumev (1841–1901), although both emigrated and performed their Bulgarian dramas in exile. Early drama in Bulgaria was a platform for nationalistic pride and patriotic protest against Turkish rule. Directly following liberation from the Turks, theatrical activity increased, and by 1880 there were seven theaters in Bulgaria.

The Rumelian Theater Company, begun in 1881 by Stephen Popov (1854–1920), was the first Bulgarian acting troupe. Other groups following soon after included the Laughter and Tears Company and the Bulgarian National Theater, which opened in 1907. The most prominent playwright of the late nineteenth century was Ivan Vazov (1850–1921), and, though his plays were hastily written, he captured the patriotic fervor surrounding the liberation. During this period European influence finally made its way into Bulgaria, and their dramas were less limited in style in the years following liberation; a few examples are *Vampire*, 1901, by A. Strashimirov (1870–1937), *When the Thunder Rolls*, 1912, by P. K. Iavorav (1877–1914), and the plays of P. K. Todorov (1879–1916), who combined Bulgarian folk tales and songs into modern plays. K. Sarafov was the lead actor at the National Theater from 1915–1920. Russian influence on acting styles increased as many Bulgarian actors began studying at the **Moscow Art Theater.** In 1925 N. O. Massalitinov, who was a Russian actor and formerly director of the Moscow Art Theater's Second Studio, became director of the National Theater in Bulgaria.

Following World War II (1939–1945), Bulgarian theater output increased, partly because of the Soviet influence and the Communist support of the arts. However, with this help came the expectation that the theater would be a propagandistic tool for the Communist Party. Plays like *The Promise*, 1949, by A. Gulyashki, were presented, which dramatized the struggle of loyal Communist workers against foreigners. The Bulgarian State Theater Academy was founded in 1946 to train actors, puppeteers, and directors. When Stalin died in 1953 censorship loosened for a time, and plays critical of Communism and governmental corruption emerged, such as *Fear*, 1956, by T. Genov. However, such freedom was short-lived, and by the 1960s restrictions on the content of plays were in place again. In the 1970s a number of pantomime groups emerged, the most prominent being Studio Pantomime of Velyo Goranov. The breakdown of the Soviet Union in 1990 brought about changes in theater in Bulgaria, inspiring many small experimental groups in Sofia and smaller cities.

In 1990 parliament revoked the dominant role of the Communist Party and created a new constitution in 1991. The majority of creative enthusiasm in Bulgaria after communist control loosened was expressed through folk dancing, ballet,and music. There are also a large number of famous and talented Bulgarian opera singers as well as opera stages.

See also Soviet Union

References: Hartnoll, Phyllis. *The Oxford Companion to the Theatre.* New York: Oxford University Press, 1967; Gradev, Dimiter. *Bulgarian Puppet Theatre.* Sofia: Information Centre, 1979; Shoulov, Iosif. *The Bulgarian Theatre.* Trans. Elena Mladenova. Sofia: Foreign Language Press, 1964; Stefanova-Peteva, Kalina. "Bulgaria." In *The World Encyclopedia of Contemporary Theatre*, ed. Don Rubin, 155–168. New York: Routledge, 1994.

Bulgarian Cinema

The Bulgarian film industry was slow to develop. Its first film, *Bulgarians are Gallant*, did not come out until 1910; it was directed by Vassil Gendov. Gendov and Boris Greshov were two of the first directors in Bulgaria to pioneer the development of cinema. The film industry was nationalized by the Communist government in 1948, which meant that all films were expected to follow the style of filmmaking shaped by **socialist realism** in the Soviet Union. It was not until the mid-1960s that contemporary themes were portrayed on the screen. The first Bulgarian films to reach international success include *Sun and Shadow*, (1962) directed by Rangel Vulchanov and *The Peach Thief*, (1964) directed by Vulo Radev. There is a modern film production studio near Sofia. Directors of note from the 1970s and 1980s include Hristo Hristov, Zako Heskiya, Vulo Radev, and Rangel Vulchanov. The Bulgarian filmmaker Ivan Nichev created *After the End of the World* (1999), which serves largely as a plea for racial and religious tolerance.

References: Katz, Ephraim. *The Film Encyclopedia.* New York: Harper Perennial, 1994.

Bunraku

Japan

Traditional puppet theater with multiple puppeteers. During the second half of the seventeenth century, storytellers, musicians, and puppeteers collaborated on developing a form of puppet theater. In the 1680s a master puppeteer, Takemoto Gidayu, invited a young **Kabuki** playwright, Chikamatsu Monzaemon, to work with him. Their combined mastery over drama and performance elevated this form of puppet theater to high art. By the eighteenth century these puppets, of at least a meter in height, had movable eyes and articulated fingers, and they were able to express a wide range of emotions, from

Performers operate puppets in a Bunraku puppet performance called 1000 Cherry Trees *in Osaka, Japan. (Michael S. Yamashita / Corbis)*

tender love to violent anger. Bunraku peaked in popularity in the middle of the eighteenth century, though it is still performed in Japan as a living national treasure. Each puppet is worked by three puppeteers, all in full view of the audience. All puppeteers are traditionally male. The master puppeteer works the head and the right arm of the puppet. The assistants are dressed in all black, with only a gauze visor in the front of the hood to see through. The first assistant moves the left arm and the second assistant moves the feet. Having three people on each puppet allows for great flexibility of movements and lifelike presence. The trio move the puppet with seeming ease, as though the puppet is pulling them along. Puppets can engage in ferocious battles with swords and acrobatic feats. Puppets can also portray true love through a tender embrace.

The stage for modern Bunraku is 36 feet wide and 25 feet deep, and it requires amazingly tight choreography of the movements of the performers. The master puppeteer wears high clogs, a ceremonial costume with stiff shoulder pieces, and

no covering on his head. The narrator sits right of stage with a script before him. He projects voices for the characters on stage as well as narrating and telling what the characters are thinking. The vocal delivery requires an enormous range of pitch and intensity and is emotionally draining, as the narrator becomes each character. Stories are often domestic tragedies famous for double suicides of ill-fated lovers.

The player of the samisen, a three-stringed instrument, controls the timing of the performance like an orchestra conductor. He cues the other musicians, the puppeteers, and the narrator. He also gives musical expression to the puppet's emotions. The puppet manipulation, the narration, and the samisen music are interlocking elements that cannot be separated from the text of a play. To become a puppeteer, a young man becomes a student of a master puppeteer, whom he serves almost as one would a spiritual master, doing many menial tasks. A master and his students rigorously train with the puppets to gain fluidity and coordination of movement. It takes ten years for each member of a team to learn the aspects of his particular function and thirty years to become a master puppeteer. In the 1890s amateur clubs studying Bunraku became popular. This was the only chance for women to be involved. These clubs help the professional troupes survive, as the clubs would invite a troupe to come and perform and give lessons. The conventions for puppet gestures and movement are rigidly prescribed and are very detailed, including even such a detail as how a hand should approach the forehead.

References: Hironaga, Shuzaburo. *Bunraku: Japan's Unique Puppet Theatre*. Tokyo: Tokyo News Service, 1973; Keene, Donald. *Bunraku: The Art of the Japanese Puppet Theatre*. Tokyo: Kodansha International; New York: Harper & Row, 1973; Scott, A. C. *The Theatre in Asia*. New York: Macmillan, 1972.

Buñuel, Luis (1900–1983)
France, Mexico, Spain, United States
Filmmaker, originally from Spain, but traveled the world for fifty years making films and only occasionally returned to Spain for that purpose, because of the extreme censorship in his home country. Buñuel was heavily influenced by the **surrealism** of Paris in the 1920s. In his early films, pre-1960s, the acting was often overstated and too obvious, but it improved dramatically, as did all other aspects of his ever evolving film style. Certain characteristics of his films are consistent over his expansive film career: a surrealist's view of reality, psychological interest in the workings of the brain and sexuality, and a focus on the brutality of humankind and the hypocrisy of the Roman Catholic Church. Some of his most important films include *Viridiana*, 1961, *Belle de Jour*, 1966, and *The Obscure Object of Desire* 1977.

See also Spanish Cinema
References: Buñuel, Luis. *My Last Breath*. London: Cape, 1984; Mast, Gerald. *A Short History of the Movies*. 4th ed. New York: Macmillan, 1986.

Burbage, James
See Burbage, Richard

Burbage, Richard (1567–1619)
England
Leading English actor of **Elizabethan England**, considered to be the best during his time.

Burbage began acting at the age of eighteen. He was son of the famous James Burbage (1530–1597) who in 1576 erected The Theatre, the first permanent playhouse in **England**, and in 1577 erected the Curtain. In 1597 Richard Burbage and his brother, Cuthbert Burbage (1566–1636), built the Globe Theatre, where they formed a partnership with **Shakespeare**. As the lead actor at the company (called the Chamberlain's Men, which later became the King's Men after James I took the throne), Burbage was the first to enact many of the great Shakespearean roles, such as King Lear, Hamlet, Macbeth, Richard III, and Othello. Physically he was short and stout, but nonetheless, could summon a commanding presence on stage and was extremely versatile.

References: Chinoy, Helen Krich, and Toby Cole. *Actors on Acting*. New York: Crown, 1970; Holmes, Martin Rivington. *Shakespeare and Burbage: The Sound of Shakespeare as Devised to Suit the Voice and Talents of His Principal Player*. London: Phillimore, 1978; Stopes, C. C. *Burbage and Shakespeare's Stage*. London: A. Morning, 1913.

Burma
See Myanmar

Burning Man
United States
Formerly Black Rock Arts Festival; annual arts festival that occurs in the southwestern desert of Nevada; everyone who attends the event in this remote location is a participant. Bizarrely costumed characters stroll through the cluster of recreational vehicles, tents, and camps around the centerpiece, the four-story tall wooden man that will be burned at the climax of the event on the last night. Over its eleven-year evolution, Burning Man has become the largest venue for **performance art** and environmental sculpture in the United States.

This event is a guerrilla action meant to keep anarchy alive for humankind. In the freedom of the desert, participants can play and invent fantasies and games. Nudity and self-adornment of any kind are accepted and experimented with, from caked mud dried on a nude body to blue makeup smeared all over. Cross-dressing and sex-

A fifty-two-foot statue of a man is set on fire during the final day of the Burning Man Festival in Nevada early in September 2000. (AFP/Corbis)

ual freedom are other prominent features. Some participants create theme camps, such as a Christmas camp, in which one man impersonated Santa throughout the entire festival, singing carols and giving out gifts, all the while dressed in a full Santa costume. Improvised interactions between various characters are being created in almost every encounter between costumed participants. The festival lasts over a week, and participants must bring all the water and supplies needed with them. People must also responsibly dispose of all waste they create.

Burning Man can be viewed as an elaborate excuse to party or as a spiritual experience. It is not politically or religiously motivated. Sponsored in part by the Cacophony Society, it is explicitly not commercial. It is rather about creating a society that generates art and expression. Its goal is to make culture something you do rather than something you consume. The symbol of the burning man is left entirely open, a mystery, an experience for each to experience. It is meant to provoke and is purposefully ambiguous.

> **References:** Wieners, Brad. *Burning Man.* San Francisco: Hardwired, 1997.

Burton, Richard (1925–1984)
England, United States, Wales

Actor, originally Richard Walter Jenkins Jr., born in **Wales** to a large coal-mining family. He took the name of his schoolmaster, Philip Burton, who helped him win a scholarship to Oxford. His 1943 stage debut occurred in Liverpool performing *Druid's Rest*. He gained admiration as a fine actor in his London performance of *The Lady's Not for Burning*, by Christopher Fry 1949, and later again in a 1950 Broadway production of the same play. Throughout his career, he alternated between the film and stage acting, and between **England** and the **United States** He portrayed **Shakespeare**'s Hamlet many times through his life, in 1953 with the Old Vic Company, an offshoot of the London Old Vic Theater, at the Edinburgh Festival and in a 1964 Broadway production directed by John Gielgud, which played a record-breaking 185 consecutive productions. Burton gained the status of movie star in the 1963 film *Cleopatra*, in which he co-starred with Elizabeth Taylor, whom he later married. He starred with Taylor again in the film *Who's Afraid of Virginia Woolf?* 1966. In 1977 he starred in the film *Equus*. Though he was nominated for an Academy Award seven times, he never won.

> **References:** Sterne, Richard. *John Gielgud Directs Richard Burton in Hamlet: A Journal of Rehearsals.* New York: Random House, 1963.

Butoh
Japan

Modern dance form in which often naked performers covered in white make-up with heads shaven transform themselves into apparitions from another world through slow movement and an extreme appearance. This style was developed between the 1950s and the 1960s with the choreographers Ohno Kazuo (born in 1906) and Hijikata Tatsumi (1928–1986). In 1972 an actor, Maro Akaji, founded the first *Butoh* troupe and lent a more theatrical organization to *Butoh* style of movement. The goal of much of *Butoh* is for the performers to metamorphose into ghosts and gods from Japanese legends and myths, and to reenact the gestures of the dead as they die their deaths once again. With arms raised and eyes rolled back, performers slowly enact these deaths as though possessed.

References: Brandon, James. *The Cambridge Guide to Asian Theatre*. New York: Cambridge University Press, 1993; Pronko, Leonard Cabell. *Guide to Japanese Drama*. Boston: G. K. Hall, 1984.

C

Cai Luong

Vietnam

Light operetta popular in the 1920s. This form replaced **Hat Boi,** classical opera in the Chinese style, as the most popular entertainment with the Vietnamese people. It is financially self-sufficient, since it enjoys great popular support. The audiences are generally working-class people who idolize the star singer/actors. The famous songs are played on the radio, and the rich and famous performers are regularly written about in the newspapers. *Cai Luong* has evolved into a superior art form. The acting and singing style is highly emotional and is based on music that comes from southern Vietnamese folk songs. These beautiful melodies are charged with strong emotions. The love song *Vong Co,* written by Cao Van Lau in 1920, is still sung many times within every performance. It is a southern melody, but is equally loved in central or northern Vietnam. No actor or actress can establish a name unless able to offer a captivating rendition of this song. The plays are adapted from Hat Boi and are set either in a historical or legendary time, or in contemporary Saigon.

See also *Tuong Tao*

References: Brandon, James R. *Brandon's Guide to Theatre in Asia.* Honolulu: University Press of Hawaii, 1976; Song Ban. *The Vietnamese Theatre.* Hanoi: Languages Publishing House, 1960; Tran Van Khe. *Traditional Theatre in Vietnam.* Edited by James R. Brandon. Paris: UNESCO, 1971.

Cambodia

As a landlocked country, Cambodia has lost portions of its kingdom to expansionist neighbors. In the fourteenth century the Vietnamese state of Annam and in the eighteenth century the kingdom of Siam (Thailand) expanded into Cambodian territory.

A folk dance-drama, **Trott,** which enacts a deer hunt, is a remnant of performances from prehistoric times.

The Cambodian Khmer empire, which flourished from 802 to 1431, built awesome temples centered around its capital, Angkor, Angkor Wat being the most famous. Court entertainers for the Khmer empire developed exquisite forms of entertainment that have greatly influenced performance styles in Thailand, Burma, and Laos. **Lakon Kbach Boran** is a classical dance-drama mostly performed by women that evolved during this rich period for the arts. A masked dance-drama performed by men, **Lakon Khol,** also from this period, is characterized by robust and vigorous acting and dancing. Accompanying live performances of theater and dance is the **Pin Peat,** a traditional musical ensemble. The story most often dramatized is the **Ream Ker,** the Cambodian version of the great Hindu epic tale, the **Ramayana.**

Shadow play theater, in which shadows are cast onto a white muslin screen by cutout puppets has evolved in two forms in Cambodia. **Nang**

At the left a masked performer impersonates Hanuman, the great white monkey, attempting to win the love of a beautiful mermaid (right). Performed by the Royal Cambodian Ballet in a temple near Angkor Wat, Siem Reap, Cambodia. (Photo by Beth Osnes)

Sbek (or Sbek Thom) is a form of shadow play using huge rawhide cutout figures requiring multiple puppeteers behind the screen to manipulate the figures. Just one puppeteer manipulates all of the smaller shadow puppets used in **Nang Sbek Touch** (also known as **Ayang,** or Nang Kaloun).

From the early twentieth century there is a popular dance-drama form, **Lakon Bassak,** performed by Cambodians, with strong Vietnamese influence.

References: Brunet, Jacques. "The Cambodian Nang Sbek and Its Audience." In The Performing Arts in Asia, ed. J. R. Brandon. Paris: UNESCO, 1971; Brunet, Jacques. "The Comic Element in the Khmer Shadow Theatre." In Traditional Drama and Music of Southeast Asia, ed. Mohd. Taib Osman, 27–29. Kuala Lumpur: Dewan Bahasa Dan Pustaka Kementerian Pelajaran Malaysia, 1974; Groslier, George. "Royal Dancers of Cambodia." Asia 22, 1 (1922): 47–53, 74; Meyer, Charles. "Cambodian Dances." Nokor Khmer 3 (1970): 2–27; Mubin, Sheppard. "The Khmer Shadow Play and Its Links with Ancient India." Journal of the Malayan Branch, Royal Asiatic Society 41, 213 (July 1968): 199–204; Royal University of Fine Arts, Cambodia. "Shadow Plays in Cambodia." In Traditional Drama and Music of Southeast Asia, ed. Mohd. Taib Osman, 47–51. Kuala Lumpur: Dewan Bahasa Dan Pustaka Kementerian Pelajaran Malaysia, 1974; Yousof, Ghulam-Sarwar. "Traditional Theatre in South East Asia." Performing Arts 2 (July 1985): 37–49.

Canada

Theatrical activity has long been widely dispersed throughout the sparsely populated enormous land mass that is Canada. The first theatrical activity occurred among the many rich traditions of the indigenous people in this region, mainly in the form of rituals and ceremonies, including the **Eskimo Spirit Play,** the Canadian Pacific Coast Mystery Play and the **Kwakiutl Mystery Play.** Native American tribes and the Inuit were likely performing elaborate dances and dance dramas millennia before European invaders arrived.

The development of European theater in Canada is divided between the French theatrical tradition and the English. The English and the French fought fiercely during the eighteenth century for control of the Canadian colonies, which were rich in resources. The English ultimately won, but there are still many in French-speaking Quebec who want a separate country. The first English-speaking theater to occur in what is now Canada happened in 1583 with entertainers brought from **England** by explorer Sir Humphrey Gilbert, who even entertained the Native Americans. The first French play occurred in 1606, The Theater of Neptune in New France, which had submissive Native American characters within it to assert France's right in this new colony.

Theater in France experienced censorship and condemnation from the Catholic Church as early as the 1690s. Other than small theatrical occurrences by the gentry and dramatic readings at universities, little happened in New France, where the church was very strong; one of the first to attempt to generate some culture in French-speaking Canada was Joseph Quesnel (1746–1809), who wrote and acted for his Théâtre Société (Society Theater) in Montreal in 1789. By the nineteenth century amateur companies were starting, and they often produced patriotic plays about the French overcoming the British. Many notable French actors toured Montreal and Quebec by the end of the nineteenth century. In 1900 Julien Daoust (1866–1943) started Théâtre National (National Theater) in Montreal, where actor Fred Barry (1887–1964) got his start. An amateur company, Montreal Repertory Theatre, ran from 1930 to 1961. In the 1970s many monologists, such as Yvon Deschamps, emerged who spoke a vernacular language known as Joual, which is

French as it is spoken in Quebec. In 1977 Robert Gravel created a form of improvisational theater which he called *Ligue Nationale d'Improvisation* (National Improvisation League), parodying hockey, in which improvising actors competed against one another. The form spread to other parts of Canada, so much so that there was a "World Cup" held in 1985.

Theater in English-speaking Canada was thriving by the eighteenth century. Touring groups and stars from America and England infused excitement and a high standard into the theater scene. The first locally written play to be produced was *Acadius, or Love in a Calm*, 1774, in Halifax. Increasingly theaters were built in the nineteenth century, which inspired more theatrical production. In the next century, however, touring groups from the **United States** began to take the place of local companies. It was not until World War I (1914–1918) that amateur theater began to sprout all over the country. In the early 1930s small art theaters began a theater festival, the Dominion Drama Festival, which included both French and English plays and which lasted until 1970. In 1954 the touring Canadian Players were founded to tour all areas of Canada. Increased national subsidy of the arts in the 1950s, 1960s, and 1970s made possible many professional regional theaters across the country.

It has long been a fact of Canadian theater that many of their best actors move to England or the United States, where there are more opportunities. On the other hand, the **Stratford Festival** began in 1952 and provided good work for the many local actors who remained dedicated to the company over the years, such as **William Hutt**, Mervyn Blake (who performed in forty-one consecutive seasons with the Stratford Festival), Martha Henry, Kate Reid, and Frances Hyland.

Popular theater troupes in Canada have long been instrumental in giving voice to minority and oppressed groups in Canada. Black Theatre Canada was started in Toronto in 1974 by Vera Cudjoe to share the culture of black people with their community. A Canadian black playwright, James Weldon Johnson, wrote *Tight Rope Time*, 1984, for an all-black cast about the struggle of blacks in Nova Scotia to find their place in that culture. Native American actors and playwrights have their works produced at the Tunooniq The-atre in the Northwest Territories. In Toronto a gay company, Buddies in Bad Times, started in 1978.

In the 1980s comedy clubs and improvisational comedy sports (theater games played with sports rules) clubs provided new opportunities for actors. At this time national funding for the arts decreased notably. One financially successful work was *Tamara*, 1978, which was put on by the Necessary Angel company; in this production audience members followed one of the many characters through different rooms to follow branches of the main story. This piece later toured internationally. Another outstanding example of a financially successful theater-circus venture is the **Cirque du Soleil** (Circus of the Sun) from Quebec. In the 1980s many large-scale theaters opened in major cities, such as the Royal Alexandra Theatre in Toronto, in which Broadway and English megamusicals were staged, nearly squeezing out all other competition. The fringe theaters, such as the Chinook Theatre in Edmonton where the first Fringe Festival was held, are managing to survive the competition. The Du Maurier World Stage Festival in Toronto is the largest international festival of contemporary English-language theater in North America. Theater artists such as Robert Lepage presented at the festival in 2000. Theater artists are optimistic about getting more popular support in the twenty-first century.

See also Native American Theater
References: Bains, Y. S. *English Canadian Theatre 1765–1826*. New York: Peter Lang, 1998; Ball, John. *A Bibliography of Canadian Theatre History, 1583–1975*. Toronto: Playwrights Co-op, 1976; Ball, John and Richard Plant. *Bibliography of Theatre History in Canada: The Beginnings Through 1984*. Toronto: ECW Press, 1993; Conolly, L. W. *Canadian Drama and the Critics*. Vancouver: Talonbooks, 1987; Donohoe, Joseph, and Jonathan Weiss, eds. *Essays on Modern Quebec Theatre*. East Lansing: Michigan State University Press, 1995; Leabhart, Thomas, ed. *Canadian Post-Modern Performance*. Claremont, CA: Ponoma College Theatre Department, 1986; Leabhart, Thomas. "Cirque du Soleil." *Mime Journal* (1986): 1–7; Nardocchio, Elaine. *Theatre and Politics in Modern Quebec*. Edmonton: University of Alberta Press, 1986; Robert, Lucie. "The New Quebec Theatre." In *Canadian Canons: Essays in Literary Value*, ed. Robert Lecker, 112–23. Toronto: ECW Press, 1982; Wagner, Anton. *Contemporary Canadian Theatre: New World Visions*. Toronto: Simon & Pierre, 1986.

Canadian Cinema

Although Canada is the second-largest country in land mass, it has a relatively small population, and the amount of its film production has been very sparse until recent decades. Because of the enormous outpouring of films in the **United States** and its influence on Canada, with whom it shares a border, Canada has barely tried to compete with the glamour and big budgets of Hollywood. The documentary film is one area in which Canada has excelled, beginning in the early 1900s. The establishment of the Film Board of Canada in 1939 gave Canada a boost as one of the top countries in the production of documentaries, especially during World War II (1939–1945). Canada's first feature film was *Evangeline* in 1914, followed by the successful film *The Viking* in 1931.

Throughout the 1940s and 1950s feature films were seldom made and poorly attended. Many talented Canadian actors and directors migrated to the United States and Great Britain, where they found more opportunities and better compensation. The Canadian Film Development Corporation was established in 1967, which greatly increased feature film production, yet did little to improve the quality, with the exception of *The Apprenticeship of Duddy Kravitz* in 1974, directed by Ted Kotcheff about a young Jewish man in Montreal trying to get rich. There has been a steady exodus of Canadian comedians to the United States, such as Martin Short and John Candy (1950–1994).

In the late 1980s a few films emerged that received both domestic and international attention, such as the French-language film *Jesus of Montreal*, 1989, starring Lothaire Bluteau and directed by Denys Arcand. Other important Canadian directors include Lea Pool, Gail Singer, Jean Pierre Lefebvre, and Guy Maddin. Most recently the Egyptian immigrant Atom Egoyan has put Canadian film on the map with his devastatingly heartfelt film, *Sweet Hereafter*, 1997, which was nominated for best film at the Academy Awards. The Canadian actress Sara Polley acted in that and others of Egoyan's films, but like so many other actors, she has since moved on to Hollywood films.

See also U.S. Cinema
References: Jones, Kent. "Body and Soul: The Cinema of Atom Egoyan." *Film Comment* 34 (January-February 1998): 32–39; Katz, Ephraim. *The Film Encyclopedia.* New York: Harper Perennial, 1994; Porton, Richard. "Film Reviews: 'Felicia's Journey.'" *Cineaste* 25 (December 1999): 42–43.

Canevas
Italy

A short outline of a plot that could be used for performances of **commedia dell'arte,** improvised sixteenth- and seventeenth-century Italian comedy.

References: Rudlin, John. *Commedia Dell'Arte: An Actor's Handbook.* London and New York: Routledge, 1994.

Cantinflas (1911–1993)
Mexico

Famous comedian and clown, often referred to as the Mexican **Charlie Chaplin**, who rose from **Carpas,** a form of improvised street theater, to great fame. He could imitate various Mexican stereotypes, often satirizing class consciousness. He was known for linguistic style and could masterfully impersonate the meaningless drivel of those full of themselves. He went on to enjoy a wildly successful movie career.

The great Mexican clown Cantinflas (left) in Around the World in Eighty Days *(1956) (Kobol Collection/United Artists)*

References: Versènyi, Adam. *Theatre in Latin America: Religion, Politics, and Culture from Cortés to the 1980's.* New York: Cambridge University Press, 1993.

Cantonese Opera
See Kwangtung Hsi

Cantonese Rod Puppet Theater
China

Rod puppet theater of Kwangtung Province, originating during the reign of the eighth-century Tang dynasty emperor, **Ming Huang.** These rod puppets have enjoyed great popularity in the last few centuries, as patrons vie for troupes to perform for important ceremonies and festivals. There are two types of rod puppets in Kwangtung Province. The first type has a life-size head with movable eyes, mouth, nose, and ears. The rod extends from the puppet's neck to about waist level on the puppet. The puppeteer's right hand holds this main rod and manipulates facial movement from pegs near the bottom of the rod. The puppeteer's left hand manipulates both arms by rods attached to the puppet's hands, which extend downward and in front of the puppet. This kind of manipulation requires great strength and flexibility. The puppeteer stands below and behind the puppet. He must hold it upright for long periods of time, which is very tiring. To evoke the walking style of each puppet character, the puppeteer will actually walk like that character behind the screen, tiny steps for female puppets and robust strides for male puppet characters. The second type of rod puppet has the whole head, neck, and torso carved from one piece of wood. The arms are the only part of the puppet that moves. A long pole extends from the torso and is held by the left hand, leaving the right hand to manipulate the rods attached to the hands. Both types of rod puppet theater use opera scripts (see **Peking Opera**). The movement style for the puppets also mimics the conventions for the Peking Opera.

References: Stalberg, Roberta Helmer. *China's Puppets.* San Francisco: China Books, 1984.

Capitano
Italy

Spanish braggart, a stock character in **commedia dell'arte,** improvised sixteenth- and seventeenth-century comedy. Either a mercenary or an officer, Capitano was always a comic warrior. He stood with his feet wide apart and his chest out, and walked with large strides. His black leather half mask sported a long phallic nose. Along with his official uniform, he wore huge boots and carried a long sword.

References: Craig, Edward Gordon. "The Characters of the Commedia Dell'Arte." *The Mask* (January 1912); Rudlin, John. *Commedia Dell'Arte: An Actor's Handbook.* London and New York: Routledge, 1994.

Caribbean Theater

An account of Caribbean theater is almost completely an account of displaced people, the British, Spanish, French, and Dutch and the West African slaves, and not of the indigenous populations inhabiting the islands before foreign invasion, since the native populations on most islands were annihilated by unfamiliar diseases and by being forced into hard labor. The European settlers created huge plantations upon which they grew predominantly sugar. Labor was provided cheaply by slaves captured from West Africa. After the slaves were emancipated in the nineteenth century, other waves of immigrants arrived on the Caribbean shores with hopes of opportunity and great wealth, chiefly the Indians, Portuguese, Chinese, and Syrians.

With such a richly varied and often volatile mixture of people, theatrical activity was naturally sporadic and largely a foreign import of traveling troupes and performers throughout the seventeenth and eighteenth centuries. Amateur groups performing classics from their country of origin were also popular for an elite sector of the population. The black slaves attempted to retain their traditional performances as best they could in their new controlled environment. Elements of African performance styles emerged from underground, where these activities were forced by the white Christian minority, when these countries struggled in the twentieth century to form a theater that would be a true national expression of each country. Blacks make up the majority of the population in most Caribbean countries.

Accounts of the history of theater in the Caribbean focus predominantly upon the sparse and artistically uninteresting activities of the white minority, since these activities are documented. Documentation of Black Caribbean activities tended to come later in the twentieth century and then primarily focused on dance. Once the slaves were freed, many European theatrical forms were taken over by the black majority and transformed to express their enthusiasm for freedom. In **Jamaica** there is the Christmas tradition of parading through the streets in costume, known as **Jonkonnu,** which appears to be a mixture of European mumming and West African masquerades. The 200-year-old pre-Lenten Trinidad carnival was imported by the French in the 1780s. Masked costumed revelers performed songs, dances, and dramatics while parading down the streets. Once slavery was abolished, the black masses took over the festival and defended their right to perform in it, even to the death at times.

The popular theater of the Caribbean featured many revue-style shows, especially popular in **Cuba** before the Communist revolution, and in Jamaica in the form of the Christmas morning concerts. Solo comic performers also met with great success throughout the Caribbean. Henry G. Murray of Jamaica delivered comic stories about the customs and manners of his time in the mid-nineteenth century. Even at the present in Trinidad and Tobago individual performers of a unique form known as the Trinidad Calypso enact contemporary events in song.

Political independence came to most of the Caribbean in the 1960s, and with it a sense of nationalism and a desire to express the distinctive cultural experience of the area. Forms of expression that relied on Caribbean modes of expression, with Caribbean characters and settings, were and still are being developed in theater groups such as the Grupo Teatro Escambray in Cuba, The Theatre Guild of Guyana, The Little Theatre Movement of Jamaica, and the Trinidad Theatre Workshop.

See also Barbados; Dunham, Katherine; Haiti

References: Banham, Martin. *African Theatre Today.* London: Pitman, 1976; Bennett Wycliffe. "The Jamaican Theatre: A Preliminary Overview." *Jamaica Journal* 8, 2–3 (Summer 1974): 3–9; Fowler, Henry. "A History of Theatre in Jamaica." *Jamaica Journal* 2, 1 (March 1968): 53–59; Franklin, Lillian Cleamons. "The Image of the Black in the Cuban Theater: 1913–1965." Ph.D. diss., Ohio State University, 1982; Gibbons, Rawle A. "Traditional Enactments of Trinidad—Towards a Third Theatre." Master's thesis, University of the West Indies, 1979; Hill, Errol. *The Jamaican Stage: 1655–1900.* Amherst: University of Massachusetts Press, 1992.

Carpas
Mexico

Popular improvised theater of the nineteenth and twentieth century, often performed in a *carpa,* which is the name for a tent on a street corner or vacant lot. Itinerant performers move their collapsible stages from one town to the next, performing shows consisting of songs, skits and comedy to a lower- and middle-class audience. Plots are based on recent events or current topics of interest, and the mood of performances is determined by the subject matter. The audience and performers are able to directly relate to each other in this relaxed informal performance setting. Performers support themselves by charging a small entrance fee for their shows. Now most *Carpas* troupes have been absorbed into variety shows or circuses. As Mexico City becomes larger and more cosmopolitan, remaining *Carpas* performances are in more obscure corners of the city, but they are still an important means of expression for the common people.

A succession of famous clowns has evolved out of the *Carpas,* one of the best known being **Cantinflas,** who performed on stage and screen.

References: Versènyi, Adam. *Theatre in Latin America: Religion, Politics, and Culture from Cortés to the 1980's.* New York: Cambridge University Press, 1993; Weiss, Judith A. *Latin American Popular Theatre: The First Five Centuries.* Albuquerque: University of New Mexico Press, 1993.

Catharsis
See Poetics

Cenaculo
Philippines

Enactment of the Passion of Christ during the Holy Week, which evolved from the **Auto Sacramentale** of Spain and from the Passion Plays in Mexico. This performance usually lasts all through

Holy Week, the week preceding Easter, during which the events leading up to the resurrection of Christ from the dead are celebrated. The Last Supper, the crucifixion and the resurrection are all portrayed realistically. The person portraying Christ drags a cross through the street and is raised onto the erected cross. There are no professionally trained actors. All parts and crowd scenes are performed by villagers. The role of Christ, as well as the other principal roles, is handed down in one family. Special areas in the village are designated for the performance, but almost the whole village is traveled through by the time all of the processions and enactments are completed.

References: Aveilana, Dassy H. "The Native Theatre." *Philippine Quarterly* 1, 4 (March 1952): 60–62; Brandon, James R. *Brandon's Guide to Theatre in Asia.* Honolulu: University Press of Hawaii, 1976; Espino, F. L. "A Literal Imitation of Christ." In *Filipino Heritage: The Making of a Nation,* ed. Alfredo R. Roces, pp. 1230–1232. Manila: Lahing Pilipino Publishing, 1977; Leon, Walfrido De. "The Passion and the Passion Play in the Philippines." *College Folio* (December 1910): 55–64; Mendoza, Liwaway. "Lenten Rites and Practices." *Drama Review* 21, 3 (September 1977): 21–32.

Ceylon

See Sri Lanka

Champmeslé, Marie Desmares (1642–1698)

France

Famous French actress known as La Champmeslé, who was the leading actress of the **Comédie Française** from the time she first performed the title role in *Phèdre,* by Jean Baptiste Racine (1639–1699), in 1680, until her death. With her melodious and highly expressive voice, she established the declamatory, almost chant-like, style of acting used in performing classical tragedies. She was adored for her beauty, wit, and charm; even Racine fell under her spell and in 1670 wrote for her the play *Bérénice.* Her husband, Charles Chevillet Champmeslé was also a fine tragic actor, but his fame was overshadowed by his wife's overwhelming popularity.

References: Chinoy, Helen Krich, and Toby Cole. *Actors on Acting.* New York: Crown, 1970; Collins,

Charles William. *Great Love Stories of the Theatre: A Record of Theatrical Romance.* New York: Duffield, 1911.

Changkuk

Korea

Theatrical form with singing, dancing, and some dialogue, based on **Pansori,** a one-woman dramatization of narrative tales. Having actors and actresses take on all of the roles in a full dramatic fashion became popular with middle-class audiences in the cities in the early part of the twentieth century. Scenery is used to indicate where the action is taking place in the play. The repertory is drawn from the Pansori tales. *Changkuk* is no longer in fashion and is rarely performed.

References: Brandon, James R. *Brandon's Guide to Theatre in Asia.* Honolulu: University Press of Hawaii, 1976; Hur, Soon-Ja. "The Development of Professional Resident Theatre Companies in South Korea from the Conclusion of the Korean War." Ph.D. diss., Ann Arbor, MI: Proquest, 1991; Shim, Jung Soon. "Trends in Contemporary Culture: In Search of Diversity—Korean Theatre in the 1980's." *Korean Culture (Hanguk Munhwa)* 12, 3 (Fall 1991): 4.

Chao Tan (1915–1980)

China

Chinese film actor, grew up in Nantung. He acted on the stage and in many films before the movie *Crossroads* in 1937 made him a star. After that he remained high in the ranks of the Chinese film industry. He joined the Communist Party in 1958. However, the Red Guard ended his career because he resisted the commands of **Chiang Ching,** the wife of **Mao Tse-tung.**

References: Leyda, Jay. *Dianying: An Account of Films and the Film Audience in China.* Cambridge, MA: MIT Press, 1972.

Chaplin, Charlie (1889–1977)

England, United States

Actor, director, and writer for film, who created a universally loved tramp character who could induce both uproarious laughter and bittersweet pathos. Born in London, Chaplin lived as a destitute street urchin as a boy until he joined a troupe

Charlie Chaplin in The Tramp *(1915) (Kobol Collection/ Essenay)*

of child dancers and then performed in the theater. He was in the premiere of *Peter Pan* in 1904. Chaplin toured Europe and the **United States** with the Fred Karno company and was then discovered by American moviemakers. His first film, *Making a Living*, 1913, was not a success, but in his second film, *Kid Auto Races at Venice*, 1914, he began to develop the tramp character that later brought him fame. *The Tramp*, 1915, was Chaplin's first masterpiece, featuring the resilient vagabond character, who was both elegant and pathetic. Chaplin's talent lay in his ability to express a wide range of emotions and situations through pantomime. He moved often with the grace of a dancer but with the comic timing of a consummate comedian. In *The Kid*, 1921, and *The Gold Rush*, 1925, he infused more bittersweet sadness into his comedy. Even after the advent of sound, Chaplin continued to make silent films such as *City Lights*, 1931, since it was the medium to which his talents were best suited. However, with the advent of sound, Chaplin added to his roles as director, actor, and writer the task of composing and directing the scores for his films, such as *Modern Times*, 1936.

His personal character was scrutinized by the U.S. government during the McCarthy era because of the pacifist message in many of his films, because he had never become an American citizen, and because of his questionable morality. He had a penchant for marrying lovely teenagers, and in his four marriages, he married two sixteen-year-olds, a nineteen-year-old and, when he was fifty-four, the eighteen-year-old Oona O'Neill, daughter of playwright **Eugene O'Neill**. In 1952 he was not allowed back in the United States, and he settled in Switzerland. He continued making films, but none reached his former level of popularity or artistic achievement.

References: Maland, Charles. *Chaplin and American Culture: The Evolution of a Star Image.* Princeton, NJ: Princeton University Press, 1989; Manvell, Roger. *Chaplin.* Boston: Little Brown, 1974; Robinson, David. *Chaplin, His Life and Art.* New York: McGraw-Hill, 1985; Tyler, Parker. *Chaplin, Last of the Clowns.* New York: Vanguard Press, 1948.

Chau
India

Masked dance-drama, which developed in the seventeenth and eighteenth centuries under patronage of the royal courts. *Chau* is performed annually in April at the Chaitra Parva festival, which honors **Ardhanarishwara,** the form of the Hindu god **Shiva** portrayed as half man, half woman. The entire village of Seraikella (now part of Bihar) participates in worship and festivities during the festival, and *Chau* is performed during the last four days.

A *Chau* performance is made up of many dance-dramas, each lasting seven to ten minutes. Actors portray animals, birds, planets, trees, and seasons. Actors wear masks and do not speak or sing. Dances vary from being made up of simple dance steps to a sophisticated type of symbolic interpretation of the narrative involving difficult dance movements, which reveal inner tension through body expression. Actors can evoke a storm at sea by swaying on the level stage. Their spiral steps, whirlwind turns, and huge leaps create the feeling of a storm. The masked performer sometimes lengthens a dance, if he feels able to, by cuing the instrumentalist with a nod of his head.

The clay masks are simple, with a flat surface painted in pastel colors. Distinguishing character features are indicated on the mask subtly. A curl of the lip or a slight squint of the eyes is enough to evoke the character. Costumes are made of glittery material. Masculine characters wear full pants with a wrap around their chests, and feminine characters wear beautiful skirts with decorated shirts, jewelry, or scarves. Some characters have headpieces or other additions to indicate who they are. The sun god, for example, has a cutout of a circle with a star burst inside of it attached to his back.

The music comes from songs by famous Indian poets. The words of the songs are discarded, but the narrative content still comes out through the melody and rhythm.

Practitioners of *Chau* believe that only men have enough stamina to perform this dance-drama. Performers come from all social classes and are generally supported by the court. Training is rigorous for *Chau* performers. They must be agile and have great bodily control and incredible stamina. They must be able to evoke many different kinds of walks, from the walk of a cow while urinating to the walk of a bear. The feet and legs must be very evocative to communicate in a language of gestures and movement.

References: Gargi, Balawanta. *Folk Theater of India.* Seattle: University of Washington Press, 1966; Vatsyayan, Kapila. *Traditional Indian Theatre: Multiple Streams.* New Delhi: National Book Trust, 1980.

Chekhov, Anton (1860–1904)
Russia

One of the greatest Russian playwrights of all time. His plays give a heartfelt, tragic picture of Russian society at the end of the nineteenth century. He observed and expressed human behavior in all its subtleties with amazing accuracy. His plays, peopled by such unhappy characters, avoid being completely despairing because of the warmth with which he treats the characters. A doctor by profession, Chekhov gained success as a playwright later in life. He was greatly popular as a writer of short stories and began his writing of plays with comic one-acts. Chekhov's *The Sea Gull* flopped miserably in 1896 in an old-fashioned mounting of this play, but in 1898, under the direction of **Vladimir Ivanovich Nemirovich-Danchenko** at the **Moscow Art Theater** (MAT),

the same play was wildly received because the MAT could give it the psychological realistic acting it needed to be understood in all its subtleties. The MAT had evolved the perfect style for acting Chekhov with the help of **Konstantin Stanislavsky** and Nemirovich-Danchenko. In 1899 the MAT premiered *Uncle Vanya*, a bitterly sad but gentle play, and it also was a hit. *Three Sisters* was first produced at the MAT in 1901. When Chekhov was stuck in the Crimea fighting a case of tuberculosis, the MAT took their tour to him so that he could witness mountings of *The Sea Gull* and *Uncle Vanya*. It was during this time he first saw and admired the actress Olga Knipper, whom he later married. In 1904 the MAT produced *The Cherry Orchard*, and it immediately became his most popular play. Chekhov was impressed with the manner in which the MAT brought his plays to life, but he sometimes took them to task for the level of realism they sought, such as actors swatting at mosquitoes in *The Cherry Orchard*, or the sound of horse hoofs on a wooden bridge rendered so realistically.

Chekhov's plays have had such resilience through time because of the truthfulness with which they portray the difficulty of human communication, wasted dreams, and the monotony of life for ordinary people. His influence on dramatic literature and modern theater has been immense.

See also Chekhov, Mikhail

References: Chekhov, Anton, *Dear Writer, Dear Actress: The Love Letters of Anton Chekov and Olga Knipper,* Hopewell, NJ: Ecco, 1997; Katzer, Julius, *A. P. Chekhov,* Moscow: Foreign Language Publishing House, 1960; Pitcher, Harvey, *Chekhov's Leading Lady: A Portrait of the Actress Olga Knipper,* New York: F. Watts, 1980; Slonim, Marc. *Russian Theater, From the Empire to the Soviets,* Cleveland: World, 1961.

Chekhov, Mikhail (1891–1955)
Russia

Russian actor, acting teacher, theater director, and nephew of the playwright, **Anton Chekhov**. Joining the **Moscow Art Theater** at the age of nineteen, Chekhov began his acting career as a student of the **Stanislavsky** System, but took his own direction toward more reliance on the imagination. An outstanding craftsman, he put a level of intensity into his roles that sometimes bordered on pathological, yet he was always in control. He was irresistible when performing the tragic humor in his uncle's plays. He played an amazing diversity of roles. With each he was relentless in his search for the truth of the character.

In 1922 Chekhov and Boris Sushkevich took over a smaller experimental theater associated with the Moscow Art Theater, the First Studio, and by 1924 it became its own separate theater, The Second Moscow Art Theater. It was here that Chekhov taught young actors, and it was here, in 1924–1925, that he portrayed Hamlet as being so despairing that he bordered on derangement.

His spiritual idealism in the theater made his philosophy objectionable to Communist authorities. Chekhov left Russia for France and later moved to the **United States**, where he continued performing on the stage and in some Hollywood movies. In Hollywood Chekhov performed in several films, including *Spellbound* (1945), *Spectre of the Rose* (1946) and *Rhapsody* (1954).

> **References:** Black, Lendley. *Mikhail Chekhov as Actor, Director, and Teacher.* Ann Arbor, MI: UMI Research Press, 1987; Slonim, Marc. *Russian Theater, From the Empire to the Soviets,* Cleveland: World, 1961.

Chiang Ching and Mao Tse-tung, 1936 (Archive Photos)

Chiang Ching (1914–1991)
China

Wife of **Mao Tse-tung,** film actress, and member of "Gang of Four" during **Chinese Cultural Revolution.** She was a film actress in Shanghai during the 1930s, but not very successful. Her first marriage, 1934–1937, was to a film critic in Shanghai. Using the stage-name Lan Ping, she performed small roles in the films *Scenes of City Life* in 1935 and *Blood on Wolf Mountain* in 1936. When the war against Japan broke out in 1937 she made propaganda films. During this time she met Mao, became his mistress, and then his second wife. Mao gave her great political power. She personally selected all works to be considered revolutionary. All other works were condemned on moral grounds. Many theatrical artists, some whom she had a personal vendetta against, underwent severe persecution. By 1965 she had suppressed the last **Peking Opera** performance and replaced it with revolutionary drama. She was on the Central Steering Committee for the Film Industry. Through her work on this committee she system-

atically avenged herself on anyone in the industry with whom she had bad relations. Ultimately she was responsible for closing China's film studios in 1966. After Mao's death and the end of the Cultural Revolution in 1976, she was tried by the people and punished for all the atrocities committed during the Cultural Revolution. She reportedly committed suicide in jail on May 14, 1991.

Childress, Alice (1920–1994)
United States

Actress, playwright, and director. Childress grew up in Harlem, New York, and was active in theater from a early age. Childress gained theatrical experience first with the New York Negro Unit of the Federal Theater Project at the Lafayette Theater in Harlem during the late 1930s. She wrote, directed and acted for the **American Negro Theater**, also in Harlem. There she performed in Abram Hill's *On Striver's Row* (1941) and Theodore Browne's *Natural Man* (1941). Perhaps her most notable performance was in *Anna Lucasta* (1944) by Philip Yordan. Her *Gold Through the Trees* (1952), a musical review, was the first time an African American woman was professionally produced. Her play *Trouble in Mind* (1955) is about a veteran black actress refusing to play an insulting stereotypical role as a "darkie" in a play. She also wrote *Wedding Band* (1972–1973).

See also **African American Theater**
References: Jennings, La Vinia Delois. *Alice Childress.* New York: Twayne, 1995.

Chile

Before the Spanish took control of Chile in the mid-1530s, indigenous populations included the Araucanian people in the south and peoples under the influence of the Inca empire in the north. Little is know of theatrical activity before colonization, after which theater popular in Spain at that time was performed sporadically in the major cities of Valparaiso, Santiago, and Concepción. There were probably also religious performances of the Loa, **Auto Sacramentale,** and **Sainete,** all originally from Spain.

During the eighteenth and nineteenth centuries, a performance form called *Tonadilla* throve, a lively mixture of dance, music, and some dramatic sketches. This new form of musical folklore satirized public affairs. It mixed rural and urban musical elements to create a new form for its popular audience. In the beginning of the nineteenth century a popular form of entertainment was the **Chingana,** a kind of irreverent comic performed by the common people to satirize their colonial oppressors. This form was resurrected and further developed in the 1970s. A phenomenon known as the Workers Theatre Movement lasted from about 1912 to 1933. From 1880 to 1930, nitrate mines partially owned by British companies brought many poor workers out into the northern desolate parts of Chile. Miserable working conditions inspired those influenced by socialist ideas to organize cultural outlets to educate the workers and inform them of their human rights. By 1931 there were fifteen amateur theater groups in the city of Iquique alone, all doing performances by and for the workers. This movement took off throughout Chile—workers enacting their own vision of how they believed their world should be.

Attempts to search for a "national soul" of Chile were first made by a group of writers referred to as the "Generation of 1927," with dramas by such authors as Germán Luco Cruchaga (1894–1936). This search was kept alive in Chile through the rest of the twentieth century by theater groups such as Teatro Experimental.

When the glory of **Argentina**'s theater began to fade in the 1940s, the hot spot for South American theater became Santiago, Chile. The famous actress Margarita Xirgu (1888–1969) left Spain in the 1930s and began an acting school in Santiago, giving a foreign influence and her great expertise to local actors. Her school later merged with the Teatro Nacional (National Theater). Two important theatrical institutions in the development of theater in Chile have been Instituto del Teatro de la Universidad de Chile (The Theater Insitute of the University of Chile), founded in 1941 by Pedro de la Barra (1912–1976), and Teatro de Ensayo (Test Theater), founded in 1943 by Pedro Mortheiru (1919–1994) and Fernando Debesa (whose actors toured to Paris and Madrid in 1961).

Latin American liberation theater, theater aimed at giving a voice and dignity to the poor of Latin America, attained great expression in Chile in the late 1960s and 1970s. The government under Eduardo Frei Montalva, 1964–1970, and Salvador Allende Gossens, 1970–1973, subsidized an enormous amount of university theater that addressed the needs of the urban and rural poor. Many socially conscious theater pieces were televised.

All that freedom and idealism ended abruptly in 1973 with the installation of the brutal Augusto Pinochet Ugarte regime in 1973. Covert acts of censorship, such as the anonymous burning of a theater producing politically critical plays, and overt mass killings occurred under this regime, which lasted until the 1980s. Some theater artists fled, such as Alejándro Sieveking and Bélgica Castro, leaders of the Chilean troupe **Teatro del Angel.** Other theater artists continued progress in Chile under this government. For the most part, performances were forced out of theaters and into church basements, neighborhoods, and demonstrations in which the actors became the oppressed, telling their own stories in an artful way.

In 1988 the Pinochet rule officially ended, bringing to a close seventeen years of military dictatorship. Prospects for theatrical artists appear to be good, and many of them, such as Alejándro Sieveking, easily step from the theater to television and film.

The work of Alfredo Castro has succeeded in infusing new direction in contemporary theater in Chile with his nonrealistic plays *Historia de la Sangre* (Story of Blood) (1992) and *Los Dias Tuertos* (Twisted Days) (1993). Throughout the 1990s Andrés del Bosque has directed Teatro Circo Imaginario (Imaginary Circus Theater) and performed as a clown. The group has achieved prominence through its trademark of highly skilled dramatic spectacles. In film, Patricio Guzmán created *Chile, Memoria Obstinada* (Chile, Obstinate Memory) (1995), a document providing a striking portrait of recent historical events in Chile and the aftermath.

References: Boyle, Catherine M. *Chilean Theater, 1973–1985: Marginality, Power, Selfhood.* Cranbury, NJ: Associated University Presses, 1992; Chanan, Michael. *Chilean Film.* London: British Film Institute, 1976; Hautzinger, Sarah. "Chile: Street Theater Takes Risks." *NACLA Report on the Americas* 21, 4 (July–August 1987): 10–11; Thomas, Charles Philip. "Chilean Theater in Exile: The Teatro del Angel in Costa Rica 1974–1984." *Latin American Theatre Review* 19, 2 (Spring 1986): 97–101; Versènyi, Adam. *Theatre in Latin America: Religion, Politics, and Culture from Cortés to the 1980's.* New York: Cambridge University Press, 1993.

China

Theater in China flourished for centuries during times of unchanged social order. As one of the oldest civilizations in the world, China had a tradition of dynastic rule that lasted from 2000 B.C. until the beginning of the twentieth century. It was predominantly an agrarian nation, and the life of the common person changed little as feuding families and even outside invasions conquered and declared their own dynasties. The opulent courts of the royal families patronized a host of theatrical entertainers. In the nineteenth century, the old civilization collapsed under pressure from western influences, internal population growth, and colonial infiltration. Theater and film in China changed drastically under the Communist government. All of the arts were expected to promote and support the ideals of the revolution,

and they were to be about and for the common person.

The leading religions in China are **Buddhism,** Taoism, and various forms of ancestor worship. Confucianism has been the dominant code of conduct since the fourth century B.C. This ethical code discourages the mingling of the sexes, making it impossible for males and females to perform in theater together. A long tradition of female impersonators, who perfected their art, believing they surpassed actual women in their understanding the feminine mystique, grew out of this custom. Homosexuality became an acknowledged part of being a **Wakashù,** a young boy who impersonated female characters. For this reason, among others, the social rank of the actor was looked down upon in society.

The **Chinese New Year** holiday was an important source of employment for actors. During this season farmers found their only chance during the year to relax and enjoy some entertainment. Elders in each village would arrange for troupes to come and perform in temporary structures.

Ming Huang, an eighth-century emperor of the Tang Dynasty (A.D. 618–907), was a dedicated patron of the arts. He started the first official training school for actors, the **Pear Garden,** in the eighth century to train court entertainers. This establishment of a school and his royal patronage contributed greatly to the development of later Chinese forms.

During Mongol rule in China, 1279–1368, Chinese scholars who were denied any other employment turned to drama to make a living. They created **Yuan Chu** (or Yuan Drama) which featured singing, dialogue, and stories ranging in theme from romances to supernatural tales. Another form of drama existing during this time was **Kun Chu,** classical drama from the south of China. These refined and elite dramas had over forty acts and took days to perform. **Li Yu** was a poet and theater practitioner in the seventeenth century who performed dramas for wealthy patrons. Because he traveled with women who were in his troupe, he was viewed as having loose morals.

The Chinese theatrical form most well known throughout the world is the **Peking Opera.** This highly refined opera reached its peak of expression in the nineteenth century as an indivisible synthesis of music, the spoken word, and gestures. In the late 1800s, the Empress Dowager **Cixi,** last ruler of the Ching Dynasty, regularly supported the arts by ordering Peking Opera performances for palace entertainment. Plays are divided into two categories, *Wen,* civil plays, and *Wu,* military plays. The main attraction in Peking Opera is the actors, who are always male and who always portray a certain type of character their whole life. The categories are **Sheng,** or male characters, **Tan,** or female characters, **Hualian,** robust male characters, **Chou,** comic characters, and **Ching,** painted face superhero characters. Actors must master vocal techniques, acrobatics, and the technique for manipulating **Water Sleeves,** which are white silk cuffs that hang down about two feet. The graceful movement of manipulating the cuffs up around the wrist and then letting them fall down to full length is used by the actors to enhance dramatic expression.

Mei Lan Fang was the most famous Peking Opera actor in the twentieth century. Known as "King of the Pear Garden," he nearly perfected the art of portraying the Tan by mimicking the gait of a traditional Chinese woman with bound feet (see **Foot Binding**). He trained at a famous private acting school named **Fu Lien Ch'eng.**

A rich variety of puppet theater has flourished in China alongside the human theater throughout the centuries. Since the eighth century, the **Cantonese Rod Puppet Theater** from the Kwangtung Province has delighted audiences with puppets featuring movable eyes, mouth, nose, and ears. In northern China another form of rod puppet theater developed known as **Zhang Mu.** An interesting variety of this type of puppet theater is **Da Mu Nao,** the largest type featuring puppets with large wooden skulls. The tradition of **Fu Tai Hsi** originated in the south of China in the sixteenth century. The master puppeteer, **Tou,** performs all the major roles in the drama, doing all the speaking, singing, and manipulation for the characters he represents. His assistant or apprentice, **Er,** performs all of the remaining minor roles. Also from the south of China is **Jia-li Xi,** the string puppet theater.

One of the earliest forms of Chinese shadow theater is **Qiao-Ying Xi,** a human shadow play performed during the Sung Dynasty, 960–1279. A puppet form of shadow theater still is performed

in China today by the name of **Pi-ying Xi.** Colorful shadows created by painted translucent rawhide shadow figures are cast onto the screen, which is called *Ying-chuana.*

The twentieth century in China witnessed two other significant evolutions in theater. In 1907 Chinese students studying in Japan began a new form of spoken drama, **Hua Chü,** which they used as a medium for social change toward more liberal ideals. Also, in 1934 the **China Traveling Dramatic Troupe** was founded as an artists' cooperative to present modern drama by a self-sufficient working troupe.

The triumph of the Chinese Communist revolution in the twentieth century brought enormous changes for the theater and film industry in China. **Mao Tse-tung** led the Communist Party from 1943 to 1976 and was an influential political theorist. He believed that all art should serve and promote the revolution. Accessibility of the arts to all people was another of Mao's goals for the arts. The **Chinese Cultural Revolution,** led by Mao and his wife, **Chiang Ching,** ravaged and shook China from 1966 to 1976. The officially sanctioned Red Guard openly humiliated and punished scholars and artists in an effort to rid China of any elitist practices remaining from their feudal past. The Cultural Revolution ended with Mao's death in 1976, but Communism is still the ruling form of government in China.

Mao's wife, Chiang Ching, was a not very successful movie actress in her earlier years. Thus, when she was given political power in directing the cultural changes in the arts, she personally avenged herself on any enemies in the film industry. A talented film actor, **Chao Tan,** was one actor whose career ended because of Chiang Ching. Other talented film performers include **Ruan Ling,** an actress from 1910 to 1935 who developed an original blend of naturalism and stylization in her acting style, and **Pai Yang,** an actress of stage and film who helped raise the status of women in Chinese society. The Chinese film industry has regained a firm standing since the Cultural Revolution, but it continues to be subject to government censorship.

References: Howard, Roger. *Contemporary Chinese Theatre.* Hong Kong: Heinemann, 1978; Hsu, Tao-Ching. *The Chinese Conception of the Theatre.* Seattle: University of Washington Press, 1985; Hymes,

Jo Ann. *Asia through Film: An Annotated Guide to Films in the University of Michigan Audio-Visual Education Center.* Ann Arbor: Center for Japanese Studies, University of Michigan, 1976; Lent, John A. *Asian Film Industry.* Austin: University of Texas Press, 1990; Leyda, Jay. *Dianying: An Account of Films and the Film Audience in China.* Cambridge, MA: MIT Press., 1972; MacKerras, Colin. *Amateur Theatre in China 1949–1966.* Canberra: Australian National University Press, 1973; Mast, Gerald. *A Short History of the Movies.* 4th ed. New York: Macmillan, 1986; Obraztsov, Sergei Vladimirovich. *The Chinese Puppet Theatre.* Trans. J. T. MacDermott. London: Faber and Faber, 1961; Scott, A. C. *The Theatre in Asia.* New York: Macmillan, 1972; Stalberg, Roberta Helmer. *China's Puppets.* San Francisco: China, 1984; Yang, Daniel Shih-P'eng. "The Traditional Theatre of China in Its Contemporary Setting: An Examination of the Patterns of Change within the Peking Theatre since 1949." Ph.D. diss., University of Wisconsin, 1968.

China Traveling Dramatic Troupe

An organization founded by Tang Huaiqiu in 1934 to present modern drama. The aim was to have an independent theater organization that presented new dramas and was financially self-sufficient. There were no salaries for the actors and technicians, just board and lodging. This organization was a training ground for many talented modern artists. The organization disbanded in 1937 with the outbreak of the war with Japan. Their seminal performance was *Thunderstorm* by Tsao Yu, a psychological portrait of a Chinese family with decaying morals.

References: Scott, A. C. *The Theatre in Asia.* New York: Macmillan, 1972.

Chinese Cultural Revolution (1966–1976)

Mao Tse-tung's reform movement to maintain the purity of the Communist revolution. The Red Guard was given power by Chairman Mao to search the country for anything counterrevolutionary and destroy it. This included books, anything Western, anything elitist. Counterrevolutionary persons or materials were at the capricious judgment of these youths. Those they condemned suffered humiliation, and punishments were severe. Many artists and scholars committed suicide. **Peking Opera** was changed radically, as it was made into an instructional propaganda tool to instruct the masses on the value of Communism. The "Gang of Four" was a commission that decided what entertainment was not to be condemned. Only five revolutionary modern plays were allowed, *Taking Tiger Mountain by Strategy, Sea Harbor, Raid on White Tiger Regiment, Shajiabang,* and *Red Lantern.* Two revolutionary modern ballets were allowed, *Red Detachment of Women* and *White Haired Girl.* The revolutionary Peking Opera featured hunters or peasant girls as heroes rather than princes or scholars. Realism was observed in all sets and costumes. Most symbolic gestures and movements were banished, but, at critical moments, the Peking Opera stylization would come out in the actors. In order to use Peking Opera acrobatic stunts, actors would try to make logical situations within the plays for hand-to-hand combat. For instance, two opponents would run out of bullets and thus need to engage in a physical dual featuring flips, leaps, and other tricks. The Cultural Revolution ended with Mao's death in 1976 and the Gang of Four (see **Chiang Ching**) was tried and condemned for the atrocities committed during the revolution. Her death sentence was changed to a life sentence in 1983.

References: Mackerras, Colin. *Chinese Theatre in Modern Times, from 1840 to the Present Day.* Amherst: University of Massachusetts Press, 1975; Peking Opera Troupe of Shanghai. *Taking Tiger Mountain by Strategy.* Peking: Foreign Language Press, 1971; Scott, A. C. *The Theatre in Asia.* New York: Macmillan, 1972.

Chinese New Year

Holiday held during the first fifteen days of the old lunar calendar. This season was an important source of employment for established actors. Actors were overworked, and services were constantly in demand. In China, which has primarily been an agricultural society, this was the only time for ordinary people to enjoy leisure. It was one of the few reliefs from labor in the fields for villagers. The elders of a given village would arrange to have a theatrical troupe perform on a temporary stage, usually erected in a dry riverbed. The performance would have a religious motive, to give thanks for a good harvest and ward of any disaster.

References: Scott, A. C. *The Theatre in Asia.* New York: Macmillan, 1972.

Chinese *Wayang*

Singapore

Expression used to indicate Chinese opera in Singapore (see **Peking Opera**). *Wayang* is used colloquially to mean going to see any kind of performance in Singapore. There are many opera troupes in Singapore performing a variety of styles from the south of China, Hokkien, Cantonese, and others. Sometimes troupes add popular songs to appeal to younger audiences. Performances usually take place in Buddhist temples or in an empty lot near a street in town or in a village.

See also *Wayang Kulit*

References: Brandon, James R. *Brandon's Guide to Theatre in Asia.* Honolulu: University Press of Hawaii, 1976.

Ching

China

Painted face character type in **Peking Opera.** *Ching* characters are superheroes from historic legends. They wear thick makeup on their faces, which communicates much about the disposition of the character. White makeup with thin black lines indicates treachery in a character. Black makeup indicates that a character is straightforward and good, if not a little stupid. Red makeup indicates bravery and dignity in a character. Yellow makeup indicates a clever and deceptive character, such as a sly politician. Symmetrical makeup on both sides of an actor's face indicates that the character is good and honest. There are four categories for characters in Peking Opera, **Sheng,** male; **Dan,** female; *Ching,* painted face; and **Chou,** clown. There are two categories of painted face characters; **Wen-Ching** is a civil character, not engaged in the armed forces, who sings a lot but seldom fights, and **Wu-Ching** is a militant character who does a lot of fighting and very little singing.

References: Chia-Chien, Chu. *The Chinese Theatre.* Trans. James A. Graham. London: John Lane, 1922; Scott, A. C. *The Theatre in Asia.* New York: Macmillan, 1972; Yang, Daniel Shih-P'eng. *An Annotated Bibliography of Materials for the Study of the Peking Opera.* 2d ed. Wisconsin China Series. Madison: University of Wisconsin, 1967.

Ching-I

China

Virtuous woman role in **Peking Opera.**

See also Tan

Chingana

Chile

Popular entertainment combining dramatic sketches, music, and dance, extremely popular in the beginning of the nineteenth century at restaurants and inns. Mulattos or mixed-caste actors performed irreverent comic farces that mocked all the colonial authorities held most sacred. These dramatic sketches often satirized the clergy, depicting scenes of them "caught in the act" with a female companion, and were humorous but serious in their critical intent. Performances usually took place in the open air on a patio, with a boisterous and dangerous atmosphere surrounding performances. Drinking, gambling, and even occasional knife fights were not uncommon and eventually attracted the attention of the authorities, who imposed some censorship on *Chingana* performances, which virtually disappeared by the end of the nineteenth century.

The form was resurrected in the 1970s and updated to serve the needs of the Teatro de Base (Base Theater) movement, which is theater designed to be created by the lower-class audience it serves. Contemporary performances of *Chingana* are richly varied and include various combinations of dance, music, songs, poetry, theater, audiovisual support, and even games. Interspersed throughout performances are testimonials, stories, and jokes, all focused on one theme pertinent to the lives of the spectators. Usually three to five people perform these *Chingana,* with two of those people serving as animators or guides who connect one event to the next. The performers encourage the audience to be involved. They can criticize anything, demand something be done over differently, or even get up and act something out themselves. The goal is for the audience to leave with newfound confidence in their ability to affect their own world and new skill for doing so.

References: Hautzinger, Sarah. "Chile: Street Theater Takes Risks." *NACLA Report on the Americas* 21, 4

(July–August 1987): 10–11; Versènyi, Adam. *Theatre in Latin America: Religion, Politics, and Culture from Cortés to the 1980's.* New York: Cambridge University Press, 1993.

Chiton
Greece

Greek dress worn by actors of the ancient theater, generally worn ankle-length by female characters and above the knee by male characters.

> **References:** Brooke, I. *Costume in Greek Classic Drama.* London: Methuen, 1962; Gullberg, Elsa. *The Thread of Ariadne: A Study of Ancient Greek Dress.* Goteborg: P. Astrom, 1970; Hope, Thomas. *Costumes of the Greeks and Romans.* New York: Dover, 1962; Houston, Mary Galway. *Ancient Greek, Roman and Byzantine Costume and Decoration.* London: A. & C. Black, 1947; Johnson, Marie. *Ancient Greek Dress.* Chicago: Argonaut, 1964.

Choregos
Greece

Wealthy citizen appointed by the state to pay for expenses incurred in producing the plays of one specific playwright for the **City Dionysia,** a religious festival in honor of the Greek god, **Dionysus.** Each year three sponsors, or *choregoi* (plural form of *choregos*), were selected from among the wealthiest citizens in Athens to pay for the productions of the three playwrights selected to take part in the competition. Lots were drawn to determine which sponsor got which playwright. Beyond carrying out a civic duty, sponsors took an active interest in productions, since they also received a share in the prize money if their playwright was victorious. As financial backer, the choregos paid the wages of fifteen men in the chorus, hired musicians, paid for any scenery or special effects needed, hired a trainer for the chorus if the playwright himself could not perform the task, and paid for the costumes for each form of play presented.

> **References:** Arnott, Peter D. *The Ancient Greek and Roman Theatre.* New York: Random House, 1971; Bieber, Margarete. *The History of the Greek and Roman Theater.* Princeton, NJ: Princeton University Press, 1961; Taylor, David. *Acting and the Stage.* Boston: George Allen & Unwin, 1978; Webster, Thomas Bertram Lonsdale. *The Greek Chorus.* London: Methuen, 1970.

Chorodidaskalos
Greece

Teacher or leader of the chorus in ancient Greek theater.

> **See also** Greek Chorus
> **References:** Arnott, Peter D. *The Ancient Greek and Roman Theatre.* New York: Random House, 1971; Bieber, Margarete. *The History of the Greek and Roman Theater.* Princeton, NJ: Princeton University Press, 1961; Webster, Thomas Bertram Lonsdale. *The Greek Chorus.* London: Methuen, 1970.

Chou
China

Comic clown stock character in **Peking Opera.** As these characters joke, they do incredibly skillful scenes of mime and acrobatics. They are often featured in domestic farces, which sometimes act as curtain raisers. They wear white patches of makeup on the their nose. Facially they appear more realistic than the **Hualian,** a robust male stock character who also wears makeup. There are two kinds of clowns, **Wen-Chou,** who are civil clowns, often scholars, and **Wu-Chou,** who are militant clowns, sometimes thieves, and always fight. The eighth-century Tang emperor **Ming Huang** played the Chou role, which has given great prestige and many privileges to the actors who also play this role.

> **References:** Chia-Chien, Chu. *The Chinese Theatre.* Trans. James A. Graham. London: John Lane, 1922; MacKerras, Colin. *Rise of the Peking Opera, 1770–1870: Social Aspects of the Theatre in Manchu China.* Oxford: Clarendon Press, 1972; Scott, A. C. *The Classical Theatre of China.* London: Allen & Unwin, 1957; Yang, Daniel Shih-P'eng. "The Traditional Theatre of China in Its Contemporary Setting: An Examination of the Patterns of Change within the Peking Theatre since 1949." Ph.D. diss., University of Wisconsin, 1968.

Chutti
India

White plaster beard worn by male characters in **Kathakali,** a form of dance-drama. A paste made of rice powder and lime juice is applied to the actor's face from his ears to his chin in successive layers. The entire application process takes three to four hours, during which time the actors usually sleep. Since *Kathakali* is so physically demanding, performers have a chorus that sings for them. It would be nearly impossible for an actor to speak while in *Chutti* because the plaster would crack and fall from the face.

References: Gargi, Balawanta. *Theatre in India.* New York: Theatre Arts, 1962; Varadpande, Manohar Laxman. *Krishna Theatre in India.* New Delhi: Abhinav, 1982.

Cibber, Colley (1671–1757)
England

English actor, playwright, and theater manager. Cibber first acted at Drury Lane in 1690 and was successful as a comic actor. He later helped manage the Theatre Royal at Drury Lane in 1710. As an all-around man of the theater, he wrote many sentimental comedies such as *Love's Last Shift*, 1696, in which he starred. He wrote an autobiography, *Apology for the Life of Mr. Colley Cibber, Comedian*, which comments on the art of acting. He was acting in the early part of the eighteenth century when exaggerated acting was in vogue. His wife, Susanna Maria Arne (1714–1766), was an actress, as were their two children, Theophilus Cibber (1703–1758) and Charlotte Clarke (1710–1760).

References: Chinoy, Helen Krich, and Toby Cole. *Actors on Acting,* New York: Crown, 1970; Cibber, Colley. *An Apology for the Life of Colley Cibber.* Ann Arbor: University of Michigan Press, 1968; Cibber, Colley. *Careless Husband: An Appreciation of Colley Cibber, Actor and Dramatist.* New York: Haskell House, 1967.

Cirque du Soleil (Circus of the Sun)
Canada, United States

Outstanding circus that uses no animals, but instead highly trained performers in circus, dance, and theater to create artistic productions that communicate feeling as well as spectacle. Born in 1984 in Quebec, Cirque du Soleil is a conglomerate of a lot of smaller street performance companies; it emerged from the Festival of Street Players. The goal is to infuse the best of theater and dance into the circus. The performers transform acrobatic stunts into fluid dancelike motion. Each production communicates some theme through pantomime, music, dance, and design. Individual

Members of Cirque du Soleil in We Reinvent the Circus in Santa Monica, California. (Neal Preston/Corbis)

pieces are laced together, usually by a group of idiosyncratic clowns. There is never a dull moment on stage, as entrances fall upon the heels of exits.

The Cirque started touring Quebec, then all of Canada, then came to Los Angeles in 1988. Since that time, the enterprise has grown immensely to include a permanent aquatic show, *O*, in Las Vegas, Nevada, and a show entitled *La Nouba* at Disney World. As new shows are created, such as *Quidam*, in 1998, and *Dralion*, in 1999, they tour extensively around the world.

References: Abrams, Steve. "Cirque du Soleil." *Puppetry Journal* 49 (Summer 1998): 19; Lampert-Greaux, Ellen. "Underwater Delights: Luc Lafortune Gives the Cirque du Soleil an Aquatic Glow at Bellagio." *Lighting Dimensions* 23, 1 (January 1999): 46–51, 72, 74; Leabhart, Thomas. "Cirque du Soleil." *Mime Journal* (1986): 1–7; Renner, Pamela. "The Zone of Fantastic Reality: Cirque du Soleil Takes Clowning in a New Direction." *American Theatre* 16 (December 1999): 28–30; Sloat, Susanna. "Cirque du Soleil—'Quidam.'" *Attitude—The Dancer's Magazine* 13 (Fall 1998): 78–79.

City Dionysia
Greece

The most lavish of the **Dionysia,** festivals honoring the Greek god **Dionysus.** Some of the greatest dramatic works known to Western history were first presented in the dramatic contests that were the highlights of the City Dionysia. The playwrights **Aeschylus, Sophocles,** and **Euripides** each competed in the contest many times; each playwright presented three tragedies and one **satyr play.** In 534 B.C. **Thespis,** traditionally considered to be the creator of drama, was the first to win the dramatic contest at the City Dionysia.

People traveled from far away by sea and land to attend this seven-day festival in late March. This was an excellent opportunity for the Athenians to show off their great wealth and rich culture.

The order of events was most likely as follows. On the first day all of the contestants were assembled in preparation for the contests. The second day began with a grand procession through the city of all contestants and important officials. Sacrifices were made to Dionysus, and then the first competitions, of choral odes sung and danced by large

numbers of men and boys, took place. Lively singing and dancing in honor of Dionysus, known as **Komos,** was performed as a procession around the town. The first two days there were probably also dithrambic contests among the ten tribes of Athens, which each had a men's and a boy's chorus.

The next three days were dedicated to the dramatic competition, which began early in the morning to take advantage of the daylight to illuminate the stage and actors. Each of these three days had the same schedule. One of the three playwrights presented all four of his plays, three tragedies and one satyr play, in the span of about six hours. After a meal break, a comic playwright would present one comedy. Starting around 487 B.C. there was an entire day dedicated to comedy, in which five comedies, each by a different playwright, were presented. However, during the Peloponnesian War (against Sparta) the day for comedy was canceled. It must have been an exhilarating, if not exhausting, experience for the audience to witness so many works of such great quality and depth in such a short amount of time.

On the final day of the festival there was the judging of best playwright and actor in both tragedy and comedy. Prizes were awarded.

See also Dithyramb
References: Bieber, Margarete. *The History of the Greek and Roman Theater.* Princeton, NJ: Princeton University Press, 1961; Pickard-Cambridge, Arthur Wallace. *The Theatre of Dionysus in Athens.* Oxford: Clarendon, 1946; Simon, Erika. *Antike Theater (The Ancient Theatre).* Trans. C. E. Vafopoulou. New York: Methuen, 1982; Taylor, David. *Acting and the Stage.* Boston: George Allen & Unwin, 1978.

Cixi, née Yehonala, Empress Dowager (1835–1908)
China

Last ruler of the Ching Dynasty (1644–1911) and a supporter of the arts. She was the best-known imperial enthusiast of the theater. Until she died in 1908, she regularly ordered **Peking Opera** troupes to her palace for entertainment. Being invited to perform for the palace was a great professional honor as well as a frightening affair. Since actors were of too low a social class to ride in a carriage, they had to travel by foot to the palace even in the winter. The performing conditions were equally dismal, with only a cold cramped space in which to perform. If they made a mistake while performing, the physical punishment was very harsh.

References: Scott, A. C. *The Theatre in Asia.* New York: Macmillan, 1972.

Ckumkpa
Nigeria

A play in which masked boys and men of the village's secret society dramatize actual or purported events in the village and neighboring settlements; performed by the Afikpo, an Igbo group in southeastern **Nigeria.** A satirical style marks these performances. Actual names of people being satirized are used. Between skits younger boys of the society, dressed as girls, dance about the performance space. The primary appeal of this dance involving female impersonation, however, is the ability of the male performer to skillfully imitate female movements.

Among the variety of new skits enacted in a performance, there is one skit performed near the end of a program that remains constant. In it a young man dressed in a raffia skirt with a young woman's hairdo moves out of the group of seated masked performers. He wears a white mask that is sculpted to represent a female face with a child sitting on top of the mask's face. Another masked performer impersonates her mother. While the "young girl" dances in a feminine style, the mother brushes her clean with a handkerchief. The seated performers begin to yell out the names of girls of marriageable age. Different performers approach the mother and daughter, representing men who want to marry the girl. The skit lasts until the young female accepts one of the men for marriage.

References: Atigbi, I. A. *Nigeria Traditional Festivals: A Guide to Nigeria Cultural Safari.* Lagos, Nigeria: Nigerian Tourist Association, 1972; Nkwoh, Marius. *Igbo Cultural Heritage.* Onitsha, Nigeria: University Publishing, 1984; Ottenberg, Simon. "Afikpo Masquerades: Audience and Performers." *African Arts* 6, 4 (1973): 32–36.

Clown
Burma, Cambodia, China, England, Italy, Java, Malaysia, Mexico, Thailand, United States

Comic type of character that appears in a variety of theatrical performances. Using physical pranks, clumsiness that often turns into a visual surprise (and actually requires great agility), and mimicry, clown characters delight audiences around the world. It is a common device to use clown skits between the acts of serious theater to relieve the dramatic tension. Comic characters seem uniquely able to diffuse conflict by mocking the seriousness of the situation and to relieve anxiety by mocking whatever threatens. Clown characters are so attractive because they seem to be free of the social constraints and the common need for dignity that bind everyone else.

There is evidence of clowns in the earliest recorded forms of theater in many part of the world. In **Native American theater,** clowns are commonly featured, often masked and with healing powers. The characters in Old Comedy, the earliest form of Greek Comedy, are essentially clowns because of their use of physical humor. The *Vidushaka* is a jester (in other words, a clown character) in Indian Sanskrit drama. Throughout Asia clowns feature prominently, often interpreting the high language of the drama through their dialogue with refined characters. In Burma the theatrical form **Zat Pwe** features many clowns. The clowns in the Malaysian **Mak Yong** dance drama are the only male performers in an otherwise all-female cast. The Chinese **Wen-Chou** and **Wu-Chou** are two types of clowns in the **Peking Opera.**

The primary clown character in the Southeast Asian shadow puppet theater is uniquely significant as a manifestation of the highest spiritual power. In the Javanese **Wayang Kulit** this character is called **Semar.** Disguising his splendor by smearing mud all over his body, he poses as a servant to the other Hindu gods and intermingles in their stories. In **Malaysia** this same character, named **Pak Dogol,** has a sidekick named **Wak Long** whom he created out of mud. In **Thailand** this clown of supernatural origin is **Nang Talung,** and in **Cambodia, Ayang.**

In **Elizabethan England** playwrights such as **Shakespeare** wrote hilarious comic scenes for clownlike characters and made striking use of fools, as jesters were called. The wise fool can often speak the truth to a ruler that no one else would dare to utter. In **Italy** during the sixteenth and seventeenth centuries the clown character was developed into specific types, known by the general name of **Zanni. Cantinflas** was a Mexican comedian in the twentieth century who rose to great fame from improvised street theater. In the **United States** the great Depression, from the late 1920s to the 1930s, inspired many versions of the pathetically comic tramp character, such as those done by Emmet Kelly (1898–1979) and silent film star, **Charlie Chaplin**. In recent years the circus clown has been resurrected as high art by the Canadian group **Cirque du Soleil** (Circus of the Sun), which performs all over the world.

> **References:** Kelly, Emmet. *Clown*. New York: Prentice-Hall, 1954; Videbaek, Bente. *The Stage Clown in Shakespeare's Theatre*. Westport, CT: Greenwood, 1996; Winkler, Elizabeth. *The Clown in Modern Anglo-Irish Drama*. Frankfurt: P. Lang, 1977.

Cocteau, Jean (1889–1963)
France

Playwright and film director, whose eclectic contributions to the arts involved Greek tragedies, ballet, and film. One of his first collaborations was writing the script for the surrealist 1917 piece *Parade* for the Ballet Russe, a piece for which Pablo Picasso (1881–1973) designed the sets and costumes. In this highly experimental venture, Cocteau combined circus acts with pantomimes and sideshows that occurred simultaneously with no seeming interrelation. In these productions, actors, sometimes dressed in cubist costumes, were rather moving elements of scenery than individuals acting out a story. Cocteau wrote other dramas for ballets, such as *Les Mariés de la Tour Eiffel* (The Wedding on the Eiffel Tower).

Cocteau turned next to staging the Greek myths, such as *Orpheus*, 1926, in which he introduced modern elements with a fantastical twist. One of his goals in production was to make the ancient stories seem familiar. In 1932 he presented *La Machine Infernale* (The Infernal Machine) based on the Greek tragedy *Oedipus Rex*. After World War II, Cocteau dedicated his writing to the cinema, with such successes as *Le Sang d'un Poète* (The Blood of a Poet), 1932, and *Beauty and the Beast*, 1945. Each of his films had its own distinctive style: *Les Parents Terribles* (The Terrible Parent), 1948, was naturalistic in its acting style and production, while *Orphée*, 1950, was poetic and symbolic.

Cocteau died of a heart attack upon hearing that his friend Edith Piaf had died.

See also Surrealism
> **References:** Armes, Roy. *French Film*. New York: Dutton, 1970; Brockett, Oscar. *Century of Innovation: A History of European and American Theatre and Drama since 1870*. Englewood Cliffs, NJ: Prentice-Hall, 1973; Katz, Ephraim. *The Film Encyclopedia*. New York: Harper Perennial, 1994; Martin, John W. *The Golden Age of French Cinema, 1929–1959*. Boston: Twayne, 1983; Sadoul, Georges. *French Film*. London: Falcon Press, 1953.

Colombia

Prior to Spanish colonization in the 1530s, the territory that is now Colombia was peopled by the Chibcha and other cultures. Portions also fell under the authority of the Inca empire. With the Spanish also came their traditional sacred dramas and some secular elitist dramas. Some of the educated colonial elite were self-critical, such as Colombian playwrights Luis Vargas Tejada (1802–1829) and José Fernández Madrid (1788–1830), author of the tragedy *Guatimoc* (c. 1824–1825), which deals with the last days of the Aztec emperor and his revenge on the Spanish. In their writing they idealized the American Indian, arguing for an end to colonial rule. They utilized local settings and characters in their dramas, even thought they still wrote in the neo-classical style.

Latin American liberation theater, theater created to give voice and dignity to the poor of Latin America, was created in Colombia above all by **Enrique Buenaventura**, with his company Teatro Experimental de Cali (Experimental Theater of Cali) from the 1960s through the 1990s. He developed models for creating theater that expressed the point of view of a Latin American who was freed from colonial oppression. Following Buenaventura's example, Santiago García (born in 1929) and his company, La Candelaria (The Candlemas), continued creating liberation theater through the 1990s.

See also Inca Theater
> **References:** Bibliowicz, Azriel. "Be Happy Because Your Father Isn't Your Father: An Analysis of Colombian *Telenovelas*." *Journal of Popular Culture* (Winter 1980): 476–485; Versènyi, Adam. *Theatre in Latin America: Religion, Politics, and Culture from Cortés to the 1980's*. New York: Cambridge University Press, 1993; Weiss, Judith A. *Latin American Popular Theatre: The First Five Centuries*. Albuquerque: University of New Mexico Press, 1993.

Colombina

Italy

Female maid and **Zanni** stock character in **commedia dell'arte,** improvised Italian sixteenth- and seventeenth-century comedy. As personal maid and confidante to the **Innamorata,** the female lover, Colombina was always meddling in the affairs of the young lovers with the best intentions. Always attractive, she was sharp and gossipy, flirtatious and quick footed. **Arlecchino,** a comic male stock character, was usually her sweetheart, and she often wore a colorful patchwork dress to match his attire. She was a likable character and often took the audience into her confidence. She wore a low-cut dress with a mop cap, an apron, and no mask.

> **References:** Craig, Edward Gordon. "The Characters of the Commedia Dell'Arte." *The Mask* (January 1912); Rudlin, John. *Commedia Dell'Arte: An Actor's Handbook.* London and New York: Routledge, 1994.

Comedia

Spain

A dramatic formula created by the playwright Lope de Vega (1562–1635), a premier writer of the Spanish Golden Age. Pedro Calderón de la Barca (1600–1681) refined Lope's formula for the *comedia,* and it remained popular throughout the seventeenth and eighteenth centuries. Seemingly infinite varieties of *comedia* were developed, beginning in the early sixteenth century with *comedia a fantasía,* the comedy of invention, and *comedia a noticia,* plays of observation. Another variety was the *comedia en capa y espada,* the cloak and sword play, a kind of comedy in which the main actor played an aristocratic character who wore a cloak and carried a sword. By the second half of the eighteenth century, two more types of comedia were developed to cater to the audience's love of spectacle, *comedia de magia,* magic show, and *comedia heroica,* heroic comedy, a fusion of marches, scene changes, and complicated plots.

> **References:** McKendrick, Melveena. *Theatre in Spain: 1490–1700.* New York: Cambridge University Press, 1989; Polito, Antonio. *Spanish Theatre: A Survey from the Middle Ages to the Twentieth-Century.* Salt Lake City: Department of Languages, University of Utah, 1967; Wadely, Donald Ray. *Lope de Vega and the*

Elizabethans. Ann Arbor, MI: University Microfilms, 1977, 29645107.

Comédie Française

France

French national theater, founded in 1680 by Louis XIV when he ordered the union of the troupe called the Hôtel de Bourgogne with **Molière**'s troupe. A permanent company of actors that exists to this day, the Comédie works as a cooperative society of actors, in which each member holds a share of the company. It is a theater run by actors on a democratic basis. New members, known as *pensionnaires,* are admitted on a probationary basis. After the dismissal, retirement, or death of a member, a pensionnaire can become a *sociétaire,* a full member of the company.

The Comédie Française is the oldest national theater of the Western world; almost every notable French actor has made his or her mark there, and most notable contributions to the art of French theater can be traced to its stage. Notwithstanding the fact that many inauthentic and flamboyant styles of acting were perpetuated at the Comédie, it set such a standard for excellence that it is perhaps the most important national theater of all time. As a somewhat conservative establishment throughout the centuries, it has served as a source of opposition to theatrical reformers such as **Jacques Copeau** and **André Antoine**.

> **See also** Lecouvreur, Adrienne
> **References:** Gautier, Jean Jacques. *Le Comedie Francaise.* Paris: Wesmael-Charlier, 1964; Lancaster, Henry Carrington. *The Comedie Francaise, 1701–1774: Plays, Actors, Spectators, Finances.* Philadelphia: American Philosophical Society, 1951.

Comic Acting in Ancient Greece

See Greek Comedy

Commedia dell'Arte

Italy

Improvised Italian comedy performed by groups of trained and highly skilled actors, who each portrayed a stock character; they traveled together, performing a repertory of plays, each play consisting of only a skeletal script, which

Commedia dell'arte *performance at the Chinese Theater in Tivoli Gardens, Copenhagen, Denmark. (Bob Krist/Corbis)*

performers fleshed out through their witty and ingenious improvised creations. This brashly spirited performance style originated in the sixteenth century, in Venice and Lombardy, from popular street theater, where professional jugglers, acrobats, and actors entertained without scenery or stage machinery, relying solely upon their skill and sharp wits to hold an audience. Deeper roots of commedia dell'arte seem to be in the **mime** and the **Atellana,** both of ancient Rome, and in medieval dramas. In the middle of the seventeenth century Italian improvised comedy reached the summit of its popularity. The inspiration declined for the next hundred years, at the end of which, *commedia dell'arte* disappeared.

Actors of *commedia dell'arte* are exceptional in the history of Western theater because they trusted so radically in spontaneity. Since performances were mostly improvised, they were attuned to the spirit of those witnessing the show. An actor would dedicate his or her entire life to perfecting one role. Such endurance in applying oneself to the creation of a single persona was unprecedented and has not since been surpassed in Western the-

ater. Commedia actors were ultimately dependent upon each other. The very best improvising actor can only play as well as his or her partner can respond. A company of actors is only as good as its weakest actor. Although commedia troupes were famous for their comedies, they did at times present serious dramas and tragedies, which attests to their mastery of the art of acting, as even comic character actors could declaim in verse with eloquence.

Stock characters of *commedia dell'arte* fall into a variety of different categories. The most famous type is the masked comic servant character known as the **Zanni,** which includes **Arlecchino** and **Brighella.** The female comic servant stock character, and only female Zanni, is **Colombina.** The old man characters include the duped father and husband, **Pantalone,** the parasitic and bombastic doctor, **Dottore,** and the Spanish braggart, **Capitano.** The young and attractive lovers were the **Innamorati,** whose exploits in coming together were often the focus of a production. The male lover, the *Innamorato,* has had many proper names made famous by various actors, such as Silvio, Fabrizio, and Aurelio. The female lover, the Innamorata, has had names such as Isabella, Angelica, and Silvia.

Commedia troupes were made up of professional actors who banded together under contract to tour amicably together sharing profits, expenses, and even ownership of the horse that pulled their wagon. The entire theatrical endeavor of production was in the hands of the actors themselves. Actors were historians, theorists, stage managers, storytellers, directors, and playwrights. Famous companies such as Gelosi, of which the famous actress **Isabella Andreini** was a member, were sought after and adored in Italy and France. Some troupes even performed in England and Spain. The number of actors in a touring company was small, usually just ten to twelve, with twice as many men as women.

Troupes not only performed in the streets, where they probably originated, but also were invited into the great courts. Their lively entertainment was most likely a welcome relief compared to the neoclassic plays performed by academicians popular in the sixteenth century. Costumes for the stock characters became somewhat set and identified characters for the audience, such as the colorful diamond-shaped patchwork costume for Arlecchino, or the red pants and dark cloak for Pantalone. Most characters wore masks that eventually evolved to being just half masks, covering only the forehead, cheeks, and nose. Most masks were shaped out of black leather, with many of the old men characters sporting long hooked noses. Characters such as the Innamorati, the young lovers, did not wear masks, but the combination of their heavy makeup and their exaggerated expressions resulted in a masklike effect.

A short outline of a plot that could be used for a performance was called **Canevas.** The subject of these usually centered around two young lovers whose coming together is initially opposed, but is made possible through some plotting by the servant characters attached to the young man on their master's behalf. Interspersed throughout a commedia performance were many **lazzi,** interludes of short comic business, of which there was a standard repertory consisting of physical pranks, jokes, surprise actions, and tricks. The performers themselves often provided the music. The comic character Brighella carried with him a

mandolin, which he would play while he danced and sang.

Actors of *commedia dell'arte* did not rely entirely upon improvisation. Training included learning fixed rhetorical phrases, jokes, and even entire monologues or dialogues that could be used when appropriate. Stock situations arose again and again, such as praising the beauty of a lover or berating a disobedient servant. The same poetic praises and clever insults were recycled and continually improved upon.

References: Chinoy, Helen Krich, and Toby Cole. *Actors on Acting.* New York: Crown, 1970; Groves, William McDonald. "The Commedia Dell'Arte and the Shakespearean Theatre: A Study of the Relevance of Applying Commedia Dell'Arte Techniques to Shakespearean Production." Ph.D. diss., Ann Arbor, MI: Proquest, 1983; Heck, Thomas. *Commedia Dell'Arte: A Guide to the Primary and Secondary Literature.* New York: Garland, 1988; Herrick, Marvin T. *Italian Comedy in the Renaissance.* Urbana: University of Illinois Press, 1960; Oreglia, Giacomo. *The Commedia dell'Arte.* Trans. Lovett Edwards. New York: Hill and Wang, 1968; Rudlin, John. *Commedia Dell'Arte: An Actor's Handbook.* London and New York: Routledge, 1994; Schwartz, Isidore Adolphe. *The Commedia Dell'Arte and Its Influence on French Comedy in the Seventeeth Century.* Paris: H. Samuel, 1933.

Commedia Erudita
Italy

Italian learned comedy, believed to have begun at the end of the fourteenth century, well established by the middle of the sixteenth century. These scripted comedies written in both prose and verse were usually modeled on the work of the two ancient Roman comic playwrights, **Plautus** and **Terence,** whose work had been rediscovered during the Renaissance. Performers were most often amateur intellectuals and dignitaries, but sometimes students and young men studying for the priesthood. This form was contemporary with **commedia dell'arte,** the popular improvised masked comedy, but actors of *commedia erudita* wore elaborate costumes rather than masks. Performances took place on the private indoor stages of the courts and were exclusively for an upper-class audience.

Commedia erudita had its roots in **Latin humanistic comedy,** Italian comedies and **Rappresentazioni**

Sacre, sacred representations dramatizing Christian mysteries and miracles, as well as in the work of the ancient Roman playwrights.

> References: Duchartre, Pierre-Louis. *The Italian Comedy* (Comedie Italienne). Trans. Randolph Weaver. New York: Dover, 1966; Herrick, Marvin T. *Italian Comedy in the Renaissance.* Urbana: University of Illinois Press, 1960; Rudlin, John. *Commedia Dell'Arte: An Actor's Handbook.* London and New York: Routledge, 1994.

Confrérie de la Passion (Brotherhood of the Passion)

France

Amateur troupe, formed in Paris in 1402, that performed religious dramas. In 1518 the *Confrérie* was given exclusive rights to perform in Paris, but by 1570, rather than performing plays, it had become an umbrella organization charging all other troupes a tax for rights to perform in Paris. The troupe also had control of the only theater of Paris at the time, the famous Théâtre de l'Hôtel de Bourgogne. The *Confrérie* controlled theater in Paris until 1675, when it lost its monopoly, disbanding soon thereafter.

> References: Axton, Richard. *European Drama of the Early Middle Age.* London: Hutchinson, 1974. 1974; Bevington, David. *Medieval Drama.* Boston: Houghton, 1975; Chinoy, Helen Krich, and Toby Cole. *Actors on Acting.* New York: Crown, 1970; Vince, Ronald W. *Ancient and Medieval Theatre: A Historiographical Handbook.* Westport, CT: Greenwood, 1984.

Copeau, Jacques (1879–1949)

France

French actor and director. Copeau founded the Théâtre du Vieux-Colombier in 1913, which began a new epoch in French theater. Here he reduced theater to its most essential ingredients, utilizing a simplicity that is quite striking, given the context of his time. He relied primarily on language and on actors, whom he regarded as servants to the written text. His life was one of searching for his own idea of "pure" theater. In his holistic search for a pure performance by an actor, he and his company rigorously exercised their minds, bodies, and voices, always in an effort to serve the text of the play.

After producing French plays in New York from 1917 to 1919, he returned to Paris and started an acting school connected to the Vieux-Colombier. After his retirement in 1924 he was followed by some of his actors and performed with them at fairgrounds farces similar to those done by the **commedia dell'arte,** attempting to escape from all that was superficial and insincere in theater at the time.

> References: Borgal, Clement. *Jacques Copeau.* Paris: L'Arche, 1960; Copeau, Jacques. *Copeau: Texts on Theatre.* Ed. and trans. John Rudlin and Norman H. Paul. New York: Routledge, 1990.

Corpus Christi

A Christian festival celebrated on the Thursday after Trinity Sunday, about two months after Easter. The feast was celebrated for the first time in 1247. In 1264 it was added to the religious calendar by order of Pope Urban IV, and by 1317 its celebration had spread throughout the world, wherever Christians practiced their faith. The purpose of the feast was to celebrate the new teaching that the body of Christ was actually present in the Host, the consecrated bread taken by believers in the sacrament of Communion. By the end of the fourteenth century the feast of Corpus Christi featured processions and pageants in which the Host was publicly displayed through the streets of the town.

Professional guilds of merchants and craftsmen such as carpenters and butchers soon began competing with each other in creating plays that would be performed on the feast of Corpus Christi. Many religious leaders encouraged performances of pageant drama in the streets and marketplaces during the festival to keep drama from being performed in the churches, a practice many deemed vulgar. Corpus Christi plays, which were cycles of mystery plays covering the Old and New Testaments, were performed at the feast of the Corpus Christi in the early summer, mainly in France, Germany, England, and Spain. Throughout the world, Corpus Christi processions still occur, many of which include the performance of religious plays.

> References: McKendrick, Melveena. *Theatre in Spain: 1490–1700.* New York: Cambridge University Press, 1989.

Coryphaeus
Greece

Leader of the **Greek Chorus** in ancient Greek theater.

> **References:** Bieber, Margarete. *The History of the Greek and Roman Theater*. Princeton, NJ: Princeton University Press, 1961; Rehm, Rush. *Greek Tragic Theatre*. New York: Routledge, 1992; Webster, Thomas Bertram Lonsdale. *Greek Theatre Production*. London: Methuen, 1970.

Cothurnus
Greece, Italy

Flat calf-length boots worn by actors in ancient Greece drama; originated from the tall buskin, a laced boot worn by participants in rituals honoring the Greek god **Dionysus.** Only later, in Roman theater, or perhaps as early as the Hellenistic age, did these boots evolve into platform shoes to make the actor appear larger.

> **References:** Bieber, Margarete. *The History of the Greek and Roman Theater*. Princeton, NJ: Princeton University Press, 1961; Gullberg, Elsa. *The Thread of Ariadne: A Study of Ancient Greek Dress*. Goteborg: P. Astrom, 1970; Taplin, Oliver. *Greek Tragedy in Action*. Berkeley: University of California Press, 1978.

Craig, Edward Gordon (1872–1966)
England

Innovative scenic designer, director, actor, and son of actress **Ellen Terry**. Craig developed the concept of reduced settings, using columns, screens of various sizes, arches, and simple architectural elements, often in gigantic scale. He wanted the theater to be suggestive of life rather than a concrete representation of life.

As a youth Craig was an actor for more than ten years under the direction of **Henry Irving**. He was reputed to be a talented actor, but his passion was for creating new theater. He became a stage designer and stopped acting in 1897. Design opportunities carried him all over Europe and Russia, to Italy, the Moscow Art Theater, the Royal Theater in Copenhagen, and, in 1903, to the Imperial Theatre in London. In 1906 he moved to Florence and there founded a theater journal called *The Mask* and created an acting school.

Craig advocated a "total theater," which melded together the roles of designer and director. He was against star actors, instead believing that actors should be subordinate to the director, almost as a puppet is to a puppeteer. Craig collaborated with **Stanislavsky** on a production of *Hamlet* (1912), but Craig left before this starkly stylized production was completed because he and Stanislavsky had such different attitudes toward actors and acting. Craig sought an objective portrayal of humanity with masked actors, a portrayal that would wipe out the emotionality of a performance, whereas Stanislavsky was intensely interested in the actor's human process of portraying emotional truth.

> **References:** Bablet, Denis. *Edward Gordon Craig*. Paris: L'Arche, 1962; Chinoy, Helen Krich, and Toby Cole. *Actors on Acting*. New York: Crown, 1970; Eynat-Confino, Irene. *Beyond the Mask: Gordon Craig, Movement, and the Actor*. Carbondale: Southern Illinois University Press, 1987; Slonim, Marc. *Russian Theater, From the Empire to the Soviets*. Cleveland: World, 1961.

Croatia

The area that is now Croatia has been inhabited by the Croats, a south Slavic people, since the seventh century. It joined with **Hungary** in 1102, was taken by the Turks in the sixteenth century, joined with **Austria** in the nineteenth century, and became part of Yugoslavia in 1918. It claimed independence in 1991, since which time there has been extreme tension between Serbs and Croats. See **Yugoslavia** for history of theater in this area.

> **References:** Batusic, Nikola. "Croatia." In *The World Encyclopedia of Contemporary Theatre*, ed. Don Rubin, 170–184. New York: Routledge, 1994; Davis, Merry Anne. "News: International: Vassili Sulich Stages 'Oedipus' in Dubrovnik Festival." *Dance Magazine* 72, 8 (August 1998): 32; Gasparovic, Darko. "Contemporary Croatian Drama." *Bridge* 55 (1978): 120; Panovski, Naum. "Art and Performance Notes: Landscape For New Millenium: Slobodan Snajder, Croatian Playwright." *PAJ—A Journal of Performance and Art* 20, 3 (September 1998): 76–78; Schopf, Davor. "Opera around the World: Croatia—Split." *Opera* 49, 4 (April 1998): 418.

Cuba

Successive radical changes in Cuban politics have had a dramatic influence on the theater of Cuba.

When Christopher Columbus arrived in the "New World" in 1492, Cuba, then populated by the indigenous Arawak, Cibonely, and Guanahataabey people, was used as a launching point for the Spanish imperialists. During that time the native population performed fully costumed dance-dramas, which were called *Areytos* by the Spanish colonists. Reportedly, these performances originally recounted the history, religion, and culture of the society. Later Spanish soldiers taught the indigenous people to worship the Virgin Mary through these Areytos in an effort to convert them to Catholicism. These people were exterminated by disease and by being forced into hard labor by their colonizers, leaving these forms extinct.

Other than the African slaves used to work the sugar plantations, the population in Cuba comprised Spanish nobles, clergy, businessmen, soldiers, sailors, travelers, and their respective families. Beginning in the seventeenth century, theater in Cuba was a transplant of Spanish theater, which at the time included the elevated plays of Lope de Vega and popular comic farces. No local playwrights could compete with the quality of theater being imported from Spain.

The man generally hailed as the father of Cuban theater is Francisco Covarrubias (1775–1850), an actor, playwright and innovator. He was famous for his portrayal of a *negrito*, the term used for a white actor in blackface, probably before the famous roles created by Thomas Rice and Daniel Decatur Emmett in the United States. As a creator of highly original plays about humorous Cuban stereotypes of his period, he initiated the Cuban **Género Chico,** a form of popular operetta. This form became part of the basis for **Bufo** theater, a form of popular musical theater satire that emerged later in the century.

The U.S. minstrel shows that visited Havana in the late nineteenth century left a strong influence on the Cuban theater. Lavish music and dance revues that incorporated humorous character skits were popular during the first half of the twentieth century. Shows that featured Regino López as principal actor and Federico Villoch as impresario were especially popular. With the advent of the republic in 1902, the vernacular theater both peaked and began to degenerate into a pornographic "for-men-only" style of spectacular performance, which had a high appeal for the rising

influx of tourists. There were also a few elite literary theater groups at this same time that performed some of the best European plays in translation, but only to a limited audience.

In the twentieth century it was not until the advent of Fidel Castro (born 1926) and the Cuban Communist Revolution in 1959 that a national theater was given attention, which marked a resurgence of theatrical activity in Cuba. Those theater artists who feared they would have to conform their artistic expression to fit the new socialist Marxist state emigrated. Those who accepted this new direction remained and became active participants in the new cultural phase of the Revolution. Not only was ample government support available for theater, but it was considered an arm of the revolutionary process. Efforts toward a "new theater," an antibourgeois theater, were undertaken by groups such as the Grupo Teatro Escambray (Theater Group Escambray) in 1968. This group searched for a new style of performing that would speak to the common people in their own language. The collapse of the Soviet system in the 1990s has left the Cuban government limping, and thus state support of theater has proportionately declined.

For the most part, Cuban films produced in the 1930s, 1940s and 1950s were light musicals and comedies. Once Castro took control in 1958, a central governmental branch was established to oversee all film production. Filmmakers were encouraged to make films relevant to the social and political goals of the revolution. The film *Soy Cuba* (I am Cuba) (1964) is a representative example of a film of this era, showing the beauty and innocence of Cuba blended with leftist propaganda. Many revolutionary films depict the United States as the enemy to the revolution. Independent filmmakers struggle with freedom of expression, distribution and funding. As recent as 1999, some independent Cuban filmmakers have entered into coproduction with the United States and Europe which increased distribution and funding but dilutes the strength of the message.

References: Banham, Martin. *African Theatre Today.* London: Pitman, 1976; Edwards, Flora Mancuso. "The Theater of the Black Diaspora: A Comparative Study of Black Drama in Brazil, Cuba and the United States." Ph.D. diss., New York University, 1975; Franklin, Lillian Cleamons. "The

Image of the Black in the Cuban Theater: 1913–1965." Ph.D. diss., Ohio State University, 1982; Palls, Terry Lee. "The Theatre in Revolutionary Cuba: 1959–1969." Ph.D. diss., University of Kansas, 1974; Pereira, Joseph R. "The Black Presence in Cuban Theatre." *Afro-Hispanic Review* 2, 1 (January 1983): 13–18.

Cultural Revolution
See Chinese Cultural Revolution

Cushman, Charlotte (1816–1876)
United States
Considered first great actress of the American stage to be born in the **United States**. Cushman was full of power and passion; her masculine features and voice often resulted in her playing male parts, though she also excelled in villainous or strong female roles. She had originally intended to be an opera singer in breeches parts, as young male roles played by women are called. She began acting in 1836 as Lady Macbeth; her performance was described as "horribly fascinating and incredible." Other famous roles included Nancy Sykes in *Oliver Twist*, Mrs. Haller in *The Stranger*, and Queen Katherine in *Henry VIII*. Opposite her beautiful younger sister, Susan Cushman (1822–1859), Charlotte even performed Hamlet and Romeo.

> **References:** Merrill, Lisa. *When Romeo Was a Woman: Charlotte Cushman and Her Circle of Female Spectators.* Ann Arbor: University of Michigan Press, 1999.

Czech Republic
The area of the present-day Czech Republic has a long history of cultural richness. Bohemia was the name of the western part of the area, and at the time of Bohemia's greatest power, in the fourteenth century, its capital, Prague, was the cultural center of Central Europe. In 1918 the Czechs joined **Slovakia** to become Czechoslovakia. In 1948, the Communists took power and the country became part of the Soviet bloc. In 1993 the two became two separate states once again.

Early Czech theater consisted of liturgical plays, first performed in the thirteenth century, which sometimes had within them elements of secular farces. By the sixteenth century there were plays in the vernacular focusing on contemporary life and history. In 1620 intellectual dramas and court performances were brought to an abrupt halt following the coming to power of the Habsburgs at the battle of Bia Hora. For over 150 years the only theater in the area consisted of foreign troupes from Italy or German-speaking territories and comedic Christmas plays performed in the villages.

Theatrical activity resumed in the late eighteenth century, as theaters were built and the managers of these theaters encouraged more Czech productions among the still plentiful foreign touring productions. By the mid-nineteenth century there were several semiprofessional companies of Czech actors in Prague. In 1859 Prokops, the first Czech touring company, formed. There were also puppet groups producing plays and many newly formed amateur acting groups. In 1862 a private theater for Czech drama, the Provisional Theater, was erected. In 1883 the National Theater arose on the same site. Acting styles were shifting during this time from a heavy and powerful delivery toward more dramatic realism. Also during the late nineteenth and early twentieth centuries, J. J. Kolar, actor and producer, brought **Shakespeare** to the Czech stage and found the actor Jaroslav Kvapil (1868–1950), who masterfully interpreted the many great Shakespearean roles. Kvapil helped form a new generation of actors, including the elegant leading lady Anna Sedlackova and his wife, Hana Kvapilova, whose delicate and subtle approach to acting was highly effective.

Socialist theater got its start in Prague in 1921, influenced by the USSR. World War II (1939–1945) crushed Czech theater. When theatrical activity resumed in 1945, it was overseen by national interests, which were in turn overseen by the USSR, and many new theaters were built in the cities and villages. However, strict censorship was enforced. In the decades following World War II, J. Svoboda made great advancements in scene design. Many small experimental theater groups emerged and were kept afloat by the actors themselves. The theater was generously subsidized but also strictly censored to insure adherence to Communist ideals. Prior to 1968 some artistic freedom was tolerated, and groups were started such as Theater Behind Gates in 1965. However, once the Warsaw Pact troops invaded the country in 1968, artistic freedom was over, and artists were silenced by force or fled the country. Throughout the 1970s oppositional theater existed in the provinces through the work of amateur groups. Also "cellar" or "apartment" theater became popular. These were hidden performances in private residences, sometimes featuring famous actors or actresses such as Vlasta Chramostova. Once the Soviet Union began weakening, the government began to loosen its control on cultural activities. In 1989 the Communist government was gone, and playwright Vaclav Havel became president of Czechoslovakia. In 1993 Havel was elected president of the Czech Republic.

Many kinds of theater now thrive in the Czech Republic. In 1999 the traditional rod puppets of the Czech Republic were used by The Czechoslovak-American Marionette Theatre to enact a performance called *Golem* about Jews in the Prague Ghetto in the sixteenth century.

References: Cerny, Jindrich. "Czech Republic." In *The World Encyclopedia of Contemporary Theatre*, ed. Don Rubin, 196–200. New York: Routledge, 1994; Fencl, Otakar. *The Czechoslovak Theatre Today*. Prague: Artia, 1963; Galloway, Doug. "Obituaries: Frantisek Vlacil." *Variety* 373, 13 (15 February 1999–21 February 1999): 74; Goetz-Stankiewicz, Marketa. *The Silenced Theatre: Czech Playwrights without a Stage*. Toronto: University of Toronto Press, 1979; Hartnoll, Phyllis. *The Oxford Companion to the Theatre*. New York: Oxford University Press, 1967; "Backstage: Vaclav Havel on the Town: Dinner and a Play." *Washington Post*, 15 September 1998, E; Major, Wade. "AFM Reviews: 'Prague Duet.'" *Box Office* 135, 1 (January 1999): 51; Staub, Nancy. "Reviews: 'Golem.'" *Puppetry Journal* 50, 3 (Spring 1999): 20–21; Trensky, Paul. *Czech Drama since World War II*. White Plains, NY: Sharpe, 1978.

Czechoslovak Cinema

Czech Republic, Slovakia

The first Czech film production studio, Kinofa, was started by a stage director, Antonin Pech (1874–1928). He produced several theatrical shorts and a *Faust* in 1912. *The Bartered Bride* was produced by Max Urban in 1913 and starred his wife, the actress Andula Sedlackova. The creation of Czechoslovakia in 1918 inspired much artistic flowering. However, it took until nearly the end of the silent film era for Czechoslovakian films to reach the quality of imported films.

One of the most popular films to emerge from the 1930s was *Extase/Ecstasy*, 1933, starring the beautiful and sensual Hedy Kiesler (later known as Hedy Lamarr). The early 1940s were difficult for the film industry due to World War II (1939–1945). Invading Germans used the studios for the Nazi cause during wartime. In 1945 the film industry was nationalized, and the rest of the 1940s were fruitful. Czechoslovakian film won international acclaim when *The Strike* (1947) won the Grand Prize at the Venice Film Festival. In the 1950s the Communist government imposed strict censorship, dictating that all films adhere to the style of **socialist realism.** By the end of the 1950s conditions eased and *September Nights*, 1957, a film critical of Stalin, was produced. In the 1960s a group of talented and enthusiastic young film directors created many experimental films, and so film played its part in the era of liberalization known as the Prague Spring. Some films to emerge during this period include *Diamonds of the Night* (1964) directed by Jan Nemec, *Daisies*, (1966), and *Closely Watched Trains*, (1966) directed by Jiri Menzel.

The invasion of Czechoslovakia by Soviet forces and troops from the other Warsaw Pact nations in 1968 brought an abrupt ending to this artistic expression and exuberance. Great filmmakers such as Frantisek Vlacil were banned from making feature films. Extreme and harsh censorship ensued until the breakdown of the Soviet Union. Film in the 1990s has enjoyed artistic freedom. In 1999 writer-director, Petr Zelenka created an absurdist black comedy called *Buttoners*. Roger Simon directed *Prague Duet*, 1999, superbly acted by Gina Gershon and Rade Serbedzija.

References: Holloway, Ron. "Communiques: The Karlovyvary Film Festival." *Cineaste* 24, 1 (December 1998): 86–87; Katz, Ephraim. *The Film Encyclopedia*. New York: Harper Perennial, 1994; Lentz, Harris. "Obituaries: Frantisek Vlacil, 74—January 28, 1999." *Classic Images* 286 (April 1999): 57; Major, Wade. "AFM Reviews: 'Prague Duet.'" *Box Office* 135, 1 (January 1999): 51; Richards, Terry. "Film Reviews: 'Buttoners.'" *Film Reviews* 563 (February 1999): 37.

Czechoslovakia

See Czech Republic; Slovakia

D

Da Mu Nao

China

Largest type of puppet used in **Zhang Mu,** Chinese rod puppet theater, literally means "large wooden skull."

References: Stalberg, Roberta Helmer. *China's Puppets.* San Francisco: China Books, 1984.

Dagelan

Java

Rural improvised comedy. This form is popular in the countryside of central Java. It usually centers around dramatizing some humorous domestic situation. The acting style is broad, with plenty of physical humor.

References: Brandon, James R. *Brandon's Guide to Theatre in Asia.* Honolulu: University Press of Hawaii, 1976.

Dalang

Indonesia, Malaysia

Puppet master of the **Wayang Kulit,** traditional shadow puppet theater. A *dalang* is a one-man show extraordinaire. He manipulates all the puppets single-handed, performs all songs, dialogue, and narration, and leads the orchestra. The *dalang* sits behind the screen with a light hanging in front of his face. When he passes flat rawhide puppets in front of the light, shadows appear on the screen. The puppet master has ultimate control over a performance. He decides which parts of an episode should be given emphasis or skipped and when songs or pure orchestral music are to be performed. The performance is not realistic, since generally only one or two puppets can be moved at one time. Puppets are held from the bottom by a rod, and the articulated limbs are manipulated by separate rods. The puppet master manipulates the puppets stylistically before the light to create expressionistic shadow effects and also to give an indication of a character's status and disposition.

Since the Hindu gods portrayed in these dramas are believed to manifest themselves in the shadows, a *dalang* must have mastery over these spirits that come to earth. He must be able to show proper homage and to control the evil gods, to ensure that they do not get loose into the village. These spiritual forces are called upon in the many healing rituals associated with Wayang Kulit, over which the *dalang* presides.

In Malaysia performances generally occur in a raised hut, with a screen as the front wall and a room for the puppet master and his orchestra inside. In Java and Bali, performances generally occur in temples, and a screen is erected, behind which the performers situate themselves. A puppet master sits cross-legged about an arm's length away from the screen. He either has the puppets arranged around him on the floor or has an assis-

A dalang (shadow puppet master) manipulates puppets in a Wayang Kulit *(shadow puppet theater) performance in Java, Indonesia. (Charles & Josette Lenars/Corbis)*

tant or two handing him the puppets. The *dalang* will describe in his narration the location for the action in the drama. Sometimes a rawhide cutout building or tree will be used to set the scene. A few properties, such as small letters or knives that fit into the hand of a puppet, are attached to rods held by puppets when needed.

Puppet masters tend to specialize in certain episodes from the great Hindu epic tales, the **Ramayana** and the **Mahabharata.** Theoretically speaking, if requested, they could perform any portion from these vast stories. Since there are no scripts, a *dalang* improvises the song, dialogue, and narration during the performance, often making clever references to local current events that correspond with the action of the story. Long comic interludes that sometimes take hours are now quite customary. These are invariably led by the clown characters, **Semar** in Indonesia, or **Pak Dogol** in Malaysia. To be a real crowd-pleaser a puppet master must have a quick wit and a dexterous hand to manipulate visual pranks. The *dalang* uses a wooden clapper placed either beneath his knee or on the side of his puppet case to cue the **game-lan,** a traditional orchestra. The connection between a *dalang* and his orchestra is very close. The musicians seem to be able to read the puppet master's mind, as they all spring to action just as he claps out the starting rhythm.

Training to be a *dalang* takes many years of dedication and a natural inclination toward the form itself. There are schools in Java where an aspiring puppeteer can study, but these have developed quite recently. The traditional training method is to apprentice with an established *dalang*. In Malaysia a student usually becomes a musician for the puppet master's orchestra and is gradually taught the *Dalang Muda*, opening ceremony, which he performs at the beginning of a performance. There is a secret knowledge that a teacher imparts to only a trusted student of many years. This knowledge concerns the spiritual aspects of performance and ritual incantations needed to ensure a successful performance.

A true *dalang* is said to have the **Agin,** which literally means "the wind," but translates as "to be deeply moved by a performance." Once a performer has the Agin, he must perform regularly to exercise it lest he become ill. A few women have trained to become puppet masters, but there are no cases of women becoming prominent performers. In Malaysia there are very few young people training to become puppet masters. Islamic conservatism discourages practicing a Hindu-based art form. In Java, where Islam is practiced in a more relaxed fashion, *dalang* are numerous and some even enjoy star status. In Bali, where Balinese Hinduism is still practiced, there are many *dalang* who are an integral part of society.

References: Brandon, James. *Theatre in Southeast Asia.* Cambridge, MA: Harvard University Press, 1974. Osnes, Mary Beth, "Malaysia's Evolving Shadow Puppet Theatre." *Asian Theatre Journal* 9 (Spring 1992): 112–116; Sweeney, P. L. *The Ramayana and the Malay Shadow-Play.* Kuala Lumpur, Malaysia: National University of Malaysia Press, 1972; Wright, Barbara Ann Stein. "Wayang Siam: An Ethnographic Study of the Malay Shadow Play of Kelantan." Ph.D. diss., Ann Arbor, MI: Proquest, 1980.

Dama
Mali

Death anniversary ceremonies held every two to three years in a Dogon village to honor important people who have died. Masked dances are a prominent feature of these ceremonies. The Dogon live in the north central part of Mali, physically isolated by mountains and cliffs. Outside forces have been slow coming, but Islam, Christianity, and modernization are exerting an influence. The masked dances are performed by members of *Awa*, a secret association made up of circumcised males in a village. Performers go on a retreat about three months before a ceremony to prepare. Middle-aged men serve as the masters of ceremonies and the dance masters. The are approximately seventy-eight different masks used in a variety of dances. The wooden masks are carved to represent birds, mammals, people, and reptiles, among other things. The purpose of these productions is to lead the souls of the recently deceased to their final resting place and to bless their passage to the rank of the ancestors. These performances rarely occur today.

See also *Baga Bundo*

References: Griaule, M. *Masques Dogons.* Paris: Institut d'Ethnologie, 1938; Imperato, Pascal James.

"Contemporary Adapted Dances of the Dogon." *African Arts* 5, 1 (1971): 28–33, 68–71.

Dan
See Tan

'dan Kama
Niger, Nigeria

Term for an itinerant comic performer who is a sort of poet, solely dedicated to praising food. He is a juggler, a dancer, a player with words; all his actions are motivated by his obsession with food. With a chorus providing music, he performs a series of songs in succession, all thematically based on food. He is an exuberant uninhibited performer and even snatches food from nearby vendors with his wooden sword while performing. 'Dan *Kama* performers must be spontaneous and quick-witted, since most of what they perform is improvised. Each performer has a stock of physical gags and jokes that he uses again and again, slightly modified to fit each occasion. He must have a receptive sense of the audience's attention and an ability to manipulate it skillfully if he is to hold an audience. A hitched-up pair of trousers with no shirt constitutes his costume, and he always carries with him a wooden sword, as well as a tambourine, which he uses to catch money and cola nuts.

In recent years the main feature of a 'dan *Kama* performance has been parodies of popular songs heard on the radio. This art has declined since World War II with the advent of television and motion pictures, but it has not died out. These comic poets are sometimes featured on radio and television in Nigeria.

References: Beik, Janet. *Hausa Theatre in Niger: A Contemporary Oral Art.* New York: Garland, 1987; Chaibou, Dan-Inna. "La Theatralite en Pays Hawsa." Université Nationale de Côte d'Ivoire, 1978–1979.

Dashavatar Kala
India

Dance-drama enacting all ten incarnations of **Vishnu-Krishna** in a single performance. *Dashavatar* literally means ten incarnations. The tradition of staging the *Dashavatar* dates from the tenth century, but in the beginning of this tradition dance was the only medium used. When dramatic elements were later added, it became known as *Dashavatar Kala* (see **Kala**).

Each performance has a ritual opening, in which a statue of the temple deity is taken on procession amidst dancing and singing. The image of the deity is worshipped and given offerings before the performing begins.

The **Sutradhara,** the narrator, is present throughout the play, providing unity of action by explaining what is occurring between scenes. The story of Vishnu's eighth and most important incarnation as **Krishna** is acted out elaborately because it has the greatest mass appeal. Some of the other incarnations are just mentioned in the songs of the Sutradhara.

The setting for performances is the assembly hall of a temple on festival occasions. Actors wear masks made out of either papier-mâché or wood. The masks themselves are worshipped. Krishna wears a gold-embroidered jacket, and if he is being portrayed as a young man, he carries a flute. Each troupe arranges its own script by selecting songs written by various poets and stringing them together in a logical order. Actors improvise dialogue between songs, sometimes receiving cues from the Sutradhara.

References: Varadpande, Manohar Laxman. *Krishna Theatre in India.* New Delhi: Abhinav, 1982.

Dasi Attam
India

Bharata Natyam, classical female temple dance, was formerly known by the term *Dasi Attam,* the dance of the **Devadasi**s. The term *Bharata Natyam* came into general use, perhaps, to disassociate dance from disreputable practices. British colonists in India did not approve of the practice of the Devadasis having sexual relations with the holy men of the temples. The British were also disturbed by the highly charged sensualism in the Indian dance forms.

References: Massey, Reginald, and Jamie Massey. *Dances of India.* London: Tricolour, 1989.

Davis, Bette (1908–1989)
United States

American film actress. Born Ruth Elizabeth Davis, she rose to the top of the film industry by sheer determination. Davis began by performing in school productions and amateur stock theater. During her first professional acting job in New York, the director fired her after the first night. During the late 1920s she performed off-Broadway with the Provincetown Players as well as on Broadway. Once in Hollywood, she gained positive attention with early films such as *The Man Who Played God,* 1932, and *Of Human Bondage,* 1934. Her acting ability continued to improve, even though the quality of films she acted in remained inconsequential and banal. Still her dynamic presence brought her an Oscar for *Dangerous,* 1935. Women in America were especially drawn to her on the screen for the fiery self-assurance she projected and her confident ambition. Davis won another Oscar for *Jezebel* (1938). She remained strong on the artistic front, ever growing in her craft, as was obvious in *All About Eve,* 1950. She remained active until the end of her life, even performing in *Wicked Stepmother* in 1989, the year of her death.

References: Higham, Charles. *Bette: The Life of Bette Davis.* New York: Macmillan, 1981; Robinson, Jeffery. *Bette Davis, Her Film and Stage Career.* New York: Scribner, 1982.

Dean, James (1931–1955)
United States

Short-lived film actor, who was the hero of the countercultural rebel movement among young Americans in the 1950s. He started by performing on the stage in New York, even sitting in on classes at the **Actors Studio,** and ended his stint in New York by performing in *The Immoralist* in 1954 on Broadway. After playing a few bit parts in films in Hollywood, he burst onto the scene with the emotionally charged film *East of Eden* in 1955, in which he portrays one of two brothers who are rivals for their father's affection. Dean became and remains the image of cool, with his turned-up collar, his tilted head, and a cigarette in his mouth with smoke going into his eyes. He had a shocking emotional honesty and bareness in his performances. Dean gave his seminal performance in *Rebel without a Cause* in 1955, as an alienated youth struggling for esteem and connection. He performed with **Elizabeth Taylor** in his last film, *Giant,* in 1956. Dean permanently cast himself as the symbol for disenfranchised youth by dying in a car crash at his peak; never plagued by old-age or compromise, he remains a pure hero of youthful independence from the status quo.

References: Hofstede, David. *James Dean: A Bio-Bibliography*. Westport, CT: Greenwood, 1996; McCann, Graham. *Rebel Males: Clift, Brando and Dean*. New Brunswick, NJ: Rutgers University Press, 1993; Roth, Beulah. *James Dean*. Corte Madera, CA: Pomegranate Artbooks, 1983.

Decroux, Etienne (1898–1963)

France

Mime performer and actor who taught and performed worldwide. He studied with the French director **Charles Dullin**. Decroux developed a systematic language of gesture and physical expression. His work revived interest in mime.

See also Mime; Ancient Mime; Ancient Pantomime

References: Felner, Mira. *Apostles of Silence: The Modern French Mimes*. Rutherford, NJ: Fairleigh Dickinson University Press, 1985; Montanaro, Tony. *Mime Spoken Here: The Performer's Portable Workshop*. Gardiner, ME: Tilbury House, 1995; Niedzialkowski, Stefan. *Beyond the Word: The World of Mime*. Troy, MI: Momentum, 1993.

Dench, Judi (1934–)

England

English actress of stage and screen. Dench's first major theater role was as Ophelia in *Hamlet* in 1957, at the Old Vic, a famous theater in London. In 1961 she joined the **Royal Shakespeare Company,** where she has continued to perform. She has long been the primary actress for director Peter Hall, performing the title female role in *Antony and Cleopatra*, 1987. She has also directed for the Renaissance Theatre Group. As an actress, she is extremely versatile, with a soft expressive voice and an intelligence that shows through her performances. She has acted in many films such as *Four in the Morning*, 1965, *A Room with a View*, 1986, *A Handful of Dust*, 1988, and *Shakespeare in Love*, 1999, for which she won an Oscar. She has also portrayed "M," James Bond's boss, in *Golden Eye*, 1995, *Tomorrow Never Dies*, 1997, and *The World Is Not Enough*, 1999.

References: Miller, John. *Judi Dench: With a Crack in Her Voice*. New York: Welcome Rain, 2000; Zucker, Carole. *In the Company of Actors: Reflections on*

the Craft of Acting. New York: Theatre Arts/Routledge, 1999.

Deneuve, Catherine (1943–)

France

French film actress. Deneuve has been one of France's leading film stars since the 1960s. In 1992 she won an Academy Award for her performance in *Indochine*. As both her parents were actors, Deneuve made her screen debut when only thirteen. Her allure as an actress can be attributed to her exquisite beauty and her detached manner. She has played a wide range of characters, from a mentally disoriented woman in *Repulsion* (1965) to the seemingly mild and innocent yet strangely erotic wife in *Belle de Jour* (1967).

References: Katz, Ephraim. *The Film Encyclopedia*. New York: Harper Perennial, 1994.

Deng Xi

See Pi-ying Xi

Dengaku

Japan

Consists of songs and dances performed by country people as part of the harvest celebration in the early thirteenth century. This form of rural entertainment had a closer connection with ordinary village people of Japan than **Sarugaku,** a kind of variety show from the thirteenth century. Stomping and mimicking straddling rice on two mud mounds, as is the position taken when harvesting or planting rice, was part of the dance. This kind of material was drawn from the daily chores of the performers when involved in a successful harvest. Eventually troupes traveled to cities to perform. In this way performers from low social origin had contact with the refined culture of those who sponsored them.

References: Scott, A. C. *The Theatre in Asia*. New York: Macmillan, 1972.

Denmark

Denmark is the only Scandinavian country with what might be considered a typically European theater history, beginning with medieval religious drama. Popular in the late Middle Ages were Easter plays and plays based on the lives of saints. By the seventeenth century, the courts were presenting rich and lavish productions of **Ballet de Cour;** the most opulent, performed by court amateurs impersonating a story of the Roman gods, occurred in 1634 for the wedding of the son of Christian IV. The story was designed allegorically to pay tribute to its sponsors. Throughout the seventeenth and eighteenth centuries, bands of itinerant players from other European countries were welcomed into the courts and were sometimes offered extended stays. Their visits brought theatrical influence from Europe to the Danish theater scene.

There were no vernacular plays in the seventeenth century until the work of the Norwegian-born Ludvig Holberg (1684–1754), the first to write Danish comedies, and Johannes Ewald (1743–1781), who wrote the first tragedies in Danish. In 1722 Denmark's first permanent theater was established in Copenhagen for the primary purpose of producing plays in the national language. Other theaters in the provinces were toured regularly by the Royal Theater. The Danish Royal Theater, founded in 1748, was the first national theater in Denmark. Years before the theater's opening, René Magnon de Montaigu was dedicated to assembling a talented band of actors, including his wife and many university students, who later formed the resident company at the Danish Royal Theater. In the mid-eighteenth century the court troupe of Christian VII excelled because of its talented performers, Henry de la Tour, Elisabeth-Marguerite le Clerc, and Marie-Rose-Chatérine Cléricourt, all inspired by the French style of acting, which included intensely expressive gestures and poses.

The beginning of the nineteenth century was dominated by Romantic drama. In 1825 P. A. Heiberg created a comic revival when he presented Denmark's first vaudevillian-style farce, disliked by critics but loved by audiences. In 1829 Hans Christian Anderson wrote the comedy *Love on St. Nicholas Tower* to support the movement. The brightest acting talent of this era was the comic actress **Johanne Luise Heiberg**.

Productions of **Shakespeare**'s works have enjoyed a long history in Denmark, one of the first countries to translate his plays. The great actor,

Peter Foersom (died in 1817), translated many Shakespearean plays, including *Hamlet,* in which he performed the title role in 1813. In the nineteenth century, Olaf Poulsen (1849–1923) was the greatest Danish actor of Shakespeare. He was skilled as a comic actor, and his renditions of Falstaff and Bottom were popular. In the early twentieth century Karl Mantzius staged many of Shakespeare's plays in an Elizabethan setting, with himself playing the leading roles.

Modern drama came to Denmark in the late nineteenth and twentieth centuries with the influence of **Henrik Ibsen**. In 1917 Betty Nansen, a famous Danish actress who performed in many Ibsen and **Strindberg** plays, created the Betty Nansen Theater in Copenhagen for the production of literary plays. **Bertolt Brecht** spent six years in Denmark (1933–1939) during his exile from Germany, and he was greatly influenced by Scandinavian acting styles and was personally fascinated by Poul Reumert, the leading male actor in Denmark at the time.

Private theaters have thrived in Copenhagen since the nineteenth century, culminating in the success of the New Theater, which by the 1950s rivaled the national theater in quality of acting and production qualities. After 1945 repertory theaters outside the capital increased in number and popularity. A small influential experimental theater, Fiolteatret, was established in 1962, with a repertory of mostly absurdist dramas. The 1970s marked the beginning of a national commitment toward subsidizing theatrical development. Experimentation continues, by enthusiastic artists such as Peter Langdal, whose iconoclastic productions of classics have shocked and impressed audiences through the 1980s and 1990s.

See also Absurdism; Romanticism; Scandinavian Theater; Vaudeville

References: Barba, Eugenio. *Beyond the Floating Islands.* New York: PAJ Publishers, 1986; Christoffersen, Erik Exe. "The Presence Radiated By the Actor-Dancer: On ISTA (International School of Theatre Anthropology)." In *Nordic Theatre Studies: Yearbook For Theatre Research in Scandinavia,* 47–52. Copenhagen: Munksgaard, 1989; Johanne Luise Heiberg. *Et Liv Gjenoplevet I Erindringen.* 5th ed. 4 vols. Copenhagen: Niels Birger Warmberg, 1973–4; Kvam, Kela. "Betty Nansen: A Unique Figure in Danish Theatre." In *Nordic Theatre Studies: Yearbook For Theatre Research in Scandinavia,* ed. Kela Kvam, 69–78. Denmark: Institute for Theatre Research, University of Copenhagen, 1988; Kvam, Kela and Janet Szatkowski. "Denmark." In *Nordic Theatre Studies: Yearbook For Theatre Research in Scandinavia*, 23–33. Copenhagen: Munksgaard International, 1989; Marker, Frederick. "The Actor in the Nineteenth Century: Aspects of Rehearsal and Performance in the Prenaturalistic Theater in Scandinavia." *The Quarterly Journal of Speech* 51 (1965): 177–189.Marker, Lise-Lone, and Fredrerick Marker. *Ingmar Bergman: A Life in the Theater*. New York: Cambridge University Press, 1992; Marker, Frederick, *A History of Scandinavian Theatre*, Cambridge: Cambridge University Press, 1996; Risum, Janne. "Towards Transparency: Soren Kierkegaard on Danish Actresses." In *Nordic Theatre Studies: Yearbook For Theatre Research in Scandinavia*, ed. Kela Kvam, 19–30. Copenhagen: Institute for Theatre Research, University of Copenhagen, 1988; Torppedersen, B. "Theater in Denmark." *Revue du Cinema* 353 (1980).

Depardieu, Gérard (1948–)
France

French film actor. The principal leading man in French films since the early 1980s. As a teenager Depardieu was a juvenile delinquent, taking up acting only as a form of therapy. He made his first film when only sixteen and then pursued acting on television and on the stage. He effectively plays an amazing range of characters, from the sensitive poet in *Cyrano de Bergerac* (1990), to the powerful artist, Rodin, in *Camille Claudel* (1988). He is an unlikely sex symbol, with his rough facial features and broad physical build, but his screen presence is both commanding and compassionate.

References: Katz, Ephraim. *The Film Encyclopedia.* New York: Harper Perennial, 1994.

Deus ex Machina
Greece

The Latin translation of a Greek term; literally, "god from a machine." This term indicates both a mechanical device used in ancient Greece to fly actors portraying gods onto the stage and, because of the way that mechanical device was often used, a literary device in which characters are rescued at the last moment by some improbable stroke of luck that is not in keeping with the drama.

An elaborate system of booms and derricks was used to fly actors portraying Olympian gods down onto the stage to intervene in human affairs, most often rescuing the protagonist from a seemingly insoluble dilemma. In the **Poetics,** Aristotle states that the use of this device should be reserved for those occasions when intervention by the gods is in keeping with the character of the play, and not just used as an easy to wrap up the plot. The playwright **Euripides** was criticized for relying on the *deus ex machina* far too heavily. Half of his tragedies end in this manner.

References: Arnott, Peter D. *Greek Scenic Conventions in the Fifth Century* B.C. Westport, CT: Greenwood, 1978; Bieber, Margarete. *The History of the Greek and Roman Theater*. Princeton, NJ: Princeton University Press, 1961; Halleran, M. R. *Stagecraft in Euripides.* London: Croom Helm, 1985; Seale, D. *Vision and Stagecraft in Sophocles.* London: Croom Helm, 1982; Taplin, Oliver. *The Stagecraft of Aeschylus.* Oxford: Clarendon Press, 1977; Taplin, Oliver. *Greek Tragedy in Action.* Berkeley: University of California Press, 1978.

Deuteragonist
See Tragic Acting in Ancient Greece

Devadasi
India

Formerly a class of women dedicated to serve a Hindu temple, as handmaidens to the gods, they are seen as being symbolically married to a specific deity. Their duty is to dance at the temple and in processions celebrating religious festivals. A carved figure found in the Indus Valley suggests that there were ritual female dancers in India as early as 2500 B.C. A formal caste of temple dancers arose in the ninth and tenth centuries. The dance training for these girls began at the age of seven and lasted approximately seven years before a girl gave her first solo performance (see **Arangetram**). Temple prostitution for the Brahman class developed from this tradition. These girls were taught to read, an exceptional women's skill until modern times. The puritanical influence of Islam, which started as early as the eleventh century, and of British colonists, beginning in the eighteenth century, led to seeing the practice of temple-supported *Devadasis* as immoral. In 1948 female dancing in temples was outlawed, and the *Devadasi* class was disgraced. Recently efforts to restore the dignity of these women have been initiated. *Devadasis* are being used more and more to teach and save the traditional arts they once perfected.

See also *Bharata Natyam; Dasi Attam*

References: Marglin, Frederique Apffel. *Wives of the God-King: Rituals of the Devadasis of Puri.* New York: Oxford University Press, 1989; Massey, Reginald, and Jamie Massey. *Dances of India.* London: Tricolour, 1989; Scott, A. C. *The Theatre in Asia.* New York: Macmillan, 1972.

Dewa Muda

Malaysia

Local Malaysian story about the adventures of *Dewa Muda*, literally means "young god." This story is the primary story used in **Mak Yong,** a form of dance-drama performed mostly by women.

References: Yousof, Ghulam-Sarwar. *The Kelantan "Mak Yong" Dance Theatre: A Study of Performance Structure.* Ann Arbor, MI: Proquest, 1976.

Diderot, Denis (1713–1784)

France

Philosopher, dramatist, and theorist who served as a spokesman for the rising bourgeoisie of France in the eighteenth century. Within a twenty-year span he completed his *Encyclopédie*, containing the most advanced ideas of his day. On the subject of acting he wrote the controversial *Le Paradoxe sur le Comédien* (The Paradox of Acting) in 1773, in which he demanded that the actor be devoid of sensibility. His extreme argument for no emotional involvement on the part of the actor raises important questions for the art of acting. He claims that an actor full of feeling could not possibly repeat a performance night after night and that the actor's task is to exactly render the outward signs of feelings and emotions so that the audience feels what the play is communicating. Diderot believed that the finest example of his prescription for acting was presented by the English actor **David Garrick**.

References: Diderot, Denis. "The Paradox of Acting." In *Masks or Faces*, ed. William Archer. New York: Hill and Wang, 1957.

Dietrich, Marlene (1901–1992)

Germany, United States

German actress who emigrated to the **United States** and became a celebrated star of the silver screen in such films as *The Blue Angel*, 1930, *The Devil Is a Woman*, 1935, and *Touch of Evil*, 1958. She was known for her sultry glares and her supreme control. Her sphinxlike beauty made her a perfect femme fatale. She began her acting career as a chorus girl in German revues, but by 1922 was studying serious theater under **Max Reinhardt**. She worked in silent films beginning in 1928 and in 1930 had the starring role in *Pinzessin Olala*, the first talking movie made in Germany. When the Nazi party came to power in Germany in 1933, Dietrich emigrated to Hollywood. During the war she worked against Nazi control by making anti-Nazi broadcasts in Germany and by entertaining American troops fighting in the war.

References: Frewin, Leslie. *Blond Venus: A Life of Marlene Dietrich.* London: MacGibbon and Kee, 1955; Manvell, Roger, ed. *International Encyclopedia of Film.* New York: Crown, 1972; Spoto, Donald. *Blue Angel: The Life of Marlene Dietrich.* New York: Doubleday, 1992; Wollenberg, Hans. *Fifty Years of German Film.* New York: Arno, 1972.

Dikir Barat

Malaysia

Choral chanting of Koranic verses and other improvised material. This form is thought to have developed in the Patani region in southern Thailand and to have been brought to Kelantan on the east coast of peninsula Malaysia in the twentieth century. Probably it was developed by young men during harvest time who would shout back and forth to each other to pass the time. It is performed by two teams who take turns singing in response to each other. Each team is led by a **Tukang Karut,** who creates the song as he sings it, one line at a time. The chorus repeats what he sings accompanying themselves on tambourines. The content is humorous and even vulgar at times. It is greeted with great enthusiasm by predominantly Muslim audiences. The Indonesian version of this form is called *Kasida*.

References: Wright, Barbara Ann Stein. "Wayang Siam: An Ethnographic Study of the Malay Shadow Play of Kelantan." Ph.D. diss., Ann Arbor, MI: Proquest, 1980.

Marlene Dietrich portrays Lola, a sultry singer, in The Blue Angel *(1930). (Kobol Collection/UFA)*

Dionysia

Greece

Religious celebration dedicated to the Greek god **Dionysus.** There were four such festivals each year in Athens, beginning with the **Rural Dionysia** in December, then the **Lenaia,** the Anthesteria, and the **City Dionysia.** During this festival, a form of revelry known as a **Komos** was performed in honor of Dionysus. Aristotle believed that comedy evolved from the comic improvisations of the revel's leader.

The Lenaia, celebrated in January, featured performances of comedy, though tragedies were also presented. In February at the Anthesteria the year's new wine was drunk. No dramas were performed at this celebration. The last and by far the grandest of all the Dionysia was the City Dionysia in March–April, at which great dramas were performed in honor of Dionysus and in competition for prizes.

References: Arnott, Peter D. *Public and Performance in the Greek Theatre.* New York: Routledge, 1989; Bieber, Margarete. *The History of the Greek and Roman Theater.* Princeton, NJ: Princeton University Press, 1961; Butler, James. *The Theatre and Drama of Greece and Rome.* San Francisco: Chandler, 1972; Taylor, David. *Acting and the Stage.* Boston: George Allen & Unwin, 1978.

Dionysian Artists

Greece

A union of all Ancient Greek theater personnel, made up of many guilds; can be traced to the early third century B.C. The union included actors of tragedy, comedy, and satyr plays; dramatic, epic, and lyric poets; persons who trained actors and the chorus, costumers, stage managers, musicians, and chorus members. These guilds were considered to be religious organizations, since all performances were sacred and in honor of the gods, and thus they were highly respected. Members did not have to serve in the military or pay taxes.

References: Bieber, Margarete. *The History of the Greek and Roman Theater.* Princeton, NJ: Princeton University Press, 1961; O'Connor, John Bartholomew. *Chapters in the History of Actors and Acting in Ancient Greece.* Chicago: University of Chicago Press, 1908; Taylor, David. *Acting and the Stage.* Boston: George Allen & Unwin, 1978; Walton, Michael. *Greek Theatre Practice.* Westport, CT: Greenwood, 1980.

Dionysus
Greece

Greek god of wine. Born, according to the most widely accepted version of the myth, in Thebes of Zeus and the Theban princess Semele, Dionysus is the only Greek god whose parents were not both divine. However, Dionysus eventually raised his mother to Mount Olympus where, though still a mortal, she resided with the gods. It is no surprise that the god of wine should have inspired so many dramatic works in his honor. The effect of wine on humans allows them to feel larger than themselves and thus able to impersonate others. The **Dionysia** were four celebrations in honor of Dionysus that occurred each year in ancient Greece, three of which featured dramatic contests.

Also known as the sufferer, Dionysus was associated with the grapevine, which was cut and pruned to a gnarled stump before each winter, but always came back to life with fresh green

A relief marble sculpture of Dionysus discovering Ariadne on Naxos. (The Art Archive/Musée du Louvre Paris/Dagli Orti)

shoots each spring. Followers of Dionysus took this as assurance that the soul lives on after the death of the body.

> References: Bell, Robert E. *Place-Names in Classical Mythology: Greece.* Santa Barbara, CA: ABC-CLIO, 1989; Boswell, Fred, and Jeanetta Boswell. *What Men or Gods Are These? A Genealogical Approach to Classical Mythology.* Metuchen, NJ: Scarecrow Press, 1980; Hamilton, Edith. *Mythology.* New York: New American Library, 1969; Parada, Carlos. *Genealogical Guide to Greek Mythology.* Jonsered: P. Astroms Forlag, 1993.

Dithyramb
Greece

Hymn celebrating and giving honor to the Greek god **Dionysus.** The name dithyramb means double birth, alluding to Dionysus's birth first from his human mother, Semele, and then from the thigh of Zeus. A musician from the beginning of the sixth century B.C., Arion, is credited with being the first to compose a dithyramb and give it a name. Arion costumed the male performers who sang the verses as **satyrs,** which led to the development of dramatic impersonation.

> References: Bieber, Margarete. *The History of the Greek and Roman Theater.* Princeton, NJ: Princeton University Press, 1961; Walton, Michael. *Greek Theatre Practice.* Westport, CT: Greenwood, 1980; Webster, Thomas Bertram Lonsdale. *The Greek Chorus.* London: Methuen, 1970.

Documentary Theater
Germany, United States

A type of dramatic production developed in Germany in the 1950s, based on recent or historical events, that resembles a documentary in style and content. The highly charged political theater of **Erwin Piscator** was influential in the formation of this genre. In the **United States** the Living Newspaper greatly developed this form. Another highly influential talent in this genre was the playwright **Peter Weiss.**

> References: Filewod, Alan. *Collective Encounters: Documentary Theatre in English Canada.* Toronto: University of Toronto Press, 1987; Holderness, Graham, ed. *The Politics of Theatre and Drama.* New York: St. Martin's, 1992; Willett, John. *The Theatre of Erwin Piscator: Half a Century of Politics in the Theatre.* London: Eyre Methuen, 1978.

Dominus Gregis
Italy

Producer and usually lead actor of a play in ancient Roman times, literally "master of the flock," as a flock of sheep was a Roman term used to indicate a troupe of actors. After establishing a contract with the magistrate organizing the festival, this producer was responsible for every aspect of a production. He chose all of the actors, rehearsed and paid them, and hired musicians to play background music during the performance. A playwright sold a play to the *Dominus Gregis* for a certain amount and received no more money if it was produced again, but he also ran no risk if the play flopped.

> **See also** Ludi
>
> References: Arnott, Peter D. *The Ancient Greek and Roman Theatre.* New York: Random House, 1971; Bieber, Margarete. *The History of the Greek and Roman Theater.* Princeton, NJ: Princeton University Press, 1961; Taylor, David. *Acting and the Stage.* Boston: Allen & Unwin, 1978.

Dottore
Italy

Foolish old lawyer, doctor, or ridiculous scholar; stock character of **commedia dell'arte,** improvised sixteenth- and seventeenth-century comedy. A pseudo-intellectual, he always spoke in a highly affected pedantic manner. In the story lines he was either a friend or a rival of **Pantalone;** either way they were always together. Dottore was as grand in size as Pantalone was scrawny and made large gestures that took up much of the room around him. He was always out of money and thus a parasite. He could be identified by his long black cloak, black half mask, and hat with a broad upturned brim. This character greatly inspired **Molière,** the French comic playwright and actor of the neoclassical age.

> References: Craig, Edward Gordon. "The Characters of the Commedia Dell'Arte." *The Mask* (January 1912); Rudlin, John. *Commedia Dell'Arte: An Actor's Handbook.* London and New York: Routledge, 1994.

Drama Gong
Bali

Spoken drama; a new form of theater in Bali, though still based on traditional stories. There is no dance. All acting is quite realistic. The costumes are beautifully ornate, much like traditional Balinese performing costumes. The music of the **gamelan,** the traditional orchestra, is used.

References: Brandon, James R. *Brandon's Guide to Theatre in Asia.* Honolulu: University Press of Hawaii, 1976.

Drew Family
See Barrymore Family

Dulac, Germaine (1882–1942)
France
French silent film director who promoted "pure cinema," free from the influence of literature, visual arts, and the stage. Dulac created what some regard as the first truly feminist film, *La Coquille et le Clergyman* (The Seashell and the Clergyman), 1927, written by **Antonin Artaud**, which is also a masterfully acted psychological film. These late 1920s films were a part of what is called the second avant-garde. Dulac and her husband owned their own production company. Her career and her artistic experiments ended with the advent of sound.

References: *Armes, Roy. French Film. New York: Dutton, 1970; Dulac, Germaine. Ecrits sur le Cinema: 1919-1937. Paris: Editions Paris Experimental, 1994; Katz, Ephraim. The Film Encyclopedia. New York: Harper Perennial, 1994.*

Dullin, Charles (1885–1949)
France
Actor, director, and manager who worked passionately for truth in acting. In 1913 he was given his start as an actor by **Jacques Copeau** at the Théâtre du Vieux-Colombier. From 1921 to 1938 he directed the Théâtre de l'Atelier. Dedicated to nurturing and training actors, Dullin became an important force behind the careers of many notable French actors. Opposed to the beautiful rhetorical tradition preceding him, Dullin rallied for simplicity and sincerity in acting. He also preferred simple settings and avoided excessively rich decors for his stagings. In the task of realizing the playwright's vision, Dullin believed that instinct was an actor's greatest tool. He is primar-

ily remembered as an actor, but as a director he made great strides toward a poetic simplicity, in contrast to the overemphasis on stage business of the Naturalists at the time.

See also Naturalism
References: Arnaud, Lucien. *Charles Dullin.* Paris: L'Arche, 1952.

Dunham, Katherine (1910–)
Caribbean, United States
A dancer, dance ethnologist, and a choreographer. Dunham was born of a black Caribbean father and a French-Canadian mother near Chicago. Trained as a dancer, she was led toward the dances of the Caribbean in hopes of discovering her own cultural heritage. Many scattered Caribbean blacks had migrated to the mainland, and her work helped forge a link between their shared cultural past and their present urban reality.

She spent the year 1937–1938 in the Caribbean islands on a Rosenwald fellowship for research and wrote the book *The Dances of Haiti,* on **Haiti** and other islands of the Caribbean. Because

Katherine Dunham and Vanoye Aikens in Dunham's ballet L'Ag 'Ya at the Prince of Wales Theater in London, 1948. (Archive Photos)

of her blood tie to Africa and the Caribbean, she was able to witness, record, and participate in both social dances and religious rituals.

Upon returning to the **United States,** she both performed in and choreographed nine Broadway shows, including *Cabin in the Sky,* and several films, including *Stormy Weather.* With earnings from work of this kind, she financed her school and company. She combined her ethnological research with her original creativity to create three successive revues: *Carib Song* (1945), *Bal Nègre* (1947), and *Caribbean Rhapsody* (1948). She adapted actual rituals for the stage as she represented everyday life in primitive communities of the Caribbean. She herself trained her dancers in classical ballet with Central European, Caribbean, and African elements.

One piece entitled *Shango* (1945), a mixture of dance and ritual, features elements from Yoruba cult worship similar to rituals still taking place in **Nigeria.** The initial dances in the piece lead to a ceremonial sacrifice to Shango, thunder god of the Yoruba people. The boy enacting the sacrifice is momentarily possessed by Damballa, the snake god, under the control of the officiating priest. At the conclusion, the boy is triumphantly carried

through the village on a huge sacred drum. Dunham first created another piece, entitled *Rites de Passage* (1943), to illustrate her lecture at Yale University on "An Anthropological Approach to the Theater." The work concerns a young man in a primitive community being initiated into adult life and a man and woman falling in love, all against the backdrop of daily activities in village life.

References: Alcide, Marie-Jose. "Theatrical and Dramatic Elements of Haitian Voodoo." Ph.D. diss., City University of New York, 1988; Buckle, Richard. *Katherine Dunham: Her Dancers, Singers, Musicians.* London: Ballet Publications, 1949; Clark, Veve A. "Contemporary Forms of Popular Theatre in Haiti." *Ufahamu* 12, 2 (1983): 93–100; Dunham, Katherine. *Dances of Haiti.* Los Angeles: Center for Afro-American Studies, 1983; Grimard, Luc. "Historical Existence of the Haitian Theatre." *World Theatre* 16, 5–6 (1967): 534–535; Pompilus, Pradel. "Tendencies of the Haitian Theatre." *World Theatre* 16, 5–6 (1967): 534–536.

Duse, Eleonora (1858–1924)
Italy

Internationally known Italian actress. Born of a theater family, she began acting as a young girl.

A priest attempts a healing by the laying of hands in the Dutch film Spetters (1980). (Kobol Collection/VSE/Endemol)

During her time, Italian theater was in the shadow of **Italian opera.** Playwriting was unexceptional, and star actors performed in a highly affected, flamboyant style. Troupes were forced to tour constantly to survive. She won audiences over to the realistic mode of acting with her subtle, yet intensely emotional, portrayals of characters. Able to reveal the inner hopes and inner conflicts of characters she portrayed, Eleonora displayed great psychological insight.

She was superb as the lead character in many plays by **Henrik Ibsen,** playing, for example, Hedda Gabler in the play by the same name and Nora in *A Doll's House.* She gained the admiration of the playwright **Anton Chekhov** when she performed in Russia in 1881. Because of ill health she retired in 1913, but for financial reasons returned to the stage in the 1920s. She died in Pittsburgh while on an American tour.

See also Bernhardt, Sarah

References: Noccioli, Guido. *Duse on Tour: Guido Noccioli's Diaries, 1906–1907.* Trans. Giovanni Pontiero. Amherst: University of Massachusetts Press, 1982; Weaver, William. *Duse: A Biography.* San Diego, CA: Harcourt Brace Jovanovich, 1984.

Dutch Cinema

The Dutch film industry was slow to get started. One of the first films to compete with foreign imports was *The Black Tulip,* 1921. From that time until the 1970s the documentary film was the major mode of filmmaking. The filmmaker Paul Verhoeven has made the largest contribution to Dutch film, with *Spetters,* 1980, and *The Fourth Man,* 1983; he then moved on to Hollywood, where he created such popular works as *Robocop,* 1987 and *Basic Instinct,* 1992. Many Dutch actors have gone on to gain international acclaim, including Rutger Hauer, Renee Soutendjik, and Johanna ter Steege. In 1999 the International Film Festival in Rotterdam enjoyed its twenty-eighth year in existence.

References: Katz, Ephraim. *The Film Encyclopedia.* New York: Harper Perennial, 1994; Kehr, Dave. "The Discreet Charm of Rotterdam." *Film Comment* 32, 2 (March-April 1999): 68–69.

E

Eastwood, Clint (1930–)
Italy, United States

American actor and director who got his start on television in the Western series *Rawhide*, in which he starred from the late 1950s into the 1960s. True fame came in Italy, where he starred in the **spaghetti westerns** directed by Sergio Leone, *A Fistful of Dollars*, 1964, *For a Few Dollars More*, 1965, and *The Good, The Bad and the Ugly*, 1966. In these violent films he created and established the role he played in most of his subsequent movies, that of a silent, stoic man, self-sufficient and often a reluctant hero. His long legs, sandy wind-blown hair, squinting eyes and nearly expressionless lips became his trademark. Back in the **United States** his most popular film, *Dirty Harry*, 1971, stirred up controversy because of its excessive violence.

Eastwood gained respect as a director with the making of a film based on the life of jazz musician Charlie Parker, *Bird*, 1988; his dark Western *Unforgiven*, 1992, which he both directed and starred in, won the Oscar for Best Picture.

> **References:** Gallafent, Edward. *Clint Eastwood: Filmmaker and Star.* New York: Continuum, 1994; Schickel, Richard. *Clint Eastwood: A Biography.* New York: Knopf, 1996.

Edinburgh Festival
See Scotland

Eglogas
Spain

Dramatic form, first written by Juan del Encina (1469–1529) in the early sixteenth century, consisting of verse dialogues between rustic characters, usually shepherds. Encina wrote on the themes of religious holy days such as Easter, contemporary issues, and love, and he even performed in his own plays. Other dramatists also used this form and eventually expanded upon it to create the Spanish form of **Comedia.**

> **References:** McKendrick, Melveena. *Theatre in Spain: 1490–1700*, New York: Cambridge University Press, 1989.

Egypt

The theatrical tradition in Egypt is exceptional; Egypt may have had the first drama known to the world, and it has been for centuries a leader in talent and creative energy in the Middle East. Egyptian civilization in the fertile Nile valley dating from 5000 B.C. enjoyed great wealth and cultural brilliance, especially during the dynasties of pharaohs from 3200 B.C. to 341 B.C. Many rich theatrical traditions flourished during this time, which gave homage to the Egyptian gods and kings. In 332 B.C., when Alexander the Great of Macedonia conquered Egypt, he introduced Greek and Roman culture, which became widely popular. In the early seventh century Muslim

Arabs invaded Egypt, bringing an abrupt halt to all theatrical activity except the *Fasl Mudhik,* crude farcical skits. From the thirteenth century on, an indigenous Egyptian style of **Arabic shadow puppet theater** evolved. European-influenced modern theater developed, predominantly in the nineteenth century, and the Egyptian film industry got a strong start in the early twentieth century.

Ancient texts from the Early Dynastic Period (3100–2686 B.C.) suggest that Egypt has the oldest traditions of drama known in the world. These include the Pyramid Texts, dramas about specific king's deaths, and the Ramesseum Dramatic Papyrus, which contains a ritual play about the legend of Osiris. This drama had forty-six scenes, which were performed at places along the Nile and viewed by the king while he cruised down the river on a boat. During the Old Kingdom (2686–2181 B.C.), ritual dramas flourished that celebrated each king symbolically becoming Horus, son of Osiris and Isis. Also the Memphite Drama was evidently performed during an annual festival that took place on the first day of spring. From 2500–500 B.C., the Abydos Passion Play, a ritual play centering on themes of creation and regeneration, was regularly performed.

Egypt has been a major force in the vitality and creation of modern Arab theater, because of the Egyptian creative zest and because Egyptian troupes toured heavily throughout Arab-speaking lands. Reportedly, French actors came to Egypt after the Napoleonic invasion, and a French theater was founded in the early nineteenth century. Italian troupes were most active touring in Egypt in the first half of the nineteenth century. The opera they brought with them became widely popular, and the other most popular forms were musical plays and comedies. One of the first actors to start a troupe during the British occupation (1882–1922) was Sulaimaan al-Qirdaahi, a Syrian immigrant who lived until 1909. He introduced the first women, including his own wife, onto the stage at the Opera House in Cairo, a practice already in vogue in **Syria**. **Salama Hijazi** was the first great Muslim actor associated with modern Arab theater, especially known for stressing the musical element and for introducing the practice of touring in Arab-speaking countries. After World War I, modern burlesques, influenced by foreign revues during war time, became popular in Egypt.

The Egyptian government has been supportive of the development of modern Arab theater by awarding prizes, granting scholarships for foreign study, supporting dramatic schools, and subsidizing dramatic theater troupes and actors. In 1935 the National Theatre opened. Egypt grew to a new artistic maturity in the 1960s, but progress was halted by new censorship laws enacted by President Sadat in 1973.

Egypt has dominated the film industry throughout the Arab world since its inception. Egypt's first full-length feature, *Layla,* about an abandoned pregnant woman, was produced by its star, stage actress 'Aziza Amir (1901–1952), and screened in 1927. When sound was introduced to film in the early 1930s, music became an important component of Egyptian films. Top singers from the stage, such as Muhammad 'Abd al'Wahhab and Umm Kulthum, starred in many stories written around their songs. The first serious historical movie was presented in 1934 by actress-producer Assia Daghia, *Queen Shagar al-Durr,* set in Cairo in the Middle Ages. Director Kamal Slim gave Egyptian audiences a taste of neorealism in 1940 with *Determination,* shot in the streets of Cairo and incorporating the real actions of daily life in the city. Egypt's exports throughout the Arab world depend on the overwhelming popularity of musical comedies and melodramas. In the 1950s especially, a rigid star system evolved for actors, with Faten Hamama and her husband 'Umar Sharif as the most popular screen actors.

Many Free Theaters emerged in the 1970s appealing mostly to young audiences. In the same decade many of Egypt's best actors turned away from the stage to work in film; the Cairo International Festival for Experimental Theater was established in 1988. Commercial theater continues to thrive into the twenty-first century. Although the government withdrew much of its financial support for the film industry in the early 1990s, many excellent films have been made, including *The Vagabonds* (1985) and *Kit Kat* (1991).

See also Italian Neorealism

References: Awad, Ramsis. *Shakespeare in Egypt.* al-Qahirah, Egypt: al-Hayah al-Misriyah al-Ammah lil-Kitab, 1986; Kahle, P. "The Arabic Shadow Play in Egypt." *Journal of the Royal Asiatic Society of*

Great Britain and Ireland (1940): 21–34; Khan, Mohamed. *An Introduction to the Egyptian Cinema.* London: Informatics, 1969; Landau, Jacob. *Studies in the Arab Theater and Cinema.* Philadelphia: University of Pennsylvania Press, 1958; Moreh, S. "The Arabic Theatre in Egypt in the Eighteenth and Nineteenth Centuries." *Etudes Arabes et Islamiques* 3 (1975): 109–113.

Ekhof, Konrad (1720–1778)
Germany

Considered by his contemporaries to be the greatest German actor of his time. Though of slight build, he had a commanding presence because of the confident manner in which he moved and the rich quality of his voice. In 1739 he joined the Friedrich Schonemann Company and remained the lead actor for seventeen years. He developed naturalistic styles of acting. In 1753 he founded the first German school for acting, the Academy of Acting, although it didn't last long. Beginning in 1801 he acted for a short time at the Court Theater in Weimar under **Goethe**.

> **See also** Naturalism
> **References:** Chinoy, Helen Krich, and Toby Cole. *Actors on Acting.* New York: Crown, 1970; Williams, Simon. *German Actors of the Eighteenth and Nineteenth Centuries: Idealism, Romanticism, and Realism.* Westport, CT: Greenwood, 1985.

Ekkyklema
Greece

A low platform on wheels used in ancient Greek theater to show interior scenes. Since the setting for plays portrayed the exterior of buildings, the *ekkyklema* would be rolled out from the central doors of the **skene,** or scene building, with actors upon it in a tableau. The audience was to imagine that the scene was still inside. This was a stage device for making visible the action of a play and was most often used to reveal some violent or dramatic act that occurred offstage. It was not the custom to show the sometimes horrifying violence that occurred in the Greek plays on the stage. However, the results of these violent acts, most often slain bodies, were revealed on the *ekkyklema*.

> **References:** Bieber, Margarete. *The History of the Greek and Roman Theater.* Princeton, NJ: Princeton University Press, 1961; Halleran, M. R. *Stagecraft in Euripides.* London: Croom Helm, 1985; Seale, D. *Vision and Stagecraft in Sophocles.* London: Croom Helm, 1982; Taplin, Oliver. *Greek Tragedy in Action.* Berkeley: University of California Press, 1978.

Elizabethan England

The Elizabethan age stands out in theater history as having seen the evolution of an alive and vigorous national theater, created by extraordinary playwrights, superb actors and directors, and a ready audience. This was an era when the imagination was allowed free rein on an unrestricted stage amidst minimal stage mechanics. Never before or since, perhaps, has so much been conjured in the imagination of the audience with so little. Queen Elizabeth, for whom the era was named, lived from 1533 to 1603 and was queen of **England** and **Ireland** from 1558 to 1603. During her reign there emerged a national secular theater performed by professional actors, such as **Richard Burbage**. The relatively crude plays of the Middle Ages were replaced by plays that were in part inspired by the rediscovery of the classic texts from Greece and the new use of the ancient models from both Greece and Rome by the humanists of the Renaissance, yet still kept the vitality of the native farces and comedies. These influences worked together to create an era of dramatic literature that was sophisticated in its ideas but still had a raucous vitality that rendered it appealing to the widest audience, including the educated and the uneducated, the nobility, the middle class, and the working class. This golden age of theater continued, with some changes, into the reign of Elizabeth's successor, James I (1603–1625), and did not completely end until the outbreak of the English Civil War.

In the earliest days of Queen Elizabeth's reign, boy actors enacted the works of court writers, which glorified their queen. Later itinerant vagabond actors sought out patronage from the court, during which time the court theater and private theaters began to flourish. The main dramatists of this time were **Christopher Marlowe**, **William Shakespeare**, and Ben Jonson (1572–1637), all of whom explored aspects of the human experience with new depth and precision.

A model of the Globe Theatre as built by Richard and Cuthbert Burbage in London in 1599. (Adam Woolfit / Corbis)

The two most successful companies were The Chamberlain's Men (later The King's Men) and The Admiral's Men (later Prince Henry's Men). Each company consisted of a group of professional male actors who collectively owned their theaters and commissioned playwrights to write plays for them. Profits on performances were shared. Young boys apprenticed with a theater and portrayed female roles, since there were no female actors in England until 1656. The theater buildings, the most famous of which were the Fortune, the Swan, and the Globe, were built on the outskirts of the city. These multilevel circular (or octagonal) structures held thousands of spectators, all focused on a thrust platform stage that was both simple and versatile. Sunlight lit the unroofed theater, and minimal stage scenery and props were used. The performance style was uninterrupted platform playing, meaning that one scene followed directly on the heels of the previous one. Characters would establish where they were through their dialogue or with a simple

prop. For example, a character entering the stage with a lantern would convey that it was night. Actors were among tight small theater groups who consistently worked together and often portrayed more than one role in a play. Short runs of plays were the norm.

The reign of James I was known as the Jacobean era (because Jacobus is the Latin form of James), and theater continued to flourish. James was an ardent supporter of the arts but did impose some restrictions on the theater. This was nothing new since under Elizabeth, Ben Jonson spent some time in jail for his part in a play considered subversive. He sponsored many elaborate masques, lavish theatrical fantasies, which used full stage settings and machinery for special effects for the first time in England; the greatest of these masques were the result of collaboration between Ben Jonson and the designer Inigo Jones (1573–1652). Such performances were of course aimed only at the nobility and the royal family. Private indoor theaters, which catered to the upper classes, also became more important during the Jacobean era, and even more so under the reign of James's son, Charles I (1625–1649). A national theater that appealed to all classes was less and less the reality.

Those called Puritans, who wanted to complete the reform of the English church and purify it of all traces of practices that were not clearly prescribed in the Bible, had always opposed the theater. Under James and Charles they became more and more powerful, opposing also the unlimited power of the crown and gaining power in Parliament. Finally civil war broke out, in 1642, and Parliament, in control in London, closed the theaters. Theater did not return until the Restoration of Charles I's son in 1660, but even then, could not regain the same level of excellence or the audience to support it.

References: Baker, Henry Barton. *English Actors from Shakespeare to Macready.* New York: H. Holt, 1879; Bradley, David. *From Text to Performance in the Elizabethan Theatre.* New York: Cambridge University Press, 1992; Edgecombe, David. *Theatrical Training during the Age of Shakespeare.* Lewiston, NY: Edwin Mellen Press, 1995; Hattaway, Michael. *Elizabethan Popular Theatre: Plays in Performance.* London: Routledge and Kegan Paul, 1982; Nicoll, Allardyce. *The English Theatre: A Short History.* London: Nelson, 1936.

Emmeleia

See Greek Chorus

England

One of the most theatrically accomplished nations in the world, with a rich history of great actors, playwrights, and directors. Performers, mimes, and storytellers no doubt traveled throughout England even during the early Middle Ages, of which so little is known that they are called the Dark Ages. As far as recorded history is concerned, theater was first presented within the church walls, with priests performing most of the parts. These performances were all religious in content. Eventually they moved out into the churchyard and then into the marketplace, where they became increasingly secular and humorous so as to please their audience. By 1210 a papal edict forbade priests from performing, since shows were becoming increasingly lewd. Shows were also by this time performed in the vernacular instead of Latin.

Trade guilds took over the theater, and their theatrical activities were at their height from 1300 to 1450. They performed plays based on Bible stories or the lives of saints. There are many cycle plays, a group of plays about a central theme or figure, from this time as well, such as the York cycle and the Chester cycle. The great cycles of scriptural plays are so called because each tells the whole story of humanity as presented in the Bible, from the Fall till the Last Judgment. Each guild was responsible for all aspects of production for one play in the cycle, the whole of which was usually performed on a religious holiday such as **Corpus Christi.** Each play had its own pageant wagon, and the wagons were drawn from one location to the next through town, presenting to a different audience at each location. These plays, performed by paid actors, were religious in theme, but they were not without their humorous elements. Noah's wife, for example, was a favorite humorous character; she is shown refusing to go on board the ark if her friends have to be left behind.

Another form of religious drama was the **morality play,** first performed at the end of the fourteenth century. These plays were moral allegories, most often about a person either strug-

gling with or receiving aid from different allegorical characters such as Kindness, Good Deeds, and Ignorance. During the late fifteenth and early sixteenth century the interlude developed, a brief, usually comic, dramatic piece, often presented during a feast. These plays were often performed purely for entertainment; they may also reflect the elitist, intellectual values of Renaissance humanism; in any case, they took the drama in a secular direction. Under the Tudor monarchs of the sixteenth century, traveling actors were severely looked down upon and would be punished for performing plays unless under the protection of nobility. These laws were still in effect at the beginning of **Shakespeare**'s time.

Even during the golden age of theater in **Elizabethan England**, English Puritans (as those were called who wanted to complete the reform of the English church, purifying it of the ritual and hierarchy of the Roman Catholic Church) were fighting the immorality of the theater. Their triumph came in 1642, when civil war broke out between Parliament and Charles I (r. 1625–1649). As a war measure, Parliament closed the theaters, and they remained closed until Charles II (1630–1685; r. 1660–1685) was restored to the throne in 1660. The theater of the Restoration Age began with great energy, but it was no longer in any sense the national theater of Elizabethan England. The dramatists catered to the nobility and the court, were influenced by French neoclassicism, rejected the freedom in staging of Shakespeare's day as barbarous, yet went in for the kind of wit, often laced with sexual innuendo, that have made Restoration comedy the most enduringly popular product of the age. One advancement was the introduction of actresses to the English stage, a convention that Charles brought back from France, where he had taken refuge for part of the war and again after his father was defeated, captured, and beheaded by Parliament and he himself had failed in his attempt to regain his kingdom.

In 1660 two playhouses were allowed by the king, the Duke of York's Company and the King's Men, which remained the case until 1843. Star actors such as Thomas Betterton (1635–1710) and his wife, Mary Saunderson (died in 1712), became more important than playwrights in Restoration theater. After them came Barton Booth (1681–1733), Elizabeth Barry (1658–1713), and

Colley Cibber. Acting during the first part of the eighteenth century was formal and full of exaggerated gestures. **David Garrick** and **Charles Macklin** were two of the first to replace the declamatory style of acting with a more natural style based on authentic actions. Sarah Kemble Siddons (1755–1831), who was elegantly simple in her approach, and her brother John Philip Kemble (1757–1823), who was well-mannered and cold, contributed to the further development of acting at the end of the eighteenth century.

In the nineteenth century a more naturalistic style of acting became the norm. Stage settings also became more realistic box sets, all placed generally behind a proscenium arch. Great actors of the nineteenth century include Edmund Kean, Junius Brutus Booth (1796–1852), Charles Kemble (1775–1854), and Eliza O'Neill (1791–1872). In the later part of the nineteenth century the actor-manager **Henry Irving** directed at the Lyceum Theatre and created excellent works with such fine performers as **Ellen Terry**. Terry's son, **Gordon Craig**, went on to become an influential stage designer and theorist. **Oscar Wilde**'s witty drawing room comedies were as popular as he himself was in society. At the turn of the century, many smaller independent experimental theater groups, impressed by the realism they saw on the continent, tried to create a native realism. The playwright **George Bernard Shaw** took the lead in this movement, following Ibsen's lead in writing plays, often brilliant comedies, that took up controversial social topics. Light opera was taken to new heights at the end of the nineteenth century by the duo **Gilbert and Sullivan.**

At the beginning of the twentieth century, playwriting was dominated by fairly conventional well-made plays and stagings of the classics. It saw the development of popular traditions such as music halls, Christmas pantomimes, and the puppet theater of **Punch and Judy**. Also for a popular audience, **Joan Littlewood** created a tradition of collective collaboration in England with her Theatre Workshop in the 1930s through the 1960s. The majority of the theater being created at this time, however, appealed to the upper-middle class. Two of the greatest actors to emerge from this type of theater were **John Gielgud** and **Laurence Olivier**, who both made enormous

(though very different) contributions to theater and film throughout their careers.

Two national theaters were established, the **Royal Shakespeare Company,** from the Shakespeare Memorial Theatre**,** which was formed in 1879 at Stratford-upon-Avon, and the National Theatre, from the Old Vic, a famous London theater that opened in 1818. Olivier became the first artistic director of the National Theatre in 1962. Peter Hall (born in 1930) took over artistic direction in 1988 and moved the company to a new theater in London's South Bank district. The actor **Derek Jacobi** got his start at the National Theatre.

The mood of playwriting changed drastically with *Look Back in Anger* (1956) by **John Osborne**, the first of the group known as the angry young men, who attacked the rigidity of the class structure. Conservative values and traditional forms of doing theater were continually challenged through the 1960s by works such as *Marat/Sade* directed by **Peter Brook** at a workshop called the Theatre of Cruelty (influenced by the radical concepts of **Antonin Artaud**) at the Royal Shakespeare Company. It was here that the actress **Glenda Jackson** got her start. The most commercially successful and broadly popular work to come out of England in the 1970s and 1980s has been the musicals of **Andrew Lloyd Webber**. A true "actor's" theater was created in the 1980s with **Kenneth Branagh**'s Renaissance Theatre Company, where **Emma Thompson** also performed. Throughout the 1990s and into the twenty-first century, England continues to be a powerful force in theater. Extremely diverse in its output, English theater ranges from experimental and progressive to mainstream production of the classics and musicals. The Nualas group in London created and performed a work of performance art, *The Big Shiny Dress Tour* (1999), the Tamasha Theatre Company presented an Indian musical spoof *Fourteen Songs, Two Weddings and a Funeral* (2001) in London. The Oxford Stage Company revived the David Storey play *The Contractor* (2001) at the Derby Playhouse in Oxford, England.

See also United Kingdom Cinema
References: Ansorge, Peter. *Disrupting the Spectacle: Five Years of Experimental and Fringe Theatre in Britain.* London: Pitman, 1975; Baker, Henry Barton. *English Actors from Shakespeare to Macready.* New York: H. Holt, 1879; Beadle, Richard. *The Cambridge Com-*

panion to *Medieval English Theatre*. New York: Cambridge University Press, 1994; Brander. *Actors and Actresses of Great Britain and the United States: From the Days of David Garrick to the Present Time*. New York: Cassell, 1886; Nicoll, Allardyce. *The English Theatre: A Short History*. London: Nelson, 1936; Noble, Peter. *British Theatre*. London: British Yearbooks, 1946; Price, Cecil John Layton. *The English Theatre in Wales in the Eighteenth and Early Nineteenth Centuries*. Cardiff: University of Wales Press, 1948; Taylor, John Russell. *Anger and After: The Angry Theatre: New British Drama*. New York: Hill and Wang, 1969.

Entremés
Spain

Spanish term describing a brief dramatic or non-dramatic diversion performed during full-length plays throughout the sixteenth and seventeenth centuries. An *entremés* was typically a comic or satirical skit, which usually came between the acts of a play and most often ended in singing and dancing. A comic *loa*, or prelude, preceded a play and was usually shorter and more varied in content than the *entremés*. In a loa a single performer would introduce a play, beg for attention for the coming production, talk about the actors, or even explain innovations in the play the audience is about to see. These diversions were sometimes the main attraction for less sophisticated audiences and were later developed into one-act plays.

> **References:** McKendrick, Melveena. *Theatre in Spain: 1490–1700*. New York: Cambridge University Press, 1989.

Epic Theater
Germany

A term for a type of political theater advocating the reform of society to fit Socialist ideals; made widely known through the work of **Bertolt Brecht**, but formulated earlier by theater artists such as **Erwin Piscator** in the late 1920s. Epic theater challenges the audience to think and actively consider their social plight. The epic actor serves as a sort of narrator, almost commenting on the character he or she is portraying during the very act of portraying the character. The actor does not lose him or herself in the character, but instead remains actively conscious of all that is happening. Epic theater seeks the alienation effect; in other words, it is an anti-emotionalist type of drama, in which the audience is purposefully kept from identifying with the characters and the suspense of the plot, yet is expected to remain alert and thinking.

> **References:** Chinoy, Helen Krich, and Toby Cole. *Actors on Acting*. New York: Crown, 1970; Speirs, Ronald. *Bertolt Brecht*. New York: St. Martin's, 1987; Weideli, Walter. *The Art of Bertolt Brecht*. New York: New York University Press, 1963; Willett, John. *The Theatre of Erwin Piscator: Half a Century of Politics in the Theatre*. London: Eyre Methuen, 1978.

Epidaurus
Greece

An outdoor theater in southern Greece designed by the architect Polykleitos about 340 B.C. Since antiquity this structure has been considered to be the most harmonious and beautiful theater of the classical age. Today the stage building made of stone is almost completely destroyed, but the seating, in which each seat had an equally good view of the orchestra, is much as it was when first constructed. The stage was raised and altered somewhat during the Hellenistic age.

> **References:** Bieber, Margarete. *The History of the Greek and Roman Theater*. Princeton, NJ: Princeton University Press, 1961; Tomlinson, Richard Allan. *Epidauros*. Austin: University of Texas Press, 1983.

Episkenion

See Hellenistic Theater

Er
China

Assistant puppeteer for **Fu Tai Hsi**.

Eskimo Spirit Play
Canada, Greenland, United States

Spirit play enacted by a shaman and other actors. The first Eskimo tribes, which include the Inuit, traveled across the Bering Strait at least 5,000 years ago to inhabit the coasts of Alaska, northern parts of Canada, and parts of Greenland. Shamans (called *Angakok*) in Eskimo culture can be female as well as male. This person must perform in many ways during healing rituals, by mimicking animals and spirits, performing in masks, and pantomiming different interactions. A major spirit play is the Sedna festival, done over three days each fall, which reenact the ritual-myth of a mermaid spirit, Sedna. With the help of a shaman, performers enact spearing Sedna, as she rises through a hole in the ice, and drag her on a line. Some spirit plays are performed in winter igloos specially made for performances, rectangular or circular, with a special acting area and seating.

References: Buller, Edward. *Indigenous Performing and Ceremonial Arts in Canada: An Annotated Bibliography of Canadian Indian Rituals and Ceremonies.* Toronto: Association for Native Development in the Performing and Visual Arts, 1981; Fitzhugh, William. *Inua: Spirit World of the Bering Sea Eskimo.* Washington, DC: Published for the National Museum of Natural History by the Smithsonian Institution Press, 1982.

Esperento

Spain

A dramatic method, sometimes translated as "absurd," which is an innovation of the Spanish playwright, Ramón del Valle-Inclán (1869–1936). In this method, the norms of theater are distorted, and reality is presented in a ruthless and uncompromising vision as a grotesque deformation of European civilization. Vall-Inclán's plays *Divine Words*, 1913, and *Lights of Bohemia*, 1920, most vividly demonstrate this method.

See also Spain

References: Edwards, Gwynne. *Dramatists in Perspective: Spanish Theatre in the Twentieth Century.* Cardiff: University of Wales Press, 1985; Holt, M. "Twentieth Century Spanish Theatre and the Canon," *Anales de la Literatura Espanola Contemporanea* 17, 1–3 (1992): 47–54.

Estonia

The Estonians are ethnically and linguistically closely related to the Finnish people. Estonian culture has been challenged historically, as Estonia has been colonized by the Danes, the Swedes, the Poles, and the Russians. Still a fierce pride emerged when the Ests were freed from serfdom in 1819, and a cultural revival resulted, in which folk songs, dances, and stories were celebrated

nationally. In 1939 Estonia lost its independence to the former Soviet Union and remained under its control until 1991, when it again gained independence.

The Estonia Theater in Tallinn is presently hugely popular, presenting traditional Estonian theater and dance, ballet, and opera. An original Estonian opera, *Puhh*, was performed in 1995. Estonian theater artists now seek to create their own voice, using the work of such playwrights as Artur Alliksaar (1923–1966) who wrote *The Nameless Island*, 1966, an anti-Stalinist fable. Alliksaar was censored during his lifetime and was not published until after his death. He was highly influential on an entire generation following his death.

See also Finland; Latvia; Lithuania

References: Slodkowski, Andrew, director and producer. *Baltic States.* San Ramon, CA: International Video Network, 1992; Straumanis, Alfreds. *Confrontation with Tyranny: Six Baltic Plays with Introductory Essays.* Prospect Heights, IL: Wavelands, 1977; Straumanis, Alfreds. *Fire and Night, Five Baltic Plays.* Prospect Heights, IL: Waveland, 1986; Vesilind, Priit. "The Baltic Nations." *National Geographic* 178, 5 (November 1990): 2–36.

Ethiopia

Ethiopia has a thriving popular theater and a rich cultural past. However, their theater is hardly known outside its borders, primarily because nearly all works are performed in the local language, Amharic. Coptic Christianity became Ethiopia's dominant religion in the fourth century. Indigenous forms of acting and dancing were suppressed as early as the sixth century, but certain church-created arts were encouraged, such as priestly dances and oral poetry. Amhara is the dominant culture in Ethiopia, but many other cultures were incorporated into the nation during conquests in the nineteenth century. Performance forms of these people are little known but are believed to include many dramatic forms of dance, storytelling, and ritual enactments.

Modern theater in Ethiopia got its jumpstart from Haile Selassie when he ascended to the throne in 1930. He continued to be both highly supportive and controlling of theatrical activity. The revolution of 1974 led to an expansion of theater as a tool for widespread politicization under the new military council. By the 1980s the government was enacting more censorship control over the theater, but in the early 1990s some liberalization of the theater began. Currently many urban theater groups are presenting greatly varied improvised productions for profit.

References: Banham, Martin. *African Theatre Today.* London: Pitman, 1976.; Eshete, Aleme. *The Cultural Situation in Socialist Ethiopia.* Paris: UNESCO, 1982; Levine, D. N. *Wax and Gold: Tradition and Innovation in Ethiopian Culture.* Chicago: University of Chicago Press, 1965; Pankhurst, E. Sylvia. *Ethiopia: A Cultural History.* Essex, UK: Lalibela House, 1955.

Euripides (485–406 B.C.)
Greece

Last of the great ancient Greek tragic playwrights; considered to be a "philosopher among poets." Educated as a free thinker, he was less reverent in his use of the Greek myths than other playwrights. Euripides elevated human values and concerns over those of the gods. Some say that he destroyed the religious meaning of tragedy by focusing excessively on human psychology. Through his plays he criticized Athenian politics and society, especially the treatment of women as inferior. Ten of the eighteen surviving plays by Euripides focus on women. Euripides created thoroughly developed female characters, something not done by his predecessors.

In addition to creating new subject matter for tragedy, Euripides made many other theatrical innovations. His dialogue was more colloquial and more human than that of his contemporaries. The **skene,** or scene building, could represent many things in Euripides' plays, for example, a rural shrine or a hut. The thought was often more unified than the action in his plays, and he often resorted to bringing a god on stage (called by the Romans the **deus ex machina,** or god from the machine) at the end of his plays to restore the balance and bring about the ending that his audience expected. His many innovations cost him popularity and acceptance in his own time. It was not until after his death that his works became popular and widely performed.

Euripides may have written as many as ninety-two plays, but only eighteen survive. The better-known works include *Medea,* 431, *Cyclops* (the only surviving satyr play), 423, *The Trojan Women,* 415, *Electra,* 417, and the *Bacchae,* 405.

References: Bates, William Nickerson. *Euripides: A Student of Human Nature.* Philadelphia: University of Pennsylvania Press, 1930; Bieber, Margarete. *The History of the Greek and Roman Theater.* Princeton, NJ: Princeton University Press, 1961; Blaicklock, E. M. *The Male Characters of Euripides: A Study in Realism.* Wellington: New Zealand Press, 1952; Decharme, Paul. *Euripides and the Spirit of His Dramas.* New York: Macmillan, 1906; Greenwood, Leonard Hugh Graham. *Aspects of Euripidean Tragedy.* New York: Russell & Russell, 1972; Halleran, M. R. *Stagecraft in Euripides.* London: Croom Helm, 1985; Murray, G. G. A. *Euripides and His Age.* New York: Oxford University Press, 1946; Norwood, Gilbert. *Essays on Euripidean Drama.* Berkeley and Los Angeles: University of California Press, 1954; Taplin, Oliver. *Greek Tragedy in Action.* Berkeley: University of California Press, 1978; Zuntz, G. *The Political Plays of Euripides.* Manchester: Manchester University Press, 1955.

Existentialism
France

A philosophical movement resulting from the horrors of World War II, from a crisis of conscience, from the thought that perhaps this is a godless universe if so much human destruction can occur. Existentialism was born of this questioning and based on the idea that each human creates his or her own meaning in life "to exist." Existentialists assert that the human self is nothing but what that individual human creates, and that individual is ultimately responsible for his or her actions in this creative process. Humans must create morality in the absense of a god that reveals itself. According to this view humans must accept the responsibility of the freedom that choice entails. The first to bring these ideas to the public consciousness and the theater was Jean-Paul Sartre (1905–1980) with plays such as *Huis-Clos* (No Exit), 1944. Related to this movement is **Absurdism,** especially through the work of Samuel Beckett (1906–1989) with his drama *Waiting for Godot,* 1953.

References: Gordon, Lois. *The World of Samuel Becket.,* New Haven, CT: Yale University Press, 1996; Sartre, Jean Paul. *Being and Nothingness: An Essay on Phenomenological Ontology.* New York: Washington Square Press, 1966.

Expressionism

Germany

An artistic movement begun in Germany in the early part of the twentieth century, first in the visual arts, then in theater and film. The goal of expressionism is to communicate a particular inner experience of life through an exaggerated and stylized outward realization. Expressionists believe they are transcending reality through a heightened portrayal of life.

The Beggar, written by Reinhard Sorge (1892–1916) in 1912, is considered the first expressionistic play. Georg Kaiser (1878–1945), another expressionistic playwright, wrote plays, such as *Gas I* and *Gas II,* that were criticized for their clipped language and highly stylized characters. **August Strindberg** in his later life wrote impassioned plays influenced by expressionism. Some expressionistic plays were presented on bare stages using strong lighting effects to create the setting and relying on actors to evoke the heightened reality of the play. Staging, when used, was generally placed at exaggerated angles, with deep recesses to create shadows, and was intentionally nonrealistic.

In film, expressionism is characterized by an acting style that externalizes emotions strongly and graphically, almost to the level of being grotesque. The setting is usually angular, with extreme contrasts, and the lighting is nonrealistic, with deep shadows predominating. A few prime examples of German expressionism in film are *The Cabinet of Dr. Caligari,* 1919, *Nosferatu,* 1922, and *Waxworks,* 1924. German expressionism was highly influential, and its techniques continue to be used.

References: Eisner, Lotte. *The Haunted Screen: Expressionism in German Cinema.* Berkeley: University of California Press, 1969; Katz, Ephraim. *The Film Encyclopedia.* New York: Harper Perennial, 1994; Patterson, Michael. *The Revolution in German Theatre: 1900–1933.* London: Routledge and Kegan Paul, 1981.

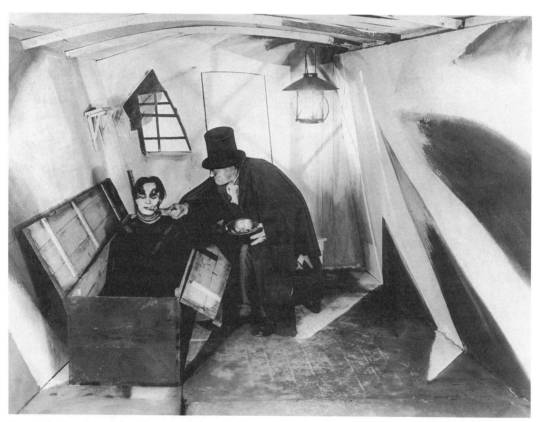

Exaggerated angles and deep shadows characterize the design for the expressionistic film Cabinet des Dr. Caligari (Cabinet of Dr. Caligari) (1919). (Kobol Collection / Decla-Bioscop)

F

Fagfagto
Philippines

Enactment of war by men of Bontac tribe. The Bontac tribe lives in the mountains of central Luzon, an area almost completely inaccessible to outsiders. This drama enacts the rivalry between different tribes and their protection of cultivated land. During this daylong war play, two groups throw stones at each other while holding crudely made shields. This is performed in the early summer to celebrate the planting of crops, mostly sweet potatoes.

> References: Aveilana, Dassy H. "The Native Theatre." *Philippine Quarterly* 1, 4 (March 1952): 60–62; Brandon, James R. *Brandon's Guide to Theatre in Asia.* Honolulu: University Press of Hawaii, 1976; Constanlino, Josefino. "Early Drama Forms in the Philippines." *Philippines Quarterly* 1 (1961): 34–36.

Farce
England, France

A genre of comedy originally developed from the interlude in the French **mystery play** of the Middle Ages such as the play Maistre Pierre Pathelin, performed in 1470. A farce is a humorous play that delights in the devices of obvious and physical comedy, such as mistaken identities, pratfalls, and the concealed person. This genre was popular in the seventeenth century, and again in the nineteenth century, with the plays of Georges Feydeau (1862–1921). Elements of farce still delight audiences of contemporary comedies, films, and television situation comedies.

> References: Axton, Richard. *European Drama of the Early Middle Age.* London: Hutchinson, 1974; Bermel, Albert. *Farce: A History from Aristophanes to Woody Allen.* New York: Simon and Schuster, 1982; Bevington, David. *Medieval Drama.* Boston: Houghton, 1975; Redmond, James. *Farce.* New York: Cambridge University Press, 1988.

Fasl Mudhik
Egypt

Farcical skits, usually consisting of vulgar jesting with indecent actions, performed in public places in Cairo or at private festivals before weddings or circumcisions, probably dating back at least to the ninth century. These farces, performed by *Mohhab-bazeen*, or players of crude and ridiculous farces, usually centered on a servant character as protagonist duping his master and having an affair with his master's wife. Plays nearly always ended with one of the characters getting whipped. In one production a British officer was completely made a fool, beaten on many occasions throughout the play, and then whipped at the end. Themes ridiculing officials accepting bribes were also enthusiastically received by audiences.

Fasl Mudhik declined in popularity when Western influence infiltrated the Middle East, but appeal to uneducated audiences in the cities still persisted. In the nineteenth century these farces were still being performed throughout the countryside and now are extremely rare.

References: Landau, Jacob. *Studies in the Arab Theater and Cinema.* Philadelphia: University of Pennsylvania Press, 1958; Moreh, S. "The Arabic Theatre in Egypt in the Eighteenth and Nineteenth Centuries." *Etudes Arabes et Islamiques* 3 (1975): 109–113.

Fastnachtspiel
Denmark, Germany, Norway, Sweden

Popular **farces**, also known as Shrovetide farces, recorded as early as 1430. During carnival, or Shrovetide, the Fastnachtspiel emerged as a popular form of entertainment. The carnival setting in medieval Scandinavia was one of merrymaking and masquerades. The *Fastnachtspiel* was carried to Scandinavia by German merchants and was performed by itinerant actors using the simplest staging, sometimes performing outside in a clearing in the forest or in the large hallway of a home. The structure of a performance began with the lead actor, the Preco, coming forward to give a summary of the action and to introduce the characters. Following that actors freely moved from one imaginary location on the playing stage to another, dramatizing a light farce. At the conclusion, the Preco would come forward to deliver a final speech and beg refreshment for the actors from the host.

References: Marker, Frederick. *A History of Scandinavian Theatre.* Cambridge: Cambridge University Press, 1996.

Fay, William (1872–1947)
Ireland

Irish actor. Fay and his brother Frank both trained with Maud Randford at her dramatic school in Dublin early in their careers. They later headed an amateur theater group in Ireland that attracted the attention of poet and playwright William Butler Yeats (1865–1939). Together they created the Irish National Theatre and in 1903 toured London and won the admiration of a wealthy arts enthusiast, Miss A. E. F. Hornimann, who gave them the theater in Dublin that later became the **Abbey Theatre.** William portrayed the lead male roles in many of the Abbey Theatre's early works, such as

Bartley in *Riders to the Sea*, 1904, and Christopher Mahon in *The Playboy of the Western World*, 1907, both by John Millington Synge (1871–1909). Fay was capable of the kind of authentic impersonation of Irish folk culture that made the peasant dramas at the Abbey so successful. Fay and his brother eventually split with the Abbey because of a disagreement over acting decisions. Fay went on to London and the **United States**, where he directed Irish plays in New York and Chicago.

References: Chinoy, Helen Krich, and Toby Cole. *Actors on Acting.* New York: Crown, 1970; Fraizier, Adrian. *Behind the Scenes at the Abbey.* Berkeley: University of California Press, 1990; Hunt, Hugh. *The Abbey: Ireland's National Theatre, 1904–1978.* Dublin: Gill & Macmillan, 1979.

Federal Theater Project
United States

A project of the U.S. government begun in 1935 as part of Roosevelt's New Deal; created primarily to provide jobs for unemployed actors, directors; and designers during the Depression. The project employed over 10,000 at its peak. These employed artists created a variety of productions from theatrical plays, to operas, to puppet shows, to **vaudeville.** Audiences could attend these shows free, or at a very low price. The benefits of this program spread to nearly every state, not just New York, and to all cultural groups, as in the all African American production *Swing Mikado*, 1939.

The Living Newspaper was the most controversial part of the FTP. This **documentary theater** of the 1930s, staffed by a mix of unemployed actors and newspaper workers, was socially critical, often through satire. They championed civil rights and government action to combat poverty and subsidize housing and health care. Successful works created include *Triple-A Plowed Under*, 1936, and *One-Third of a Nation*, 1938. The director of the FTP was Hallie Flanagan (1890–1969), who encouraged new works on socially significant topics. She was eventually accused of being a Communist, a serious charge at the time, which led to the end of the FTP in 1939.

References: Flanagan, Hallie. *Arena: The History of the Federal Theatre.* New York: B. Bloom, 1940; Fraden, Rena. *Blueprints for a Black Federal Theatre, 1935–1939.* New York: Cambridge University Press, 1994; Kazacoff, George. *Dangerous Theatre: The Federal Theatre*

Project as a Forum for New Plays. New York: P. Lang, 1989.

Fellini, Federico (1920–1993)
Italy

Italian twentieth-century filmmaker. Fellini began as an apprentice to film directors of **Italian neo-realism,** a movement characterized by working-class actors caught in an oppressive society. However, his own inclinations led him toward making flamboyant movies full of mystery, magic, and circus imagery. The primary theme of most of his movies is the tension between sensuality and spirituality. Fellini's wife, Giulietta Masina, stars in some of his best movies, including *La Strada,* 1954, and *Nights of Cabiria,* 1956. Her spirited disposition, coupled with her sparkling eyes and playful smirk, lent great warmth to her characterizations. Fellini often peopled his movies with actors engaged in circus stunts and revelry as background. He reveals a fascination with beauty that borders on the grotesque. Thus, many of his actors appear garish and exaggerated. In one of Fellini's best-known films, *8½,* the actor Marcello Mastroianni portrays a film director laboring to make the very film that is being made, exposing the boundary between reality and fiction. In the end the protagonist is swept away in a dream of a circus parade made up of all the characters in the movie and people from his personal memories. This conclusion seems to demonstrate Fellini's vision of art and life swirling together in the same circus-like vision.

References: Betti, Liliana. *Fellini: An Intimate Portrait.* Boston: Little, Brown, 1979; Bondanella, Peter, ed. *Federico Fellini: Essays in Criticism.* New York: Oxford University Press, 1978; Fellini, Federico. *Fellini on Fellini.* New York: Delacorte, 1976.

Female Impersonation
Africa, China, Europe, Japan, United States

Throughout the world, in Africa, Asia, Europe, and the Americas, female impersonation by male performers has been a common and reoccurring phenomenon. This practice evolved in most cultures because it was deemed unacceptable to have women performing on a stage in public. Women were thought to arouse male desire, which would threaten the stability of a society based on the family structure. Perhaps it was also a method of keeping women without power and submissive. Young boys most often took the parts of females because of their slender builds and high voices. However, they seem to have historically excited as much lust in men as their female counterparts would have, as can be seen in *Kabuki,* for example. There is also a long history in Western theater of older men portraying older women, even when women were allowed on the stage, for sheer comic value.

In the sub-Sahara region of Africa in rural areas where traditional performances occur, such as the **Ckumkpa** in Nigeria, women rarely perform in predominantly theatrical performances. In the *Chumkpa,* young boys satirize women through skillful female impersonation, carefully mimicking a female walk and mannerisms. Though women are heavily involved in African dance, theatrical performance done by all-male secret societies and masquerades rarely allow women.

Throughout Asia in centuries past, women have historically been allowed to dance but rarely to perform in theatrical presentations. In the highly refined Chinese **Peking Opera, Tan** is the name for female character roles. This is further broken down into Ching-I, the virtuous woman role, Hua-Tan, the coquette female role, and Wu-Tan, the militant female or amazon role. The famous *Tan,* **Mei Lan Fang,** is said by his admirers to have been able to portray the essence of woman better than any actual woman. In the Japanese Kabuki, the term for female roles is **Onnagata.** The tradition of female impersonation in Japan continued into the film era until the mid-1920s, the name for the role being **Oyama.** In **Java** there is a realistic contemporary dramatic form, **Ludruk,** including female impersonators, who are used because it is believed the dance within the drama is too rigorous for female performers.

Female impersonation has provided humor, titillation, and shocks in the **U.S. cinema,** with such classics as *Some Like It Hot,* 1959, and *Tootsie,* 1982.

References: Ferris, Lesley. *Crossing the Stage: Controversies on Cross-Dressing.* New York: Routledge, 1993; Senelick, Laurence. *The Changing Room: Sex, Drag, and Theatre.* New York: Routledge, 2000.

Finland

Finland is sometimes considered a part of Scandinavia, mainly because Sweden controlled Finland from 1154 to 1809 and greatly influenced Finnish culture and theater. From 1809 to 1917 Finland was an autonomous grand duchy within the Russian Empire, and it then had continuous interaction with the Soviet Union. The effect on Finland of this relationship was negative at first, but grew to be increasingly beneficial to Finland until the collapse of the USSR in 1991. Theatrical links with Russia are likely, but scholarship has yet to confirm this claim. Finns have a long history of asserting independence from Scandinavia and Russia, and their fierce spirit has been dynamically expressed in theater created in their native language throughout the twentieth century.

Formal theater was first recorded in Finland at the newly founded university, the Academy of Abo Turku, in 1640, when students performed a kind of Latin humanist drama, sometimes referred to as Abo Theater. Throughout the remainder of the seventeenth century student actors performed university dramas. The eighteenth-century theater scene in Finland was dominated by touring Swedish acting groups.

In the nineteenth century a clear division developed between the Finnish-speaking and the Swedish-speaking theaters. In the first half of the twentieth century, the major conflict in Finnish theater was between those speaking Finnish and those speaking a higher, more literary form of Swedish. The goal of unification has never been fully realized.

The Finnish-speaking National Theater was founded in 1872, predominantly through the inspiration of Kaarlo Bergbom (1843–1906) and his sister Emilie (1834–1905). Together they created a strong group of actors, including Ida Aalberg (1857–1915) and Adolf Lindfors (1857–1929). Oskari Vilho (1840–1883) is affectionately known as the father of Finnish acting. Quality Finnish plays were written in the nineteenth and twentieth centuries, starting with Aleksis Stenvall (1834–1872). In 1902 the Finnish National Theater obtained its first permanent playhouse. Theater in Finland today is mostly performed in Finnish, and many professional companies flourish. New plays are being written by some recent playwrights: Paavo Haavikko

(born 1931), Inkere Kilpiners (born 1926), and Viejo Meri (born 1928). Notable directors include Eino Kalima and Arvi Kivimaa, who have worked at the Finnish National Theater.

The Swedish-speaking National Theater was founded in 1916. Before this time Carl Gottfried Seuerling (1727–1792) and his wife brought the classic plays from Europe to Finland. Exceptional Finnish performers in the Swedish-speaking National Theater were Marie Silfvan (1802–1865) and Erik Lindstrom (born 1906). More recently the innovative director Vivica Bandler ran the Swedish-speaking theater Lilla Teatern (Little Theater). Jack Witikka and Rolf Langbacka are exceptional recent directors.

In the 1980s and 1890s, the rise of the collective theater movement has been a major force in the continued development of Finnish Theater.

See also Latin Humanistic Comedy

References: Bandler, V. "The Cry From an Island in the Cliffs (The Theater Scene in Finland and Sweden)." *Theater Heute* 21, 10 (1980); Hartnoll, Phyllis. *The Oxford Companion to the Theatre.* New York: Oxford University Press, 1967; Helavuori, Hanna-Leena and Irmeli Niemi. "Finland." In *Nordic Theatre Studies: Yearbook for Theatre Research in Scandinavia,* 41–45. Copenhagen: Munksgaard, 1989; Lacy, Suzanne. "Finland: The Road of Poems and Borders." *Journal of Dramatic Theory and Criticism* 5, 1 (Fall 1990): 211–222; Langbacka, Ralf. "Brecht in Finland." *The Brecht Yearbook* 20 (1995): 128–133; Marker, Frederick. *A History of Scandinavian Theatre.* Cambridge: Cambridge University Press, 1996; Meserve, Mollie Ann, and Walter J. Meserve. *A Chronological Outline of World Theatre.* New York: Feedback Theatre & Prospero Press, 1992; Robinson, Horace. "A Brief Visit to Theater in Finland." *Players Magazine* 40 (1964): 176–177.

Foot Binding

China

Tradition of binding feet of young Chinese women to demonstrate refinement and increase sexual appeal. Perhaps the custom of foot binding was developed during the Tang dynasty in the sixth century by court dancing girls who did a sort of tap dance in a small space. Although the exact date of this custom's inception is unknown, the custom of foot binding was well in place by the ninth century. Women with bound feet have a

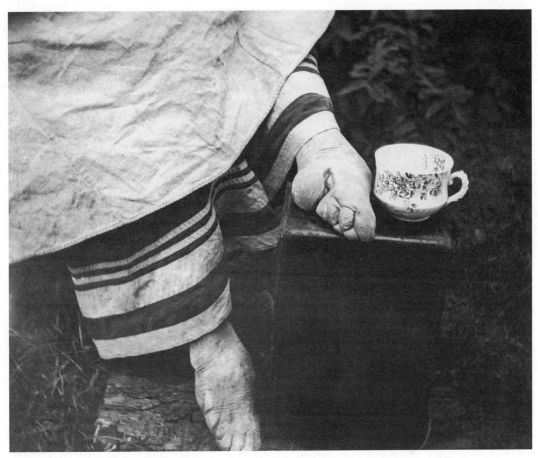

Disfigured feet of a Chinese woman whose feet had been bound. (Bettmann/Corbis)

teetering step that causes them to sway from side to side with a hip movement regarded as highly erotic. Male actors of female roles in **Peking Opera,** called **Tan,** have perfected this gait. They use a special device bound to their own feet to aid them in this manner of walking. This device is a small wooden block to which the actor's foot is securely bound. The wooden block is shaped to resemble the hoof-like form of a woman's bound foot. The actor would characteristically have one hand on his hip and hold a handkerchief coquettishly. Even though reasons a woman could not appear on stage were moral ones, it's also the case that a woman's portrayal of the female character would have been inferior to a man's because of her physical disability, namely her deformed feet. Male actors were able to develop techniques for imitating women that were theatrically more powerful and visually more exciting than would have been possible for real women with bound feet, who were unable to walk very far or for a very long time. The Manchus, nomadic Mongoloid people of Manchuria, who conquered China in the seventeenth century, outlawed foot binding, but they were unable to enforce such a law and eventually withdrew it. Since the **Chinese Cultural Revolution,** 1966–1976, the technique of impersonating women with bound feet has been banished from the stage because it represents the feudalistic values rejected by Communist thinking.

References: Scott, A. C. *The Theatre in Asia.* New York: Macmillan, 1972.

Forman, Richard (1937–)
United States

Theater director, designer, writer, and producer of avant-garde works; founder, in 1968, of The Ontological Hysterical Theater. His work rebelled against traditional theatrical conventions; instead, it mapped the very act of imagining, progressing along one thought and then changing gears without a logical reason to do so. His first production, *Angelface*, in 1968, included discordant speech and actions, performed mostly by inexperienced actors. Much of his work prior to 1975 was primarily concerned with putting an object or actor on stage for observation. *Total Recall*, 1970, involved actors who were directed to show no emotion and to speak dialogue that seemed random. The higher aim of these performances was to force the audience into another manner of thinking and processing information.

Other performances include *Pandering to the Masses*, 1975, *Penguin Touquet*, 1981, and *Film Is Evil: Radio Is Good*, 1987. Forman became director of the upstairs theater at St. Mark's Church in New York in 1991, where he has produced many of his own works and the work of others.

References: Bigsby, C. W. E. *A Critical Introduction to Twentieth-Century American Drama*. New York: Cambridge University Press, 1985.

France

The history of theater in France is one led predominantly by actors, who often acted as playwrights, directors, and managers. Outstanding actors took a lead role in setting standards of excellence, advancing their medium to match the advancement of human thought, and experimenting with theatrical conventions. Many leading French theater artists of the twentieth century also contributed to **French cinema.**

Although traveling performers no doubt entertained throughout medieval France, the first recorded French performance is in 1283, with the folk play *Le Pièce de Théâtre de Robin et Marion* (The Play of Robin and Marion). The first secular drama, recorded as occurring in the late thirteenth century, is *Adam de la Halle* (Adam of the Market). **Farce** is a genre of comedy that developed from the interlude in the French **mystery play** of the Middle Ages (1470). Among many other troupes, one amateur troupe of performers, the **Confrérie de la Passion (Brotherhood of the Passion)**, performed religious dramas in Paris from the fourteenth through the sixteenth cen-

turies and controlled the French theater scene in the seventeenth century.

French theater reached its first high point in the seventeenth century, elevated by the outstanding tragedies of Pierre Corneille (1606–1684) and Jean Baptiste Racine (1639–1699) and the comedies of **Jean-Baptiste Poquelin Molière** (1622–1673). Molière did more to inspire excellence in the art of acting, playwriting, staging, and intelligent satire than any other French theater artist before or since. He thrilled audiences, both royal and common, with his natural style of comic acting.

The **Comédie Française,** founded in 1680, is still a cooperative society of actors making up the French national theater, which, since its inception, has attracted and "made" many of France's star actors. The centuries in French theater history are marked by outstanding and highly influential actors such as **Marie Desmares Champmeslé**, **Adrienne Lecouvreur**, Lekain (Henri Louis Cain, 1728–1778), **François Talma**, and **Sarah Bernhardt**. After the French Revolution, the Romantic movement inspired many great writers for the theater, especially Alexandre Dumas (1803–1870) and Victor Hugo (1802–1885), the success of whose plays was enhanced by the fame of well-known actors. During the nineteenth century new theaters opened to end the monopoly of the Comédie-Française, such as the Odéon, another government theater. The shift to **naturalism** prompted by authors like **Henrik Ibsen** and Emile Zola (1840–1902) made obsolete the stylized acting of the most prominent actors. **André Antoine** developed hugely influential new naturalistic acting styles, which included the use of low voices, occasional backs to the audience, colloquial ways of speaking, and complete absorption in the character. This new movement demanded that actors focus less on their style of declamation and vocal abilities and more on the content of the play, serving the play with natural vocal expression and realistic acting.

The beginning of the twentieth century saw an enormous sweep of energetic reformers, actor-directors such as **Lugné-Poe, Jacques Copeau**, and **Charles Dullin**, who worked to do away with all that was considered false in French theater. **Jean Cocteau**, primarily a playwright and filmmaker, was a leader of an artistic movement known as

surrealism which sought to present a reality above or within the surface reality.

Perhaps one of the most influential theater theorists in the twentieth century, **Antonin Artaud** still stands as a prophetic spokesman for pure and essential theater. In the 1930s Artaud published a series of essays promoting a "Theater of Cruelty," in which the audience is assaulted out of its apathy and metaphorically raped by a performance. He strove for a primitive vision of theater that communicated beyond language. His vision, though never fully realized, has been a guiding point for many theater artists.

Absurdism and **existentialism** are two post–World War II movements that asserted that the world is inherently irrational and created dramas in which characters strive to construct meaning from the rubble of human existence.

Many French theater artists attempted to break out of the typical mold of theater centered in Paris serving an elite audience. **Jean Vilar** presented classics to a popular audience in Paris. The government began subsidizing the decentralization of theater in the late 1940s, supporting the work of **Roger Planchon** in the provinces for example. More recently, **Ariane Mnouchkine** created a theater commune, the Théâtre du Soleil (Theater of the Sun), that produces innovative theater in nontraditional spaces.

France was home to a revival of the ancient performance form **Mime** with the work of **Etienne Decroux,** who developed a language of gestures. **Marcel Marceau**, regarded as the greatest mime performer of his time, continued this tradition. **Jean-Louis Barrault** integrated his expertise in mime into many innovative theater performances.

Fernando Arrabal (b. 1932), the most notable French playwright of the 1960s, wrote absurdist plays such as *Pique-nique en Campagne* (Picnic on the Battlefield) (1959), and more ceremonial, "free theater" plays such as *L'Architecte et l'Empereur d'Assyrie* (The Architect and the Emperor of Assyria) (1967). During the 1960s in France, dissatisfaction with the conservative Comédie-Française and the partial breakdown of the Odéon and TNP (Théâtre National Populaire) caused theater groups to perform in nontraditional spaces such as cafes, the streets, and artistic centers, a tradition which has continued to enliven the French theater scene on a grassroots level.

Other recent popular theater groups include the Théâtre de la Salamandre and Théâtre National de Strasbourg. Both created innovative theater works through the 1970s and 1980s. In 1983 the production of Michel Vinaver's *L'Ordinaire*, a play about cannibalism, at the Comédie-Française demonstrated that the Old Guard of the Comédie is making attempts to take in the new talent that is emerging. Alternative theater continues to thrive in France. Cirque d'Hiver (Circus of the Winter) is an innovative circus that performed for several months in Paris in 2001. Musical street theater groups, such as Cirque de la Mer starring Luc Zalay, are finding great success in France touring the country and performing music, short comical skits, and jokes, mostly at outdoor festivals. In puppet theater, the play *La Bataille de Stalingrad* (The Battle of Stalingrad) was presented at the Tblisi Theatre in Paris in 2000. This World War II piece of puppet theater is described as an intimately scaled piece.

See also Diderot, Denis; Romanticism; Well-Made Play

References: Axton, Richard. *European Drama of the Early Middle Age.* London: Hutchinson, 1974; Carlson, Marvin. *The French Stage in the Nineteenth Century.* Metuchen, NJ: Scarecrow Press, 1972; Chinoy, Helen Krich, and Toby Cole. *Actors on Acting.* New York: Crown, 1970; Gaensbauer, Deborah, *The French Theater of the Absurd,* Boston: Twayne, 1991; McCormick, John. *Popular Theatres of Nineteenth-Century France.* New York: Routledge, 1993; Williams, A. R. "Eighty Years of Elegance and Excellence." *Americas* 39, 5 (September–October 1987): 14–19.

Free Southern Theater
United States

Theater founded in 1963 by John O'Neal and Gilbert Moses (1942–1995) (both African American actors and directors) and **Richard Schechner**; a product of the civil rights movement. Based in New Orleans, the theater traveled to small black communities, many of which had never seen theater before. Their first performance was the thought-provoking *In White America*, and then they did a comedy, *Purlie Victorious*, by an African American writer, Ossie Davis. This was at a time when segregated seating at movies and theaters was still enforced or when African Americans were not allowed in theaters at all. Thus, FST was the only theater available to many African American communities. In the beginning they took up donations at their performances and existed on a meager budget, while still maintaining high artistic standards; later they received large grants.

References: Bigsby, C. W. E. *A Critical Introduction to Twentieth-Century American Drama.* New York: Cambridge University Press, 1985.

French Cinema

The history of cinema is generally acknowledged as beginning in 1895, when two French brothers, Louis and Auguste Lumière, projected their films, usually scenes of real life, for a paying audience. This established the prominence and influence of French cinema throughout film history. The first female film director was a French woman, Alice Guy (1873–1968), once the secretary of Léon Gaumont, who by 1900 was head of the world's largest studio, Gaumont Studios. Another early pioneer of French film and rival to Gaumont was Charles Pathé, who in 1908 contributed financially to a film company named Film d'Art (Art of Film) that produced films of stage productions starring famous stage actors who performed at the **Comédie Française,** including even the famous **Sarah Bernhardt**.

After World War I, French film began to exhibit the sophisticated artistic qualities it has since continued to develop. Two of the early proponents of avant-garde art films were Louis and **Germaine Dulac**, who directed a number of experimental silent films. Two of the primary creators of French film in the 1920s and 1930s were René Clair (1898–1981), and Jean Renoir (1894–1979), who acted in his own film *La Grande Illusion* (Grand Illusion), 1937. Renoir filmed *Toni*, 1935, on location in the village of Les Martiques and utilized nonprofessional actors.

The actor Jean Gabin (1904–1978) best exemplified the poetic realism that dominated the French cinema in the late 1930s. Prior to the outbreak of World War II, France was at the forefront of quality film production, but that lead was badly jarred by German occupation from 1940 to 1944. Many actors were recruited for service in the war, and many of France's leading filmmakers emigrated to Hollywood. A major talent in the late 1940s was Jean Cocteau, who created an eclectic array of visually stunning films. **Jacques Tati** emerged as a wildly talented comic actor and director in the 1940s and 1950s.

France's next influential movement was called *La* **Nouvelle Vague,** or the New Wave. Talented young filmmakers rebelled against what they perceived to be the stagnation of the old guard. **Luis Buñuel**, a Spanish-born filmmaker, created some masterly films in France in the 1960s including *Belle de Jour*, 1967, starring the leading French actress **Catherine Deneuve**.

Competition from Hollywood plagued French cinema throughout the 1970s and afterwards. However, the creation of films of high artistic quality continues, with such talented filmmakers as Diane Kurys, who directed *Entre Nous* (Between Us), 1983, and Luc Besson, who directed *La Femme Nikita* 1990. French actors of great range and talent such as **Gérard Depardieu** and Juliette Binoche are famous throughout the world and appear in the films of many nations.

See also Italian Neorealism

References: Armes, Roy. *French Film*. New York: Dutton, 1970; Bandy, Mary Lea. *Rediscovering French Film*. Boston: Little Brown, 1983; Bazin, André. *French Cinema of the Occupation and Resistance*. New York: Fredrick Ungar, 1981; Butcher, Maryvonne. "France's Film Renascence." *Commonweal* (January 8, 1960): 414–416; Graham, Peter. *The New Wave*. Garden City, NY: Doubleday, 1968; Katz, Ephraim. *The Film Encyclopedia*. New York: Harper Perennial, 1994; Martin, John W. *The Golden Age of French Cinema, 1929–1959*. Boston: Twayne, 1983; Sadoul, Georges. *French Film*. London: Falcon Press, 1953; Thiher, Allen. *The Cinematic Muse: Critical Studies in the History of French Cinema*. Columbia: University of Missouri Press, 1979.

Fu Lien Ch'eng
China

Most famous actor training school for **Peking Opera** during the late nineteenth and early twentieth centuries. The school was privately owned by a businessman with a love for theater and music. Only male students between the age of seven and twelve were admitted to the school, and only with consent of the owner. Students had to be physically suited for performing, strong, agile and physically attractive. Once accepted, the boys were separated from their parents, who signed a contract permitting the school to have complete control over their sons for the next seven years. Students were not allowed to quit. Most students were from professional acting families, so they had no choice but to pursue acting. There was no real way out of their social caste. After five years a student was reassessed, and it was determined whether the child had a chance of making it as a performer. If not, he was trained in makeup or costumes, or as a musician. Actors had an austere lifestyle, with strictly controlled diet and activities. There was no general education in the history or aesthetics of Peking Opera, just performance practice and training. Teachers led the students through unrelenting drills with their voices and through rigorous physical training in movement and acrobatics. After graduating from the school, almost all of the students would continue training with a private teacher. **Mei Lan Fang** (1894–1961), the most famous actor of Peking Opera, graduated from this school and left a detailed description of its aims and organization in his memoirs.

References: Kalvodova, Sis, and Vanis Kalvodova. *Chinese Theatre.* Trans. Iris Urwin. London: Spring House, 1957; Scott, A. C. *The Theatre in Asia.* New York: Macmillan, 1972.

Fu Tai Hsi
China

Hand puppets from southern China. It is believed that hand puppets first appeared in the sixteenth century in Fujian, southern China. The approximately 16-inch-long puppets are constructed around a cotton glove shell into which the puppeteer's hand is inserted to control the puppet. The legs are stuffed cotton with carved wooden feet attached at the bottom. The puppeteer's forefinger reaches into the hollow head to control it. The hands for the puppet are also carved from wood and can sometimes hold little properties. The master puppeteer, **Tou,** performs all the major roles and does most of the speaking and singing. The assistant, **Er,** usually an apprentice to the master, performs minor roles. The backstage area must be painstakingly organized for quick transitions of puppets to maintain the flow of a performance. A puppeteer controls one puppet on

each hand, perfectly coordinating jabs, spins, and jumps. Fujian puppeteers are famous for their lifelike portrayal of animals. A tiger puppet may leap ferociously and then stop to scratch its fleas. The stage for performances is elaborately carved from wood with two levels. It is 6 feet wide and 7 feet high with windows, panels, and doors. Inside it has space for two puppeteers. In the 1950s larger, more open stages replaced traditional types, allowing ten or more puppeteers to perform together. Taped music and theatrical lighting were also added for special effects. The costume and makeup on the puppets is the same as the **Peking Opera.** Puppeteers must begin training young before the tendons in the hand become inflexible. This is necessary because the thumb controls one arm and the last two fingers the other arm. To make the shoulders appear even on the puppet, the hand must be very flexible. Students train with a master puppeteer to learn to move the head of the puppet subtly, so that the movements are not jerky or overdone.

References: Stalberg, Roberta Helmer. *China's Puppets.* San Francisco: China Books, 1984.

Fugard, Athol (1932–)
South Africa

Internationally known South African playwright, whose work exposes the harsh social realities for all South Africans, blacks and whites. He participated as an actor and director in many of his own early productions, so that the dialogue was often developed during rehearsals. Though he is white himself, two of his first plays, *No Good Friday,* 1958, and *Nongogo,* 1959, had all-black casts. He also created plays in sympathy with poor whites in South Africa, and his play *People Are Living There,* 1963, had an all-white cast.

In 1961 he produced *Blood Knot* at the Dorkay House in Johannesburg, performing one of the lead roles himself. He collaborated with black actors in New Brighton in 1963 and formed a theater group, the Serpent Players. The actors who created *Sizwe Bansi Is Dead* in 1972 with Fugard met with extraordinary international success. Their efforts inspired many groups to experiment with improvisational methods for creating dramas and discovering their own voice, rather than following the set European and American models of theater. His work *Master Harald and the Boys* premiered at the Yale Repertory Theater in New Haven in 1982.

In the 1990s his work became more actively engaged with the political situation, with plays such as *My Children, My Africa*, 1989, and *Playland*, 1992. His plays are still widely performed by universities and theaters around the world. The film *Boesman and Lena*, 2000, starring Danny Glover and Angela Bassett, is based on the play by Fugard.

References: Banham, Martin. *African Theatre Today.* London: Pitman, 1976; Kavanagh, Robert. *Theatre and Cultural Struggle in South Africa.* London: Zed, 1985.

Futurism
France, Italy

Artistic movement created by Filippo Tommaso Marinetti (1876–1944) when he published his futurist manifesto in Paris in 1909. Impressed with industrialization, artists in this movement sought to embody the energy and speed of machines in artistic forms. Futurists were a band of young people who sought a complete break with the past. They valued aggressiveness to such an extent that they idealized war. During the 1920s its theories became identified with Fascism.

In theater futurists denounced contemporary practices and advocated change, in hopes of capturing the dynamism of modern life. They proposed a synthetic form of drama characterized by being very brief and having a rapid succession of disparate attractions. Playwrights wrote *Sintesi*, short scripts intended to capture the essence of a mood, emotion, condition, or situation. The actors in these plays performed disconnected tasks or actions, often simultaneously, and used nonverbal sounds. Psychological characterization was minimized and nearly obliterated.

The postwar futurist, Enrico Prampolini, went so far as to call for a theater with no human actors. He proposed that colored gas and luminous forms should take the place of humans, claiming that light and gas are better at evoking the mysterious spiritual forces with which theater should concern itself.

The futurist movement brought about an examination of some fundamental aspects of theater, such as the use of the arena (the circus ring especially), barriers between audience and performers, and the use of modern multimedia technology.

References: Kirby, Michael. *Futurist Performance.* Trans. Victoria Nes Kirby. New York: E. P. Dutton, 1971; Marinetti, Filippo Tommaso, Emilio Settimelli, and Bruno Corra. "The Synthetic Futurist Theatre." In *Art and the Stage in the Twentieth Century*, ed. Henning Rischbieter. Greenwich, Connecticut: New York Graphic Society, 1968; Prampolini, Enrico. "The Futurist Pantomime." In *Art and the Stage in The Twentieth Century*, ed. Henning Rischbieter. Greenwich, CT: New York Graphic Society, 1968; Prampolini, Enrico. "Futurist Scenography." In *Total Theatre*, ed. E. T. Kirby. New York: E. P. Dutton, 1969.

G

Gamelan

Indonesia, Malaysia

A traditional Southeast Asian orchestra, made up of gongs, cymbals, drums, and sometimes a melodic reed instrument, used to accompany traditional dance and drama.

Ganesha

India

Elephant-headed Hindu god, known as the remover of obstacles, son of the Hindu god **Shiva** and his female consort, Parvati. He is most often shown with four arms, each hand holding one of his attributes, and accompanied by a mouse, who removes obstacles too large for Ganesha. Many Indian theatrical performances begin with invocations to Ganesha.

> **References:** Aherne, Consuelo Maria, Paul Kevin Meagher, and Thomas C. O'Brien., eds. *Encyclopedic Dictionary of Religion.* 3 vols. Washington, D.C.: Corpus Publishers, 1979; Eliade, Mircea, ed., *The Encyclopedia of Religion.* 16 vols. New York: Macmillan, 1987; Varadpande, Manohar Laxman. *Krishna Theatre in India.* New Delhi: Abhinav, 1982.

Garrick, David (1717–1779)

England

English actor, writer, theater manager, and playwright. Garrick began as a wealthy wine merchant who enjoyed performing in amateur plays.

His first large role was the lead in **Shakespeare's** *Richard III,* which made him an immediate success. In 1742 he was invited to Drury Lane, oldest and most famous of London's theaters, where he played many leading roles, including the title roles in *Hamlet* and *King Lear.* Garrick was a friend to **Charles Macklin** and in love with the talented actress Peg Woffington (1714–1760).

As an actor he was versatile and had a natural grace in his stage movements. He was a naturalistic actor in a time of stilted declamation and stylized stage movement. He drew his inspiration from life and nature and observed the world around him for insight into his characters. In 1747 he became director of Drury Lane, where he played many of the great roles to high acclaim until 1776, when he retired. He is also responsible for removing spectators from the stage, where previously the rich had sat to observe performances and to be seen.

> **References:** Matthews, Brander. *Actors and Actresses of Great Britain and the United States from the Days of David Garrick to the Present Time.* New York: Cassell, 1886; Oman, Carola. *David Garrick.* London: Hodder and Stoughton, 1958.

Gaucho

Argentina, Uruguay

The cowboy of South America, a character that developed in Argentina and Uruguay, first through poetry in the early nineteenth century, then novels, and finally on the stage in a popular genre known as **Teatro Gaucho.** The gaucho always operates alone in his demand for justice. He is proud and most often silent. He became a symbol of Argentine and Uruguayan independence as the rural individual and rebel who stands in solitary opposition to such forces as colonization and a controlling institutionalized government that would regulate his life.

References: Versènyi, Adam. *Theatre in Latin America: Religion, Politics, and Culture from Cortés to the 1980s.* New York: Cambridge University Press, 1993; Weiss, Judith A. *Latin American Popular Theatre: The First Five Centuries.* Albuquerque: University of New Mexico Press, 1993.

Gaulan Kala

India

Oldest and most popular form of drama about **Krishna,** the eighth and most important incarnation of the Hindu god **Vishnu,** in the Gomantaka region in south India. Both male and female children enact the various sports of Krishna as a young boy. The **Sutradhara,** the narrator, opens the show with a song explaining the glory of Krishna and the value of worshipping him. Then there is a play based on the naughty pranks of Krishna as a child, such as his getting caught stealing butter or his flirtations with the **Gopis,** or milkmaids. Two *Gopis* act as jesters. Their interplay creates much humor. The child performers generally sing in verse with minimal dialogue. There is none of the eroticism in *Gaulan Kala* that is usual in other dance-dramas focusing on Krishna.

References: Varadpande, Manohar Laxman. *Krishna Theatre in India.* New Delhi: Abhinav, 1982.

Gelede

Benin, Nigeria

Masked dance drama, in which male and female *Gelede* characters portray the physical characteristics distinctive to each gender. The *Gelede* is said to belong to women, though both male and female characters are performed only by men. It is dedicated primarily to the great-grandmothers of the community. Though *Gelede* could be viewed primarily as a dance, there is dramatic impersonation occurring, namely the portrayal of social roles for men and women and the attributes of each gender.

A performance commences with young boys, *Gelede*-to-be, who are so small they must hold the mask with both hands while they dance. The audience enthusiastically receives these performers-in-training. After the children perform, the older and more accomplished performers take turns performing, progressing from teenaged dancers to, finally, the master dancers. Each dancer enters from one side of the oval-shaped clearing used as the performance space and progresses toward the drummers at the opposite side. Through the choreography the crowd witnesses how the male aggressively consumes the space with his dance and movements, flaunting his unrestrained power. He exhibits a great variety of stamping movements while maintaining a wide stance. In his exuberant performance he whirls and jumps full turns in the air. The female character maintains a narrow stance. Her controlled and channeled movements have purpose and move her more directly toward the drums. She performs with great strength and speed. At times two identical characters emerge and mirror each other's movements. Each performer is portraying the *Ase*, or life force, of each gender, which communicates the differences between the two, his Ase strong and obvious, hers, mysterious, hidden, and covertly powerful.

Beginning at noon, performances occur in the center of the main market. An oval-shaped performance area is maintained by "crowd controllers," men armed with large sticks or palm branches, needed because the audience crowds toward the performers as the excitement mounts. The masks are carved from wood and balanced on the head. The male *Gelede* character wears a paneled garment that spins outward when he turns with great speed, whereas the female *Gelede* character has her torso tightly wrapped in fabric. All performers hold horsetail whisks in each hand to emphasize the reach of the arm.

The drums do more than accompany performances. They have a dialogue through rhythm with the performers, each responding to the other and following each other's lead. The drums are tuned to evoke the sounds of the human voice. The basis for *Gelede* choreography is the *Eka*, which is a drum phrase that imitates the vocal patterns of the Yoruba language, thus communicating social commentary, the beauty of the language, and even humor.

References: Atigbi, I. A. *Nigeria Traditional Festivals: A Guide to Nigeria Cultural Safari.* Lagos, Nigeria: Nigerian Tourist Association, 1972; Drewal, Henry John. "Efe: Voiced Power and Pageantry." *African Arts* 7, 2 (1974): 26–29, 58–66, 82–83; Ekwuema, Lazarus E. N. "Nigerian Performing Arts, Past, Present and Future, with Particular Reference to Igbo Practice." *Presence Africaine* 92, 2 (1975): 195–213.

Gendai-geki
Japan

A type of Japanese film based on modern life. There many subgenres: **Shomin-geki** (middle-class comedy), Mother Picture (focused on a mother-children relationship), Wife Picture (depicting the hardships of marriage for a woman), Nonsense Picture (farcical comedy), and Youth Picture (depicting the wild antics of youth, like American beach movies of the 1950s and 1960s).

See also Ozu, Yasujiro; Kurosawa, Akira
References: Mast, Gerald. *A Short History of the Movies.* 4th ed. New York: Macmillan, 1986.

Género Chico
Cuba, Dominican Republic

A dramatic form that originated in Spain as an abbreviated version of the light opera called **Zarzuela;** based on a contemporary theme with the same kind of alternation of dialogue and music as an operetta. *Género Chico* developed in Cuba in the early nineteenth century and even earlier in the Dominican Republic. The name comes from the Spanish generic term for a short one-act play. This form was naturalized to Cuban tastes by Francisco Covarrubias (1755–1850) in the early nineteenth century. The plots were based on Cuban customs and situations of the period. These performances attracted a popular audience from the lower and middle class and became the basis for **Bufo** theater, which emerged later in the century.

See also Cuba
References: Banham, Martin. *African Theatre Today.* London: Pitman, 1976; Palls, Terry Lee. "The Theatre in Revolutionary Cuba: 1959–1969." Ph.D. diss., University of Kansas, 1974.

Genet, Jean
See Absurdism

George II, Duke of Saxe-Meiningen (1826–1914)
Germany

German director and scenic designer, considered to be the first modern director to have worked toward ensemble acting. In 1874 the duke established an acting troupe in the minor principality of Saxe-Meiningen that was to have a major influence on the development of Western theater. He proved that having one director, for whom he used the French term *régisseur*, who could give a unified interpretation of a play, was superior to having all of the action of a play revolve around a few star performers, which was the norm in his day. Succeeding in getting the star actor out of the spotlight and integrating him or her into the action of the drama, he and his first-rate troupe of actors worked toward true ensemble playing. They sought to find a vital connection between all of the actor's movements in connection with the stage design. The rehearsal process was extensive, and the director attended to the smallest details of stage action, including crowd scenes, which were carefully choreographed. The Duke's wife, Ellen Franz, was responsible for coaching the actors on the interpretation of their lines. Excellent discipline was demanded of the entire company. Costumes were historically accurate.

The Meiningen Company toured throughout most of Europe and inspired both **Konstantin Stanislavsky** and **André Antoine**.

References: Carlson, Marvin. *The French Stage in the Nineteenth Century.* Metuchen, NJ: Scarecrow Press, 1972; Chinoy, Helen Krich, and Toby Cole. *Actors on Acting.* New York: Crown, 1970; Patterson, Michael. *The Revolution in German Theatre: 1900–1933.* London: Routledge and Kegan Paul, 1981; Williams, A. R. "Eighty Years of Elegance and Excellence." *Americas* 39, 5 (September–October 1987): 14–19.

Georgia

An independent nation that was a part of the **Soviet Union** from 1922 until the USSR dissolved in 1991. Georgia has a long rich theater history, with close ties with Russian theater, beginning in the nineteenth century. Many leading actors and directors of Georgia trained in Russia. The Soviet Union encouraged theater. The thirteen theater companies in Georgia in 1913 had expanded to forty-eight theater companies by 1938. In 1921 the Rustavelli Theater was established in Tbilisi in a climate of artistic flourishing and rapid growth in the arts. One of the great theater artists and teachers of the time was K. A. Mardzhanishvilli. One of the founders of modern Georgian theater was the richly expressive actress Vera Iulianovna Andzhaparidze (born in 1900). In addition to being an accomplished actress of both comic and tragic roles, she directed the Mardzhanishvilli Theater in Tbilisi from 1957 to 1959. By 1960 there were twenty operating theaters in Georgia, most of which performed in Georgian. The Georgian acting style has been greatly influenced by Russian trends, particularly **Stanislavsky**. Great agility and expressiveness in many actor's movements is due to the ballet training made available to them. Georgian folk dancing and their ancient musical traditions are a great pride for Georgians and are still performed today to celebrate their past and present culture.

See also Soviet Cinema

References: Hartnoll, Phyllis. *The Oxford Companion to the Theatre.* New York: Oxford University Press, 1967; Speake, Graham. *Cultural Atlas of Russia and the Former Soviet Union.* London: Andomeda Oxford, 1998.

German Cinema

Film in Germany has varied greatly since its inception, experiencing a 1920s golden age, complete government domination during the Nazi regime, and another artistic flowering in the late 1960s. The early years of silent films in Germany produced unexceptional works, which often lost out in popularity with German audiences to imports from the **United States**, France, and Italy. The famed stage director **Max Reinhardt** lent the medium of film some credibility when he directed a few early silent films. In 1914, when World War I broke out, film production in many other European countries decreased. German film companies were no longer plagued by competition from imports, which gave a boost to their industry. Film actors to emerge during this time include Emil Jannings (1884–1950) and Pola Negri (1894–1987).

When the war ended in 1918, a decade of quality filmmaking began. Primary influences on the films of this era were the artistic movement known as **expressionism** and the theater of Max Reinhardt. Robert Wiene's *The Cabinet of Dr. Caligari*, 1919, was one of the first highly expressionistic Germany films, characterized by a nightmarish excursion into the twisted mind of its protagonist. Another classic German expressionistic film is *Nosferatu*, 1924, directed by F. W. Murnau. Reinhardt influenced German film through his use of light and shadow, his impressive ability to create convincing crowd scenes, and his creation of the kind of intimate drama known as the *Kammerspiel*, or the chamber play. At the end of the 1920s the advent of sound brought on a decline in the artistic quality of German films. Early talkies were predominantly romantic dramas or light musicals. One exceptional early movie of the sound era was *The Blue Angel*, 1930, directed by an American in Germany, Josef von Sternberg, starring **Marlene Dietrich** (1901–1992) in one of her first film performances.

When the Nazis took control of Germany in 1933 they likewise began controlling the film industry and were quick to use it to promote their ideology. All Jews were banned from the industry, and liberals were strongly discouraged from continuing their work. Censorship preceded the complete takeover of the film industry by the Nazis in 1942. Lavish amounts of funding were poured into the making of propagandistic films, including the documentary *Triumph of the Will*, 1935, by Leni Riefenstahl. Another film of hers, *Olympia*, 1938, was a more covertly propagandistic film, as it idealized and beautifully presented the body of the Arian athlete.

In 1945, at the end of World War II, directors who had been prominent under Nazi rule were blacklisted. In response to the devastation of war, Germany produced many films—known as "rubble films"—dramatizing the deterioration of cities and social conditions. East and West Germany officially separated in 1949, and their respective film industries grew in separate directions. In East Germany many films dealt with issues of hardship for the lower, working class, such as *Our Daily Bread*, 1949, written and directed by King Vidor. West Germany produced mostly films of low artistic merit that were meant for light entertainment. Many film actors gained fame, some even international, during this post-war time including Horst Buchholz, Romy Schneider, Maria Schell, and Maximilian Schell.

The Junger Deutscher Film, or Young German Cinema, did not emerge as a powerful artistic force until the late 1960s. An enthusiastic group of young filmmakers protested to the government for support, but did not receive this until 1968, when a government-sponsored film institute was established in Berlin. These filmmakers, such as Werner Fassbinder, Werner Herzog, and Wim Wenders, were united in their ideological stance, opposing the affluent bourgeois way of life of West Germany while searching for a more communal idealistic way of living.

Since the 1960s, production of German films has lagged behind that of other European countries, and competition from Hollywood films still plagues the German industry. Still, quality films were produced in the 1980s and 1990s by Agnieszka Holland, Doris Dorrie, Vadim Glowna, and Michael Klier. The 1990 unification of East and West Germany led to increased production of films and the enrichment of the artistic quality of these films, thanks to pooled resources and excitement over unification.

References: Brauerhoch, Annette. "VIPER: The Twelfth International Film and Video Convention, Lucerne." Screen 33 (Autumn 1992): 321–3; Eisner, Lotte. The Haunted Screen: Expressionism in German Cinema. Berkeley: University of California Press, 1969; Katz, Ephraim. The Film Encyclopedia. New York: Harper Perennial, 1994; Kracauer, Siegfried. From Caligari to Hitler: A Psycological History of the German Film. New York: Noonday, 1959; Manvell, Roger, ed. International Encyclopedia of Film. New York: Crown, 1972; Wollenberg, Hans, Fifty Years of German Film, New York: Arno, 1972.

Germany

Germany is a central European nation, originally composed of numerous states with a common language and traditions; it was not united into a country until 1871. At the end of World War II (1939–1945), Germany was split into two countries, the Federal Republic of Germany (or West Germany) and the German Democratic Republic (or East Germany), and it remained divided until 1990. Germany has been a powerful theoretical and creative force in the development of Western theater.

One of the first known forms of secular theater in Germanic areas was the **Fastnachtspiel,** a kind of farce that was a mix of religious drama and native Germanic elements from pagan rituals. Farces of this kind were often performed at carnivals traditionally preceding Lent, or by youths in villages, in which case in-jokes played a large part in the humor. It is believed that there was very little separation of audience and performers and that both joined in a final round dance at the conclusion of the show.

Some of the first actors in Germany moved from performing religious plays in the church to form guilds by the fourteenth century. Guilds were professional organizations of tradespeople such as cobblers or carpenters who sometimes sponsored and themselves participated in theater productions. One of the best-known guilds in Germany was that of the Mastersingers. Their chief dramatist, Hans Sachs (1494–1576), wrote hundreds of folk comedies, and Sachs himself trained the actors, who were tradesmen performing in their spare time. Thus, these actors were able to maintain their good standing as respectable citizens.

By 1550 Jesuit schools began performing instructive teachings that included some dramatic spectacle. As the Jesuits continued performing these plays, often dramatizing the lives of saints, they increasingly made concessions in their moral rigidity to appeal to popular taste and eventually included even scenes of violence. One performance in 1640 featured a dummy figure of Jezebel being torn to pieces by dogs.

Germany was late to develop a national theater with professional actors, mainly because of the devastation caused by the Thirty Year War (1618–1648), which left a divided Germany that still performed medieval religious plays and secular farces. By the seventeenth century, many touring groups from **Italy, England,** and **France** encouraged local groups to form and improve their skill. The comic character **Hanswurst** appeared in many farces.

In the eighteenth century, **Friedrike Caroline Neuber** raised the standard of "good taste" on the German stage, ridding the theater of its former vulgarity (though not without a struggle with popular audiences), and providing instead more elevated dramas, mostly adapted from French plays. **Johann Wolfgang von Goethe** was the most celebrated intellectual of his time in Germany, and indeed in all Europe. Together with the playwright **Friedrich von Schiller** he created a kind of theater at the Duchy of Weimar that emphasized beauty and harmony on the stage. The great actor **Konrad Ekhof** performed for a brief time at their theater.

At the beginning of the nineteenth century, the Burgtheater, founded half a century earlier, became one of the finest theaters in Europe under the management of Joseph Schreyvogel (1768–1832). He attracted the best German-speaking actors of the time. By the mid-nineteenth century, the trend toward realistic acting was beginning, with fidelity to real life as its goal. A true director's theater began near the end of the nineteenth century with the work of the Duke of Saxe-Meiningen, who stressed ensemble acting and did away with the idea that all aspects of a performance should be subservient to one star actor, as was the case before. This movement toward theatrical unity was advanced farther by **Richard Wagner**. Freie Buehne (The Free Stage) was a naturalistic group of actors, including Emanuel Reicher (1849–1924), which was modeled after **André Antoine**'s Théâtre Libre, formed in 1889, a highly influential group in promoting realistic acting even though it only lasted three seasons.

Max Reinhardt gained international recognition for the high quality of his many eclectic productions. Once in the **United States** he married the actress **Helene Thimig**. Another important innovator of modern German theater of the early twentieth century was **Gustav Grundgens**. The artistic movement known as **expressionism** began in Germany in the early part of the twentieth century and greatly influenced German theater and **German cinema. Erwin Piscator** and **Bertolt Brecht** were inspired by social ideas that radically changed the way they presented theater. They wanted an **epic theater,** one that did not allow the audience to be swept away by sentimental emotions, but instead kept them alert and examining the social situations of the characters.

Brecht used a style of acting aimed at producing what was known as the **alienation effect** to achieve this desired end. Brecht's wife, **Helene Weigel**, is said to have best exemplified this style of acting. Piscator developed **documentary theater,** which was carried on by **Peter Weiss**.

The rise of the Nazi party in 1933 and the coming of World War II (1939–1945) had a devastating effect on German theater. Most of Germany's top theater practitioners, many of whom were Jewish, fled the country. The Nazis did, however, permit a specifically Jewish theater, which continued up until the climax of the persecution of the Jews began in 1941; After World War II actors in West Germany gathered back together at the Zurich Playhouse, which lasted into the 1950s. In 1947 the Ruhr Festival was started to encourage the coal miners of the area to interact with their own culture. In the 1960s the notion of a *Volkstheater*, or a theater for the people, became popular. Many theaters tried to democratize the way in which theater was created by allowing actors and designers to have input into artistic decisions in a sort of collective. Perhaps the most influential theater in the 1970s and 1980s was in Berlin, the Playhouse on the Hallenschen Ufer, begun in 1962 by Peter Stein, who gathered a talented and dedicated group of actors around himself.

After World War II theater in East Germany began as early as 1945, with returning actors such as Ernst Busch (1900–1980) and Gustav von Wangenheim (1895–1975). Bertolt Brecht, Helene Weigel, and Erich Engel (1891–1966) founded the Berliner Ensemble in 1949, upon the request of the East German government, in order to use theater to promote ideals of social justice, peace, and democratic renewal. In the 1950s Stalinist cultural policies began to dictate following the tenets of **socialist realism,** against the wishes of many theater artists who wanted to develop their own style of theater. In the 1960s, at the Deutsches Theatre (German Theater) in Berlin, Benno Besson contributed to the development of a Russian realistic style of acting, inspired by **Stanislavsky**. In the 1970s, as governmental control over artistic output increased, many top actors and artists left East Germany. For those who stayed, the theater became a powerful tool for protest and demonstration against oppression.

The reunification of East and West Germany in 1990 has brought about a new enthusiasm for collaborative works. Theater artists in former East Germany have struggled to discover their role in this new governmental setting, since they have lost their vital role as spokespersons for the oppressed.

See also Nazi Germany's Jewish Theater; Reiniger, Lotte

References: Carlson, Marvin. *The French Stage in the Nineteenth Century.* Metuchen, NJ: Scarecrow Press, 1972; Chinoy, Helen Krich, and Toby Cole. *Actors on Acting.* New York: Crown, 1970; Loney, Glenn. "Germany Sings." *TCI* 29 (February 1995): 10–11; Patterson, Michael. *German Theatre Today: Post-War Theatre in West and East Germany, Austria and Northern Switzerland.* London: Pitman, 1976; Prudhoe, John. *The Theatre of Goethe and Schiller.* Totowa, NJ: Rowman and Littlefield, 1973: Williams, Simon. *German Actors of the Eighteenth and Nineteenth Centuries: Idealism, Romanticism, and Realism.* Westport, CT: Greenwood, 1985.

Ghana

The traditional theatrical roots in Ghana richly feed the modern flowering of new theatrical creations. One older traditional form is the **Bedu,** a masked dance-drama performed by the Nafana people during one lunar month out of the year known as the "dance moon." Another traditional source of theater comes from storytelling, such as the *Anansesem,* or spider stories. Ceremonies and festivals with theatrical elements also lend to the current richness of Ghanaian theater. The *Aboakyer,* a deer-hunting festival in Winneba, is a festival of misrule, which provides an occasion for licensed mischief, many dramatic skits, and much parodying of important figures in the community.

Ghana's most exciting theatrical creation of this century is the **Trios,** or concert parties. These are professional touring theater groups that improvise comic plays based on themes pertinent to the lives of the general populace.

References: Antubam, Kofi. "Arts of Ghana." *United Asia* 9, 1 (1957): 61–70; Banham, Martin. *African Theatre Today.* London: Pitman, 1976.; Kedjanyi, John. "Observations on Spectator-Performance Arrangements of Some Traditional Ghanaian Performances." *Research Review* (Legon) 2, 3 (1966): 61–66; Kennedy, Scott. *In Search of African Theatre.* New York: Scribner, 1973; McHardy, Cecile. "The Performing Arts in Ghana." *Africa Forum* 1, 1 (Summer 1965): 113–117; Opoku, A. A. *Festivals of Ghana.* Accra: Ghana Publishing, 1970; Williams, Drid. "The Dance of the Bedu Moon." *African Arts* 2, 1 (1968): 18–21.

Gielgud, John (1904–2000)
England

English actor, whose grandmother, Kate Terry, and aunt, **Ellen Terry**, were great actresses. Gielgud began acting at seventeen and by twenty-five was the leading male performer at the Old Vic Company, a famous London Theater, where he performed the lead role in many works by **Shakespeare** and others. Gielgud performed the title role in *Hamlet* over 500 times during his life. In 1935–1936 Gielgud performed in *Romeo and Juliet* over 180 times; he and **Laurence Olivier** traded off the roles of Mercutio and Romeo. In 1945 he began directing and was particularly successful with his production of *The Lady's Not for Burning* (1949) by the popular playwright Christopher Fry. His theatrical performances are far too numerous to mention all of them. In 1958 he created a solo work featuring many Shakespearean characters, *Ages of Man,* which he toured internationally to great acclaim.

As an actor he was known for his intelligence and awareness. Not as physical as some of his other male contemporaries, he projected a more refined style. Vocal expressiveness and remarkable range were most prominent in his work. He performed in numerous films, including *Julius Caesar,* as Cassius in 1953 and later in the title role in 1970, *The Shoes of the Fisherman,* 1968, *Murder on the Orient Express,* 1974, *Chariots of Fire,* 1981, *Gandhi,* 1982, and *The Power of One,* 1992. Gielgud won an Oscar in the comedy *Arthur,* 1980, as Dudley Moore's butler. He played Prospero in a richly ornate film based on Shakespeare's *Tempest, Prospero's Books,* 1988, directed by Peter Greenaway.

On his ninetieth birthday in 1994, the Globe Theatre in London became the Gielgud to honor his contribution to English theater.

References: Chinoy, Helen Krich, and Toby Cole. *Actors on Acting,* New York: Crown, 1970; Gielgud, John. *Gielgud: An Actor and His Time.* New York: C. N Potter, 1980; Harwood, Ronald. *The Ages of Gielgud: An Actor at Eighty.* New York: Limelight, 1984.

Gilbert and Sullivan
England

Famous librettist and composer duo who created light operas together from 1871 to 1896. William Gilbert (1836–1911) wrote the lyrics and Arthur Sullivan (1842–1900) was the composer in their collaborations, which began with *Thespis*, 1871. Another early work was *Trial by Jury*, 1875. They gained fame with *HMS Pinafore*, 1878 and *The Pirates of Penzance*, 1879. Other works include *Princess Ida*, 1884, and *The Mikado*, 1885, set in Japan. Their operas were known for their outstanding musical quality and topsy-turvy plots. The film *Topsy Turvy*, 2000, directed by Mike Leigh, focused on the separate lives of Gilbert and Sullivan their relationship, and the staging of *The Mikado*. It also gives insight into the acting life of the late nineteenth century in England.

Giri
Japan

Code of honor for a **samurai** warrior.

Gish, Lillian (1896–1993)
United States

American actress of the stage and silent films, often considered the best actress of her era. Both Gish and her sister, Dorothy Gish (1898–1968), began acting as children in melodramas on the stage. She toured as a child with companies, sometimes with her mother and sister and sometimes alone, to supplement their meager family income. Their big break came when the two sisters and their mother were cast in D. W. Griffith's *An Unseen Enemy*, 1912. Lillian became Griffith's favorite heroine, and her physical frailty, combined with spiritual strength and tenacity, came to typify the Victorian female of his sentimental films. These implausible melodramatic films, such as *Orphans of the Storm*, 1922, were elevated through the richly creative acting talent of Gish. Since these were silent films, she relied heavily upon her physical expression of emotions and her communicative facial expressions. She performed many of her own stunts, even riding an ice block down a frozen river.

Lillian directed her sister Dorothy in the film *Remodeling Her Husband*, 1920, and Dorothy married

Winnie Melville and Derek Oldham during the first act of a 1929 London production of Gilbert and Sullivan's Mikado at the Savoy Theater. (Hulton-Deutsch Collection/Corbis)

James Rennie, her co-star of that film, in 1920. Lillian went on to perform in the films *La Bohême* and *The Scarlet Letter*, both in 1926. By the 1930s she returned to the Broadway stage and performed Ophelia opposite **John Gielgud** in the title role of *Hamlet*. Gish never married and kept her private life away from the public eye.

> **References:** McCaffrey, Donald. *Guide to the Silent Years of American Cinema*. Westport, CT: Greenwood, 1999; Oderman, Stuart. *Lillian Gish: A Life on Stage and Screen*. Jefferson, NC: McFarland, 2000; Wagenknecht, Edward. *Lillian Gish: An Interprtation*. Seattle: University of Washington, 1927.

Gita Govinda
India

Operatic dance-drama, mostly in southern India, in Orissa, and also in Kerala, where this form is known as **Ashtapadi Attam**. A chorus of singers perform narration and songs enacted on stage by dancers. The dramatic action of each performance revolves around **Krishna,** the eighth and most important incarnation of the Hindu god **Vishnu,** and Radha, Krishna's favored milkmaid, coming together. Sexual union is seen as a metaphor for blissful union with God.

A performance opens with a song invoking the gods, after which a beautiful dancer enters and scatters flowers on the stage. She then interprets a song through dance, exits, and the drama begins. Jayadeva (born early twelfth century) wrote the poetic dramas most popular in *Gita Govinda*. His lyrical style of writing is a near perfect vehicle for song, dance, and language.

References: Varadpande, Manohar Laxman. *Krishna Theatre in India.* New Delhi: Abhinav, 1982.

Goethe, Johann Wolfgang von (1749–1832)
Germany

German playwright, poet, intellectual, and theorist, who established a vogue for an idealized form of acting for the classical stage to lend grace and dignity to the theater. His best-known plays are *Faust* (Part 1), 1808, and *Faust* (Part 2), 1830. In 1775 Goethe was invited to the Duchy of Weimar and became extremely active with the duke's amateur theater group. From 1791 to 1817 he was director for the Weimar Court Theater, during which time he attempted to infuse dignity into the art of theater and the occupation of acting. Goethe collaborated with **Friedrich von Schiller** from 1794 until 1805, when Schiller died. Together they created a style of acting for the classical movement based on simplicity, harmony, and dignity.

Goethe wanted to create an idealized artificial beauty on the stage. Because the actors he had at his disposal were lacking in talent and creativity, he devised "Rules for Actors" spelling out how to speak, move, and gesture. Strict rules of conduct were enforced for his actors off the stage too. In fact these rules even extended to the conduct of the audience, which would be reprimanded by Goethe himself during a performance if they transgressed the rules. Goethe's rules for acting were carried on for generations, the popularity of them fueled by the fame of Goethe himself. Theater artists in later times had to argue long and hard to deconstruct this artificial and external approach to acting.

References: Carlson, Marvin. *The French Stage in the Nineteenth Century.* Metuchen, NJ: Scarecrow Press, 1972; Chinoy, Helen Krich, and Toby Cole. *Actors on Acting.* New York: Crown, 1970; Goethe, Johan Wolfgang von. "Rules For Actors (1803)." *Quarterly Journal of Speech Education* 13, 3 (June 1927): 247–256, 259–264; Goethe, Johann Wolfgang von. *The Autobiography of Johann Wolfgang Von Goethe.* Trans. John Oxenford. New York: Horizon Press, 1969; Goethe, Johann Wolfgang von. *Correspondence between Goethe and Schiller.* Trans. Liselotte Dieckmann. New York: P. Lang, 1994; Prudhoe, John. *The Theatre of Goethe and Schiller.* Totowa, NJ: Rowman and Littlefield, 1973; Reed, Terence. *The Classical Centre: Goeth and Weimar.* New York: Barnes & Noble, 1980.

Gogol, Nikolay (1809–1852)
Russia

Playwright, theorist. When in school as a young man, Gogol was active in theater. In 1828, when he moved to Saint Petersburg, he hoped to become an actor but failed. He wrote many comedies, but the only one to reach success (and cause great controversy) was *The Inspector General*, 1836, a comedy of errors about a small corrupt town that mistakes an opportunistic traveler for the inspector general. The only thing that saved this play from the censors was the fact that the emperor liked it. This play is one of the first realistic comedies from Russia. Gogol also wrote *The Marriage* in 1833. His writing coincided with a time when acting styles in Russia were becoming more realistic. Gogol believed that a director should be actively involved in the process of the actors, drawing out the inner life of the play and balancing all the parts. He also called for truthfulness in theatrical representation.

See also Russia

References: Gogol, Nikolai. *The Theater of Nikolay Gogol: Plays and Selected Writings.* Trans. Milton Ehre and Fruma Gottschalk. Chicago: University of Chicago Press, 1980; Popkin, Cathy. *The Pragmatics of Insignificance: Checkov, Zoshchenko, Gogol.* Stanford, CA: Stanford University Press, 1993; Slonim, Marc. *Russian Theater, From the Empire to the Soviets.* Cleveland: World, 1961.

Goldberg, Whoopi (1949–)
United States

American film actress capable of hilarious comedy and touching drama. Originally named Caryn

Actress Whoopi Goldberg in the starring role of Sarafina! (1982) (Courtesy of Hollywood Pictures)

Johnson, Goldberg began performing as a child and attended the High School for the Performing Arts in New York. Her big break came with her one-woman show *Spook Show,* in which she impersonates a wide variety of characters, from a young African American girl wishing for long soft hair, to an urban black man visiting the Anne Frank museum in Germany. She weaves them all together into a heartfelt and humorous consideration of race and humanity. Her first screen appearance was in *The Color Purple,* 1985, for which she received acclaim. As a supporting actress in *Ghost,* 1990, she won an Academy Award. In a pure comedic role, she made *Sister Act,* 1991, and the sequel, *Sister Act II,* 1993. She performed in the movie *Sarafina!,* 1992, about **South Africa.** With her wild hair and round spectacles, her exuberance and keen sense of timing have made her one of the great comedians of the twentieth and twenty-first centuries.

References: Stuart, Andrea. "Making Whoopi: Andrea Stuart Explores the Extraordinary, and Unlikely, Success of Whoopi Goldberg." *Sight and Sound* 3 (1993): 12–13.

Gopal Kala
India

A form of drama about **Krishna,** the eighth and most important incarnation of the Hindu god **Vishnu,** in the Gomantaka region, south India; usually performed in the morning after an evening performance of **Dashavatar Kala,** a form of drama about the ten incarnations of **Vishnu-Krishna,** the Hindu god. The story dramatized tells of a demon disguised as a cowherd boy who was sent to kill Krishna. The demon mixes with the **Gopis,** milkmaids, and plays games with them. The demon is killed by Balarama, another incarnation of Vishnu-Krishna, before he can do Krishna any harm.

A performance begins as the **Sutradhara,** the narrator, invokes Lord **Ganesha,** an elephant-headed Hindu god. Then the chorus sings about the games being played by the Gopis. Performers in two groups, one led by Krishna, the other by the demon, challenge each other with riddles presented in song for two hours. This sung duel culminates as the demon lifts Balarama onto his shoulders and starts running away. Balarama hits him on the head with a fatal blow of the fist. The Sutradhara and his chorus then sing a song of Krishna. The final act is that a pot of milk and curd is broken and the contents shared with the audience.

Only performers playing Krishna, Balarama, and Pralambha wear makeup and costumes. All others perform in simple street clothing.

References: Varadpande, Manohar Laxman. *Krishna Theatre in India.* New Delhi: Abhinav, 1982.

Gopis
India

Young milkmaids. In stories about the life of **Krishna,** the eighth and most important incarnation of the Hindu god **Vishnu,** the *Gopis* often gather around him, unable to overcome their extreme attraction to him. They are present in **Ras Lila,** a Krishna dance-drama, and in most other forms that dramatize Krishna tales.

References: Varadpande, Manohar Laxman. *Krishna Theatre in India.* New Delhi: Abhinav, 1982.

Gray, Spalding (1941–)
United States

Actor, playwright; most known for his humorous autobiographical one-man shows, which he tours with extensively. Gray began as an actor at the Alley Theater in Houston. In 1969 he joined **Richard Schechner**'s Performance Group. He later broke from the group and began working with Elizabeth LeCompte and the Wooster Group on the Rhode Island Plays, such as *Sakonnet Point, 1975, Rumstick Road,* 1977, and *Nayatt School,* 1978, all based largely on autobiographical material. He went on to begin performing solo works, such as *Sex and Death at the Age 14, Swimming to Cambodia,* and *Monster in the Box,* which he tours extensively to popular crowds in large venues. When performing these he utilizes minimal setting, usually an oversized chair and table upon which he places his script, which he refers to while performing. His performance style is conversational and unaffected, more like storytelling or solo comedy than acting. In 1988 he successfully performed the role of the Stage Manager in *Our Town* at the Lincoln Center.

References: Bigsby, C.W.E. *A Critical Introduction to Twentieth-Century American Drama.* New York: Cambridge University Press, 1985; Gray, Spalding. *Impossible Vacation.* New York: Knopf, 1992; Gray, Spalding. *Swimming to Cambodia.* New York: Theatre Communication Group, 1985; Salz, Melissa. "Theatre of Testimony: The Work of Emily Mann, Anna Deavere Smith and Spalding Gray." Ph.D. diss., University of Colorado, 1996.

Greece

From the sixth to the third centuries B.C. one of the greatest civilizations of the ancient world evolved, above all in Athens, to lead the world in art, politics, philosophy, and science. Greek civilization, including **ancient Greek theater,** was spread throughout much of the Middle East and western Asia by Alexander the Great, king of Macedonia, and, after his death in 323 B.C., by the Hellenistic kings who ruled over the different parts of his empire. Greece was absorbed into the Roman Empire between the second and first centuries B.C. and remained part of the Byzantine Empire after the split of the Roman Empire in the fourth century A.D. The country was taken over by the Ottoman Turks in 1460 and was under control of the Ottoman Empire for 350 years. During this time the shadow puppet theater of Turkey, *Karagoz,* was adapted by Greek theater practitioners to become *Karagiozis.* Greece won its independence from the Turks in 1827. Various Western powers sponsored leaders for Greece, none of which were well accepted by the people. Political instability characterized the Greek political situation until the 1950s, when Greece adopted a new constitution designed to create a stable government.

During Byzantine and Turkish rule, Greece did not have a national theater. Following Greece's independence from the Ottoman Empire, the Theatron Scontzopulos was opened in 1835, but it was dominated by traveling French and Italian companies. Many Greek theater ensembles and opera companies found a home in 1930 when a national theater was founded. A romanticized ideal of their classical past and perhaps a desire to reclaim some pride after the debilitating effect of World War II led Greece to a revitalization of classical theaters such as **Epidaurus** in the 1970s. In these preserved structures many contemporary directors revive the classic works of ancient **Greek tragedy** and **Greek comedy.**

References: Arnott, Peter D. *The Ancient Greek and Roman Theatre.* New York: Random House, 1971; Bieber, Margarete. *The History of the Greek and Roman Theater.* Princeton, NJ: Princeton University Press, 1961; Ley, Graham. *A Short Introduction to the Ancient Greek Theater.* Chicago: University of Chicago Press, 1991.

Greek Chorus

A group of men who sang and danced choral odes, especially those that divided the acts of an ancient Greek drama; these odes may be descended from the **dithyramb,** a kind of hymn honoring **Dionysus.** The chorus originally had approximately fifty men, but the playwright **Aeschylus** reduced the number. Members of the chorus remained in the orchestra, a large circular area between the audience and the stage, throughout the entire play. Functioning as an ethical and social framework for a drama, the chorus often represented members of the community. For example, in *Oedipus Rex,* by **Sophocles,** the chorus is a group of concerned citizens, and in *Medea,* by **Euripides,** the chorus is a group of important women of Corinth. Choruses were an important element of many community events in ancient Greece, contributing a richness to any ceremony at which they performed. Thus, it was quite natural and effective to have a chorus play such an integral role in dramatic performances. There were choruses for tragedies, comedies, and **satyr plays.**

The structure of **Greek tragedy** included a prologue, the episodes (or agons), and the *exodos*. Between each structural element, the chorus performed different songs: *parodos* was the general name given to songs sung while moving onto the stage, and the *stasimon* was sung between episodes while standing still. In some plays, the chorus sang a choral ode set in a pair of stanzas called the strophe and the antistrophe; the former was sung as the chorus moved from right to left, the latter as they moved back to the right. The chorus would also sing or chant a dialogue with the chorus leader. Almost nothing is known about the music, other than that the lyrics were sung by the entire chorus in unison, probably with one note to each syllable.

During a production the chorus remained still when not performing: That is, they did not act like a crowd scene to provide a naturalistic background for the drama. The *coryphaeus*, the leader of the chorus, who was probably distinguished by costume, occasionally spoke dialogue with the actors on the stage. The function of the chorus was to give advice to the characters, express opinions, and ask questions. The chorus was the ideal spectator and set the overall mood of the performance. Not only adding movement and spectacle, their songs and dances also served an important rhythmic function. The choral dancing was done in formation of either a rectangle or a circle. Believed to be predominantly solemn, the style of dance was dignified, but at times could have become wild and nearly ecstatic. *Emmeleia* is the name given to a solemn choral dance performed during a tragedy. The chorus's movements were expressive and mimed the moods, emotions, and content of the accompanying songs through use of the hands, arms, body position, and feet movements.

Choruses practiced for months before a production. A *choregos* was a wealthy citizen who paid for all expenses of a performance, including payment to chorus members. He also paid the *chorodidaskalos*, the teacher of the chorus.

See also Greek Comedy

References: Bieber, Margarete. *The History of the Greek and Roman Theater.* Princeton, NJ: Princeton University Press, 1961; Taplin, Oliver. *Greek Tragedy in Action.* Berkeley: University of California Press, 1978; Webster, Thomas Bertram Lonsdale. *Greek Theatre Production.* London: Methuen, 1970.

Greek Comedy

Ancient Greek comedy most likely evolved from the Komos, dancing and antics of gay revelers in honor of the Greek god **Dionysus.** From the fifth century onward comedy in Greece developed through three distinct periods: Old, Middle, and New Comedy. It was at the **Lenaia,** one of the religious festivals dedicated to Dionysus, that comedy was first improvised and then, in the first half of the fifth century B.C., given literary form. Comedy was allowed into the grandest religious festival, the **City Dionysia,** in 487.

Lasting from 486 to 400 B.C., Old Comedy focused on farce and physical humor. Embodying some far-fetched idea, these plays commented on contemporary society in clever ways, sometimes by ridiculing famous individuals or by exposing the absurdity of government policies. The visual humor largely depended upon physical pranks, such as erect phalluses emerging from the costumes of male characters. The only surviving works of Old Comedy are by the great comic playwright **Aristophanes.**

Middle Comedy, from which there are only pieces of scripts, lasted from 400 until 330 B.C. and was never considered even in times of antiquity to be more than a feeble reflection of Old Comedy. Much less political than its predecessor, Middle Comedy tended to focus on themes from daily life. Individual resemblances to public figures were avoided, and humor was instead drawn from physical imperfections, shameless behavior, bawdy flirtations, and old age.

The New Comedy of the playwrights **Menander,** Philemon, and others replaced Middle Comedy in about 330 B.C., during the early years of the Hellenistic Age, if that period is thought of as beginning when Alexander the Great came into power in 336. Since Athens was no longer an independent democracy, there was not the same freedom of speech as Aristophanes had enjoyed. Thus, plays from this era focused on the middle class and their shortcomings in social manners. In a polished and refined style of humor, social vices such as vanity were attacked rather than individuals. A popular theme was children outwitting their parents to marry by choice, usually with the help of a quick-witted servant or slave.

Comedy was first performed voluntarily by nonprofessional actors, who were always male.

Thus, the number of actors in a drama was not limited. An independent contest for best comic actor was introduced at the Lenaia in about 442 B.C., and not until 325 B.C. at the City Dionysia. After this time, the number of actors performing comedies was limited to three, since the state would pay the salaries for only that many. Actors had to play several roles, using masks and costumes to distinguish the various characters.

Costuming in Old and Middle Comedy was designed to make the actor appear comical. Padded bodysuits, which probably evolved from those used by the **padded dancers** who reveled for Dionysus in the sixth century, were worn under costumes to make the actors appear short and fat. Since a limited number of actors performed a play, there would not have been time to change much more than a mask when an actor had to change character. Thus, both male and female characters wore the padding. Male characters wore short tunics and cloaks that didn't extend much below the waist. To great comic effect, a large leather phallus was strapped to the waist and protruded out of the short male costume. Sometimes it was strapped up to try to hide it, and it was let loose when jokes were made about it. The phallus was a symbol of fertility associated with the worship of the Greek god Dionysus. Masks worn by actors featured exaggerated facial expressions, with big mouths, and sometimes humorously mimicked important citizens.

New Comedy abandoned these greatly exaggerated costumes, discarding the indecent phallus and stuffed bodysuits. The grotesque masks were preserved only for some of the lower-class characters, such as soldiers and slaves.

Musical accompaniment for comedies was performed on flutes, clappers, and a guitar-like instrument called a cithara. The licentious and wild **Kordax,** complete with whirling jumps and clashing buttocks, was the style of dance typical of Old and Middle Comedy performances.

References: Bieber, Margarete. "The Statuette of an Actor of New Comedy." *Bulletin of the Art Museum, Princeton University* (1951): 4–12; Bieber, Margarete. *The History of the Greek and Roman Theater.* Princeton, NJ: Princeton University Press, 1961; Cornford, F. M. *The Origins of Attic Comedy.* London: Edward Arnold, 1914; Ehrenberg, Victor. *The People of Aristophanes: A Sociology of Old Attic Comedy.* New York: Barnes & Noble, 1974; Rees, K. "The Three-Actor Rule in Menander." *Classical Philology* 5 (1910): 291–302; Sandbach, F. *The Comic Theatre of Greece and Rome.* New York: Norton, 1977; Taylor, David. *Acting and the Stage.* Boston: George Allen & Unwin, 1978; Webster, Thomas Bertram Lonsdale. "The Costume of the Actors in Aristophanic Comedy." *Classical Quarterly* 5 (1955): 94.

Greek Tragedy

The first Greek tragedy was created in the middle of the sixth century B.C. by Thespis, when he distinguished himself from the chorus as a character and entered into dialogue with the chorus during the performance of an ode in honor of **Dionysus,** thus creating dramatic confrontation. In the fifth century B.C., which was the golden age for Greek tragedy, great works by the poets **Aeschylus, Sophocles,** and **Euripides** were written, and some of them survive today, providing a measure by which all Western dramas are judged. As the quality of dramatic literature decreased in the fourth century B.C., the quality of Greek classical tragic acting reached its peak.

Once actors distinguished themselves from the chorus, a structure of Greek tragedies evolved into an elaborate series of alternations between dialogue performed by actors and choral odes (lyric poems sung by the chorus), each part developing the dramatic action or responding to it. The recurring structural features include the following: The prologue introduces the conflict by telling of the action that occurred prior to the opening of the play. Not all tragedies have a prologue, but the next feature is present in all tragedies; the *parodos* opens the drama proper with the entrance of the chorus. Of the extant plays, this portion varies in length from 20 to 200 lines; the chorus introduces itself, provides exposition, and sets the proper mood. A series of three to six episodes, or *agons,* follows, during which the main action is developed. The episodes consist of dialogue between actors, and between actors and the chorus. Between the episodes, the chorus performs choral songs known as *Stasima.* The final feature, the *exodos,* reveals the conclusion of the drama, after which all characters and the chorus depart from the performance area.

There are many other recurring stylistic features of Greek tragedies. The dramas commence just prior to the climax, and only the final part is dramatized, a device known as a late point of attack. Physical violence in the dramas is almost always committed off stage and only after its completion are the results revealed to the audience, usually on what is called the *ekkyklema*, a platform on wheels. Most often there is a unity of time, place, and action, meaning that the drama occurs in real time, with no breaks and no change of location. Greek myths and history form the subject matter for Greek tragedies. Playwrights were free to alter these stories as they wished and could invent motivations for the characters.

Three male actors performed all character roles and often had to play more than one role in a play, ranging in type from royal to coarse and from masculine to feminine. Because the state paid the expenses for only three actors to perform in each drama, physical and vocal versatility was a must for actors. There is no evidence besides the remaining scripts for what happened in the action of the play, and there are almost no stage directions in the scripts, since the playwright himself was usually the director.

Since tragedy descended from Dionysian rituals, costumes worn for tragedy retained three essential elements for such rituals, to symbolize continued devotion to Dionysus: the sleeved robe, the *cothurnus*, a flat calf-length boot, and the mask. The floor-length robes with long sleeves are believed to have been lavish, made of fabric designed in colorful swirls, stars, and circles. Special character types had other accoutrements to identify them; warriors wore armor, and people in mourning wore black. The heel of the cothurnus was flat originally; it became a platform shoe later in the history of Greek theater, in order to make the actor appear larger.

A masterfully crafted mask covered the entire head of the tragic actor. These masks were usually made of linen, but sometimes cork or wood was used. Lifelike hair billowed from the top of the mask, surrounding the solemn expression of the face. There were openings for the eyes, so that the actor could see, and for the mouth, which not only allowed the actor's voice to be heard, but amplified it. The facial expression of the mask could not change, but, due to the size of the audience, subtle expressions of the face would not have been visible. This suited Greek dramas, since

they were not trying to communicate the psychological nuances of characters so much as the ethos of their heroic characters, which a visually static mask could consistently assert.

Musical accompaniment was performed by a flute that sounded like an oboe or clarinet in tone, a lyre, a trumpet, and various forms of percussion. Only rarely was music used apart from words sung by the chorus. The choral dance that accompanied their singing was expressive rhythmical movement.

Greek tragedies focused on the protagonist, who was always a person of noble birth. This person was at the mercy of his or her *moira*, or fate, of which he or she did not have a complete understanding. The **anagnorisis,** the moment of recognition of destiny, was most often the climax of the play. Aristotle, in his theoretical work on theater, the *Poetics*, wrote that it was most satisfying for the audience if this recognition occurred at the same instant that the tragic hero's fortune reversed, known as peripeteia. The most perfect example of this conjunction of peripeteia and anagnorisis was, according to Aristotle, to be found in *Oedipus Rex*, by Sophocles.

References: Bieber, Margarete. *The History of the Greek and Roman Theater.* Princeton, NJ: Princeton University Press, 1961; Else, G. F. *The Origin and Early Form of Greek Tragedy.* Cambridge, MA: Harvard University Press, 1965; Ferguson, John. *A Companion to Greek Tragedy.* Austin: University of Texas Press, 1972; Kitto, H. D. F. "The Dance in Greek Tragedy." *Journal of Hellenic Studies* 75 (1955): 36–41; Rehm, Rush. *Greek Tragic Theatre.* New York: Routledge, 1992; Shister, Famic Lorine. "The Portrayal of Emotion in Tragedy." *American Journal of Philology* 66 (1945): 377–397; Taplin, Oliver. *Greek Tragedy in Action.* Berkeley: University of California Press, 1978.

Grotowski, Jerzy (1933–1999)
Poland

Theater innovator and director who was influenced by his training in Cracow, Moscow, and China. Brought up in the **Stanislavsky** tradition, Grotowski had great respect for Stanislavsky and worked to continue his research on the physical action involved in acting. He became the champion of the idea of a "poor theater," in which the actors and the theater are freed from financial restrictions because of a vow of poverty. Poverty gave the luxury to work on a performance for as long as a year and to perform it to very small audiences. Poverty also demanded minimal stage trickery, and so allowed for a direct and profound connection between the audience and the performer. His theater was a laboratory, and his productions were investigations into the relationship between the actors and the audience.

In 1959 Grotowski became manager of Theater Laboratory, which moved to Wroclaw in 1965. He began his work believing in the primacy of the director but later shifted his focus to the actor. His was a psychotherapeutic morality theater rather than a theater for entertainment. Through extreme and arduous physical exercises, his actors gained mastery over their expressive capacity. All this was done to remove the blocks between the actor and his or her pure expression. This process demands that the actor surrender to a role, as a sort of sacrificial offering to the audience. Grotowski articulates his theories and experiences in his 1968 book, *Towards a Poor Theatre*.

He toured to the United States and Europe with his famous works *Akropolis* and *The Constant Prince*. In 1976 Grotowski disbanded the Laboratory Theatre but continued practical research on actors. In 1986 the workshop of Jerzy Grotowski was founded in Pontedera, Italy. In 1996 Grotowski changed the name to Workcenter of Jerzy Grotowski and Thomas Richards. In 1987 Richards created the "opus" (as it is referred to) *Downstairs Action* (1987) and the "opus" *Action* (1994), both experimental, mostly non-narrative pieces. Grotowski's influence on the development of modern theater has been outstanding.

References: Chinoy, Helen Krich, and Toby Cole. *Actors on Acting.* New York: Crown, 1970; Richards, Thomas. *At Work with Grotowski on Physical Actions.* New York: Routledge, 1995; Wolford, Lisa. *Grotowski's Objective Drama Research.* Jackson: University Press of Mississippi, 1996.

Group Theater
United States

Collective theater in New York from 1931 to 1941, started by Harold Clurman (1901–1980), Cheryl Crawford (1902–1986), and Lee Strasberg (1901–1982), that stressed ensemble acting and sought to present plays with social significance. These three former members of the Theater Guild wanted to establish a group of dedicated actors who would train according to the Method, based on the teachings of **Stanislavsky** of the **Moscow Art Theater.** The unifying goal of this theater was the belief that a point of view was necessary for the actors, directors, and designers of a show, and that the actors should all train in their craft in the same way to realize this vision in true ensemble acting.

Young American actors first learned the Method from two Stanislavsky students, Richard Boleslavsky and Maria Ouspenskaya, who worked at the American Laboratory Theater. At the Group Theater, Strasberg was the primary acting teacher. He is known for having developed his own interpretation of the Russian Stanislavsky System and turned it into the distinctively American Method. He utilized many improvisational exercises to get actors to portray true emotions. He relied heavily upon emotional recall and the actor's own life experience to inform insight into the character. This training forced the actors to go deeply into themselves. When **Stella Adler** returned from studying with Stanislavsky overseas, she said that the Group was relying too heavily on these elements introduced by Strasberg, which caused a rift among the Group. Strasberg left in 1937 and continued working and teaching with the **Actors Studio.**

Committed to social realism, the Group chose as their primary playwright Clifford Odets (1906–1963), who wrote *Awake and Sing* and *Waiting for Lefty,* both produced in 1935. One important actor with the Group from the beginning was Morris Carnovsky (1897–1992), who appeared in *The House of Connelly,* 1931, among many other productions. As an actor he was known for speaking in a rich voice and exuding a sense of ease.

References: Demastes, William. *Beyond Naturalism: A New Realism in American Theatre.* New York: Greenwood, 1988; Gassner, John. "The Group Theatre, In Its Tenth Year: A Critical Estimate." *Theatre Arts* 24 (1940): 729; McBride, Murdoch. "For Actors Studio's 50th Year, A Group Theatre Retrospective." *Back Stage* 39, 17 (24 April 1998–30 April 1998): 3, 49; Mordden, Ethan. *The American Theatre.* New York: Oxford University Press, 1981.

Grummelot
Italy

A term, originally from the French, referring to the creation of a flow of sounds to suggest a continuation of speech even though simply one is only babbling; used by players of **commedia dell'arte,** improvised sixteenth- and seventeenth-century Italian comedy. The onomatopoeic continuation of sounds that resemble speech, when combined with gestures, gives the onlooker the impression of having witnessed a polished and well-rounded speech. The ability to create this illusion was the basis of improvisational performing in *commedia dell'arte*.

References: Rudlin, John. *Commedia Dell'Arte: An Actor's Handbook*. London and New York: Routledge, 1994.

Grundgens, Gustav (1899–1963)
Germany

Actor, director, and a prominent innovator in modern German theater. Beginning as an actor, Grundgens got his first notable roles with Ziegel's Company in 1923, where he performed the lead role in *Danton's Death* in 1928. He joined the Berlin National Theater in 1932 where he both acted and directed. At the Deutsches Schauspielhaus (German Theater) in Hamburg, he directed many innovative modern works. He was, perhaps, most famous for his portrayal of Mephistopheles in the play *Faust* by **Goethe**. As an actor, he was renowned for his wit, grace, and elegance, which won him many sophisticated roles that commanded the attention of all who witnessed him.

References: Chinoy, Helen Krich, and Toby Cole. *Actors on Acting*. New York: Crown, 1970; Patterson, Michael. *German Theatre Today: Post-War Theatre in West and East Germany, Austria and Northern Switzerland*. New York: Pitman, 1976.

Guomundsdóttir, Stefania (1876–1926)
Iceland

Actress of the Icelandic stage, credited with ushering in a new age of artistic growth and excellence in Iceland. Known as Frú Stefania, she was not the first actress to perform on the stage in Iceland, since women are reported to have performed in Iceland since 1839, except in grammar schools where it was not allowed. She had her debut at the age of sixteen and impressed the crowds with her vivacity and charm. She started as an actress of light comedies but developed into a dramatic actress capable of expressing the complex emotions found in the European classics. Her career lasted thirty years, during which time she performed many of the great roles from plays by **Henrik Ibsen** and other playwrights.

She is noted for her extraordinary flexibility of expression. Reviews of her performances often mentioned her charm and radiance. After 1923 she managed the Reykjavik Theater Company. When she visited Copenhagen to perform, reviews compared her favorably with the best Europe had to offer. She is credited as the first great actor of either gender to emerge from the Icelandic settlement.

References: Einarsson, Sveinne. "Frú Stefania: The First Icelandic Actress." In *Nordic Theatre Studies: Yearbook for Theatre Research in Scandinavia*, ed. Kela Kvam, 41–48. Denmark: Institute for Theatre Research, University of Copenhagen, 1988.

Gustav III (1746–1792)
Sweden

King of Sweden from 1771 to 1792 and enlightened patron of the arts, theater being his primary passion. Other Scandinavian monarchs had influenced and supported theater but never to the level of Gustav, who participated in selecting the plays to be presented, casting, writing, and often acting. He was a champion for Swedish theater in its native tongue, a theater no longer dominated by French imports. He was highly interested in historical and nationalistic drama and wrote many such plays himself or with a collaborator. The Royal Opera was formed under his direction in 1773, performing the ambitious tragedy *Orpheus and Eurydice* by C. W. Gluck in the same year. In this theater a highly emotional French-inspired acting style with graphic physical language was employed. Costumes became more evocative of the character being played, rather than replicas of the popular court dress of the time.

As an actor, Gustav enjoyed performing some of the great heroic roles, such as the title role in Voltaire's *Genghis Khan*, until counselors persuaded him for political reasons to desist from such public exploits. Hundreds of actors, singers, musicians, and dancers in residency presented operas, spoken dramas, and ballets at his court theater in Drottningholm, while outside beautiful spectacles were performed as pageants. From all over Europe he acquired the greatest talent in scenic design, acting, and architecture.

This momentum of theatrical growth came to an abrupt halt in 1792 at a masked ball at the Royal Opera when an assassin's bullet killed Gus-tav. His death marked the end of royal involvement in Swedish theater.

See also **Royalty and World Leaders as Actors**

References: Marker, Frederick, *A History of Scandinavian Theatre*, Cambridge: Cambridge University Press, 1996; Mattsson, Inger, ed. *Gustavian Opera: An Interdisciplinary Reader in Swedish Opera, Dance, and Theatre 1771–1809*. Stockholm: Royal Swedish Academy, 1991; van Boer, Bertil, ed. *Gustav III and the Swedish Stage*. Lewiston, NY: E. Mellen, 1993.

H

Haiti

Originally inhabited by the Arawak, the island now known as Haiti was first visited by Westerners in 1492 when Christopher Columbus stepped onto its shores. In the next century, Western enslavement and foreign diseases killed the entire population of the Arawak. A predominantly African slave-based agricultural society followed, until slavery was abolished in 1794. France had colonized Haiti until a general uprising of slaves in 1791, which led to the country's independence in 1804. Extreme political instability during the last two centuries has made for much hardship for the 95 percent black population of Haiti.

Though more than 80 percent of Haiti is Christian, the majority also practice Voodoo, there called Vodun. Dance, which often includes theatrical elements, is the most vibrant expression of the Vodun religion in Haiti. Many aspects of Haitian dance-drama were brought from Africa with the slave trade. The *Meringue* is a Haitian dance form that recollects a folk story about a famous Haitian general injured in war who found the strength to limp off the battle field once he heard the Vodun drums. In this couples dance performers imitate his limp.

Another dance form with strong dramatic features is the *Ghèdé*, an overtly sexual dance performed by a dancer possessed by the personification of death, known as Ghèdé, and his devotees. Death as a character is a jokester, one who deranges things and takes situations lightly. He dresses in a black tailcoat and skirt, a stovepipe hat, and sunglasses. The performer possessed by Ghèdé speaks the language of the dead and of old Africa in a nasal voice to his dancing devotees and audience. The dance is brisk and gay with much hip swaying.

A dancer possessed by the Vodun deity Asaka, the deity of the mountains and the fields, performs the *Asaka*. Thus, the dance is performed in the garb of a mountain peasant—smock, hat, and knapsack—and in his dance he imitates planting and sowing the ground. He moves awkwardly and crudely to evoke the mountain people.

See also Caribbean Theater; Dunham, Katherine
References: Dunham, Katherine. *Dances of Haiti*. Los Angeles: Center for Afro-American Studies, 1983; Lekis, Lisa. "The Dance As an Expression of Caribbean Folklore." In *Caribbean: Its Culture*, ed. A. Curtis Wilgus, 43–73. Gainesville: University of Florida Press, 1955; Metraux, Alfred. *Black Peasants and Voodoo*. New York: Universe, 1960; Murphy, Joseph M. *Working the Spirit: Ceremonies of the African Diaspora*. Boston: Beacon, 1994; Nunley, John, and Judith Bettelheim, eds. *Caribbean Festival Arts*. Seattle: University of Washington Press, 1988.

Haka
New Zealand

All-male dance performed by the **Maori** of New Zealand, which celebrates the Maori ideal of masculinity. The purpose may be to perform a war

A Vodun (Voodoo) ceremony performed in Port-au-Prince, Haiti, 1969. (Raymond Buckley/Fortean Picture Library)

dance, in which case all the performers carry a weapon with apparent deadly intent, or the dance may be used to welcome guests who are visiting the island.

The dancing consists of synchronized foot stamping with the arms extended and the fingers quivering while the dancer's tongue hangs out and his eyes roll. A huge chorus of men accompanies the dancing with its thunderously loud rhythmic singing; an amazing sight and sound to behold. No wonder Europeans have long been fascinated by this dance form.

> References: Barlow, Cleve. *Tikanga Whakaaro: Key Concepts in Maori Culture.* New York: Oxford University Press, 1991; Dansey, Harry. *The Maori in Colour.* London: Reed, 1973.

Hakawati
Iran, Turkey

A dramatic one-man storytelling tradition performed in Arabic; very similar to the Turkish **Meddah.** Performers enliven their impassioned tales with gestures and amusing imitations of behavior and speech. When the performer impersonates different characters, only headdresses are changed,

since there is no time to change clothes. A handkerchief and a club are used to aid performer's mimicry and sound effects. *Hakawati* is still performed in the early twenty-first century, though much less frequently than in previous centuries.

> References: Landau, Jacob. *Studies in the Arab Theater and Cinema.* Philadelphia: University of Pennsylvania Press, 1958; Moreh, S. "The Arabic Theatre in Egypt in the Eighteenth and Nineteenth Centuries." *Etudes Arabes et Islamiques* 3 (1975): 109–113.

Hanamichi
Japan

Runway platform going between the audience and the stage in **Kabuki,** popular dramatic form of the seventeenth century.

> See also **Hashigaakari**
>
> References: Ernst, Earle. *The Kabuki Theatre.* New York: Oxford University Press, 1956. Reprint, Honolulu: University Press of Hawaii, 1974.

Hanswurst
Austria, Germany

Comic character in German-speaking theater; considered to have been created by an Austrian,

Josef Anton Stranitzky. Many improvised comic interludes in farces were centered around Hanswurst. The character was as outrageously popular with the people as he was shunned by the aristocracy. Wearing a red jacket, a ruffled collar, yellow trousers, and a pointy green hat, this character was imitated by many subsequent comedians. Hanswurst scenes were popularly used as a comic counterpart to the serious action of a play. The development of the character was influenced by the Italian **Arlecchino** character in **commedia dell'arte** and by the English clown Pickelherring.

Hanswurst was considered a vulgar element in German theater by the eighteenth-century reformers such as **Friedrike Caroline Neuber**. She expelled him from the German stage, even holding a ceremony at Leipzig in 1737 during which she symbolically burned him to death.

> **References:** Prudhoe, John. *The Theatre of Goethe and Schiller.* Totowa, NJ: Rowman and Littlefield, 1973; Scheit, Gerhard. *Hanswurst Und Der Staat.* Wein: Deuticke, 1995; Van Abbe, Derek Maurice. *Drama in Renaissance Germany and Switzerland.* Parkville: Melbourne University Press, 1961.

Hanuman
South Asia

The great white monkey, a beloved character from the Hindu epic tale, the **Ramayana.** Hanuman is beloved by all audiences that witness performances including his adventures and amazing feats. A favorite among all ages, he has special powers, such as amazing strength, the ability to fly, and a keen strategic sense. He is depicted in the **Wayang Kulit,** traditional Southeast Asian shadow puppet theater, in **Ketjak,** Balinese monkey dance, in **Kathakali,** Indian dance-drama, and in many other Hindu-inspired performance form.

Hapa Haole
Polynesia

Form of **hula,** Hawaiian dance that interprets lyrics through gestures, that has been greatly influenced by Christian ideas and Western culture and literally means "half-white *Hula.*" This form is generally performed only by hip-swaying women for tourists visiting Hawaii.

> **References:** Brandon, James. *The Cambridge Guide to Asian Theatre.* New York: Cambridge University

An Indonesian dancer portraying Hanuman, the great white monkey, in a scene from the Ramayana. (Lindsay Hebberd /Corbis)

Press, 1993; Dean, Beth. *South Pacific Dance.* Sydney: Pacific Publications, 1978.

Happening
United States

A performance event, often improvised, which contains elements of everyday life arranged artistically; often void of character, plot, or conflict; begun as a movement in the 1960s. Often outrageous and confrontational, these events are meant to raise questions on art and society. The name "happening" was taken originally from a piece by Allan Kaprow called *18 Happenings in 6 Parts*, 1959. These happenings often occur in nontraditional performance spaces such as streets or museums and are closely related to the visual arts. Most often untrained performers are used, as they are sometimes better than trained actors at performing mundane tasks without emoting. Happenings often require the performer to join in as almost a sculptural element rather than a psychologically complex individual or character. Though happenings still occur, the term is dated.

References: Bigsby, C. W. E. *A Critical Introduction to Twentieth-Century American Drama.* New York: Cambridge University Press, 1985; Johnson, Ellen, ed. *American Artists on Art from 1940 to 1980.* New York: Harper & Row, 1982; Sandford, Mariellen, ed. *Happenings and Other Acts.* New York: Routledge, 1995.

Hashigaakari
Japan

Bridgeway leading to the stage in **Noh,** masked dance-drama of medieval Japan. The *Hashigaakari* is used only for entrances and exits. It has three pine saplings along the length of the bridgeway, which serve as visual markers for the actors, who have limited sight because of the masks they wear.

See also *Hanamichi*
References: Ernst, Earle. *The Kabuki Theatre.* New York: Oxford University Press, 1956. Reprint, Honolulu: University Press of Hawaii, 1974; Scott, A. C. *The Theatre in Asia.* New York: Macmillan, 1972.

Hat Boi
Vietnam

Classical opera. Hat Boi was inspired by contact with the Chinese as early as the thirteenth cen-

tury. Troupes flourished under court sponsorship as a favorite type of court entertainment until the time of Emperor Tu Duc (1847–1883). Also small troupes would travel from one village to the next with their costumes and equipment in tow, performing wherever they could draw an audience. The plays, music, costumes, and makeup were changed slightly from the conventions for the **Peking Opera** in order to reflect Vietnamese tastes. Movement style and acting conventions are still very much like the Peking Opera. Only a few chairs and sometimes a table are used to evoke any setting needed for a performance. The ornate costumes and dramatic makeup identify for the audience the character type and sometimes even the specific character. Stories are taken from famous Chinese stories that teach Confucianism. In this century the popularity of Hat Boi is declining rapidly. The Vietnamese people see it as inaccessible and esoteric. There still are a few historical live performances in the north or shown on television.

See also *Tuong Tao*
References: Brandon, James R. *Brandon's Guide to Theatre in Asia.* Honolulu: University Press of Hawaii, 1976.

Hat Cheo
See Hat Boi

Hawaii
See Hula; Mele; Polynesia

Heiberg, Johanne Luise (1813–?)
Denmark

Née Hanne Patges, the leading comic actress in Denmark for over forty years. Her husband, P. A. Heiberg (1758–1841), was a playwright and theatrical innovator who championed the comic revival in 1825. Many considered her to be the finest actress in all of Europe. She was credited with idealizing nature in her performances, synthesizing the real with the beautiful.

In 1826 at the age of thirteen she began her career in a vaudevillian comedy written by her husband-to-be. He continued to write roles tailored for her. Her comic partner was the much older man, Rosenkilde. She was extraordinarily expressive facially, physically, and vocally. In her roles she was both flirtatious and self-assured. She is said to have been fiercely independent in the rehearsal process, during which she focused on the inner truth of the character to lead her to the appropriate outward expression. After retiring from acting in 1864 she went on to become the resident stage director at the Danish Royal Theater beginning in 1867, a position she held for seven years.

References: Johanne Luise Heiberg. Et Liv Gjenoplevet I Erindringen. 5th ed. 4 vols. Copenhagen: Niels Birger Warmberg, 1973–4; Marker, Frederick. A History of Scandinavian Theatre. Cambridge: Cambridge University Press, 1996.

Hellenistic Theater
Greece

Hellenistic theater can be thought of as beginning with the reign of Alexander the Great, who came to power in 336 B.C. Alexander conquered the Persian Empire and extended his reign to India and Egypt, building cities and promoting Greek culture wherever he went. The favorite type of drama for Hellenistic audiences was New Comedy, and not tragedy as it was for Athenian audiences the century before. The playwrights became less important in the theater, and the spotlight was shone on the actors instead, since the quality of writing had gone down, while the quality of acting had steadily increased. Thus, architectural changes occurred during this time to create a highly distinguished and visible acting space for these prized actors. The most dramatic change in setting was that the stage was raised to a height of 8–13 feet. Other innovations include the Proskenion, the facade of the lower story of the scene building, and the Episkenion, the facade of the second story of the scene building. The renovations made on the theater at Epidaurus in Southern Greece are an excellent example of Hellenistic architecture.

See also Greek Comedy

References: Arnott, Peter D. The Ancient Greek and Roman Theatre. New York: Random House, 1971; Bieber, Margarete. The History of the Greek and Roman Theater. Princeton, NJ: Princeton University Press, 1961; Ley, Graham. A Short Introduction to the Ancient Greek Theater. Chicago: University of Chicago Press, 1991; Sifakis, G. M. Studies in the History of Hellenistic

Drama. London: Athlone, 1967; Tomlinson, Richard Allan. Epidauros. Austin: University of Texas Press, 1983.

Henson, Jim (1936–1990)
United States

Puppeteer who created and performed many of the lovable and zany characters of Sesame Street, The Muppet Show, and the many Muppet movies. Henson began performing puppet shorts for a television show called Afternoon, where he first collaborated with Jane Nebel, whom he later married. In 1955 he created a television show called Sam and Friends, which ran successfully until 1961 and featured his creatures, basic hand and rod puppets that he called Muppets, known for their bizarre and slightly dangerous comedy. Frank Oz joined Henson's company in New York in 1963. In 1969 they created a radical new concept for children's programming with Sesame Street, an educational television show featuring such characters as Big Bird, Ernie, Bert, Oscar the Grouch, Cookie Monster, and Grover.

Due to his irreverent humor and anarchistic performance style, Henson's puppets appealed to adults. In 1975 Henson's Muppets began appearing in the groundbreaking television show Saturday Night Live. The Muppet Show began on television in 1976 and offered a style of puppetry that suited an adult audience, with new characters such as the Swedish Chef, Dr. Teeth, and many more. Henson began making Muppet movies in 1979. Frank Oz was the sole performer of Miss Piggy, and Henson was of Kermit. Together they made movie history in their many adventures as unlikely lovers. Henson died in 1990, but his contribution to contemporary American puppetry lives on in Muppet movies still being made and in the International Festival of Puppet Theater held at the Joseph Papp Public Theater in New York which began in 1992.

References: Finch, Christopher. Jim Henson, The Art, The Magic, The Imagination. New York: Random House, 1993.

Hijazi, Salama (1855–1917)
Egypt

First great Muslim actor to be associated with modern Arab theater. The greatest impact Hijazi had on Arab theater was that, because he was more a singer than an actor, he made the musical element the center of attention. He also started the practice of touring to other Arabic-speaking lands.

As a young man, Hijazi was praised for his ability to recite the Koran and for his popular songs. He was influenced by European theatrical touring troupes he witnessed. He performed in the troupe of Iskandar Farah (1898–1958) for eighteen years, where he excelled in musical dramas and gained the admiration of the public. In 1905 in Cairo, he started his own troupe, called The Arab Theater (Dar al-tamthil al-arabi), in which he performed until his death.

References: Landau, Jacob. *Studies in the Arab Theater and Cinema.* Philadelphia: University of Pennsylvania Press, 1958; Moreh, S. "The Arabic Theatre in Egypt in the Eighteenth and Nineteenth Centuries." *Etudes Arabes et Islamiques* 3 (1975): 109–113.

Hilarotragoedia
Italy

Hilarious tragedy, a parody of tragedy given literary form in 300 B.C. in Syracuse. Actors in this popular genre of farce were called **Phlyakes,** or gossips. Mythological subject matter was parodied by these plays, using a mix of serious and gay elements. There probably was some use of stock characters as well as mythological characters. Heracles (or Hercules) was a favorite hero of this genre and was featured in many of the plays of which we have knowledge. Only fragments of scripts exist. Much of what is known about this form has been derived from vase paintings of scenes from these plays.

References: Arnott, Peter D. *The Ancient Greek and Roman Theatre.* New York: Random House, 1971; Bieber, Margarete. *The History of the Greek and Roman Theater.* Princeton, NJ: Princeton University Press, 1961; Simon, Erika. *Antike Theater* (The Ancient Theatre). Trans. C. E. Vafopoulou. New York: Methuen, 1982.

Hindi Movies
India

Popular Indian movie style; romances, fantasies, or adventures, acted in a melodramatic and exaggerated style with lively songs and dances. Hindi movies are named after Hindi, the language spoken in them. These films cater to almost all of India, since the majority of the population understands Hindi, except in the south of India. Throughout the world, wherever there are sizable pockets of Indian people, there usually are Hindi movies at the local cinemas and on the television stations. The birth of Indian films dates back to the early 1900s. The first Hindi talkie was produced in 1931. Since the 1980s, India has been the world leader in the number of films produced each year, with at least 800 per year.

The plot for a Hindi movie is formulaic, and actors portray almost stock characters. The movies are always a war between good and evil characters, with the good group triumphant in the end and the evil group humiliated in defeat. In each cast there is the handsome male lead, the beautiful female lead (sometimes an expert in Martial Arts), the evil male or female antagonist, and the overweight clownish character. There are few concessions made to realism. Between scenes dance numbers erupt, with the leads gyrating their hips suggestively in the middle of a field. The dancing is acrobatic, enticing, and impressively vigorous, considering the numbers are shot outdoors in the hot midday sun. Catchy songs accompany these dances, which usually last five or ten minutes. Sometimes the heroine changes saris in different shots of a single song sequence, just to show how wealthy she is and how free her spirit is to express itself. The films themselves range from being one and a half to two and a half hours long.

The Hindi film industry is centered in Bombay. The movie stars, almost idolized, are popular throughout the entire nation. The major audience for a standard Hindi film is drawn from the middle- to lower-middle-income groups. However, even those below the poverty line will do all they can to save enough money to see the first showing of a new release.

See also Theologicals
References: Barnouw, Erik, and S. Krishnaswamy. *Indian Film.* New York: Columbia University Press, 1963; Chakravarty, Sumita. *National Identity in Indian Popular Cinema.* Austin: University of Texas Press, 1993.

Hinduism
India

Predominant religion of India, based on the **Vedas,** literature which developed from 1400–

400 B.C. By the beginning of the Christian era the actual worship of the Vedic gods was superseded by worship of the Hindu trinity, made up of Brahma, the creator, **Vishnu,** the preserver, and **Shiva,** the destroyer. Nevertheless, the Vedas are still revered as the most sacred of scriptures, given by revelation. This trinity predominates over a pantheon of Hindu gods numbering in the thousands who have mixed powers, good and bad, creative and destructive.

Hindu beliefs include a deep respect for all living things and belief in reincarnation. After a human dies, Hindus believe that the soul is reborn in a higher life form if the human has lived well, and in a lower life form if the human has been evil.

Hindu society is fragmented by belief in the caste system; the caste one belongs to is held to depend on one's relationship with the divine. The highest caste, the Brahmans, are considered to be the most favored by the divine. Kshatriyas, powerful merchants and landowners, make the second caste, and Vaisyas, artisans and farmers, make the third caste. Separate from them are the Sudras and the untouchables, who are generally serfs and laborers.

Hinduism has long been a rich inspiration for a myriad of theatrical expressions. Due to missionary zeal, Hinduism also exists throughout much of Asia (see entries on Indonesia, Malaysia, Nepal, and India) and has inspired the cultures.

References: Aherne, Consuelo Maria, Paul Kevin Meagher, and Thomas C. O'Brien, eds. *Encyclopedic Dictionary of Religion.* 3 vols. Washington, DC: Corpus Publishers, 1979; Brandon, James R. *Brandon's Guide to Theatre in Asia.* Honolulu: University Press of Hawaii, 1976; Eliade, Mircea, ed., *The Encyclopedia of Religion.* 16 vols. New York: Macmillan, 1987.

Hira-Gasy
Madagascar

A kind of improvised dramatic sketch, which includes song and dance; in which the community focuses on specific social problems and attempts to find a solution through the performance event. A *Hira-Gasy* performance involves about twenty peasant actors, known as *Mphihira-Malagasy.* In the eighteenth century Queen Ranavalona called *Hira-Gasy* performers to her court to entertain her and her European guests. Some of these

Europeans, soldiers and missionaries, got so carried away at these spirited displays, they joined in the dancing. Parodying foreigners' movements has been an integral part of *Hira-Gasy* performances ever since. *Hira-Gasy* served the French government when they replaced the monarchy in 1896. Following political turmoil in the early 1970s, *Hira-Gasy* returned to the villages where it is still performed.

References: Banham, Martin. *African Theatre Today.* London: Pitman, 1976; Cornevin, Robert. *Le Theatre en Afrique Noire et a Madagascar.* Paris: Le Livre Africain, 1970; Kent, Raymond. *From Madagascar to the Malagasy Republic.* New York: Praeger, 1962.

Hitchcock, Alfred (1899–1980)
England, United States

Film director in **England** and the **United States;** master of the suspense thriller. In 1920 Hitchcock entered the film business, doing odd jobs, and he worked his way up to assistant director and then, in 1925, to director. One of his first films, *The Lodger,* 1926, was a suspense drama, the genre for which he became famous. Hitchcock appeared as an extra in this film out of necessity, but he continued to appear in his own films as an extra as a practical joke. Hitchcock's wife, Alma Reville, collaborated with him on many of the screenplays he directed. His next big success and England's first synchronous sound movie was *Blackmail,* 1929.

Hitchcock became an international figure in 1934 with his thriller, *The Man Who Knew Too Much.* His last great film made in England was *The Lady Vanishes,* 1938, after which he moved to Hollywood. His first movie in the United States, *Rebecca,* 1940, a psychological suspense drama, was a huge success, winning the Academy Award for best picture. His next picture *Suspicion,* 1941, starred Joan Fontaine and Cary Grant (1904–1986). He experimented with many film techniques. In *Rope,* 1948, for example, he experimented with continuous shooting, only editing when the camera needed to be reloaded. Some of Hitchcock's best films include *Rear Window* 1954, *Vertigo,* 1958, and *Psycho,* 1960.

Hitchcock was a masterful technician with film and an innovator of many techniques. His technical mastery contributed to his recognizable visual style, which was highly effective at heightening the dramatic effect of his movies. He was a careful director, planning out each shot and scene. He offended many actors by treating them as just one of the many elements in a mise-en-scène rather than as "stars."

References: Phillips, Gene. *Alfred Hitchcock.* Boston: Twayne, 1984; Ryall, Tom. *Alfred Hitchcock and the British Cinema.* Atlantic Highlands, NJ: Athlone, 1996.

Homer
Greece

Greek poet who composed the two great epic poems the **Iliad** and the **Odyssey.** Generally believed to date from no earlier than 1000 B.C., and perhaps as late as the eighth century B.C., these epics serve as the first written record of Greek mythology. The epic is the earliest Greek literary form, followed by **Lyric** and then drama. **Greek Tragedy** derived its stories of the gods and heroes from the Homeric epics, as well as from other epics now lost, and even **Greek Comedy** drew on these stories to some extent, or at least relied on the audience's thorough knowledge of them.

Homer was the basis of Greek education, and performances of Homer were extremely popular.

References: Hamilton, Edith. *Mythology.* New York: New American Library, 1969; Scott, John Adams. *Homer and His Influence.* Boston: Marshall Jones, 1925; Wace, Alan John Bayard. *A Companion to Homer.* New York: St. Martin's, 1962.

Hong Kong

Money making and trade are the main focus of modern Hong Kong. Since Hong Kong has long been a British colony, there is a strong British and Western influence; nevertheless, the fact that 95 percent of the population is Chinese means there is much Chinese-style theater performed regularly in Hong Kong. *Kwangtung Hsi* (or *Yueju*), Cantonese opera sung in the southern Chinese dialect, is performed often in Hong Kong, using many of the same conventions used in Peking Opera.

The most prominent professional spoken drama is created by the Hong Kong Repertory Theatre, formed in 1977 and subsidized by the Urban Council. There are also many modern Chinese amateur theater troupes and troupes that

Elaborately costumed singers perform in a Cantonese opera in Hong Kong. (Travel Ink/Corbis)

perform Western-style dramas. The Hong Kong Academy for Performing Arts is the first school in Hong Kong dedicated exclusively to training theatrical artists: designers, directors, actors, technicians, and playwrights. It was established in 1985. A big boost for the arts was the completion of the Cultural Complex, built in the 1980s, which houses a concert hall and a theater for drama. In 1997 China reclaimed control over Hong Kong from Great Britain.

References: Brandon, James R. *Brandon's Guide to Theatre in Asia.* Honolulu: University Press of Hawaii, 1976; Brandon, James. *The Cambridge Guide to Asian Theatre.* New York: Cambridge University Press, 1993; Howard, Roger. *Contemporary Chinese Theatre.* Hong Kong: Heinemann, 1978; Mackerras, Colin. *Chinese Theatre in Modern Times, from 1840 to the Present Day.* Amherst: University of Massachusetts Press, 1975.

Hopkins, Anthony (1937–)
England, United States, Wales
Actor born of a working-class Welsh family who has become a well-respected actor of the London and New York stage and achieved superstar status in Hollywood for his Academy Award–winning performance in *Silence of the Lambs* in 1991. Hopkins made his stage debut in 1960 at the Library Theatre in Manchester and first appeared on the London stage in 1964 in **Shakespeare**'s *Julius Caesar*. Hopkins joined the National Theatre Company in London in 1967 and through the late 1960s and 1970s was a leading actor there. In 1974 he came to New York to perform *Equus*. In the **United States** he acted in many television movies and Hollywood films. He returned to the English National Theatre in 1985 to portray the newspaper tycoon in *Pravda*. After his haunting portrayal of a serial killer in *Silence of the Lambs*, Hopkins has acted in a wide variety of films, such as *Mission Impossible*, 2000, *Titus*, 1999, *Nixon*, 1995, and *Remains of the Day*, 1993. He resurrected the Hannibal character in *Hannibal*, 2000.

References: Callan, Michael. *Anthony Hopkins: The Unauthorized Biography.* New York: Scribner, 1994.

Hsias
China
Young male role in **Peking Opera,** a subcategory of **Sheng,** the category of male characters in the Peking Opera.

Hsii
China
Middle-aged male character type in **Peking Opera,** a subcategory of **Sheng,** the category of male characters in the Peking Opera.

Hua
China
Coquette female role in **Peking Opera**; a category of **Tan,** female character in Peking Opera.

Hua Chü
China
Spoken Chinese drama begun in 1907 by a group of Chinese students in Japan who were members of the Spring Willow Society in Tokyo. It gained a serious following in 1917 and was seen as a medium for literary and social change. They performed translations of Western dramas by such authors as Alexandre Dumas and Henrik Ibsen, and Western-style original Chinese dramas. The principal dramatists, Tian Han and Hong Shen, paved the way for future artists in the 1920s. They eventually founded theater companies and drama schools. The production quality and level of acting in Hua Chü was generally considered amateurish, but the form was still appealing to students and social advocates. In 1937, when the Japanese invaded China, the theater became a tool for propaganda, promoting nationalism and patriotism.

References: Brandon, James R. *Brandon's Guide to Theatre in Asia.* Honolulu: University Press of Hawaii, 1976; Howard, Roger. *Contemporary Chinese Theatre.* Hong Kong: Heinemann, 1978; Mackerras, Colin. *Chinese Theatre in Modern Times, from 1840 to the Present Day.* Amherst: University of Massachusetts Press, 1975; Scott, A. C. *The Theatre in Asia.* New York: Macmillan, 1972.

Hualian
China
Painted face robust male stock character in **Peking Opera.** Every visual and vocal element of performance for a Hualian serves to demonstrate his power. The vocal technique is characterized by tremendous range and volume. Each Hualian role in a play has its own costume, makeup, gestures

and form of speech. Only superb actors can make even subtle changes in the way a character is performed. Once a change is accepted by the public, it becomes the standard for other actors to follow in the future. An actor must shave his forehead to have room on his head for the complicated makeup pattern. The design of the makeup exaggerates the ferocity of the eyebrows and the sneer of the mouth with circular lines that originate from the nose area and move outward. Disposition of a character is indicated by design and color of makeup. White makeup indicates ferocity or danger; black, honesty, integrity and maybe a bit of stupidity; red, loyalty, courage and dignity; blue, stubbornness and ferocity; faded pink and gray, old age; green, demons and outlaws; and gold, gods and immortals. Beards can indicate success for a character if long and full, refinement if tripartite, and divine nature if red or blue. An actor often sweeps his beard with a stylized gesture of the hand. The costume is huge in order to create an impressive presence. It has long square sleeves and a huge headpiece.

Hula
Polynesia

Hawaiian dance form from pre-Christian times, performed by both men and women, that utilizes expressive gestures to visually interpret lyrical accompaniment. Originally *hula* was performed by men at temple services to honor the gods. It was supported by nobles. In the early nineteenth century Hawaii was converted to Christianity, traditional religion was banned, and performances of *hula* were discouraged by missionaries. There has been a revival of *hula* since the late nineteenth century, but Christian ideas and Western influences have greatly changed this dance from its original form and purpose.

The strong and physical male *hula* was associated with training in the martial arts and thus included the use of weapons. Female *hula* was characterized by a much more graceful style. The hips and feet of the female dancers would respond to the musical rhythm, as the arms and hands interpreted the lyrics through graceful gestures. Performing often in temples, male *hula* performers wore leaf decorations as costumes, and the women generally wore skirts made of grass. The

content of the chanted lyrics comprised the stories of nobles, historical events, or simply praise for the gods. Chanters often beat an instrument made of a gourd and played bamboo rattles. There was also a drum with a sharkskin drumhead that provided a strong rhythmic accompaniment.

Performers of *hula* were serious and dedicated students who studied at special *hula* dance schools before performing publicly. These schools were usually housed in a temple to the goddess of dance, Laka.

Now *hula* is generally known as a sensual hip-swaying dance performed for tourists visiting Hawaii and is found in hotel lobbies rather than temples. *Hapa Haole*, which literally means "half-white *hula*," is the term given to this form of *hula*.

See also **Mele; Mele Hula; Mele Oli**

References: Beckwith, Martha W. *The Kumulipo: A Hawaiian Creation Chant*. Honolulu: University Press of Hawaii, 1972; Brandon, James. *The Cambridge Guide to Asian Theatre*. New York: Cambridge University Press, 1993; Charlot, John. *Chanting the Universe: Hawaiian Religious Culture*. Honolulu: Emphasis International, 1983; Dean, Beth. *South Pacific Dance*. Sydney: Pacific Publications, 1978.

Hun Krabok
Thailand

Rod puppet theater. *Hun Krabok* is a simplified descendant of *Hun Luang* of the eighteenth and nineteenth centuries. Little is known about this earlier tradition except that they used sophisticated three-foot-high puppets, almost as big as **Bunraku** puppets of Japan. They had complex internal string mechanisms; and it took as many as three people to operate one puppet. The Hun Krabok rod puppets of the twentieth century are smaller and easier to operate, yet even so the number of people who can operate them has decreased significantly. The puppets are carved from wood with cloth clothing. They have gold tiered crowns on their heads with the puppet's fingers sloping upward, both of which are distinctively Thai characteristics. Since the puppet's face can show no emotion, the puppeteer must endow a puppet with life and emotions through movement and vocal delivery. He or she must interpret the role to the fullest. One puppeteer, Chuen Sakulkaew, reported that she portrayed an evil jealous puppet character so well that the next morning the noodle vendor refused to sell her any of his ware. The repertory comes from a wide variety of Thai literary sources, including local legends and episodes from the **Ramukien,** the Thai version of the Indian epic tale, the **Ramayana.** There are only a few older troupes remaining in Bangkok and surrounding areas. It is likely that when these troupes are gone, this art form will become extinct.

References: Bunnag, Tej. "Hun Krabook: Thai Classical Puppets." *Impact Magazine*, October 16, 1971; Montri, Tramote. "Thai Puppeet Show." *Silpakorn* 4, 2 (1960): 48–54; Redwood, John Elkert. "The Siamese Classical Theatre." *Educational Theatre Journal* 5 (1952): 100–105.

Hung
China
Peking Red-faced male role in **Peking Opera,** a category of **Sheng,** male character in Peking Opera.

Hungarian Cinema
Film development in Hungary got an early start in the twentieth century but was slow to lead anywhere worthy of note. The first movie house opened in 1905 in Budapest and featured mainly light comedies and exaggerated melodramas with little artistic quality. The oppressive government of the 1920s forced many of Hungary's leading actors and directors, including Peter Lorre (1904–1964), Mischa Auer (1905–1967), Bela Lugosi (1882–1956), and Martha Eggerth, to flee the country. The first film of quality to be produced in Hungary after that mass exodus of talent was *Somewhere in Europe/It Happened in Europe* (1947). In 1948 the film industry was nationalized by the Communist government, after which film production increased as did censorship. By the 1960s and 1970s films centered on relevant contemporary themes emerged, under the direction of a vivacious "new wave" of directors. In the 1990s film production and its popularity with audiences has declined. The fall of the Communist government, which meant the loss of its subsidization, is one contributing factor. The film *One Winter Behind God's Back* (1999), written and directed by Togay Can, offers an examination of life in a mountain backwater during a time of profound change.

References: Katz, Ephraim. *The Film Encyclopedia.* New York: Harper Perennial, 1994.

Hungary
There is evidence of liturgical drama dating back to the eleventh century in Hungary, including **mystery play**s. Jesuit theater in the sixteenth and seventeenth century was performed in schools by students and priests. Traveling troupes from Italy and German-speaking territories performed in the homes of nobility and the wealthy throughout the seventeenth and eighteenth centuries. The first, though short-lived, Hungarian theater company was established in Buda in 1790 by Frenc Kazinczy (1759–1831) and Laszlo Kelemen (1760–1814). The great Hungarian actress Johanna Dery (1793–1872) performed at a different theater, which opened in 1792 in Kolozsvar.

In the Hungarian struggle for cultural independence from the Habsburg culture of the Austro-Hungarian empire, one of the major accomplishments of the Hungarian people was the establishment of a national theater. In 1837 the first Hungarian theater opened in Pest, and in 1840 it became the National Theater and received state subsidy. A popular playwright who created an entire set of lovable Hungarian peasant characters was Karoly Kisfaludy (1788–1830). Some of his most popular plays were *Partutok*, 1825, and *Csalodasok*, 1924. A second Hungarian-language theater opened in the 1860s, the People's Theater, which was directed by Gyorgy Molnar (1830–1891). In 1864 the first school for actor training opened, the School of Dramatic Art. The best-known and talented actors of this time, many of whom emerged from this school, were Lujza Blaha (1850–1926), Vidor Kassai (1840–1928), Mari Jaszai (1850–1926), and Emilia Markus (1862–1949). The Vigszinhaz Theater, founded in 1896, was home to a naturalistic style of acting.

World War II (1939–1945) caused economic hardship for the theater in Hungary, yet following the war theaters flourished for decades. Under a new nationalized system of theater, actors enjoyed a high standard of living, with permanent employment as well as a guaranteed salary and pension. Some outstanding schools were founded in the 1950s, including the Academy of Dramatic Art (reorganized in 1957) and the Institute of

Theatrical Studies. Currently in Hungary there are numerous professional theater companies and thousands of amateur groups. Theater has flowered in Hungary since the Soviet era ended. Many plays by Hungarian playwrights have been produced, such as *The Glass Slipper* (1998) by Ferenc Molnar and the avant-garde play *The Price of Gold* (1999), written and directed by Géza Bereményi. Puppet theater also flourishes, such as *The Tragedy of Man* (1999) directed by Dezso Garas at the Budapest Puppet Theater. The Madach theater in Budapest was rebuilt and in 2000 presented *Cats* by **Andrew Lloyd Webber.**

See also Naturalism

References: Hartnoll, Phyllis. *The Oxford Companion to the Theatre*. New York: Oxford University Press, 1967; Klein, Holgar, and Peter Davidhazi, eds. *Shakespeare and Hungary*. Lewiston, NY: Edwin Mellen Press, 1996; Malyusz, Edith Csaszar, ed. *The Theater and National Awakening*. Atlanta: Hungarian Cultural Foundation, 1980; Nagy, Peter. "Hungary." In *The World Encyclopedia of Contemporary Theatre*, ed. Don Rubin, 427–450. New York: Routledge, 1994; Szekely, Csilla. "American Dramas on the Hungarian Stage, 1918–1965." *Hungarian Studies in English* 3 (1967); Szekely, Gyorgy. "A Theatrical Guide to Hungary." *Theatre Research/ Recherches Théâtrales* 9, 1 (1967): 5-14.

Hutt, William (1920–)

Canada

Canadian actor dedicated to remaining in Canada at a time when many talented actors and directors left for **England** or the **United States** for more promising opportunities and steady employment. Born in Toronto, Hutt began acting in high school and amateur theater. After serving in World War II (1939–1945), he began acting at the Hart House theater under the direction of Robert Gill, and at the Bracebridge Playhouse. As it was difficult for Canadian actors to secure full-time employment, Hutt worked summer stock at Niagara Falls Summer Theatre in 1950. In 1952 he began acting with the Canadian Repertory Theatre and that same year joined the **Stratford Festival.**

As an actor, Hutt approaches roles more analytically than emotionally. He is a proficient technical actor who excels at brittle comedy that portrays little emotion. He is able to portray a melancholy wisdom with his acting, always holding back, only revealing a portion of the depths he feels. He portrayed Lear in a *King Lear* production (1961–1962) set in the Northern Canadian Inuit culture. He also played a superb Lady Bracknell in **Oscar Wilde**'s *Importance of Being Earnest* in 1975. Hutt toured London and performed on Broadway in 1964 in *Tiny Alice*. From 1976 to 1980 he was artistic director of the Theatre London in **Canada**. He continues to act well into his older years, performing in the film version of Eugene O'Neill's *Long Day's Journey into Night* (1996).

References: Garebian, Keith. *William Hutt: A Theatre Portrait*. New York: Mosaic Press, 1988; Portman, Jamie. *Stratford: The First Thirty Years*. Toronto: McClelland & Stewart, 1989.

I

Ibsen, Henrik (1828–1906)

Norway

Playwright, pioneer of the modern theater and champion of a true Norwegian national theater, who sought to present a truthfulness to nature in his plays. The social topics he dealt with were highly controversial in his time. Perhaps because of his insightful explorations of the human condition and the poetic impact of his writing, his works have endured well through the years and are still often performed throughout the world. His influence on the development of modern Western drama is enormous. He integrated relevant social themes into highly realistic portrayals of the human struggle.

Many regard the publication of Ibsen's first play, *Catilina*, 1850, as the beginning of modern Western drama. In 1851 Ibsen became resident playwright, and later director, acting instructor, and equipment facilitator, at the Ole Bull in Bergen, Norway. As a director Ibsen was keenly interested in the visual aspects of the setting of a scene and in the total dramatic arrangement. He also expanded the role of the director by getting the authority to supervise the actors' interpretations of their roles, especially when producing his own plays. Norwegian actress Laura Gundersen (1832–1898) and Swedish actress Elise Hwasser masterfully performed many of Ibsen's early modern female characters.

Ibsen's 1864 play *The Pretenders* marked the last time he took an active role in the practical aspects of a production. Because of his vast practical experience in the theater in his earlier life, Ibsen wrote his dramas in such a way as to give the actors tangible expressions for the underlying emotional and psychological experiences of the character. He wrote with the live production of his work in mind. Ibsen stated that he wanted his audience to feel as if they were witnessing real life when they watched his plays. He demanded naturalness from his actors to succeed in bringing his characters to life.

Ibsen left Norway in 1864, beginning twenty-seven years of traveling. After writing *Brand*, 1866, and *Peer Gynt*, 1867, he turned to writing realistic plays centered on contemporary social issues, many of which were controversial, such as a woman's place in marriage (*A Doll's House*, 1876) and venereal disease (*Ghosts* 1881). He provided some of the most substantial and juicy roles for both male and female actors in the modern theater, such as the lead roles in both *Hedda Gabler*, 1890, and *The Master Builder*, 1892.

The actor **August Lindberg**, a contemporary of Ibsen's, gave marvelous naturalistic portrayals of many of Ibsen's lead male characters. William Bloch directed many of the premieres of Ibsen's works and was an advocate for naturalistic acting.

References: Heiberg, Hans. *Ibsen: A Portrait of the Artist.* Trans. Joan Tate. London: Allen and Unwin, 1969; Ibsen, Henrik. *The Correspondence of Henrik Ibsen.* Trans. Mary Morison. London: Hodder and

Stoughton, 1905; Lucas, F. L. *The Drama of Ibsen and Strindberg*. New York: Macmillan, 1962; Marker, Frederick. *A History of Scandinavian Theatre*. Cambridge: Cambridge University Press, 1996; Meyer, Michael. *Henrik Ibsen*. Garden City, NY: Doubleday, 1971.

Iceland

Iceland is a volcanic island settled by the Vikings in the ninth century. It was under Norwegian rule in the thirteenth century, and in 1380 was conquered by Denmark, which then controlled all of Scandinavia. The Icelandic people, generally a homogeneous mixture of descendants of Norwegians and Celts, did not gain their independence until 1918. The creative genius of Iceland seems to have expressed itself more richly in its literary sagas than in its theater, which is largely a derivative of Scandinavian theater. In the twentieth century, actors and theatrical practitioners began to create a distinctly Icelandic theater of quality in their native language.

There is no evidence of medieval theater in Iceland, even though Christianity was introduced in the year 1000. Iceland's rich literary traditions make no clear reference to theatrical activity. One possible candidate, however, is an old Icelandic dance named *Vikivaki*. Some claim the name indicates a dance done to keep people awake during vigils, thus suggesting the possibility of acting in the churches in the Middle Ages. The oldest trace of Icelandic theater is a record of a 1740 performance known as the *Herranott*. The Herranott began with a procession, followed by a satirical sermon delivered by a fake bishop. The event included the adoration of an effigy, usually a puppet. The Herranott is a transplant, a mutation of a European tradition.

During the nineteenth century, amateur theater societies existed mainly in the capital Reykjavik and other coastal villages. Trade unions often contributed to the theater at this time. Sigurour Guomundsson (1833–1874) used the theater in his fight for national independence. He wanted plays performed in the Icelandic language only, not the fashion at the time, and his insistence greatly encouraged the development of native Icelandic dramatic literature. Actors visiting from Denmark positively influenced the somewhat low quality of Icelandic acting. Iceland's first great actress, **Stefania Guomundsdóttir** (known as Frú Stefania), and the famous actor Arni Eiriksson appeared at this time.

The founding of the Reykjavik Theater Company (Leikfelag Reyjavikur) in 1897 was a turning point for Icelandic theater, an event that increased the quality of acting and inspired more ambitious projects. A leading lady with the RTC, Gunnborunn Hallorsdottir, left the company in 1905 to perform popular light revues, returning to the "legitimate" stage twenty-five years later to perform older character roles.

The first national theater opened in 1950 with a permanent company of about fifteen actors, who perform both Icelandic plays and some European and American imports. The School of Dramatic Arts is an actor training facility attached to the theater. Audience attendance is generally high. The National Theater complex hosts touring companies from around the world, who perform theater as well as ballet and opera. Currently there are many active amateur theater groups, innovative performances and festivals in Iceland. Active directors and actors in Reykjavik currently include Sunna Borg, Sigridur Thorvaldsdottir and Helga Thorberg.

References: Einarsson, Sveinne. "Frú Stefania: The First Icelandic Actress." In *Nordic Theatre Studies: Yearbook for Theatre Research in Scandinavia*, ed. Kela Kvam, 41–48. Denmark: Institute for Theatre Research, University of Copenhagen, 1988; Einarsson, Sweinn. "Icelandic Theatre History: Some Questions." In *Nordic Theatre Studies: Yearbook for Theatre Research in Scandinavia*, 91–94. Copenhagen: Munksgaard, 1989; Marker, Frederick. "The Actor in the Nineteenth Century: Aspects of Rehearsal and Performance in the Prenaturalistic Theater in Scandinavia." *Quarterly Journal of Speech* 51 (1965): 177–189; Marker, Frederick. *A History of Scandinavian Theatre*. Cambridge: Cambridge University Press, 1996; Woods, Leigh. "Theater in Iceland: The Quest for National Identity." *Scandinavian Review* 73, 3 (Autumn 1985): 55–63.

Iliad
Greece

Greek epic poem by **Homer,** believed to have been composed between the eighth and eleventh century B.C., that tells of the last few days of the Trojan War, focusing on the disastrous results for

A painting by the French artist Carle Vernet (1758-1836) of a scene from Homer's Iliad depicting games in honor of the funeral of Patroclus. (The Art Archive/San Carlos Museum Mexico City/Dagli Orti)

the Greeks of Achilles' withdrawal from the contest. This glorious account provides much of the dramatic material for **Greek Tragedy,** and even, at least indirectly, for **Greek Comedy.**

See also *Odyssey*

References: Hamilton, Edith. *Mythology.* New York: New American Library, 1969; Scott, John Adams. *Homer and His Influence.* Boston: Marshall Jones, 1925; Wace, Alan John Bayard. *A Companion to Homer.* New York: St. Martin's, 1962.

Imbongi
South Africa

Professional praisesinger, usually linked to a powerful Zulu chief. These performers of *Izibongo,* poems in praise of an individual chief, a clan, an inanimate object, or even cattle, dramatize the qualities of their subject using a narrative enhanced through mime and dance. These narrative poems vary in length to suit the occasion and tell of the special qualities, deeds, and skills of the person, animal, or thing being praised. The *Imbongi* perform their poems at great speed and loudly. Their voice is at a high pitch and is delivered with great intensity. Rarely can the *Imbongi* remain still while performing, but strides back and forth the length of the performing area. The spe-

cial costume worn by performers varies. One such costume reportedly had long horns fixed on the performer's forehead. This *Imbongi* acted like a bull clawing at the ground with his horns, shouting praises and leaping in the air.

These performances are still done at special ceremonies and important events.

References: Cornevin, Robert. *Le Theatre en Afrique Noire et a Madagascar.* Paris: Le Livre Africain, 1970; Larlham, Peter. *Black Theater, Dance, and Ritual in South Africa.* Ann Arbor, MI: Proquest, 1985.

Inao
Thailand

Thai term for **Panji tales,** pre-Islamic tales of Prince Panji.

References: Brandon, James. *Theatre in Southeast Asia.* Cambridge, MA: Harvard University Press, 1974; Faulder, Dominic. "Thailand's Puppet Theatre." *Sawasdee* 18 (August 1989): 14–20.

Inca Theater
Peru

Inca civilization was indigenous to Latin America; the Incas once had a kingdom centered in the Andes Mountains of present-day Peru, extending northward through Ecuador and southward to central **Chile**; it was conquered by Spanish invaders in the early sixteenth century. Also included in the Inca domain was about half of Bolivia and part of northwest **Argentina.** Information on pre-Columbian theatrical activity of the Inca people is severely limited; Spanish Christian missionaries destroyed many books on indigenous theater, and the Incas themselves had a custom of destroying old records, in order to start fresh when a new ruler took power. The limited information available seems to indicate that Inca and **Mayan theater** was quite similar to that of the more northern Aztec, and so mostly of the religio-theatrical kind.

The Inca had innumerable gods, with the sun god taking precedence over them all. The Inca also had a highly stratified society with a strong aristocracy. Theater served as an important tool for acknowledging and reasserting the power of both of these intertwined systems; the sun was believed to be the ancestor of the Inca people. In order to support the status quo, the subjects were encouraged to perform dances and songs celebrating the great exploits of their king. After a victorious battle, warriors often, as best they could, reenacted the battle in which they had triumphed. These enactments were of a highly practical nature, confirming the primacy of the emperor and glorifying the warrior-actors.

Ritualistic performances were also enacted for the fertilization of both the earth and of women. The Quechua in Peru had one such rite, in which a warrior portraying the sun's messenger, adorned with beautifully colored feathers and carrying a lance, ran into the center of the public plaza. There he was awaited by four warriors who, once touched by the first warrior's lance, ran outward in four directions, representing the four corners of the Inca empire. This performance was believed to ritually purify the state.

See also Aztec Theater; Mexico; Quetzalcóatl

References: Markham, Sir Clements. *Incas of Peru.* London: Smith, Elder, 1910; Usigli, Rodolfo. *Mexico in the Theater.* Trans. Wilder P. Scott. University, MS: Romance Monographs, 1976; Versènyi, Adam. *Theatre in Latin America: Religion, Politics, and Culture from Cortés to the 1980s.* New York: Cambridge University Press, 1993.

India

The variety, mastery, and vibrancy of Indian theater are almost overwhelming. **Hinduism,** the religion practiced by most Indians, is perhaps the greatest inspiration to dramatic expression known to the world. The two great Hindu epic tales, the *Mahabharata* and the *Ramayana,* are exciting stories of adventure packed full of spiritual refinement and philosophical wisdom.

Based on the sacred texts, the **Vedas,** the religion Hinduism recognizes three principal gods, Brahma, the creator, **Vishnu,** the preserver, and **Shiva** (or Siva), the destroyer. Vishnu's best-known incarnation is **Krishna,** best known as a flirtatious young lover but also a wise statesman in his later years. Devotees of Krishna see Krishna and Vishnu as synonymous and usually refer to them as **Vishnu-Krishna.** The image of Shiva as *Nataraja,* Lord of the Dance, features Shiva doing the cosmic dance that sets all of creation in motion, and so it is a powerful symbol for all performers. Another form of Shiva is *Ardhanarishwara,* in which he is depicted as half man and half woman, demonstrating a beautiful union of two opposing forces. A pantheon of other lesser Hindu gods exists and inspires the arts. The elephant-headed god, **Ganesha,** is called upon in most invocations at the beginning of performances because he is believed to be the remover of obstacles. *Natya Sastra* is an ancient Hindu text on dramaturgy that gives detailed instruction on every element of the performing arts. Classical Indian performances are most often presented in theater halls, called *Koothambalams,* attached to Hindu temples.

The oldest known classical drama in India is **Sanskrit drama,** which flourished from 100 B.C. to A.D. 1200. Other theatrical forms that evolved from it survive, as well as some Sanskrit scripts, but the exact conventions for staging Sanskrit drama are lost to history. *Vidushaka* is the name for the clown or jester character in Sanskrit drama, who evolved from the clowns of older folk dramas. Originally the narrator for Sanskrit drama, the *Sutradhara* is now present in many forms of traditional Indian drama, in which he introduces characters, controls entrances and exits, and comments on the action of a performance. **Kudiyattam** (or *Kutiyattam*), is an ancient style of presenting Sanskrit plays from south India. Careful interpretation of each line takes up to twenty minutes. Both this form and Sanskrit drama were for the elite upper-classes who understood Sanskrit.

From the sixteenth to the eighteenth century in India **Ram Lila,** a pageant play based on the life of Rama, hero of the *Ramayana,* emerged. A popular opera from Northeast India, **Jatra,** is energetic in dramatizing original plays. **Chau,** a masked dance-drama in which actors portray animals, forces of nature, or trees, nonverbally interprets beautiful tales through movement.

One of India's oldest forms of classical female solo dance is **Odissi,** which is dignified and sensual. Similar to this is **Bharata Natyam** (formerly called **Dasi Attam**), which originated in the eighth century A.D. in south India. This devotional female solo temple dance joins pure rhythm with depiction of spiritual union in a celebration of movement and drama. *Abhinaya* are gestures that express a particular **Bhava,** a feeling or emotion. *Nritya* is the term for expression of sentiment or mood in classical Indian dance, and *Nritta* is the term for pure, nonnarrative dance. The debut performance for a young dancer is called **Arangetram.** The classical female Indian dancer has at her disposal **Adavus,** the basic rhythmic units of dance with specific tempos and set movement, and **mudras,** symbolic gestures that have been codified into a language of gesture. Through her pureminded execution the dancer can create **rasa,** a joyous spiritual experience aroused by artistic expression, for herself and her audience.

Devadasis, Hindu temple maids, are a class of women dedicated to temple ceremonies. They were the first temple dancers, and their lineage still supplies many of the best dancers, even though they were expelled from temples in 1948 due to pressure from the British. **Shantala,** a queen from south India in the twelfth century, is the earliest known *Bharata Natyam* dancer, suggesting that the women of court also performed temple dances. The most famous *Bharata Natyam* dancer of the twentieth century was **Balasaraswati,** who raised the social status of dancers by her unquestionable elegance and mastery.

In the eighteenth century, **Kathakali**, an all male dance-drama from Kerala State, evolved. The main attraction of this form is virtuoso acting, characterized by a fiercely emotional acting style. The actors wear huge headpieces and dramatic makeup with layered rice paste beards called **Chutti.** Around that same time, **Bhavai** developed as a rural drama featuring eight to ten skits about uplifting secular themes linked together by a narrator.

Two important folk theater traditions from India are **Nautanki,** a folk opera of Northwest India that mixes Islamic and Hindu culture, and **Terrukutta** (or *Therukoothu*), a folk opera performed in the streets of Southeast India. In this form, which enacts tales from the great Hindu epics, the **Kattiakaran** serves as the stage manager and narrator, and the **Komali** provides much of the humor and acrobatic feats as the clown character.

Krishna drama has been realized throughout the centuries in India in a variety of different forms. **Jagar** is an early folk drama, which enacts the myth of Krishna killing two demons. Another of the earliest forms of Krishna worship was performed by the **Kathaks,** a class of storytellers who enacted stories of Krishna seated on the floor in temples, using beautiful gestures. From this tradition of Kathaks there developed in the sixteenth century **Ras Lila.** In this dance-drama an actor portraying Krishna dances with the **Gopis,** young milkmaids who are in love with Krishna, and scenes from Krishna's life are enacted. There is much humor in **Krishna Parijat,** which is a folk theater based on episodes from Krishna's life.

Of the Krishna drama that stresses the element of dance there are many examples. **Kuchipudi** evolved in the fourteenth and sixteenth centuries as an offering to Krishna and is a mixture of singing, drama, and complicated rhythmic dancing. **Kathak** is a classical dance of north India with erotic themes that was especially enjoyed in the Muslim courts from the sixteenth through the nineteenth centuries. A dance-drama about Krishna performed in the tradition of Kathakali is called **Krishnattam.**

In the form of operatic dance-dramas devoted to Krishna there are **Ankai Nat** and **Gita Govinda** (called *Ashtapadi Attam* in Kerala). Both enact scenes from the life of Krishna. **Yakshagana** is a folk opera from Mysore State honoring Krishna, which is colorful and energetic. An enticing opera from the eighteenth century, **Tamasha,** features sexually suggestive songs and dances based on Krishna's flirtations and love affairs.

Kala is a branch of Krishna drama from the south of India that combines many performance elements, such as song, dance, drama, and music. Separate forms are **Gaulan Kala,** Krishna drama performed by children, **Gopal Kala,** Krishna drama performed in the morning, and **Dashavatar Kala,** Krishna drama depicting the ten incarnations of Vishnu-Krishna.

Alongside the human theater, there has been a rich and diverse history of puppet theater. An ancient form of shadow puppet theater from Orissa that employs simple rough puppets made of rawhide is known as **Ravanachhaya. Tholu Bommalata** is another form of shadow puppet theater from the third century B.C., about which little is known. Two other forms of shadow puppet theater from India are **Mysore Shadow Puppet Theater**, from Mysore, and **Tholu Pava Koothu,** from Kerala State. Most often shadow play performances are presented on platform stages, called **Koothu Madams,** attached to Hindu temples.

Two musical forms of drama in India in the nineteenth century were **Natya,** English-style melodrama performed by Indian troupes, and **Surabhi,** which was performed by traveling troupes in small rural villages.

The film industry in India is one of the most prolific in the world. The majority of the films produced in India are **Hindi Movies,** a popular Indian movie form in the Hindi language. These romantic films feature an exaggerated melodramatic acting style that perfectly suits the "good versus evil" adventure stories. Interspersed between scenes in the movies are dance routines with romantic songs, nearly bursting at the seams with energy. Another lesser but popular genre of film consists of **Theologicals,** movies in which actors bring the Hindu deities and their stories to life.

References: Awasthi, Suresh. "Shadow Plays of India and Their Affinities with the Shadow Plays of Southeast Asia." In *Traditional Drama and Music of Southeast Asia,* ed. Mohd. Taib Osman, 112–119. Kuala Lumpur: Dewan Bahasa Dan Pustaka Kementerian Pelajaran Malaysia, 1974; Chakravarty, Sumita. *National Identity in Indian Popular Cinema.* Austin: University of Texas Press, 1993; Gargi, Balawanta. *Theatre in India.* New York: Theatre Arts, 1962; Gargi, Balawanta. *Folk Theater of India.* Seattle: University of Washington Press, 1966; Massey, Reginald, and Jamie Massey. *Dances of India.* London: Tricolour, 1989; Shah, Panna. *The Indian Film.* Bombay: Motion Picture Society of India, 1950; Varadpande, Manohar Laxman. *History of Indian Theatre.* New Delhi: Abhinav, 1987; Varadpande, Manohar Laxman. *Krishna Theatre in India.* New Delhi: Abhinav, 1982; Vatsyayan, Kapila. *Traditional Indian Theatre: Multiple Streams.* New Delhi: National Book Trust, 1980; Wells, Henry Willis. *The Classical Drama of India: Studies in Its Values for the Literature and Theatre of the World.* New York: Asia Publishing House, 1963.

Innamorati
Italy
Young lover characters in **commedia dell'arte**, the Italian improvised comedy popular during the sixteenth and seventeenth centuries. The male *Innamorato* and the female *Innamorata* are characters of high status, but they are forced to conspire with the lower classes, usually their own servants, to remedy their hopeless romantic situations. Compared to the many other stock characters in the commedia, these two roles were played straight, but they still required a performer to possess wit, decorum, and charming language skills. With a musical way of speaking, these characters were always quoting poetry and speaking metaphorically about love. Their walk was almost like that of a ballerina with an airy graceful way, with movements exaggerated to parody the affectations of the wealthy. These characters were meant to look young and attractive, so actors of these roles dressed in the latest fashions. Actresses playing the part would change costumes many times during a show to show off their lovely wardrobes. Heavy makeup was worn, which allowed aging actresses to portray this role even into their sixties.

References: Craig, Edward Gordon. "The Characters of the Commedia Dell'Arte." *The Mask* (January 1912); Rudlin, John. *Commedia Dell'Arte: An Actor's Handbook.* London and New York: Routledge, 1994.

Intermezzo
Italy
A musical interlude in a play during the Middle Ages, which became during the Renaissance an entity of its own characterized by a light dramatization including music, dancing, and choral singing. By the seventeenth century, the Intermezzo had dissolved into new forms, such as ballet, comic opera, and melodrama.

See also Ballet de Cour

References: Herrick, Marvin T. Italian Comedy in the Renaissance. Urbana: University of Illinois Press, 1960; Marker, Frederick. A History of Scandinavian Theatre. Cambridge: Cambridge University Press, 1996; Smith, Ed. "Special Reports: The Performing Arts in Jamaica: Theater." Black World 23 (July 1974): 47–48, 73–77.

Ionesco, Eugène

See Absurdism

Iran

Theater in Iran, from the Middle Ages to the present, has consisted mainly of puppet theater and some traveling acting companies. In 1750 there were several improvised theater forms in Iran with an acting style similar to the *commedia dell'arte,* improvised sixteenth- and seventeenth-century Italian comedy. *Hachalakbazi,* which literally means "play of the bald," denounced dishonest wealthy people; *Baqqal Bazi,* which literally means "play of the grocer," was based on antics between a miserly grocer and his ignorant servant; and in *Ruband Bazi,* which literally means "plays of the mask," actors performed on stilts.

In 1823 there is the first report of *Ruhozi,* a form of Persian comedy which means "over the pool," in which a stage was built over a tank in an open courtyard. The two main characters were Siyah "the black," an actor in blackface impersonating a former slave, and a wealthy man named Haji. Translations of European works performed in traditional Western style have been popular since the 1950s. Currently there are a few private theaters in Teheran. From 1850 into the twentieth century serious censorship problems have greatly limited theatrical activity.

The first Iranian feature film was made in 1948. The output of films steadily increased to almost a hundred films a year, mostly low-budget comedies and action films. Outstanding filmmakers include 'Abbas Kiya Rustami, Bahman Farmanara, and Daryush Mehrju'i, who made serious works with lasting meaning. Because of tighter censorship, films in Iran in the 1990s were mainly educational.

References: Cachia, P. "The Dramatic Monologues of Al-Ma'arri'." Journal of Arabic Literature 1 (1970):

129–136; Landau, Jacob. Studies in the Arab Theater and Cinema. Philadelphia: University of Pennsylvania Press, 1958; Meserve, Mollie Ann, and Walter J. Meserve. A Chronological Outline of World Theatre. New York: Feedback Theatre & Prospero Press, 1992; Moreh, Shmuel. Live Theatre and Dramatic Literature in the Medieval Arab World. New York: New York University Press, 1992; Mostyn, Trevor, and Albert Hourani, eds. The Cambridge Encyclopedia of the Middle East and North Africa. New York: Cambridge University Press, 1988; Rosenthal, Franz. Humor in Early Islam. Westport, CT: Greenwood, 1976.

Iraq

Signs of an Arab theater, besides **Karagoz,** Turkish shadow puppet theater, began at the end of the nineteenth century. British influence has been pervasive in the areas of acting style, playwriting, stage settings, and costumes. Otherwise theatrical practices in Iraq closely follow the Egyptian model in musical dramas and in the way European plays are adapted into Arabic. In the twentieth century the Iraqi government has demonstrated its interest in promoting Arab theater by sending actors such as Haqqi'l-Shibli to study dramatic arts in Paris, by giving acting troupes tax breaks, and by sponsoring awards for playwriting. Many amateur and a few professional acting troupes are active in Baghdad and elsewhere. Artistic progress was made in the 1940s and 1950s due to the exceptional work of actor-director Sami 'Abd al-Hamid, as well as Yusuf al-'Ayni and Qasim Muhammad. The 1968 revolution in Iraq established it as a modern nation-state. The 1970s and 1980s were lively years for theater with many thriving professional and amateur theaters. War with Iran through much of the 1980s and isolation from the international theater scene throughout the 1990s has had a negative influence on their theater. Many talented theater artists, such as the actress Meriam Abbas, left Iraq in the 1980s because of the war. She has recently performed in Patrick Marber's play, *Closer* (1998) in Vienna.

Many Egyptian films are popular and widely viewed in Iraq, but extreme Muslims generally regard cinema as having a negative effect on public morals. There have been well-intentioned attempts by the state to create a film industry in Iraq, but no great success has been achieved, and the film industry is still in its infancy compared to neighboring countries such as **Algeria** and **Egypt.**

See also *Ta'ziya*

References: Baram, Amatzia. *Culture, History, and Ideology in the Formation of Bathist Iraq, 1968–89.* New York: St. Martin's, 1991; Hadethy, Waleed H. "Educational Theatre in Iraq: Elementary and Secondary Levels." Ph.D. diss., University Microfilms, 1986; Landau, Jacob. *Studies in the Arab Theater and Cinema.* Philadelphia: University of Pennsylvania Press, 1958; Moreh, S. "The Arabic Theatre in Egypt in the Eighteenth and Nineteenth Centuries." *Etudes Arabes et Islamiques* 3 (1975): 109–113.

Ireland

Ireland is an island with two distinct political units, the southern portion, the Republic of Ireland, which is autonomous, and Northern Ireland, which is still under the British Crown, though it is partially self-governing. In the twelfth century the English invaded Ireland and encountered the Gaelic culture and language, which had a strong literary tradition but no signs of live theater. The English brought with them religious dramas, which continued in Ireland throughout the Middle Ages.

Nothing exceptional arose from Ireland until the Irish Dramatic Movement began in the late nineteenth century, primarily inspired by two playwrights, the poet William Butler Yeats (1865–1939) and Augusta Gregory (1852–1932). Finally Irish playwrights were writing about Irish subject matter. By 1901 Irish actors, instead of the customary English actors, from the Irish National Dramatic Society performed these plays. The **Abbey Theatre** became their home in 1904 and became internationally known as a repertory company of outstanding quality. Irish nationalism was strong at the beginning of the

The Abbey Theatre in Dublin, Ireland. (Bettmann/Corbis)

twentieth century. Theater artists wanted to discover an authentic Irish culture, which they believed could be found in peasant life, Irish myth and folklore. One playwright who got his start at the Abbey Theatre was **Sean O'Casey,** who wrote realistically of Dublin's poor. When audiences rejected his political views he moved to London. His departure foreshadowed the conservatism that dominated the theater from the late 1920s to the 1950s. The work performed at the Abbey Theatre at that time was rural playwrights writing conventional works idealizing Irish rural living and a conservative moral code.

In 1928 the Gate Theatre opened in Dublin, which complemented the Abbey Theatre well since it offered a much wider range of works and exposed the Irish to classic works from the ancient Greeks to **Shakespeare** and **Anton Chekhov.** Their standard of presentation was as high as any of the best European theaters. The company, Longford Productions, begun in 1936, performed at the Gate Theatre half the year and toured the provinces the other half. It was run without government subsidies by Lord Longford, who was dedicated to staging quality plays regardless of their potential to break even at the box office. It continued after his death in 1960 under the management of his widow, the Countess of Longford.

Begun in 1904, the Ulster Theatre was for Belfast in the north what the Abbey Theatre was for Dublin in the south. The Ulster produced new plays about life in Northern Ireland and was a training ground for many actors. The group revived from a slump in the 1950s when they invited two popular comic actors, James Young and Jack Hudson, to join their group. Also in the north, Hubert Wilmot founded the Belfast Arts Theatre in 1947, where stimulating productions from local, European, and American sources were performed for small audiences. Beginning in the 1950s many alternative productions that could not gain acceptance at the more established theaters were presented in "basement theaters," often literally the basements of large homes. In Dublin the Pike Theatre was the most famous of these, begun by a married couple, Carolyn Swift and Ahan Simpson.

In 1957 the first Dublin International Theatre Festival took place, which brought in new plays and ideas of staging to a rather stifled, isolationist environment in Ireland. In the 1960s modernization took hold of Ireland, and a thriving amateur theater ensued. In 1969 tension mounted in the north between separatist Catholics and Protestants who wanted to retain ties to Great Britain. This conflict still keeps Northern Ireland in a constant state of unrest. Many plays have this conflict as their theme, for example, *The Freedom of the City,* 1983, by Brian Friel, a leading Irish playwright.

Arts funding increased in the 1970s, as did the interest in theater by the prospering middle class. In the 1980s there was a lot of development in theater and a number of new performance festivals. In 1990 a cultural renaissance was under way, and since then innovations have abounded. For example, in 1992 the MacNas Theatre Company in Galway performed a show centered on Irish mythology in the streets. Many new playwrights are emerging, such as Gary Mitchell, who wrote *In a Little World of Our Own,* 1997, and Patricia Burke Brogan, who wrote *Eclipsed,* 1998. The Friel Festival was held in Dublin in 1999 to honor Irish playwright Brian Friel, whose work has been internationally performed.

References: Barbour, Sheena, ed. *Irish Performing Arts Yearbook.* London: Rhinegold, 1992; Chinoy, Helen Krich, and Toby Cole. *Actors on Acting,* New York: Crown, 1970; Fitz-Simon, Christopher. *The Irish Theatre.* Thames & Hudson: London, 1982; Kilroy, Tom. "A Generation of Irish Playwrights." *Irish University Review* 22, 1 (Spring/Summer 1992): 135–41; Morash, Christopher. "Ireland." In *The World Encyclopedia of Contemporary Theatre,* ed. Don Rubin, 467–495. New York: Routledge, 1994; Worth, Katharine. *The Irish Drama of Europe from Yeats to Beckett.* Atlantic Highlands, NJ: Humanities Press, 1978.

Irish Cinema

Many of the first Irish films were nationalistic in nature and shown to locals in music halls. In 1909 the first movie house was built in Dublin. The British government censored what could be shown, and it banned *Ireland, A Nation,* 1914, from being shown in **Ireland,** though it was shown in the **United States.** After the south of Ireland gained freedom from Great Britain, a period of isolated development ensued. Foreign films were mostly kept out of Ireland, and the advent of sound did not come until 1933, with *The Voice of Ireland*.

For decades the quality and quantity of Irish produced films lagged behind the rest of Europe, primarily due to foreign competition, internal censorship inspired by the Roman Catholic Church, and lack of funds. It was not until the 1980s that Ireland gained any kind of international success, and that came with movies like *My Left Foot*, 1989 about a man with cerebral palsy who becomes a great writer and painter by using only his left foot. Noted Irish actors such as Donald McCann, Gabriel Byrne, and Brenda Fricker also gained recognition. National support for Irish films increased in the 1990s, as a school for film and the Irish Film Center were created. A consistent stream of quality films has ensued such as *The Commitments*, 1991, *The Crying Game*, 1992, and *A Love Divided*, 1999.

References: Hill, John. "Contemporary Irish Cinema: Filming in the North." *Cineaste—America's Leading Magazine on the Art and Politics of the Cinema* 24, no. 2–3 (March 1999): 26–27; Katz, Ephraim. *The Film Encyclopedia*. New York: Harper Perennial, 1994; Petropoulos, Constantina. "Byrne, Gabriel." *Current Biography* 60, 5 (May 1999): 5–7; Power, Paul. "Contemporary Irish Cinema: The Irish Are Rising Again: Profiles of New Filmmaking Talent." *Cineaste* 24, 2–3 (March 1999): 74–75.

Iroquois False Face

Canada, United States

Masked dance drama of the Iroquois performed using wooden masks, called False Faces in English, worn by the Society of False Faces in the prevention and cure of illness. The False Faces participate in three kinds of ceremonies within the year, the spring or autumn purging ceremony known as the Traveling Rite, private feasts, and the Midwinter Festival. Husk Faces, performers wearing masks made of corn husks, perform as heralds for the False Faces when they go through a village purifying. False Face masks are carved from wood and have hair of horsehair and are painted. Some masks have small bags of Indian tobacco attached to the top, indicating that the mask has been compensated for a cure or appeased by its owner.

In the Traveling Rite, False Face performers go through houses frightening away disease spirits, shaking their turtle shell rattles to scare away the spirit of sickness. An unmasked singer leads their procession through the houses of the village, singing to quiet the winds, upon which they believe sickness is transmitted. Along the way they accept donations of tobacco.

The False Face Society is popular among the Iroquois and has many members. When wearing the mask, the member of the society is believed to have special powers such as being able to hold hot coals without getting burned. The traditional way to carve a False Face mask is to begin carving the mask while the wood is still a living part of the tree. Tobacco is burned beneath the carving area to transfer the healing power into the wood. The Iroquois are now centered in upstate New York and southern Ontario.

References: Fenton, William. *The False Faces of the Iroquois*. Norman: University of Oklahoma Press, 1987; Wagner, Anton. *Contemporary Canadian Theatre: New World Visions*. Toronto: Simon & Pierre, 1986.

A traditional mask for the Iroquois False Face ceremony (Milwaukee Public Museum)

Irving, Henry (1838–1905)
England

Actor-manager in England in the nineteenth century and the greatest classical actor of his day. Irving moved to London from Cornwall when he was still young to work, study, and begin training as an actor. In 1856 he moved to Edinburgh for a few years to gain some performing experience before returning to London. In London he joined the Lyceum Theatre in 1856, where he gained fame with his tender performance of Hamlet in 1874. Irving played many famous roles that he kept in repertory for years, such as Mathias in *The Bells* by Erckmann-Chatrian.

By 1878 Irving became actor-manager at the Lyceum Theatre. The female lead who regularly played opposite him was **Ellen Terry.** They were regarded as the best male and female actors of their day. Irving staged and starred in many of **Shakespeare**'s plays, such as *Hamlet, Othello,* and *The Merchant of Venice.* As manager of the Lyceum Theatre for thirty years, Irving made long tours with his company of actors to the **United States.**

> **References:** Chinoy, Helen Krich, and Toby Cole. *Actors on Acting.* New York: Crown, 1970; Craig, Edward Gordon. *Henry Irving.* New York: Longmans, Green, 1930; Irving, Laurence. *Henry Irving: An Actor and His World.* London: Faber and Faber, 1951.

Isinyago
Mozambique, Tanzania

The Makua tribe's name for a masklike costume that covers the entire body of the performer or performers. Also the name for the masked dance, performed by other tribes as well, such as the Yao and the Makonde. Various animals are created by constructing costumes made of elaborate bamboo frames that are covered with grass and rags. Dancers perform from inside the structure, giving the animal its powerful dance through the way they manipulate the structure. Beasts too small for a man to hide in are manipulated like puppets. Performances occur on dark nights between the quarter and half moon so that females and uninitiated boys will not be able to see the mechanics of the costumed performer, but there will still be enough illumination for the performance to be visible.

Representations of real animals, such as elephants and pigs, are made into costumes, as well as representations of animals not known to exist, such as the fire-carrier. The fire-carrier beast is portrayed by a dancer on whom numerous glowing bark strings are tied. He spins as he dances, creating a beast of fire. His dance does not last long, for obvious reasons, but receives by far the most enthusiastic response from the audience. In modern performances of *Isinyago*, bicycles and motorcars are portrayed as well as colonial agents, who are classified as beasts.

In preparation for a performance, several days are set aside to secretly construct the costume of the animal. A clearing is made by cutting down trees and plants for the performance, and a road is constructed from it to the village, both of which must be stump-free so that performers don't stumble and fall, thus destroying the illusion during the performance. The structure of a performance begins as the sponsor, or primary artistic creator of the animal, elaborately introduces the animal to the crowd. He tells them of how far the beast traveled to arrive in their village. The beast them emerges from the bushes and enters the ring dancing. Songs are sung telling about how fierce or dangerous the beast is. The shouts of the audience cue the performers inside the frame where the audience is so that they don't run into any members of the audience and reveal the secret. The entire beast costume is burned after a performance, so that curious women and children cannot learn the secrets of the performance.

See also *Midimu*

> **References:** Wembah-Rashid, J. A. R. "Isinyago and Midimu: Masked Dancers of Tanzania and Mozambique." *African Arts* 4, 2 (1971): 38–44.

Israel

Supportive audiences and government subsidization have led to a thriving Israeli theater since the independent state of Israel was established in 1948. Prior to that time Palestinian Arabs who lived in that area while under British rule, which began in 1917, had a theater of their own, modeled predominantly after the **Arab theater** in Egypt. Palestinian playwrights during this time included Nasri'l-Jauzi and Jamil Bahri.

Leading Israeli companies since independence include the Habimah National Theater and the Cameri Theatre, both in Tel Aviv, and the Khan Theatre in Jerusalem. Because the country is so small, companies tour with ease. This prosperous environment allows actors and directors to enjoy steady employment with one company for years. Much of the culture in Israel has been imported from Europe. Israeli playwright Nissim Aloni, working mostly in the 1960s and 1970s, assimilated European influences into an essentially Israeli modern idiom with such plays as *The Gypsies of Jaffa* (1971). Other writers, including Hanakh Levin, Yehoshua Sobol, and Aloni, write in a non-naturalistic manner, which invites a highly stylized form of acting, with characters played in broad strokes, almost like cartoon characters. Israeli actors and audiences alike delight in parody, slapstick, and physical humor. The Habimah Theatre was founded in 1917 in Moscow to perform plays in Hebrew and then moved to Palestine in 1928. In 1932 the company settled in Tel Aviv and was declared the Israeli National Theatre in 1958. In the 1980s the Fringe Theater Festival was established to promote new talent and experimental theater.

The first feature film produced in Israel, *Hill 24 Does Not Answer*, was directed by British director Thorold Dickinson in 1955. The indigenous Israeli film industry progressed with the work of filmmaker Ephrayim Kishon, with his movie *Salah* (1964), starring Hayim Topol. Low-budget melodramas and low-grade comedies dominated the 1970s. The Israel Film Center, formed in 1969, did however give funding and support for quality films with a thoughtful serious content. The Israeli film industry produced several successful films in the 1990s, including *Summer with Erika* (1991) and *Tel Aviv Stories* (1992).

References: Abramson, Glenda. *Modern Hebrew Drama.* New York: St. Martin's, 1979; Kahansky, Mendel. *The Hebrew Theatre: Its First Fifty Years.* New York: Ktav, 1969; Landau, Jacob. *Studies in the Arab Theater and Cinema.* Philadelphia: University of Pennsylvania Press, 1958; Mostyn, Trevor, and Albert Hourani, eds. *The Cambridge Encyclopedia of the Middle East and North Africa.* New York: Cambridge University Press, 1988.

Italian Neorealism

An artistic movement in Italian film that occurred after World War II, featuring a raw and honest view of society's effects on the disenfranchised masses. After decades of making only light comedies, musicals, histories, and Mussolini-inspired propaganda films, Italian film makers found freedom after the overthrow of Mussolini and the exit of the Nazis, and that freedom unleashed their creativity. Because post-war conditions made highly polished studio films nearly impossible, filmmakers like Roberto Rossellini turned to the streets to find locations, as in his film *Open City*, 1945. In lieu of professional actors, who were scarce, laborers and peasants were the actors. For the seminal neorealist film *The Bicycle Thief*, 1948, the director Vittorio De Sica claims that an American producer would have rewarded him handsomely if he had cast Cary Grant in the lead role. Instead he cast a young metalworker with no acting experience to portray the desperate father searching the city for his stolen bike.

The principles of neorealism call for sweat rather than sparkle, the common man rather than Hollywood idols, reality rather than idealized illusion. The central theme of neorealist films was the effect of the immense sociological forces on ordinary human beings, forces that shaped their existence. But far from being fatalistic, these films for the most part show the enduring strength of the human spirit. By 1950 in Italy the focus had shifted from the struggle within society to more psychological inquiry, and neorealism had run its course.

See also Egypt
References: Mast, Gerald. *A Short History of the Movies.* 4th ed. New York: Macmillan, 1986.

Italian Opera

Richly produced dramas in which music plays a dominant role; developed in Florence when in 1597 two noblemen, Ottavio Rinuccini and Jacopo Peri, created and produced the first opera, based on the story of Daphne. They were attempting to revive what they believed to be classical Greek theater. The popularity of opera was stimulated by the opening in 1637 of the first public opera house in Venice. In the seventeenth century Italian-style opera spread to Austria, Germany,

Brussels, Amsterdam, and Warsaw, and by the eighteenth century opera had spread to England, Spain, Stockholm, and St. Petersburg.

Actor-singers in opera can communicate emotionally charged and complex ideas and feelings to an audience because at their disposal are the melodic phrase, rhythm, harmony of their own singing, and the tone and feeling of the instruments in the orchestra. It is no wonder that stories of strong emotion distilled to their purest form are often associated with Western opera. Not only can music elaborate the words sung by the actor-singer, but a performer can pose silently while the orchestra communicates explicitly the course of an inner monologue. As a general rule, music is given more importance than the words in an opera. Thus, performers must be singers first and good actors second, so that the quality of acting is usually below the standard acceptable in the spoken theater.

Famous operatic composers include Wolfgang Amadeus Mozart (1756–1791), **Richard Wagner** (1813–1883), and Giuseppe Verdi (1813–1901). Composers continue to create operas throughout Europe and the United States, believing that the medium of opera still holds unthought-of possibilities, as demonstrated by modern composers such as Kurt Weill (1900–1950). However, many operagoers shun operatic innovations and prefer the classics from the seventeenth, eighteenth, and nineteenth centuries.

References: Kimbell, David. *Italian Opera*. New York: Cambridge University Press, 1991; Nicolaisen, Jay. *Italian Opera in Transition, 1871–1893*. Ann Arbor, MI: Proquest, 1980; Sternfeld, Fredrick William. *The Birth of Opera*. New York: Oxford University Press, 1993; Weaver, William. *The Golden Century of Italian Opera From Rossini to Puccini*. London: Thames and Hudson, 1980.

Italy

The early history of Italian theater gives us some of the finest and most highly developed styles of acting, namely in classical Roman times and during the sixteenth and seventeenth centuries, with the *commedia dell'arte*. The centuries following are not nearly as exceptional in their accomplishments. During the eighteenth century the plays of Carlo Gozzi and Carlo Goldoni delighted audiences. Virtuoso acting and traveling troupes dominated the nineteenth century theater scene. It seems the artistic excellence of Italy did not fully reemerge until the advent of the motion picture, in which Italy continues to excel.

Rome became a major power in Italy around 500 B.C. and during the fifth century the Greek model of classical theater was assimilated into Roman culture to create Roman ancient drama. Theatrical activity during medieval times included the **Maggio,** a rural Italian drama named after the month of May, which celebrated the rites of Spring. Sacred dramas in Italy that dramatized the Christian mysteries and miracles were known as **Rappresentazioni Sacre;** they date back to the thirteenth century. **Latin humanistic comedy** was Italian comedy written in Latin during the fourteenth and fifteenth centuries. Learned comedy from the fourteenth, fifteenth and sixteenth centuries, known in Italy as **commedia erudita,** was based on classical models. A true actor's theater, **commedia dell'arte,** dominated the outdoor and court stages during the sixteenth and seventeenth centuries. A troupe of highly skilled trained actors improvised comedy and delighted audiences with clever repartee and acrobatic stunts.

In the seventeenth, eighteenth, nineteenth centuries **Italian opera** overshadowed spoken drama in Italy with its artistic achievements and visual spectacles.

Theater in Italy in the early twentieth century featured one great playwright, **Luigi Pirandello,** who challenged conventional playwriting, and one great actress, **Eleonora Duse,** who rose above the flamboyant acting style of her time to achieve sincerity and truth in her performing. Artists under the banner of **futurism,** an artistic movement of this same time, sought to embody the energy and speed of machines in artistic forms.

Italy entered the motion picture industry with huge silent spectacles in the 1910s. During Benito Mussolini's rule as dictator of Italy, 1922–1943, escapist comedies, romantic musicals, and pro-Mussolini propaganda films were abundant. Italian filmmakers experienced a new artistic freedom after the overthrow of Mussolini following World War II. **Italian neorealism** examined the effect of society on the common man in a raw and honest fashion. After this period of painfully realistic films, Italy turned to a more psychological approach to filmmaking, much like the rest of

Western Europe. Directors such as **Federico Fellini** (1920–1993), Michelangelo Antonioni (born in 1912), and Bernardo Bertolucci (born in 1940) reacted to neorealism with their own varied personal creations. Film and theater director and designer Franco Zeffirelli (born in 1923) succeeded in bringing the expansiveness of romantic and baroque theater and opera to both film and stage, exciting renewed interest in **Shakespeare** and other European classics in a broad twentieth-century audience. The excellence of Italian film continues to develop and expand the art of filmmaking.

See also Roman Theater, Ancient

References: Jarratt, Vernon. *The Italian Cinema.* New York: Macmillan, 1951; Leprohon, Pierre. *Italian Cinema.* New York: Praeger, 1972; Manvell, Roger. *New Cinema in Europe.* New York: Dutton, 1966; Rondi, Gian. *Italian Cinema Today.* New York: Hill and Wang, 1965; Smith, Winifred. *Italian Actors of the Renaissance.* New York: Coward-McCann, 1930.

J

Jackson, Glenda (1936–)

England

English actress of theater and film, who got her start in 1964 as an actress in the Theatre of Cruelty workshop, which was a part of the **Royal Shakespeare Company.** This collaboration led to her performing the role of Charlotte Corday in *Marat/Sade*, directed by **Peter Brook**, in which she became well known for her haunting performance as the beautiful young murderess. As an actress she is emotionally direct and honest, with an independent spirit that has kept her from an alliance with just one theater company, instead, moving about performing the title role in **Ibsen**'s *Hedda Gabler* (1975) at the Royal Shakespeare Company, *Stevie* in 1977 on the West End in London, and **Brecht**'s *Mother Courage* in 1990 in Glasgow.

In 1971 Jackson performed in Ken Russell's film *The Music Lovers*, for which she won an Academy Award. She was given a second Academy Award for *A Touch of Class* in 1973. Jackson retired from acting in 1992 to serve as a member of the House of Commons.

References: Woodward, Ian. *Glenda Jackson: A Study in Fire and Ice.* New York: St. Martin's, 1985.

Jacobean England

See Elizabethan England; England

Jacobi, Derek (1938–)

England

English actor of the stage and cinema. Jacobi began acting at the Marlowe Society at Cambridge University. In 1963 he joined the National Theatre at the Old Vic, a famous London theater, where he performed many Shakespearean roles. From 1972 to 1978 Jacobi performed with the Prospect Theatre Company. At the **Royal Shakespeare Company** he performed **Ibsen**'s *Peer Gynt* in 1982–1983. He also portrayed Claudius in the popular television series *I, Claudius.* In 1992 he portrayed Byron in *Mad, Bad and Dangerous to Know.* He has been in numerous films, including *Three Sisters*, 1970, *The Odessa File*, 1974, *Enigma*, 1982, *Little Dorrit*, 1987, and *Dead Again*, 1991. In 1998 he masterfully portrayed Francis Bacon in the film *Love is the Devil.*

See also Shakespeare, William

References: Cameron-Wilson, James. "Film Reviews: "Love Is the Devil."" *Film Review* (October 1998): 25; Gudehus, Lesley. "A Half-Hour with Derek Jacobi: An Interview." *Dramatics* 60, 1 (September 1988): 16; Jacobi, Derek. "Derek Jacobi on Shakespearean Acting." *Shakespeare Quarterly* 36 (1985): 134.

Jagar

India

Early folk theater from Gomantaka region that shows influence from the cult of **Krishna,** the eighth and most important incarnation of the Hindu god **Vishnu.** The myth of Krishna killing two demons is enacted by having a girl dance while holding an image of Krishna in her hands. Two masked demon appear and are quickly slain by another incarnation of **Vishnu-Krishna.**

References: Varadpande, Manohar Laxman. *Krishna Theatre in India.* New Delhi: Abhinav, 1982.

Jamaica

Jamaica was visited by Columbus in 1494 and was ruled by Spain until the British seized control in 1655. Under Spanish rule the native population of Arawak Indians died out. Independence was gained in 1962. No theater events are recorded until the early eighteenth century, with the arrival in Kingston of the Irish actor, John Moody, who was in Jamaica from 1745–1749. He jumpstarted theatrical activity on the island, which remained an elitist, primarily imported product until 1838, when a quarter of a million black slaves were set free. The result was increased rowdiness in the theaters as well as underground black performances that were based on traditions from their native countries. One form that seems to be a result of combining European mumming and West African masquerades is **Jonkonnu,** a Christmas parade of masked costumed performers.

In the late nineteenth century the tradition, imported from New York, of portraying popular black stereotypes in blackface was adopted and adjusted to fit the Jamaican character. During that same time Henry G. Murray, who was black, began traveling the country delivering humorous stories about Jamaican customs and manners. He was so popular that, when he died in 1877, his sons continued the storytelling tradition he had started.

With the advent of the twentieth century, the challenge was to establish an indigenous style of theater that reflected the Jamaican experience with both Jamaican characters and a Jamaican setting. One popular form that emerged in the 1890s and continued until the late 1950s was the Christmas morning concert. These variety shows gave many young talented performers their start. Acts of gymnastics, singing, comedy, and improvised skits were showcased and were outra-

geously popular with working-class audiences. The coming together of two groups advanced the creation of Jamaican theater profoundly: the Little Theatre Movement of Jamaica, begun in 1941, and the Caribbean Thespians, begun in 1946. Leading actors to emerge from these groups include Mona Chin Hammond, Charles Hyatt, and Ronald Harrison.

The remainder of the century and the beginning of the next has been dominated by three types of theater, Jamaican pantomime, a variety show that is a Jamaican version of the traditional English Christmas revel; grassroots theater; and original Jamaican and Caribbean scripted plays.

References: Banham, Martin. *African Theatre Today.* London: Pitman, 1976; Bennett Wycliffe. "The Jamaican Theatre: A Preliminary Overview." *Jamaica Journal* 8, 2–3 (Summer 1974): 3–9; Fowler, Henry. "A History of Theatre in Jamaica." *Jamaica Journal* 2, 1 (March 1968): 53–59; Hill, Errol. *The Jamaican Stage: 1655–1900.* Amherst: University of Massachusetts Press, 1992; Johns, Eric. "Jamaican Renaissance." *Theatre* (Spring 1947): 35–37.

Japan

A small, somewhat isolated island, Japan has developed its own homogeneous culture and a unique aesthetic of the performing arts. In Japan there is a great variety of highly refined artistic traditions, including dance-drama, puppet theater, folk performances, musical dramas, and a thriving film industry.

Two religions have existed side by side in Japan and have each inspired the performing arts. The **Shinto** religion, an indigenous cult of the sun goddess, inspired *Kagura,* ritual dances performed for Shinto deities. **Zen Buddhism,** after making its way to Japan via China in the seventh century, had an enormous influence on Japanese arts and the Japanese aesthetic of daily living. Zen is a school of Mahayana **Buddhism** that stresses a kind of single-mindedness that is reflected in the Japanese arts by an emphasis on simplicity, serenity, and spontaneity.

A number of folk performance traditions have evolved during Japan's history. *Bugaku* was a traditional temple dance, originating in the seventh century. In the thirteenth century, songs and dances performed by country people at harvest celebrations were called **Dengaku.** In these dances, performers mimicked the stamping movements involved in harvesting rice. Around that same time, variety shows, known as *Sarugaku,* featured singing, dancing, acrobatics, and juggling to please the courts and general audiences. A strongly rhythmic dance, *Kuse,* was also popular.

During the fourteenth century, a court performer named **Kanami Kiyotsugu** introduced *Kuse* into existing *Sarugaku* dance and created a new style of dance-drama, which later came to be known as **Noh.** Kanami's son, **Zeami Motokiyo,** further developed and refined Noh drama. Because Noh became highly refined, appeal to a popular audience lessened as it increased for the court and the **samurai** warrior class. Noh, with its restrained power and understated refinement, grew to exemplify the character of Zen Buddhism, which also served as the ethical code for the samurai class. Since samurai were always ready to face death to protect their lord and honor, this melancholy poetic theater form appealed to them. Samurai had a strict code of honor called **Giri,** yet they felt **Ninjo,** sympathy in their hearts, and the conflict between the two led to many inner struggles for the samurai. If a samurai betrayed his duty or was disgraced, he was expected to commit **sepukku,** a form of suicide. These inner conflicts in the life of a samurai are the subject for many dramas in the traditional Japanese dramas.

The goal of Noh is evoke **Yugen,** which literally means the dark or obscure hidden meaning beneath the Buddhist sutras. It came to refer to the state of yearning, tinged with wistful sadness, that the audience is left with at the end of a Noh drama. In 1400 Zeami wrote **Kadensho,** a secret manual intended to pass down the professional secrets of the Noh actor to his descendants.

This masked dance-drama from medieval Japan, Noh, is traditionally performed only by men. Character types portrayed by actors include the **Shite,** or protagonist, **Waki,** or second lead, **Koken,** or stage manager, **Tsure,** or attendant to either of the two leads, **Kokata,** or child role, and **Tomo,** or walk-on role. There are typically five plays in a *Noh* program with a **Kyogen,** a comic interlude, performed during each interval between plays. The performing area is a raised square with a bridgeway leading to the stage from stage right called a **Hashigaakri.** Flanked by three pine saplings, this bridgeway is the path taken by principal Noh actors for their entrances and exits.

A more commercial dramatic form emerged in the seventeenth century to satisfy the appetites of the rising merchant class in Japan. **Kabuki** was and still remains a popular form of drama. It is unabashedly commercial in outlook and is primarily a showcase for virtuoso acting. Actors wear heavy kimonos sometimes with huge square sleeves and colorful bizarre makeup to create the striking image of a demon or god. Entering down a runway platform, called the **Hanamichi,** from the back of the theater to the stage, actors strike a **Mie,** a stylized dramatic pose, when about seven-tenths of the way to the stage. This creates great excitement and suspense in the audiences, since the actors are so close to viewers. Actors speak their own lines, but a narrator sits to the side on the stage performing narration accompanied by the **samisen,** a three-stringed instrument.

During the 1750s, a tradition of puppet theater, now called **Bunraku,** evolved, which featured multiple puppeteers manipulating each puppet. The realistic expression created by the movements of these puppets has elevated this form to that of a national treasure.

In the beginning of the development of film in Japan, many theatrical conventions were carried over. Until the 1920s, films featured **Oyama,** female impersonators, for all female characters, just as Kabuki and Noh utilize female impersonators. Also a **Benshi,** or storyteller, served as a live narrator at showings of films until the 1930s. This tradition is a carryover from Kabuki, in which a narrator comments on the action. Another element in film related to Noh drama is the kind of character types used. The **Tateyaku,** the powerful male lead in film, relates to the Shite character in Noh, and the **Nimaime,** the mild-mannered male second lead in film, relates to the Waki character in Noh.

Leading film directors in Japan have been **Akira Kurosawa,** who is famous for Western-style samurai films, **Yasujiro Ozu,** who made movies about the modern middle class in Japan, and **Kenji Mizoguchi,** who made period films set in Japan's past. Film types have been categorized as *Gendai-geki,* films based on modern life, **Shomin-geki,** middle-class comedies, and **Jidai-geki,** period films set in Japan's past. **Toshiro Mifune,** known for his virile portrayal of animal-like male characters, stands out as the most famous actor to emerge from the Japanese film industry.

Two notable modern developments of Japanese theater have been **Shimpa,** a melodramatic style of modern theater that is a mix of Kabuki and Western drama, and **Shingeki,** a modern Japanese dramatic form that grew out of the *Shimpa* style in order to give voice to the concerns of the left-wing proletariat in Japan.

> **References:** Bock, Audie. *Japanese Film Directors.* New York: Kodansha International, 1978; Bowers, Faubion. *Japanese Theatre.* New York: Hill and Wang, 1964; Ernst, Earle. *The Kabuki Theatre.* New York: Oxford University Press, 1956. Reprint, Honolulu: University Press of Hawaii, 1974; Immoos, Thomas. *Japanese Theatre.* Trans. Hugh Young. Originally published as *Japanisches Theater.* New York: Rizzoli, 1977; Inoura, Yoshinobu, and Toshio Kawatake. *The Traditional Theater of Japan.* New York: Weatherhill in collaboration with Japan Foundation, 1981; Keene, Donald. *Bunraku:The Art of the Japanese Puppet Theatre.* Tokyo: Kodansha International; New York: Harper & Row, 1973; Lent, John A. *Asian Film Industry.* Austin: University of Texas Press, 1990; Scott, A. C. *The Theatre in Asia.* New York: Macmillan, 1972; Waley, Arthur. *The No Plays of Japan.* London: George Allen & Unwin, 1921. Reprint, London: Unwin Hyman, 1988.

Jataka
Asia

Stories of the former births of Gautama Buddha associated with Hinayana, or Theravada, **Buddhism.** The Jataka is included in the Buddhist canon and is comprised of over 500 moral tales and simple animal stories. Some of the tales date back to before the birth of the Buddha. These stories were used by court poets and also dramatized in folk drama and popular performances. These tales originated in India, but became popular throughout Southeast Asia, spread by the travels of Hinayana Buddhist missionaries. **Lakon Bassak,** popular dance-drama of Cambodia, **Lakon Nok,** popular dance from the south of Thailand, and **Yokthe Pwe,** marionette theater of Myanmar, are all performances that dramatize the Jataka tales.

> **References:** Aherne, Consuelo Maria, Paul Kevin Meagher, and Thomas C. O'Brien, eds. *Encyclopedic Dictionary of Religion.* 3 vols. Washington, DC: Corpus Publishers, 1979; Brandon, James. *Theatre in*

Southeast Asia. Cambridge, MA: Harvard University Press, 1974.

Jatra
Bangladesh, India

Popular opera from northeastern India, in West Bengal, Assam, Bihar, and Orissa, originating in the sixteenth century in Bengal. Traveling *Jatra* troupes perform highly energized original plays to working class–audiences, who sit on the ground all around the stage. No Sanskrit is spoken or sung, only Bengali.

A *Jatra* play always starts with the climax of the story to grab the interest of the audience. The actors strive for virtuoso acting. They must be able to perform sharp changes of mood, abrupt flares of temper, and sudden drops of the spirit. Actors always perform their own singing and improvised dialogue. A prompter sits at the side of the stage with an outline of the play and suggests lines for the actors when needed. Actors not immediately involved in the action sometimes lounge along the edge of the platform stage. Vocal ability is the main criterion upon which performers are evaluated. There is some dialogue, but the focus is on the singing. Female impersonators are a part of traditional all-male troupes. They are a great attraction for an audience. In modern troupes women portray female characters.

Performances are staged in an open space outside, on a raised platform with rampways leading to it through the audience. One light on a pole at each of the four corners of the stage illuminates the acting area. The only property on stage is a chair, which can represent a throne, a tower, steps, or whatever else is needed. All other properties, like swords, capes, or letters, are carried on and off stage by actors. Makeup is used creatively for dramatic effect. For example, a demon character paints white fangs on his upper lip and a black spiked beard on his chin.

New plays are written for almost every performance. Subjects for dramas are diverse, drawing for example on domestic issues, political criticism, historical happenings, and movie plots. Musical accompaniment is made up of drums, cymbals, bells, flute, clarinet, harmonium, and four trumpets.

References: Brandon, James R. *Brandon's Guide to Theatre in Asia.* Honolulu: University Press of Hawaii, 1976; Gargi, Balawanta. *Folk Theater of India.* Seattle: University of Washington Press, 1966; Vatsyayan, Kapila. *Traditional Indian Theatre: Multiple Streams.* New Delhi: National Book Trust, 1980.

Java
Indonesia

The most densely populated island in Indonesia, Java is a rich haven for the performing arts. Highly refined forms of dance-drama and shadow puppet theater stand out worldwide for their sophistication and grace. A warm beautiful climate and gracious populace create an environment in which the magical Hindu epic tales performed by masters animate the imagination of the spectators. Even though the majority of the Javanese people are Muslim, Hindu mythology still defines their national character and world view. There are even textbooks for children in public school on the Hindu characters in the epic tales, the **Mahabharata** and the **Ramayana,** as performed in the shadow puppet theater.

One of the oldest known forms of drama in Java is **Wayang Beber.** From the fourth or fifth century, this is a form of storytelling in which a narrator unrolls a scroll that is wrapped around a pole with one hand while winding the other end of the scroll with the other hand onto a pole. The pictures of the story on the scroll follow the storyteller's dramatization. This tradition of using a visual aid for telling the great Hindu tales was elaborated upon by **Wayang Kulit,** the general term for shadow puppet theater in Southeast Asia. The Wayang Kulit is a magical combination of intricately designed rawhide puppets casting shadows onto a screen, hypnotic music from a **gamelan,** the traditional orchestra, and one puppet master, known as a **dalang,** dramatizing a tale from the *Mahabharata* or the *Ramayana.* A local god-clown character who was integrated into the Hindu epics is **Semar,** who serves as translator and critic of the ancient Jawa language used by the high and refined characters.

There are many specialized forms of shadow puppet theater, which evolved from *Wayang Kulit* to perform other stories but share almost identical performance conventions. **Wayang Madya** enacts

the tales of East Javanese kings. Dramatizing the **Panji tales** is the **Wayang Gedog** shadow puppet theater. **Wayang Djawa** enacts stories about Prince Diponegoro who was famous for rebelling against the Dutch in the nineteenth century. Two types that use wooden puppets instead of the carved rawhide variety are **Wayang Klitik,** which uses flat wooden puppets, and **Wayang Golek,** which uses carved three-dimensional puppets. The **Menak** is a Javanese cycle of stories about the famous Islamic hero, Amir Hamzah, which is dramatized in *Wayang Golek.* Shadow puppet theater has also been utilized by the government for propaganda purposes, since it is a format intimately familiar to the rural population of Java. **Wayang Suluh** was performed during the Indonesian revolution against the Dutch in 1945–1949. Once the revolution was successful, **Wayang Pantja Sila** was developed to promote nationalism. The five main puppet characters in the drama represented the five principles of the new revolution.

There are several varieties of dance-drama that have evolved through the centuries in Java. Performed both in Javanese courts and in villages, **Wayang Topeng** is a masked dance-drama that blends dance styles from classical Indian dance and Javanese mask dances to dramatize the Panji tales, pre-Islamic stories about Prince Panji. In the dance-drama **Wayang Wong,** styled after the Wayang Kulit shadow puppet theater, the performers mimic the stylized movements of the shadow puppets. **Ketoprak,** a dance-drama based on strong rhythmic stamping, became a popular craze in the early 1900s. In the romantic dance-opera, **Ardja,** attractive young women performed dramas through song and dance, mostly at temple festivals. The most recent dance-drama form is **Sendratari,** which is condensed into a short format with no speaking and was created to appeal to foreign tourists.

Dramatic performance that do not include dance have also evolved in Java, but to a less refined level than Javanese dance-dramas. **Dagelan** is an improvised comedy form about humorous domestic situations from central Java, performed in the rural countryside. Also a form of comedy, **Ludruk** is realistic contemporary drama performed by men and female impersonators. From the capital city, Jakarta, **Lenong** is an improvised theater form performed in the streets. A loosely defined serious dramatic form, which borrows from many Western forms, has gone through three different names as the political climate has shifted. It was first named *Komedie*, then *Toneel* (the Dutch word for drama), and then it was changed to the Indonesian word for drama, **Sandiwara,** in the 1980s.

References: Bandem, I Made. "Notes on the Development of the Arja Dance Drama." *Indonesia Circle* 3 (March 1983): 28–32; Brandon, James. *On Thrones of Gold.* Cambridge, MA: Harvard University Press, 1970; Brandon, James. *Theatre in Southeast Asia.* Cambridge, MA: Harvard University Press, 1974; Brandon, James R. *Brandon's Guide to Theatre in Asia.* Honolulu: University Press of Hawaii, 1976; Guritno, Pandam. *Wayang Kebudayaan Indonesia Dan Pancasila.* Jakarta: Penerbit Universitas Indonesia, 1988; Hatley, Barbara. "Wayang and Ludruk: Polarities in Java." *Drama Review* 15, 3 (1971): 88–101; Hatley, Barbara. "Ketoprak: Performance and Social Meaning in a Javanese Popular Theatre Form." Ph.D. diss., University of Sydney, 1985; Kam, Garret. "Wayang Wong in the Court of Yogyakarta: The Enduring Significance of Javanese Dance Drama." *Asia Theatre Journal* 4, 1 (1987): 29–51; Keeler, Ward. *Javanese Shadow Plays, Javanese Selves.* Princeton, NJ: Princeton University Press, 1987; Ludwig, Ruby Ornstein. "Wayang Wong, the Javanese Classical Theatre." *World Music* 18, 1 (1976): 15–22; Moebirman. *Wayang Purwa.* Jakarta: Yayasan Pelita Wisata, 1973; Peacock, James. "Javanese Folkdrama and Social Change." Ph.D. diss., Harvard University, 1965; Peacock, James. "Comedy and Centralisation in Java: The Lubruk Plays." *Journal of American Folklore* 80, 318 (October–December 1967): 345–356; Ludwig, Ruby Ornstein. "Wayang Wong, the Javanese Classical Theatre." *World Music* 18, 1 (1976): 15–22; Ulbricht, H. *Wayang Purwa: Shadows of the Past.* Kuala Lumpur, Malaysia: Oxford University Press, 1970; van der Kroef, Jusuts M. "The Roots of Javanese Drama." *Journal of Aesthestics and Art Criticism* 12 (March 1954): 318–327; Yousof, Ghulam-Sarwar. "Traditional Theatre in South East Asia." *Performing Arts* 2 (July 1985): 37–49.

Jia-li Xi
China

String puppet theater of Chuan-chow, southern China. The marionette theater became highly developed and sophisticated during the Tang dynasty, A.D. 618–907. It was brought to the south of China as early as the tenth century. Jia-li Xi literally means "theater of auspicious rituals." Ritual and spiritual observances are an important part of this form. Folk religions in China believe that the world is crowded with spirits that are quick to inhabit any object. Thus puppets are always kept locked away with their heads stored separate from their bodies. This ensures that spirits are unable to inhabit the puppets. A strict ritual is carried out before each performance in which the patron deity is honored and given offerings. The whole troupe chants a spell to dispel evil and create harmony. A likeness of the deity is put on a pole and called down to inhabit its puppet image. After the possessed puppet performs a purifying dance, the show begins. The show is not over until this same deity returns in puppet form to say farewell.

In a troupe there are usually four performers portraying four character types. Most troupes have over thirty puppets. The average number of strings on a puppet is sixteen, but it can go as high as thirty-two for an agile puppeteer. The puppets are manipulated by wooden controls on which there are strings leading down to the puppet. All the complicated manipulations must be executed smoothly and exactly so as not to cause even a momentary loss of the illusion of life. String puppeteers are highly regarded in society and wear an academic gown and hat. The stage is 3 feet high and 7 feet square, with a curtain hanging across the bottom of the stage half way back from the stage. There are four musicians in each troupe. The instruments are drum, bell-shaped gong, vertical bamboo flute, and cymbal. The southern-style music is simple and slow. In modern performances the stage is divided into three parallel playing areas, which create the illusion of depth. This illusion is enhanced by the use of small puppets in back and larger puppets in front.

References: Stalberg, Roberta Helmer. *China's Puppets.* San Francisco: China Books, 1984.

Jiang Qing
See Chiang Ching

Jidai-geki
Japan

Period films set in Japan's past. These films can be further divided into specific periods of Japanese history, for example, Tokugawa or Meiji (see **Japan**). During the American occupation of Japan after World War II, these films were not allowed by American forces because they were feudalistic and militaristic. Instead, the Americans encouraged cultural reorientation films that demonstrated peaceful living and democracy.

See also Mizoguchi, Kenji; Kurosawa, Akira

References: Mast, Gerald. *A Short History of the Movies.* 4th ed. New York: Macmillan, 1986.

Jones, James Earl (1931–)

United States

Actor of the stage, film, and television. His father, who was once a prizefighter, was also an aspiring actor. James got his break on Broadway in 1957 and continued to perform in New York with the New York Shakespeare Festival, among others. He won a Tony award for his acting in the play *The Great White Hope*, 1966–1968, which was made into a film in 1970. He starred in the film *The Man*, 1972, in which he portrayed the first black president of the **United States**. Jones is well remembered for his portrayal of the lead in *Paul Robeson*, 1977, on Broadway.

His rich "voice of God" vocal quality has led him to many vocal roles, including Darth Vader in *Star Wars*, 1977. In 1986 he won another Tony award for his performance in *Fences* on Broadway. Jones continues to perform in made-for-television movies and in popular films such as *Patriot Games*, 1992.

References: Jones, James Earl. *James Earl Jones: Voices and Silences.* New York: Scribner, 1993.

Jonkonnu

Caribbean

Christmas tradition dating back to the eighteenth century, in which masked performers in elaborate costumes proceed down the public streets accompanied by fife and drum. The performers use heavily disguised voices if they speak at all and never remove their masks in public. Characters such as Devil, Cow Head, Belly Woman, and Actor Boy are portrayed. It seems likely that this tradition is a result of the mixture of European mumming and West African masquerades.

References: Banham, Martin. *African Theatre Today.* London: Pitman, 1976; Bettelheim, Judith.

James Earl Jones plays a fighter in The Great White Hope (1970). (Kobol Collection/20th Century Fox)

"Jonkonnu and Other Christmas Masquerades." In *Caribbean Festival Arts*, 39–71. Seattle: University of Washington Press, 1988; Fowler, Henry. "A History of Theatre in Jamaica." *Jamaica Journal* 2, 1 (March 1968): 53–59.

Jordan

British influence pervades the theater of the nineteenth and twentieth centuries, in acting style, playwriting, stage settings, and costumes. Dramatic output is limited in Jordan. One of the few published plays from Jordan, *The Prisoner*, was written in 1933 by Muhammad Mamish. There are a few acting companies, all of which are amateur, and they have generally been short-lived, as was, for example, the Theatrical Renascence Troupe. Most have been located in the capital city Amman and in Ram-Allah.

See also **Syria**

References: Cachia, P. "The Dramatic Monologues of Al-Ma'arri'." *Journal of Arabic Literature* 1 (1970): 129–136; Landau, Jacob. *Studies in the Arab Theater* and Cinema. Philadelphia: University of Pennsylvania Press, 1958; Moreh, S. "The Arabic Theatre in Egypt in the Eighteenth and Nineteenth Centuries." *Etudes Arabes et Islamiques* 3 (1975): 109–113; Mostyn, Trevor, and Albert Hourani, eds. *The Cambridge Encyclopedia of the Middle East and North Africa.* New York: Cambridge University Press, 1988.

Kabuki

Japan

Popular dramatic form of seventeenth-century Japan. Kabuki developed with an unashamedly commercial outlook, taking from other theater forms whatever would draw an audience. The rising merchant class wanted a form of entertainment better suited to their tastes than **Noh,** the classic masked dance-drama. Kabuki was invented by a woman, Okuni, in 1596, and became associated with loose women and prostitution. When women were no longer allowed to perform in 1629, young boys took the roles, but this was still considered too titillating and was banned in 1652. Thus, it came to be that fat older men with shaven heads and blackened teeth performed all roles, leaving almost no room for sex appeal. Though authorities looked down on actors as unclean, a famous actor was often idolized by his town or his community.

In order to succeed commercially Kabuki took bits of **Noh, Bunraku** (puppet drama), dance, legends, and history, mixed with a racy and sensational style of acting. Kabuki actors regard their whole bodies as their tool for expression. They use refined techniques of expressing complex emotions through stylized and exaggerated full-body techniques that are deeply moving for a Kabuki audience. Their movement has a dancelike quality, and the meaning of the words in a song is often revealed in strong rhythmic movement.

Gestures made by the actors range from being quite literal to being beautifully evocative of some abstract sentiment. Movement by actors tends to work toward static poses rather than following fluid patterns. These dramatic poses, called **Mie,** reveal the nature of the character being portrayed. Kabuki is predominantly a showcase for virtuoso acting. All other elements of performance are subordinate to the dramatic impression created by the actor. Different types of characters are portrayed. For example, **Aragoto** is a rough character, and an **Onnagata** is a female impersonator. An actor specializes in portraying a specific type of character his whole life and is often born of a father who portrayed the same type.

The wide, shallow stage for a performance has a **Hanamichi,** a runway platform, going from the stage into the audience and all the way to the back of the theater. The runway is flush with the stage and is set to the audience's left side. This device creates tension between the audience and the performer when an actor enters. An actor usually strikes a dramatic pose, a mie, when about three-quarters of the way to the stage. The actual stage floor is usually not nailed down, providing resonance for the actor's stamping. The costumes are several layers of kimono, sometimes weighing as much as 60 pounds. The layers must be carefully arranged so that when an actor sits, moves, or poses no ungraceful costume line may occur. There are stage assistants

An actor portrays the part of the ogre of the moor in a kabuki drama, Japan. (Charles & Josette Lenars/Corbis)

who enter the stage to make adjustments on costumes. The audience accepts this as a convention and hardly notices them. Actors wear thick makeup that is almost masklike to exaggerate the nature of the character. Fierce characters have brightly colored lines curving around the eye and mouth and also wear wigs that increase their height considerably. The musical accompaniment is comprised mostly of sound effects. The wooden clappers and other instruments give musical and rhythmic expression to the movements of the actors. The narrator who sits with the musicians stage left performs all the narration and songs, accompanied by the **samisen,** a three-stringed instrument. Kabuki actors concentrate on the external appearance and impression of a character and surrender their intellectual and emotion selves to the portrayal. Before an actor enters the stage via the Hanamichi, he studies his fully costumed image in a mirror, absorbing the character. This practice is symbolic of the method of training for a Kabuki actor. The craft is learned almost completely by imitation. Traditional portrayal of characters is honored, and not until an actor is at least fifty years old is he allowed to attempt any innovations in the portrayal of a specific role.

References: Bowers, Faubion. *Japanese Theatre.* New York: Hill and Wang, 1964; Ernst, Earle. *The Kabuki Theatre.* New York: Oxford University Press, 1956. Reprint, Honolulu: University Press of Hawaii, 1974; Ernst, Earle. *The Kabuki Theatre.* New York: Oxford University Press, 1956. Reprint, Honolulu: University Press of Hawaii, 1974; Immoos, Thomas. *Japanese Theatre.* Trans. Hugh Young. Originally published as *Japanisches Theater.* New York: Rizzoli, 1977; Inoura, Yoshinobu, and Toshio Kawatake. *The Traditional Theater of Japan.* New York: Weatherhill in collaboration with Japan Foundation, 1981; Scott, A. C. *The Kabuki Theatre of Japan.* 1955. Reprint, London: Allen & Unwin, 1956; Scott, A. C. *The Theatre in Asia.* New York: Macmillan, 1972.

Kadensho

Japan

"The Book of Handing on the Flowers," a manual on secret acting techniques written in A.D. 1400 by Zeami Motokiyo, famous performer and playwright for **Noh,** the masked dance-drama of medieval Japan; intended to preserve professional secrets for a trusted son or disciple next in line to continue the performance tradition.

References: Ernst, Earle. *The Kabuki Theatre.* New York: Oxford University Press, 1956. Reprint, Honolulu: University Press of Hawaii, 1974, Inoura, Yoshinobu, and Toshio Kawatake. *The Traditional Theater of Japan.* New York: Weatherhill in collaboration with Japan Foundation, 1981, Scott, A. C. *The Theatre in Asia.* New York: Macmillan, 1972.

Kagura

Japan

Ritual dance performed to pay tribute to local **Shinto** deities. This dance honors the gods and establishes contact with them. It is performed in Shinto shrines during festivals in Japan. The dancer is either a young boy or, more often, a shrine maiden, a young girl dedicated to a specific shrine, dressed in white, the color of purity.

References: Scott, A. C. *The Theatre in Asia.* New York: Macmillan, 1972.

Kala
India

A kind of theater about **Krishna,** the eighth and most important incarnation of the Hindu god **Vishnu**; from the Gomantaka region in the south of India, it involves a variety of theatrical elements, including dance, song, instrumental music, and dialogue. The term *Kala* is originally the name of a mixture of food gathered together by the **Gopis,** milkmaids, to share with Krishna. This term eventually came to be used for a mixture of theatrical elements too.

Among the separate forms of *Kala* theater are **Gaulan Kala,** Krishna drama performed by children; **Gopal Kala,** Krishna drama performed in the morning; and **Dashavatar Kala,** drama depicting the ten incarnations of **Vishnu-Krishna.**

References: Varadpande, Manohar Laxman. *Krishna Theatre in India.* New Delhi: Abhinav, 1982.

Kantor, Tadeusz (1915–1990)
Poland

Polish director, scenographer, and painter who began directing underground theater during the German occupation of Poland in 1939. In 1956 he formed an experimental theater group, Cricot–2, in Cracow. Kantor was stimulated most as a director by the visual elements of a production. His theater performed many avant-garde plays by the Polish playwright, Stanislaw Witkiewicz. He created the first **happening** in Poland. Kantor wrote scripts loosely structured on existing works of literature. His best-known productions include *The Dead Class,* 1975, and *Wielopole, Wielopole,* 1980.

References: Cioffi, Kathleen. *Alternative Theatre in Poland 1954–89.* Canada: Harwood, 1996; Czerwinski, E. J. *Contemporary Polish Theater and Drama (1956–1984).* Westport, CT: Greenwood, 1988; Karpinski, Maciej. *The Theatre of Andrzej Wajda.* Trans. Christina Paul. New York: Cambridge University Press, 1989.

Karagiozis
Greece

Greek shadow puppet theater evolved from **Karagoz,** an Ottoman entertainment from the fourteenth century that was disseminated to the territories of the Ottoman Empire in Greece in the eighteenth century. The Greek version, *Karagiozis,* differs from the original in that it has evolved to suit the Greek national character and has been influenced by Christianity and European culture.

From a repertory of hundreds of texts passed from one generation to the next orally, a single puppet master speaks all dialogue and narration from memory and also does the majority of puppet manipulation. Two apprentice puppet masters manipulate secondary puppets, make sound effects, and carry out the scene changes. An elongated rectangular screen is set up outdoors at night in a clearing, and behind it the puppets are manipulated. The screen is made of white cloth and is generally 18 feet wide and about 5 feet high. The screen is held taut by a wooden and stone structure that raises the screen a few feet off the stage floor, which is itself, raised about one foot. There is a shelf just below the bottom of the screen backstage, about 1.5 feet deep, that is used to hold the lights and as a walkway for the puppets. About ten shelf lamps are evenly spaced along this shelf about 1 foot away from the screen. The puppet manipulators stand behind the screen manipulating the puppets against the screen using 20–inch-long sticks. The audience sees only the shadows of the puppets. These shadows appear crisp and not distorted because they are held close to the screen. Since the puppets are translucent and painted, the shadows appear brightly colored. Three overhanging lamps complement the standing lamps by creating an even wash of light over the entire screen to cast the set pieces in clear shadow. Sometimes these set pieces are attached to the screen and sometimes two preset screens are used that are rigged on a pulley system to be changed when the action of the play shifts.

Comic and irreverent, the most common type of *Karagiozis* play consists of a series of stock scenes related loosely to some central theme enacted by a set of approximately twenty-five stock characters. The main character, named *Karagiozis,* is a humpbacked fool-hero who dresses in rags as a poor Greek and disrupts the world of the rich and powerful. Other type characters represented are the nagging wife, the street urchin, the idiotic intellectual, and the Jewish merchant. *Karagiozis* was traditionally handed down to each successive generation as an oral tradition from an elder master to his apprentices. The traditional Turkish plays from *Karagoz* were mixed with Greek historical material to create plays through which the Greek people could come to know their new emerging national identity.

The sound effects created by the assisting apprentice puppet masters were usually simplistic, such as a hand clap to indicate a slamming door or hitting a piece of tin to evoke the sound of thunder. The assistants also created simple lighting effects. A traditional performance at a time when *Karagiozis* was highly popular would have been accompanied by singers and an orchestra, but contemporary performances usually resort to using recorded music on a tape player.

The influence of the motion picture and other forms of modern entertainment has nearly wiped out this theater form. Whereas in the 1950s *Karagiozis* players traveled all across Greece performing in villages and cities, now performances can only rarely be found and then only in large cities such as Patras and Athens. *Karagiozis* stories have been rendered into comic book art and are sold alongside Mickey Mouse comic books. By the late 1950s, *Karagiozis* had become entertainment for children, featured sometimes in short fifteen-minute episodes on television.

References: Myrsiades, Linda S. *The Karagiozis: Heroic Performance in Greek Shadow Theater.* Hanover, NH: University Press of New England, 1988; Myrsiades, Linda S. *Karagiozis: Culture and Comedy in Greek Puppet Theater.* Lexington: University Press of Kentucky, 1992.

Karagoz
Turkey

Popular folk form of shadow puppet theater from the fourteenth century A.D. *Karagoz* has both an urban and a rural flavor to its humor and performance style. It was popular in the Turkish capital, Istanbul, and in popular festivals held throughout the mostly rural Ottoman lands. The roots of this tradition extend back in time to the **Mime** performances from ancient Rome and to fool lore. Middle Eastern countries taken over by the Ottoman Empire, including **Egypt, Syria,** Persia, **Tunisia,** and **Algeria,** have a history of *Karagoz* shadow puppet theater being performed as early

as the seventeenth century. *Karagoz* made its way into occupied Greece possibly as early as the eighteenth century and evolved into a similar form, named **Karagiozis.**

The main puppet character, after whom the form was named, is *Karagoz*, a crude clown character. Other characters include Hacivat, a pseudo-intellectual petty bourgeois, and Zenne, a female character. The word *Karagoz* originally meant "black eyes," referring to Turkish gypsies.

In order to evade the Islamic prescription that no artistic representations of humans should be made, since it is believed that Allah is the only creator, theatrical practitioners from the Ottoman empire designed shadow puppets that represented the human being as a shadow. Holes were cut into the shadow puppets to allow the spirits to escape, rendering *Karagoz* an allowable art form in an Islamic world. This form having escaped prohibition, because of the narrow margin between the real and the shadow world, it has enjoyed a certain freedom from the normal social constraints on behavior. It has often been viewed as being anarchistic, and its characters enjoy the freedom of speech of a court jester or a court fool.

The style of humor is often obscene and charged with sexual innuendo. Male shadow figures often wear a phallus, as was done in ancient **Greek comedy.** The setting for these performances is the carnival, where the distinctions between performers and audience are blurred and all become participants.

References: Esslin, Martin. *The Encyclopedia of World Theater.* New York: Charles Scribner's Sons, 1977; Martinovitch, Nicholas. *Turkish Theatre.* New York: Theatre Arts, 1933; Myrsiades, Linda S. *The Karagiozis: Heroic Performance in Greek Shadow Theater.* Hanover, NH: University Press of New England, 1988; Myrsiades, Linda S. *Karagiozis: Culture and Comedy in Greek Puppet Theater.* Lexington: University Press of Kentucky, 1992.

Kathak
India

Classical dance of North India, closely associated with the cult of **Krishna,** the eighth and most important incarnation of the Hindu god **Vishnu.** *Kathak* developed from the performances of the **Kathaks,** storytellers who sat in temples and sang songs about Krishna, embellishing them with gestures. When Muslim kings ruled India, especially between the sixteenth and nineteenth centuries, *Kathak* became a court dance and incorporated more erotic than religious themes. *Kathak* is performed by both men and women and can be a solo or group dance. This energetic and technically demanding dance features consecutive whirling pivots, intricate footwork, complex stamping rhythms; the acting of the dancers brings the story to life.

The dance begins by invoking the gods, followed by *Nritta*, non-narrative pure dance. Next there is sometimes *Nritya*, a dance interpreting a song about Krishna through graceful gestures and **mudras,** hand gestures that make up a symbolic language. The dancer elaborates on the meaning of each word to bring out the deep emotive content. Then a dancer improvises a conversation with both the musicians and the audience. If the performance is particularly appealing to the audience, the audience will respond with loud shouts and applause.

References: Brandon, James R. *Brandon's Guide to Theatre in Asia.* Honolulu: University Press of Hawaii, 1976; Varadpande, Manohar Laxman. *Krishna Theatre in India.* New Delhi: Abhinav, 1982.

Kathakali
India

All-male dance-drama from Kerala State, dating back to the seventeenth and eighteenth century. It is derived from **Kudiyattam,** an ancient style of presenting Sanskrit plays, but is much more alive and accessible for an audience. Through dance and pantomime, actors interpret the songs in a fiercely emotional acting style. Gestures and facial expressions with symbolic meaning are executed with incredible speed and accuracy by actors as they powerfully enact a scene. Dressed in enormous headpieces, dramatic makeup, and huge full skirts, the actors seemingly become gods and demons assembled for a cosmic battle. Two singers perform all songs for the actors, who neither speak nor sing, since the dancing and acting are so physically demanding. All songs are in the vernacular language, Malayalam. There are many troupes in Kerala performing *Kathakali* almost nightly during the winter and the spring.

A performance of Kathakali in Kerala, India. (Alison Wright/Corbis)

The acting style is not impersonation but embodiment. Once an actor has "stepped into character" he does not speak. The range of emotions traveled in a performance is enormous. Actors emit tender love during a romantic scene and fierce hatred during a battle. Dramatic interpretation through dance and gesture is more important than the spoken word in *Kathakali*. A play that could be read in twenty minutes takes three to four hours to perform. An actor stands with his feet wide apart and his knees bent. He keeps his weight on the outer edges of his feet so that his energy may not be sucked out of him by the earth.

Actors execute impressive leaps, jumps, and spirals during their dances. With their entire bodies, performers speak a codified symbolic language. There are numerous mudras, symbolic gestures. For the limbs there are 64 mudras, nine for the head, eleven for casting a glance, six for the eyebrows, and four for the neck. While moving, a performer predominantly follows his hands with his eyes. It is believed by practitioners that the heart and the mind follow the eyes to the hands and that then **rasa,** aesthetic spiritual joy, is created.

Huge headdresses and swirling full skirts are worn by the male characters. Female characters wear very plain costumes compared to the dazzling costumes of their male counterparts. Most male characters also wear a **Chutti,** a white beard formed from a paste made of rice powder and lime juice, layered from the ears to the chin of the performer. The actor usually dozes off as it is being applied, since the process takes three to four hours. Once it is on, an actor rarely speaks, both because he is in character and to keep it from cracking. Colorful makeup identifies the character's identity and disposition. Green makeup is used for gods and heroes, red for violent characters, yellow for simple mortals, and black for demons.

Episodes from the **Ramayana** and the **Mahabharata,** the two great Hindu epics, form the basis of the repertory, along with other legends. The texts are only sung. Musical accompaniment is performed by a gong, cymbal, and two drums played with great speed and strength.

Training for *Kathakali* is incredibly rigorous. Boys start their training very young and are subjected to a strict schedule of physical and dramatic training. They must practice sharp quick movements with the eyes while holding their eyes open larger than one would think possible. Only religious believers can be motivated to pursue this performance form because they are not guaranteed an income, or even three meals a day. Today the Kerala Kalamandalam, the state academy for the performing arts of Kerala, provides full-time training for *Kathakali*.

See also *Krishnattam*

References: Anand, Mulk Raj. *The Indian Theatre.* London: D. Dobson, 1950; Brandon, James R. *Brandon's Guide to Theatre in Asia.* Honolulu: University Press of Hawaii, 1976; Gargi, Balawanta. *Theatre in India.* New York: Theatre Arts, 1962; Jones, Clifford Reis, and Betty True Jones. *Kathakali: An Introduction to the Dance-Drama of Kerala.* New York: Theatre Arts, 1970; Varadpande, Manohar Laxman. *Krishna Theatre in India.* New Delhi: Abhinav, 1982; Wells, Henry Willis. *The Classical Drama of India: Studies in Its Values for the Literature and Theatre of the World.* New York: Asia Publishing House, 1963.

Kathaks
India

Storytellers who relate stories of **Krishna,** the eighth and most important incarnation of the Hindu god Vishnu, in temples. Storytellers sit on the temple floor to sing and translate the meaning of songs through beautiful gestures. **Kathak,** the classical dance of north India, emerged from this form.

References: Varadpande, Manohar Laxman. *Krishna Theatre in India.* New Delhi: Abhinav, 1982.

Kattiakaran
India

Stage manager and narrator for **Terrukutta,** folk opera. A male always performs this role; he enters after the invocation dance to introduce himself and the action in the drama that is to follow. He remains a prominent figure throughout the drama, commenting on events and describing the setting. The *Kattiakaran* is similar to *Sutradhara,* the stage manager of a **Sanskrit drama.**

References: Gargi, Balawanta. *Folk Theater of India.* Seattle: University of Washington Press, 1966.

Kazakhstan

See Soviet Cinema; Soviet Union

Kebyar

Bali

Solo male dance. This relatively recent development is only about fifty years old. It was developed by a young man named Mario, with talent enough to combine the robust masculinity of the **Baris,** the male war dance, with the grace and delicacy of **Legong,** the female dance drama. The *Kebyar* is performed in a squatting *Baris* position, with emphasis on facial expressions and arm movements. This form of dance responds to and visually interprets musical moods.

References: Brandon, James R. *Brandon's Guide to Theatre in Asia.* Honolulu: University Press of Hawaii, 1976; Covarrubias, Miguel. *Bali.* New York: Oxford University Press, 1972.

Kente, Gibson (1932–)

South Africa

South African playwright and director. Kente was extremely successful as one of the first black entrepreneurs who created popular melodramatic musicals, known as Township Musicals, about life in black townships. In 1967 he became the first black producer of theater in South Africa. For twenty-five years he produced one box-office hit after another. He drew upon popular cultural expression and created performances with incredible energy and professionalism. His works were primarily addressed to the people of the townships. Even in the 1980s he was almost unknown to the white theater scene.

A strict director and choreographer, Kent continually demanded the best performance from his actors. Being in one of his productions was tantamount to undergoing the most rigorous theater training program.

He was not overtly political in his works early on, usually opting, instead, for more light-hearted themes. However, in the 1970s as the Black Consciousness Movement began to assert the rights and dignity of the black populace, even Kente introduced stronger political themes into his works, most pronounced in his play *How Long?*, 1971. Kente has since turned to film and television production as a more secure and profitable option.

References: Banham, Martin. *African Theatre Today.* London: Pitman, 1976; Coplan, David. *In Township Tonight! South Africa's Black City Music and Theatre.* New York: Longman, 1985.

Ketjak

Bali

Monkey dance. *Ketjak* was created in the 1930s, and now at least six village troupes perform it regularly. The monkey chorus is from traditional trance-dances. The dance numbers were added to appeal to tourist audiences. One to two hundred men sit in a series of tight rows forming one circle. They rapidly chant the sounds made by a monkey, "Ketjak," in varying rhythms. One or more leaders give vocal cues to help coordinate the chorus. The chorus sways back and forth in unison, sometimes even lying back so that the heads of those in one row rest on the people sitting behind them. The general effect is hypnotic and trance-inducing. In the cleared center area of the circle a few young women enact scenes from the **Ramayana** in pantomime and dance. Usually the only light source is a many-branched candelabra. This is placed in the center of the circle around which the girls dance. Often a masked actor portraying **Hanuman,** the great monkey, will pounce into the action too. For costumes the men wear black–and–white–checkered sarongs with a red tie around their waists. The women are in traditional Balinese dance costumes. They wear gold headpieces adorned with flowers, sarongs with tight bodices made of long strips of golden cloth wrapped around the chest, and gold ornamental wings at the elbows and wrists.

References: Brandon, James. *Theatre in Southeast Asia.* Cambridge, MA: Harvard University Press, 1974; Brandon, James R. *Brandon's Guide to Theatre in Asia.* Honolulu: University Press of Hawaii, 1976; McKean, Philip F. "From Purity to Pollution? The Balinese Ketjak (Monkey Dance) as Symbolic Form in Transition." In *Imagination of Reality: Essays in Southeast Asian Coherence Systems,* ed. A. L. Becker and Aram A. Yengoyan, 293–302. Norwood, NJ: Ablex, 1979.

Ketoprak

Java

Dance-drama form popular in the 1920s. In 1914 an official of the court of Surakarta, a city in Java,

Dancers perform the Ketjak, or monkey dance, in Bali. (Wolfgang Kaehler/Corbis)

was intrigued by the sound and the rhythm of peasant women singing as they stamped on rice in the hollow of a log. He brought a hollow log into his home and practiced creating various stomping sounds and rhythms, adding other musical instruments like flute, drum, and tambourine. From this research he developed dances he called *Ketoprak* (*ketok* literally means "to knock"). He gave private showings in his home. A veritable craze developed by the 1920s, as new troupes popped up everywhere. Stories based on Javanese history and legends began to be dramatized using dance and dialogue. In Yogjakarta the dramatic aspects, portraying specific characters and the telling of a story, are stressed, and spoken dialogue is a major portion of a performance. In Surakarta dance is prominent. Musical accompaniment is provided by the rhythm of the hollow log, tambourine, flute and drums, all joined by a **gamelan,** the traditional ensemble. For a few decades Western musical instruments were used, but they are not used now.

References: Brandon, James. *Theatre in Southeast Asia.* Cambridge, MA: Harvard University Press, 1974; Brandon, James R. *Brandon's Guide to Theatre in Asia.* Honolulu: University Press of Hawaii, 1976; Hatley, Barbara. "Ketoprak: Performance and Social Meaning in a Javanese Popular Theatre Form." Ph.D. diss., University of Sydney, 1985; Hood, Mantle. "The Enduring Tradition: Music and Theatre in Java and Bali." In *Indonesia*, ed. Ruth McVey. New Haven, CT: Yale University Press, 1963.

Khoi
South Africa

Traditions of dance, mime, and narrative enactment dating back more than 6,000 years, performed by the nomadic San communities that travel throughout the vast areas of semidesert terrain in the Cape Province.

References: Banham, Martin. *African Theatre Today.* London: Pitman, 1976; Cornevin, Robert. *Le Theatre en Afrique Noire et a Madagascar.* Paris: Le Livre Africain, 1970; Larlham, Peter. *Black Theater, Dance, and Ritual in South Africa.* Ann Arbor, MI: Proquest, 1985.

Khon
Thailand

Masked dance-drama performed by men for the Thai court. *Khon* probably evolved from **Nang Yai,** a shadow play performance where dancers move in profile with large cutout shadow figures. There is a historical account of a birthday celebration given for King Rama Tibodi II in 1515. There dancers mimicked the sideways two-dimensional movements of Nang Yai performers. As Khon is performed today, two narrators seated to the side speak the narration and dialogue as actors pantomime the action. Actors perform powerful dances, especially in warrior scenes. The performance style is broad and masculine in nature. There are nightly stylized battles with a kind of acrobatic combat that ends in a group pose. Warriors proceed in a stately fashion onto the stage. All movement is formal and stylized. Performers used to wear heavy makeup, possibly inspired by the Indian **Kathakali** makeup. Then masks with headpieces that were gold and tiered to a high point were worn. In contemporary performance only demons and monkey characters wear masks. The repertory is drawn from the Thai version of the **Ramayana,** the **Ramakien.** Khon is very much like the Cambodian **Lakon Khol.** Presently women portray female characters and refined male characters, such as Rama and his brother, Laksamana. They do not wear masks. The soft elements of **Lakon Nai** have been added to Khon, smoothing its former rough masculine edge. Today only the Thai National Theatre knows how to perform Khon.

References: Brandon, James. *Theatre in Southeast Asia.* Cambridge, MA: Harvard University Press, 1974; Brandon, James R. *Brandon's Guide to Theatre in Asia.* Honolulu: University Press of Hawaii, 1976; Dhani Nivat, Prince. *The Khon.* Bangkok: Sivaporn, 1962; Redwood, John Elkert. "The Siamese Classical Theatre." *Educational Theatre Journal* 5 (1952): 100–105; Sariman, Chua. "Traditional Dance Drama in Thailand." In *Traditional Drama and Music of Southeast Asia,* ed. Mohd. Taib Osman, 165–171. Kuala Lumpur: Dewan Bahasa Dan Pustaka Kementerian Pelajaran Malaysia, 1974; Yupho, Dhanit. *Classical Siamese Theatre.* Trans. P. S. Sastri. Bangkok: Hatha Dhip, 1952; Yupho, Dhanit. *The Khon and Lakon.* Bangkok: Department of Fine Arts, 1963; Yupho, Dhanit. *Khon Masks.* Thai Culture, New Series. Bangkok: Fine Arts Department, 1968.

Kich Noi
See Thoai Kich

Kiyotsugu Kanami (1333–1384)
Japan

Earliest developer of **Noh** drama. Kanami lived from performing **Sarugaku,** a kind of variety show from the thirteenth century. As a performer he was exposed to the refined ways of the court in his mature life and tried to shape his art according to that aesthetic. Kanami introduced a strongly rhythmic dance known as **Kuse** to what was called Noh drama. Kanami's son, **Zeami Motokiyo,** continued the development of this new refined dance-drama and became a famous playwright, actor, and theorist.

References: Bowers, Faubion. *Japanese Theatre.* New York: Hill and Wang, 1964; Inoura, Yoshinobu, and Toshio Kawatake. *The Traditional Theater of Japan.* New York: Weatherhill in collaboration with Japan Foundation, 1981; Immoos, Thomas. *Japanese Theatre.* Trans. Hugh Young. Originally published as *Japanisches Theater.* New York: Rizzoli, 1977; Scott, A. C. *The Theatre in Asia.* New York: Macmillan, 1972; Waley, Arthur. *The No Plays of Japan.* London: Allen & Unwin, 1921. Reprint, London: Unwin Hyman, 1988.

Kkoktu Kaksi
Korea

Glove puppet theater, in which comedy is the primary focus. Only one puppeteer manipulates the puppets, one on each hand, with his arms raised over his head. He speaks for the lead character, and a speaker from the orchestra performs the voices for all of the minor characters. The simple stage is used to hide the puppeteer from the audience. The repertory is based on plays used for masked plays (see **Sandae**). The stories make fun of nobles, enact love games between young women and priests, and make fun of marital affairs. Plenty of bawdy pranks and physical humor are performed by the puppets to delight a rural audience. The musical accompaniment is provided by an oboe, drums, gong, and an instrument like a fiddle.

References: Brandon, James R. *Brandon's Guide to Theatre in Asia.* Honolulu: University Press of Hawaii, 1976.

Knipper, Olga (1870–1959)
Russia

Accomplished actress of the **Moscow Art Theater,** known for her masterly interpretations of **Anton**

Olga Knipper performing as Irina in Tolstoy's play Tsar Fedor Ioannovich (1898). Opposite Knipper is I. M. Moskvin, portraying Tsar Fedor. (Austrian Archives/Corbis)

Chekhov's female lead characters and also as his wife. She was an exemplary representative of **Stanislavsky**'s method of acting. She is said to have been an artist who labored over her preparations for a role, its outward manifestation, and each detail. She left Russia after the Revolution of 1917 and became the director of the Moscow Art Theater in Prague.

References: Chekhov, Anton. *Dear Writer, Dear Actress: The Love Letters of Anton Chekov and Olga Knipper.* Hopewell, NJ: Ecco, 1997; Maugd-Soep, Carolina. *Chekhov and Women:Women in the Life and Works of Chekhov.* Columbus, OH: Slavica, 1987; Pitcher, Harvey. *Chekhov's Leading Lady: A Portrait of the Actress Olga Knipper.* New York: F. Watts, 1980; Schuler, Catherine. *Women in Russian Theatre.* London: Routledge, 1996; Slonim, Marc. *Russian Theater, From the Empire to the Soviets.* Cleveland: World, 1961.

Kokata
Japan

Child role in **Noh,** masked dance-drama of medieval Japan. Only boys portray the **Kokata** role.

References: Inoura, Yoshinobu, and Toshio Kawatake. *The Traditional Theater of Japan.* New York: Weatherhill in collaboration with Japan Foundation, 1981; Scott, A. C. *The Theatre in Asia.* New York: Macmillan, 1972.

Koken
Japan

Stage manager role in **Noh,** masked dance-drama of medieval Japan. *Koken* brings on stools for characters to sit on and various properties that characters may need. He walks on in full view of the audience.

References: Immoos, Thomas. *Japanese Theatre.* Trans. Hugh Young. Originally published as *Japanisches Theater.* New York: Rizzoli, 1977.

Kolam
Sri Lanka

Masked folk drama from southern Sri Lanka. In Sinhalese, the word *Kolam* means comic disguise, so amusement is the primary function of this form. One of the *Kolam* plays tells the story of its origin: A Queen who was in the later stages of a pregnancy desired entertainment, so the King ordered a performance, which became known as *Kolam.* Because of this story dealing with pregnancy, it is suspected that *Kolam* may have evolved from ancient pregnancy ceremonies, such as **Rata Yakuma.**

All of the characters wear masks during the opening dances and incantations to the presiding deities. Musicians chant verses about the history of each character as he or she enters individually and performs a dance. Masks are not worn during the play that follows, to allow the actors greater freedom in speaking. The stories in the plays involve kings and queens, important people from the village, demons, and even animals. Performances usually occur outdoors in a clearing and continue from sundown to sunup.

References: Brandon, James. *The Cambridge Guide to Asian Theatre.* New York: Cambridge University Press, 1993; de Zoete, Beryl. *Dance and Magic Drama in Ceylon.* London: Faber & Faber, 1957; Gunawardana, A. J. *Theatre in Sri Lanka.* Colombo: Department of Cultural Affairs, Sri Lanka, 1976; Sarachchandra, Ediriweera R. *The Folk Drama of Ceylon.* 2d ed. Colombo: Department of Cultural Affairs, 1966.

Komali

India

Buffoon or clown character in **Terrukutta,** folk opera. This character has much freedom during a performance to yell at the audience and to ridicule kings and princes. He performs many impressive and comical physical stunts to amuse the audience.

> **References:** Gargi, Balawanta. *Folk Theater of India.* Seattle: University of Washington Press, 1966.

Komedie

See Sandiwara

Kommissarzhevskaya, Vera (1864–1910)

Russia

Russian actress who created symbolic and poetic works in the theater. She acted under **Stanislavsky**'s direction in 1891 and then toured with provincial companies, acted in comedies and performed in **vaudeville.** In 1896 she joined the company of the Alexandrinsky and excelled there for six years. Feeling stifled working under others, she opened her own theater, Kommissarzhevskaya Theater, in 1904 in Saint Petersburg. She hired **Vsevolod Meyerhold** as her director and acted the leading female role in many of his antirealistic productions. She played Melisande in *Pelléas and Melisande*, by Maurice Maeterlinck (1862–1949), and the title role in **Henrik Ibsen**'s *Hedda Gabler.* In her acting she portrayed a much larger hidden meaning within a play than was apparent in the lines, and she was known for her use of symbolist techniques. Trouble between her and Meyerhold grew because she believed actors were the true essence of the theater and he wanted actors to behave almost like marionettes. She asked him to leave, and soon after, in 1909, her theater closed.

She was physically small, frail, and somewhat unearthly, yet she had a powerful presence on the stage. Her low melodious voice entranced her audiences. She was particularly effective at portraying women in great distress. She was said by some to have always played herself, since her personal life was so tumultuous. Her personal instability led to uneven performing: Some nights she was filled with passion; other nights she was pale and listless. She toured the Americas and Russia for a brief time, then caught smallpox and died in 1910. Thousands attended her funeral in Saint Petersburg.

> **See also** Symbolism
>
> **References:** Gregor, Joseph. *The Russian Theatre: Its Character and History with Especial Reference to the Revolutionary Period.* Philadelphia: J. B. Lippincott, 1929; Schuler, Catherine. *Women in Russian Theatre.* London: Routledge, 1996; Slonim, Marc. *Russian Theater, From the Empire to the Soviets.* Cleveland: World, 1961.

Komos

Greece

Gay singing and dancing in honor of the Greek god **Dionysus.** First developed during the festival called the Rural Dionysia, the *Komos* later was performed during the evening on the first day of the Athenian festival called the **City Dionysia,** with the revelry carrying on late into the night. It is believed that **Greek Comedy** evolved from the *Komos,* since the word comedy means the song of the *Komasts,* the gay revelers. According to Aristotle, the *Komos* sang mocking songs abusing the unpopular important figures in a town, while also teasing and mocking the spectators. *Komasts* did not want to be recognized while doing this, so they wore masks to disguise themselves. Among the most popular types of masks were those resembling various animals, like those worn by the **Greek chorus** in many plays by **Aristophanes,** such as *The Birds* and *The Frogs.*

> **References:** Bieber, Margarete. *The History of the Greek and Roman Theater.* Princeton, NJ: Princeton University Press, 1961; Cornford, F. M. *The Origins of Attic Comedy.* London: Edward Arnold, 1914; Taylor, David. *Acting and the Stage.* Boston: George Allen & Unwin, 1978.

Koothambalams

India

Theater halls attached to Hindu temples for the presentations of live plays.

> **See also** *Koothu Madams*
>
> **References:** Awasthi, Suresh. "Shadow Plays of India and Their Affinities with the Shadow Plays of Southeast Asia." In *Traditional Drama and Music of Southeast Asia,* ed. Mohd. Taib Osman, 112–119. Kuala Lumpur: Dewan Bahasa Dan Pustaka Kementerian Pelajaran Malaysia, 1974.

Koothu Madams
India

Platform stage attached to a temple for presentation of shadow plays, such as **Tholu Bommalata, Tholu Pava Koothu, Mysore Shadow Puppet Theatre,** or Orissa Shadow Puppet Theatre, all rawhide shadow puppet plays.

> **See also** *Koothambalams*
> **References:** Awasthi, Suresh. "Shadow Plays of India and Their Affinities with the Shadow Plays of Southeast Asia." In *Traditional Drama and Music of Southeast Asia*, ed. Mohd. Taib Osman, 112–119. Kuala Lumpur: Dewan Bahasa Dan Pustaka Kementerian Pelajaran Malaysia, 1974.

Kora
Niger

Hausa religious ceremony in which performers become possessed by various spirits in order to expel evil spirits from the village. It occurs the last day before the Islamic month of fasting, Ramadan, which is a time when such non-Islamic ceremonies are forbidden. The event begins as the musicians, the initiates of the Bori spirit possession cult, and the spectators gather at the house of the head of the cult. Each initiate in turn becomes possessed by a particular spirit when the appropriate music for that spirit is played. At the start, initiates are costumed in a way appropriate to the spirits they anticipate becoming. Once possessed, performers dance, gesture, and move as the spirit demands. All involved move from place to place throughout the village, wherever an evil spirit dwells. At each location performers engage in a battle against the bad spirit, which usually resides in a rocky outcrop, using arrows and knives to drive the spirit away. At the final place a calf is sacrificed in private by the initiates. The performers, overcome by fatigue, need only cough three times for the benevolent spirits to know they should depart their beings. With the guarantee of a new peaceful year to come, all involved continue to celebrate and dance well into the night.

This tradition is being eliminated by Islam in most Hausa regions.

> **References:** Beik, Janet. *Hausa Theatre in Niger: A Contemporary Oral Art*. New York: Garland, 1987; Chaibou, Dan-Inna. "La Theatralite en Pays Hawsa." Université Nationale de Côte d'Ivoire, 1978–1979.

Kordax
Greece

Wild and licentious dance typical of ancient **Greek comedy** that featured whirling jumps and dancers clashing their buttocks together.

> **References:** Bieber, Margarete. *The History of the Greek and Roman Theater*. Princeton, NJ: Princeton University Press, 1961; Butler, James. *The Theatre and Drama of Greece and Rome*. San Francisco: Chandler, 1972; Sandbach, F. *The Comic Theatre of Greece and Rome*. New York: Norton, 1977.

Korea

Due to Korea's physical location, China has been influential on the style and content of Korea's cultural expression. Buddhist faith (see Buddhism) and a government modeled on Chinese Confucian systems have been in place in Korea for over a thousand years. Japan, a continual outside threat to Korea, finally colonized Korea in 1910, destroying much of the indigenous culture. When Japan surrendered in World War II, Korea was divided into two zones: The north became a Communist state aided by the former Soviet Union, and the south became a primarily agricultural republic, occupied until 1949 by the United States. After many attempts, the two halves of Korea are still not reunited.

In the seventeenth century a court entertainment called **Sandae** began to be presented at Buddhist celebrations. After the demise of court sponsorship for this all-male masked dance-drama, the form became much cruder and is now only performed by traveling troupes. Regional styles of *Sandae* include *Yangju Sandae* and *Pongsan Sandae*.

One folk art that has taken two different forms is based on a story called *Pansori*. The older form, also named *Pansori*, is a one-woman performance in which the performer sings, dances, and acts out all of the roles. *Changkuk* is a theatrical form that evolved from the former in the early part of the twentieth century, in which actors and actresses take on the roles in the story and enact the drama. A folk art in the form of glove puppet theater in Korea is **Kkoktu Kaksi.** Many humorous pranks and jokes are enacted by just one puppeteer, who manipulates all of the puppets.

Modern Korean drama, **Shingkuk,** started in 1908 with a group of Korean students studying in Japan. The plays they presented grew in seriousness as the audience support for such a form increased. The city of Seoul is presently the center for experimental and quality theater in Korea. The Korean theater enjoys generous governmental support.

> **References:** Hur, Soon-Ja. "The Development of Professional Resident Theatre Companies in South Korea from the Conclusion of the Korean War." Ph.D. diss., Ann Arbor, MI: Proquest, 1991; Lee, Duhyun. *Pongsan Mask Dance-Drama: Korean Pongsan Mask Dance: Drama Troupe.* Seoul: Korean Culture and Arts Foundation, 1983; Shim, Jung Soon. "Trends in Contemporary Culture: In Search of Diversity—Korean Theatre in the 1980's." *Korean Culture (Hanguk Munhwa)* 12, 3 (Fall 1991): 4; Van Leest, Hyung-a-Kim. "Political Satire in Yangja Pyolsandae Mask Drama." *Korea Journal* 31, 1 (Spring 1991): 87.

Koutsai Hsi
Taiwan

Taiwanese opera, a regional form of Chinese opera that originated in southern Fujian Province and was introduced to Taiwan in 1662. Basic stage conventions for *Koutsai Hsi*, such as costumes, makeup, movement, musical accompaniment, and acting style, were adapted from the Peking Opera. The style of singing in *Koutsai Hsi*, which literally means "the drama of songs," is adapted from Taiwanese ballad singers. Singing patterns unique to Taiwan, known as the "Wailing Tune" and "Seven-Word Tune," characterize the musical element in *Koutsai Hsi*. After having been suppressed by the Japanese during their occupation of Taiwan until the 1940s, *Gozai Xi* is now the most popular form of theatrical entertainment in Taiwan.

> **References:** Brandon, James. *The Cambridge Guide to Asian Theatre.* New York: Cambridge University Press, 1993.

Krio Theater
Sierra Leone

Popular urban theater performed in Krio, the lingua franca of Sierra Leone, based on English, which developed out of the interaction between freed slaves, Europeans, and the indigenous people all settled around the capital city, Free-town. Thomas Decker is credited with pioneering Krio theater through his promotion of Krio in literary works. Recognition was given to his efforts with the success of his translation of **Shakespeare**'s *Julius Caesar* into Krio in 1964. Julian John developed Krio theater further by writing original works in Krio that integrated song and dance.

It is primarily a working class theater: The characters in Krio dramas are drawn from the lower classes, and issues pertinent to working people are explored. Dole Charley's Krio play, *Fatmata*, 1977, introduced a new style of Krio theater, in which a narrator and chorus performed the story through song and narration, while actors dramatized the story nonverbally through dance and gesture.

> **References:** Abraham, Arthur. *Cultural Policy in Sierra Leone.* Paris: UNESCO, 1978; Akar, John. "The Arts in Sierra Leone." *Africa Forum* (Fall 1965): 87–91; Banham, Martin. *African Theatre Today.* London: Pitman, 1976.

Krishna
India

The eighth and most important incarnation of the Hindu god Vishnu. The most human of the Hindu pantheon, Krishna is a lover, a statesman, and a yogi. Tales of his youth include numerous naughty pranks, such as stealing butter and flirting with the milkmaids to keep them from their work. He is a playful and sensual god who is portrayed in all accounts as being irresistible to women. The female devotee's desire for Krishna is generally interpreted as an allegory of the soul's longing for union with the divine.

A surge of Krishna worship occurred all over India in the fourteenth and sixteenth centuries, which inspired many new forms of dance and drama such as **Krishna Parijat,** folk theater, and **Krishnattam,** dance-drama.

Krishna cult devotees think of Krishna as synonymous with Vishnu and refer to him as Vishnu-Krishna. In the Hindu epic tale the **Mahabharata,** Krishna is an older philosopher and statesman who sides with the good Pandava brothers. His philosophical discourse on the battlefield, in which he explains the need to act without attachment to the results of the action, is

The Indian god Krishna dances with the lotus flower in the rain while accompanied by three female musicians in this seventeenth-century depiction. (*The Art Archive/Marco Polo Gallery Paris/Dagli Orti*)

often published separately from the rest of the epic, and is known as the Bhagavad Gita (literally, the Song of the Blessed Lord), one of the most revered Hindu texts.

See also Shiva

References: Brandon, James R. *Brandon's Guide to Theatre in Asia.* Honolulu: University Press of Hawaii, 1976; Byrski, Maria Christopher. *Concepts of Ancient Indian Theatre.* New Delhi: Munshiram Manoharlal, 1974; Varadpande, Manohar Laxman, and Sunil Subhedar, eds. *The Critique of Indian Theatre.* Atlantic Highlands, NJ: Humanities Press, 1982; Varadpande, Manohar Laxman. *Krishna Theatre in India.* New Delhi: Abhinav, 1982.

Krishna Parijat
India

Folk theater based on the life of Krishna, the eighth and most important incarnation of the Hindu god **Vishnu,** from the early nineteenth century in northern Karnataka. This form of theater tells the story *Parijat Harana,* which includes the conflict of Krishna when caught between two jealous wives fighting for the *Parijat* flower. There is much humor in these performances. Women portray female characters instead of the young boys who so often play these roles in other forms of Indian theater. Performers wear ordinary street clothing for costumes.

References: Varadpande, Manohar Laxman. *Krishna Theatre in India.* New Delhi: Abhinav, 1982.

Krishnattam
India

The story of Krishna, the eighth and most important incarnation of the Hindu god **Vishnu,** performed in the tradition of **Kathakali,** Indian dance-drama. From Kerala and performed mostly on religious holidays, this form takes eight nights to perform. Actors perform the cycle of eight Krishna plays, which starts with the birth of Krishna. This cycle was first written by a Zamorin king named Manaveda in the seventeenth century in the classical Sanskrit language. Almost all theatrical elements are similar to those in *Kathakali,* including setting, costumes, music, and performance style.

Since Krishna is viewed as refined and alluring, this dance-drama is also refined and romantic in style. There are no clowns or jesters. Drumming announces that a performance is about to begin. All dialogue and song is performed by a chorus seated on the side of the stage. The actors on the stage enact through dance the lines sung by the chorus. This allows the actors to concentrate on their dancing. The vigorous style of dance is too demanding to allow a performer to also deliver lines and sing. Dance scenes include choreographed battles and scenes of Krishna dancing with the **Gopis,** milkmaids. A favorite dance involves Krishna dancing on the hood of a serpent to pacify him with the rhythm of his feet. This dance includes many swift turns, whirls, and jumps.

The setting for the drama is a Hindu temple. Some characters wear painted masks and others wear elaborate makeup. Chutti is a rice paste applied to the chin and cheeks of an actor in successive circular flat layers. It is complemented by red, black, or white makeup designs on the face of the actor. For costumes men wear full ankle-length skirts and high crowns. The female *Gopis* wear saris, white makeup, and long flowing cloth on their heads. There is much gold embellishment on all of the costumes. The crown for the actor playing Krishna has a peacock feather. The only stage properties are a few wooden stools. Two large oil lamps made of brass light the acting area. Performances are generally held in the courtyard of the temple or an a stage constructed outside the temple for non-Hindus to view the performance.

A handsome boy who lives in the temple is called upon to portray Krishna. To purify themselves, actors fast for a day before performing. Some devoted audience members do the same.

References: Brandon, James R. *Brandon's Guide to Theatre in Asia.* Honolulu: University Press of Hawaii, 1976; Varadpande, Manohar Laxman. *Krishna Theatre in India.* New Delhi: Abhinav, 1982.

Kuchipudi
India

Dance-drama named after the village in Andra Pradesh from which it came. *Kuchipudi* evolved during the fourteenth and sixteenth centuries during a time when worship of **Krishna,** the eighth and most important incarnation of the Hindu god Vishnu, was increasing. Brahman boys of Kuchipudi were the first performers of this form. Even today it is still expected of these boys to perform *Kuchipudi* as a sort of offering to Krishna. Formerly the performers were all male; only recently have women become important as performers. Robustly performed, *Kuchipudi* is a synthesis of singing, drama, and complicated rhythmic dancing. Sensual longing and religious devotion are combined in *Kuchipudi* by portraying passionate longing for Krishna by female devotees. Physical union between man and woman is seen as a near perfect metaphor for union with the divine.

A performance is led by one or two *Sutradhara,* narrators, who comment on the story, describe scenes, and introduce characters before they enter. They also double as comedians, who humorously comment on the action. In some cases, a pair of dancers perform together, and in others *Kuchipudi* is performed as a solo dance. A dancer-actor must be able to perform dialogue, sing, and dance with equal skill. The main emphasis of the dancing is footwork that is incredibly fast and rhythmically exacting. There are dance sections of both *Nritya,* which is the expression of sentiment or mood through movement, and *Nritta,* which is nonnarrative, pure dance that is a direct response to rhythm and music. The style of dance is often compared to *Bharata Natyam,* classical Indian female temple dance, but the style of *Kuchipudi* is much more sensual and supple. *Kuchipudi* also has a vigor of motion and an exaggeration of technique, which was probably a result of the early and long-standing influence of Kuchipudi male dancers.

Performances begin with worship of Ganesha, the elephant-headed Hindu god, after which the *Sutradhara* sings invocations to a host of Hindu gods. When the main characters enter and dance for their first time, the *Sutradhara* sings about their background, function, and role in the story. Main characters enter from behind a curtain held up by two people, which they dramatically clutch, peek over, and dance behind. This device creates great suspense, as actors play a sort of peekaboo to entice the audience.

Male actors who portray female characters are beautifully dressed in saris with black makeup to enhance their eyes and eyebrows. Accessorized with gold jewelry, they appear quite realistically to be attractive females. Stories for performances are usually about Satyabhama, wife of Krishna, who is jealous of another woman's love for Krishna. Stories are delivered through song, dialogue, and narration. The musical accompaniment is performed in syncopated rhythms that match and accent the complicated footwork of the dancer's stamping.

There is an interesting dance in which a dancer balances on the edge of a round brass bowl with his feet while also balancing a full pot of water on his head. While singing a song, he skillfully turns in circles without spilling any water.

Training usually begins at the age of seven and continues for several years. Presently only a few Kuchipudi troupes still perform in India.

References: Brandon, James R. *Brandon's Guide to Theatre in Asia.* Honolulu: University Press of Hawaii, 1976; Gargi, Balawanta. *Theatre in India.* New York: Theatre Arts, 1962; Massey, Reginald, and Jamie Massey. *Dances of India.* London: Tricolour, 1989; Samson, Leela. *Rhythm in Joy.* New Delhi: Lustre Press, 1987; Varadpande, Manohar Laxman. *Krishna Theatre in India.* New Delhi: Abhinav, 1982.

Kudiyattam
India

Ancient style of presenting Sanskrit plays (see **Sanskrit Drama**), from Kerala State in the south of India, by temple performers who claim their lineage goes back to Sutra, the narrator of the Hindu epic tale, the **Mahabharata.** Classical Sanskrit plays are recited by actors who interpret and enhance the meaning of each line using elaborate gestures and facial expressions. One line of verse can take twenty minutes to convey. Actors often sit for hours as they perform. A single act from a play can take several days to perform. The audience is quite sophisticated, since they must understand Sanskrit and be attentive to subtle interpretations of the classics. *Kudiyattam* was replaced almost completely by **Kathakali,** a form of dance-drama, in the eighteenth century.

Performances take place near temples. Oil lamps placed between the actors and the audience illuminate the performing area. Performers wear elaborate costumes. Hypnotic and repetitive music is performed by oboes and huge clay-pot drums. *Kudiyattam* is rarely performed today, and there are only a few actors still alive who know this tradition.

References: Brandon, James R. *Brandon's Guide to Theatre in Asia.* Honolulu: University Press of Hawaii, 1976; Scott, A. C. *The Theatre in Asia.* New York: Macmillan, 1972; Varadpande, Manohar Laxman. *Krishna Theatre in India.* New Delhi: Abhinav, 1982; Vatsyayan, Kapila. *Traditional Indian Theatre: Multiple Streams.* New Delhi: National Book Trust, 1980.

Kun Chu
China

Classical southern Chinese drama. These plays are over forty acts long and take days to perform. Over a thousand plays survive today. A minor character starts a performance with a synopsis of the play. Unlike **Yuan drama**, in which only one actor can sing, Kun Chu allows any of the actors in it to sing. A bamboo flute accompanies soft melodies sung in a gentle style. The rhyming scheme changes throughout the play. The language is refined and poetic, making Kun Chu an entertainment for the elite classes. Historically, Kun Chu has been the entertainment for the upper class and **Peking Opera** for the middle and lower class. It is still performed today but is much less popular than Peking Opera.

Kunqu
See Kun Chu

Kurosawa, Akira (1910–1998)
Japan

Japanese film director. Kurosawa is a director with great stylistic imagination. He is more well known in the West than any other Japanese director and was greatly influenced by Western films. His **samurai** warrior films are closely related to American Westerns. Characters in his films often represent types that demonstrate something about the human race rather than the psychology of any one person. He attempts to convey a philosophical view on the human condition. He is the only leading Japanese director to create effective films in both the **Jidai-geki,** period films set in Japan's past, and **Gendai-geki,** films based on modern life. In 1951 he won the Grand Prize at the Venice Film Festival for *Rashomon.* Other important films by Kurosawa include *Seven Samurai* (1954), *Yojimbo* (1961), *The Lower Depths* (1957), *Throne of Blood* (1957), *Dodes Ka-den* (1970), *Dersu Uzala* (1975), *Kagemusha* (1980), and *Dreams* (1990).

References: Bock, Audie. *Japanese Film Directors.* New York: Kodansha International, 1978; Mast, Gerald. *A Short History of the Movies.* 4th ed. New York: Macmillan, 1986.

Kuse
Japan

Strongly rhythmic dance from medieval Japan. *Kuse* had an influence on the development of **Noh,** masked dance-drama form.

References: Immoos, Thomas. *Japanese Theatre.* Trans. Hugh Young. Originally published as *Japanisches Theater.* New York: Rizzoli, 1977; Ortolani, Benito. *The Japanese Theatre: From Shamanistic Ritual to Contemporary Pluralism.* New York: E. J. Brill, 1990; Scott, A. C. *The Theatre in Asia.* New York: Macmillan, 1972.

Kutiyattam
See Kudiyattam

Kwagh-hir
Nigeria

Puppet show performed by the Tiv people in Benue state. This lively contemporary form has established roots in the Tivland culture. Competitions between different puppet troupes of the villages still entertain rural audiences, who gather to witness the highly complex and animated puppets. The playlets performed depict modern life in Tivland and frequently use biting satire to criticize various social customs. Each troupe has a chorus of female singers and a sizable traditional orchestra accompanying their performances.

References: Banham, Martin. *African Theatre Today.* London: Pitman, 1976; Ekwuema, Lazarus E. N. "Nigerian Performing Arts, Past, Present and Future, with Particular Reference to Igbo Practice." *Presence Africaine* 92, 2 (1975): 195–213.

Kwakiutl Mystery Play
Canada

A Native American mystery play performed by the Kwakiutl; one of the most spectacular ceremonies in the world, involving a multitude of special effects. In the Cannibal Spirit performance the story dramatized is of a hero who kills the Cannibal's three great bird spirits, the Raven, the Hohok, and the Crooked Beak, and, finally, the Cannibal. The hero returns to the village acting as though he is possessed by the Cannibal spirit. Armed with masks, whistles, and other things obtained in the wild, he bursts into the longhouse, biting at anyone who comes too close. Frenzied, he hops about in a crouching posture. Assistants have to restrain him with ropes as he proceeds to dance four times around the fire. He then runs behind a screen, changes his mask, and reappears to dance around the fire as the Raven. He does this sequence with each of the birds and finally once more with the Cannibal.

Performers are supposed to be possessed by a spirit when performing, but to maintain awareness of their surroundings and their task at hand. Within these performances, outstandingly advanced and creative special effects are employed. Actors in a fight scene conceal animal bladders filled with blood that are burst by an opponent's blade at just the right moment, accented by horrific screams of pain. Quartz crystals are used to refract light beautifully within the longhouse. Puppets, sometimes manipulated by strings, are used in many varieties.

One of the deeper meanings beneath this performance is the view of reality and illusion as being a paradox, an examination of how all human beings perform behind a variety of masks everyday.

See also Nootka Mystery Play

References: Buller, Edward. *Indigenous Performing and Ceremonial Arts in Canada: An Annotated Bibliography of Canadian Indian Rituals and Ceremonies.* Toronto: Association for Native Development in the Performing and Visual Arts, 1981; Drucker, Philip. *Kwakiutl Dancing Societies.* Berkeley: University of California Press, 1940; Wagner, Anton. *Contemporary Canadian Theatre: New World Visions.* Toronto: Simon & Pierre, 1986.

Kwangtung Hsi
China and Hong Kong

Traditional Chinese opera sung in the southern Chinese dialect Cantonese; also called Cantonese Opera. Using basically the same theatrical conventions as **Peking Opera,** this form is a beautiful combination of singing with stylized movements and gestures. This form was often performed in the south of China before the Communist Revolution and is currently presented often in Hong Kong.

The acting style in *Kwangtung Hsi* is slightly more toned down than it is in Peking Opera, and there are no acrobatic stunts. Sets are usually a series of three-dimensional painted drops or pieces of scenery. The costumes are ornate, with glittering trim and large headdresses. The makeup conventions are the same as Peking Opera. Rather than strong and strident, as in Peking Opera, the music in *Kwangtung Hsi* is soft and has popular appeal.

References: Brandon, James R. *Brandon's Guide to Theatre in Asia.* Honolulu: University Press of Hawaii, 1976; Howard, Roger. *Contemporary Chinese Theatre.* Hong Kong: Heinemann, 1978; Scott, A. C. *The Theatre in Asia.* New York: Macmillan, 1972.

Kyogen
Japan

A comic interlude between each of the five types of plays performed during an evening of **Noh,** masked dance-drama of medieval Japan; literally means "mad words." *Kyogen* plays provide comic relief from the serious plays of the Noh program. A *Kyogen* is always based on an inconsequential incident, such as a servant trying to steal wine from a slow-witted master. These plays are so popular that there are presently troupes that perform only *Kyogen* plays.

References: Scott, A. C. *The Theatre in Asia.* New York: Macmillan, 1972.

Kyrgyzstan

See Soviet Cinema; Soviet Union

L

Lakon Bassak
Cambodia

Popular dance-drama form, literally "Theater of the Bassak." This form was created in the early part of the twentieth century by Cambodian performers living in Southern Vietnam near the Bassak River. There are both Cambodian and Vietnamese performance elements present in a performance. However, the two influences remain separate, with one following the other rather than the two being blended together to create one new style. There are influences from **Peking Opera** and Cambodian dance. The dance in this form evolved from **Lakon Kbach Boran,** a court performance, but was changed to suit the middle- and lower-class audience for the *Lakon Bassak.* The costumes are a mix of Cambodian and Vietnamese traditions. The clown characters wear a white butterfly patch on their faces as they do in Vietnam. The formal wear for princes and princesses is based on Cambodian court costumes. The repertory is drawn from the **Jataka,** tales of former births of Gautama **Buddha,** and local legends. The musical accompaniment is provided by a traditional orchestra, **Pin Peat.** There are also songs accompanied by Vietnamese-style strings and cymbals. Many professional troupes perform in Phnom Penh, Battambang, and other provincial towns.

References: Brandon, James. *Theatre in Southeast Asia.* Cambridge, MA: Harvard University Press, 1974; Brandon, James R. *Brandon's Guide to Theatre in Asia.* Honolulu: University Press of Hawaii, 1976; Groslier, George. "Royal Dancers of Cambodia." *Asia* 22, 1 (1922): 47–53, 74.

Lakon Jatri
Thailand

Southern Thai dance-drama enacting **Manora,** a story from the **Jataka,** stories of former births of Gautama **Buddha.** It is the oldest known form of Thai dance-drama. It started as a dance form greatly influenced by Indian classical dance and later was changed to enact some stories from **Buddhism.** There are some very unusual Indian dance movements found in this style, such as a backbend where the dancer's head appears between the legs, which are a remnant of the style of Thai dancing before it was refined by court influence. The *Manora* story, about a mythical bird-princess, can be performed over the span of many nights. Traditional performances would have three male performers who acted and sang. One man played the male hero parts. The second played all the female parts. The third played the animal and clown, usually wearing a mask as the clown. Performers must be able to dance gracefully, sing, act, mime, and deliver dialogue. The long solo dances are quite refined and graceful. Musical accompaniment is provided by a flute, drums, and cymbal. This form is very similar to the Malaysian

Manora. The traditional format is no longer followed. Performances are more like variety shows today. Women are often cast in female roles now and sometimes even play the refined male hero role.

References: Brandon, James R. *Brandon's Guide to Theatre in Asia*. Honolulu: University Press of Hawaii, 1976; Brandon, James. *Theatre in Southeast Asia*. Cambridge, MA: Harvard University Press, 1974; Sariman, Chua. "Traditional Dance Drama in Thailand." In *Traditional Drama and Music of Southeast Asia*, ed. Mohd. Taib Osman, 165–171. Kuala Lumpur: Dewan Bahasa Dan Pustaka Kementerian Pelajaran Malaysia, 1974; Yupho, Dhanit. *The Khon and Lakon*. Bangkok: Department of Fine Arts, 1963.

Lakon Kbach Boran
Cambodia

Classical dance-drama performed mostly by women. The earliest mention of classical dance performance in Cambodia appeared in the seventh century in a Sanskrit inscription. The Khmer empire (802–1431) ruled over a great part of Southeast Asia. Their court performers developed performance forms of exquisite purity and sensuality during this time. The style was very sensual during Khmere rule, complete with swinging hips and bare breasts. The Thai invasion ended the Khmere empire. *Lakon Kbach Boran* was stolen by the Thai invaders and changed to suit the tastes of the court in Thailand. This form was later reintroduced to Cambodia from Thailand.

In *Lakon Kbach Boran*, long dramatic episodes are interspersed with nondramatic group dances. Women portray hero roles, princes and princesses, and demons. Men portray old man roles and clowns. Boys portray monkeys. There are two types of dance. In the narrative dancing, performers pantomime the meaning of the song lyrics. The second type consists of patterns of nonnarrative dance. The feet gently touch the floor in continuous patterns that flow effortlessly from one pose to another. There are seven basic hand positions, which are modified from Indian dance (see **Bharata Natyam**). The rowdy pranks of the clown characters provide a great contrast to the grace and composure of the female performers.

Costumes include headdresses adorned with flowers, elaborate jewelry around the neck and wrists, and a snug silk bodice with a pleated skirt. Some Thai influence is evident in the addition of tall tiered crowns, epaulettes at the shoulder, and metallic embroidered cloth. Performers used to wear white makeup to hide facial expressions, but now natural makeup is worn. The repertory is drawn from the **Ramayana, Panji tales** (or **Inao** tales), the legend of the Prince of the Golden Sea Shell, and other tales. Musical accompaniment is a traditional **Pin Peat** orchestra. The National Khmer Classical Ballet Troupe, managed by the University of Fine Arts in Phnom Penh, is the only group able to perform this form now. However, their style is a Thai creation based on the former Khmer style, not the original.

References: Brandon, James. *Theatre in Southeast Asia*. Cambridge, MA: Harvard University Press, 1974; Brandon, James R. *Brandon's Guide to Theatre in Asia*. Honolulu: University Press of Hawaii, 1976; Groslier, George. "Royal Dancers of Cambodia." *Asia* 22, 1 (1922): 47–53, 74; Meyer, Charles. "Cambodian Dances." *Nokor Khmer* 3 (1970): 2–27.

Lakon Khol
Cambodia

Masked dance-drama performed by men. This was originally a court dance-drama and enjoyed the patronage of the king. However, this support was halted abruptly in the late nineteenth century when a leading performer kicked one of the king's wives in anger. Performers of this form were stolen during the Thai invasion and brought to Thailand to entertain the court. The Thai **Khon** form probably developed from this. This form was later reintroduced into Cambodia. This highly ceremonial form has a robust and vigorous dance and acting style. Two narrators sit with the orchestra and chant the dialogue and verses. There are no actual songs. The repertory is drawn from the **Ramayana,** especially the episodes of Sita's kidnapping and the final battle scene. Musical accompaniment is provided by a traditional **Pin Peat** orchestra. As recently as the 1970s there were two troupes reported to be performing, one at the Wat Sway temple near Phnom Penh, and another at Battambang.

References: Brandon, James. *Theatre in Southeast Asia*. Cambridge, MA: Harvard University Press, 1974; Brandon, James R. *Brandon's Guide to Theatre in Asia*. Honolulu: University Press of Hawaii,

1976; Groslier, George. "Royal Dancers of Cambodia." *Asia* 22, 1 (1922): 47–53, 74; Meyer, Charles. "Cambodian Dances." Nokor *Khmer* 3 (1970): 2–27.

Lakon Nai
Thailand

Court dance-drama performed by women. Thai classical dance is basically an adaptation of Cambodian court dances. *Lakon Nai* dates back to the fourteenth century, when the Thai army invaded Angkor in Cambodia and captured Cambodian musicians and dancers from their court. The first female performers were part of the Thai king's private harem. Only special guests of the king could see them perform. There are no male performers, since members of the harem could not be left alone with young men to rehearse. A chorus of women sing verses from a seated position while others dance to the music. Performers speak their own dialogue while on stage. Women perform both male and female roles. The dance is made up of synchronized movement in choreographed patterns. Small steps and graceful arm gestures flow elegantly from one pose to another. The facial expression of the dancers is set in a welcoming smile. The type of robust, less refined movement used in **Lakon Nok** was replaced with a slower, more elegant style of dance to suit the tastes of the court.

Lakon Nai evolved to the point where women were enacting dramas of significant magnitude and complexity using a sort of alphabet or language of dance. Gestures and movements are used as symbols to communicate complex emotions and actions. Costumes consist of high gold tiered headpieces, bare feet, wristbands of gold, and sleeveless fitted dresses of crisscrossing fabric with a front pleated sarong-type skirt. The most popular story used for the repertory are the **Inao** tales, which is the Thai term for the **Panji tales.** A highly regarded written version of the Panji tales was composed by King Rama II (1809–1824) expressly for *Lakon Nai*. The musical accompaniment is called **Pin Peat.** This ensemble is made up of bamboo xylophones, bronze bowls, oboe, cymbals, and drums.

Lakon Nai is very much like the Cambodian **Lakon Kbach Boran** in its movement style, musical accompaniment, and costuming.

References: Brandon, James. *Theatre in Southeast Asia.* Cambridge, MA: Harvard University Press, 1974; Brandon, James R. *Brandon's Guide to Theatre in Asia.* Honolulu: University Press of Hawaii, 1976; Sariman, Chua. "Traditional Dance Drama in Thailand." In *Traditional Drama and Music of Southeast Asia,* ed. Mohd. Taib Osman, 165–171. Kuala Lumpur: Dewan Bahasa Dan Pustaka Kementerian Pelajaran Malaysia, 1974; Redwood, John Elkert. "The Siamese Classical Theatre." *Educational Theatre Journal* 5 (1952): 100–105; Yupho, Dhanit. *Classical Siamese Theatre.* Trans. P. S. Sastri. Bangkok: Hatha Dhip, 1952.

Lakon Nok
Thailand

Popular drama from the South; name literally means "drama from Southern Provinces." This form evolved from **Lakon Jatri,** the oldest known form of Thai dance-drama. Long pure dance numbers were taken out. Dance was only used in dramatic action for *Lakon Nok.* The intent of performances was no longer religious. These changes occurred because popular audiences wanted quick action, accessible language, plenty of comedy, and no more long dance sequences. The upper class enjoyed this form as well as the lower classes. In the nineteenth and twentieth centuries many plays were written by members of the royal family, including King Rama II, who wrote plays in the early 1800s. The repertory consisted of local legends and **Jataka** stories, tales of former births of Gautama **Buddha.** The musical accompaniment is similar to that used for Lakon Jatri, but melodic instruments were added. Many professional troupes performed until World War II, when this form died out. There are no troupes performing today.

References: Brandon, James. *Theatre in Southeast Asia.* Cambridge, MA: Harvard University Press, 1974; Brandon, James R. *Brandon's Guide to Theatre in Asia.* Honolulu: University Press of Hawaii, 1976; Sariman, Chua. "Traditional Dance Drama in Thailand." In *Traditional Drama and Music of Southeast Asia,* ed. Mohd. Taib Osman, 165–171. Kuala Lumpur: Dewan Bahasa Dan Pustaka Kementerian Pelajaran Malaysia, 1974; Redwood, John Elkert. "The Siamese Classical Theatre." *Educational Theatre Journal* 5 (1952): 100–105; Yupho, Dhanit. *Classical Siamese Theatre.* Trans. P. S. Sastri. Bangkok: Hatha Dhip, 1952.

Langren Ju

Taiwan

Modern theater in Taiwan seems to have begun in 1911, when a Japanese director recruited local actors to stage several productions. Since the actors he attracted also had rough reputations as thieves and scallions, this form was called *Langren Ju*, literally "Ruffian Drama." This initial effort inspired local drama troupes to produce Chinese and Taiwanese dramas on an amateur basis.

When the Republic of China government fled to Taiwan in 1949 during the Communist takeover in mainland China, many theatrical artists, including actors, playwrights, and directors, went with them. This influx of trained professionals who had performed **Hua Chü,** spoken Chinese drama, on the mainland, gave new energy to the modern drama being presented in Taiwan.

> References: Brandon, James. *The Cambridge Guide to Asian Theatre.* New York: Cambridge University Press, 1993; Scott, A. C. *The Theatre in Asia.* New York: Macmillan, 1972.

Lao

China

Old man character type in **Peking Opera,** a subcategory of **Sheng,** the category of male characters in Peking Opera.

Laos

The performing arts of Laos have been strongly influenced by Thai and Cambodian forms. An almost completely Buddhist nation (see **Buddhism**), Laos is made up of the Thai-speaking Lao people, the Hmong, and other tribes. Laos was predominantly ruled by its more powerful neighbors, Thailand and Vietnam, until 1893, when France claimed it as a protectorate. After being occupied by the Japanese during World War II, Laos gained autonomy and is now a Communist state.

Other than less elaborate copies of Thai and Cambodian classical dance, the main theatrical activity in Laos is a popular style of comic opera known as **Mohlam Luong** (or *Mohlam Mu*). Comic characters shine in their amazing physical pranks, in performances characterized by an otherwise somewhat amateurish style. **Mohlam** is a lively style of folk singing performed by traveling troupes, who belt out racy songs about romance and love. This form heavily influenced the musical style in *Mohlam Luong*.

> References: Bachfield, August. "Theatre in Siam." *Erdball* 2 (1928): 335–377; Brandon, James R. *Brandon's Guide to Theatre in Asia.* Honolulu: University Press of Hawaii, 1976; Sariman, Chua. "Traditional Dance Drama in Thailand." In *Traditional Drama and Music of Southeast Asia*, ed. Mohd. Taib Osman, 165–171. Kuala Lumpur: Dewan Bahasa Dan Pustaka Kementerian Pelajaran Malaysia, 1974; Yousof, Ghulam-Sarwar. *Southeast Asian Traditional Performing Arts: A Preliminary Bibliography.* Penang, Malaysia: Southeast Asian Studies Program, 1990.

Latin American Cinema

Cinema in Latin America has greatly shaped popular culture in the many countries making up this diverse region. From political propaganda to diverting comic skits, Latin American films have been continuously produced since the 1920s. Because of censorship and oppressive governments, many of the most artful Latin American films have been more popular in foreign lands, namely Europe and the **United States.**

From the inception of film in Latin America, imported products from the United States and Europe have dominated the market, taking up 90 to 95 percent of the screen time. Even those films made in Latin America often mimicked their foreign competition. In Brazil some filmmakers who were making Westerns used an Anglo-Saxon pseudonym. However, even in the silent-film era, an indigenous film culture began to develop, to the extent that in Mexico silent-film actresses became national icons. Into the 1920s and 1930s many documentary films were produced and even censored because of their powerful, often critical content. Working-class culture was often a theme of silent films, such as with the Argentine film *La Muchacha de Arrabal* (Neighborhood Girl) in 1922.

With the advent of sound films in the early 1930s, a tradition of imported U.S. culture gained a stranglehold throughout much of Latin America. Domestic films that were nevertheless popular often contained some specific regional element that had widespread appeal, such as tango, a popular musical genre. The Argentine star Carlos Gardel (1887–1935) made several tango movies

Carlos Gardel in the film Big Broadcast of 1936 (1935). (*Kobol Collection/Paramount*)

before continuing his career in Europe. In 1935 the golden age of Mexican cinema began, due in part to state support of studios. Throughout the 1940s a studio system flourished, along with its major stars, such as Maria Félix (1906–1983), Pedro Armendáriz, and Dolores Del Rio (1906–1983), and even **Cantinflas,** the popular theater entertainer who moved to film. In Brazil a popular musical film style developed known as *Chanchadas.* An example of this is *Moleque Tião* (Kid Tião), 1943, which featured the great black comedian and actor Grande Otelo.

Throughout the 1950s studio-produced films decreased in both number and quality generally throughout Latin America. The Cinema Novo (New Cinema), a film movement in Brazil begun in the late 1950s, is synonymous with modern Brazilian cinema. A movement known as Nuevo Cine (New Cinema), named after a film festival in Chile in 1967, began in an attempt to fill the void left by the decline of studio films. Attempting to create a "cultured cinema," these artists created

films that combined indigenous themes with a personal style, such as the Brazilian *O Pagador de Promessas* (The Given Word), 1962, the Argentinean *Paula la Cautiva* (The Captive Paula), 1963, and the Mexican *Tiempo de Morir* (A Time to Die), 1965. The acting style was often a documentary-like realism, which attempted to communicate long-hidden social realities. These filmmakers were greatly influenced by **Italian neorealism.** Some directors, such as the Brazilian Glauber Rocha, the Argentinean Fernando Solanas, and Octavio Getino, Cuban Julio Garcia Espinosa, and Bolivian Jorge Sanjiés, took this social goal even farther and aimed to provoke a heightened political awareness. Their films, however, were celebrated mostly at international film festivals and not in their home countries because of political suppression.

In the 1970s the governments in many Latin American countries encouraged a quality film industry, with the strongest residing in Cuba. Directly after the Cuban Revolution in 1959 Fidel

Castro declared cinema the most important socially useful art, which simultaneously encouraged and controlled film. The Cuban government created the Institute of Cinematic Art and Industry (ICAIC), to which many leftist Latin American filmmakers fled to escape persecution in their home countries. In 1979 an annual Festival of New Latin American Cinema was begun in Cuba as a showcase and marketplace for Latin American films. The Cuban situation has suffered in recent years, due to the collapse of its socialist allies.

Brazilian commercial film production from the 1970s tended to put out films featuring raucous and rowdy performances of slapstick comedy and a *Pornochanchada*, a pornographic version of the earlier form *Chanchada*, slap-stick comedy. Economic hard times adversely affected the film market throughout Latin America in the late 1980s, although many filmmakers stand out as having created quality work, filmmakers such as Brazilian Ruy Guerra and Argentine Fernando Solanas. Many female directors also succeeded during these hard times, Brazilian Suzana Amaral, Argentine María Luisa Bemberg, and Mexican María Novaro. In recent times, the advent of affordable video equipment has converted some filmmakers to video productions instead.

References: Armes, Roy. *Third World Film Making and the West*. Berkeley: University of California Press, 1987; Burns, Bradford E. *Latin American Cinema: Film and History*. Los Angeles: UCLA Latin American Center, 1975; Burton, Julianne. *Cinema and Social Change in Latin America: Conversations with Filmmakers*. Austin: University of Texas Press, 1986; Chanan, Michael. *Chilean Film*. London: British Film Institute, 1976; King, John. *Magical Reels: A History of Cinema in Latin America*. London: Verso, 1990; Mosier, John. "Film." In *Handbook of Latin American Popular Culture*, ed. Harold E. Hinds and Charles M. Tatum, 173–189. Westport, CT: Greenwood, 1985; Pick, Zuzana M. *Latin American Filmmakers and the Third Cinema*. Ottowa: Carleton University, 1978; Trelles Plazola, Luis. *South American Cinema: Dictionary of Film Makers*. Rio Piedras: Editorial de la Universidad de Puerto Rico, 1989; de Usabel, Gaizka S. *The High Noon of American Films in Latin America*. Ann Arbor, MI: Proquest, 1982.

Latin American Liberation Theater

A form of theater that is inspired by liberation theology, which seeks to give a voice and dignity to the poor. This movement is rooted in a long-standing dissatisfaction with the plight of the poor from all sectors of society in Latin America, but it was first articulated and disseminated in 1973 in *A Theology of Liberation*, by Gustavo Gutiérrez. Liberation theater enables an audience to speak for itself, outside the imposed colonial models that have oppressed the common people of Latin America for centuries. Actors are usually drawn from the community itself. Acting out roles in improvised sketches serves as a tool for understanding one's own oppression and creates situations in which individuals/actors can discover solutions to their societal problems. It is a clear reaction against and rejection of foreign models of theater.

Liberation theater is best known through the work of the Brazilian director and innovator **Augusto Boal,** who developed his techniques beginning in the early 1970s. Others working in this same model are **Enrique Buenaventura** of **Colombia** and **Alan Bolt** of Nicaragua.

References: Albuquerque, Severino João. *Violent Acts: A Study of Contemporary Latin American Theatre*. Detroit, MI: Wayne State University Press, 1991; Boal, Augusto. *Theater of Oppression*. Paris: La Decouverte, 1985; Gutiérrez, Gustavo. *A Theology of Liberation*. Maryknoll, NY: Orbis, 1973; Quiles, Edgar. "The Theatre of Augusto Boal." Ph.D. diss. Ann Arbor, MI: University Microfilms, 1981; Versènyi, Adam. *Theatre in Latin America: Religion, Politics, and Culture from Cortés to the 1980's*. New York: Cambridge University Press, 1993; Weiss, Judith A. *Latin American Popular Theatre: The First Five Centuries*. Albuquerque: University of New Mexico Press, 1993.

Latin American Theater

Nowhere in the world has the imposition of a colonial power wrought so much cultural devastation over so large an area as in Latin America. What little information we have from pre-Columbian times that was not destroyed by zealous Spanish Christian missionaries alludes to many rich ritual-theater traditions, which had in common a close connection to nature and its cycles. There is evidence of highly organized and evolved performance traditions in **Inca theater, Mayan theater,** and **Aztec theater.**

Control over what is now know as Latin America began in the early sixteenth century with the arrival of the Spaniard Hernán Cortés in **Mexico** in 1519. Upon arrival in the "New World," Cortés adapted and improvised theatrically, assuming the role of the god **Quetzalcoátl** in order to help in his conquest, just as the friars who directly followed him adapted and improvised theatrically in order to help in their conversion of the indigenous people to Christianity. Toward the end of the sixteenth century the Christian missionary theater begun by the friars had almost totally disappeared, as had an enormous portion of the indigenous population. According to most sources war, disease, exploitation, and brutality killed off more than 90 percent of the indigenous population in the century following the conquest thus indigenous theater also disappeared. True, there are indigenous elements in some Latin American theater subsequent to this period, even elements in the indigenous language. However, these elements are alienated from their roots and lack the religious inspiration from which they were born, and are thus far less meaningful.

The theater in **Argentina, Chile, Mexico, Colombia,** and **Brazil** that developed after colonization was primarily modeled after European theater, with the most exceptions occurring in the realm of popular drama, intended for popular audiences. **Latin American liberation theater** developed in the 1970s out a desire to give voice and dignity to the poor of Latin America. It seeks to allow an audience to speak for itself of its own oppression, outside the confines of the imposed colonial models. **Latin American cinema** has been an important expression of Latin American culture, with a great variety of styles and artistic aims. The arts in many Latin American countries still suffer from a lack of support and even censorship, due to unstable governments that are largely a product of the oppressive colonial model, which merely transferred power to the wealthy elite when the various countries gained independence.

References: Franco, Jean. *On Edge: The Crisis of Contemporary Latin American Culture.* Minneapolis: University of Minnesota Press, 1992; Luzuriaga, Gerardo. *Popular Theater for Social Change in Latin America: Essays in Spanish and English.* Los Angeles: UCLA Latin American Center Publications, 1978; Mujica, Barbara. "Encore for a National Treasure." *Americas* 43, 2 (1991): 50–53; Phelan, John Leddy. *The Millennial Kingdom of the Franciscans in the New World: A Study of the Writings of Geró Nimor de Mendieta* (1525–1604). Berkeley: University of California Press, 1956; Taylor, Diana. *Theatre of Crisis: Drama and Politics in Latin America.* Lexington: University Press of Kentucky, 1991; Taylor, Diana. *Negotiating Performance: Gender, Sexuality, and Theatricality in Latin America.* Durham, NC: Duke University Press, 1994; Versènyi, Adam. *Theatre in Latin America: Religion, Politics, and Culture from Cortés to the 1980's.* New York: Cambridge University Press, 1993; Weiss, Judith A. *Latin American Popular Theatre: The First Five Centuries.* Albuquerque: University of New Mexico Press, 1993; Woodyard, George W., and Vicky Wolff Unruh. "Latin American Theatre Today: A 1992 Conference in Kansas." *Latin American Theatre Review* 26, 2 (Spring 1993): 6–8.

Latin Humanistic Comedy
Italy
Italian comedies written in Latin from the fourteenth and fifteenth centuries. These plays were written and generally performed by intellectuals who knew classical models of drama. However, their dramas were much cruder than their classical prototypes. The subject matter included student life at early universities, folk tales, and issues of daily life. Since the plays were episodic, the action of the dramas shifted freely from place to place over long periods of time. No exceptional works of Latin Humanistic comedy remain, but this form was an important influence on the development of Italian comedy.

See also *Commedia Erudita*
References: Duchartre, Pierre-Louis. *The Italian Comedy (Comedie Italienne).* Trans. Randolph Weaver. New York: Dover, 1966; Herrick, Marvin T. *Italian Comedy in the Renaissance.* Urbana: University of Illinois Press, 1960.

Latvia
Latvia's history largely parallels that of Estonia, being characterized by multiple occupations by Germans, Swedes, and Lithuanians, and then Russian rule. In the nineteenth century Latvia experienced a cultural revival, primarily through the effort of Johann von Herder who encouraged interest in Latvian folklore and compiled the epic poem *Lacplesis* from Latvian legends. Latvia has long been a rather cosmopolitan port city, which naturally led to a mix in population. A cultural life

has thrived there that is comparable to that found in many more central European cities. In 1918 Latvia gained independence, only to lose it again to the Soviet Union in 1940. During an abortive Soviet coup, Latvia declared independence in 1991.

Janis Rainis (1865–1929), who mostly wrote plays of Latvian mythology and history, was the greatest Latvian playwright of his age. He wrote *Fire and Ice*, a drama based on the national epic (written by Andrejs Pumpurs [1841–1902] about folk heroes), first performed at the New Theater of Riga in 1911. The Latvian National Theater in Riga has been open since the beginning of the twentieth century, and Latvian independence was declared on its stage in 1918. This theater offers in-house rigorous training and sponsors many experimental works. Since independence from the Soviet Union in 1991 the national consciousness that was never eradicated by Soviet dominance is finding its voice and expression through the arts. Latvian folk songs, known as *Dainas*, are extremely popular and central to the expression of the national character. They influence all of the other performing arts.

Opera in Latvia began in the eighteenth century at the palace of the ruling family in the Duchy of Kurzeme. Traveling troupes began performing in Riga in 1760. German influence increased, and they brought their opera to Latvia with them. By 1883 the first Latvian composer, Jekabs Ozols (1863–1902), began presenting his work. The Latvian Opera Company began in 1912 and continued under Soviet rule under the name of the Soviet Latvian Opera Company. The Latvian National Opera continues to flourish.

In cinema, there are many directors and writers using film as a tool for preserving and inspiring the Latvian spirit. Alexander Ivanov's film *Homewars with a Victory*, 1947, portrays Latvians as passionate revolutionaries. Rolands Kalnins, one of Latvia's best film directors of the 1960s and 1970s, created *Ceplis*, 1972. In the 1990s, cinema was energized by the newly gained independence. In 1998 the Latvian National Film Center provided over (US)$1 million to fund four feature films and coproductions with other nations.

See also Estonia; Lithuania

References: Slodkowski, Andrew, director and producer. *Baltic States*. San Ramon, CA: International Video Network, 1992; Straumanis, Alfreds. *Confrontation with Tyranny: Six Baltic Plays with Introductory Essays*. Prospect Heights, IL: Waveland, 1977; Straumanis, Alfreds. *Fire and Night, Five Baltic Plays*. Prospect Heights, IL: Waveland, 1986; Vesilind, Priit. "The Baltic Nations." National Geographic 178, 5 (November 1990): 2–36.

Lazzi
Italy

Comic business invented by the **Zanni** comic servant stock character in **commedia dell'arte,** improvised sixteenth- and seventeenth-century Italian comedy. These humorous bits contributed nothing to the progression of the plot but were highly entertaining, astonishing in their physical execution, and extravagant in their conception. Usually involving some acrobatic stunt combined with some clever gag, a *lazzo* was sometimes used to pick up the lagging energy of a performance. Although usually superfluous, the *lazzo* was sometimes used to connect or bridge the action of the drama.

References: Rudlin, John. *Commedia Dell'Arte: An Actor's Handbook*. London and New York: Routledge, 1994.

Lebanon

The early history of Lebanon is one with that of **Syria,** since Syria then comprised present-day Syria, Lebanon, **Israel,** and **Jordan.** Beginning in the eighteenth century there was strong French influence in Lebanon, since French forces were present to defend the rights of Christians in the area, and with them came French touring theater troupes. Egyptian theater troupes also toured the area, spreading their influence wherever they performed. In the nineteenth century **Arab theater** began to rival French theater.

From the end of World War II to the early 1970s was a prosperous time for Lebanon, and the city of Beirut became a wealthy, cultured city, where there was a healthy amount of theatrical activity. Civil war broke out in 1975, making it difficult for theaters. Some individuals worked to keep theater alive despite the war, such as Nabih Abu'l-Husn. Group efforts were made by Roger 'Assaf's **Hakawati** troupe, which worked to revive the ancient art of storytelling in a modern theatrical manner.

On the contemporary scene, Playwright Tayyib al-Siddiqi creates plays, combining a mixture of ritual and burlesque with political undertones, which are lively and colorful spectacles. He collaborated with leading Lebanese actress Nidal Ashqar in creating an Arab Actors' Company, the first such pan-Arab venture, which brought together many talented leading Arab actors. There first production was 1001 Nights in Suq Ukaz.

In cinema, coproductions with European and American film studios since the end of the civil war have saved the Turkish film industry based in Beirut. Arab makers of serious films have an eye on the European and international market. The success of filmmakers such as Burhan 'Alawiyya, Roger Assaf, Rafiq Hajjar, and Jocelyn Sa'b has given new hope and incentive to Lebanese filmmakers.

References: Cachia, P. "The Dramatic Monologues of Al-Ma'arri'." *Journal of Arabic Literature* 1 (1970): 129–136; al-Khozai, Mohamed. *The Development of Early Arabic Drama*. London and New York: Longman, 1984; Landau, Jacob. *Studies in the Arab Theater and Cinema*. Philadelphia: University of Pennsylvania Press, 1958; Mostyn, Trevor, and Albert Hourani, eds. *The Cambridge Encyclopedia of the Middle East and North Africa*. New York: Cambridge University Press, 1988.

Lecouvreur, Adrienne (1692–1730)
France

French actress, famous for her emotional portrayals of tragic roles. Her acting style, inspired by pure emotion, was enthusiastically received, even though academic diction was the norm at the time. She was with the **Comédie Française** for thirteen years, where she starred in the leading female roles of such works as Phèdre, 1670, by Jean Baptiste Racine (1639–1699) and Tite et Bérénice (1970) by Pierre Corneille (1606–1684). Her acting was based on simplicity, not the showy artifice that had in France been the standard for decades preceding her. Speaking from the heart, she reportedly showed great feeling and emotional truth. She also argued for historically accurate costumes.

References: Richtman, Jack. *Adrienne Lecouvreur: The Actress and the Age*. Englewood Cliffs, NJ: Prentice-Hall, 1971; Williams, A. R. "Eighty Years of Elegance and Excellence." *Americas* 39, 5 (September–October 1987): 14–19.

Legong
Bali

Dance-drama traditionally performed by three girls, usually under the age of twelve or thirteen, but can be performed by one or many. This form is the ultimate in expressing a delicate femininity. The performance begins with a sequence of pure dance in which the narrative tale is not advanced, as one performer strikes a dramatic pose and, at a cue from the music, proceeds directly into a brisk and lively dance. As the other two join in they flutter fans and execute intricate patterns of movement. They have incredible control over the sharp movement of their eyes as separate from the movement of their heads and necks. During the more dramatic portion of the performance, the girls pantomime the story, using a very economical style of action. There is usually a storyteller to the side delivering the dialogue and narration.

Performances usually take place in the late afternoon under a canopy. The costumes are made up of wrap skirts with a corset-like bodice made up of many layers of strips of cloth. There is a golden headpiece adorned with flowers and a golden collar with a narrow apron of cloth extending over the chest. The girls wear thick powder on their faces, with a white dot between their darkly drawn eyebrows. The repertory is drawn from stories named *Lasem* and *Semaradhana*. Musical accompaniment is performed by a Balinese **gamelan,** the traditional orchestra. Girls start very young to train for *Legong*, since they must retire by twelve or thirteen years of age. The technical perfection required by this form takes years of physical training and practice. The most common method for transmitting this dance is that a teacher, who is usually a former dancer or an orchestra leader, is invited to a village to teach the technique and actual dances. *Legong* performers are held in high esteem in Balinese society. They do not have to do heavy chores and sometimes even marry princes.

References: Brandon, James R. *Brandon's Guide to Theatre in Asia*. Honolulu: University Press of Hawaii, 1976; Covarrubias, Miguel. *Bali*. New York: Oxford University Press, 1972; Hood, Mantle. "The Enduring Tradition: Music and Theatre in Java and Bali." In *Indonesia*, ed. Ruth McVey. New Haven, CT: Yale University Press, 1963; de Zoete, Beryl, and Walter Spies. *Dance and Drama in Bali*. London: Faber & Faber, 1938.

Young Balinese dancers perform the Legong dance in Ubud, Bali. (Photo by J. P. Osnes)

Lenaia
Greece

One of four **Dionysia,** festivals in honor of the Greek god **Dionysus**; it was celebrated in Athens in January and the beginning of February. It was at this festival that **Greek comedy** was first improvised. Once comedy was given literary form, it was presented at this festival from the first half of the fifth century B.C. on. Tragedies were added about fifty years later, approximately in 442, but comic plays were always the primary focus of the Lenaia. Two tragedians and five comic playwrights were selected to present plays each year, with prizes for the best comic and tragic actor and playwright. This festival was only attended by Athenians, since it was too difficult for foreign visitors to travel by sea in the winter. Local audiences were very loyal, often sitting for hours on cold and sometimes wet stone seating in the open air to witness the performances.

References: Bieber, Margarete. *The History of the Greek and Roman Theater.* Princeton, NJ: Princeton University Press, 1961; Cornford, F. M. *The Origins of Attic Comedy.* London: Edward Arnold, 1914; Pickard-Cambridge, Sir Arthur Wallace. *Dramatic Festivals of Athens.* 2d ed. Oxford: Clarendon, 1962; Taylor, David. *Acting and the Stage.* Boston: George Allen & Unwin, 1978.

Lenong
Java

Improvised street theater performed in Sudanese in and around the city of Jakarta.

References: Brandon, James R. *Brandon's Guide to Theatre in Asia.* Honolulu: University Press of Hawaii, 1976.

Li Yu (1611–1680)
China

Poet and theater practitioner of the seventeenth century. After failing the government examination for a post in the civil service, Li Yu lived by writing and producing dramatic works. He had patrons who were wealthy officials. He traveled with his troupe of singing girls, and they performed plays, mostly in the homes of high officials who would house all of them as well. He was viewed as being decadent and as having loose morals because he interacted so closely with female performers.

References: Scott, A. C. *The Theatre in Asia.* New York: Macmillan, 1972.

Libya
See Arab Theater

Likay
Thailand

Popular opera performed at fairs and temple festivals, and in public theaters in urban places. Most often performances tended to occur in rundown disreputable theaters. The form began in the early twentieth century, as unemployed court performers tried to make a living staging court dramas after learning only the basics of acting and dancing. Performers were generally untrained and not excessively talented. Performers would strike poses upon entering and exiting, based on their idea of classical dance. A court audience would have thought this performance ridiculous, but it had an enormous appeal to the popular audience for whom court performances were inaccessible. Likay was extremely popular in the 1920s and 1930s. This was the first style of theater in Thailand in which men and women appeared on stage together. The repertory was drawn from parts of the **Ramakien** (Thai version of the **Ramayana**), **Inao** stories (Thai version of **Panji tales**), and other court plays. In later years, stories from court were not used. **Pin Peat** is the name of the musical ensemble that accompanied the operas. Only one Likay troupe was reported to remain in the 1970s, suggesting that this form may be extinct within a few decades.

References: Bachfield, August. "Theatre in Siam." *Erdball* 2 (1928): 335–377; Brandon, James. *Theatre in Southeast Asia.* Cambridge, MA: Harvard University Press, 1974; Brandon, James R. *Brandon's Guide to Theatre in Asia.* Honolulu: University Press of Hawaii, 1976; Roosman, R. S. "Cross-Cultural Aspects of Thai Drama." *Journal of Oriental Literature* 8 (January 1967): 43–51; Rutnin, Mattani, ed. *The Siamese Theatre: Collections of Reprints from Journals of Siam Society.* Bangkok: Siam Society, 1975.

Likay dancers applying makeup before a performance in Bangkok, Thailand (Lindsay Hebberd/Corbis)

Lindberg, August (1846–1916)
Norway, Sweden

Swedish actor, best known for his naturalistic portrayals of the leading male characters in the plays of Henrik Ibsen, many of which he premiered. Lindberg first gained a name for himself as an actor touring Sweden performing plays by **Shakespeare**. By 1882 he had founded his own traveling theater company. He was a director at the Royal Opera in Sweden from 1906 to 1915 and then became an actor and director at the Royal Dramatic Theater in Stockholm.

Lindberg's son, Per Lindberg (1890–1944), studied under the German director **Max Reinhardt**. Per experimented with many expressive modes of staging, using angular frames and minimal structures to evoke a setting for performances of such plays as *Hamlet*.

References: Marker, Frederick. *A History of Scandinavian Theatre.* Cambridge: Cambridge University Press, 1996.

Lithuania

Lithuania differs from its neighbor, **Latvia,** with whom it shares a similar language, in that it remained its own ruler until 1795, when it was absorbed into **Russia.** Prior to that Lithuania had a union with Poland that lasted four centuries, which is why Lithuania is predominantly Catholic. With Catholicism came Jesuit Theater, which still occurs on the streets, performed with rustic costumes and folk music. In 1921 Lithuania gained independence, only to lose it again in 1940 to the former Soviet Union. In 1991 Lithuania gained its independence once again.

Drama has never been the dominant genre in Lithuanian literature or folk culture. Because folk songs are such a strong form of expression, the emphasis on rhythm and rhyme carries over into their literature. Many plays are written in verse, challenging the actors to act naturally while speaking in verse and to move in rhythm to the iambic pentameter.

During the 1920s and 1930s, the Lithuania State Theater at Kaunas throve as a center of creativity and artistic quality. Playwright Balys Sruoga (1896–1947), who mostly focused on Lithuanian history and the struggles for independence, was a part of this golden age. With his play *Kazimieras Sapiega* (Casimir Sapiega; 1942), he sought to strengthen the spirit of the common person of Lithuania. However, in 1943 Sruoga and other Lithuanian intellectuals were arrested and sent to a concentration camp. He survived for two years, only to be released to the postwar horrors that faced Lithuania. Later many powerful dramas focused on the Soviet control over Lithuania, such as Justin Marcinkevicius's *Mindaugas*, 1969, performed first at the Lithuanian State Academic Drama Theater. Since the Soviet era the work of director Eimuntas Nekrosius has stood out as bringing Lithuanian theater to fruition. His production of *Hamlet* (1999) was hailed for its stark design, including all-metal props, a bare black stage, and a perennial rain drizzling throughout the performance. A film by Valdas Navasaitas, *Kiemas* (The Courtyard; 1999), was reviewed at the Cannes Film Festival in France.

References: Slodkowski, Andrew, director and producer. *Baltic States.* San Ramon, CA: International Video Network, 1992; Straumanis, Alfreds. *Confrontation with Tyranny: Six Baltic Plays with Introductory Essays.* Prospect Heights, IL: Waveland, 1977; Straumanis, Alfreds. *Fire and Night, Five Baltic Plays.* Prospect Heights, IL: Waveland, 1986; Vesilind, Priit. "The Baltic Nations." *National Geographic* 178, 5 (November 1990): 2–36.

Littlewood, Joan (1914–)
England

English actress and director who began a tradition of collective collaboration in **England**. In the 1930s Littlewood did work at a theater collective in Manchester with dramatist and folk singer Ewan McColl, promoting socialist ideals in performances that were often considered documentaries. In 1945 Littlewood and McColl began the Theatre Workshop, an experimental left-wing theater group that presented both classical and modern works in a new, robust style. In 1953 the Theatre Workshop was based at the Theatre Royal, Stratford East, London. The Theatre Workshop was concerned with working-class issues and tried to reach a broader spectrum of British society, including a working-class audience. Performances were created collectively with the actors. Actors in her group found her to be both passionate and autocratic.

Littlewood is credited with bringing Brechtian techniques to England. Her production of **Bertolt Brecht**'s *Mother Courage and Her Children* in 1955 was highly successful. The Theatre Workshop's musical documentary *Oh! What a Lovely War*, 1963, was a political and irreverent play about World War I. Littlewood however, had left the Theatre Workshop in 1961 because she was disappointed that the group was seeking commercial success rather than staying true to their radical political ideals. The Theatre Workshop disbanded soon after she left. Since 1975 Littlewood has lived and worked in France.

References: Goorney, Howard, and Ewan MacColl. *Agit-Prop to Theatre Workshop: Political Playscripts 1930–50.* Dover, NH: Manchester University Press, 1986; Tynan, Kenneth. *A View of the English Stage 1944–63.* London: Davis-Poynter, 1975.

Living Newspaper
See Federal Theater Project

Living Theater
United States

Experimental Off-Broadway theater company begun in 1948 in New York by a married couple, Julian Beck (1925–1985) and Judith Malina (born in 1926). Born out of respect for poetic language, the group began performing works by poets such as **Jean Cocteau** (1889–1963) and William Carlos Williams (1883–1963), who wrote *Many Loves*, 1959. The Living Theater became a theater company that unified art, politics, and lifestyle. Upon establishing a permanent theater in 1959, the Living Theatre performed two of its most successful productions: *The Connection*, 1959, about a group of drug addicts, included actors panhandling in the audience during intermission to challenge the traditional audience-performer relationship, and *The Brig*, 1963, exposed the brutal treatment of prisoners in U.S. Marine Corps prisons.

In 1963 the Living Theater was evicted from its theater for tax evasion and went into self-imposed exile in Europe as an anarchistic commune. It toured Europe from 1964 to 1968 with many productions, most notably *Antigone*, 1967, in which the action was placed in the Vietnam War. When it returned to the **United States** in 1968, it was much freer in its expression than before. Its audiences were witnessing real events, free expressions of sexuality, politics, and ritual. Actors, instead of pretending, aspired to achieving a natural state of being in front of an audience, in that way portraying their authentic selves. After Beck died in 1985, Malina continued work with the Living Theatre, collaborating with Hanon Reznikov. The Living Theatre had a huge influence on experimental theater in the 1960s and beyond.

References: Bigsby, C. W. E. *A Critical Introduction to Twentieth-Century American Drama.* New York: Cambridge University Press, 1985; Biner, Pierre. *Living Theatre.* New York: Horizon, 1972; Brown, Kenneth. *The Brig: A Concept for Theatre or Film.* New York: Hill and Wang, 1965.

Livius Andronicus (240–204 B.C.)
Italy

Playwright of the first important works in Latin, who lived from 240–204 B.C., came as a child to Rome. He became a slave, and later a freedman and tutor. Because he had command of both Latin and Greek, he became the first translator of the Western world, translating the works of **Sophocles, Euripides,** and **Greek Comedy** into Latin. He was responsible for many innovations in the theater, one being that he separated gesture and action from speech. The tragic orator stood and spoke in a full-length tragic robe while another masked actor enhanced the words through movement and gesture, which opened the way for the further development of **mime** and **pantomime.** Livius also acted in his own plays.

References: Bieber, Margarete. *The History of the Greek and Roman Theater.* Princeton, NJ: Princeton University Press, 1961; Chinoy, Helen Krich, and Toby Cole. *Actors on Acting.* New York: Crown, 1970.

Loa
See Entremés

Ludi
Italy

Official holidays on which plays were presented, associated with the state religion and given in honor of the gods. The most important of the *Ludi* were the **Ludi Romani.** These festivals were celebrated in the Circus Maximus, the oldest building for games in Rome. There were always stage plays followed by circus performances. During the empire, 27 B.C.–A.D. 476, interest in stage plays declined, and interest in the flashy spectacle of the circus performances and games increased.

References: Bieber, Margarete. *The History of the Greek and Roman Theater.* Princeton, NJ: Princeton University Press, 1961.

Ludi Romani
Italy

Oldest of the **ludi,** official holidays on which plays were presented, associated with the state religion and given in honor of the gods. Established in the sixth century B.C., the *Ludi Romani* were in honor of Jupiter and occurred in September each year. The first presentation of a tragedy and a comedy in Rome was instituted by **Livius Andronicus** at the *Ludi Romani.*

References: Arnott, Peter D. *The Ancient Greek and Roman Theatre.* New York: Random House, 1971; Bieber, Margarete. *The History of the Greek and Roman Theater.* Princeton, NJ: Princeton University Press, 1961.

Ludruk
Java

Realistic contemporary drama performed by men and female impersonators. This form has its roots in a traditional folk dance of invulnerability, a demonstration of strength and magical powers, called *Ludruk Bendang.* This was an exhausting dance that enacted the entire cycle of life for a human. The dance was followed by the presentation of offerings. Only men performed the roles because it was so physically demanding. Later the dancers began to borrow more contemporary adventure stories, and by the 1950s there were professional troupes. There are still traditional dances performed at the opening of the performance, and songs and dances are interspersed between scenes. The acting style is realistic and not nearly as demanding as it used to be, yet men still perform the female roles. This form is looked on as being strange, even perverse, by the general public because it includes female impersonators. The repertory consists of contemporary plays, mostly comedies based on domestic situations. **Gamelan** (the traditional orchestra) music accompanies performances.   *Ludruk* is performed mostly in Surabaya in East Java.

References: Brandon, James. *Theatre in Southeast Asia.* Cambridge, MA: Harvard University Press, 1974; Hatley, Barbara. "Wayang and Ludruk: Polarities in Java." *Drama Review* 15, 3 (1971): 88–101; Leonard, Dorothy. "Ladies of Ludruk." *Orientations* 5, 4 (April 1974): 3–4; Peacock, James. "Javanese Folkdrama and Social Change." Ph.D. diss., Harvard University, 1965.

Lugné-Poe (1869–1940)
France

French actor and director, who was a leading theatrical innovator in the beginning of the twentieth century. As the director and lead actor of the Théâtre de l'Oeuvre from 1893 to 1929, he was the first to bring to the French stage the great modern plays from all over Europe, including plays by **Henrik Ibsen, August Strindberg,** and Maxim Gorky (1868–1936). An excellent actor, he also had great insight as a director and continually experimented with new ideas for staging.

References: Jasper, Gertrude Rathbone. *Adventures in the Theatre: Lugne-Poe and the Theatre de L'Oeuvre to 1899.* New Brunswick, NJ: Rutgers University Press, 1947; Robichez, Jacques. *Lugne-Poe.* Paris: L'Arche, 1955.

Luxembourg

Luxembourg is a very small country situated between **Belgium, France,** and **Germany.** French and German influence has been very strong in the theater of Luxembourg, but since World War II (1939–1945), plays in the native language, Letzeburgesch, have rivaled the popularity of imported plays. Since 1970 many new companies have formed, such as Théâtre Ouvert Luxembourg (Open Theater Luxembourg) and Théâtre du Centaure (Centaur Theater). Beginning in 1985 the City of Luxembourg formed the Théâtre des Capucins de la Ville de Luxembourg, which presents many new productions by a variety of semiprofessional companies. Because of the small size of this country, there are very few professional actors, and it is difficult for theater companies to stay together. In film Luis Galvao Teles' melodramatic work *Elles* (1998) focuses on the issue of aging among women in their forties. The government is making efforts to increase film production and to increase foreign coproductions, such as the Luxembourg/Belgian/French film *La Promesse* (The Promise; 1999), directed by Luc and Jean-Pierre Dardenne.

References: Olinger, Marc. "Luxembourg." In *The World Encyclopedia of Contemporary Theatre,* ed. Don Rubin, 569–570. New York: Routledge, 1994.

Lyric
Greece

Song to the accompaniment of the lyre, a stringed instrument in the harp family, considered to be the second literary form that developed after the epic and before drama. **Greek**

tragedy may have grown out of choral lyrics, which were sung and danced by a chorus, and choral lyrics were certainly an important part of both tragedy and comedy.

See also Greek Chorus; Greek Comedy.

References: Bieber, Margarete. *The History of the Greek and Roman Theater.* Princeton, NJ: Princeton University Press, 1961; Scott, William Clyde. *Musical Design in Aeschylean Theater.* Hanover, NH: Published for Dartmouth College by University Press of New England, 1984.

M

Macedonia

The area that is now Macedonia in Southeast Europe was ruled by Muslim Turks from 1389 to 1912 and was then mostly absorbed by Serbia in 1918. The founder of the Macedonian theater was Vojdan Cernodrinski (1875–1951), who ushered in the wealth of European dramatic literature. Until the 1940s almost all plays were performed in the Serbian language and not until the late 1940s and 1950s were plays written in Macedonian. Dimce Trajkovski (1888–1978) was the first professional actor of the twentieth century in Macedonia; in 1933 he started his own company, the Little Skopje Theater. He then became a member of the Macedonian National Theater in Skopje once World War II ended in 1945.

Macedonia declared its independence from Yugoslavia in 1991. See **Yugoslavia** for history of theater in this area.

References: Aleksiev, Aleksandar. *Founders of Macedonian Drama.* Skopje: Misla, 1972; Siljan, Rade. *Macedonian Drama: The Nineteenth and Twentieth Centuries.* Skopje: Makedonska Kniga, 1990; Stefanovski, Risto. *The Theatre in Macedonia.* Skopje: Misla, 1990; Stefanovski, Risto. *The Theatre in Macedonia.* Skopje: Misla, 1990.

Macklin, Charles (1697–1797)
England, Ireland

English actor and playwright. Born in Ireland, he began as a strolling performer in Ireland and then **England**. Macklin introduced naturalistic acting into an era when declamation and formalism was the rule. In 1733 he began performing at Drury Lane, oldest and most famous of London's theaters, where he was able to put his naturalistic style of acting into practice. Macklin is most remembered for being the first to perform the role of Shylock in **Shakespeare**'s *Merchant of Venice* as a tragic character rather than a comic one. He is also remembered for his volatile temper; most notably, he killed another actor during a dispute over a wig and then proceeded to urinate in the fatal wound he had given in an attempt to clean it.

He formed his own company in 1744. When teaching actors, he encouraged them to speak the great lines of tragedy conversationally, rather than in a singsong rhythm. Macklin introduced the idea of historically accurate costuming in 1772 when he performed Macbeth in Scottish clothing.

References: Appleton, William Worthen. *Charles Macklin: An Actor's Life.* Cambridge, MA: Harvard University Press, 1960; Cooke, William. *Memoirs of Charles Macklin.* London: J. Asperne, 1806.

Madagascar

Located in the Indian Ocean east of Mozambique, Madagascar is the fourth largest island in the world. The people of Madagascar are a mixture descended from Africans and Indonesians.

The country was ruled by the indigenous Merina monarchy before it became a French colony from 1896 to 1967. In Madagascar there still exist indigenous performances, mainly in the form of the **Hira-Gasy,** improvised sketches. For many centuries there have been highly developed verbal arts in Madagascar such as riddling, proverbs, and a kind of wordplay known as *Hainteny.* Of these verbal arts, a children's conversation game, **Tomabo,** most closely approaches a theatrical performance.

In the nineteenth to early twentieth centuries, theater in the Malagasy language thrived through the scripted works of national playwrights Tselatra Rahaonah and Arthur Rodlish. Theater in French has also been performed during and beyond colonial times. In the 1990s it enjoyed widespread popularity through the works of playwrights such as David Jaomanoro and Charlotte Rafenomanjato.

> **References:** Banham, Martin. *African Theatre Today.* London: Pitman, 1976; Bloch, Maurice. *Ritual, History, and Power: Selected Papers in Anthropology.* Atlantic Highlands, NJ: Athlone, 1989; Cornevin, Robert. *Le Theatre en Afrique Noire et a Madagascar.* Paris: Le Livre Africain, 1970; Haring, Lee. *Verbal Arts in Madagascar: Performance in Historical Perspective.* Philadelphia: University of Pennsylvania Press, 1992; Kent, Raymond. *From Madagascar to the Malagasy Republic.* New York: Praeger, 1962; Ruud, Jorgen. *Taboo: A Study of Malagasy Customs and Beliefs.* New York: Humanities, 1960.

Maggio
Italy

Rural Italian drama called simply "May," since it is rooted in the ancient rites of spring. This native type of theater was most likely a medieval form developed before the revival of the ancient Roman classics in the sixteenth century. *Maggio* originated as a mere dialogue between a few country dwellers performing mostly comic scenes. Plays had free form, since the country audience did not demand a sophisticated script. A performance began with a prologue performed by a special actor who gathered the attention of the audience, prepared them for the production, and gave praises to the glory of Spring.

> **References:** Herrick, Marvin T. *Italian Comedy in the Renaissance.* Urbana: University of Illinois Press, 1960; Nicoll, Allardyce. *Masks, Mimes and Miracles: Studies in the Popular Theatre.* London: G. C. Harrap, 1931.

Mahabharata
India, Southeast Asia

Hindu epic tale originating from India (400–100 B.C.). The *Mahabharata* includes a cast of hundreds, but centers around two sets of cousins, the virtuous Pandavas and the evil Kauravas. Through an unfair gambling match with dice, the Pandavas are exiled into the forest. When the Kauravas deny their cousins their rightful inheritance of the kingdom, a mighty war ensues, in which the Pandavas are victorious. The Bhagavad Gita is a famous episode in this tale, which is about sacred duty and other philosophical issues. The *Mahabharata* is four times as long as the **Ramayana** and is much more complex, both philosophically and intellectually. The *Mahabhrata* is the inspiration for many dramatic forms. In Javanese **Wayang Kulit,** traditional shadow-puppet theater, the complex issues of sacred duty, responsibility to family, and fate are explored in great depth through scenes from the *Mahabharata.* In India the dance-drama **Kathakali** enacts the whole range of the drama, from the most violent scenes, as when Bima devours an enemy while possessed by demons, to the most honorable scenes between the Pandavas and their advisor, **Krishna,** an incarnation of the Hindu god **Vishnu.**

> **References:** Narayana, Birendra. *Hindi Drama and Stage.* Delhi: Bansal, 1981.

Mai Komo
Niger, Nigeria

Praisesinger; male solo performer who incorporates poetry, vocal impersonation, gesture, and music to communicate the qualities and glory of the hunter or chief he is praising. It is traditionally believed by the Hausa people of Niger and Nigeria that for a hunter to kill an animal he must have both physical prowess and secret knowledge regarding how to overcome the strong spirit of the animal being hunted. Praisesingers follow behind important hunters as they proceed toward a hunt and build them up, increasing their confidence and foretelling their success.

The praisesinger mimes certain gestures of characters in the story, but just enough to evoke the action in the imagination of the audience. He also changes his voice to distinguish between straight narrative and when characters are speaking, using appropriate vocal qualities for each character. Most perform material passed down to them, along with poems of their own creation. These poems often tell a story in which the hunter or chief performs some heroic deed or amazing feat, such as hunting down an elephant to be used as a sacrifice for a religious festival. Praisesingers often include themselves in the story, portraying themselves as cowards to further exemplify the glory of their subject. Performers accompany themselves on a guitar-like instrument called the *Komo* or the *Gurumi*. The music emphasizes intense moments in the story.

Since hunting has declined in recent years, many praisesingers have had to diversify their repertoire and have taken up other forms of praisesinging.

See also *'dan Kama*

References: Beik, Janet. *Hausa Theatre in Niger: A Contemporary Oral Art.* New York: Garland, 1987;

Chaibou, Dan-Inna. "La Theatralite en Pays Hawsa." Université Nationale de Côte d'Ivoire, 1978–1979.

Mak Yong
Malaysia

Traditional Malay dance-drama performed mostly by women, also the name of the leading female role within this form. *Mak Yong* is thought to be the creation of females attached to the Malay court of Patani, southern Thailand, perhaps as early as the seventeenth century. Performances last a few nights, from sundown till the early morning hours. *Mak Yong* serves as a healing ritual. The role of the lead Mak Yong is that of an entertainer and spirit medium. However, more than 90 percent of the shows are for entertainment alone. Ten or more female dancers perform all of the major roles, with men usually playing the two clown roles. The women dance, sing, and perform improvised dialogue. The action takes place in the round, with all nonactive cast members sitting casually around the outside of the circle. Actors are considered to be off-stage or members of the

The traditional Malaysian dance-drama, Mak Yong, being performed in Kuala Lumpur, Malaysia. (Photo by Beth Osnes)

chorus when not in the central acting space. The highlight of a performance is the graceful circle dance performed by the lead women and the chorus. The dancing of the women is characterized by slow synchronized movement of the hands. Hand gestures are like the Indian *mudra*. However, the meaning of the hand movements usually is not known by the performer or the audience. Hands are often held in front of the chest with palms out and fingers extended upward. Isolated movement of one or more fingers in this position is typical. *Peran* is the name for the male clown character, who is more a wise fool than a foolish clown. These characters perform difficult stylized dances involving turns, steps, and poses.

The performance space is an open 12-foot by 16-foot structure made of bamboo with a mat-covered floor. The women's costumes are usually a typical Malay sarong with a fitted long-sleeved shirt. The *Mak Yong* character wears a high tiered headpiece, with tassels above the ears and glittery ornamentation up to the peak of the headpiece. The chorus women usually wear their hair back, with flowers and gold hair ornaments. The male clown characters usually wear baggy clothing with a vest. There are very few if any properties. The place where the action occurs is usually established through the dialogue, since there is no set. The repertory for performances is mainly from **Dewa Muda** stories, but there are also some **Manora** stories that have been absorbed into the Mak Yong repertory. There are many improvised comic interludes, usually between the lead female and a clown character. Actors must be aware of their audience. They must be able to sense whether people are restless or engaged and be able to shorten or lengthen an episode accordingly. The musical accompaniment is generally the same as for the **Wayang Siam** but with all cues given by the lead female performer. There are gongs, drums, a reed instrument, and the *rebab*, a three-stringed instrument. This form survives only in Kelantan and Trengganu and is rarely performed today.

See also *Manora*

References: Wright, Barbara Ann Stein. "Wayang Siam: An Ethnographic Study of the Malay Shadow Play of Kelantan." Ph.D. diss. Ann Arbor, MI: Proquest, 1980; Yousof, Ghulam-Sarwar. *The Kelantan "Mak Yong" Dance Theatre: A Study of Performance Structure*. Ann Arbor, MI: Proquest, 1976; Yousof, Ghulam-Sarwar. "Feasting of the Spirits: The Berjamu Ritual Performance in the Kelantanese Wayang Siam Shadow Play," *Journal of Malaysian Studies* 1 (June 1983): 95–115.

Malaysia

Islam, Hinduism, and cultural influence from Malaysia's neighbors, mainly Thailand and Java, have all been strong, resulting in a richly diverse variety of performing arts in Malaysia. West Malaysia, on the Malay peninsula, is located directly on a trade route, between the Strait of Malacca and the South China Sea, so contact with spice traders and seafaring people of all nations has been a facet of Malay life as far back as the recorded history of this area. The center of early activity, the Kingdom of Malacca, previously Hindu, was converted to Islam on a grand scale in the fourteenth century. British influence grew during the eighteenth century, until the Malay states became British protectorates in the late nineteenth century. It wasn't until 1963 that Malaysia became completely self governing, gaining control over Sabah and Sarawak on the island of Borneo. Now a country of Muslim Malays, mostly Buddhist Chinese, Hindu Indians, and the native people of Borneo, Malaysia must work to tolerate cultural diversity.

One of the most prominent theater forms on the peninsula is the **Wayang Kulit** shadow puppet theater in all of its regional varieties. A single puppet master, known as a **dalang,** manipulates all of the flat rawhide puppets, casting shadows on a muslin screen from behind. He trains many years, learning the repertory, the great Hindu epic tales, the **Mahabharata** and the **Ramayana,** which he must know by heart. Upon his graduation, a *dalang* receives from his teacher his **Pelimau,** a ceremonial bath with limes. Telling the traditional tales is often sidetracked by the escapades of the two local clown characters, **Pak Dogol** and **Wak Long,** who have been assimilated into the Hindu tales. Local varieties of Wayang Kulit include **Wayang Melayu** (or *Wayang Jawa*), which is an aristocratic form from the north featuring Javanese-style puppets. Another local variety is **Wayang Siam** from the northeast, which is robustly performed to suit the tastes of its rural village audience. Accompanying most traditional live theater and dance performances in Malaysia is a **gamelan** orchestra, which in Malaysia is made up of drums, gongs, cymbals, and a melodic reed instrument called a **serunai.**

Believed to have evolved during the seventeenth century, **Mak Yong** is a dance-drama performed mostly by women. The lead woman, called *Mak Yong,* is an entertainer and a spirit medium. Along with two male clowns and a chorus of women, she sings, dances, and improvises dialogue. One local story that is dramatized is the **Dewa Muda,** a story about the adventures of *Dewa Muda,* literally "young god."

Performed by Thai immigrants in the north of the peninsula is **Manora,** a dance-drama. The story dramatized is of the same name, about a bird princess named Manora and is from the **Jataka,** a collection of stories about the former incarnations of Gautama **Buddha.** Inspired by Javanese shadow play is an improvised form of drama, performed by traveling troupes, named **Bangsawan.** Since Islam does not allow dramatic representations, the only Islamic performance with even minimum theatrical elements is **Dikir Barat,** choral chanting of Koranic verses and other improvised material. Two teams, each with a leader known as **Tukang Karut,** take turns singing in response to each other.

References: Brandon, James. *Theatre in Southeast Asia.* Cambridge, MA: Harvard University Press, 1974; Matusky, Patricia. "Music in the Malay Shadow Puppet Theater (Volumes I and II)." Ph.D. diss., Ann Arbor, MI: Proquest, 1980; Matusky, Patricia. "Musical Instruments and Their Function in the *Wayang Siam* of Malaysia." *Performing Arts* 3 (August 1986): 18–25; Osnes, Mary Beth. "A Survey of Shadow Play in the Malaysian Traditional Shadow Puppet Theatre." Ann Arbor, MI: Proquest, 1992; Osnes, Mary Beth. "Shadow Puppet Theatre in Malaysia: Many Traditions, One God," *Quest* (Spring 1994): 70–73, 89; Sweeney, P. L. *The Ramayana and the Malay Shadow-Play.* Kuala Lumpur: National University of Malaysia Press, 1972; Sweeney, P. L. Amin. *Malay Shadow Puppets: The Wayang Siam of Kelantan.* London: British Museum Publications, 1980; Winstedt, Richard O. *The Malays: A Cultural History.* Singapore: Graham Brash, 1981; Yousof, Ghulam-Sarwar. *The Kelantan "Mak Yong" Dance Theatre: A Study of Performance Structure.* Ann Arbor, MI: Proquest, 1976; Yousof, Ghulam-Sarwar. "Traditional Theatre in South East Asia." *Performing Arts* 2 (July 1985): 37–49.

Mali

The richness of theatrical tradition in Mali extends from ancient history into the present. One of many important theatrical ceremonies in Mali is the **Dama,** a death anniversary ceremony held every few years in villages of the Dogon people. Performed as a part of *Dama,* the **Baga Bundo** is a rite performed by masked dancers in honor of someone important in the community that has died. There are also initiation ceremonies for young adolescents that include theatrical performances such as *Do,* which is performed by masked men for the initiates only. The **Tyi Wara,** a dance that glorifies agriculture, features performers covered with strips of fiber wearing headpieces resembling antelope horns dancing for an enraptured crowd.

Mali has a significant modern theater in French and also theater groups that are engaged in creating a precolonial performance style that has its roots in early Mali culture. Innovations in performing with puppets has been done with the Bamana Youth Theater of Mali in the late 1980s. Another puppet group from Mali performed with giant animal figures at the Puppeteers of America Festival of the Millennium in 1999 in Seattle, Washington. Malian playwright, Sotigui Kouyate, wrote *La Voix du Griot* (The Griot Voice) and performed it in the United States in 1999. Kouyate's own name is linked to the griots, a caste entrusted with keeping and teaching of native oral tradition. Malian filmmaker Cheick Oumar Sissoko has created many films including *La Genèsse* (Genesis) (2000).

References: Banham, Martin. *African Theatre Today.* London: Pitman, 1976.; Cornevin, Robert. *Le Theatre en Afrique Noire et a Madagascar.* Paris: Le Livre Africain, 1970; Imperato, Pascal James. "Contemporary Adapted Dances of the Dogon." *African Arts* 5, 1 (1971): 28–33, 68–71.

Mamet, David (1947–)
United States

Playwright, controversial for his use of profanity, writing style, and sexual language; one of America's leading writers for the stage, and a master at drawing out the poetic qualities of everyday language. Mamet was born in Chicago and bases much of his work on his experiences there. He moved to the East Coast to complete a graduate degree in Vermont. Upon returning to Chicago he reached success with *Sexual Perversity in Chicago* in 1974. The same year he reestablished in Chicago a group he had started on the East Coast, St. Nicholas Players.

American Buffalo, set in Chicago, opened in New York in 1977 and won much recognition, as well as the Drama Critic's Circle Award. In this play he focuses on three nearly inarticulate characters caught in a linguistic idiom that seems to serve the passing of time more than communication. Other works include *A Life in the Theater*, 1977, *Edmond*, 1982, *Glengarry Glen Ross*, 1983, and *Oleanna*, 1992. William Macy, an actor who has appeared in numerous Mamet productions, is exemplary at communicating Mamet's ideas in an acting style that relies on the power of the words.

References: Bigsby, C. W. E. *David Mamet*. New York: Methuen, 1985; Brewer, Gay. *David Mamet and Film: Illusion/Disillusion in a Wounded Land*. Jefferson, NC: McFarland, 1993; Heilpern, John. *How Good Is David Mamet, Anyway? Writings on Theatre—and Why It Matters*. New York: Routledge, 2000.

Mani-rimdu

Nepal

An outdoor three-day dance-drama performed by Buddhist monks for the **Sherpas,** a rural people of northeastern Nepal. It is believed to have descended from Tibet, the ancient homeland of the Sherpas. Enacting the triumph of good over evil, *Mani-rimdu* reinforces traditional Buddhist beliefs and serves as a ritual form of worship. With Mount Everest as the backdrop for the outdoor stage, this colorful event unfolds in a strict order that has been adhered to since the beginning of recorded history in this region. This festival, which centers on the performance of *Mani-rimdu*, occurs each November at Tengpoche and each May at Thami. Dedicated audiences brave the outdoor temperatures, which drop to as low as ten degrees below zero during the November performance. Performers must fight exhaustion while dancing in heavy masks and costumes, since they perform at an elevation of 14,500 feet, where there is 50 percent less oxygen than at sea level.

The opening day of the festival is the Life-Consecration rite in which there are prayers, chants, and a procession by the lamas. During the second day, a drama in thirteen acts is performed from mid-morning till soon after sundown. Each of the acts lasts about twenty minutes and is an independent unit, consisting of group dances and two short improvised comic dramas. For example, in the dance named *Dur-bdag*, dancers dressed as skeletons destroy an effigy of evil. Ritually blessed foods are distributed to audience members between each act. The third and last day features rituals that symbolize the final destruction of evil forces in the region. This rite, performed by the chief abbot of the monastery, ensures protection from evil for the Sherpas until the next performance.

The acting style is ruled by religious tradition, so much so that there is no tolerance for individual experimentation, except with the clown characters who perform on the second day. Starting with a rough scenario, the two clowns, named Mi-tshe-ring and Rtogs-Idan, perform their story using dialogue, the only time dialogue is used in the festival. Bordering on making fun of the very idea of religious worship, they make jokes based on local events and happenings with great freedom.

Performances take place within the monastery compound, in the courtyard, in a space about 30 feet square. Sometimes covered with a wooden structure to protect the audience from the elements, this area can accommodate up to 400 people. Brightly colored pants, tunics, and ponchos of silk are tied at the waist on performers. The costumes and ornaments that actors wear have specific symbolic meaning. For example, a sword may represent the power of a specific god, and a certain color may designate a particular deity. Designed to represent specific deities, mythological characters or humans, large masks are worn by performers. The mask that represents a manifestation of Padmasambhava (founder of Tibetan Buddhism) appears outrageous, with bulging eyes, fangs, huge nostrils, skulls sticking out on the sides, and wild tufts of black hair billowing from the top.

The lyrics of the chanting in the performances are highly symbolic, referring often to the Buddhist pantheon. The obscurity of the language greatly enhances the ethereal quality of the performances. The musicians sit either on the courtyard floor or in a balcony in the wooden structure assembled for honored audience members. Ten-foot-long brass horns are the most unique instruments used to accompany the performances. There are also cymbals, a hand drum, and a trumpet made from a human thigh bone. The singing is chanted by lamas in deep throated tones. Usually seven lamas and the main abbot chant the Buddhist scriptures from their seats on the balcony. A red curtain is drawn in front of them and not opened until they perform.

Mani-rimdu is the only type of organized theatrical entertainment in Sherpa society.

References: Brandon, James. *The Cambridge Guide to Asian Theatre*. New York: Cambridge University Press, 1993; Fantin, M. *Mani Rimdu, Nepal, the Buddhist Dance Drama of Tengpoche*. Singapore: Toppan; New Delhi: distributed by the English Book Store, 1976; Jerstad, Luther G. *Mani-Rimdu: Sherpa Dance-Drama*. Seattle: University of Washington Press, 1969; Manandhar, J. K. *Nepal, Legend and Drama*. Banepa Wankhya: Sukha Veti Manandhar, 1982.

Manora
Malaysia, Southern Thailand

A dance-drama that tells a story from the **Jataka,** stories of the previous births of Gautama **Buddha.** Thai immigrants in Kedah, Kelantan, and Perlis; the northern states of Malaysia; perform this folk tradition in southern Thai dialect. A troupe is made up of mostly Thai performers. Malays often supply the music and portray the clown characters. A traditional performance lasts three days and nights. During the day preliminary contact is made with the spirits by a medium on behalf of the person sponsoring the performance. At night the story about the bird-princess, *Manora,* is dramatized in successive episodes. Three actresses play the major roles, with two or more actors portraying clowns. Stylistically there is much borrowing from **Mak Yong** such as the movement style and performance structure. Sometimes masks are worn by male performers. The costumes are elaborate. The chestplate is adorned with beads, and wings are worn at the hip. The usually golden headpiece is called *Kecopong* and is tall and tiered.

The story is about Manora, the lovely daughter of King Kinnara, who is of a mythical race of bird people. She is captured by an earthly kingdom and falls in love with the prince of the land. Because she is feared for her magical powers, she is condemned to be burned while her beloved is away at war. Magically she ascends back to her heavenly home just before her certain death. Her prince defies all obstacles and finds her at the peak of the Himalayas, where they are happily reunited. This traditional drama is rarely performed today.

See also *Lakon Jatri*

References: Brandon, James. *Theatre in Southeast Asia*. Cambridge, MA: Harvard University Press, 1974; Wright, Barbara Ann Stein. "Wayang Siam: An Ethnographic Study of the Malay Shadow Play of Kelantan." Ph.D. diss., Ann Arbor, MI: Proquest, 1980.

Mao Tse-tung (1893–1976)
China

Political theorist, Chinese head of state, 1949–1959, and Communist Party chairman from 1943 to 1976. When the Communist Party took control in 1949 the government ruling China at the time fled to Taiwan. Most famous artists remained in Mainland China, and many took government positions in cultural development. At the Yenan Forum in 1942 Mao publicly declared his principles regarding the place of art and literature in society. He said that art is valid only if it is devoted to the communist political cause. Art and literature are a component in the revolution. Education and art should not be reserved for the elite class, but should exist for the peasants and workers. The proletariat and the artists must be indoctrinated with the same beliefs, Mao said. Reforms in existing Chinese drama, mainly **Peking Opera,** were enacted slowly, since the Chinese people were so attached to the drama as it was. Political consciousness had to be changed before the structures of drama could be changed. The star system was abolished. Local forms of theater were revived and sponsored by the state, which allowed for great security for actors. By the 1960s Mao's leadership ability and his policies toward the arts were openly criticized. In the theater he was criticized in a play entitled, *Hai Jui Dismissed*. For his effect on theater from 1966 until his death, see **Chinese Cultural Revolution.** Mao died in 1976, and the Chinese Cultural Revolution ended with his death.

See also Chiang Ching

References: Howard, Roger. *Contemporary Chinese Theatre.* Hong Kong: Heinemann, 1978; Scott, A. C. *The Theatre in Asia.* New York: Macmillan, 1972; Yang, Daniel Shih-P'eng. "The Traditional Theatre of China in Its Contemporary Setting: An Examination of the Patterns of Change within the Peking Theatre since 1949." Ph.D. diss., University of Wisconsin, 1968.

Maori
New Zealand

Originally Polynesian people who moved to the uninhabited island now called New Zealand in the fourteenth century A.D. The Maori language is a part of the Austronesian or Malayo-Polynesia family of languages and is considered by Maoris to be the basis of the performing arts. Expression through oratory, singing, storytelling, or chanting is not considered a separate entity from dance or music. Rather than focusing on the divisions within the arts, Maori art is valued for its ability to express common concerns of the Maori community by mixing among the available artistic media. The typical Maori artist is not a lonely introspective outsider to the community, but rather an involved and valued member of the community.

The orator in a Maori village is an honored and vital person who, through the art of oratory, can discuss politics, inspire the people to fight for a cause, or honor someone who has died. This position is attained only through years of practice and a thorough knowledge of modes of address, of decorum, and of classical songs and chants.

Music, though seen as essential by the Maori, is considered secondary to the words of a song. The manner of singing before European influence was more a rhythmical flow of words than actual singing in a Western sense. The singing was almost chantlike; the variations in the tune were in subtle quarter tones, and stress was laid on the length of the vowel sound in a word, as that indicates meaning. Since Europeans have lived in New Zealand, the Maori have adopted elements of Western-style music that appeal to them. A catchy tune such as "In the Mood' was adapted into a lament for the dead by making the tempo slower and the whole song more solemn. The guitar and ukulele are Western instruments that were gladly adopted by the Maori, as both are quite portable and good for accompanying singing.

Before European influence, drama was never performed alone, but it was considered to be an important element of most dance traditions. The vigorous posture dance, **Haka,** is performed only by men, either as a war dance or as a dance to welcome guests. Accompanied by a gentle lyrical song, the **Poi** is a woman's dance during which performers twirl balls attached to strings. Since the coming of European influence, another posture dance has developed, the **Action Song,** which is performed by both men and women, who perform body and hand movements in response to the lyrics.

Most forms of singing and dancing are learned by the Maori at a young age through participation in public events or at school.

Ever since Western-style amateur drama was established in New Zealand in the 1920s and 1930s, Maori actors have been involved. In the 1930s many Maori also acted before the camera, playing important roles in the early films of Rudall Hayward, a New Zealand film director, entitled *Te Kooti's Trail* and *Rewi's Last Stand.* However, it was not until the 1970s that Maori actors were given anything but two-dimensional "native" roles in films made in New Zealand. In the theater, after a large group of Maori actors performed in a successful staging of *Porgy and Bess,* they formed the New Zealand Maori Theatre Trust in 1966. The Trust served to train actors and inspire professional standards in the presentation of traditional and contemporary Maori arts and culture. After a group from the Trust went on a world tour in 1970, the group became inactive. However, it succeeded in integrating talented Maori actors into mainstream theatrical activity in New Zealand.

References: Barlow, Cleve. *Tikanga Whakaaro: Key Concepts in Maori Culture.* New York: Oxford University Press, 1991; Barber, Laurie. *New Zealand: A Short History.* Auckland: Century Hutchinson, 1989; Dansey, Harry. *The Maori in Colour.* London: Reed, 1973; Metge, Joan. *The Maoris of New Zealand Rautahi.* Boston: Routledge & Kegan Paul, 1976.

Marceau, Marcel (1923–)
France

French mime who inspired a great revival of interest in the art of mime and is popularly re-

French mime artist Marcel Marceau as his character "Bip" in a September 2000 performance in Paris. (AFP/Corbis)

garded as the greatest mime artist of his time. He began as an actor, studying primarily with experimental theater directors, such as **Charles Dullin**, **Jean-Louis Barrault**, and **Etienne Decroux**. After working in mime for some time, in 1946 Marceau debuted his character Bip, a white-faced melancholy clown, whom he portrayed for the rest of his life. He established a school for the art of mime, the Ecole de Mimodrame de Paris.

In his many skits, his Bip faces and overcomes everyday situations and, by doing so, draws the extraordinary from ordinary occurrences. Alone on a bare stage, Marceau could fill an entire scene by his own actions and reactions to imaginary forces and objects. His focus and precision in doing simple tasks, such as exploring the inside of an imaginary box, are the qualities that impressed his audience so strongly. In silence he was able to portray some of the primary emotions and attitudes common to humankind.

He also created mime-dramas, such as *Mort avant l'aube* (Death before the Dawn), 1947, and *Jardin Public* (Public Garden), 1949, in which he portrayed ten different characters. He appeared in the film *Silent Movie*, 1976, directed by Mel Brooks, in which none of the actors spoke except, ironically, Marceau.

See also Ancient Mime; Mime
References: Felner, Mira. *Apostles of Silence: The Modern French Mimes.* Rutherford, NJ: Fairleigh Dickinson University Press, 1985; Marceau, Marcel. *Meet*

Marcel Marceau. Videocassette. Sandy Hook, CT: Video Yesteryear, 1999 (original 1965); Martin, Ben. *Marcel Marceau, Master of Mime.* New York: Paddington, 1978.

Marlowe, Christopher (1564–1593)
England
Playwright in **Elizabethan England,** a contemporary of **William Shakespeare**. Marlowe studied in Cambridge University on a scholarship and then moved to London, where he began writing for the theater. His first successful play *Tamburlaine the Great,* 1587, was praised for its gorgeous verse. His most famous play was *The Tragical History of Doctor Faustus,* 1589, based on the German legend of a scholar who sells his soul to the devil in exchange for earthly power. He also wrote *The Jew of Malta,* 1590, about an acquisitive Jewish merchant named Barabas, and a history play, *Edward II,* 1592. Marlowe was killed in 1593 during a quarrel in a tavern. Though he wrote for the theater for only six years, his contribution to the blossoming of drama that began under Elizabeth I was enormous.

References: Hattaway, Michael. *Elizabethan Popular Theatre: Plays in Performance.* London: Routledge and Kegan Paul, 1982; Marlowe, Christopher. *The Life of Marlowe and the Tragedy of Dido, Queen of Carthage.* New York: Gordian, 1966.

Marx Brothers
United States
Comedic family of zany brothers who performed in **vaudeville** and on Broadway before becoming world-famous film actors in their own movies from the late 1920s through the 1940s. Their mother, Minna Schoenberg, came from a long line of stage performers and launched her boys on their career as a vaudeville music ensemble. They switched to comedy and finally made it to Broadway in 1924 with *I'll Say She Is*, followed by *The Coconuts,* 1925, which they made into a film in 1929, and *Animal Crackers,* 1928, which they made into a film in 1930.

Once on the screen, their absurd slapstick comedy was outrageously appealing to both refined and unrefined audiences. Their antics usually involved one of the brothers kicking, tripping, tweaking, or bopping another of the brothers. The brothers included Groucho (1890–1977), master of improvised insults and roving eyes, Harpo (1888–1964), the round-faced silent brother, who usually wore a curly red wig, Chico (1886–1961), who explained Harpo's jokes in a thick Italian accent, and Zeppo (1901–1979), who played the romantic lead in their early works. One of their best films is *Duck Soup*, 1933. The last film in which the comic team worked together was *Love Happy*, 1950.

> **References:** Adamson, Joe. *Grocho, Harpo, Chico, and Sometimes Zeppo; A History of the Marx Brothers and a Satire on the Rest of the World.* New York: Simon and Schuster, 1973; Tiersma, Peter. *Language-Based Humor in the Marx Brothers Films.* Bloomington: Indiana University Linguistics Club, 1985.

Masks

Africa, Bali, Burma, Cambodia, Canada, Caribbean, Greece, India, Indonesia, Italy, Japan, Korea, Thailand, United States

A mask is a material object covering a performer's face either partially or fully, which may or may not extend beyond the face, and which represents a character. Perhaps it is because masks are frozen in posture, like the dead, that they are so often used as a link to ancestors and the spiritual world. The mask is usually created to hold within its design the essence of a spirit, god, or legend, and it visually communicates that being's most salient characteristics. By animating the mask through movement and voice, the performer can make that character present and thereby create a connection with the ancestral past or the spirit world.

Masks are most effective at portraying mythological characters, which often have only a few prominent characteristics. Masks are not good at portraying psychologically complex characters, which may explain why they have not been used much in modern Western-style theater. With the use of masks, one performer can portray several roles in one performance, simply by changing masks. An audience is forced to actively imagine that a performer and the mask are one moving entity. An audience feels an aesthetic thrill when it momentarily believes the two are one, joined through the art of performing.

Wearing a mask allows the performer to partially disengage from the audience, since the performer is hiding behind some facial or bodily covering. This isolation enhances the performer's ability to enter into trance, which is often a necessary ingredient in portraying a god or spirit. Devotees believe that, in these instances, a god or spirit is made manifest and is performing through the body of the performer, who is a sort of totem or channel.

Performing with a mask introduces many challenges for the performer. Expressiveness must be conveyed through the entire body rather than just the face. A mask often hinders breathing, and the performer's body easily overheats. Often vision is partially impaired, so greater spatial awareness is needed. Larger masks are cumbersome and difficult to balance. The performer must serve the portrayal of the masked character by suiting movement and vocalization to it. Often performers hold the mask in their hands and contemplate it before putting it on. In some traditions, such as Japanese **Noh,** they regard themselves masked in a mirror before performing.

Throughout Asia masks are almost exclusively used to portray gods and legends in ceremonies or ritual performances involving worship, such as the Japanese **Bugaku,** a masked temple dance dating back to the seventh century. The **Zat Gyi** of Burma, the **Khon** of Thailand, the **Lakon Khol** of Cambodia, the **Wayang Topeng** and the **Wayang Wong** of Bali and Java, and the **Sandae** of Korea are all masked dance-dramas. The **Dashavatar Kala** is an Indian masked performance enacting all the incarnations of the Hindu god Vishnu.

Western traditions that utilize masks began with Greek classical tragic acting and later appeared in Italy in **commedia dell'arte,** an improvised street theater from the sixteenth and seventeenth centuries that used partial masks for stock characters. In Jamaica and the Caribbean the Christmas celebration **Jonkonnu** features masked performers and dates back to the eighteenth century. Throughout Native American performances, masks are used such as in the **Iroquis False Face.** Many experimental groups, such as the **San Francisco Mime Troupe,** have used masks to great effect. Contemporary designers such as **Julie Taymor** have reintroduced the use of mask in popular performances.

In Africa masks for performance range greatly in size and design. Many masks are revered and stored in special houses when not in use. Mixed with music, dance, and dramatic content, masked performances in Africa are an exuberant expression of their culture and beliefs. In Nigeria the **Abua Masquerade** is a masked dance with many dramatic elements. The *Gelede* is the Yoruba masked dance-drama celebrating the different genders and their respective characteristics. In Malawi the **Nyau Masks** are used in rituals by the Nyau society. Known as the "moon dance," the *Bedu* masked drama is enacted on the Ivory Coast and in Ghana by the Nafana people. Huge horned head pieces that cover the entire body are used by the people of Mali in the *Tyi Wara* to honor the god of farming. In Nigeria the *Chumkpa* includes female impersonation by masked boys and men. In Sierra Leone the **Sande Masks** are worn by prepubescent girls during female initiation ceremonies. In Tanzania and Mozambique, **Midimu** is the general term for masks, of which there are many varieties.

The tradition of masking the face of a performer is practiced all over the world. Covering the identifiable face of the performer with another face is perhaps the most instinctual way of becoming another person, spirit, or animal. Masking presents a unique challenge to the audience to actively imagine the character being performed as real. The mask can be a plaything to delight children, a frightening device to induce terror, even a tool for political satire.

References: Emigh, John. *Masked Performance*. Philadelphia: University of Pennsylvania Press, 1996; Nicoll, Allardyce. *Masks, Mimes and Miracles*. London: G. C. Harrap, 1931.

Matano
South Africa, Zimbabwe
Dramatic performances that usually convey some valuable message; performed at female initiation schools for Venda girls. These schools, of which Domba is the most important, initiate girls into cultural life and prepare them for sexual maturity and marriage. The schools are said to have been started two centuries ago by Chief Nzhelele, though many Venda people believe this tradition to be older. School sessions can last from three months to two years. During this time girls perform a variety of ritual songs and dances. The

girls, however, are merely spectators for *Matano*. Male master teachers at the initiation schools arrange and perform all of the *Matano*.

Almost always shown at night, these performances employ mime, dance, and even clay models, such as a clay cobra to represent the penis during the sexual act, to communicate various elements of the stories. Many of the lessons in these performances prepare girls for the act of lovemaking, warning them of the pain of first insertion, and tell them of the changes that their bodies will undergo, such as menstruation and breast development.

A *Matano* named *Mitotombudzi* or "The Locust," begins with a great bonfire in the center of the acting area. Two grass-covered figures appear suddenly out of the darkness, stepping high from side to side in rhythm to the music. Both the male and the female figures, both performed by men, wear grass "skirts" over their shoulders and hips as well as a grass mask with four large grass antennae. The figure representing the male also has an enormous phallus made of grass, with which he simulates intercourse with the female figure.

Another *Matano* named *Nyalilo* was most criticized by Christian missionaries since it was a mime show representing actual people having intercourse. Initiates were told to kneel facing outside the circle while performers arranged themselves under a blanket in the center performing area. When the girls faced center the performers mimed copulation, though fully dressed, under the blanket. The *Matano* has continued into the twenty-first century.

References: Blacking, John. "Songs, Dances, Mimes and Symbolism of Venda Girls' Initiation Schools." *African Studies* 28, 3 (1969): 149–191; Cornevin, Robert. *Le Theatre en Afrique Noire et a Madagascar*. Paris: Le Livre Africain, 1970.

Mayan Theater
Belize, Guatemala, Mexico
Mayan civilization, indigenous to Latin America, once supported a kingdom spanning parts of present-day **Mexico,** most of Guatemala, and Belize; it was conquered by Spanish invaders in the early sixteenth century. The Mayans believed that the organization of the universe dictated that good always defeated evil, and they performed

many rituals and religio-theatrical ceremonies that demonstrated that belief. One example is the dramatization of *El Baile de los Gigantes*, or Dance of the Giants, a story from the *Popul Vuh*, the Mayan sacred text. Two boys, each twelve years of age, portrayed the young Sun and the young Moon, who allied themselves with the White Giant. They engaged in a mighty battle against the Black Giant. There were five movements to the performance, and often the action was interrupted so that the characters could do homage to the Sun. At the climax, the young Sun cut off the head of the Black Giant, asserting the dominance of good over evil.

The Mayan culture also claims the only extant script of a play from pre-Columbian times in Latin America, the *Rabinal Ach*. The play centers around two enemy warriors, one of whom is taken prisoner by the other and is ultimately sacrificed for not humbling himself before the enemy's leader. The structure of the play is a series of formal challenges interspersed with dance and music. Actors wore intricately carved wooden masks and colorful plumage that indicated their character. Since the masks were heavy and the actors had to continue singing during all of the dances, the lead actors were replaced two or three times during a performance. The formal qualities of the *Rabinal Ach* are believed to be quite similar to those of **ancient Greek theater** before the adding of the third actor, because both styles of drama consist of two actors engaging in a conflict on stage, interrupted at specific moments by a chorus, who most likely sang a few necessary phrases of commentary on the action.

> **References:** Usigli, Rodolfo. *Mexico in the Theater*. Trans. Wilder P. Scott. University, MS: Romance Monographs, 1976; Versènyi, Adam. *Theatre in Latin America: Religion, Politics, and Culture from Cortés to the 1980's*. New York: Cambridge University Press, 1993; Weiss, Judith A. *Latin American Popular Theatre: The First Five Centuries*. Albuquerque: University of New Mexico Press, 1993.

Mechane

Greece

Literally *machine* in ancient Greek; see **Deus ex Machina**.

> **References:** Arnott, Peter D. *Greek Scenic Conventions in the Fifth Century B.C.* Westport, CT: Greenwood,

1978; Halleran, M. R. *The Origins of Attic Comedy*. London: Croom Helm, 1985; Taplin, Oliver. *Greek Tragedy in Action*. Berkeley: University of California Press, 1978.

Meddah

Turkey

Tradition of storytelling in Turkey dating back to the fourteenth century, when *Meddah* provided entertainment in the courts of the sultans. Through the centuries, this form was still performed in the courts but also, eventually, in cafes for lower-class audiences as well. Thought to first have been about Muslim saints, *Meddah* later became secularized because of Islam's disapproval of theatrical imitation. Throughout the second half of the twentieth century this form continued to decline.

A solo performer, also called a *Meddah*, sits on a chair telling stories from memory. The stories are usually comedies about lower-class people, with some kind of moral message running through the parable. The *Meddah* can create excellent caricatures of stereotypical characters drawn from Turkish society and is able to imitate all dialects of the characters in the drama. Due to the quick pacing of the shows, the *Meddah* only has time to change headdresses to indicate which character is speaking, a fez for a Turk, or a high cap for a Persian. He also makes his own sound effects vocally, such as gurgling sounds for drinking. Depending on the audience, shows usually last two to three hours.

In the nineteenth century a *Meddah* would often run his own coffee house, at which he would perform. Tickets would be sold at the door, and admission would include a coffee and a sweet treat. At this time European tourists in Turkey were attracted to this form, so shows were sometimes performed in French instead of Turkish. Performers delighted in satirizing and criticizing officials and governmental decisions, but by the second half of the nineteenth century the usually liberal *Meddah* could be subject to censorship of their political views. Thus a *Meddah* still performs with a short heavy club and a handkerchief around his neck as a promise of obedience, a holdover from the days when, if a performer were to make a slip and criticize the sultan the authorities could choke him with his own handkerchief or beat him with the club.

References: Landau, Jacob. *Studies in the Arab Theater and Cinema*. Philadelphia: University of Pennsylvania Press, 1958; Martinovitch, Nicholas. *Turkish Theatre*. New York: Theatre Arts, 1933; Moreh, Shmuel. *Live Theatre and Dramatic Literature in the Medieval Arab World*. New York: New York University Press, 1992.

Mei Lan Fang (1894–1961)
China

Famous **Peking Opera** actor in the twentieth century known for his mastery of the traditional female character, **Dan.** He reached a level of mastery in performing that led him to be known as King of the **Pear Garden,** famous training school for opera performers. He introduced many innovations in stage practice and gave new dignity and respect to his profession. He traveled internationally and created a passion for Chinese theater through his performances. He attended the school of **Fu Lien Ch'eng** and left a detailed description of its aims and organization in his memoirs. Each morning he would begin vocal exercises at five o'clock to strengthen his lungs and voice control. Then for the rest of the day he would work with a teacher on words and melodies of famous plays. Repetition was the manner of perfecting his art. In 1920 he made films for the first time, with the Commercial Press, entitled *Spring Fragrance Disturbs the Study* and *Heavenly Maiden Strews Blossoms*. During a 1935 performance in Moscow, Sergei Eisenstein made a film, thought to be lost, of Mei's best scenes. He remained in China during the **Chinese Cultural Revolution** and even received a high government position, rare for an actor. Ironically, even though he was a female impersonator, he did much to allow women to perform on the stage. He took women as pupils and created a new school where women could study with a man to learn to portray women! The trend of using only modern revolutionary themes in operas, as promoted by the Communist government, did away with the style of acting he refined and taught.

References: Leyda, Jay. *Dianying: An Account of Films and the Film Audience in China*. Cambridge, MA: MIT Press., 1972; Scott, A. C. *The Theatre in Asia*. New York: Macmillan, 1972.

Chinese actor Mei Lan Fang, famous for playing female roles. (Bettmann/Corbis)

Melanesia

The name given to a group of islands in the Pacific Ocean by European explorers; literally, "black islands," referring to the color of the skin of those who inhabited the islands. Cultural diversity characterizes Papua New Guinea, Irian Jaya, Vanuatu, New Caledonia, and the Solomon Islands, all part of the Pacific region known as Melanesia. Contact with Western Christian missionaries during the nineteenth and early twentieth centuries radically changed the indigenous arts of Melanesia. Most religious practices done before Western contact that included ritualistic and theatrical elements were banned as "heathen" by the missionaries and are now extinct. However, it is known that miming through dance was very common throughout Melanesia and that use of masks believed to be manifestations of spirits was also a common element of performances.

References: Brandon, James. *The Cambridge Guide to Asian Theatre.* New York: Cambridge University Press, 1993; Dean, Beth. *South Pacific Dance.* Sydney: Pacific Publications, 1978; Kaeppler, A. "Movement in the Performing Arts of the Pacific Islands." In *Theatrical Movement: A Bibliographic Anthology,* ed. Robert Fleshman. Metuchen, NJ: Scarecrow, 1986; Kneubuhl, V. "Traditional Performance in Samoan Culture." *Asian Theatre Journal* 4, 2 (1987): 166–176; Oliver, D. *A Solomon Island Society.* Cambridge, MA: Harvard University Press, 1955; Tausie, Vilsoni. *Art in the New Pacific.* Suva: Institute of Pacific Studies in collaboration with the South Pacific Commission, 1980.

Mele

Polynesia

Chanting of traditional Hawaiian poetry for pre-Christian performances. This form was a powerful cultural expression that told of the people's shared history and the genealogy of their rulers, and gave expression to shared emotions and feelings. There are two types of *Mele*: **Mele Oli** is a solo performance on a religious theme, and **Mele Hula** is accompanied by dance movements. It was believed that singers of *Mele* received their songs by divine inspiration.

See also *Hula; Polynesia*

References: Beckwith, Martha W. *The Kumulipo: A Hawaiian Creation Chant.* Honolulu: University Press of Hawaii, 1972; Brandon, James. *The Cambridge Guide to Asian Theatre.* New York: Cambridge University Press, 1993; Charlot, John. *Chanting the Universe: Hawaiian Religious Culture.* Honolulu: Emphasis International, 1983.

Mele Hula

Polynesia

Chanting of pre-Christian Hawaiian poetry performed with dance movements and often accom-

panied by musical instruments such as gourds, bamboo rattles, and drums.

See also *Hula; Mele*

References: Beckwith, Martha W. *The Kumulipo: A Hawaiian Creation Chant.* Honolulu: University Press of Hawaii, 1972; Brandon, James. *The Cambridge Guide to Asian Theatre.* New York: Cambridge University Press, 1993; Charlot, John. *Chanting the Universe: Hawaiian Religious Culture.* Honolulu: Emphasis International, 1983.

Mele Oli

Polynesia

Solo chanting of traditional pre-Christian Hawaiian poetry, often based on religious themes. There is usually no musical accompaniment.

See also *Hula; Mele; Mele Hula*

References: Beckwith, Martha W. *The Kumulipo: A Hawaiian Creation Chant.* Honolulu: University Press of Hawaii, 1972; Brandon, James. *The Cambridge Guide to Asian Theatre.* New York: Cambridge University Press, 1993; Charlot, John. *Chanting the Universe: Hawaiian Religious Culture.* Honolulu: Emphasis International, 1983.

Menak

Java

Javanese cycle of stories about the adventures of Amir Hamzah, a famous Islamic hero who converted much of Arabia to Islam through holy battle and through his own noble example.

See also *Wayang Golek.*

References: Brandon, James. *Theatre in Southeast Asia.* Cambridge, MA: Harvard University Press, 1974; Osnes, Mary Beth. "A Survey of Shadow Play in the Malaysian Traditional Shadow Puppet Theatre." Ann Arbor, MI: Proquest, 1992.

Menander (342–291 B.C.)

Greece

Playwright of New Comedy. Menander was very popular in his own time and highly regarded by Roman playwrights, who borrowed from him widely, translating his work into Latin. Only one play survives in its entirety, *The Bad-Tempered Man,* along with fragments of other works. He received an excellent education as a young man and was good friends with the philosopher Epicurus, who deeply influenced his comedies. In 321 he wrote his first play, and he eventually wrote more than a hundred. Menander's scripts for New Comedy and the scripts of **Aristophanes** for Old Comedy are the only works of **Greek comedy** that remain.

Menander's plays were about ordinary people from the wealthy bourgeoisie of Athens, who were often portrayed realistically, complete with delicate character shades and vivid individual traits. Since Athens was a province of Macedonia and no longer an independent democracy, as it had been in Aristophanes's time, freedom of speech was greatly curtailed. Menander could not engage in the satire on contemporary politics that Aristophanes had mastered.

The role of the **Greek chorus** was no longer important in New Comedy. In fact, Menander's plays do not even include words for musical interludes, making his plays seem quite modern.

References: Bieber, Margarete. *The History of the Greek and Roman Theater*. Princeton, NJ: Princeton University Press, 1961; Rees, K. "The Three-Actor Rule in Menander." *Classical Philology* 5 (1910): 291–302; Sandbach, F. *The Comic Theatre of Greece and Rome*. New York: Norton, 1977; Webster, Thomas Bertram Lonsdale. *The Greek Chorus*. London: Methuen, 1970.

The Method
See Group Theater

Mexico

Prior to Spanish occupation of Mexico, indigenous traditions of dance, drama, festivals, and theatrical rituals throve. Numerous civilizations flourished during that time, chief among them being the Aztec, Mayan, Olmec, and Toltec, as well as the less sophisticated cultures of many nomadic tribes. In 1519 the Spaniard Hernán Cortés was welcomed into what is now Mexico City as the Aztec god **Quetzalcóatl,** in a highly theatrical display, thereby setting the trend of the Spaniards' use of theater to penetrate and conquer the indigenous people of Mexico. Most of what we know regarding pre-Columbian theater is based on accounts of early sixteenth-century Spanish missionaries who documented the extraordinary religious and cultural traditions they witnessed. One example of such an account is from the sixteenth century, documenting a festival at Cholula

in honor of the deity Quetzalcóatl. There were great dances on a central patio in the temple. On a raised stage in the middle of the patio, which was 30 feet square, humorous skits were performed. The setting was decorated with arches of roses and branches. After the people feasted, the performers ascended the stage, all pretending to be sick or deaf or lame or blind and asking health from the idols as they came. To conclude, a great *Mitlte*, or dance, was performed involving all the performers. Other than performances giving praise and homage to the gods, dance-dramas glorifying hunting, agriculture, and warfare were also common. Some of these performances existed among the indigenous people until the second half of the nineteenth century, although they were greatly altered after their conversion to Christianity.

Between the years of the conquest and the end of the sixteenth century, Spanish missionaries were responsible for an incredible wave of conversion to Christianity. The primary tools used were religious performances in the native language, which the missionaries learned promptly upon arrival. These performances were mostly adaptations of Spanish *Autos Sacramentales* enacting scenes from the Bible. As in most world theaters at that time, it is assumed that no women performed on the stage, but that young boys portrayed all female roles. Performances were staged lavishly, as is evident from an account of a performance in Tlaxcalanl in 1538 that was an *auto sacramentale* based on the story of Adam and Eve in paradise. Their home was adored with golden fruit, every kind of bird, animals both real and portrayed by costumed actors, and four enormous fountains.

This trend of performances of enormous proportions was also documented in Mexico City in 1539; a show written and directed by Spanish priests was performed, enacting the conquest of Jerusalem and the conquest of Rhodes. In the latter show, hundreds of "commanders" richly costumed rode through town on horses, and ships traveled through the plaza awaiting a fully cast Turkish ambush. Casts of hundreds were drawn from the indigenous populations. The scale and grandeur of these displays must have gone a long way in impressing the converted with the power of the Spanish and the glory of their past. We know that Indian performers incorporated some of their former religious dances, rites, and costumes into these performances because of a document in 1544 by Bishop Zumárraga prohibiting just that.

By the end of the sixteenth century, the theater formerly performed inside the churches moved out into the streets and underwent many changes, one of which was the evolution of professional actors (which seems to indicate the advent of women on the stage). One example of this newly evolved theater was a pantomime performance of the stages of the Passion (the sufferings of Christ between the Last Supper and his death on the cross), begun by Franciscan Fray de Gamboa, which was done on Good Friday. This performance is still enacted in rural parts of Mexico at present.

Not much original theatrical activity occurred from the sixteenth to the eighteenth century, besides sporadic performances of European plays and special performances to celebrate the viceroy's birthday. The only authentically Mexican playwright who stands out during this time is Sor Juana Inés de la Cruz (1651–1695), who provided many great roles for Mexican actors. There was one exceptional play during this time, *Ollantay*, performed in 1780 before Tupac Amaru, the last great Inca rebel against Spanish rule, it was quickly banned by the Spanish viceroy.

The eighteenth century cemented the tradition of foreign actors performing foreign plays, one reason being that royalties didn't need to be paid for a foreign script. There were a few outstanding Mexican-born actor managers (although even they were of Spanish descent); among them were Esteban Vela, reportedly a great actor, who began managing the Coliseum as a successful theater in 1731, and Ana Mara de Castro, who took over the same theater after Vela's death. She was highly acclaimed as an actress for her energy, elocution, the vividness of her actions, her sweet singing voice, and an outrageous wardrobe. From the end of the eighteenth century onward, the feudal custom of theatrical family dynasties began and caused the near death of dramatic conservatories, since any outsiders were considered to be intruders.

Censorship and governmental regulations began to be more present in the theater in the eighteenth century. The viceroyalty introduced many ordinances regulating the theater in the 1770s, the strangest of which was a law that a border be built on the front edge of the stage so that the actress's feet could not be seen. Plays at the beginning of the nineteenth century were strictly censored by the Holy Office for any progressive thinking that questioned religious teachings. Plays such as *The Sensitive Negro*, a Mexican melodrama that became very popular, was censored in 1809 because it encouraged the insurrection of slaves against their masters.

Mexico gained independence from Spain in 1810, but the weight of the colonial mentality kept an indigenous theater from taking off. A growing revulsion for Spaniards, beginning in 1821, culminated with their being forced out of Mexico, which emptied the theaters, since most of the actors were foreign. The need for actors led to an abundance of talented Mexican actors coming to the stage, who were seen as dignified and exciting by the public even though, in order to survive in their profession, they had to simultaneously work as dancers and singers. Their names and incomes were highly publicized. Exceptional examples of actors from this time are Victorio Rocamora, the leading musical man, and leading ladies Luz Vallecillo and Agustina Montenegro.

The twentieth century brought a rejuvenated Mexican theater after centuries of dependence on Spain and Europe; this renewal has its true origin in Virginia Fábregas, who began acting in the 1890s alongside Spanish actor Leopoldo Burón. She consistently demonstrated a higher vision and a thirst for learning. In works she was involved with, the public found elegance, effective staging, innovative scenery, and thoughtful intelligent acting. Also popular in both the nineteenth and twentieth centuries were shows of improvised comedy known as **Carpas,** in which the great Mexican comedian **Cantinflas** got his start.

Religious spectacles and theatrical rituals persist until the present throughout villages in Mexico. These are usually performed by villagers with no theatrical training and improvised on a scenario based on a Bible story. One example, **Las Tres Caídas de Jesucristo,** *Jesus Christ's Three Falls,* reenacts Christ's Passion. There are also numerous dance-dramas based on religious themes and enactments of the religious miracles of the "New

World," such as the appearance of the Virgin of Guadalupe.

Beginning in the 1920s, *Teatro de Masas* (Theater of the Masses), performed in huge open-air theaters, was created through government sponsorship. In this kind of theater, ambitious theatrical works of enormous proportions reenacted Mexican history, always ending in the glorious Mexican Revolution (1910), which was seen as a sort of secular salvation for the masses.

One such play, *Liberación (Liberation)*, 1929, by Efrén Orozco Rosales (1903–1973), dramatizes the most important moments in Mexican history to instill pride and increase awareness among Mexican people. The piece calls for a cast of 1,235 people and culminates with the Mexican Revolution. Sometimes Aztec ceremonies were recreated, using enormous casts in a like fashion, thus rejecting colonial history and asserting Aztec nobility. Many government efforts sought to revitalize indigenous theatrical forms as a way of casting off colonial dominance and as a way of claiming their shared past.

In the 1960s and 1970s there was the creation of the Teatro Campesino (Peasant's Theater), which linked education and theater through approaches used by practitioners of **Latin American liberation theater,** theater designed to give dignity and a voice to the poor of Latin America. One of the best examples of this effort is Transhumante, a theater group organized in the late 1960s named after the Transhumante Indians, a nomadic tribe from central Mexico. The group taught drama and performed in factories and church halls. Although based in Mexico City, they toured in a trailer truck converted into a traveling theater.

The Institute for Community Development (IMDEC) has also used theater as a tool for social change in urban areas. Theater is used as a means of raising the community's consciousness regarding issues such as health care, housing, and workers' rights. One group of students sponsored by IMDEC created a performance of the Stations of the Cross during Holy Week that depicted Christ's carrying of the cross. Instead of having an actor portray Christ, they had industrial workers repeatedly being beaten down by injustice and oppression as they "carried their cross." Productions by IMDEC involve audience participation in the creating and molding of their pieces, so that the plays truthfully depict the audience's own experience with injustice and oppression. All efforts are to provide a catalyst toward positive action and improvements for the poor communities of Mexico.

References: Costantino, Roselyn. "Theatre in Mexico: New Challenges, New Visions." *Latin American Theatre Review* 28, 2 (Spring 1995): 132–140; Donahue, Francis. "Toward a Mexican National Theater." *Revista/Review Interamericana* 19, 3–4 (1989): 29–40; Macotela, Fernando. "Mexican Popular Cinema of the 1970s: How Popular Was It?" *Studies in Latin American Popular Culture* 1 (1982): 27–34; Michel, Manuel. "Mexican Cinema: A Panoramic View." *Film Quarterly* 18, 4 (Summer 1965): 46–55; Usigli, Rodolfo. *Mexico in the Theater.* Trans. Wilder P. Scott. University, MS: Romance Monographs, 1976; Versènyi, Adam. *Theatre in Latin America: Religion, Politics, and Culture from Cortés to the 1980's.* New York: Cambridge University Press, 1993; Weiss, Judith A. *Latin American Popular Theatre: The First Five Centuries.* Albuquerque: University of New Mexico Press, 1993.

Meyerhold, Vsevolod (1874–1940)
Russia

Director, actor, innovator, born Karl Theodore Kazimir Meyergold. Meyerhold studied acting under **Nemirovich-Danchenko** and performed several parts at the **Moscow Art Theater.** Though he greatly admired Nemirovich-Danchenko and **Stanislavsky**, he left the MAT in 1902 because his artistic inclinations were more nonrealistic, symbolic, and experimental. In 1905, Stanislavsky asked Meyerhold to direct the Studio, an appendage to the MAT, where he immediately began creating works whose settings were the reverse of naturalistic. Meyerhold wanted the overall aesthetic to communicate the content and feel of the production, with the actor subservient to this aim. His appointment to head the Studio was quickly terminated.

In 1906 **Vera Kommissarzhevskaya** invited Meyerhold to direct her new theater, which was the center of the leftist movement in the arts and of nonrealistic theater. Here he created a total stage aesthetic that conveyed a mood and feeling visually, and he then expected the actors to work to become a part of that visual unit. He had the actors move and speak in a slow, almost ritualistic fashion. Great actors such as Kommissarzhevskaya could find no place for themselves in his vision and were not able to realize his ideals, and his audience seldom appreciated or understood his efforts. He directed many plays by symbolist playwrights such as Maurice Maeterlinck (1862–1949). He achieved great success with his production of *The Little Showbox*, 1906, even acting the role of Pierrot himself. Ultimately, however, Meyerhold and Kommissarzhevskaya differed so drastically in their idea of acting that she asked him to leave.

In 1907 he was appointed director-producer of the Imperial Theater. At this pivotal point in his development, he turned from symbolism to experimenting with a circus-like show of the comically grotesque. He emphasized the actor's physical training, the body, the voice, and the movements, and glorified the actors of the Italian *commedia dell'arte.* Between 1908 and 1917 Meyerhold was known as one of Russia's greatest theater directors. After the Revolution of 1917, he became the universally recognized leader of the new forms of theatrical expression and a member of the Communist Party, which embraced him as an innovator of new forms to further the revolution. He was given freedom to realize his most extravagant productions. In 1918 he staged Vladimir Mayakovsky's *Mystery Bouffe*, a futurist political farce. In 1922 he directed *The Magnificent Cuckold*, by Fernand Crommelynck, utilizing his system of **bio-mechanics** on a constructivist set occupied by ramps, wheels, and a trapeze. In his athletic and highly physical system of biomechanics, Meyerhold attempted to demonstrate that human communication in essence is conveyed through gesture, action, and attitude.

Throughout his life, he spoke out for artistic freedom. In 1937 his theater was closed because he did not create productions that were in the obligatory style, **socialist realism.** He was later arrested, and many believe he was taken prisoner and shot in 1940. Other accounts say he lived until 1942.

See also Naturalism; Symbolism

References: Braun, Edward. *Meyerhold: A Revolution in Theatre.* Iowa City: University of Iowa Press, 1995; Gladkov, Aleksandr Konstantinovich. *Meyerhold Speaks, Meyerhold Rehearses.* Trans. Alma Law. Amsterdam: Harwood Academic, 1997; Hoover, Marjorie. *Meyerhold: The Art of Conscious Theater.* Amherst: University of Massachusetts Press, 1974; Slonim, Marc. *Russian Theater, From the Empire to the Soviets.* Cleveland: World, 1961.

Micronesia

The name given to a group of more than two thousand islands in the northwestern Pacific Ocean by European explorers; literally, "small islands." The Federated States of Micronesia, Yap, Chuuk, Pohnpei, and Kosrae, along with the Mariana Islands, Marshall Islands, Beleu (Palau), Kiribati, and Nauru, are dispersed across almost two thousand miles. There are eight primary languages in this ethnically diverse area, further divided by regional dialects. Spain claimed sovereignty from 1565 to 1899 over the Caroline Islands, after which Germany bought the islands. Following World War I, the islands were granted to Japan to use for agricultural development. After World War II, the United States administered the islands as the United Nations Trust Territory of the Pacific. Independence was gained in 1986.

Traditional performing arts in Micronesia tend to involve poetry, spoken or as song lyrics, and dance rather than drama. There are a few examples of dramatic elements contained within dance performances or rituals. Often dancers will impersonate animals, such as a frigate bird or an iguana. Dancers also mime such activities as rowing a canoe, fighting, or lovemaking. Acting out the spirit world through dance, poetry, and chanting tends to be the primary goal of most Micronesian performing arts.

References: Brandon, James. *The Cambridge Guide to Asian Theatre.* New York: Cambridge University Press, 1993; Browning, M. "Micronesian Heritage." *Dance Perspectives* 43 (Autumn 1970): 7–49; Dean, Beth. *South Pacific Dance.* Sydney: Pacific Publications, 1978; Kaeppler, A. "Movement in the Performing Arts of the Pacific Islands." In *Theatrical Movement: A Bibliographic Anthology*, ed. Robert Fleshman. Metuchen, NJ: Scarecrow, 1986; Tausie, Vilsoni. *Art in the New Pacific.* Suva: Institute of Pacific Studies in collaboration with the South Pacific Commission, 1980.

Midimu

Mozambique, Tanzania

General name for face masks that are used in performances in Tanzania and Mozambique. There are numerous varieties of masks in this category, including a helmet-type mask, small masks that cover only the face, and extended masks. An example of an extended mask is the *Amwalindembo,* or young pregnant woman. In this performance a performer wears a mask that covers the face and extends down in a sort of sculpted torso mask depicting large breasts and a very pregnant stomach. The performer dances sluggishly about, demonstrating the discomfort of pregnancy. In Tanzania there are masked stilt dancers, or *Midimu ya Muha,* of the Makonde tribe, who perform on high stilts, dramatizing various aspects of community life, ranging from the hazards of honey collecting to courting a girl. Each scene performed in an evening performance has its own song and rhythm.

All performers are males and are usually members of a secret society that organizes performances. In all types of *Midimu* masked performances there is a great deal of secrecy concerning the identity of the masked dancer. Performers tell their relatives that they must go on a long journey during the time of the performance, so the identity of performer is not known. The initiated men of the society are believed to have a fellowship with spiritual mysteries and beings. The women and uninitiated boys are kept from knowing the secrets of the performances and, thus, the spiritual mysteries.

In recent times masked dancing in general has become commercialized, and the spiritual significance of the performance has changed in character.

See also *Isinyago*

References: Wembah-Rashid, J. A. R. "Isinyago and Midimu: Masked Dancers of Tanzania and Mozambique." *African Arts* 4, 2 (1971): 38–44.

Mie
Japan
Stylized pose used to great dramatic effect in **Kabuki,** popular Japanese dramatic form of the seventeenth century. An actor strikes a *Mie* as a defensive pose with one arm raised above the head and the body either leaning back on one bent leg or balancing on one foot. He wears a fierce facial expression with the corners of his mouth down and his eyes wide open. The ultimate expression of the Kabuki style of physical movement is expressed through an actor striking a *Mie.*

References: Ernst, Earle. *The Kabuki Theatre.* New York: Oxford University Press, 1956. Reprint, Honolulu: University Press of Hawaii, 1974.

Mifune, Toshiro (1920–1997)
Japan
Famous Japanese film actor from the 1950s into the 1980s. He most often portrays the **Tateyaku,** a type character, as a sensual, virile, exuberant male animal. He is popular for his roles, where he displays total disregard for social conventions. He swats at bugs and scratches indiscriminately. He played the bandit in *Rashomon* and starred in many other films by **Akira Kurosawa.**

See also John Wayne, *Tateyaku*

References: Bock, Audie. *Japanese Film Directors.* New York: Kodansha International, 1978; Mast, Gerald. *A Short History of the Movies.* 4th ed. New York: Macmillan, 1986.

Miller, Arthur (1915–)
United States
One of America's greatest playwrights, who created such heart-wrenching American tales as the Pulitzer Prize–winning *Death of a Salesman,* 1949, with the tragic American character, Willy Loman. His first successful play was *All My Sons* in 1947. *The Crucible,* 1953, is about the seventeenth-century Salem witch trials, a barely disguised metaphor for the McCarthy-era anticommunist fervor that so resembled a witch-hunt. Miller was married to **Marilyn Monroe** from 1955 to 1961 and wrote the screenplay of *The Misfits,* 1961, specifically for Monroe (her last film). Miller's next play, *After the Fall,* 1964, is believed to have been influenced by his failed relationship with Monroe. His later plays, such as *Playing for Time,* 1981, and *The Last Yankee,* 1992, have not enjoyed the same popular success as his early work.

References: Moss, Leonard. *Arthur Miller.* Boston: G. K. Hall, 1980; Nelson, Benjamin. *Arthur Miller: Portrait of a Playwright.* New York: McKay, 1970.

Mime
France, United States, Italy
A purely physical form of artistic expression that originates from the **ancient mime** and **ancient**

pantomime of the Greeks and the Romans. Ancient mime performances became so lewd in nature that by the fifth century the Roman Catholic Church forbade the performances and excommunicated all mime performers. Mime emerged in the Italian improvised theater of the sixteenth and seventeenth centuries, the *commedia dell'arte,* in which there was much physical humor. "Dumb shows" were also popular in Elizabethan and Jacobean times and were performed within spoken dramas.

Modern mime follows no strict conventions and can include a single performer on a bare stage or many performers enacting a scene with setting and props. Music usually plays an important role in a performance, enhancing the mood and emotions of the wordless scenes. The famous mime artist Jean-Gaspard Deburau lived from 1796 to 1846. The great French revival of mime as a popular art form was headed by **Etienne Decroux,** followed by **Marcel Marceau.** Many innovative French theater artists, such as **Jean-Louis Barrault**, studied mime and incorporated it into their productions. Mime has thrived for hundreds of years as a popular form of street entertainment, delighting audiences with its simplicity, cleverness and elegance.

References: Felner, Mira. *Apostles of Silence: The Modern French Mimes.* Rutherford, NJ: Fairleigh Dickinson University Press, 1985; Montanaro, Tony. *Mime Spoken Here: The Performer's Portable Workshop.* Gardiner, ME: Tilbury House, 1995; Niedzialkowski, Stefan. *Beyond the Word: The World of Mime.* Troy, MI: Momentum Books, 1993.

Ming Huang (713–756)
China
Emperor of Tang dynasty (A.D. 618–907) and dedicated patron of Chinese theater. Ming Huang started the **Pear Garden,** which was the first official training academy for actors, dancers, and singers. The emperor himself played the clown role, **Chou,** in **Peking Opera.** Because the role became associated with the emperor, the Chou actor enjoys many comforts and special considerations. For example, the Chou actor gets the number one trunk to store costumes and supplies in when on the road. Also, no other actors can start applying their makeup before the clown.

References: Kalvodova, Sis, and Vanis Kalvodova. *Chinese Theatre.* Trans. Iris Urwin. London: Spring House, 1957; Scott, A. C. *The Theatre in Asia.* New York: Macmillan, 1972.

Minstrel
United States
An indigenous form of entertainment in the **United States** that enjoyed the peak of its popularity from 1840 to 1880; made up of lively and sentimental songs, soft-shoe dancing, and comic skits, all in a style that parodied southern African Americans. White performers applied black makeup that unkindly exaggerated the facial features of African Americans. The songs and skits were based on stereotypical portrayals of African Americans and plantation life. The form's beginning is attributed to Thomas D. Rice, who performed the Jim Crow character in 1828, wearing blackface and playing the banjo. Minstrels grew to include four performers, which included the white-faced leader, Mr. Interlocutor, and two "end-men," Mr. Tambo and Mr. Bones. Minstrel performers were most often northern whites with little direct experience with southern African Americans. Thus their portrayals were gross exaggerations and largely fictional.

Performers usually sat in a semicircle, with each playing an instrument, such as tambourine, violin, banjo, and a rhythmical instrument known as bones. A standard format was introduced by a troupe leader named E. P Christy; it began with wandering performers being invited to sit down and begin an instrumental and song section. Comic repartee by the "end-men" often interrupted this section. The second portion consisted of specialty acts, and the third of a comic sketch of a plantation scene, a parody of a Shakespearean scene or a melodrama.

By the 1850s black performers had adopted the format of the minstrel show and began to perpetuate the stereotypical depiction of African Americans. A black group called Callender's Georgia Minstrels, which featured the comedian Billy Kersands and Haverly's Coloured Minstrels, was a huge success. African American minstrels were the first popular performance groups to introduce female performers. The minstrel was an excellent training ground for many actors, black and white, such as Al Jolson (1886–1950), Sam Lucas, Billy McLain, and Eddie Cantor, whose careers survived longer than the popularity of the minstrel.

Great Britain had a great love affair with American-style minstrels in the late nineteenth and early twentieth centuries and had their own troupes such as the Moore and Burgess Minstrels. Since tastes and sensibilities have evolved in the United States and abroad, both minstrels and blackface in general have become very rare and are largely viewed as being insulting and racist.

> **References:** *Early Minstrel Show.* (Sound recording.) New York: New World Records, 1985; Fletcher, Tom. *100 Years of the Negro in Show Business.* New York: Burdge, 1954; Mahar, William. *Behind the Burnt Cork Mask: Early Blackface Minstrels and Antebellum American Popular Culture.* Urbana: University of Illinois Press, 1999; Slide, Anthony. *Early American Cinema.* Metuchen, NJ: Scarecrow,1994.

Miracle Play
Europe
A medieval type of religious play dramatizing the life and martyrdom of a saint and the miracles that saint may have performed. The most famous miracle plays are about the Virgin Mary. Plays for specific saints were performed in cathedrals and abbeys on that saint's feast day. In **England** plays of this kind are sometimes called **mystery play**s.

Mizoguchi, Kenji (1898–1956)
Japan
Japanese film director. Mizoguchi's career was at its peak just as Kurosawa's was beginning. He specialized in **Jidai-geki,** period films set in Japan's past. He gave a view of the past as seen through folk legends, fairy tales, and paintings. He evoked the manner of living from the past. He was drawn to the combination of art and nature and delighted in the view of life in the past as frozen in drawings. In his movies many of his protagonists are artists. His films are classical in structure and display a Japanese sense of symmetry. Important films by Mizoguchi include *Taki no Shiraito* (1933), *The Story of the Last Chrysanthemum* (1939), *Utamaro and His Five Women* (1953), *Sansho,* and *Ugetsu.*

> **See also** Ozu, Yasujiro
> **References:** Bock, Audie. *Japanese Film Directors.* New York: Kodansha International, 1978; Mast, Ger-

ald. *A Short History of the Movies.* 4th ed. New York: Macmillan, 1986.

Mnouchkine, Ariane (1939–)
France
Director; founder and director of the Théâtre du Soleil (Theater of the Sun), a theatrical commune consisting of about forty artists who create innovative theatrical works in nontraditional spaces. Dedicated to extremely high standards, this group has been admired throughout the world. The Théâtre du Soleil resided at the Cirque d'Hiver (Theater of the Winter) in Paris until 1968 and has since worked in many nontraditional theater buildings. During their production of **Shakespeare**'s *A Midsummer Night's Dream,* they peopled the fairy world with timid human creatures who crawled over every available surface in the performance space. They created a sensation with a work of environmental theater, entitled 1789, first performed in Milan in 1970 and then moved to Paris. It was performed in a wide-open space, and the audience was cast as the mob and stood in the center of the performance space as the French Revolution was enacted around them on various platforms. Numerous devices were used, sometimes in unison, such as mime, sideshows, music, puppets, and dialogue. The actors then separated the audience into groups that were encouraged to join in the celebration when a huge effigy of Louis XVI was destroyed.

> **References:** Champagne, Lenora. *French Theatre Experiment since 1968.* Ann Arbor, MI: UMI Research Press, 1984.; Kiernander, Adrian. *Ariane Mnouchkine and the Theatre du Soleil.* New York: Cambridge University Press, 1993; Richardson, Helen Elizabeth. "The Theatre du Soleil and the Quest for Popular Theatre in the Twentieth Century." Ph.D. diss. Ann Arbor, MI: University Microfilms International, 1991.

Modrzejewska, Helena
Poland
Polish actress of humble origin who began acting with a third-rate troupe run by Gustav Zimajer, but quickly rose to fame as Poland's leading actress, performing brilliantly in both comic and tragic roles. She gained elegance and sophistication and mingled with the nobility and intellectu-

als. In 1876 she emigrated to the **United States** and toured widely. Modrzejewska returned to Poland from 1878 to 1879 to tour with her own newly formed company. Contemporaries said that her soft, sweet voice deepened as she grew older into a more mature voice with more warmth and emotional resonance, allowing her to play villains like Lady Macbeth. In 1881 she moved to London and in 1889 began touring extensively. Her most famous roles include the title role in *Adrienne Lecouvreur,* by Eugène Scribe, and Nora in *A Doll's House,* by **Henrik Ibsen**. Along with **Sarah Bernhardt**, and **Eleonora Duse**, Modrzejewska was in her time considered one of the leading actresses in the Western world.

> **References:** Csato, Edward. *The Polish Theatre.* Warsaw: Polonia Publishing, 1963.

Mohhabbazeen

See *Fasl Mudhik*

Mohlam

Laos

A lively style of folk singing accompanied by a reed panpipe. *Mohlam* troupes travel from village to village singing racy songs about romance and lovemaking. *Mohlam* inspired **Mohlam Luong,** musical dramatic performances.

> **References:** Brandon, James R. *Brandon's Guide to Theatre in Asia.* Honolulu: University Press of Hawaii, 1976.

Mohlam Luong

Laos

A popular style of comic opera. Performing troupes of **Likay,** popular light opera in Thailand, came to Laos from the south. They put their plays to **Mohlam,** a lively style of singing in Laos accompanied by a reed panpipe. *Mohlam Luong* performers improvise dialogue about local news and intrigue in between songs. There are usually 15–20 performers in a *Mohlam Luong* troupe. The acting is usually amateurish, but the comic characters are quite skillful with both improvised jokes and physical humor. The actors' stamina in delivering long sung passages is impressive.

> **References:** Brandon, James R. *Brandon's Guide to Theatre in Asia.* Honolulu: University Press of Hawaii, 1976.

Mohlam Mu

See *Mohlam Luong*

Moira

See Greek Tragedy

Moldova

The Moldovans are Romanian in language and culture. Moldova theater traditions date back to medieval times, when religious dramas linked to rituals and mysteries were performed. A distinct folk theater tradition had developed from folk practices and carnivals by the eighteenth century. Moldova was under Soviet control almost exclusively from 1924 until independence was declared in 1991. There is believed to have been some performances of religious dramas and some forms of folk drama in Moldova during the Middle Ages. Other than sporadic visits from Russian theater troupes, theater did not begin to emerge until early the twentieth century with performances by amateur troupes. Once the Soviets gained control in the 1920s, all artistic expression was forced to conform to Soviet ideology. Soviets opened a theater in Tirapol in 1933 to propagate these views and values. The Likuritch National Puppet Theater opened in 1945. After Stalin's death in 1953, the Romanian language, which had been suppressed in Moldavia previously, was allowed again, and the staging of Romanian plays became popular, such as those by Vasile Alecsandri (1821–1890). Control of the theater became harsher in the late 1960s and did not ease until the late 1980s. As Moldova works to regain its cultural identity, many young artists are enjoying the freedom of expression denied for decades.

> **See also** Romania; Soviet Cinema; Soviet Union
> References: Cheianu, Constantin. "Moldova." In *The World Encyclopedia of Contemporary Theatre,* ed. Don Rubin, 593–595. New York: Routledge, 1994.

Molière, Jean-Baptiste Poquelin (1622–1673)

France

Actor, director, and playwright who contributed a canon of excellent comedies and a high standard of comedic acting, both of which stood as a measure of excellence for centuries to follow. Molière was educated for a law career but had long loved the theater. He joined the theater group of the Béjart family, Les Enfants de Famille (The Children of Family), who later changed their name to L'Illustre Théâtre (The Illustrious Theater). Early on in his acting career he changed his name so as not to disgrace his family. In 1658, Molière's group, over which he had assumed artistic leadership, was summoned to perform for the court of Louis XIV. His troupe captivated the audience with their delightfully performed farces and was rewarded with being able to perform in the theater called the Petit Bourbon.

Molière stressed natural speech for his actors and often satirized the actors of his rival theater, the Hôtel de Bourgogne, for their bombastic style of acting. Molière's success was with comedies, as he did not excel as a tragic actor earlier in his career. He was able to please audiences so effectively with his comedy in part because of the influence of the popular Italian theater form, the **commedia dell'arte.** Though he was triumphantly successful as a playwright, actor, and director, he lived during fiercely competitive times, and success was not without its controversy and pain. His enemies spread vicious rumors about his personal affairs, such as accusing him of marrying his own daughter. He was not popular among those in power because his plays so often exposed the hypocrisy of members of the aristocracy. Nevertheless, his company was under the king's direct protection.

His most famous plays are Tartuffe, 1664, Le Misanthrope, 1666, and Le Malade Imaginaire (The Imaginary Invalid), 1672. During a performance of the latter play, Moliére, playing the hypochondriac, had a seizure and died a few hours later. As was common for French actors at that time, he was buried at night with a humble service, far from befitting the enormous contribution he had made to French theater.

References: Chinoy, Helen Krich, and Toby Cole. *Actors on Acting.* New York: Crown, 1970; Dussane, Beatrix. *An Actor Named Moliere (Comedier Nomme Moliere).* Trans. Lewis Galantiere. New York: C. Scribner's Sons, 1937; Hall, H. Gaston. *Comedy in Context: Essays on Moliere.* Jackson: University Press of Mississippi, 1984; Mander, Gertrud. *Jean Baptiste Moliere.* Velbert: Friedrich, 1967.

Monroe, Marilyn (1926–1962)
United States

Legendary American actress and film star in the 1950s and early 1960s. Born Norma Jean Mortenson, Monroe had a turbulent childhood with no father, a mother in a mental institution, and many different foster homes, some of which were abusive. Her acting career began after she modeled for a pinup poster for soldiers in World War II. In this manner she got noticed by Hollywood, and Hollywood virtually re-created her, shaping her into the American icon we recognize as Marilyn Monroe. Her career slowly took off in the early 1950s with films such as *As Young as You Feel,* 1951, and *Gentlemen Prefer Blondes,* 1953, peaking with *The Seven Year Itch,* 1955. To break out of the stereotypical role as the breathless blonde, Monroe went to New York and began studying with Lee and Paula Strasberg at the **Actors Studio.** Her development as an actress showed in her next film, *Bus Stop,* 1956, in which she demonstrated comic ability. Her film *Some Like It Hot,* 1959, was a smash, as was *The Misfits,* 1961, which was written especially for her by her husband of the time, playwright **Arthur Miller.** Overcome by illness, depression, and drug addiction, Monroe was found dead by her housekeeper in August of 1962 and is believed to have committed suicide.

References: Rollyson, Carl. *Marilyn Monroe: A Life of the Actress.* Ann Arbor, MI: UMI Research Press, 1986; Steinem, Gloria. *Marilyn.* New York: New American Library, 1987.

Monty Python
United Kingdom

English comedy group, successful in the 1960s and 1970s, who produced the BBC television show *Monty Python's Flying Circus* and many feature films. Their over-the-top comedy was based on the outstanding talent of the six performers, Graham Chapman (1941–1989), John Cleese, Terry Gilliam, Eric Idle, Terry Jones, and Michael Palin. They became a hit in the United States and continue to enjoy an almost cult following. They took absurd and ridiculous situations to the extreme and could be seriously silly better than nearly any other comedy group. Their films include *And Now*

All six members of the Monty Python team on location in Tunisia to film Monty Python's Life of Brian. From left to right are John Cleese, Terry Gilliam, Terry Jones, Graham Chapman, Michael Palin, and Eric Idle. (Archive Photos)

for Something Completely Different, 1972, Monty Python and the Holy Grail, 1974, The Life of Brian, 1979, and Monty Python's The Meaning of Life, 1983.

> **References:** Chapman, Graham. The Complete Monty Python's Flying Circus. New York: Pantheon, 1989; Thompson, John. Monty Python: Complete and Utter Theory of the Grotesque. London: BFI Publishing, 1982.

Morality Play
Europe

A medieval type of religious drama in Europe, probably originating in the late fourteenth century, in which the forces of good and evil fight for the soul of a human being through allegorical characters. Some of the most famous morality plays are The Castle of Perseverance (1400–1425), Mankin, (1465–1470), and Everyman, in about 1500.

Morocco

Before the Arab influence dominated Morocco beginning in the seventh century, Roman theater and culture influenced the area. It is assumed that many Moroccans performed in Roman dramas given the many ruins of Roman theater buildings throughout the country. After the seventh century, many theatrical festivals and performance forms were developed as a means of expression in an Islamic country. Sultan al-Tulba (The Student Sultan) is a week-long celebration in which a young performer pretends to be sultan for a week while the entire community plays along. The halqa (circle) is a centuries-old storytelling tradition in which spectators are invited to act out certain portions of the performance. Many dramatic dances that have traveled to Morocco—probably from other lands—during the last few centuries include gnawa, a drumming and chanting dance of African origin, and the aissawa, done for Sufi religious purposes incorporating snake charmers and music-induced trances performed by members of the Sidi Aissa sect.

From 1912 until independence in 1956, Morocco was divided into two protectorates—one French and one Spanish. Each of these European countries brought with them a mild influence of their theater traditions. Moroccans began doing western-style theater in the 1920s in schools and theater groups. By the 1950s many theater groups thrived, such as the al-Masrah al-Tala'ee (Growing Theater) in Casablanca. The country's first professional theater, al-Ma'moura (National Theater), was founded in 1954. Perhaps the most influential person in Moroccan theater in the 1950s, 1960s, and 1970s was Tayeb al-Seddiki, who translated many works, wrote theater pieces, and also experimented with many traditions. An actor, writer, and director, Nabil Lahlou, has been very influential in the 1980s because of his innovative productions.

In the film industry many young filmmakers who have received training in Europe have been successful at persuading European backers to join in coproductions. As a result, more films have been made recently in Morocco, **Tunisia,** and **Lebanon** than ever before.

References: Landau, Jacob. *Studies in the Arab Theater and Cinema.* Philadelphia: University of Pennsylvania Press, 1958; Moreh, S. "The Arabic Theatre in Egypt in the Eighteenth and Nineteenth Centuries." *Etudes Arabes et Islamiques* 3 (1975): 109–113; Mostyn, Trevor, and Albert Hourani, eds. *The Cambridge Encyclopedia of the Middle East and North Africa.* New York: Cambridge University Press, 1988.

Moro-moro
Philippines

Folk play, in which a Christian prince defeats a Muslim prince. The first play was written in 1637 by a Spanish Jesuit priest to religiously instruct the people of the Philippines. By the eighteenth century plays of this sort were regularly performed on saints' days and various festivals in the villages. There is a great contrast between the bloody fight scenes, in which the Christians triumph over and slaughter the Muslim army, and the tender romantic scenes of love between the Christian prince and his beloved. There are hun-

dreds in each cast, and rehearsals go on for months for a single performance. The actors are attractive young people from the village. Since they are not trained performers, actors often need prompting on their lines during a performance. The acting style is formalized, in imitation of medieval times, full of chivalry and grandeur. *Moromoro* contains some elements of Filipino pre-Christian dramatic styles, despite opposition by Catholic missionaries. The plays are set in elaborate facsimiles of palaces and castles arranged on a stage. Performers travel from the stage to the church square and back to the stage again, with the audience following close behind. The texts for plays are written in verse by local priests or learned villagers. The plays are exclusively romantic love stories mixed with elements of fairy tales. Honor and love are central themes. In each play the Christian forces triumph over the advances of the Muslim empire. Musical accompaniment is provided by a brass band playing battle tunes and marches. *Moro-moro* has been considered old-fashioned by Philippine people since the 1970s. It is no longer popular in the cities and is almost extinct in the villages.

See also Spain

References: Reyes, Francisca, and Leonor Orosa Gaquingco Aquino. *Philippine Folk Dances.* 5 vols. Manila: Kayamanggi, 1953–1966; Aveilana, Dassy H. "The Native Theatre." *Philippine Quarterly* 1, 4 (March 1952): 60–62; Brandon, James R. *Brandon's Guide to Theatre in Asia.* Honolulu: University Press of Hawaii, 1976; Constanlino, Josefino. "Early Drama Forms in the Philippines." *Philippines Quarterly* 1 (1961): 34–36.

Moscow Art Theater
Russia

Famous Russian theater and actor training facility that opened in 1898, begun by **Konstantin Stanislavsky** and **Vladimir Ivanovich Nemirovich-Danchenko**. The period from 1898 to the 1917 Revolution was the most fertile time for the Moscow Art Theater (MAT), with abundant activity and a fresh and revolutionary way of realistically portraying the inner truth of a play. The MAT company took a trip abroad from 1922 to 1924, at which time they gained worldwide recognition for their achievements in realistic theater. The Communist party viewed the MAT as being associ-

Anton Chekhov (center) reading his play The Seagull *to players of the Moscow Art Theatre, including actor and director Stanislavsky, who is sitting on Chekhov's right, 1898. (Archive Photos)*

ated with bourgeois values but tolerated it because of its high professional ratings. By the 1930s the MAT had become a sort of national academy, a home for psychological realism, which was seen as conservative to many by that time.

Stanislavsky and Nemirovich-Danchenko established workshops for experiments that did not suit the main theater. The first was the Studio, begun in 1905 under the direction of **Vsevolod Meyerhold**, which later closed because Meyerhold's aesthetic principles clashed with Stanislavsky's. Later in 1912 the First Studio of the MAT was started, with Leopold Sullerzhitsky in charge. Some outstanding actors during this time were Evgeny Vakhtangov (1883–1922), **Mikhail Chekhov**, and Serafima Birman. In 1917, the year of the Revolution, Vakhtangov took over the First Workshop associated with the MAT. Stanislavsky saw Vakhtangov as the successor of his work with actors. Vakhtangov brought outstanding standards to his work, which was technically nearly flawless but also had a human touch that lent warmth to his productions. After Vakhtangov's death in 1922, Mikhail Chekhov and Boris Sushkevich

took over the First Studio. In 1924 it became its own theater, called the Second Moscow Art Theater, later renamed the Theater of Gorky.

Stalin took the MAT under his wing and regarded it as a national treasure. He wanted them to do only the classics, which soon left the MAT stagnant and unchanging. In 1998 the MAT celebrated its 100th anniversary. The MAT continues to do only the classics. It remains a frozen relic, a home for the great Russian repertoire.

References: Gauss, Rebecca, *Studio of the Moscow Art Theatre from 1905–1927*, Ph.D. diss., University of Colorado, Ann Arbor, MI: UMI, 1997, 37888530; Slonim, Marc. *Russian Theater, From the Empire to the Soviets.* Cleveland: World, 1961; Stenberg, Douglas, *From Stanislavsky to Gorbachev: The Theater-studios of Leningrad.* New York: P. Lang, 1995; Worrall, Nick. *The Moscow Art Theatre.* New York: Routledge, 1996.

Motokiyo Zeami (1363–1443)
Japan

Son of **Kanami Kiyotsugu,** who developed **Noh** drama. Zeami was a ***Sarugaku*** player with his father for the court and gained great favor from the shogun. Early in his life he was exposed to refined culture, even though as an actor he was of low social origin. Zeami continued the work of his father, and the word Noh came into use during his lifetime. He created a refined, understated, and restrained style of expression that was at the same time powerful. The appeal to popular audiences declined, but it increased for the **samurai** warrior class who provided patronage and protection for performers. Zeami wrote the most highly regarded plays for Noh, in which even low characters spoke in highly refined language so that there would be nothing in the performances to offend the ears of his court patrons. As an actor Zeami was considered to be the best of his era, and his reputation grew so much that he brought the status of actors nearly to the level of the samurai class. In 1400 he wrote **Kadensho,** *The Book of Handing on the Flowers,* which is a secret manual intended to preserve professional secrets, enabling a son or disciple next in line to continue the family tradition. The book includes practical knowledge, as well as writing on the nature and aesthetic principles for Noh. There is also a chapter on *Kashu,* how to achieve *Hana,* literally "flower," usually translated as "beautiful moment." Sadly, Zeami had no successor, since his only son died.

> **References:** Bowers, Faubion. *Japanese Theatre.* New York: Hill and Wang, 1964; Immoos, Thomas. *Japanese Theatre.* Trans. Hugh Young. Originally published as *Japanisches Theater.* New York: Rizzoli, 1977, Inoura, Yoshinobu, and Toshio Kawatake. *The Traditional Theater of Japan.* New York: Weatherhill in collaboration with Japan Foundation, 1981, Scott, A. C. *The Theatre in Asia.* New York: Macmillan, 1972, Waley, Arthur. *The No Plays of Japan.* London: Allen & Unwin, 1921. Reprint, London: Unwin Hyman, 1988.

Mudras

India

Hand gestures associated with specific meanings; they serve as a symbolic language in classical Indian dance.

> **See also** *Bharata Natyam; Kathak; Odissi*
> **References:** Massey, Reginald, and Jamie Massey. *Dances of India.* London: Tricolour, 1989; Samson, Leela. *Rhythm in Joy.* New Delhi: Lustre Press, 1987.

Muqaddam

See Arabic Shadow Puppet Theater

Myanmar

Until the summer of 1989, the country Myanmar was known as Burma. The Burmese Buddhist monarchy has a long history of suffering foreign invasion; Burma was invaded by the Mongol empire in the thirteenth century, the Chinese in the fourteenth century, the British and French in the nineteenth century, and the Japanese in the 1940s. International isolation imposed in the late 1940s by the Burmese socialist government rendered Burma so closed to the Western world that not even Coca-Cola or McDonalds was present there. The Burmese military government seized power in a harsh crackdown on prodemocracy organizations in 1988. It voided the election of Aung San Suu Kyi and her party and placed her under house arrest. Myanmar's military government, State Law and Order Restoration Council (SLORC), is responsible for extreme human rights abuses. Two comedians, U Pa Pa Lay and U Lu Zaw, of an *Anyein Pwe* troupe were in prison from 1996 until mid-2000 for simply making a joke about the government.

Because of Burma's location, it has borrowed culturally from India to the west, Thailand to the east, and China to the north. However, Burmese performance style remains very much its own, characterized by joyful, carefree, and energetic turns, leaps, and kicks. Burmese clown characters easily take over traditional performances for up to an hour doing stunts of physical comedy and pratfalls. **Pwe** is the generic term for any kind of performance in Burma. The word appears in the name of many Burmese theater forms.

Along with Buddhism, there are remnants of spirit worship in the form of **Nats,** the name for Burmese spirits. Many early forms of theater were centered on these spirits. **Nibhatkhin** was a form of theater perhaps originally based on spirit plays, it but evolved toward secular themes. Evolved from *Nibhatkhin* is **Nat Pwe,** a spirit medium dance. The most important dance in the performance, that in which the future is told, is performed by a **Natkadaw,** a female spirit dancer who is considered to be a wife to a *Nat.* Basically an adaptation of Thai court dramas, **Zat Gyi** is a masked dance-drama performed for the Burmese courts from 1750 to 1850. Accompanying traditional live performances is an orchestra called a **Saing,** comprised of drums, gongs, bells, cymbals, a reed instrument, and a xylophone.

A highly developed form of marionette theater, **Yokthe Pwe,** began in the fourteenth century as an amusement for children. This form grew more and more sophisticated in the number of strings used to manipulate the puppet, and the dramas used also grew in depth and magnitude. **Apuodaw** is the name of one of the most complicated string puppets.

More modern creations of theatrical forms include **Anyein Pwe,** a variety show of dancing, comedy, and traditional and Western music. Based on Burmese legends, **Zat Pwe** is a dance-drama in which the movement is a combination of classical Thai dance, Burmese dance, and Western ballet brought by the colonists. Evolved from Zat Pwe is **Pya Zat,** a modern dance-drama form that is contemporary in style but set in the past.

References: Ba Han. "The Evolution of Burmese Dramatic Performance and Festival Occasions." *Guardian* 13, 9 (September 1966): 18–24; Brandon, James. *Theatre in Southeast Asia.* Cambridge, MA: Harvard University Press, 1974; Derkeke, U Ba Cho. "The Burmese Marionette Stage." *Asian Horizon* 1 (1948): 51–56; Htin Aung, U. *Burmese Drama: A Study with Translations of Burmese Plays.* Calcutta: Oxford University Press, 1937; Moe Kyaw Aung. "Burmese Marionettes for Modern Audiences." *Forward* 6 (1967): 17–20; Parry, David. "The Burmese Theatre." *Eastern World* 3 (December 1949): 29–31; Ramasubramaniam, V. "The Mediaeval and the Pre-Modern Burmese Theatres." *Bulletin of the Institute of Traditional Cultures* (January–June 1974): 106–117.

Mysore Shadow Puppet Theater
India

Shadow puppet theater from Mysore and parts of Maharashtra State. From behind a muslin screen puppeteers slowly manipulate shadow figures between the screen and a flame. Seated on the other side of the screen, the audience sees only the flickering shadows of the figures as they move in and out of view. A **Sutradhara,** a narrator, stands to the side of the shadow screen, narrating the performance. Instrumental music enhances both his storytelling and the movement of the puppets. The stories dramatized are from the **Ramayana** and the **Mahabharata,** the two great Hindu epic tales.

Shadow figures are carved out of one piece of rawhide, 2 to 3 feet high, with no articulated limbs. Either one or many characters are represented in the shadow figures in a dramatic pose befitting their disposition. Thin colorful paints are used to decorate the figures so that the light passes through the rawhide shadow figure making the shadow itself appear in color.

Because of the limited range of motion possible with these shadow figures, they are generally held close to the muslin screen by the puppeteers, so that the audience sees a sharp distinct shadow image. This creates a pictorial effect that complements the storytelling.

See also *Ravanachhaya*
References: Awasthi, Suresh. "Shadow Plays of India and Their Affinities with the Shadow Plays of Southeast Asia." In *Traditional Drama and Music of Southeast Asia,* ed. Mohd. Taib Osman, 112–119. Kuala Lumpur: Dewan Bahasa Dan Pustaka Kementerian Pelajaran Malaysia, 1974.

Mystery Play
Europe

A medieval type of religious play written in the vernacular, that was spoken, not sung, and performed outdoors. Subjects for these dramas were taken from the Bible, but coarse humor was injected as well. Mystery plays were presented over more than one day in cycles. In the later fourteenth century these plays were performed by members of trade or craft guilds on converted wagons known as pageant wagons. Mystery plays were sometimes called **miracle plays** in **England,** although these usually revolved around the life of a saint.

N

Nadagama
Sri Lanka

Christian folk theater introduced to Sri Lanka in the late eighteenth century by Catholic missionaries. These dramatizations of heroic stories involving love and war are performed in a mixture of the Tamil and Sinhalese languages. Originally they told only religious stories intended to spread the faith, but later, nonreligious stories were added, and the popularity of *Nadagama* throve along the entire western coast of Sri Lanka during the eighteenth and nineteenth centuries.

The *Pote Gura*, the presenter or narrator, begins a performance by singing incantations to the Christian saints to bless the performance. After the presenter has introduced the drama he introduces each character as he or she enters, asking each humorous questions. The jester is always the first to enter, then a wise man, two fortunetellers, and finally the king. After the characters from the court enter in ceremonial song and dance, the drama can finally begin. A traditional play takes seven nights, from after sundown till midnight, to perform completely.

The stage for *Nadagama* performances is a raised semicircular platform placed in a public place in a village. A roof protects the acting area from the elements. The audience sits on the ground or in chairs all around the platform. Additional vocal music is provided vocally by two singers who repeat the lines of songs sung by the *Pote Gura*. On the opposite side of the stage the instrumentalists sit, playing drums, cymbals, a violin, and a harmonium.

References: Brandon, James. *The Cambridge Guide to Asian Theatre.* New York: Cambridge University Press, 1993; Goonatilleka, M. H. *Nadagama: The First Sri Lankan Theatre.* Delhi: Sri Satguru, 1984; Gunawardana, A. J. *Theatre in Sri Lanka.* Colombo: Department of Cultural Affairs, Sri Lanka, 1976.

Nai Nang
Thailand

Term designating puppet master of **Nang Talung,** shadow puppet theater, **Nang Yai,** large shadow figure theater, and **Hun Krabok,** rod puppet theater.

See also *Dalang*
References: Dhani Nivat, Prince. "The Dalang." *Journal of the Siam Society* 43, 2 (1955): 113–135.

Nang Kaloun
See Nang Sbek Touch

Nang Rabam
See Nang Yai

Nang Ram
Thailand

Dance version of **Nang Yai,** shadow theater using huge 5-foot-high shadow figures.

Nang Sbek
Cambodia

Shadow play using huge cutout shadow figures. There are six to eight performers, who manipulate the shadow figures, holding them high over their heads while moving behind and in front of a huge backlit screen. Two narrators sit to the side and perform dialogue and chant verses. The shadow figures are as much as 6 feet high and 5 feet wide. They can portray an entire scene, including three to four characters with some setting around them such as walls, trees, or water. Scenes are based on the relief sculptures on the Khmer temple, Angkor Wat, built A.D. 1112–1152. The order in which the shadow figures are carried onto the stage corresponds to the development of the story being told. The main characters, Rama, Sita, and Laksamana, each warrant their own puppet. The shadow figure and performer are seen first in shadow as they enter behind the screen. Then they pass in front of the screen and are seen in silhouette. Performer and puppet become one moving image as they dance together.

The screen is 30 feet wide and at least 15 feet high. A large fire behind the screen provides the only light source. The repertory is drawn exclusively from the **Ramayana.** Musical accompaniment is performed by a traditional **Pin Peat** orchestra. The type of music being played indicates a fighting scene, a love scene, or a scene of traveling.

There is a village near Battambang where *Nang Sbek* is still performed in its ancient form, but the performers are quite advanced in age. They have no one to take their place when they are gone. There is also a troupe of dancers at the University of Fine Arts in Phnom Penh that can perform it.

See also *Nang Yai*

References: Brandon, James. *Theatre in Southeast Asia.* Cambridge, MA: Harvard University Press, 1974; Brandon, James R. *Brandon's Guide to Theatre in Asia.* Honolulu: University Press of Hawaii, 1976; Brunet, Jacques. "The Cambodian Nang Sbek and Its Audience." In *The Performing Arts in Asia,* ed. J. R. Brandon. Paris: UNESCO, 1971; Royal University of Fine Arts, Cambodia. "Shadow Plays in Cambodia." In *Traditional Drama and Music of Southeast Asia,* ed. Mohd. Taib Osman, 47–51. Kuala Lumpur: Dewan Bahasa Dan Pustaka Kementerian Pelajaran Malaysia, 1974.

Nang Sbek Touch
Cambodia

Shadow puppet theater, literally "theater of small hides," also called *Ayang* or *Nang Kaloun.* One puppet master manipulates various rawhide puppets while sitting behind a screen. The shadows of these two-dimensional figures are cast onto the screen by a petroleum lamp that hangs in front of the puppeteer's face. The technique of performance is similar to the Thai shadow puppet theater, **Nang Talung,** and the Malaysian shadow puppet theater, **Wayang Siam.** Performances take place in a small hut raised several feet off the ground on wooden posts. There is a muslin screen in the wall facing the audience. The flat rawhide puppets are carved. Separate pieces for the arms and legs are loosely attached to the body of the puppet to allow for movement. A thin rod of wood is used to support the body of the puppet, and other rods are attached to the hands and feet of the puppets to control their movement. The puppets are modeled after figures in bas-relief sculpture found on Angkor Wat, the Khmer Buddhist temple in Angkor. The further from Angkor a puppet performance is, the cruder the puppets appear, due to the lack of direct contact with the design model.

References: Brunet, Jacques. "The Comic Element in the Khmer Shadow Theatre." In *Traditional Drama and Music of Southeast Asia,* ed. Mohd. Taib Osman, 27–29. Kuala Lumpur: Dewan Bahasa Dan Pustaka Kementerian Pelajaran Malaysia, 1974.

Nang Talung
Thailand

Traditional shadow puppet theater of Southern Thailand; literally, *Nang* means leather and *Talung* is a shortened form of Pattalung, a southern city where shadow puppet shows are popular. There is a sizable Malay population in Southern Thailand, so the shadow puppet traditions of both countries share many of the same attributes and have developed together. *Nang Talung* is primarily for entertainment, but can also used as a healing ritual or a way to appease the gods. Performances are usually done in temple grounds, but may also be sponsored privately at homes for weddings, funerals, and other special occasions. No village festival would be complete without a performance, which begins a few hours past dusk and lasts until dawn. A puppet master, or **Nai Nang,** sits behind a white muslin screen with a light hanging just before his face. He passes puppets between the light and the screen, casting a shadow for the audience to see. There is a banana log at the foot of the screen, which serves as a stand for puppets that are on stage but not being held by the puppet master. The **Pin Peat** orchestra sits around the puppet master and supplies musical accompaniment for the puppet action, singing, narration, and dialogue.

These puppets depicting only one character are much smaller than in **Nang Yai,** Thai shadow theater using 5-foot-high shadow figures that can depict many characters. The puppets are designed to look like dancers from **Lakon Nai,** Thai court dance-drama performed by women, or **Khon,** Thai masked dance-drama. They are carved from rawhide and colored with a thin paint to leave them translucent when cast in shadow, thus, making the shadow appear in full color. There are wooden rods that are halved and placed over the puppet to lend it structural support and to serve as a handle for the puppet master. There are thin rods attached to the end of an articulated arm on a puppet. These puppets are smaller than in other places in Southeast Asia, more like the **Pi-ying Xi,** Chinese shadow puppet theater. The repertory is drawn mostly from the **Ramakien,** Thai version of the Hindu epic, the **Ramayana,** but also from Thai literary sources and historical sources. There is a local god-clown character who is of supernatural origin, like **Pak Dogol** in the Malaysian **Wayang Siam,** shadow puppet theater of Northern Malaysia. Music is provided by a Pin Peat orchestra, consisting mostly of drums, cymbals, and gongs.

Training to become a puppet master is done by the apprentice system, since there are no formal schools. There are more female puppet masters in Thailand than in other areas of Southeast Asia. Rare performances of day-time Nang Talung do occur. These are performed in the late afternoon, without a screen, using colored puppets made of thicker leather. Here the actual puppets are seen by the audience rather than just the shadows. The performance conventions are very much the same.

See also Pi-ying Xi

References: Brandon, James R. *Brandon's Guide to Theatre in Asia.* Honolulu: University Press of Hawaii, 1976; Dhani Nivat, Prince. "Nang Talung." *Journal of the Siam Society* 47 (1959): 181; Montri, Tramote. "Thai Puppeet Show." *Silpakorn* 4, 2 (1960): 48–54; Rutnin, Mattani. "The Role of Shadow Play in Modern Thai Society." *Bangkok Post Sunday Magazine* (November 17, 1974): 13–14; Rutnin, Mattani. "Nang Talung and Thai Life." *East Asian Cultural Studies* 15 (March 1976): 45–52; Sweeney, P. L. *The Ramayana and the Malay Shadow-Play.* Kuala Lumpur: National University of Malaysia Press, 1972; Sweeney, P. L. Amin. *Malay Shadow Puppets: The Wayang Siam of Kelantan.* London: British Museum Publications, 1980.

Nang Yai
Thailand

Shadow play using large shadow figures as tall as 5 feet. The first record of shadow puppet theater in Thailand is 1458, soon after the Thai invasion of Cambodia. Thus, it is likely that Thai shadow play came from Cambodia. Performances occur on national holidays, at funerals, and at other important happenings, such as weddings. Two narrators seated to the side of the screen perform all narration and dialogue, as up to twelve performers holding the shadow figures move in front of and behind a huge screen that is backlit with a flame. The performers who are moving in the same style as the figures they hold alternate being in shadow and silhouetted. In most other forms of shadow-puppet theater in Southeast Asia, the puppeteer tries not to let any part of himself cast a shadow. In this form, the human performers are intentionally visible. An entire scene is carved into the large rawhide shadow figures, including one or two characters and their surroundings. For example, one shadow figure may feature the monkey Angkut holding the slain body of Ravana's son over his head, with trees in the background and a border around the entire scene. There are no articulated arms or jaws. The hide is painted heavily so as to cast a dark shadow.

Shadow figures are at least 4 feet high and usually in a square shape with rounded edges. Two poles are cut down the center, and the hide figure is inserted down the length of each pole. The poles are sewn to the rawhide, framing the figure between the two poles. The lower parts of the poles form handles for the stage manipulators. Performers must strike the appropriate pose with the shadow figures over their heads to signify each scene. Manipulators keep time with their feet to the music. The performer manipulating the shadow figure evokes so much of the action of the drama that the shadow figure's function is often reduced to merely identifying the human performer's role. The repertory is drawn from the **Ramakien,** the Thai version of the Hindu epic, the **Ramayana.** Nang Yai is very much like the Cambodian **Nang Sbek.** It is believed that the Thai masked dance-drama **Khon** developed from Nang Yai. **Nang Ram** (or Nang Rabam) is a variation of Nang Yai accompanied by dance.

References: Brandon, James. *Theatre in Southeast Asia.* Cambridge, MA: Harvard University Press, 1974; Brandon, James R. *Brandon's Guide to Theatre in Asia.* Honolulu: University Press of Hawaii, 1976; Montri, Tramote. "Thai Puppet Show." *Silpakorn* 4, 2 (1960): 48–54; Rutnin, Mattani. "The Role of Shadow Play in Modern Thai Society." *Bangkok Post Sunday Magazine* (November 17, 1974): 13–14; Rutnin, Mattani. "Nang Yai: The Thai Classical Shadow Play and the Wat Kanon Troupe of Rajburi." *East Asian Cultural Studies* 15 (March 1976): 53–59.

Nat

Myanmar

General term for an animistic spirit in Burma. There are many dances and spirit plays dedicated to one or more of the thirty-seven Nats known in Burma. Two examples of performances for Nats are **Nibhatkhin,** a spirit dance-play, and **Nat Pwe,** a spirit medium dance.

References: Brandon, James. *Theatre in Southeast Asia.* Cambridge, MA: Harvard University Press, 1974.

Nat Pwe

Myanmar

Spirit medium dance. This ritual performance evolved from **Nibhatkhin,** spirit plays. Performers contact spirits of objects and natural phenomena to gain direction and guidance. The most important dance is performed by a female spirit medium dancer. She is called a **Natkadaw,** or **Nat** wife. In Myanmar animistic spirits are referred to as Nats. During performance the Nat goes into the

performer's body while she is dancing and gives her the vision to see the future. Audiences are usually more interested in hearing of the future than in witnessing the dance. This ritual is never performed for tourists.

References: Brandon, James R. *Brandon's Guide to Theatre in Asia.* Honolulu: University Press of Hawaii, 1976.

Nataraja

India

Image of the Hindu god **Shiva** as the "Lord of the Dance," the dance from which all destruction and creation originates. Dancing his fierce cosmic dance, Shiva balances on one foot, which shows his connection to the earth, while his other foot is lifted from the earth, showing his release from this world. Iconographic images of Nataraja show Shiva with four arms: In his upper arms he holds a drum, which symbolizes sound and creation, and in the other a flame, which symbolizes the final destruction. His lower right hand makes a mudra, a symbolic gesture, which means "fear not," and his left lower arm gracefully points to his lifted foot, reminding the worshipper of his release from the earth. Dancing in a ring of flames, he stands triumphantly on the dwarf of ignorance.

This form represents both a universal equilibrium and the continual play of movement and rhythm.

References: Aherne, Consuelo Maria, Paul Kevin Meagher, and Thomas C. O'Brien, eds. *Encyclopedic Dictionary of Religion.* 3 vols. Washington, DC: Corpus Publishers, 1979; Eliade, Mircea, ed., *The Encyclopedia of Religion.* 16 vols. New York: Macmillan, 1987; Vatsyayan, Kapila. *Traditional Indian Theatre: Multiple Streams.* New Delhi: National Book Trust, 1980.

Native American Theater

Canada, United States

Native American theater, occurring in hundreds of distinct cultures, often as rituals, was the first dramatic expression to take place in North America. Deeply tied to the cycles of the earth and the forces of nature, dramatic rituals and ceremonies provide an entry into the spiritual and mythical realms of existence for these communities. There is incredible diversity within Native American

The Apache Devil Dance held near Gallup, New Mexico in 1940 during an Inter-Tribal Ceremonial. (Bettmann/Corbis)

theater, since it is an essential element of so many cultures that occupied such large and diverse areas throughout the Americas.

Colonization by Europeans proved to be devastating for Native American culture. Christian missionaries, who followed explorers to the "New World," severely disapproved of these indigenous forms of worship and considered them blasphemous and sometimes even devil worship. As the **United States** and **Canada** formed, Native Americans suffered war, foreign disease, relocation onto reservations, and a loss of the connection with their native lands that informed their way of life and spiritual reality. Many rituals and ceremonies were outlawed or severely discouraged. As these bans lifted in the 1930s and 1940s, the damage had largely been done. Younger Native Americans schooled in European-style schools lost their traditional ways of being in nature. Many dances, songs, and prayers were forgotten by all but the very old. Nevertheless, much has been preserved and is still treasured.

Despite the rich variety and the many differences among Native American performances, some general similarities do exist. Nearly all dramatic enactment is integrally tied in with dance and music. Not only that, dramatic enactments most often are not the primary elements in Native American performance; rather they serve the entire event by contextualizing the action and providing a focus of attention, as with the Navajo *Shootingway*. A common way of integrating outside intruding forces, whether Indian or European, that threaten the tribe's way of life is to mock them, as in the Pueblo **Tewa Ritual Performance** or the Cherokee **Booger Dance.** Denigrating parodies of this nature make the outsider seem less threatening and powerful. Many ceremonies that contain dramatic elements prepare members of the tribe for special events, such as a hunt, or celebrate life changes, such as puberty as does, for example, the Apache **Sunrise Ceremony.** There are many examples of male societies, such as the Comanche Little Ponies, the Kiowa Gourd Clan and the **Iroquois False Face,** that hold within their membership secret spiritual knowledge and the tradition of many dances and dance dramas. One of the most important purposes of Native

American performances is to provide connection with the spiritual world, as with the Apache Crown Dancing. Examples of spirit plays and **mystery play**s include the **Eskimo Spirit Play, Nootka Mystery Play** and the **Kwakiutl Mystery Play.**

One part of the continent that has its own distinctive traditions is Alaska. In 1741 Russia claimed Alaska, later selling it to the United States in 1867. It became a state in 1959. However, long before this foreign activity, indigenous people inhabited this region. There are five main cultural or ethnic groups native to Alaska, the Inupiat, who perform the elaborate Wolf Dance, the Yupik, who perform the masked dances and songs of the Bladder Feast, the Alutiiq/Aleut, Athabascan and the Tlingit, Haida, and Tsimshian of Southeastern Alaska. The Bladder Feast of the Yupik involves masked dancers who perform to honor and return the life force back into all the animals hunted the previous year. The animal's bladders, made into balloons, are cleaned, treated, and returned to the water, where they are believed to regain life.

Dramatic plays in the Western sense, that is scripted presentational plays, are not an indigenous part of Native American culture. However, enough Native Americans have been educated in the Western model and have assimilated into Western culture that dramatic works have become an outlet of expression. These plays are perhaps more accessible to a mixed-race audience than the indigenous rituals, ceremonies, and dance dramas. Hanay Geiogamah wrote the play *Body Indian*, 1972, which was performed at La Mama, an experimental theater club in New York. Geiogamah started the Native American Theater Ensemble in the early 1970s, performing works such as *49*, 1975, which takes place in the past and the present, joined by the figure of a night walker who can pass through time. In 1987 Geiogamah and Barbara Schwei formed the American Indian Dance Theater, which brought together the best dancers in America. They present shortened versions of traditional dances such as the Zuni Buffalo Dance and the Apache Crown Dance.

The powwow has become a strong force in reviving interest among Native Americans and other Americans in traditional Indian dances and dance dramas. Derived from the Narragansett, an eastern Algonquian language, the term powwow was adopted into the English language to refer to an Indian gathering or council. Native Americans have come to use the term to refer to a secular event or gathering that features singing and dancing by assembled groups. Many different dances are performed at one event. Dances, often containing some dramatic elements, that are performed for non-Indian audiences are often not the same ones performed at powwows for an all-Indian audience—powwows include more sacred dances. The competitions and the social excitement of these events have attracted many younger Native Americans toward mastering the traditional forms. These events, including the Red Earth Powwow in Oklahoma City and the Gathering of Nations in Albuquerque, are an opportunity to express pride and affirm identity.

Native American film has been very slow to develop, although there is a long history of Indian stereotypes being portrayed in Hollywood. Sometimes actual Native Americans were used, especially in crowd or battle scenes, but often white actors in makeup would portray any speaking roles. The 1998 movie *Smoke Signals* was the first all-Indian-made movie to reach success. It is about two boys, Victor and Thomas, portrayed by Adam Beach and Evan Adams, on the Idaho Coeur d'Alene reservation, who come to understand the death of Victor's father. A successful Native American actress, Irene Bedard, also performs in the film.

References: Broom, Leonard, and Frank Speck. *Cherokee Dance and Drama.* Norman: University of Oklahoma Press, 1983; D'Aponte, Mimi Gisolfi. *Seventh Generation: An Anthology of Native American Plays.* New York: Communications Group, 1999; Fenton, William. *The False Faces of the Iroquois.* Norman: University of Oklahoma Press, 1987; Heath, Sally. "The Development of Native American Theatre Companies in the Continental U.S." Ph.D. diss., Ann Arbor MI: UMI, 1995; Jenkins, Linda. "The Performances of the Native Americans as American Theatre." Ph.D. diss., University of Minnesota, 1975.

Natkadaw
Myanmar

Lead dancer in **Nat Pwe** performance; literally means "*Nat* wife." The *Natkadaw* is a professional dancer-medium who becomes possessed by a **Nat,** a Burmese animistic spirit, while dancing and, as a result, can see into the future.

See also Nibhatkhin

References: Brandon, James. *Theatre in Southeast Asia.* Cambridge, MA: Harvard University Press, 1974; Brandon, James R. *Brandon's Guide to Theatre in Asia.* Honolulu: University Press of Hawaii, 1976.

Naturalism
Europe

An artistic movement led by Emile Zola (1849–1902), who in 1881 wrote a theoretical treaties on naturalism, *Le Naturalisme au Théâtre* (Naturalism in the Theater). The movement held that since individuals are shaped by their environment, only by ruthlessly depicting the ugly and discordant aspects of the modern environment could modern life be properly dramatized. Henri Becque (1837–1899) wrote a naturalistic play called *Le Vautour* (The Vultures) in 1882, and Maxim Gorky (1868–1936) wrote *The Lower Depths* in 1905. The movement had an enormous impact throughout Europe, but was centered in Paris. **André Antoine** of the Théâtre Libre was a great teacher of naturalistic acting and did much to establish naturalistic drama in France.

References: Brockett, Oscar. *Century of Innovation: A History of European and American Theatre and Drama since 1870.* Englewood Cliffs, NJ: Prentice-Hall, 1973; Zola, Emile. *Le Naturalisme au Théâtre.* Paris: E. Fasquelle, 1912.

Natya
India

Melodrama inspired by English melodramas but performed by Indian troupes. This form began in the nineteenth century and is now almost extinct. The performance style was extremely exaggerated. The singing was of poor quality and extreme volume. Accompaniment was provided by raucous band music.

References: Brandon, James R. *Brandon's Guide to Theatre in Asia.* Honolulu: University Press of Hawaii, 1976; Gargi, Balawanta. *Theatre in India.* New York: Theatre Arts Books, 1962; Yajnik, Ramanial Kanaiyaial. *The Indian Theatre.* London: Allen and Unwin, 1933.

Natya Sastra
India

A text that conveys authoritative teaching on the dramatic art, believed to be from the Hindu god Brahma, who created four distractions for humans that would take their minds away from greed and sensual pleasure. Legend has it that these four distractions—speech, song, mime, and **rasa,** or aesthetic bliss—were made known to a sage, Bharata, who then wrote the *Natya Sastra* to teach the right use of these distractions. He then taught all the information to his hundred sons, thus bringing the arts from heaven to earth. No exact date of its writing is known; it is believed, however, that various authors throughout the centuries modified the text, probably between the third and the eighth centuries. The text as it now exists is completely in Sanskrit. Exhaustive in detail, the *Natya Sastra* prescribes theatrical architecture, music, aesthetic principles, hand gestures, and much more. **Kathakali,** a form of dance-drama, and **Bharata Natyam,** classical female temple dance, are two of many Indian performance forms prescribed by the *Natya Sastra.*

References: Gargi, Balawanta. *Theatre in India.* New York: Theatre Arts, 1962; Scott, A. C. *The Theatre in Asia.* New York: Macmillan, 1972; Wells, Henry Willis. *The Classical Drama of India: Studies in Its Values for the Literature and Theatre of the World.* New York: Asia Publishing House, 1963.

Nautanki
India

Folk opera of northwest India, in Uttar Pradesh, Rajasthan, and Punjab, that mixes characteristics of Hindu and Islamic culture. Believed to have evolved from the performances of ballad singers; in fact, many verses in *Nautanki* are from old ballads. These fast-paced plays glorify noble bandits, brave fighters, and sincere lovers. The language is simple, direct, and forceful. The acting style is energetic and filled with action, and there are many fight scenes.

A performance begins with songs to deities. Then *Ranga,* the stage manager and director, sings about the story to be performed and ushers in the characters. Actors who are not in a scene sit on the side of the platform and are ignored as invisible by the audience. If the audience is large, performers will walk to each side of the platform and sing each line over again to each side, in order to reach the most remote limits of the audience. Performers burst into sequences of vigorous dancing at the culmination of a song. The exploding rhythm of the kettledrum drives on the dancers. Traditionally boys perform all female roles. Their high voices suit the demands of female impersonation.

Performances take place on a 3-foot-high platform, with the audience sitting all around. The costumes are not faithful to any time period. Actors wear contemporary clothing mixed with Western and traditional Indian styles. Munshiji, the clown, wears his brightly patched coat backward and has a funny hat. He makes jokes about local gossip and scandals. Musical accompaniment is performed by a harmonium, a clarinet, and a kettledrum. The drum is used very theatrically to accent important lines, sharp movements, and entrances and exits.

References: Brandon, James R. *Brandon's Guide to Theatre in Asia.* Honolulu: University Press of Hawaii, 1976; Gargi, Balawanta. *Folk Theater of India.* Seattle: University of Washington Press, 1966.

Nazi Germany's Jewish Theater

The coming to power of the Nazi party in Germany in the 1930s was devastating to all German Jews, and that included those active in the theater. There was, however, a surprisingly active Jewish theater that continued producing a great many works of quality in Germany throughout the 1930s and early 1940s, up to the climax of the persecution of the Jews. German Jews such as **Max Reinhardt** were not allowed to participate in the German theater they had worked to create. Some, such as Reinhardt, fled the country, but most Jewish theater artists stayed. The expulsion of the Jews from public and private theaters created an enormous void, such that many non-Jewish actors gained employment.

The treatment Jewish actors received under the Nazi state was influenced by an edict that was promulgated throughout the fragmented German states in the late 1700s. At that time, actors were accorded the status of *Beamten*, or civil servants, and they performed in state-subsidized state theaters. In 1933 the government of Adolf Hitler forced the retirement of all non-Aryan government employees, which included Jewish actors. German Jews could not even perform in commercial or private theaters because of the creation of the Reich Cultura Chamber in 1933, a sort of cultural union that did not allow Jews membership. The government branch of culture asserted that Jewish actors could not effectively portray German characters.

Dr. Kurt Singer (1885–1944) created the Kulturbund Deutscher Juden, or the Cultural Union of German Jewry, which was approved by the Nazi government in 1933 with the condition that it be only for Jews. It was later stipulated that this group produce only works written by Jews. Censorship of their productions was extreme. The Propaganda Ministry of the Third Reich encouraged the organization because they believed it would help ease foreign criticism of their treatment of Jews. Kulturbund D. J. was an extremely prolific organization that produced a wide array of dramas and had on its stage most of the finest actors of Germany. By 1941, in its last year, the Kulturbund performed light escapist comedies to relieve the bitter reality faced by the Jews. In 1941 all the artists and administrators of the Kulturbund were arrested, taken to work camps, and later death camps. Very few survived.

References: Eichberg, Henning. "The Nazi *Thingspiel*: Theatre for the Masses in Fascism and Proletarian Culture." *New German Critique* 11 (Spring 1977): 133–150; Gadberry, Glen. "Nazi Germany's Jewish Theatre." *Theatre Survey* 21, 1 (May 1980): 15–32; Kvam, Wayne. "On Stage in the Third Reich: An Unrecorded Letter." *Theatre Survey* 28 (November 1987): 102–105; London, John, ed. *Theatre under the Nazis.* New York: Manchester University Press, 2000.

Nemirovich-Danchenko, Vladimir Ivanovich

Russia

Cofounder of the **Moscow Art Theater** (MAT) with **Konstantin Stanislavsky**, teacher, director, playwright, and critic. During the 1880s he was a dramatist and a theater critic and began teaching at the Philharmonic Dramatic School. In 1896 he won the Griboyedov prize for the play, *The Worth of Life.* Ironically, he felt the judges should have given the prize to *The Sea Gull* by **Anton Chekhov**, who later became the most important playwright for the MAT. In 1898 Nemirovich-Danchenko and Stanislavsky started the MAT because of their shared passion for creating truthful theater, free from pretence and artificiality. Both agreed in promoting a theater of authentic emotion, even though they disagreed at times on other matters, such as style of acting and selection of specific plays for production. Other than carrying out some organizational duties, Nemirovich-Danchenko devoted himself to directing at the MAT. He directed *The Sea Gull* in 1898 after the play had failed in other theaters. Even Stanislavsky was not convinced of the play's merits. Yet the MAT's *Sea Gull*, where form and content had a near perfect match, was the new type of play needed to display the style of truthful acting so desired by Nemirovich-Danchenko and Stanislavsky.

In 1900 and 1901 Nemirovich-Danchenko directed **Ibsen** in a way that introduced some symbolist staging. Through the 1910s and 1920s he continued to focus on directing, even as Stanislavsky was veering off toward creating his system for acting and his acting theories. In 1919 Nemirovich-Danchenko founded a music studio where he developed new production styles for operas, and in 1926 this theater was named after him. By the 1930s the MAT was a well-established and world-renowned institution that stayed within the confines of psychological realism, which it performed better than any other theater. After Stanislavsky's death in 1938, Nemirovich-Danchenko continued as director of the MAT until his own death.

References: Gauss, Rebecca, *Studio of the Moscow Art Theatre from 1905–1927*, Ph.D. diss., University of Colorado, Ann Arbor, MI: Proquest, 1997, 37888530; Nemirovich-Danchenko, Vladimir, *My Life in the Russian Theatre*, New York: Theatre Arts, 1968; Slonim, Marc. *Russian Theater, From the Empire to the Soviets*. Cleveland: World, 1961.

Nepal

Though dwarfed by its neighbors, India and China, the kingdom of Nepal enjoys the splendor of the Himalayan mountain range as its backdrop. As the birthplace of the **Buddha,** Nepal was predominantly Buddhist until 1769, when the country was united under the Gurkhas, who made

Crowds watch a dance performance at the Thyangboche Monastery in Nepal during the festival of Mani Rimdu. (WildCountry/Corbis)

Hinduism the official religion, although there continued to be Buddhist groups. In more recent years, tourism by those wishing to mountain climb and trek has infiltrated this predominantly isolationist country.

The colorful **Mani-rimdu** is a dance-drama performed outdoors for three days twice a year for the **Sherpas** by the Buddhist monks. As the only type of organized theater for the rural Sherpa people, *Mani-rimdu* enjoys great popularity as a form of entertainment, instruction, and worship. There is a very small amount of modern theater, which is primarily confined to Kathmandu.

> **References:** Brandon, James. *The Cambridge Guide to Asian Theatre.* New York: Cambridge University Press, 1993; Ducan, M. H. *Harvest Festival Dramas of Tibet.* Hong Kong: Orient, 1955; Fantin, M. *Mani Rimdu, Nepal, the Buddhist Dance Drama of Tengpoche.* Singapore: Toppan; New Delhi: distributed by the English Book Store, 1976; Jerstad, Luther G. *Mani-Rimdu: Sherpa Dance-Drama.* Seattle: University of Washington Press, 1969; Manandhar, J. K. *Nepal, Legend and Drama.* Banepa Wankhya: Sukha Veti Manandhar, 1982.

Nero (37–68)

Italy

Named emperor of Rome in A.D.54; pupil of the Roman tragic playwright and philosopher, **Seneca.** Nero may have performed portions of tragic monologues on the stage. When he presented himself in the Theater of Dionysus on the **Acropolis,** which he had rebuilt in honor of himself and the Greek god **Dionysus,** Nero wore a theatrical costume and probably performed. He portrayed gods, heroes, and heroines. In one role he reportedly even mimicked the screams of a woman in labor.

> **References:** Bieber, Margarete. *The History of the Greek and Roman Theater.* Princeton, NJ: Princeton University Press, 1961; Chinoy, Helen Krich, and Toby Cole. *Actors on Acting.* New York: Crown, 1970.

Netherlands

The Republic of the Netherlands was founded in 1579. Secular theater had an early start, dating from the fourteenth century, with evidence of dramas based on themes of medieval chivalry and romance. The Netherlands' most significant contribution to Western theater in the Middle Ages was the first version of the **morality play** *Everyman.* In 1638 the Schouwburg Theater opened in Amsterdam and offered a wide repertoire. By 1655 they had a troupe of professional actors, which continued through the centuries with a high standard of acting. In 1800 a more natural style of acting was introduced by the actor and teacher Marten Corver. The Royal Society of Netherlands Theater was in existence from 1876 to 1932 and produced literary masterpieces by French authors and **William Shakespeare,** attracting leading actors such as Louis Bouwmeester. Joost van den Vondel (1587–1679), a playwright predominantly, had great influence on the development of Jewish theater in Amsterdam in the seventeenth century, though his contribution to mainstream theater was also substantial.

The nineteenth century was dominated by foreign troupes touring the Netherlands. After World War II there have been many permanent theater companies in Amsterdam, including Tilburg, The Hague, and Arnhem. In Haarlem and Utrecht, Con Hermus (1889–1953) was director of a theater called Comedia, which began in 1945 and lasted until 1953. In the 1950s subsidies from the government became available for theater groups in all areas, urban and rural. In an effort to discover a truly indigenous drama, as opposed to producing imported works from **France,** the **United Kingdom,** and the **United States,** many small experimental groups began, such as Test, which was run by Kees van Iersel from 1956 to 1962. This group inspired many other groups to start creating new works toward the same goal of creating a theater uniquely of the Netherlands.

Social unrest among the young reached the Netherlands, as it did most of Europe and the United States, in the 1960s. In 1965 a theater called Theatre Aside was founded without government subsidies as a voice for this movement of discontent. Avant-garde groups from all over the world were invited to Amsterdam by subsidized theater groups. There was much protest against traditional bourgeois theater in the 1970s by young theater artists calling for the creation of a true people's theater. To this end, performances of traditional elitist plays were sabotaged and their actors bombarded with tomatoes during curtain calls. One example of the creation of a theater for all people was the Work Theater, which ran from 1970 to 1985 and created works communally and democratically, making them an influential model for others to follow. They rarely performed in proper theaters, but rather in schools and clubs and on the streets.

In the 1990s there were two distinct types of theater being presented: Classical works with a modern interpretation and extreme works created by the radical fringe. The latter often performed at the Summer Festival, 1986–1990, which was a gathering place for a wide variety of alternative theater.

References: Brandt, George, ed. German and Dutch Theatre, 1600–1848. New York: Cambridge University Press, 1993; Davidson, Michael. "Opera around the World: Netherlands—A Human "Ring," Amsterdam." Opera 50, 10 (October 1999): 1214–1216; Franses, Philip Hans. "Theatre-Going in Rotterdam, 1802–1853: A Statistical Analysis of Ticket Sales." Theatre Survey 39, 2 (November 1998): 73–97; Frey, Martin. Kreatieve Marge: Die Entwicklung des Niederlandischen Off-Theatres (The Creative Fringe: The Development of Dutch Off-Theatre). Vienna: Bohlau, 1991; Gieling, Lia. "Netherlands." In The World Encyclopedia of Contemporary Theatre, ed. Don Rubin, 596–613. New York: Routledge, 1994; Kehr, Dave. "The Discreet Charm of Rotterdam." Film Comment 32, 2 (March-April 1999): 68–69; Korenhof, Paul. "In Review: From around the World—Amsterdam." Opera News 63, 10 (April 1999): 86–87; Ogden, Dunbar H. Performance Dynamics and the Amsterdam Werkteater. Berkeley: University of California Press, 1984.

Neuber, Friedrike Caroline (1697–1760)
Germany
Actress and theater manager; credited with ushering in modern German theater. Neuber raised the standard of German acting and replaced the common vulgar farces with repertory drawn from French dramas. She and her husband, Johann, acted for several companies before founding their own company in 1727. She trained their actors to portray the grand heroic characters from French tragedies. These actors were pushed beyond their former skills at vulgar and crowd-pleasing improvisational comedy. The actors had to memorize long passages in verse. Many of her actors throve

under her tutelage. She was passionately involved in rehearsals. She even aided the social standing of her actresses by having them live with her.

Not all of her reforms were lasting, and German theater turned back to staging many crude farces starring the comic character **Hanswurst,** but an indelible impression had been made that influenced the development of German theater.

References: Chinoy, Helen Krich, and Toby Cole. Actors on Acting. New York: Crown, 1970; Williams, Simon. German Actors of the Eighteenth and Nineteenth Centuries: Idealism, Romanticism, and Realism. Westport, CT: Greenwood, 1985.

New Zealand
Located in the south Pacific Ocean just southeast of Australia, New Zealand was first settled around the fourteenth century A.D. by the **Maori,** who came from neighboring islands in Polynesia. Dutch visitors landed on the island in the seventeenth century. Captain James Cook landed on its shores a century later to claim the island for Great Britain, and Christian missionaries soon followed. The Maoris suffered continual displacement under the British, and many bloody wars ensued over land disputes. New Zealand has been an independent state within the British Commonwealth since 1907. The Maoris make up less than 10 percent of the total population presently, but they remain a cohesive culture and so will be treated in their own entry.

Theater for New Zealand inhabitants of European descent was nearly nonexistent in the early twentieth century. What cultural activity did exist was largely derivative from slightly outdated European traditions. There were some attempts to establish a professional national theater group in the 1950s, but none of these was successful. Starting in the 1950s a few metropolitan theater groups stayed together and regularly produced works. However, they rarely produced works written by New Zealanders, and thus the plays did not have great appeal or interest for the audiences of New Zealand. One notable exception to this trend was the drama of Bruce Mason (1921–1982): The Pohutukawa Tree, a play about the clash of lifestyles between Europeans and Maoris, and The End of the Golden Weather, which was a solo work performed by Mason himself.

See also Polynesia

References: Archey, Gilbert. "Polynesia, Polynesian Cultures." EWA 11 (1966): 438–466; Barber, Laurie. *New Zealand: A Short History*. Auckland: Century Hutchinson, 1989; Barrow, Terence. *Art and Life in Polynesia*. Wellington, NZ: Reed, 1972; Brandon, James. *The Cambridge Guide to Asian Theatre*. New York: Cambridge University Press, 1993.

Nibhatkhin

Myanmar

Secular plays that were said by performers to be spirit plays. In the sixteenth century these dance-plays evolved, incorporating the style of Indian dance. Professional performers traveled around in troupes claiming to be "spirit dancers," dancers possessed by animistic spirits. However, their plays were quite secular in content. They called their performances spirit plays as an excuse for using religious holidays to perform their plays. The clown character was the central character, and bawdy physical humor abounded in performances. **Nat Pwe,** the Burmese spirit medium dance performance, descended from this tradition.

References: Brandon, James. *Theatre in Southeast Asia*. Cambridge, MA: Harvard University Press, 1974; Brandon, James R. *Brandon's Guide to Theatre in Asia*. Honolulu: University Press of Hawaii, 1976.

Niger

Theater in Niger has a rich and varied history that has led to a thriving contemporary popular theater, but little modern theater in the literary sense. There is a long history of **Mai Komo,** or praise-singers. These male solo performers heap praise upon a chief or hunter through poetry, acting, and music. **'dan Kama** were and still are itinerant comic performers who are solely dedicated to praising food. The Hausa culture has a long rich history of spirit-possession cults, such as the Bori, and exorcisms, such as the **Kora.** Ritual performers in a Kora act as good spirits that battle the evil spirits that reside throughout the community.

During the period of French colonization, European-style theater was limited to a few clubs, such as the **Amicale,** that created plays in French. However, these highly elitist organizations disappeared with colonization.

Since independence, many popular theatrical styles have flourished. Some forms are developed and produced by **Samariyas,** local youth groups that organize theatrical productions to spur political action, and some by independent troupes. One of the two primary new forms, **Wasan Kwaikwayo,** or *Teyatur*, is improvised theater that is primarily performed in urban centers and began in the 1970s. The other recent form is the African ballet, which are theatrical performances that feature song and dance.

See also African Ballets

References: Banham, Martin. *The Cambridge Guide to Africa and Caribbean Theatre*, ed. Errol Hill Martin Banham, George Woodyard, and Olu Obafemi. New York: Cambridge University Press, 1994; Beik, Janet. *Hausa Theatre in Niger: A Contemporary Oral Art*. New York: Garland, 1987; Cornevin, Robert. *Le Theatre en Afrique Noire et a Madagascar*. Paris: Le Livre Africain, 1970; Chaibou, Dan-Inna. "La Theatralite en Pays Hawsa." Université Nationale de Côte d'Ivoire, 1978–1979; Kofoworola, Ziky, and Yusef Lateef. *Hausa Performing Arts and Music*. Lagos: Department of Culture, Federal Ministry of Information and Culture, 1987.

Nigeria

Nigeria comprises many traditional cultures and much cultural diversity; there are over a hundred different languages spoken in the country. Nigeria dominates theatrical genius in West Africa and arguably in all of Africa. This dramatic talent is not a reflection of one people, but, rather, is distributed among many peoples, such as the Yoruba, the Ijaw, and the Ibo.

The scope of theatrical variations is enormous in Nigeria, ranging in scale from a **Mai Komo,** a solo praisesinger who bestows glory on a chief or hunter, to the full-scale dramatic performance of the *Ozidi* saga by the Ijo people, which takes years to rehearse and takes over the whole village in which it is performed. Masquerades are found in great abundance and are highly refined forms in their many incarnations throughout Nigeria. In the **Abua Masquerade,** masked performers represent water spirits in order to clear out the evil from the past year to prepare for the new year. The *Gelede* features a male and a female masked *Gelede* character, both performed by men, who enact the most salient characteristics unique to each gender.

Other theatrical forms include **Ckumkpa,** which are plays performed by males of the Afikpo and Igbo people in which actual or reported events are dramatized. The **Kwagh-hir** puppet show is just one example of the use of puppets to dramatize tales. Many traveling performers weave their way through various parts of Nigeria, entertaining audiences. The 'yankama are traveling minstrels who perform satirical plays and songs. Perhaps one of the most unusual touring performer is the **'dan Kama,** an itinerant comic performer solely dedicated to praising food.

Though many traditionally based forms are still performed, new forms are emerging and continue to develop. The **Wasan Kwaikwayo** is a popular improvised theatrical form that began in the 1970s, predominantly for a popular urban audience. Similar but more heavily focused on dance and music is the Ballet (see **African Ballets**), a kind of theatrical dance performance inspired by indigenous cultures. The trend in modern Nigerian theater is toward a "total theater," in which elements such as masks, music, dance, movement, incantation, and wordplay interact to create a highly expressive product that combines traditional ingredients with a contemporary artistic impulse. The internationally recognized Nigerian playwright **Wole Soyinka** actively integrates age-old African traditions with the modern experience in his plays.

References: Banham, Martin. *African Theatre Today.* London: Pitman, 1976; Harper, Peggy. "Dance in Nigeria." In *Dance in Africa, Asia and the Pacific: Selected Readings,* ed. Judy Van Zile, 148–163. Manoa: University of Hawaii at Manoa, 1976.

Nimaime
Japan

Mild-mannered male type character in Japanese cinema. The term *Nimaime* literally means "second lead," and the character is similar to the character type often portrayed by American actors such as Henry Fonda and Montgomery Clift. The *Nimaime* character is mild and kind, with a slight physique. The **Tateyaku,** or "first lead," is robust and bold with a well-developed physique. The *Nimaime* corresponds to the **Waki,** the second actor in **Noh** masked dance-drama.

References: Bock, Audie. *Japanese Film Directors.* New York: Kodansha International, 1978; Mast, Ger-

ald. *A Short History of the Movies.* 4th ed. New York: Macmillan, 1986.

Ninjo
Japan

Term for human sympathy in a **samurai** warrior.

References: Bowers, Faubion. *Japanese Theatre.* New York: Hill and Wang, 1964; Immoos, Thomas. *Japanese Theatre.* Trans. Hugh Young. Originally published as *Japanisches Theater.* New York: Rizzoli, 1977.

Noh
Japan

Masked dance-drama from medieval Japan. **Kanami Kiyotsugu** (1333–1384) was a famous **Sarugaku** player who gained the favor of the young shogun, Yoshimitsu. Kanami's son, **Zeami Motokiyo** (1363–1443), also a performer, grew up under the patronage of the shogun and lived in the refined royal setting. Kanami took the popular forms of entertainment, changing and refining them to create Noh. He introduced a strongly rhythmic dance, **Kuse,** into sung dramas, which gave both dramatic tension and a focus to the performances. After his father's death, Zeami created a restrained but powerful style of expression on the basis of the innovations begun by his father. The appeal of this form for popular audiences was not nearly as great as that of the popular forms it came from, but for the nobility and **samurai** warrior class it had a much greater appeal.

Highly conventionalized gestures and posturing communicate the substance of much of the play. There is no concession to naturalism, and representational movements, such as weeping, are all formalized. Dance is the dominant feature of most plays. There are different dance forms for different characters. The two principal actors in any Noh drama are **Shite,** the protagonist, who always wears a mask, and **Waki,** the second actor, who never wears a mask. Other characters include **Koken,** a stage manager who brings on stools and props, **Tsure,** an attendant to either of the two leads, **Kokata,** a child role, and **Tomo,** a walk-on role. Though these characters can be of either sex, only male performers perform all roles. Each type of character has its own techniques, and actors specialize in one or another of

A mask maker carves wooden masks for Noh theater. He is working on one modeled after the face on his television screen. (Nik Wheeler/Corbis)

these types. Leading actors are both singers and dancers, and it is around their characterizations that the play evolves. A typical feature of Noh dancing is the sliding step. Actors move about the stage with their feet close together and parallel, without raising their heels, only lifting the toes. Stamping is another feature, in which the knee is lifted waist high and the foot is brought down squarely on the ground with control and precision. There are resonant pots under the stage in set places to give these stamps an even more powerful effect. Actors can maintain control of balance and movement when performing huge leaps as demons or warriors.

The goal of Noh is to evoke **Yugen,** dark or obscure hidden meaning beneath the surface of the Buddhist sutras. The dignified form of beauty that expresses this meaning is characterized by gentleness and aristocratic refinement. The symbol for Yugen is a swan with a flower in its bill. Noh performers intentionally withhold part of their energy during a performance, in order to leave the audience wanting more. Even the beat of the drums in the musical accompaniment is intentionally off rhythm a bit. This creates a longing in

the audience for perfection. The audience is supposed to feel a sadness in their hearts. The fourteenth century audience were samurai warriors, and they were always ready to face death at a moment's notice. Noh creates in its audience an exquisite state of yearning that the performers believe characterizes human life.

The stage is a square raised platform with four pillars, one at each corner, supporting a canopy. There is a bridgeway on stage right, the **Hashigaakari.** This is used only for entrances and exits. It has three pine saplings along its length, which serve as markers for the actors on the bridgeway. The masks worn by some of the characters only allow for limited vision, so various visual reference points, like the trees and pillars, are used by the actors in order to gracefully move about. There is a mirror room backstage off the bridgeway, where the lead actor puts on his mask and meditates on his image, preparing for his performance. Strict silence is observed in the mirror room. A curtain at the beginning of the bridgeway is flung open suddenly when an entrance is made. Costumes are bulky to make the actor's body appear sculpted on stage. Actors appear to be symbolic visions, not grounded in time or space. They wear only white stockings on their feet. The mask for *Shite* is usually small and white with a neutral expression. The skill of an accomplished actor can transform his bulky build with double chin bulging out under a mask into the presence of a timid young maiden. Properties are kept to a minimum, and simple objects are used to evoke many things. For example, a fan may be a cup of tea or a letter.

A typical Noh program includes five types of plays performed in the following order: a God Play (the hero is a god or goddess), a Warrior Play (the hero is a famous medieval warrior), a Woman Play (the hero is a woman and wears a big wig), a Frenzy Play (the hero is a mad woman), and a Demon Play (the hero is supernatural, and there is much vigorous dancing). In between each play is a **Kyogen,** a comic interlude, to relieve tension and provide comic relief. These interludes have become so popular that there are troupes that do only *Kyogen* plays.

The language in the Noh plays is poetic and full of double meanings, with many allusions to classical Japanese poetry. The musical accompaniment is provided by three drummers and a flutist. A singing chorus and a leader chant some of the play, serving a narrative role and sometimes chanting the lines for a principal character who may be dancing. Actors sing solo passages. It is mandatory that an actor portray the same type of role that his father portrayed. There is no room for advancement, meaning that if one inherits the role of *Waki,* one can never advance to the lead role of *Shite.* Training begins in the crib, where the baby hears his father training and starts memorizing. There is little study of acting theory or plays for a student. Students learn by imitating their teachers, without questioning why it is done as it is. Noh is chiefly supported now by amateurs who form clubs, go to all performances, and invite master performers to come and instruct them. Women can now learn to perform Noh through involvement in one of these clubs. Noh is now regarded as a national treasure.

References: Bowers, Faubion. *Japanese Theatre.* New York: Hill and Wang, 1964; Fenollosa, Ernest, and Ezra Pound. *Noh: The Classical Noh Theatre of Japan.* Originally published as *Noh.* New York: New Directions, 1916. Reprint, Westport, CT: Green-

wood, 1977; Immoos, Thomas. *Japanese Theatre.* Trans. Hugh Young. Originally published as *Japanisches Theater.* New York: Rizzoli, 1977; Inoura, Yoshinobu, and Toshio Kawatake. *The Traditional Theater of Japan.* New York: Weatherhill in collaboration with Japan Foundation, 1981; Scott, A. C. *The Theatre in Asia.* New York: Macmillan, 1972; Waley, Arthur. *The No Plays of Japan.* London: Allen & Unwin, 1921. Reprint, London: Unwin Hyman, 1988.

Nootka Mystery Play
Canada

Native American dramatic event performed on the northwest coast of Canada; may have originated with the Nootka and then been transmitted to the Kwakiutl and other tribes. The event takes the entire winter, five months, to perform and is made up of many smaller plays and dances dedicated to various spirits. The event opens on the first night of the winter season with a meeting at the longhouse, a community house, for the performers to paint their faces and dance. On subsequent nights the spirit plays begin. The plays dramatize a hero leaving the tribe and getting captured by a spirit, who take its victim into its own lair in the wilderness. After time the hero captures the spirit's power and brings it back to the community, demonstrating that new power through song and dance.

Near the end of the winter season the community performs a four-day resurrection ritual, which includes clowns performing obscene antics. Next is the group singing and drumming, known as "The Calling." Those who had been captured into the spirit world are shaken back into this reality by the music and return to the community to show their new power. On the final day there is a great feast. The Mystery Play serves as a method of transmitting the basic cultural values to the society.

See also Kwakiutl Mystery Play

References: Buller, Edward. *Indigenous Performing and Ceremonial Arts in Canada: An Annotated Bibliography of Canadian Indian Rituals and Ceremonies.* Toronto: Association for Native Development in the Performing and Visual Arts, 1981; Drucker, Philip. *Kwakiutl Dancing Societies.* Berkeley: University of California Press, 1940; Wagner, Anton. *Contemporary Canadian Theatre: New World Visions.* Toronto: Simon & Pierre, 1986.

Norway

The early history of Norwegian theater is closely tied to the development of **Scandinavian theater.** In Norway, as early as 1617, the Lutheran church encouraged humanistic theater in schools so that students would learn high morals and polite behavior. Some of the plays performed were revisions of plays from ancient Rome and Greece and some, based on biblical stories from the Old Testament, were written by local schoolmasters.

During the eighteenth century, control of the theater passed from royalty to the private sector, with popular audiences willing to support theater. Near the end of the eighteenth century, amateur dramatic societies began to flourish in Norway. In 1827 the first permanent playhouse, the Christiania theatre, was established, housing a permanent company of Norwegian professional actors.

These developments led the way to a true Norwegian theater, brought finally to fruition by two native sons and talented playwrights of Norway, Bjornstjerne Bjornson (1832–1910) and **Henrik Ibsen.** Bjornson is most remembered as a playwright, but he was also a theorist, political activist, innovator, and director. Actors who worked under him gave testimony to his effectiveness in conveying the very essence of a character he had written. His important contribution to the development of modern theater were succeeded by the work of Ibsen who brought Norwegian theater to the attention of the Western world and was a pioneer of the modern theater.

A new National Theater was erected in Norway after the Christiania theater was demolished in 1899. An alternative theater, Norway Teater, was established in Oslo in 1913, where plays were performed in a Norwegian language based on peasant dialects, rendering the theater independent of Danish influence. Opportunities for actors increased when the Folk Theater opened in 1933 and again in the 1950s when a private theater in Olso, the New Theater, began to rival the Norwegian National Theater. In 1945 some young Norwegian actors started the Studio Theater in Oslo, modeled after the studio established by **Konstantin Stanislavsky** in Russia. They held that actors, creative artists in their own right, should not submit themselves to controlling directors.

Opposition to the conventional theater was led by **Eugenio Barba**, who started the Odin Theater in Oslo in 1964 and two years later moved to Denmark. There are two competing National Theaters in Oslo, as well as smaller more experimental theaters such as the New Norse Dialect Theater, where Peter Palitzsch directed such dramas as *Mother Courage*, 1986, by **Bertolt Brecht**. Currently the BAK Troupe, an alternative to the established "safe" theaters, works on expanding modes of expression in theater.

References: Arntzen, Knut. "New Theatre in Norway: From Group Theatre to Project Theatre." *Scandinavia* 31, 2 (Nov. 1992): 187–202; Bergman, Ingmar. *Images: My Life in Film.* Trans. Marianne Ruuth. New York: Arcade, 1994; Gladso, Svein. "Norway." In *Nordic Theatre Studies: Yearbook for Theatre Research in Scandinavia,* 34–40. Copenhagen: Munksgaard, 1989; Marker, Frederick. *A History of Scandinavian Theatre.* Cambridge: Cambridge University Press, 1996; Meyer, Michael. *Henrik Ibsen.* Garden City, NY: Doubleday, 1971.

Nouvelle Vague

France

Literally, "New Wave," an artistic movement within French cinema that began in 1958 with the work of film directors François Truffaut (1932–1984), Claude Chabrol, Jean-Luc Godard, Eric Rohmer, and Jacques Rivette. In contrast to French cinema before this time, their work is characterized by having a strong personal viewpoint. The French actress Brigitte Bardot (1934–1969) began her career in a New Wave film by Roger Vadim (1928–2000), *Et Dieu Créa la Femme (And God Created Woman)*, 1956, proving that even an experimental film, if coupled with sex appeal, can have economic success. International recognition for the movement came with Truffaut's film *Les Quatres Cents Coups (400 Blows)*, 1959, and *Hiroshima Mon Amour (Hiroshima My Love)*, 1959, by Alain Resnais.

References: Butcher, Maryvonne. "France's Film Renascence." *Commonweal* (January 8, 1960): 414–416; Graham, Peter. *The New Wave.* Garden City, NY: Doubleday, 1968; Katz, Ephraim. *The Film Encyclopedia.* New York: Harper Perennial, 1994; Monaco, James. *The New Wave: Truffaut, Godard, Chabrol, Rohmer, Rivette.* New York: Oxford University Press, 1976; Siclier, Jacques. "New Wave and French Cinema." *Sight & Sound* 30, 3 (Summer 1961): 116–120; Slide, Anthony. *The International Film Industry: A Historical Dictionary.* New York: Greenwood, 1989; Weightman, J. G. "New Wave in French Culture." *Commentary* (September 1960): 230–240.

Nyau Masks
Malawi

The Nyau society of Malawi is an ancient organization for males of the Maravi, people of the Lake Malawi area. For centuries members have carved wooden masks that have been used to animate religious traditions and rituals. Masked dances occur at *Chinamwali*, a girl's puberty ceremony, and during *Maliro*, funeral services.

Masked performers portray many things, from ancestors or spirits to personifications of undesirable character traits and animal characters. An individual performer portrays the first type of animal character, which is often the *Lebwede*, a monkey-like character, who wears a small mask made of hardened leather or hide molded over a frame. Strips of cloth hang from the mask to hide the performer's head. This character is mischievous. His goal while performing is to chastise participants in the female puberty ceremony by teasing them. The other larger animal character, such as an antelope or elephant, requires more than one performer. Structured frames covered with cloth are animated by a pair of dancers who move inside the framework. These characters are usually only seen by female initiates because they are newly made for each occasion, used for performance only at night, and then immediately burned.

The masks for most characters are carved from wood and are usually the size of the human face. Features on the mask communicate the identity and nature of the character. For example, the *Thamu-Thamu*, or drunkard, wears a mask that has an open mouth with drooping lips to show he is intoxicated. All single-performer masked figures wear long flowing robes that cover every part of the body except the hands and feet. There is a female masked character that performs a dance that is an anti-Christian parody of the Virgin Mary, as an attack on the alien religion.

References: Banham, Martin. *African Theatre Today.* London: Pitman, 1976; Blackmun, Barbara, and Matthew Schoffeleers. "Masks of Malawi." *African Arts* 4 (1972): 36–41, 69, 88.

O'Casey, Sean (1880–1964)
Ireland

Irish dramatist who depicted the lives of the poor Irish in the slums of Dublin during the 1910s and 1920s. O'Casey's upbringing was poor, and he later taught himself to write and read and worked many manual jobs. His first work, *The Shadow of a Gunman*, was staged at the **Abbey Theatre** in 1923. After the success of his next play, *Juno and the Paycock*, 1924, O'Casey was able to focus solely on his writing. *The Plough and the Stars*, 1926, caused a riot because of its controversial subject matter. His next play *The Silver Tassie*, 1928, was an antiwar play, which the Abbey Theatre refused to produce because William Butler Yeats (1865–1939), influential because he was one of the founders, felt it was too harsh and didactic. O'Casey angrily left for London in a self-imposed exile. He kept writing, but the strength of his work decreased when he was estranged from his homeland, as can be seen in works such as *Red Roses for Me*, 1942.

References: Fitz-Simon, Christopher. *The Irish Theatre*. London: Thames & Hudson, 1982; Kilroy, Tom. "A Generation of Irish Playwrights." *Irish University Review* 22, 1 (Spring/Summer 1992): 135–141.

Oceania

A term given to the Pacific region; usually divided into three different groupings, named by early European explorers.

See also Melanesia; Micronesia; Polynesia

Odissi
India

One of the oldest forms of female solo dance in India, usually only performed in the state of Orissa in the east of India. It is very similar to **Bharata Natyam** but is softer, more curved and sensual. A dancer begins an evening's show by performing an invocation dance behind a curtain, which is held up by two people. After the curtain is removed, she performs a dance pantomiming different modes of praying to Shiva, for example, offering flowers or burning incense. Each mode of prayer is ended with a section of complex rhythmic dancing. The next section features beautiful poses and eye movements that interpret the music. The recital ends in a joyous dance in a quick tempo, in which the drummer and dancer play off each other as the intensity and speed increase. A 9–foot-long silk sari of a bright color serves as the costume. The dancer wears a fitted blouse with jewels sewn on it, along with golden earrings, hair ornaments, choker, long necklace, wristbands, and arm bands to further ornament her. Her hair is worn either in a bun or braided down the back. She wears a design on her forehead in the center and outlines her eyes in black. Drums, cymbals, flute, and sometimes a violin provide musical accompaniment. Earlier in the history of this form, dancers used to sing while dancing, but now a singer sits with the musicians and performs the lyrics for the dancers.

Training begins with eight basic body positions and movements called *Belis*. There are specific positions for rising, jumping, sitting, walking, and spinning.

References: Brandon, James R. *Brandon's Guide to Theatre in Asia*. Honolulu: University Press of Hawaii, 1976; Marglin, Frederique Apffel. *Wives of the God-King: Rituals of the Devadasis of Puri*. New York: Oxford University Press, 1989; Massey, Reginald, and Jamie Massey. *Dances of India*. London: Tricolour Books, 1989.

Odyssey
Greece

Greek epic poem by **Homer,** believed to have been composed between the eighth and eleventh century B.C., that recounts the adventures of Odysseus as he journeys home to Ithaca following the end of the Trojan War. The adventures and accounts of characters in this poem provide much of the dramatic material for **Greek Tragedy,** and even, at least indirectly, for **Greek Comedy.**

See also *Iliad*

References: Hamilton, Edith. *Mythology*. New York: New American Library, 1969; Scott, John Adams. *Homer and His Influence*. Boston: Marshall Jones, 1925; Wace, Alan John Bayard. *A Companion to Homer*. New York: St. Martin's, 1962.

Olivier, Laurence (1907–1989)
England

One of the best-regarded and most versatile actors in the English-speaking world during the twentieth century. Olivier was born in Dorking and performed in school plays as a child. His father encouraged him to become an actor. He studied at the London Central School of Drama and Speech. In 1926 Olivier joined Sir Barry Jackson's Birmingham Repertory Theatre for two years and in 1929 appeared in New York on Broadway. His first film appearance was in 1930, but he didn't gain widespread acceptance until the mid-1930s. In 1935 he performed **Shakespeare**'s *Romeo and Juliet* with **John Gielgud**, with the two of them alternating the roles of Romeo and Mercutio. In 1937 he joined the Old Vic, a famous London theater, and began by starring in a controversial production of *Hamlet*. In 1944 Olivier was made codirector of the Old Vic and there played the title roles in **Henrik Ibsen**'s *Peer*

Laurence Olivier and Vivian Leigh in the stage version of Antony and Cleopatra *(1951) (Kobol Collection)*

Gynt and Shakespeare's *Richard III*. Meanwhile, he became a Hollywood heartthrob, with many film roles that won high praise, such as Heathcliff in *Wuthering Heights* (1939).

When World War II (1939–1945) broke out Olivier served in the Royal Navy and directed and starred in a film version of Shakespeare's *Henry V* (1944), so well designed to stir national pride that it has been called a propaganda film, as well as other films with the same goal. His *Hamlet* (1948), in which he starred, won him Best Picture and Best Actor at the Academy Awards. He continued to perform in films and numerous plays, such as *The Entertainer* (1957), by **John Osborne**. In 1963 he became director of **England**'s National Theatre Company. Due to ill health his final stage performance was in 1974, but he continued to work in film and television.

He was knighted in 1947 and in 1971 took his seat in the House of Lords. In his private life, he was first married to the actress Jill Esmond (1908–1990), then in 1940 to Vivien Leigh (1913–1967) (with whom he performed some of his best roles), and finally in 1961 to actress Joan Plowright.

References: Burton, Hal. *Great Acting*. New York: Bonanza Books, 1967; Chinoy, Helen Krich, and

Toby Cole. *Actors on Acting.* New York: Crown, 1970; Darlington, William Aubrey. *Laurence Olivier.* London: Morgan-Grampian, 1968; Olivier, Laurence. *On Acting.* New York: Simon and Schuster, 1986.

O'Neill, Eugene (1888–1953)
United States

One of the greatest American playwrights; son of actor James O'Neill (1846–1920), who made his career playing the title role in *The Count of Monte Cristo.* Eugene grew up in the theater, with an acting father and a shy devout Catholic mother, who became addicted to morphine after Eugene's birth. He portrayed his own bleak home life in *Long Day's Journey Into Night,* 1957. As a young man he dropped out of college to work at sea and led a nearly vagabond life in Europe and the **United States.** He suffered through alcohol addiction, an attempted suicide, and tuberculosis. As a form of therapy, he began writing in 1912 and was produced by the Provincetown Players. His first full-length play was *Beyond the Horizon,* in 1920, for which he was awarded a Pulitzer Prize. He also won Pulitzers for *Anna Christie,* 1922, *Strange Interlude,* 1928, and *Long Day's Journey Into Night.* O'Neill wrote *Desire Under the Elms,* 1924, phonetically in a thick New England accent. It is a heavily symbolic play about the effect of the forces of the earth and nature on a father, his young bride, and his son. Other plays include *Mourning Becomes Electra,* 1931, his only comedy, *Ah! Wilderness,* 1933, and *The Iceman Cometh,* 1946. His tragic personal life deeply affected his writing, and his picture of humanity is often bleak. He offered what many consider to be the first serious distinctive voice in American dramatic literature. He provided American actors with some of the most substantial roles by a native playwright. He won the Nobel prize for literature in 1936.

> **References:** Carpenter, Frederic. *Eugene O'Neill.* New York: Twayne Publishers, 1964; Manheim, Michael, ed. *The Cambridge Companion to Eugene O'Neill.* New York: Cambridge University Press, 1998; Shipley, Joseph. *The Art of Eugene O'Neill.* Seattle: University of Washington Book Store, 1928.

Onkos
Greece, Italy

High hairstyle featured on masks for **Greek tragedy** and **Roman tragedy** to make the actor appear larger, first used around 500 B.C. This archaic hairdressing brought forward the ends of the long twisted tresses and built them up over the brow.

> **References:** Bieber, Margarete. *The History of the Greek and Roman Theater.* Princeton, NJ: Princeton University Press, 1961; Gullberg, Elsa. *The Thread of Ariadne: A Study of Ancient Greek Dress.* Goteborg: P. Astrom, 1970; Hope, Thomas. *Costumes of the Greeks and Romans.* New York: Dover, 1962; Houston, Mary Galway. *Ancient Greek, Roman and Byzantine Costume and Decoration.* London: A. & C. Black, 1947; Johnson, Marie. *Ancient Greek Dress.* Chicago: Argonaut, 1964.

Onnagata
Japan

Female impersonator in **Kabuki,** popular dramatic form of the seventeenth century. The need for men to portray female roles arose out of the government decree that women were not allowed to perform on the stage. As Kabuki developed, male actors successfully learned to evoke the ideal qualities of femininity. Contemporary Kabuki audiences still prefer to have male actors play female roles, because they believe that if a woman were to play woman's roles it would bring the performance too close to reality and the distinction between actor and character would be lost.

Open Theater
United States

Off-Off Broadway experimental theater company, started in 1963 in New York by Joseph Chaikin (born in 1935), who used to be a part of the the **Living Theater,** and Peter Feldman. Trained actors with experience were the creative agents in this group, encouraged to viscerally explore and improvise around a given topic, theme, or idea. A dramatist would finalize a script based on what they had all done together; in this way the group collectively created scripts. In their plays actors portrayed many roles. There were minimal settings and no makeup, and street clothing was worn for costumes.

Their first full-length play was *Viet Rock,* 1966, scripted by Megan Terry based on workshops exploring the idea of aggression. Other works include the ceremonial *Serpent,* 1968, *Terminal,* 1969, *Mutation Show,* 1971, and *Nightwalk,* 1973. After 1970 the Open Theatre performed mostly at universities and prisons until it disbanded in 1973.

References: Bigsby, C. W. E. *A Critical Introduction to Twentieth-Century American Drama.* New York: Cambridge University Press, 1985; Chaikin, Joseph. "The Open Theatre." *Carleton Drama Review* 9, 2 (Winter 1964): 191; Horwitz, Simi. "Face to Face: Joseph Chaikin Directs Arthur Miller: 'Making Ordinary Moments Extraordinary.'" *Back Stage* 39, 3 (16 January 1998–22 January 1998): 5, 33.

Orta Oyunu
Turkey

Literally, "play in the middle," referring to the fact that these dramatic performances took place in the middle of a public square. The earliest mention of this form appears in the twelfth century. The acting style is quite similar to ancient mime, so it is thought that it was probably brought to Turkey through Byzantium. Because Turkey maintains a close relationship with Venice, *Orta Oyunu* is also believed to have been influenced by the **commedia dell'arte,** improvised sixteenth- and seventeenth-century Italian comedy. Throughout history this theater form has entertained Turks from the highest sultans to the lowest strata of society.

Most of the actors portray many different stock characters within the course of one play. The two actors playing the leads only portray that one character throughout the course of the entire drama because they rarely leave the acting area. These characters are Pishekiar, the chief actor and clever conjurer, and Kavuklu, the second actor, whose name means "man with large wadded hat," a comic servant or trader. Their dialogue is a humorous counterpoint to the drama being acted out. Other stock characters include Zenne, a female role always played by a man with a high voice wearing special makeup, and Zampara, the elegant lady's man.

Performances take place in an oval acting area, about 90 feet by 40 feet, roped off from the audience, who sit on the ground all around, except for the women, who are separated by a veiled structure to hide them from public view. The only decor is a screen indicating the location of the action, which is placed opposite the one entrance. An orchestra that accompanies performances sits outside the acting area; it includes a horn called a *Zurna,* double drum, and sometimes a lute, violin,

dulcimer, and flute. Music cues the actor's entrances, and all actors sing a special song called a *Hava* when entering.

Performances commence with a lively dance accompanied by the orchestra, performed by all characters except Pishekiar, Kavuklu, and Zenne. After the other characters exit, Pishekiar enters, greets the audience, and announces the play. The action continues uninterrupted, alternating between a separate dialogue between the two main characters and the acting out of the drama.

Historically Orta Oyunu actors were very liberal with political satire and criticism, but they were not censored until the end of the nineteenth century. Theater, such as Orta Oyunu, is tolerated in this Islamic country and modern Western theater is even encouraged, seemingly defying Islam's rule against the performing arts.

References: Landau, Jacob. *Studies in the Arab Theater and Cinema.* Philadelphia: University of Pennsylvania Press, 1958; Martinovitch, Nicholas. *Turkish Theatre.* New York: Theatre Arts, 1933; Moreh, Shmuel. *Live Theatre and Dramatic Literature in the Medieval Arab World.* New York: New York University Press, 1992.

Osborne, John (1929–)
England

English playwright and actor, whose first play to be produced, *Look Back in Anger,* 1956, initiated a new style of playwriting, known by its attack on middle-class conservative values. Osborne's protagonist was the archetypal angry young man, the antihero of the "new wave." In *The Entertainer,* 1960, **Laurence Olivier** portrayed the seedy hero Archie Rice in its opening. Osborne also wrote *A Patriot for Me,* 1969. He has written for film and television and won an Oscar for Best Screenplay for *Tom Jones,* 1964.

References: Carter, Alan. *John Osborne.* Edinburgh: Oliver & Boyd, 1969; Tynan, Kenneth. *A View of the English Stage 1944–63.* London: Davis-Poynter, 1975.

O'Toole, Peter (1932–)
England

English actor in theater and film. Born in Ireland, O'Toole began acting at the Bristol Old Vic, where he performed from 1955 to 1958, and then joined the Shakespeare Memorial Company in

1960. O'Toole soared to fame when he starred in the film *Lawrence of Arabia*, 1962. His blond hair and chiseled thin face, and an ability to portray characters who balanced between sanity and madness made him an intriguing new talent. His next films include *Lord Jim*, 1965, and *The Ruling Class*, 1972, in which he portrays a compelling Christ-like aristocrat. Ill health kept him largely inactive in the 1970s, but he came back in 1980 with *The Stunt Man*, in which he portrayed a villainous movie director. He continued to make some appearances on stage, in **George Bernard Shaw**'s *Man and Superman* on the West End in 1982, for example, portraying John Tanner successfully. In 1992 he appeared in the film *Rebecca's Daughter*, *Fairy Tale: A True Story*, 1997, and *Joan of Arc*, 1999.

References: O'Toole, Peter. *Loitering with Intent*. New York: Hyperion, 1992.

Oyama
Japan

Female impersonator in Japanese films. Women did not appear in Japanese films until the mid-1920s. The convention of having men play female roles tended to keep cinema tied to its theatrical roots, **Noh,** masked dance-drama, and **Kabuki,** a popular Japanese dramatic form, in both of which male actors impersonated female characters. The cinema paid the price in loss of realism. These male actors fought the extinction of their *Oyama* roles by calling a strike in 1922 when they realized they were to be replaced by women. This disrupted film production for a short time, but they were indeed replaced within a few years.

References: Mast, Gerald. *A Short History of the Movies*. 4th ed. New York: Macmillan, 1986.

Ozu, Yasujiro (1903–1963)
Japan

Japanese film director. Ozu, a contemporary of **Mizoguchi,** specialized and excelled in **Shomin-geki,** movies, about the modern middle-class. He focused on the form of life itself; the central social processes, eating at home or out, gossiping, men at a bar, and so on. His movies are made up of endless dialogue. Visually there are no camera tricks. The results resemble made-for-TV movies. His subjects, style, actors, and even titles are very much alike in every film. He displays a subtle understanding of Japanese character and creates quiet comedies. He demonstrates that warm human interactions occur in the midst of cold sterile surroundings and that pleasantries and convention are what allow us humans to live together in peace. Important films by Ozu include *I Was Born But . . .* (1932), *Late Spring* (1949), *Early Spring* (1956), *Late Autumn* (1960), *End of Summer* (1961), and *An Autumn Afternoon* (1962).

References: Bock, Audie. *Japanese Film Directors*. New York: Kodansha International, 1978; Mast, Gerald. *A Short History of the Movies*. 4th ed. New York: Macmillan, 1986.

P

Padded Dancers

Greece

Dancers wearing a thickly padded jersey undergarment on the torso under their costumes to make them appear comically plump. These performers probably represented **satyrs** in attendance on the Greek god **Dionysus.** Throughout the Greek world, early in the sixth century, there were choruses of padded dancers, who may have also been called *Komasts,* or revelers. Padded dancers may have worn a phallus and had a masked leader. Their costumes are similar to those used for Old Comedy, the form that emerged in Athens in the fifth century, perhaps from the revels of these dancers.

> **See also** Greek Comedy; *Komos*
>
> **References:** Bieber, Margarete. *The History of the Greek and Roman Theater.* Princeton, NJ: Princeton University Press, 1961; Cornford, F. M. *The Origins of Attic Comedy.* London: Edward Arnold, 1914; Kitto, H. D. F. "The Dance in Greek Tragedy." *Journal of Hellenic Studies* 75 (1955): 36–41.

Pageant Play

Europe, India

A type of religious drama in which a parade or public spectacle illustrates the history of a faith or its gods. In medieval Europe Christian pageant plays usually took place on performance wagons, which had dressing rooms in the lower half and a performance space on the top in the open air.

Later in the medieval period in Europe the term pageant play was also applied to secular entertainments that took place on traveling wagons during festivals. In **India** the **Ram Lila** is a pageant play based on the life of the hero Rama, an incarnation of the god Vishnu.

Pai Yang (1920–)

China

Famous Chinese actress of film and theater in the early twentieth century. She got her training and made her mark as a part of the **China Traveling Dramatic Troupe** in their performance of *Thunderstorm* by Tsao Yu. Though no outstanding films survive from this era, these early films did a lot to dispel prejudices about women in the theater and in public life by showing respectable female characters portrayed by women instead of female impersonators.

> **References:** Leyda, Jay. *Dianying: An Account of Films and the Film Audience in China.* Cambridge, MA: MIT Press, 1972.

Pak Dogol

Malaysia

God-clown character in the **Wayang Kulit,** traditional shadow puppet theater. Legend has it that Pak Dogol is a high god from heaven who decided to come to earth to inquire after the state of

Two Malaysian clown characters, Wak Long (left) and Pak Dogol (right), in a Wayang Siam (shadow puppet theater) production. Only the shadows cast by the rawhide puppets are visible to the audience. (Photo by Beth Osnes)

humanity. Upon arriving on earth he realized that he was so bright, both physically and spiritually, that he would blind humans, so he went to the stream and covered his body in mud. He then created his sidekick, **Wak Long,** also out of mud, so he would not get lonely. The mud gave Pak Dogol boils all over, especially his behind. He is a witty character who often exposes the folly of the gods by devising practical solutions to their holy quests. He passes himself off as a servant to the gods and never reveals his true identity as a god himself. The puppet of Pak Dogol is made of a thick rawhide and is painted black. He has a movable jaw, and both arms are articulated. His buttocks are bulbous, and his big stomach protrudes over his sarong. This puppet is used extensively in healing rituals, as it is believed to have spiritual powers. It is stored in a high place when not in use so that no one will step over it and incur bad luck.

References: Osnes, Mary Beth. "A Survey of Shadow Play in the Malaysian Traditional Shadow Puppet Theatre." Ann Arbor, MI: Proquest, 1992; Sweeney, P. L. *The Ramayana and the Malay Shadow-Play.*

Kuala Lumpur: National University of Malaysia Press, 1972.

Pakistan

Pakistan was formed in 1947, consisting of East and West Pakistan, formerly the majority Islamic areas of India; the majority of Indian Muslims from elsewhere in the country immigrated to Pakistan. After a long separatist struggle, in 1971 East Pakistan became the autonomous nation of Bangladesh. Since Pakistan is an Islamic state, theater has not been encouraged; any kind of representation of human life is forbidden by Islamic law, since Allah is believed to be the only creator.

However, there is a history of theater in the Urdu language, and it most accurately traces the history of theatrical development in Pakistan. The production *Inder Sadha*, which is a play in verse with dancing, music, and elaborate costumes, was created in 1853 for the royalty of the Kingdom of Oudh. A few years later the British deposed the extravagant king who had sponsored the theatrical event, but the music from that show remained popular long after that time.

Right after independence in 1947, modern theater in Pakistan was created by a few dramatic clubs in colleges and universities. Mostly translations of Western dramas were produced. Presently the Pakistani government seems to be encouraging the development of original Urdu drama; a new law exempts plays from entertainment tax, and the president has made state awards for outstanding theater achievements. As a result, there are now several semiprofessional theater groups that tour around the country presenting plays.

References: Brandon, James. *The Cambridge Guide to Asian Theatre.* New York: Cambridge University Press, 1993; Hyder, A. R. Z. "'A Small House beside a Highway': A Play for Television with an Essay, Development of Drama and Theatre in East Pakistan." Master's thesis, University of Hawaii, 1968; Qureshi, M. Aslam. *Wajid Ali Shah's Theatrical Genius.* Lahore, Pakistan: Vanguard, 1987.

Palestine
See Arab Theater; Israel

Panji Tales
Southeast Asia
The Panji tales are pre-Islamic Javanese stories about Prince Panji. The tales borrow indiscriminately from the **Mahabharata,** the **Ramayana,** and other Hindu literature. The Panji tales have assimilated some Muslim stories since Islam came to Southeast Asia in the eleventh century. These tales are dramatized in many dance and dramatic forms in **Malaysia,** Sunda, **Java,** and **Bali.**

See also *Inao*
References: Brandon, James. *Theatre in Southeast Asia.* Cambridge, MA: Harvard University Press, 1974; Winstedt, Richard O. *The Malays: A Cultural History.* Singapore: Graham Brash, 1981.

Pansori
Korea
One-woman performance of a narrative tale; started in the southwest of Korea, in the Cholla Province. *Pansori* is also the name of the twelve lengthy stories used as the repertory for this performance. It is a folk art that is performed often during the harvest festival in September of each year. The performer sings while dancing and acts out a tale, playing all of the characters one after the other. It requires great skill, dramatic range, and stamina to perform. Feminine grace and strength of delivery are also necessary attributes for a performer. There were originally twelve long tales in the *Pansori* repertory, but presently only five are known. Musical accompaniment is provided by one drummer, who keeps a consistent rhythm during the dances and provides accents to the performer's spoken words.

See also *Changkuk*
References: Brandon, James R. *Brandon's Guide to Theatre in Asia.* Honolulu: University Press of Hawaii, 1976.

Pantalone
Italy
The duped father or cuckolded husband; stock character in **commedia dell'arte,** improvised sixteenth- and seventeenth-century comedy. A controlling character, he was most often a Venetian merchant who loved money and was mean to his servants. Physically he appeared thin and scrawny, with an old man's stoop. He could be identified by his costume of red pants and a dark cloak and by his half mask with a long hooked nose. This character was either played as a greedy lecher or as a ridiculously doting old man. Either way, he was always a favorite with commedia audiences.

References: Craig, Edward Gordon. "The Characters of the Commedia Dell'Arte." *The Mask* (January 1912); Rudlin, John. *Commedia Dell'Arte: An Actor's Handbook.* London and New York: Routledge, 1994.

Parodos
See Greek Chorus; Greek Tragedy

Pasku
Sri Lanka
Christian Passion play that originated in northern Sri Lanka in the late nineteenth century; performed during Holy Week. Christ's death and resurrection are dramatized by actors or by life-size statues that represent each character and are manipulated from behind a six-foot wall. Painted

scenery up to 20 feet high serves as the background. A narrator who is situated between the performers and the audience describes what is occurring in each scene for the audience. Christian church music serves as the musical accompaniment and is sometimes played on a Western-style organ.

References: Brandon, James. *The Cambridge Guide to Asian Theatre*. New York: Cambridge University Press, 1993; Gunawardana, A. J. *Theatre in Sri Lanka*. Colombo: Department of Cultural Affairs, Sri Lanka, 1976.

Pasos
See Rueda, Lope de

Passion Play
Europe, Iraq, Mexico, Philippines, Turkey

A type of play depicting the suffering and death of a prophet of a faith, usually referring to Jesus Christ, but also applicable to a descendant of the Islamic prophet Hussein, in the **Ta'ziya.** Christian passion plays are performed quite differently in the many European nations, with some being spoken in the vernacular and others being sung in Latin. In the Philippines, the **Cenaculo** is an enactment of the passion of Christ during Holy Week, which is the week preceding Easter. The Mexican **Las Tres Caídas de Jesucristo** (Jesus Christ's Three Falls) in performed on Holy Thursday, the Thursday preceding Easter.

Pastor-Bobo
Spain

Comic rustic character from the sixteenth-century Spanish theater, both religious and secular. Various renditions of this character portray him as lazy, greedy, ignorant, superstitious, obscene, or indifferent, but always rustic and foolish. *Pastor-Bobo* was a very adaptable character, used differently by many playwrights. He is recorded as an exceedingly popular character, which means that this part must have attracted some of the best performers of the time. The part demanded comic timing, physical agility (in order to enact pranks and stunts), and language skills, in order to imitate the rustic jargon known as *Sayagues*. He ap-

pears in religious sixteenth-century drama, sometimes as an ignorant sinner converted to the faith, and sometimes as a "wise fool." He also appeared in the burlesque secular farces of the sixteenth-century playwright, Lucas Fernández.

References: Brotherton, John. *The Pastor-Bobo in the Spanish Theatre before the Time of Lope de Vega*. London: Tamesis, 1975; McKendrick, Melveena, *Theatre in Spain: 1490–1700*. New York: Cambridge University Press, 1989.

Pear Garden
China

Training academy for both male and female performers, founded by the Tang dynasty (A.D. 618–907) emperor **Ming Huang** in the first half of the eighth century. It is considered the first official school of drama in China. Students of the school were known as Children of the Pear Garden. It was intended only to teach singers and dancers for elaborate court entertainments. Trainees were all paid a government subsidy. Most of the female students were concubines for the court, who were expected to be able to entertain as well as provide sexual pleasures.

References: Scott, A. C. *The Theatre in Asia*. New York: Macmillan, 1972.

Peking Opera
China

Highly conventionalized opera form that reached its peak of expression in the nineteenth century. Emperor **Ming Huang** in the eighth century was the first major patron of the Chinese theater and contributed to the development of the opera through the establishment of the **Pear Garden**, a training academy for actors and singers. Peking Opera is only one of many regional styles of opera and is a synthesis of various local styles. However, all the regional styles of opera throughout China share the same premise; they involve an indivisible synthesis of music, the spoken word, and gestures, all understood through an elaborate system of acting techniques. The Peking style stands out worldwide, mainly because of the talented actors who have taken the form to such a high level. Peking Opera is a popular entertainment form, looked down

Pupils training to be actors in Chinese classical theater productions during a class at the Peking Opera's school at Taipei, 1955 (Archive Photos)

upon by Chinese intellectuals for its cheapening of classical sources.

The primary attraction for an audience has always been the actors, who have sought perfection in a systematic form of expression. All characters are traditionally portrayed by male actors. Actors specialize in a type of role such as **Sheng,** male characters; **Dan,** female characters; **Hualian,** robust male characters; or **Chou,** comic characters. The nature of Chinese theatrical technique makes it possible for an actor to run from one performance engagement to the next. An actor is trained to play a certain type of role, and his training prepares him to step into any play requiring such a role at a minute's notice. No rehearsal is necessary.

The time and the place of action in a Peking Opera can skip about, with no concessions made for realistic portrayal of an event. There is no background setting to indicate for the audience at what place or time the drama is occurring. Since the stage is not representational, it allows for an episodic plot that quickly jumps from one imagined setting to another. The projected, almost square stage for a traditional Peking Opera performance has two curtained doors for entrances and exits. Properties are minimal and are used economically. A table may represent a bridge, an altar, or a wall. Acting conventions establish time and place within a drama. For example, an actor walks in a circle to indicate a long journey. An actor carrying an oar indicates that the character is on a boat. Much information about a character is communicated by costuming. Colors indicate character type. Yellow indicates an emperor, red a high official, blue a civilian, brown an aged person, and black a rough character. Features of the costumes enhance movement of the actors. The pheasant plumes on a general's headdress extend up to 10 feet into the air. Their subtle movements can be very expressive. Water sleeves are white silk cuffs on the sleeves that hang down about two feet. Manipulation of these is part of an actor's training, as it enhances hand movements and dramatic expression. As well as being visually pleasing, the water sleeves also have a functional value, as they are used to indicate an aside when the actor lifts his arm to his cheek. Actors wear heavy makeup with shaded lines arching over the eyebrows. The rough male character, *Hualian*, and the clown character, *Chou*, wear specialized makeup.

Plays are classified as civil, *Wen*, or military, **Wu.** They are written in a theatrical dialect of combined colloquial and literary Chinese with songs in verse. The spoken dialogue provides an opportunity for singers to rest their voices and for the story to be advanced. The speaking of a character escalates emotionally until the singer goes into a long crescendo, signaling the orchestra that a song is beginning. Strenuous training begins at age ten, or even as early as eight. Body type and talent slate a child for a particular role. Training continues on for many years. The Pear Garden was one school for actors with royal patronage. Private schools, such as the one owned by **Fu Lien Ch'eng,** also existed. From the fifth century B.C. men have played female roles, since Confucian morality discourages mingling of the sexes. Finally in 1911 actresses were introduced onto the stage.

During the **Chinese Cultural Revolution,** Peking Opera was adjusted to suit the beliefs of the Communist Party. After the death of **Mao Tse-tung** in 1976, Peking Opera regained some of its former ways. Currently Peking Opera coexists with **Hua Chü,** spoken drama. By making certain reforms, Peking Opera has remained the most popular form of entertainment in China, even during times of great social change.

References: Brandon, James R. *Brandon's Guide to Theatre in Asia.* Honolulu: University Press of Hawaii, 1976; Chia-Chien, Chu. *The Chinese Theatre.* Trans. James A. Graham. London: John Lane, 1922; Hsu, Tao-Ching. *The Chinese Conception of the Theatre.* Seattle: University of Washington Press, 1985; MacKerras, Colin. *Rise of the Peking Opera, 1770–1870: Social Aspects of the Theatre in Manchu China.* Oxford: Clarendon, 1972; Scott, A. C. *The Theatre in Asia.* New York: Macmillan, 1972; Yang, Daniel Shih-P'eng. *An Annotated Bibliography of Materials for the Study of the Peking Opera.* 2d ed. Wisconsin China Series. Madison: University of Wisconsin, 1967.

Pelimau
Malaysia
Ceremonial bath with lime water. Upon a young shadow puppeteer's graduation to the status of **dalang,** puppet master of the **Wayang Siam,** shadow puppet theater of northern Malaysia, he is washed by his teacher with water in which limes have been soaking.

References: Sweeney, P. L. *The Ramayana and the Malay Shadow-Play.* Kuala Lumpur: National University of Malaysia Press, 1972.

Performance Art
France, Germany, United Kingdom, United States
A loosely defined genre of performance that seeks to break free from the traditional constraints concerning the creation of art; became used as a phrase in the 1970s. In a performance art creation, the actor need not portray a character, nor does the piece require a plot or narrative structure. Often alternative performance places are used, such as galleries, warehouses, or street corners. Artist involved in performance art are usually interested in multiple artistic media, convey an unconventional or disturbing content, and challenge the status quo in both the art world and society at large.

Some well-known performance artists include Robert Wilson, who does opulently staged "operas," and singer Laurie Anderson, who uses multimedia and rock music to enhance her story-telling. Eric Bogosian performed a night of mono-logues, entitled *Drinking in America*, at clubs in New York, in which he portrayed a broad range of characters. Karen Finley performs solo theater pieces in which she takes on difficult issues with a brash yet effective presentational style. A Mexican American performance artist, Guillermo-Gomez Peña, performs audience-interactive commentary on the mistreatment of Mexican Americans in contemporary society. It is not unusual for him to adorn his performance space with hanging dead chickens, popular Mexican iconography, and skeletons.

> **References:** Goldberg, Rose Lee. *Performance Art.* New York: Harry N. Abrams, 1988.

Periaktoi

Greece

Revolving triangular scenic structures with a different scene on each side, used in ancient Greek drama as side decorations.

> **See also** *Pinakes*
> **References:** Bieber, Margarete. *The History of the Greek and Roman Theater.* Princeton, NJ: Princeton University Press, 1961; Halleran, M. R. *Stagecraft in Euripides.* London: Croom Helm, 1985; Seale, D. *Vision and Stagecraft in Sophocles.* London: Croom Helm, 1982.

Peripeteia

See Greek Tragedy

Petrushka

Russia

Russian puppet theater popular, from 1830 to 1930; performed throughout Russia, mostly at carnivals but also as street theater; predominantly enjoyed by the urban poor. At carnivals the Petrushka theater was usually a tent that held about 200 people, who were invariably standing packed together. It was either free or very inexpensive to enter the tent. The main character of this puppet show was Petrushka, who was a noisy, rowdy trickster and troublemaker. He and his cohorts were performed by one single puppeteer, who made up all of the dialogue extempo-

raneously, based on a skeleton plot. Sometimes a marionette, but usually a glove puppet, Petrushka had a crudely carved wooden head that had to be able to withstand many beatings in performance. The body of the puppet was made of cloth, and Petrushka's outfit was always red.

The show was performed under a tent in a booth of either wood or cloth stretched between two poles. Movement was limited with these crude glove puppets, so words took on great significance. Comedies were performed that were most often socially critical, always pushing the limits of decency and decorum. These shows were most often accompanied by a barrel-organ player with whom the puppeteer would have to share his meager earnings. The art was taught by demonstration, since there were no written scripts or formal schools. By the late nineteenth century, upper- and middle-class families began to take their children to these performances, which led to much criticism of the vulgar content by the wealthy parents.

Most Westerners know the character Petrushka through the Benois-Stravinsky ballet *Petrouchka,* first performed in 1911. The story used in the ballet is one of the most famous adaptation of a Russian dramatic tale that has been transmitted orally throughout history.

> **References:** Kelly, Catriona. *Petrushka: The Russian Carnival Puppet Theatre.* New York: Cambridge University Press, 1990.

Philippine Zarzuela

Philippines

Light opera modeled after the Spanish form of the same name. **Zarzuela** was brought to the Philippines by Spanish officials to entertain them and their families. It was eventually taken over by the Filipinos during American rule, which started in 1898. By the 1920s it had evolved to suit Filipino tastes in language, repertory, and music. Even the political tone of it was set against the colonial American forces, causing it to be banned occasionally by American officials. The music is light and melodic, and original scores are created anew for each show. It is much like musical comedy in style. There were many touring professional troupes before World War I, but now it is performed in just a few villages as a folk drama.

References: Banas, Raymundo C. *Philipino Music and Theater*. Quezon City: Manlapaz Publishing, 1969; Brandon, James R. *Brandon's Guide to Theatre in Asia*. Honolulu: University Press of Hawaii, 1976; Javillonar, Elna V. "The First Vernacular Zarzuela." *Philippine Studies* 12 (April 1964): 323–325.

Philippines

Spanish culture has so dominated the Philippines for three centuries that most traces of indigenous styles of theater and dance have been erased. Spanish conquest of the islands began in 1564 and lasted until 1898, during which time most Filipinos, other than the southwestern islanders, who were Muslim, were converted to Catholicism. The next fifty years saw U.S. rule and Japanese occupation during World War II. Finally an independent nation, the country now struggles to create a national culture that will reflect their own style and tastes.

Fagfagto, an enactment of war by men of the Bontac tribe that celebrates the planting of crops, is one of the few indigenous art forms known in the Philippines. Almost every other theatrical form known to history or practiced now has been greatly influenced by the Spanish. *Cenaculo* is an enactment of the Passion of Christ realistically portrayed during Holy Week; it was brought from Spain in the sixteenth and seventeenth centuries. Started by a Jesuit priest in the fourteenth century to instruct the native people, **Moro-moro** is a folk play in which a Christian prince defeats a Muslim prince. Modeled after the Spanish form of the same name, **Philippine Zarzuela** is light opera, which has evolved to suit the tastes of the Philippine audiences.

Modern theater is lead by the efforts of the Arena Theatre of the Philippines, which has been a community theater in Manila since the 1960s. Through branch theater groups it links rural folk theater artists with the more Western-influenced urban theater artists in Manila. This effort may be successful in creating a vibrant modern theater that is linked with the Philippines' national character.

References: Abaya, Consuelo. "The Fiesta." *Philippines Quarterly* 1, 4 (March 1952): 29–35; Reyes, Francisca, and Leonor Orosa Gaquingco Aquino. *Philippine Folk Dances*. 5 vols. Manila: Kayamanggi, 1953–1966; Aveilana, Dassy H. "The Native Theatre." *Philippine Quarterly* 1, 4 (March 1952): 60–62; Banas, Raymundo C. *Philipino Music and Theater*. Quezon City: Manlapaz, 1969; Ceballos, Patricia R. "The Fiesta Plays of Bohol." *Philippine Studies* 23 (1975): 190–222; Constanlino, Josefino. "Early Drama Forms in the Philippines." *Philippines Quarterly* 1 (1961): 34–36; Espino, F. L. "A Literal Imitation of Christ." In *Filipino Heritage: The Making of a Nation*, ed. Alfredo R. Roces, pp. 1230–1232. Manila: Lahing Pilipino, 1977; Javillonar, Elna V. "The First Vernacular Zarzuela." *Philippine Studies* 12 (April 1964): 323–325; Leon, Walfrido de. "The Passion and the Passion Play in the Philippines." *College Folio* (December 1910): 55–64; Mendoza, Liwaway. "Lenten Rites and Practices." *Drama Review* 21, 3 (September 1977): 21–32.

Phlyakes
Italy

Term used for actors in **Hilarotragoedia,** a form that parodied tragedy, and the **Phlyax Play,** rude farces; literally, gossips.

References: Bieber, Margarete. *The History of the Greek and Roman Theater*. Princeton, NJ: Princeton University Press, 1961.

Phlyax Play
Italy

Popular Roman farce from the fifth and fourth centuries B.C. that dramatized Greek legends but changed the stories to create more humor. It was acted by **Phlyakes,** which literally means "gossips," performers who, like all actors at the time, were servants of the Greek god Dionysus. The costumes were similar to those used in Greek comedy, in that characters wore padded tights the covered the body under a too-short vest that exposed the phallus the men wore. However, everything was more realistic and grotesque in this lower-class Italian farce than in Greek comedy. Some costumes even had bare breasts and navels painted onto the padding.

References: Bieber, Margarete. *The History of the Greek and Roman Theater*. Princeton, NJ: Princeton University Press, 1961; Taylor, David. *Acting and the Stage*. Boston: George Allen & Unwin, 1978.

Pi Phat
See Pin Peat

Pickford, Mary (1893–1979)

United States

Film star of the silent-screen era, dubbed "America's Sweetheart" for the sweet lovable character she most often portrayed in her films. Born Gladys Smith, Pickford became the breadwinner for her widowed mother and siblings at the age of five. She toured with various theater companies until the age of fourteen, when she convinced producer **David Belasco,** who also gave her her new name, to give her a part in *The Warrens of Virginia* on Broadway. Next she charmed the filmmaker D. W. Griffith (1875–1948), to give her a beginning to her film career. She went on to become one of the most popular stars in screen history, both in the **United States** and internationally. As an actress she was infectiously spirited, with a natural, easy way about her, as well as her trademark golden curls. As a businesswoman she was a shark, and by 1916 she was earning $10,000 a week. In 1919 she, along with **Charlie Chaplin**, Griffith, and Douglas Fairbanks (1883–1939), started United Artists Corporation. Pickford married Fairbanks amid much publicity and performed opposite him often in films.

She attempted to rebel against her good-girl image by cutting off her curls and playing a more daring role in *Coquette* in 1929. She won an Academy Award for her performance, but was not so successful in convincing her audience of her development as a performer. After a few less successful films, she retired in 1933, a child star who, like **Shirley Temple,** was not allowed to grow up by her adoring public.

> **References:** Eyman, Scott. *Mary Pickford: America's Sweetheart.* New York: D. I. Fine, 1990; Pickford, Mary. *Sunshine and Shadow.* Garden City, NY: Doubleday, 1955; Whitfield, Eileen. *Pickford: The Woman Who Made Hollywood.* Lexington: University Press of Kentucky, 1997.

Pin Peat

Cambodia, Thailand, Laos, Burma

Traditional musical ensemble, also called Pi Phat, which accompanies live theatrical and dance performances; called **Saing** in Burma. This orchestra is usually made up of six instruments, including a double-reed oboe, a set of tuned bronze bowls arranged in a semicircle, a bamboo xylophone, a large upright drum, a horizontal drum played at both ends by hand, and a small bell cymbal. Pin Peat has a hollow sound because of the contrast of the wooden xylophone and the metal cymbals and bowls.

> **See also** Gamelan
> **References:** Brandon, James. *Theatre in Southeast Asia.* Cambridge, MA: Harvard University Press, 1974; Brandon, James R. *Brandon's Guide to Theatre in Asia.* Honolulu: University Press of Hawaii, 1976.

Pinakes

Greece

Painted panels used to decorate the back of the stage in ancient Greek drama. Aristotle, in his **Poetics,** credits the playwright **Sophocles** with being the first to use painted scenery.

> **See also** Periaktoi
> **References:** Bieber, Margarete. *The History of the Greek and Roman Theater.* Princeton, NJ: Princeton University Press, 1961; Halleran, M. R. *Stagecraft in Euripides.* London: Croom Helm, 1985; Seale, D. *Vision and Stagecraft in Sophocles.* London: Croom Helm, 1982.

Pirandello, Luigi (1867–1936)

Italy

Italian playwright who was a major influence on the development of modern European drama. His plays were revolutionary for their time, breaking the customary boundaries between the audience and the performers and between the supposed reality of the world and the illusion of the theater. For instance, in his best-known play, *Six Characters in Search of an Author,* 1921, the characters appear on an empty stage searching for an author to finish their story. Many of his plays deal with the inability of humans to communicate even with themselves. He founded his own theater group in 1925, which he managed for three years.

Piscator, Erwin (1893–1966)

Germany

German director deeply committed to a socially moral theater. Piscator began acting and directing in various towns in Germany. By 1918 he was an official member of the German Communist Party and used the theater as a tool for political influ-

The Italian playwright Luigi Pirandello (center) surrounded by the cast for the play Henry the 4th, Berlin, 1925. (Bettmann/Corbis)

ence. He began directing at the Volksbuhne Theater (The People's Theater) and worked there
from 1924 to 1927, creating radical productions
that caused a stir artistically and politically. For example, he set his production of *The Lower Depths* by
Maxim Gorky (1868–1936) amid a background
of stark human suffering brought on by unem-
ployment and revolution. He experimented with
various stage machinery, film clips, newsreels,
slide projections, and audio effects to create a
total experience for his audience and heighten the
emotional impact. This approach led him to create
the theory of **epic theater,** which influenced
Bertolt Brecht.

In 1931 Piscator was arrested for not paying
entertainment tax, and he left Germany and lived
in the Soviet Union until 1938, when he moved
to New York. Here he started a school, the Dramatic Workshop, and continued directing. In
1951 he moved back to West Germany and in
1962 was appointed artistic director of the West
Berlin Volksbuhne, where he produced many

highly controversial works by playwrights such as
Peter Weiss. His influence on **documentary theater** was enormous. In 1964 he directed the first
work of this genre to receive international recognition, *The Case of J. Robert Oppenheimer*, with script by
Heinar Kipphardt (1922–1982).

References: Holderness, Graham, ed. *The Politics of
Theatre and Drama*. New York: St. Martin's, 1992;
Ley-Piscator, Maria. *The Piscator Experiment: The Politi-
cal Theatre*. New York: J. H. Heineman, 1967; Willett,
John. *The Theatre of Erwin Piscator: Half a Century of Poli-
tics in the Theatre*. London: Eyre Methuen, 1978.

Pi-ying Xi
China

Chinese shadow-figure theater (also *Teng-ying Xi*,
"theater of lantern shadows"). Shadow figure
theater exists in almost every part of China. The
origins of Chinese shadow play are unknown. It
first appeared during the second century B.C.,
used by Emperor Wu to commune with his dead

wife. After her death the emperor threatened the court magician that he must bring his beloved wife back to life. The magician made a shadow figure in her likeness, and the shadow image of her satisfied the grieving emperor. The Ming (1368–1644) and Ch'ing (1644–1911) dynasties were great periods of growth for the shadow theater.

In Pi-ying Xi the flat carved character figures are passed between a light and a screen, causing the shadow of the figure to appear on the screen. Troupes did street corner performances, as well as private performances in people's homes, which were particularly popular with women, since they could not attend public shows. The figures used for performances are not called puppets by the Chinese. The Chinese distinguish these flat rawhide character figures in a category all their own, separate from the three-dimensional puppet traditions in China (see **Cantonese Rod Puppet Theater** and **Jia-li Xi**). The shadow figures are carved out of rawhide that is semitranslucent, painted vibrant colors, and supported with thin wooden rods. The colors of the figures show through in the shadows. Their limbs are articulated. In the north and northeast parts of China the figures are only 6–10 inches tall and are very ornately carved and painted. In the south figures are larger and not so ornate. The bodies are cut into about ten to twelve pieces (less for animals) and jointed at the shoulders, elbows, knees, waist, and wrists. Figures are manipulated with wire rods attached to loops at the neck and hands. There are usually three rods to be manipulated by a master.

Traditionally, one master assisted by one apprentice performed at one time. Presently many performers work the figures behind the screen at once. A great master can move up to four figures in each hand. The performer must evoke a character through the style of movement for the figure. A female shadow figure is made to walk with a delicate sway. Fight scenes are performed in rhythm to the music. During songs the figures do not move, so that the performer can concentrate on singing. A performer must be careful never to show the rods or their hands while manipulating the puppets. The screen, Ying-chuang, is usually 5 feet wide and 3 feet high. It is usually made out of white silk. The light source is hung midway on the screen between the screen and the performers. An even diffuse light is best so that it lights the entire screen. A fluorescent light is now often used. The figures are held close to the screen while performing, so that the shadow image is not distorted and the colors in the figures are not diffused. The music for performances carries much of the emotional meaning, since the figures cannot portray emotions facially. The dramatic scripts for performances are the same as the operas for human performers.

> **See also** Peking Opera; Qiao-Ying Xi
> **References:** Stalberg, Roberta Helmer. *China's Puppets.* San Francisco: China Books, 1984.

Planchon, Roger (1931–)
France

Director, who brought innovative theater to a provincial working-class audience. In 1952 Planchon opened the Théâtre de la Comédie de Lyon, where he both directed and played the lead role in many plays. Moving to an area outside of Lyons, he founded the Théâtre de la Cité in the industrial town Villeurbanne in 1957. Here in the provinces he and his company created the first Centre Dramatique (Dramatic Center) as a theater for factory workers. Planchon offered theater directed to the taste of his audience and encouraged attendance by transporting people free to the theater. Yet, not condescending to his audience, Planchon performed sophisticated works by such playwrights as **Molière** and **Shakespeare**. His biggest success both at home and while touring was with *The Three Musketeers* by Alexandre Dumas (père) (1803–1870). He used imaginative staging including the use of turntables, film projection, and projected captions and commentary. He enjoyed a consistent and strong following in Villeurbanne, where he remained as director of Théâtre National Populaire (National Popular Theater) from 1973 until 1995, though his fame could easily have carried him elsewhere. Planchon has worked chiefly in the cinema in the 1980s and 1990s, acting in *Camille Claudel* (1988) and *Lautrec* (1998).

> **References:** Brockett, Oscar. *Century of Innovation: A History of European and American Theatre and Drama since 1870.* Englewood Cliffs, NJ: Prentice-Hall, 1973; Planchon, Roger. *Les Libertins.* Villeurbanne: Theatre National Populaire, 1996.

Plato (427–348 B.C.)
Greece

Greek philosopher. As a student of Socrates, Plato wrote most of his works in dialogue form, with Socrates as one of the voices. A man cannot be a master at any two things, Plato writes in his *Republic*, and, thus, an actor who attempts to imitate many people and things will never be able to do anything well. Plato also makes a more serious charge against the theater in the same dialogue; he presents Socrates as saying that the theater has an enormous capacity for corrupting society because it encourages indulgence in emotionality by making the audience weep at others' tragic and personal affairs and, in comedy, encourages the audience to laugh at vulgar acts of which one should be ashamed.

See also Poetics

References: Beardsley, Monroe C. *Aesthetics from Classical Greece to the Present: A Short History.* New York: Macmillan, 1966; Bieber, Margarete. *The History of the Greek and Roman Theater.* Princeton, NJ: Princeton University Press, 1961; Dukore, Bernard F. *Dramatic Theory and Criticism.* Chicago: Holt, Rinehart and Winston, 1974; Strauss, Leo. *Socrates and Aristophanes.* New York: Basic Books, 1966.

Plautus (254–184 B.C.)
Italy

Titus Maccius Plautus, often considered the best comic playwright of ancient Rome. Plautus is an original and richly amusing playwright, with a genuine instinct for theatricality. The twenty-one plays of his that survive are all based on the new form of **Greek Comedy** called New Comedy. However, Plautus added more psychological interest and cleverer wit and thus improved the playability of the more refined Greek comic plays. The native farces of Italy, such as the *Atellana,* also influenced the work of Plautus, who modeled his Greek adaptations after these rustic plays.

Many plots and character types were taken from the Greek playwright **Menander,** whose chief theme was love between a well-born young man and a courtesan who, by the end of the play, is discovered to be the respectable daughter of a citizen. His plays are known for their complicated plots, which involve misunderstandings, clever deceptions, or mistaken identity, as in the *Twin Menaechmi,* in which twin brothers who have been separated since the age of seven are finally reunited, after being in the same town for some time and being mistaken for each other.

There was no chorus in the plays of Plautus, but an integral part of the action was accompaniment by a flute and an actor chanting. Other plays by Plautus include *Cistellaria* (204 B.C.), *Stichus* (200 B.C.) and *Pseudolus* (191 B.C.).

References: Arnott, W. G. *Menander, Plautus, Terence.* Oxford, UK: Clarendon, 1975; Bieber, Margarete. *The History of the Greek and Roman Theater.* Princeton, NJ: Princeton University Press, 1961; Norwood, Gilbert. *Plautus and Terence.* New York: Cooper Square, 1963; Taylor, David. *Acting and the Stage.* Boston: George Allen & Unwin, 1978.

Poetics
Greece

The first systematic treatise on drama, written by the philosopher Aristotle between 335 and 322 B.C. The primary intent of the *Poetics* was to refute Plato's argument in *The Republic* for banishing the poets (including the dramatic poets) from an ideal community. Aristotle defends the value of dramatic poetry and theater and justifies its existence in an ideal state, arguing most famously for the positive effect tragedy has on the spectator by rousing and purging the emotions of pity and fear. Aristotle used the Greek word for purgation, catharsis, to describe this effect.

Imitation, states Aristotle, is the origin of all poetry. The object of this imitation in tragedy is human beings presented better than they are, and in comedy it is human beings presented worse than they are. Plot is the most important element of tragedy, according to Aristotle, and he sees characters as defined by what they do rather than by their psychological motivations. Aristotle gave the highest praise to the tragic poet **Sophocles,** because he handled plot so well, especially in his skillful dramatic construction of *Oedipus Rex.*

See also Greek Comedy; Greek Tragedy

References: Beardsley, Monroe C. *Aesthetics from Classical Greece to the Present: A Short History.* New York: Macmillan, 1966; Bieber, Margarete. *The History of the Greek and Roman Theater.* Princeton, NJ: Princeton University Press, 1961; Dukore, Bernard F. *Dramatic Theory and Criticism.* Chicago: Holt, Rinehart and Winston, 1974.

Poi

New Zealand

A graceful woman's dance performed by the **Maoris** of New Zealand, during which women twirl balls attached to cords. If only one ball is used, the performer twirls the ball with the right hand and hits it with the left to create a rhythm. In between each beat she touches her left hand to her head, shoulders, and hips. The rhythm created by this can imitate many sounds, including the sound of a galloping horse. The movements can imitate many common actions, such as paddling a canoe. A slow song full of emotional impact usually accompanies the dance. The costumes are usually very colorful, often consisting of a red underskirt covered by a yellow and black flax kilt with a red bodice.

> **References:** Barlow, Cleve. *Tikanga Whakaaro: Key Concepts in Maori Culture.* New York: Oxford University Press, 1991; Dansey, Harry. *The Maori in Colour.* London: Reed, 1973.

Poland

One of the first examples of drama in Poland took place in the thirteenth century in the church as a liturgical dialogue between the three Marys at the tomb of Jesus Christ. This type of liturgical drama evolved over the centuries, moving outside the church and taking on more and more secular characteristics, such as the Polish vernacular becoming more popular than Latin. Actors were deacons, priest, students, or craftsmen, who sometimes received a fee. **Mystery play**s and Passion pageants depicting the death of Christ date back to the fourteenth and sixteenth centuries. Puppet mystery plays were also popular during this time. A dramatic text, *The History of the Lord's Glorious Resurrection,* dates from the fourteenth century and was revived successfully in Poland in 1923 under Leon Schiller and again in 1961. In the sixteenth century students performed Polish translations of Roman classics in wealthy homes and even toured to other cities to pay for their schooling.

In the seventeenth century town pageants became prevalent and featured comical stock characters influenced by the Italian **commedia dell'arte,** which toured in Poland. During the seventeenth and eighteenth centuries performances took place at castles and palaces of wealthy and powerful families, some of whom created permanent theaters. Members of the families, their guests, and serfs specially trained for acting performed in these amateur productions. These serfs were the forerunners of Polish professional actors.

Augustus II created the first public place for theater in 1724, which became the Polish National Theater in 1765, managed by Woyciech Boguslawski (1757–1829), considered by many the father of Polish theater. Many actors of humble origin could gain high social standing, such as the late nineteenth-century actress **Helena Modrzejewska**. In the nineteenth and early twentieth centuries acting in Poland was a family profession. Troupes of actors lived together and often intermarried within theatrical circles. The children learned the skills of the theater as they grew. For example, Alojzy Fortunat Zolkowski (1777–1822) taught his son Alojzy Gonzaga Zolkowski (1814–1889), and both were famous comedians. Also Jerzy Leszczynski, son of a theater family, was one of Poland's greatest actors of the twentieth century until he died in 1959. **Naturalism** made its mark in Poland predominantly through the dramas written by former actress Gabriela Zapolska (1860–1921) in her comedies about current social issues.

During German and Soviet occupation, beginning in 1939, no theater was allowed, yet prison productions thrived. By the end of World War II in 1945, the Soviet government installed Communist rule. Nevertheless. experimental theater was prevalent throughout Polish urban centers from the 1950s through the 1980s; **Jerzy Grotowski**, for example, formed his famous theater laboratory and investigated the bare essence of performance free from the pressure of profit. His poor theater was one in which actors trained relentlessly to strip away the barriers that kept them from their true expression. His contribution to modern theater has been enormous. **Tadeusz Kantor** directed surrealist productions and created **happenings** with audience involvement and unusual settings. **Andrezej Wajda** crossed over between live theater and film, creating an eclectic array of quality productions. Until 1990, when Poland finally gained its independence, resistance to foreign domination was strong. That resistance throve in the theater, which, in underground performances, kept the national character alive. In 1997 *November Night*, by Stanislaw Wyspianski, was presented at the newly rebuilt Narodowy Theater in Warsaw. Opera is popular in Poland and is often presented at the Warsaw Chamber Opera and at the National Theater. The opera *Boccanegra Sails In* was performed in Warsaw in 1998. Puppet theater is also popular, with works such as *The Cage* performed by Grzegorz Kwiecinski's Fire and Paper Theater of Lodz.

See also Polish Cinema; Polish Prison Productions; Serf Theater; Surrealism

References: Braun, Kazimierz. *A History of Polish Theater, 1939–1989*. Westport, CT: Greenwood, 1996; Cioffi, Kathleen. *Alternative Theatre in Poland 1954–89*. Canada: Harwood Academic, 1996; Csato, Edward. *The Polish Theatre*. Warsaw: Polonia Publishing, 1963; Czerwinski, E. J. *Contemporary Polish Theater and Drama (1956–1984)*. Westport, CT: Greenwood, 1988; Kabikowski, Tomasz. "Performance Review: 'November Night,' by Stanislaw Wyspianski." *Theatre Journal* 50, 4 (December 1998): 518–521; Kanski, Josef. "Opera around the World: Poland-Warsaw: 'Boccanegra Sails In.'" *Opera* 49, 5 (May 1998): 580–581; Meils, Cathy. "Postmark Poland: Seven Years after the Revolutions." *American Theatre* 14 (October 1997): 90–92; Wolford, Lisa. *Grotowski's Objective Drama Research*. Jackson: University Press of Mississippi, 1996.

Polish Cinema

During the beginning of the film era, Poland was culturally rich, but economically poor, giving the nation a slow start in this budding art form. One of the first sensations was the actress Apollonia Chalupiec (1894–1987), who later became a famous Hollywood actress known as Pola Negri. By the mid-1930s a student group of avant-garde filmmakers, known as START, made advancements in Polish film production. The most famous among them was Aleksander Ford, who made *Legion of the Streets*, 1932, and *Young Chopin*, 1952.

World War II (1939–1945) devastated Polish cinema. The mandatory style of the Soviets, **socialist realism,** was demanded of Polish filmmakers in the beginning of the 1950s, but control loosened by the end of the decade, bringing forth a highly vital and creative era of cinema in Poland. Outstanding films that received international recognition included *Ashes and Diamonds*, 1958, by **Andrzej Wajda** and *Mother Joan of the Angels*, 1961, by Jerzy

Kawalerowicz. Roman Polanski, born Polish, started his career in Poland with his short film *Knife in the Water*, 1961, but later emigrated to the **United States.**

By the late 1960s conditions had worsened for Polish filmmakers because of political turmoil. Many Jews, such as Ford, left Poland because of increased anti-Semitism. Despite these pressures, resistance to rule from the Soviet Union was strong and growing in Poland. This sentiment found its expression dynamically through Polish film in the 1970s with such films as *Behind the Wall*, 1971, by Krzysztof Zanussi, *Camera Buff*, 1979, by Krzysztof Kieslowski, and Wajda's *Man of Iron*, 1981, which won the Palme d'Or at Cannes. During the 1980s censorship was extreme, as the Communist government was weakening and grasping for control until its final collapse at the end of the decade. Since the economic shifting that occurred in the early 1990s, the Polish film industry has stabilized.

Kieslowski has gained an international reputation for his enigmatic and hauntingly beautiful films, such as *The Double Life of Veronique*, 1991, and his series of three films that were symbolically about the unification of Europe *Blue, White*, and *Red*, begun in 1993. He also created a ten-part cycle of short films known as *Decalogue* that first aired on Polish television in 1988–1989. His death in 1996 was a great loss to Polish cinema. In 1998 only seventeen films were released in Poland, but 1999 produced many promising works, including *Pan Tadeusz*, by Andrzej Wajda and *With Fire and Sword*, by Jerzy Hoffman.

References: Corliss, Richard. "Show Business: Dazzling Decalogue: Krzsztof Kieslowski's 10-Part Masterpiece Finally Comes to the U.S. Thou Shalt Not Miss It." *Time* 152, 4 (July 27, 1998): 61; Karpinski, Maciej. *The Theatre of Andrzej Wajda*. Trans. Christina Paul. New York: Cambridge University Press, 1989.Katz, Ephraim. *The Film Encyclopedia*. New York: Harper Perennial, 1994; Kehr, Dave. "Kieslowski's Trilogy: Blue, White, Red." *Film Comment* 30, 6 (1994): 10–21; Meils, Cathy. "Postmark Poland: Seven Years After the Revolutions." *American Theatre* 14 (October 1997): 90–92.

Polish Prison Productions

Theatrical productions that took place in prisons, labor camps, concentration camps, extermination camps, or prisoner-of-war camps in Poland during World War II (1939–1945), when the Germans and Soviets occupied Poland. These performances were put on by prisoners for prisoners, all incarcerated for resisting foreign domination and struggling to defend Polish values and identity. Shows of amazingly high artistic quality and number were presented, some in secret, some sanctioned by the authorities in the canteens or even in the officer's camps.

The repertoire varied from Greek classics to **Shakespeare** to Polish classics. Scripts were recreated from the memory of actors who had played roles in these plays. Audience members even received handwritten programs for performances. Sanctioned productions were highly censored, and secret performances were usually native Polish works and sometimes politically inflammatory.

References: Braun, Kazimierz. *A History of Polish Theater, 1939–1989*. Westport, CT: Greenwood, 1996; Csato, Edward. *The Polish Theatre*. Warsaw: Polonia Publishing, 1963.

Polus
Greece

Famous tragic actor of fourth century B.C., praised in his day for his portrayal of Oedipus in *Oedipus Rex* and *Oedipus of Colonus*, both by **Sophocles**. He performed the lead role in *Electra*, also by Sophocles, after his own son had died, carrying an urn holding the ashes of his son during the scene when Electra thinks her brother has died. His depth of feeling is reported to have moved the audience deeply.

See also Greek Tragedy

References: Allen, James Turney. "Greek Acting in the Fifth Century." University of California Publications in Classical Philology 15 (1916): 279–289; Bieber, Margarete. *The History of the Greek and Roman Theater*. Princeton, NJ: Princeton University Press, 1961; Hunningher, B. "Acoustics and Acting in the Theater of Dionysus Eleuthereus." *Mededelingen der Nederlandse Akademie van Wetenschappen* 9 (1956);O'Connor, John Bartholomew. *Chapters in the History of Actors and Acting in Ancient Greece*. Chicago: University of Chicago Press, 1908.

Polynesia

The name given to a number of islands scattered over a vast area in the Pacific Ocean by European explorers; literally, "many islands." Polynesia is generally divided into two groups: The eastern group includes the Society Islands (Tahiti), Marquesas Islands, Austral Islands, Mangareva, Tuamotu Islands, Cook Islands, Easter Island, **New Zealand,** and Hawaii; and the western group includes Tonga, Samoa, Uvea, Futuna, Niue, Tuvalu, Tokelau, and Fiji. The goal of most traditional Polynesian performing arts is to interpret poetry through music and dance. The legs and hips of the dancer respond to the rhythm of the music, as the hands and arms elaborate on the poetic story through graceful gestures that create a visual language. As a storyteller, the dancer does not directly imitate the characters in the story, but, instead, narrates the tale. Sometimes short, usually comic, skits are improvised as interludes between these dance-stories.

Early European visitors to Tahiti told of an elaborate performance worshipping Oro, the youthful god of fertility and the god of war. The myths of this god were dramatized through dancing and chanting, with poetry as a major element. Clowning was also an important part of these performances. The sexually suggestive movements of the dancers and the human sacrifices that accompanied worship of Oro caused the cult of Oro to be banned by Christian missionaries in the early nineteenth century when Tahiti was converted to Christianity.

In Samoa, *Fa'asamoa,* or cultural life, has adapted to Christianity and modern Western culture as introduced by Christian missionaries in the early nineteenth century. Church theatricals and biblical operas are popular in Samoa in the early twenty-first century. These experiments with Christian themes often incorporate elements of pre-Christian traditional performances. The older traditions included large ensembles of performers who danced and chanted. Clown characters performed improvised skits in between dance-chant numbers. Exceptional clown performers were believed to be able to invoke the protection of the spirits, under whose guard they could make fun of even the highest chiefs.

In Hawaii the performing arts primarily served to honor the highest-ranking kings and chiefs, who are believed to have descended from the gods. These performing arts included chanted songs, poetic chanting, storytelling, and interpre-

Polynesian dancers from near Arutanga, Aitutaki, Cook Islands (Dallas and John Heaton/Corbis)

tative dance. **Mele** is the Hawaiian term for chanting, which can be of two forms: **Mele Oli** is a solo performance on a religious theme, and **Mele Hula** is accompanied by dance movements. **Hula,** an expressive dance performed to lyrical music, was performed by both men and women in pre-Christian Hawaii. The version of hula performed now in Hawaii, under Western cultural influence, is called **Hapa Haole,** literally, "half-white hula."

References: Archey, Gilbert. "Polynesia, Polynesian Cultures." *EWA* 11 (1966): 438–466; Barrow, Terence. *Art and Life in Polynesia.* Wellington, NZ: Reed, 1972; Beckwith, Martha W. *The Kumulipo: A Hawaiian Creation Chant.* Honolulu: University Press of Hawaii, 1972: Brandon, James. *The Cambridge Guide to Asian Theatre.* New York: Cambridge University Press, 1993: Charlot, John. *Chanting the Universe: Hawaiian Religious Culture.* Honolulu: Emphasis International, 1983: Dean, Beth. *South Pacific Dance.* Sydney: Pacific Publications, 1978: Kaeppler, A. "Movement in the Performing Arts of the Pacific Islands." In *Theatrical Movement: A Bibliographic Anthology,* ed. Robert Fleshman. Metuchen, NJ: Scarecrow, 1986; Tausie, Vilsoni. *Art in the New Pacific.* Suva: Institute of Pacific Studies in collaboration with the South Pacific Commission, 1980.

Poor Theater

See Grotowski, Jerzy

Portugal

Theater in Portugal dates back to at least 1193, the date of a written record of two performers, Bonamis and Acompaniado, who put on an *Arremedillum,* a comic impersonation. In the thirteenth century there is evidence of lewd comical performances in which clergy apparently took part. There is a church mandate demanding that clergy not involve themselves in these crude farces and another ruling that priestly vestments should not be worn by comic characters. By the fourteenth century there were liturgical dramas being performed. An important playwright in the late fifteenth and early sixteenth centuries was Gil

Vicente (1465–1537); he also acted in his own plays. He wrote **morality plays, *Autos Sacramentales,*** farces, and romantic comedies in both Spanish and Portuguese.

During the sixteenth century, the power of the Inquisition led to more censorship by the church. The king of Spain ruled Portugal from 1580 to 1640, which subjugated Portuguese theater to the preferred Spanish theater. By the seventeenth century, Portuguese indigenous drama was nearly dead, but commercial theater offering Spanish plays and popular comedies survived well. In the eighteenth century the introduction of **Italian opera** challenged the popularity of other theater forms. The playwright Joao Baptista de Almeida Garrett (1799–1854) helped usher in a period of drama in Portuguese that reflected the values of **Romanticism.** Garrett also founded the National Theater in 1846.

Strict governmental censorship existed from 1926 through the 1970s. In 1945 it became less powerful a force, which allowed for the creation of a new National Theater run by actress Amelia Reycolaco (1898–1990). In 1944 Francisco Ribeiro (1911–1984) began the Commediantes de Lisboa. The Teatro Estúdio do Salitre was founded in 1946. Begun in 1953, the Experimental Theater in Oporto was an important performing space for new plays. Theater was an important tool in the political revolution of 1974. After the revolution, the many new theater groups started in the 1970s were able to realize their ideals. In the 1990s low state subsidy of the arts has not hampered the theater's continued development, and new audiences have emerged to support increased production.

In film Portugal has hosted the International Encounters in Documentary Cinema in Lisbon for nine years starting in 1990. A recent film of note from Portugal is *Trafico* (1999, directed by Joao Botelho), which presents almost caricatured characters.

References: Anger, Cedric. "Cahier Critique: Balade Fune/Raire: 'Trafico' Critical Notebook." *Cahiers du Cinema* (March 1999): 66–67; Carver, Benedict. "Fine Line OKs First Picture in Two Years." *Variety* 374 (26 April 1999–May 1999): 10; Hartnoll, Phyllis. *The Oxford Companion to the Theatre.* New York: Oxford University Press, 1967; Menashe, Louis. "Communiues: Lisbon's International Encounters in Documentary Cinema." *Cineaste* 23 (April 1998): 55; Michaelis de Vasconcellos, Carolina. "Shakespeare in Portugal." *Jahrbuch der Deutschen Shakespeare-Gesellschaft* 15 (1880): 266; Montes, Carmen Marquez. "X Festival Del Sur—Encuentro Teatral Tres Continentes (10th Festival of the South—Theatrical Meeting of Three Continents)." *Latin American Theatre Review* 31 (Spring 1998): 201–204; Pierson, Colin M. "Portugal's Geraao de 70: Drama Influenced by a Changing World." *Theatre Research International* 20 (1995): 1–6.

Po-the-hi
Java, Malaysia, Singapore, Taiwan

Glove puppet theater performed for children in Buddhist temple courtyards and in the streets. *Po-the-hi* troupes travel around, residing in a village three to four days before moving on. Usually two puppeteers perform all of the characters in these adventurous dramas about heroic warriors who fight horrible monsters. Three musicians accompany the fast-paced action. Special effects created with flash powder and flames highlight peak moments in the dramas. Sometimes highly rehearsed and refined performances of *Po-the-hi* are televised on local Taiwanese television stations.

References: Brandon, James R. *Brandon's Guide to Theatre in Asia.* Honolulu: University Press of Hawaii, 1976; Howard, Roger. *Contemporary Chinese Theatre.* Hong Kong: Heinemann, 1978; Mackerras, Colin. *Chinese Theatre in Modern Times, from 1840 to the Present Day.* Amherst: University of Massachusetts Press, 1975.

Presley, Elvis (1935–1977)
United States

Rock and roll film star of the 1950s who introduced a gyrating, sexually charged performance style to the American scene, which caused mass hysteria among his young female fans and furrowed the brows of parents and assorted moral figureheads. From a humble family and raised mainly in Memphis, Tennessee, Presley burst onto the music scene in 1955 and became an overnight sensation. The next year he began to appear in films, such as *Love Me Tender,* 1956, and *Jailhouse Rock,* 1957, that were tailor-made to highlight his personality and singing talent. He continued making movies all through the 1960s and performed successfully in nightclubs and concerts in the early 1970s. Poor health due to excessive weight gain and drugs led to his premature death at forty-two. His memory lives on, and he holds an important place in the history of American popular culture.

References: Doll, Susan. *Understanding Elvis: Southern Roots vs. Star Image.* New York: Garland, 1998; Marsh, Dave. *Elvis.* New York: Rolling Stone, Times Book, 1982.

Proskenion
See Hellenistic Theater

Protagonist
See Tragic Acting in Ancient Greece

Punch and Judy
England

World-famous English puppet theater tradition, originating from Italian influence in the seventeenth century. Punch and Judy began as marionette puppets and became glove puppets by the nineteenth century. Even by 1780, the glove puppet Punch was a popular and common street show, usually performed in a wooden booth with a curtain. Mr. Punch is the antihero, a hunchback with a long hooked nose and a nasty temperament. Judy is his wife. Also featured in the show are the Hangman, the Crocodile, and Toby, Punch's dog. The show is violent and sexist, and offends many modern sensibilities, yet it has an attractive raw edge mixed with grotesque humor that is strangely appealing. It also regularly features fast action and audience interaction. Performers of this tradition of puppetry are often referred to as "professors" and usually learn to perform from family who performed before them. Percy Press, one of the most famous Punch and Judy professors, performed until his death in 1980.

By the 1950s competition from television had caused a great decline in all puppet theater in **England**. It was revived in the 1970s with the creation of a permanent venue for puppet theater, Covent Garden Piazza in London, and the founding of the Punch and Judy Fellowship in 1980.

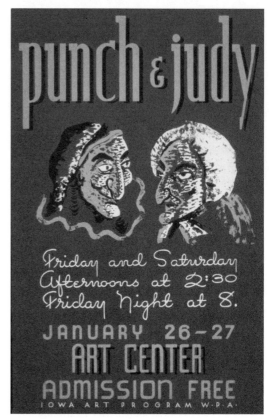

An advertisement for a performance of Punch and Judy, the humorous puppet characters (Library of Congress)

References: Fraser, Peter. *Punch and Judy.* New York: Van Nostrand Reinhold, 1970; Myers, D. H. *The Last Days of Mr. Punch.* New York: McCall, 1971; Spaight, George. *The History of the English Puppet Theatre.* London: George Harrap, 1990.

Puppeteer
Burma, Cambodia, China, Egypt, Europe, India, Indonesia, Japan, Korea, Turkey, United States

The job of a puppeteer is one of the most demanding in live entertainment. The puppeteer must be a consummate technician, with agility, endurance, and strength, and a performing artist with a keen sense of dramatic timing, vocal expressiveness, and an ability to endow an inanimate figure with lifelike movement. The responsibilities heaped on the puppeteers of some puppet forms seem crushing. The **dalang,** puppet master of the Southeast Asian shadow puppet theater **Wayang Kulit,** must manipulate all of the puppets from behind a shadow screen, enact all of their voices, improvise the version of the tale being told, conduct the **gamelan** (a traditional orchestra) behind him with a wooden clapper beneath his knee, and perform without interruption from sundown to sunup. One of the reasons this is possible for a single performer is because the conditions of performance for a *dalang* are trance inducing. The screen isolates him from his audience. He also spiritually readies himself to be a conduit through which the gods may tell their stories. To varying degrees, all puppeteers feel this kind of release from self-consciousness, both because the all-consuming task of fully animating their puppet characters, and because they are most often not visible to the audience. In this sense, though heavily burdened, puppeteers are some of the freest performers in live theater.

In Asia the occupation of puppeteer garners great respect, as with the master performers of the Japanese **Bunraku.** The Chinese performers of the string puppet theater **Jia-li Xi** are also highly regarded in society. The puppeteer of the Burmese *Yokthe Pwe* string puppet theater is also admired for his manipulation of these highly complicated puppets. Practitioners of the **Cantonese Rod Puppet Theater** must possess great strength, endurance, and dexterity. For **Fu Tai Hsi** the *Tou-shou*, the master puppeteer, and the *Er-shou*, his assistant, must develop highly flexible hands to manipulate both the puppet's arms and the head in a realistic manner. As there is often a spiritual or shamanistic aspect to puppet performances in Asia, men are almost exclusively the performers since mastery over the spirit world is traditionally a man's domain in Asia.

Other terms for puppeteers include the Thai *Nai Nang, Nang Sbek Touch* in **Cambodia,** and *Muqaddam* in **Egypt.** There are several forms of Asian puppet theaters in which the performers are visible during performance, such as the Chinese **Zhang Mu** and the Cambodian *Nang Sbek.* For the comedic **Kkoktu Kaksi** of **Korea,** the master puppeteer of this glove puppet theater speaks the lead voice and another actor performs all of the other voices.

Puppeteers in the West have rarely garnered much respect and have been largely relegated to children's entertainment. A few forms, such as the Turkish *Karagoz* and the English **Punch and Judy,** have appealed to adults through political and so-cial satire. In these cases, the puppeteers protect themselves by having politically inflammatory statements come out of the mouths of their puppets rather than their own. In the **United States** the widely popular work of **Jim Henson** and his Muppets brought puppets into mainstream America. This trend has been further developed by the American designer and director **Julie Taymor**, who created magical wild creatures for *The Lion King* on Broadway.

References: Crothers, J. Frances. *The Puppeteer's Library Guide: The Bibliographic Index to the Literature of the World Puppet Theatre.* Metuchen, NJ: Scarecrow, 1971–1983; Tillis, Steve. *Towards an Aesthetics of the Puppet: Puppetry as a Theatrical Art.* New York: Greenwood, 1992.

Puppets
Africa, Americas, Asia, Europe, United States

Two- or three-dimensional figures manipulated by a **puppeteer** that represent characters in performance in place of human actors; utilized throughout the world in dramatic presentations. Puppetry has never secured a place in mainstream adult theater in the West. It has most often been relegated to children's entertainment, even though it was championed as a form by the English designer, **Gordon Craig**. Exceptional examples from the West include the English **Punch and Judy,** the work of the American puppeteer **Jim Henson** and of theater artist **Julie Taymor**, the Native American **Kwakiutl Mystery Play** and the **Bread and Puppet Theatre.**

The art of puppetry has reached its highest refinement in Asia, most specifically with the Japanese **Bunraku,** a form that uses a masterfully carved and manipulated wooden doll puppet, and the Javanese form of the *Wayang Kulit,* shadow puppet theater. Other regional forms of the Southeast Asian *Wayang Kulit* include the Malaysian *Wayang Siam* and the *Wayang Melayu,* the Javanese *Wayang Pantja Sila, Wayang Suluh, Wayang Golek, Wayang Tengul,* Wayang Jawa, *Wayang Madya, Wayang Klitik,* and *Wayang Gedog.* In Thailand puppetry is found in the *Nang Yai, Hun Krabok, Nang Talung,* and *Nang Sbek.* In Cambodia there is the *Nang Sbek Touch* puppet theater and in Korea the **Kkoktu Kaksi.** Burma's puppet theater, *Yokthe Pwe,* highly influences its dance and other performing arts. Chinese puppetry has many forms, including the **Cantonese Rod Puppet Theater, Fu Tai Hsi, Zhang-tou Mu-ou, Jia-li Xi,** and **Pi-ying Xi.** In India puppet theaters include **Tholu Pava Koothu, Tholu Bommalata, Mysore Shadow Puppet Theater,** and *Ravanachhaya.*

People around the world delight in imitation, and much of puppetry's appeal can be attributed to this universal taste. An audience feels an aesthetic thrill when a puppet in motion appears to have life breath and be its own master.

References: Crothers, J. Frances. *The Puppeteer's Library Guide: The Bibliographic Index to the Literature of the World Puppet Theatre.* Metuchen, NJ: Scarecrow, 1971–1983; Tillis, Steve. *Towards an Aesthetics of the Puppet: Puppetry as a Theatrical Art.* New York: Greenwood, 1992.

Pwe
Myanmar

Generic term for any kind of performance in **Myanmar** (Burma).

References: Becher, Alton. "The Journey through the Night: Some Reflections on Burmese Traditional Theatre." *Drama Review* 15 (Winter 1970): 83–87; Brandon, James. *Theatre in Southeast Asia.* Cambridge, MA: Harvard University Press, 1974; Htin Aung, U. *Burmese Drama: A Study with Translations of Burmese Plays.* Calcutta: Oxford University Press, 1937.

Pya Zat
Myanmar

Modern dance-drama. Pya Zat evolved from the Burmese court dance-drama, **Zat Pwe,** although the style of the former is quite contemporary in comparison. Performances are set in the past, where a princely hero overcomes evil magicians and demons in a mysterious kingdom. A typical evening performance includes a *Pya Zat* followed by a *Zat Pwe* dance-drama.

References: Brandon, James R. *Brandon's Guide to Theatre in Asia.* Honolulu: University Press of Hawaii, 1976.

Q

Qiao-Ying Xi
China

Theater of human shadow play performed during the Sung dynasty, 960–1279. Literally meaning "Theater of Larger Shadows," Qiao-Ying Xi used as performers humans casting silhouettes on a screen. It is thought that performers sought to imitate the appearance and movement style of the leather shadow figures moving in a two-dimensional manner, **Pi-ying Xi.**

> **References:** Stalberg, Roberta Helmer. *China's Puppets.* San Francisco: China Books, 1984.

Quetzalcoátl
Mexico

Aztec god for whom an annual festival was celebrated before Spanish colonization. Forty days prior to the festival a slave without any blemishes on his body was purchased to represent the god Quetzalcoátl. The slave was costumed with a crown and a bird's beak upon his head, jewels, loincloth, and all other adornments to make him the living representation of the idol for the forty days of the festival. By day he was worshiped and expected to dance and sing in processions through the community; women and children would emerge from their homes with offerings fit for a god. He was fed opulent feasts and given garlands of roses around his neck. By night he was kept in a cage to keep him from trying to escape his doom, which was to be sacrificed to the god at the final day of the festival, the third of February. If the slave became frightened of his coming death, in which his heart was to be carved out of him and offered to the moon, he was drugged by the priests of the temple to allow him to forget his future and happily sing and dance again.

Quite fortuitously, Cortés, the Spanish explorer who conquered the Aztec nation, landed on the shores of the Yucatán in 1519, which corresponded to the date that the Aztec people believed the god Quetzalcoátl promised to return. Cortés realized he had been taken for a deity by the Aztec and their chief Moctezuma and took full advantage of it. In a theatrical display, he clothed himself completely in the clothing offered to him by the Aztec chief and was elaborately welcomed into Mexico as a god, making his subsequent victory much easier than it could otherwise have been against the fierce Aztec warriors.

> **See also** Aztec Theater
>
> **References:** León-Portilla, Miguel. *Aztec Thought and Culture: A Study of the Ancient Nahuatl Mind.* Trans. Jack Emory Davis. Norman: University of Oklahoma Press, 1963; Phelan, John Leddy. *The Millennial Kingdom of the Franciscans in the New World: A Study of the Writings of GeróNimor de Mendieta (1525–1604).* Berkeley: University of California Press, 1956; Usigli, Rodolfo. *Mexico in the Theater.* Trans. Wilder P. Scott. University, MS: Romance Monographs, 1976; Versènyi, Adam. *Theatre in Latin America: Religion, Politics, and Culture from Cortés to the 1980's.* New York: Cambridge University Press, 1993.

A portion of the *Aztec Codex Borbonicus* showing various gods, including Quetzalcoátl at the left (*The Art Archive*/Bibliothéque de *L'Assemblée Nationale Paris*/Dagli Orti)

R

Raimund, Ferdinand (1790–1836)

Austria

Considered to be the greatest Austrian comic actor of his day, who created a truly Viennese style that incorporated spectacle, songs, and a celebratory feel. Since he was not from a wealthy family, Raimund began working as an apprentice to the Viennese stage. Though a comedian, he also had a wistful sadness about him that was best expressed in the plays he wrote for himself, the most famous of which were *Das Mädchen aus der Feenwelt oder der Bauer als Millionär* (The Girl from the World of the Fairies and the Farmer as the Millionaire), 1826, and *Der Alpenkönig und der Menschenfeind*, 1828. He ended his own life.

References: Hartnoll, Phyllis. *The Oxford Companion to the Theatre.* New York: Oxford University Press, 1967; Robertson, Ritchie, and Edward Timms, eds. *Theatre and Performance in Austria: From Mozart to Je-linek.* Edinburgh: Edinburgh University Press, 1993.

Ram Lila

India

Pageant play based on the life of Rama, incarnation of **Vishnu,** a Hindu god (see **Ramayana**), originating in the sixteenth century and performed mostly in Banaras and Allahabad. *Ram Lila* takes up to thirty consecutive days to perform during the annual performance at the Dashahara festival in September and October. The Sanskrit language is used during parts of a performance, but the performance is mostly in Hindi.

The *Vyas*, the director, stands by the side of the action and prompts the actors. He is dressed in all white including his white turban. Characters speak very slowly, a syllable at a time, in order to be perfectly understood. Important to a performance are the *Ramayanis*, the chorus members, who squat in circle with small metal cymbals. They are silent when the actors sing, but after the actors finish they translate the Sanskrit into the local language. They add accent to important points of an actor's speech by yelling "hay-haah" in unison. They also describe the setting for each episode and let the audience know the inner thoughts of characters through the songs they sing. The festival ends with an enactment of Rama destroying Ravana, the evil monster. The audience is renewed for another year by Rama's victory.

The setting for a performance is the whole village. Each day the action is staged, usually on a platform in the most appropriate location in town. The audience watches from every available vantage point. The actor portraying Rama is elaborately costumed and made up, with a silver jacket, a jeweled crown, black outline around his eyes, and jewels painted on his face. Actors who play ferocious characters generally wear masks. The mask for **Hanuman,** the white monkey warrior, is most impressive, as it is made of 10 pounds of copper with a golden crown, bulging eyes, and exposed teeth.

Once an adult an actor usually plays a specific role throughout his whole life. After thirty years, actors even become known in the community by the role they portray. Actors view their portrayal of a god as an act of worship. Since there are only male performers, boys play female roles. The actor portraying Rama must be pure, with no sexual experience. A young boy starts by playing Rama's younger brother, Laksmana. Next he graduates to portraying Sita, Rama's wife, then Rama, and finally a demon, god, or other mature character.

> **References:** Brandon, James R. *Brandon's Guide to Theatre in Asia.* Honolulu: University Press of Hawaii, 1976; Gargi, Balawanta. *Folk Theater of India.* Seattle: University of Washington Press, 1966; Vatsyayan, Kapila. *Traditional Indian Theatre: Multiple Streams.* New Delhi: National Book Trust, 1980.

Ramayana
India, Southeast Asia

Hindu epic tale originating from India (400–100 B.C.). The *Ramayana* centers around the mighty Prince Rama, who is an incarnation of Vishnu, one of the three main Hindu gods (see **Hinduism**). Rama's father is tricked by one of his wives into exiling Rama to the forest for fourteen years. Rama's wife, Sita, and his faithful brother, Laksmana, accompany him. Sita is kidnapped by Ravana, the horrible forest monster, by a clever trick in which Ravana has Rama and Laksmana led away from Sita by a golden deer. Then Ravana approaches in the form of an old man, gets close to Sita, and snatches her away to his island. Rama assembles a mighty army, including **Hanuman,** the great white monkey, who is the leader of his troops. A mighty battle ensues, in which Rama rescues Sita and fulfills his destiny by killing Ravana. The *Ramayana* has inspired many dramatic performances. The *Wayang Siam,* shadow puppet theater of Malaysia, uses this story almost exclusively for its repertory. The Thai **Khon,** masked dance-drama, uses the **Ramakian,** the Thai version of the *Ramayana,* as its main source of inspiration. The Indian **Kathakali,** dance-drama, dramatizes scenes from the *Ramayana* as well as the **Mahabharata,** the other of the two central Hindu epic tales.

The Ramayana ballet being performed in a theater near the Shaivan Lara Jonggrang temple at Prambanam in Java (Photo by J. P. Osnes)

> **References:** Sweeney, P. L. *The Ramayana and the Malay Shadow-Play.* Kuala Lumpur: National University of Malaysia Press, 1972.

Ramukien
Thailand

The Thai version of the Indian epic tale, the **Ramayana.** As the *Ramayana* spread throughout Thailand, it took in many Thai characters and was adjusted to suit Thai tastes.

> **References:** Brandon, James. *Theatre in Southeast Asia.* Cambridge, MA: Harvard University Press, 1974.

Rappresentazione Sacre
Italy

Literally, "sacred representation"; a form of sacred drama in Italy dramatizing Christian mysteries and miracles, believed to date back to the thirteenth century. The origin of sacred drama is to be found in church, in the form of a song performed by the priest and the congregation. Next the clergy became the actors, performing the liturgy for the congregation, which became a passive audience. In time the dramas were performed outside the church walls by young men who were members of religious organizations. Latin was soon substituted for the vernacular language, making these dramas suitable entertainment for carnivals, a tradition that carried on into the twentieth century. The popularity of sacred dramas severely dropped, especially in urban areas, during the revival of classic drama in the fourteenth and fifteenth centuries. By the sixteenth century sacred drama further declined until at last, other than during carnivals, it was only performed in convents by and for nuns.

Actors in these dramas portrayed angels, Jesus, and Mary, with beggars mingling freely with such high characters as bishops. God was most often portrayed by a disembodied ominous voice, but the devil wore a variety of clever disguises, none of which could conceal his wicked identity. There were no **morality plays** in Italy as there were in France and England, but there were such characters in Italian sacred dramas as Peace, Truth, and Justice, each exemplifying a moral quality.

The episodic plots traversed heaven, hell, and the whole physical world, with no divisions of acts in the dramas. There was usually a prologue called an *Annunziazione*, most often performed by an angel who introduced the story, welcomed the audience, and promised spiritual rewards for those who listened well. Concluding a performance was an epilogue called a *Licenza*, also performed by an angel, who pointed out the moral lesson of the drama.

Rappresentazioni Sacre is an early example of civic theater. Important businessmen, notable poets, and even politicians were active in composing, directing, and producing these performances.

See also *Commedia Erudita*; Latin Humanistic Comedy
References: Duchartre, Pierre-Louis. *The Italian Comedy* (Comedie Italienne). Trans. Randolph Weaver. New York: Dover, 1966; Herrick, Marvin T. *Italian Comedy in the Renaissance.* Urbana: University of Illinois Press, 1960.

Ras Lila
India

Dance-drama glorifying **Krishna,** the eighth and most important incarnation of the Hindu god **Vishnu,** originating in the sixteenth century; and evolved from the performances of **Kathaks,** storytellers who sang Krishna stories and used gestures to embellish their narration. It is performed primarily in north India, mainly in the Braj area of Uttar Pradesh State, where it is believed Krishna was born. Performances are viewed as a form of prayer through religious enactment, not just as entertainment. *Ras* indicates the opening dance of the **Gopis,** young milkmaids in love with Krishna, and *Lila*, which literally means play, indicates the various plays that enact Krishna's life. Young boys perform all roles because they alone are considered pure enough for this holy enactment. Once they are in costume and makeup, they are treated like gods and are adored and worshipped. The plays are spoken or sung in Sanskrit at times, but the language most often used is Vragboli.

The first third of an evening performance is a group dance with Krishna and the *Gopis*. There are usually seven *Gopis* dancing in a circle, with Krishna and Radha, Krishna's most beloved *Gopi*, in the center also dancing. There are some historical paintings of this form that show many Krishnas, one dancing with each girl, suggesting that the god multiplied himself in order to dance with all simultaneously. The next portion of the performance is a drama enacting an episode from the life of Krishna in song and through dialogue. The most popular incidents of the life of Krishna constitute the repertory. The complete series of representations takes a month.

Performances take place in the open air on temple grounds. There is usually a raised circular dance floor, to accommodate circular dances, with a highly decorated throne behind. *Ras Mandal* is the proper name for a performance space for *Ras Lila*. The costumes cover most of the performer's bodies, from their neck to their feet, with ornate robes and skirts. The performer playing Krishna wears a high golden crown that forms a sort of sun or fan-shaped circle above his head. Braided hairpieces are added behind the ears for the performers playing *Gopis*. Swirling designs of small white dots decorate the actor's face. The eyes are outlined with a heavy black makeup. There are scarcely any props other than Krishna's flute and no scenery other than the throne. Musical accompaniment is provided by a variety of drums, cymbals, stringed instruments, reed instruments, and singers.

The performers are not formally trained, and since they are so young the performance quality is not very high.

See also Ram Lila

References: Brandon, James R. *Brandon's Guide to Theatre in Asia.* Honolulu: University Press of Hawaii, 1976; Gargi, Balawanta. *Folk Theater of India.* Seattle: University of Washington Press, 1966; Varadpande, Manohar Laxman. *Krishna Theatre in India.* New Delhi: Abhinav, 1982; Vatsyayan, Kapila. *Traditional Indian Theatre: Multiple Streams.* New Delhi: National Book Trust, 1980.

Rasa

India

Literally, sentiment, taste, or flavor; used to describe a spiritual joy experienced through witnessing a well-executed expression of emotion through drama, song, dance, or visual spectacle. The aesthetic principle of cultivating *rasa* underlies all Indian arts.

References: Brandon, James R. *Brandon's Guide to Theatre in Asia.* Honolulu: University Press of Hawaii, 1976; Gargi, Balawanta. *Folk Theater of India.* Seattle: University of Washington Press, 1966.

Rata Yakuma

Sri Lanka

A ceremony done for the safety of unborn babies, a successful birth, and to help women conceive a child if they are having trouble. Containing elements of drama and mime, this ceremony is directed toward the numerous folk deities of the island. The origin of the ceremony is not known.

The ceremony begins with offerings and invocations to an altar dedicated to the Seven Barren Queens. An exorcist chants the purpose of the ritual and the story of the Seven Barren Queens. Following this is the Twelvefold Ritual, during which seven daughters give a cloth to a representation of the **Buddha.** To end this portion, the exorcist mimes the Barren Queens wearing a similar cloth, which is also offered to the Buddha. Next the exorcist symbolically acts out the birth of a child in song and movement and presents the imaginary baby to the parents for whom the ceremony is performed.

See also Kolam

References: Brandon, James. *The Cambridge Guide to Asian Theatre.* New York: Cambridge University Press, 1993; de Zoete, Beryl. *Dance and Magic Drama in Ceylon.* London: Faber & Faber, 1957; Gunawardana, A. J. *Theatre in Sri Lanka.* Colombo: Department of Cultural Affairs, Sri Lanka, 1976.

Ravanachhaya

India

Ancient shadow puppet theater from Orissa that is the least sophisticated form of traditional shadow puppet theater in India. Puppeteers manipulate flat rawhide shadow figures behind a flame-lit muslin screen. The audience sits on the opposite side, where only the flickering shadows are visible. The **Sutradhara,** the narrator, stands to the side of the screen in full view of the audience reciting an episode from the **Ramayana,** the great Hindu epic tale. In addition to singing in between narrations, he also improvises dialogue between the characters, all the while playing a small percussive instrument.

A shadow figure is made of a whole piece of buffalo rawhide. Characters are carved out in a rough manner, posed in either a sitting or standing posture. There is very little ornamental carving done, except for perforated holes to delineate jewelry or headdresses. Rama and his younger brother, Laksamana, are usually shown in bold poses befitting warriors. Shown in a horizontal flying posture is **Hanuman,** the white monkey, who is also a fierce warrior. Scenes with multiple characters are sometimes carved into a single piece of rawhide. Since there are no articulated limbs to manipulate, the movement of the puppets is limited to entering, exiting, and swaying to the music. Most often, the puppets are held stationary behind the screen. The Sutradhara compensates for the lack of physical dramatization through dynamic descriptions of the action.

See also Mysore Shadow Puppet Theater

References: Awasthi, Suresh. "Shadow Plays of India and Their Affinities with the Shadow Plays of Southeast Asia." In *Traditional Drama and Music of Southeast Asia,* ed. Mohd. Taib Osman, 112–119. Kuala Lumpur: Dewan Bahasa Dan Pustaka Kementerian Pelajaran Malaysia, 1974.

Ream Ker

Cambodia

Cambodian version of the great Hindu epic tale, the **Ramayana.**

> **References:** Osman, Mohd. Taib, ed. *Traditional Drama and Music of Southeast Asia.* Kuala Lumpur: Dewan Bahasa Dan Pustaka Kementerian Pelajaran Malaysia, 1974.

Reinhardt, Max (1873–1943)

Austria, Germany, United States

Austrian director and actor, who gained international recognition for the high quality of his many eclectic productions and who started the vogue for attributing the success and unity of a production to the director. In 1894 Reinhardt began training as an actor under the direction of Otto Brahm (1856–1912) in his naturalistic school at the Deutsches Theater (German Theater) in Berlin where, though still a young man, Reinhardt most often portrayed old men. He then began to turn away from the naturalistic way of creating theater. He began directing productions at the Kleines Theater (Little Theater), which he founded in 1902. In 1905 he became director of the Deutsches Theater. At this time in his career, he was successfully producing, directing and acting in many of his productions, such as his directing of *The Lower Depths* in 1903, in which he also played the part of Luka.

Reinhardt was extremely eclectic in his choice of plays, from contemporary to classical, and in his manner of production, from intimate chamber theater to lavish works of great spectacle. However, even though Reinhardt experimented with the newest stage effects available, his actors were always primary—his was a true actor's theater. He was extraordinary in his ability to inspire the best performance possible from his actors, and he worked intimately with actors during the rehearsal process. He is known for having started rehearsals with a detailed production script, or *Regiebuch,* but he remained open to input from the actors.

Reinhardt was one of the first to direct the expressionistic plays being written during World War I, 1914–1918, abandoning naturalism for a more abstract portrayal of reality in which he sought to draw out the very marrow of existence.

He experimented with enormous festival productions and with ancient plays such as Sophocles's *Oedipus Rex.* In 1919 he created an actual theater to realize these grandiose ideals, the Grosses Schauspielhaus (The Grand Theater) in Berlin, an arena theater, with state-of-the-art stage mechanisms, that held 5,000 spectators. The failure of this venture led Reinhardt back to Vienna and Salzburg, where he continued producing works until he returned to Berlin and continued directing until 1933. When the Nazis took control, he fled to the **United States**, where he settled in Hollywood, married the actress **Helene Thimig**, continued directing, and established a school for acting.

Reinhardt influenced the direction of German cinema by bringing expressionistic acting to the cinema. Nearly all important actors and directors during the 1920s and 1930s in Germany trained under Reinhardt. Reinhardt directly participated in cinema with a few silent films made in Germany, such as *Sumurun* (1908) and a filming of *A Midsummer Night's Dream* (1935).

> **See also** Expressionism; Naturalism
> **References:** Carter, Huntly. *The Theatre of Max Reinhardt.* New York: B. Blom, 1964; Sayler, Oliver Martin. *Max Reinhardt and His Theatre.* New York: Brentano's, 1924; Styan, J. L. *Max Reinhardt.* New York: Cambridge University Press, 1982.

Reiniger, Lotte (1899–1981)

Germany

German performer and creator of silhouette animation who began as a student of **Max Reinhardt** in Berlin in 1916. She developed an original technique for silhouette animation and created a variety of shadow films, most often photographed by her husband, Carl Koch, whom she married in 1921. *The Adventures of Prince Achmed,* 1926, was her first full-length animation film, and it gained international success. She also created a shadow film *Cinderella* for television. She created actors for her dramas out of two-dimensional cutouts that revealed only the form of their images, thereby drawing out the essence of their characters through their stylized silhouette. She moved to England in 1950.

> **References:** Reiniger, Lotte. *Shadow Theatres and Shadow Films.* New York: Watson-Guptil, 1970.

Revel

See Komos

Roman Comedy

Italy

Roman comedy was a less-refined imitation of the **Greek Comedy** from which it drew its inspiration. The Roman playwrights adapted the works of the Greek playwright **Menander** and his contemporaries by changing the plots and characters and by introducing topical or local humor. The influence of native Italian forms of entertainment, such as the **Phlyax Play** and *Atellana,* lent a rough edge to these Greek adaptations. Roman comedy eliminated the **Greek chorus,** and the plays were not divided into episodes. **Plautus** and **Terence,** who wrote during the third and second centuries B.C., are the two most famous Roman comic playwrights.

The movements of the actors in comedy were quick and lively, especially for those who played the kind of slave character who was often running errands as a go-between in some scheme or love affair. Roman comedies still used Greek costumes (as the Romans saw them) and the Greek setting, since the plays were originally in Greek. The basic garment was a tunic of linen or wool, tied at the waist, worn in different colors to symbolize different character types. For example, the rich wore purple, and prostitutes wore yellow. Props, such as a sword for a soldier, and other details, such as a garland on the head to indicate that someone had been celebrating, also communicated to the audience what type of person a character was. Actors probably wore masks that covered the entire head, even in the earlier periods of Roman comedy. The color of the wigs attached to the masks indicated the age or type of character: white for an old man, black for a young man, and red for slaves.

Official religious and state holidays, known as **Ludi,** were the occasions for the presentations of comedies. The conditions under which comedy was presented often caused the performances to suffer. A frenzied audience would hurry to another performance site if word got out that something more exciting, like a gladiator fight, was occurring simultaneously.

References: Arnott, Peter D. *The Ancient Greek and Roman Theatre.* New York: Random House, 1971;

Beacham, Richard. *The Roman Theatre and Its Audience.* Cambridge, MA: Harvard University Press, 1992; Bieber, Margarete. *The History of the Greek and Roman Theater.* Princeton, NJ: Princeton University Press, 1961; Butler, James. *The Theatre and Drama of Greece and Rome.* San Francisco: Chandler, 1972; Cornford, F. M. *The Origins of Attic Comedy.* London: Edward Arnold, 1914; Gentili, Bruno. *Theatrical Performance in the Ancient World: Hellenistic and Early Roman Theatre.* Amsterdam: Gieben, 1979; Johnston, Mary. *Exits and Entrances in Roman Comedy.* Geneva, NY: W. F. Humphrey, 1933; Taylor, David. *Acting and the Stage.* Boston: George Allen & Unwin, 1978.

Roman Theater, Ancient

Italy

Theater in ancient Rome began with humorous native dramas, elevated itself to highly refined and sophisticated comedies and tragedies based on Greek models, and then declined into decadent shows of spectacle and comic diversion. Throughout this history, Roman actors achieved great skill in gesture and rhetorical delivery. The first phase of Roman history is the republic, 509–27 B.C., characterized by discipline, endurance, and loyalty, all qualities that made Rome a world power. **Roman tragedy,** strongly influenced by Greek models, concerned itself with these virtues and was widely popular until the end of the republic. Also inspired by Greek models was **Roman comedy,** Latin adaptations of Greek scripts that delighted in clever and farcical action. The influence of native Italian comic dramas lent a rougher edge to Roman comedies, however.

The second phase of ancient Rome was the Roman Empire, 27 B.C.–A.D. 476. As a republic, Rome had enjoyed a government with at least some elements of democratic representation. During the imperial period, all power rested with the emperor. The audiences of imperial Rome enjoyed comic spectacle and are generally characterized as being less philosophical than Romans under the republic, who were attempting to emulate ancient Greek ideals. During the empire Greek-style tragedy and comedy gave way to lower-class forms of entertainment that delighted the audience with sensational light plots and visual spectacle. The heir of tragedy became **Pantomime,** which dramatized single scenes from

The ruins of an ancient Greek theater at Taormina in Sicily, 1994 (John Heseltine/Corbis)

older plays with one masked actor who used only movements and gestures. The heir of comedy became **Mime,** which had an unmasked actor dramatizing light plots using only facial expressions and movement. The decay of the Roman Empire from within and the impact of the barbarian tribes from without led to the fall of the Roman Empire. By the sixth century A.D. Christianity had spread and gained power throughout Rome. Theaters were accused of being immoral and closed.

There was a lively variety of theatrical activity in Italy even before the growth of Rome (which was founded in 753 B.C.) and before the influence of foreign ideas and structures overtook Roman theater. Actors from this period were known as **Phlyakes,** which literally means "gossips." The **Phlyax Play** is from the fifth and fourth centuries B.C. and featured popular comic skits. From the same period evolved the **Satura,** comic drama based on scenes of daily life, **Versus Fescennini,** improvised humorous skits native to Rome, and the **Atellana,** a kind of farce full of rustic humor performed by masked actors. From before the fourth century B.C. was **Hilarotragoedia,** literally "hilarious tragedy," a parody of tragedy.

In ancient Rome most actors were slaves with no legal or religious rights. Roman actors did not enjoy the high social status that Greek actors did, who were in holy service to the gods. Roman dramas had largely lost their religious significance by the time of the Empire. Since actors were most often slaves, they could be subjected to rigorous training and strict discipline and were even beaten if they did not perform satisfactorily. Proof of the ill-treatment actors received is found in an epilogue of the play *The Casket* by **Plautus,** which says that any actors who make mistakes during the performance will get a beating.

Acting in Rome reached its peak during the first century B.C., following the peak for the highest development of Roman dramatic literature. Actors who gained star status were freed and could become citizens. Two famous Roman actors from the first century who gained great fame and wealth were **Aesop** and **Roscius.** The art of acting was highly developed during Roman times, and actors were most praised for showmanship and virtuosity. The style of acting resembled Greek classical tragic acting and the acting style in **Greek comedy.** Different kinds of plays demanded different kinds of gestures, and characters of every age and every profession had their own stylized behaviors, which the actors were obliged to reproduce. The director of acting for a production was usually the **Dominus Gregis,** the actor-manager of a theatrical company, who was the producer and usually chief actor who oversaw every aspect of a production.

Theatrical productions in ancient Rome were held at festivals for the gods known as **Ludi,** of which the **Ludi Romani** were the oldest and most important. Temporary wooden buildings were constructed for plays, until, starting in 55 B.C., these were largely replaced by permanent theaters. Romans utilized the arch as a means of support in building and did not have to rely on a hillside for support of a theater as did the Greeks. A long wooden stage represented a street; the fronts of three houses were visible, with doors on each used for entrances and exits. All action took place on the street, and since plays were originally Greek, the setting was usually meant to be Athens or some other Greek city. Roman theaters varied in a variety of ways from the Greek model from which the Romans drew their inspiration. The orchestra in Roman theaters became an exact half-circle, the stage was covered by a roof, and there was sometimes an awning for the audience. Also the stage house used by actors as a dressing room and waiting area, or *skene*, was joined with the auditorium to form a single unit of the same height. Huge amphitheaters, such as the Colosseum in Rome, were also erected during the empire for the presentation of sensational and often bloody entertainment such as gladiator fights or chariot races.

Playwrights of ancient Rome chiefly translated, with slight adaptations, Greek comedies and tragedies. **Livius Andronicus,** 240–204 B.C., wrote the first important works in Latin, translating them all from their Greek originals. Plautus, 254–184 B.C., and **Terence,** approximately 185–160 B.C., were both prominent comic playwrights. The works of **Seneca,** 5 B.C.–A.D. 65, are the only tragedies in Latin remaining from antiquity.

Whereas classical Greek theater was a holy event in honor of the gods, Roman theater catered to the taste of the public. Roman audiences at theatrical events, which included slaves, women, and children, as well as citizens, were more diverse than Greek theater audiences. Since Roman plays were presented at festivals, simultaneously with shows of juggling and acrobats, Roman playwrights had to compete for audiences with popular entertainers. It was not uncommon for an audience to leave midway through a play if rumor of an exciting fight about to commence made its way through the crowd. During the decline of the empire, the Roman audience's thirst for blood and excitement was extreme. Gory death scenes from plays were enacted, and sometimes slaves or condemned criminals were actually killed on stage as part of the dramatic action.

References: Beacham, Richard. *The Roman Theatre and Its Audience.* Cambridge, MA: Harvard University Press, 1992; Bieber, Margarete. *The History of the Greek and Roman Theater.* Princeton, NJ: Princeton University Press, 1961; Chinoy, Helen Krich, and Toby Cole. *Actors on Acting.* New York: Crown, 1970; Dorey, Thomas Alan. *Roman Drama.* New York: Basic, 1965; Gentili, Bruno. *Theatrical Performance in the Ancient World: Hellenistic and Early Roman Theatre.* Amsterdam: Gieben, 1979; Hamilton, Edith. *The Roman Way.* New York: W. W. Norton, 1932; Taylor, David. *Acting and the Stage.* Boston: George Allen & Unwin, 1978.

Roman Tragedy
Italy

Roman tragedy was modeled closely on **Greek tragedy** and flourished most during the time of the Roman Republic, 509–27 B.C., when high virtues, with which tragedy concerns itself, were more apt to be valued. The plays of Ennius, Pacuvius, and Accius from the third century B.C. were performed for more than two hundred years. Audiences knew the plays so well that they could cue actors who forgot their lines. Little is known about Roman tragedy during the republic because only fragments of scripts have survived. During the Roman Empire, 27 B.C.–A.D. 476, audiences craved coarser and more sensational forms of entertainment. **Roman comedy, mime,** and **pantomime** became more popular, until they finally replaced Roman tragedy almost completely. The great Roman tragic playwright of the first century A.D., **Seneca,** who wrote during the empire, only performed private readings of his plays for an elite and sophisticated audience, since the general population had no interest.

Costuming for Roman tragedy was designed to make the actor appear larger than life. The sole of the **cothurnus,** a mid-calf shoe worn by actors, became a high wooden bulky block of wood, and the **onkos,** the hairstyle on the tragic mask, was heightened. Roman tragic masks had wide-open mouths, large eyes, and abundant hair flowing down in twisted locks. Male characters often had beards that were wavy or curled. Earlier Roman tragic masks were often still rather serene, as Greek ones had been, but later these masks became particularly frightening, with hollow terrified eyes and wide-open mouths.

References: Arnott, Peter D. *The Ancient Greek and Roman Theatre.* New York: Random House, 1971; Beacham, Richard. *The Roman Theatre and Its Audience.* Cambridge, MA: Harvard University Press, 1992; Bieber, Margarete. *The History of the Greek and Roman Theater.* Princeton, NJ: Princeton University Press, 1961; Dorey, Thomas Alan. *Roman Drama.* New York: Basic Books, 1965; Gentili, Bruno. *Theatrical Performance in the Ancient World: Hellenistic and Early Roman Theatre.* Amsterdam: Gieben, 1979; Simon, Erika. *Antike Theater (The Ancient Theatre).* Trans. C. E. Vafopoulou. New York: Methuen, 1982; Taylor, David. *Acting and the Stage.* Boston: George Allen & Unwin, 1978.

Romania

Early theater in Romania consisted of religious ceremonies, Christian cycle plays, pagan rituals, and plays composed under the influence of the classical Greek and Roman theater. In fact, there are still ruins of a classical stage in Histria. While Romania was under Turkish influence in the sixteenth through the nineteenth century, the Turkish shadow puppet theater, **Karogoz,** was performed. Many foreign theater troupes visiting Romania during the seventeenth and eighteenth centuries interested the upper classes in theater. Royalty even created theaters in their palaces. The first formal theater performance in the Romanian language was given in Transylvania in 1782, *Achille in Sciro.* Transylvania was politically separated from the rest of Romania until 1920, but served as a cultural link between Romania and Western Europe.

The first Romanian school of drama was begun in 1834 by Ion Eliade, but it was short-lived. In 1840 the first National Theater opened in Jassy, performing, among others, the plays of Romanian playwright Vasile Alecsandri (1821–1890). A state-subsidized conservatory began in 1864. Impressive actors to emerge from the late nineteenth century include Ana Danescu and Petre Liciu. The first private theater in Romania was the Modern Theater, which throve under the direction of Alexandru Davila in the early twentieth century. Many native playwrights emerged during this time as well, such as George Mihail Zamfirescu, Victor Ion Popa (1895–1946), and Mihail Sebastian (1907–1945). Eugène Ionesco left his homeland, Romania, in 1938 for Paris, where he became famous as an absurdist playwright. His compatriot, George Ciprian, who remained in Romania, also wrote absurdist plays.

After World War II (1939–1945), there were almost 10,000 groups of amateur actors in Romania who performed short plays. During the 1940s, 1950s, and 1960s Romanian playwrights published large quantities of short plays. Romanian theaters were nationalized in 1948, when the Communist government was installed. Strict censorship ensured that nothing contrary to the Communist ideal was presented on the stage. One of the leading actresses of the time was **Lucia Sturdza Bulandra,** for whom the Bulandra Theater was named. The Bucharest Jewish State Theater has operated since the end of World War II and has its roots in the efforts of actor Avram Goldfaden, who in 1876 founded Romania's first professional Jewish Theater. Puppet theater was particularly popular for young audiences following World War II. Communist countries, in general, have used puppets as a means of education and propaganda for children. The most famous professional puppet theater is the Tandarica in Bucharest, started in 1950.

An active theater in the later part of the twentieth century is the National Theater's Sala Comedie Hall. Leading Romanian actors of the 1970s include Radu Beligan (also manager of the National Theater for a time), Cella Dima, and Victor Rebengiuc. The Romanian National Opera and the National Theater, most recently under the direction of Andrei Serban, are both still active. A recent Romanian actress of note is Rona Hartner.

References: Alterescu, Simion. *An Abridged History of Romanian Theatre.* Bucharest: Academiei Republicii Socialiste Romania, 1983; Berlogea, Ileana.

"Shakespeare in Romania." *Shakespeare Quarterly* 31 (1980): 405; Ghitulescu, Mircea. "Romania." In *The World Encyclopedia of Contemporary Theatre*, ed. Don Rubin, 682–703. New York: Routledge, 1994; Lamb, Ruth Stanton. *The World of Romanian Theatre.* Claremont, CA: Ocelot, 1976.

Romanticism
England, France, Germany

An artistic movement begun in Europe in the late eighteenth century, emphasizing the imagination and high emotions over intellect and reason. It is often seen as beginning in Germany, with the early work of **Johann Wolfgang von Goethe** and **Friedrich von Schiller.** French Romanticism in theater began in 1830 with Victor Hugo's play *Hernani.* The play was received with hostility by some of the audience because it ignored the rules of French classical drama. The controversy over that first performance is known as the "Battle of *Hernani*"; the play received enough critical acclaim that the Romantic style of writing, in which the poetic imagination is free of the strict rules of classicism, continued to command audiences in the French theater for many decades. The English Romantic playwrights were not nearly as effective as their German and French counterparts; in the late eighteenth and early nineteenth centuries William Wordsworth, Lord Byron, and John Keats did all try their hand at writing Romantic dramas, with little success.

References: Chinoy, Helen Krich, and Toby Cole. *Actors on Acting.* New York: Crown, 1970; Collins, Herbert. *Talma: A Biography of an Actor.* New York: Hill and Wang, 1964.

Roscius (126–62 B.C.)
Italy

Quintus Roscius Gallus, a famous Roman actor. Though actors in general were not held in high esteem by society in ancient Rome, individual actors could rise to great heights of fame and wealth. Specializing, as actors generally did, in certain types of roles, Roscius most often portrayed women and youths. Originally a slave, Roscius gained such distinction as an actor that he was freed from and actually became a citizen. Actors trained by Roscius gained renown just by association, rendering him a much sought-after

teacher for actors who wished to improve their craft.

References: Bieber, Margarete. *The History of the Greek and Roman Theater.* Princeton, NJ: Princeton University Press, 1961; Chinoy, Helen Krich, and Toby Cole. *Actors on Acting.* New York: Crown, 1970.

Royal Shakespeare Company
England

In 1879 the Shakespeare Memorial Theatre was created to perform the plays of **William Shakespeare** at Stratford-upon-Avon, Shakespeare's birthplace. In 1925 the company received royal patronage. It was renamed the Royal Shakespeare Company (RSC) in 1960/61 when Peter Hall (born in 1930) became the artistic director and the company acquired a London base. Hall added modern plays to the repertory and extended the season. In 1963 the Theatre of Cruelty Workshop was a part of RSC under the direction of **Peter Brook.** The RSC continues to maintain an excellent standard of productions. Most English actors

Actress and founding member of the Royal Shakespeare Company Peggy Ashcroft in the 1953 production of Antony and Cleopatra in Stratford-upon-Avon. (Archive Photos)

aspire to this company, and many of the best have been trained there.

References: Beauman, Sally. *The Royal Shakespeare Company: A History of Ten Decades.* New York: Oxford University Press, 1982; Chambers, Colin. *Other Spaces: New Theatre and RSC.* London: Eyre Methuen, 1980.

Royalty and World Leaders as Actors
Africa, France, Italy, Poland, Scandinavia, Spain, United States

Throughout the history of humankind, royalty and world leaders have strongly influenced the performing arts, whether through their condemnation or censorship, their use of them for propaganda, or their love of and direct participation in the performing arts. In some regions of the world, such as among the Asanti people of **Ghana,** it is still customary for their chief to dance before them to reassure them of his worthiness and strength as their leader. In Western European regions, having one's leader perform is much less prevalent, and if the leader does perform, the behavior is apt to be considered as unbecoming a leader. Perhaps this is because the acting profession has long been associated with prostitution and loose morals.

However, the power and euphoria a performer feels under the adoring eyes of the audience is a familiar and desirable feeling for most leaders. In ancient Rome, **Nero** (A.D. 37–68) embodied the self-infatuated tyrant who performed to please himself and expected his people to attend, most likely to avoid his wrath. As emperor of Rome from 54 to 68, he performed in the circus and portrayed through mime the incestuous sister in *Marcaris and Canace.* He once even enacted giving birth on stage. In **France,** King Louis XIV, who ruled from 1643–1715, performed as Le Roi Soleil (The Sun King) in the *Ballet de la Nuit* (Ballet of the Night) at court in 1653. The name stuck, since it seemed to fit him. During his reign he exercised his "divine right" as king quite freely and conducted his kingdom as if he were the very sun around which all his people revolved. In his palace of Versailles, Louis performed various Greek gods and many other characters in countless court ballets, in order to instill in the minds of his nobility his sovereign right to rule and his superiority by birthright to other men.

Not all royal patrons and participants in the arts were focused on only self-glorification and indulgence; some were led rather by a true passion for the arts. Philip IV, leader of Spain from 1621 to 1665, presided over the later years of the Golden Age of Spanish drama, participating as both a dramatist and an actor. In the sixteenth and seventeenth centuries in Scandinavia, the **Trionfi** was a royal procession, in which royalty would masquerade as gods of antiquity or historical heroes. When Queen Christina of Sweden was crowned in 1650, there was lavish entertainment lasting a week. During her reign she performed many roles from a peasant girl to the muse of war. **Gustav III,** king of Sweden from 1771 to 1792, was passionate about theater, involving himself in producing, casting, writing, and even acting in plays, against the judgment of his advisors, who thought it ill-befitting his rank.

Pope John Paul II, who became leader of the Roman Catholic Church in 1978, began acting in a school troupe touring parts of his native Poland. During Nazi occupation in Poland he renewed his involvement in the theater through his association with Miecyslav Kotlarczyk, a famous actor, with whom he started the Rhapsody Theatre. As a form of resistance he, then known as Karol Wojtyla, wrote and performed in inspirational plays. He was admired as an actor and even considered acting as a profession. His one published play is *The Goldsmith's Store.*

Ronald Reagan, born 1911, president of the **United States** from 1980 to 1988, was a somewhat popular grade-B actor in Hollywood films from the 1930s through the 1950s. A stanch conservative, Reagan found his good looks and experience in front of the camera useful in becoming a popular American president. His first wife, from 1940 to 1948, was actress Jane Wyman, and his second wife, from 1952 on, was Nancy Davis, also a former actress. Recently, famous actors and movie stars have been able to create wield through their political endorsements of individuals or causes, since they are revered by their public much like royalty.

References: Bartsch, Shadi. *Actors in the Audience: Theatricality and Doublespeak From Nero to Hadrian.* Cambridge, MA: Harvard University Press, 1994; Jonas, Gerald. *Dancing: The Pleasure, Power, and Art of Movement.* New York: Harry N. Abrams, 1998;

Krol, John Cardinal. *Pope John Paul II*. New York: Catholic Book Publishing, 1979.

Ruan Ling (1910–1935)
China

Chinese film actress, born in Shanghai. She was thought to be the most original actress in Chinese film history. Her style of acting was a delicate balance of naturalism and stylization. She could elevate the trashy scripts she was dramatizing to a level of mature consciousness. She was genuine, in an era of heightened melodramatic exaggeration in acting style. In the movie *New Women* (a silent film with a musical track), she played a novelist who takes her own life. This self-sufficient character who ruled her own destiny was an inspiration to Chinese women of that era. Ruan Ling-yu took her own life in 1935, in the presence of slanderous gossip that was aimed against her.

References: Leyda, Jay. *Dianying: An Account of Films and the Film Audience in China*. Cambridge, MA: MIT Press, 1972.

Rueda, Lope de (1510–1565)
Spain

Actor, dramatist, and one of the first theater managers in Spain. He began performing solo comedy pieces, traveling from one town square to the next. Greatly influenced by visiting Italian **commedia dell'arte** troupes, he formed his own company in 1554. They performed short satirical plays known as pasos, written by Rueda, which featured two or three characters speaking in dialect in a variety of comic situations.

References: McKendrick, Melveena. *Theatre in Spain: 1490–1700*. New York: Cambridge University Press, 1989; Polito, Antonio. *Spanish Theatre: A Survey from the Middle Ages to the Twentieth-Century*. Salt Lake City: Department of Languages, University of Utah, 1967.

Rukada
Sri Lanka

Marionette puppet theater performed only in the southwest of Sri Lanka. Evolved from the Christian folk theater, **Nadagama,** Rukada uses the same stories and songs and is performed on similar occasions. Most puppeteers are former Nadagama performers. The puppets themselves are 3–4 feet high and are manipulated with strings by puppeteers positioned above the puppets' performing area. The stage is divided into three different sections, all with scenic drops behind them and a front curtain to conceal scene changes. Puppeteers are hidden from view on a platform above the stage. Musical accompaniment is performed by an orchestra made up of harmonium, violin, and a *Tabla* drum.

References: Brandon, James. *The Cambridge Guide to Asian Theatre*. New York: Cambridge University Press, 1993; Gunawardana, A. J. *Theatre in Sri Lanka*. Colombo: Department of Cultural Affairs, Sri Lanka, 1976; Tilakasiri, J. *Puppetry in Ceylon*. Colombo: Department of Cultural Affairs, 1961.

Rural Dionysia
Greece

One of four **Dionysia,** religious celebrations dedicated to the Greek god **Dionysus.** Each December in ancient Greece this celebration occurred, featuring a form of revelry known as the **Komos,** performed in honor of Dionysus. It is believed that comedy evolved from this revelry.

References: Arnott, Peter D. *The Ancient Greek and Roman Theatre*. New York: Random House, 1971; Bieber, Margarete. *The History of the Greek and Roman Theater*. Princeton, NJ: Princeton University Press, 1961; Taylor, David. *Acting and the Stage*. Boston: George Allen & Unwin, 1978.

Russia

The first signs of theater in Russia date back to the eleventh century, when *Skomorokhak*, or wandering troupes, toured around the country side providing entertainment for celebrations. They were versatile performers who could juggle, sing, improvise comic stunts, recite folktales, animate puppets, and even perform with animals, most often bears. These nomadic players went in and out of favor with the church and state, banned in the fourteenth century and merely tolerated in the sixteenth and seventeenth centuries. Between the tenth and the sixteenth centuries, puppet shows were popular throughout Russia at fairs or carnivals. **Morality plays** were introduced to Russia by the Greek Orthodox Church and were performed, usually inside the church walls, as early as the sixteenth century.

There is no evidence of czarist theater until 1613, when the Romanov line built a theater for amusement. Since the royal family most likely deemed local street performers to be beneath them, they probably invited foreign groups to perform. Development of theater in Russia took a leap forward in the later half of the seventeenth century when Czar Alexey commissioned a German, Johann Gregory, to write plays and later create a theatrical school. Peter the Great (1672–1725) had ambitions of resurrecting the often persecuted theater for his own political purposes, so in 1702 in the Red Square he built the first public Russian theater and issued a law requiring all, even foreigners, to attend. Peter's daughter, Yelisaveta, invited French and Italian influence into Russia. In 1756 Russia's National Theater in Saint Petersburg was born under Yelisaveta's reign. She completely subsidized the operation and entrusted its lead to Fyodor Volkov, who was also its leading actor. After his death he was succeeded by Ivan Dmitrevsky (1734–1821). In the beginning of their careers, both men played female roles as well as male, but by mid-century actresses gained in stature. The first two important actresses were Agrafena Musina-Pushkina, wife to Dmitrevsky, and Tatiana Troepolskaya (died in 1774). In 1779 the Imperial Theatrical School for the training of actors, singers, and dancers was established. As noblemen sought to emulate the royal family in their taste for theater, many privately owned **serf theater** operations arose.

By the nineteenth century, the status of the actor had been raised, since so many noblemen and aristocrats had begun practicing the trade. Comedies were popular and more prevalent than French tragedies at the beginning of the nineteenth century. Romanticism began to affect the Russian stage during the reign of Nikolay I (1825–1855), who was an avid fan and supporter of the theater. By the 1830s and 1840s melodrama, sobbing plays, and **vaudeville** gained popularity with all but the nobility, who preferred opera and ballet. There were many divergent styles of acting throughout the nineteenth century and many great actors: the skillful and intelligent Vassily Karatyghin (1802–1853); Nadezhda Samoilov

(1818–1899), a naturally gifted comic actress; Mochalov (1880–1848), a wildly emotional actor who infused his audience with passion when he was favored by the muse; and Mikhail Shchepkin (1788–1863), who achieved great realism in creating character. Playwrights such as **Nikolay Gogol** and Alexander Ostrovsky (1823–1886) brought realism to the stage and began the desire for more realistic acting styles. On the more popular front, the puppet theater **Petrushka** was enjoyed by the urban poor at the carnivals.

The **Moscow Art Theater** (MAT), formed in 1898 by **Konstantin Stanislavsky** and **Vladimir Ivanovich Nemirovich-Danchenko,** revolutionized Russian theater with its psychological realism and ensemble playing. Their primary playwright, **Anton Chekhov,** provided the perfect form for their newly developed acting style. His nephew **Mikhail Chekhov** and his nephew's wife, **Olga Knipper,** were both exceptional actors at the MAT. **Symbolism** was influential in Russia in the early 1900s; the great actress of symbolist techniques was **Vera Kommissarzhevskaya.** Working in a similar vein was **Vsevolod Meyerhold,** whose approach was almost diametrically opposed to that of Stanislavsky and the MAT, but who emerged as a great director, always challenging accepted conventions.

The Revolution of 1917 changed the theater in Russia dramatically (see **Soviet Union**). By 1919 all theaters had come under state ownership, with Vladimir Lenin (1870–1924) as the new Communist ruler. Reacting against bourgeois theater, the government sponsored enormous spectacles, rejecting the past in favor of a better future. For example, The Storming of the Winter Palace, 1920, included eight thousand performers. So massive was the event, that directors led the action with megaphones. Russia shifted toward proletariat theater, rejecting bourgeois actors in favor of handing the means of expression to the masses and unleashing their creativity. The Protocult, a group inspired by Communist ideas, created a mainly propagandistic theater, which embraced new avant-garde forms of theater by people like Meyerhold. In the 1920s the avant-garde throve in Russia, including such movements as cubism and constructivism. During this time free theater tickets were distributed to the general public, and theaters throve. Amateur groups sprang up everywhere, in factories, villages, and military units. From 1918 into the 1920s, the common person's interest in theater was outstanding.

During the Stalinist era (1922–1953), under Joseph Stalin (1879–1953), experimentation and innovation were halted, and **socialist realism,** meant to oppose decadent Western culture and values, was introduced as the only allowable style. In 1948 the Soviet government handed control over to the theaters, and thereafter except for children's theaters, theaters were self-ruled entities. Actors in Soviet theater experienced great security. Their training was paid for by the state, and once in a permanent company, they had total job security, with no fear of the troupe being disbanded at the end of a run. The same government that limited and censored their creative expression also provided labor laws to protect their rights.

Throughout the 1960s, 1970s, and 1980s, the Taganka Theater ran counter to the Soviet regime and their policy of socialist realism. Their productions were both politically and aesthetically radical in their society and works were sometimes banned by the government.

After the fall of the Soviet Union in 1991, many theaters divided within themselves under the direction of various artistic leaders. The theater is popular with all sectors of society, as well as accessible, since ticket prices vary greatly in price from very expensive to quite cheap. The strict censorship from Communist times has ceased, making way for much artistic freedom in the theater. Presenting classics in a modern style has popular appeal with younger audiences. In 1998 Konstanin Raikin, a great comedian, presented a modern version of *Hamlet* in Moscow. In Saint Petersburg, the Mariinsky Theater is very popular and presents opera, ballet, and theater. There is also a resurgence of interest in Meyerhold and his system of bio-mechanics. An unpredictable director named Anatolia Vasiliev is popular with elite audiences. His recent work *The Cry of Jeremiah,* 1996, was performed by singers who were not trained actors. Dressed in robes the cast ceremonially performed slow, stately choreography in a simple setting, creating an ancient tone. Vasiliev worked with the performers for over a

year on this modern choral piece. In 1999 Sergei Gazarov directed Harold Pinter's *The Homecoming* at the Dzhigarkhanyan Theater, described as being a show of remarkable power, superbly acted and directed ruthlessly.

References: Gregor, Joseph. *The Russian Theatre: Its Character and History with Especial Reference to the Revolutionary Period.* Philadelphia: J. B. Lippincott, 1929; Hartnoll, Phyllis. *The Oxford Companion to the Theatre.* New York: Oxford University Press, 1967; Shvydkoi, Mikhail. "Nostalgia for Soviet Theatre—Is There Hope for the Future?" *Performing Arts Journal* 15 (January 1993): 111–119; Slonim, Marc. *Russian Theater, From the Empire to the Soviets.* Cleveland: World, 1961; Varneke, Boris. *History of the Russian Theatre, Seventeenth through Nineteenth Century.* New York: Hafner, 1971; Warner, Elizabeth. *The Russian Folk Theatre.* The Hague: Mouton, 1977; Zarhina, Regina. "Russian Theatre of the Silver Age and the World of Art Group." M.A. thesis, University of Colorado, 1996.

Russian Cinema

See Soviet Cinema

Ruzzante (1502–1543)

Italy

Italian actor and playwright, credited with greatly influencing **commedia dell'arte,** the improvised Italian comedy of the sixteenth and seventeenth centuries. Actually named Angelo Beolco, he was better known by the name of the peasant role he created for himself, Ruzzante. After a good education as a youth, Ruzzante was writing farces and acting by age eighteen. He led one of the earliest traveling companies, which performed plays he wrote with himself performing the lead role, often the clever peasant boy Ruzzante. That character is believed to have been an important influence on the **Zanni,** comic characters of the commedia dell'arte. Ruzzante is reported to have been a gifted pantomimist and an excellent improviser of comic scenes.

References: Herrick, Marvin T. *Italian Comedy in the Renaissance.* Urbana: University of Illinois Press, 1960; Rudlin, John. *Commedia Dell'Arte: An Actor's Handbook.* London and New York: Routledge, 1994.

S

Sainete

Spain

A short farce reflecting everyday life in Madrid, very popular during the seventeenth and nineteenth centuries. These short sketches in verse were usually performed between acts or at the end of a long piece of drama. The most famous writer of this type was Ramón de la Cruz (1731–1794). In his racy and lively sketches actors began to portray life more realistically than they had before. In the twentieth century this form was revived.

> **References:** McKendrick, Melveena. *Theatre in Spain: 1490–1700.* New York: Cambridge University Press, 1989; Polito, Antonio. *Spanish Theatre: A Survey from the Middle Ages to the Twentieth-Century.* Salt Lake City: Department of Languages, University of Utah, 1967.

Saing

Myanmar

Burmese term for the Cambodian **Pin Peat,** traditional musical ensemble that accompanies live theater and dance performances.

> **References:** Brandon, James. *Theatre in Southeast Asia.* Cambridge, MA: Harvard University Press, 1974.

Samariyas

Niger

Local youth groups in Niger that organize community projects. Their theatrical performances are their most visible activities. These groups existed before French rule (1900–1960), but had little social use then. *Samariyas* were revitalized during the military regime in 1974 to spur political action and national development. Troupes compete nationally in an annual competition for the National Arts Festival. They perform plays similar to **Wasan Kwaikwayo,** improvised plays in which song and dance may be present.

> **See also** African Ballets
>
> **References:** Beik, Janet. *Hausa Theatre in Niger: A Contemporary Oral Art.* New York: Garland, 1987; Chaibou, Dan-Inna. "La Theatralite en Pays Hawsa." Université Nationale de Côte d'Ivoire, 1978–1979.

Samisen

Japan

Three-stringed instrument indispensable to the accompaniment of **Kabuki,** popular dramatic form of the seventeenth century. The sounding box is covered, usually with cat skin, and a bow is used to play it. It was first used to accompany Kabuki in 1624 and immediately became popular. The samisen provides short melodic passages to accompany the narrator's voice in a performance, and it provides short pieces as interludes between the action. It is still the most prominent instrument in Japan for accompanying dance and drama.

> **References:** Ernst, Earle. *The Kabuki Theatre.* New York: Oxford University Press, 1956. Reprint, Honolulu: University Press of Hawaii, 1974.

Samurai

Japan

A member of the military aristocracy of feudal **Japan.** The warrior class became dominant in Japanese society, especially throughout the sixteenth and seventeenth centuries, since there was military rule with a shogun (military governor) as ruler. Samurai were at the top of the Confucian social class structure. They gave loyalty to a family or feudal chief and gained respect through mighty swordsmanship and martial austerities. The distinguishing mark of the samurai was that he was allowed to wear two swords. **Zen Buddhism** became identified with the ethical code for the samurai, advocating strength and mental alertness through austerity. **Giri** is the code of honor for a samurai, the most important point being supreme allegiance to one's superior, or lord. **Ninjo** is the term for human sympathy in the heart of a samurai. This sympathy and the way it causes a struggle in the heart of a samurai is the subject of many stories used for Japanese dramatic forms such as **Noh,** the classic masked dance-drama, and **Kabuki,** a popular dramatic form of seventeenth-century Japan. If a samurai betrays his duty or is disgraced, then he must commit **sepukku,** which is a way of committing suicide with a knife cut in the stomach and across the throat. The stability that prevailed during Japan's isolationist period (1603–1868) was bad for the samurai, since the merchant class rose in power, and peace left the warriors out of work.

> **References:** Ernst, Earle. *The Kabuki Theatre.* New York: Oxford University Press, 1956. Reprint, Honolulu: University Press of Hawaii, 1974; Immoos, Thomas. *Japanese Theatre.* Trans. Hugh Young. Originally published as *Japanisches Theater.* New York: Rizzoli, 1977; Scott, A. C. *The Theatre in Asia.* New York: Macmillan, 1972.

San Francisco Mime Troupe

United States

Performing group centered in San Francisco, founded by R. G. Davis in 1959; influenced by modern dance and **mime.** By 1962 the group began performing broadly political pieces outdoors, sometimes in city parks, using as their model the Italian **commedia dell'arte,** seventeenth-century improvised comedy around stock characters. Since half the face was masked, the group relied on broad gestures. In the beginning they adapted existing plays, such as **Molière's** *Tartuffe* and *L'Amant Militaire,* taking from them what was useful. They freely rewrote sections to suit their artistic aims. The political unrest surrounding the Vietnam War and the Civil Rights Movement in the 1960s fueled their enthusiasm. They employed puppets and often used them as a device to speak directly to the audience.

In 1970 the troupe shifted from using the *commedia* style to melodrama, as in the production *The Independent Female* in 1970. In the same year Davis left the company, which was rebelling against white male authority, and they became a Marxist theater group and called themselves a collective. Their first collaborative production was *The Dragon Lady's Revenge,* 1970, which was more overtly political than past work. Still politically focused, the troupe has toured extensively through the **United States,** Europe, and Central America.

> **References:** Bigsby, C. W. E. *A Critical Introduction to Twentieth-Century American Drama.* New York: Cambridge University Press, 1985; Davis, R. G. *The San Francisco Mime Troupe: The First Ten Years.* Palo Alto, CA: Ramparts, 1975.

Sandae

Korea

Male masked dance-drama that began in the seventeenth century as court entertainment for Buddhist celebrations. Since there is no longer any court sponsorship, presently traveling troupes go from village to village performing a cruder folk version of what was performed in the courts under better conditions. Bawdy humor and physical pranks abound in performances of the folk type. The all-male cast speaks dialogue and chants in between dancing. Each play begins with offerings for the local spirits and ends with a Buddhist ritual service. The style of dance is highly energetic with dancers whirling and taking huge high steps. Performers also do a limited amount of pantomime.

The costumes are simple yet colorful, with a long cotton shirt, pants, and fabric wrapped around the torso. There are different types of

The San Francisco Mime Troupe entertains a crowd in the Haight-Ashbury area of San Francisco in 1967. (Bettmann/Corbis)

masks in various regions where *Sandae* is performed. In *Yangju Sandae*, a regional style of *Sandae*, a piece of gourd in the shape of a dish, with stylized cuts into the gourd for eyes and eyebrows, is used for a mask. In the Hahoe district beautifully carved wooden masks are used. In *Pongsan Sandae*, another regional style of *Sandae*, paper masks are worn. These paper masks are burned after they are used in performance because it is believed that the spirits remain in the mask and would be dangerous to handle. In all types of Korean masked dance-drama there are about a dozen scenes in a performance. The play is usually aimed at making fun of some respectable person; it presents, for example, the antics of a nobleman, a young woman tempting an old priest to sleep with her, or a monk chasing after a young woman. Musical accompaniment is provided by an oboe, drums, and an instrument like the fiddle. *Sandae* is taught in private dance schools, at the National Classical Music Institute, and in the villages by experienced performers.

See also Buddhism

References: Brandon, James R. *Brandon's Guide to Theatre in Asia.* Honolulu: University Press of Hawaii, 1976; Lee, Duhyun. *Pongsan Mask Dance-Drama: Korean Pongsan Mask Dance: Drama Troupe.* Seoul: Korean Culture and Arts Foundation, 1983.

Sande Masks
Sierra Leone

The Sande (or Bundu Society) of the Mende people of **Sierra Leone** is a female initiation organization, one of the oldest in West Africa. Female initiates, usually prepubescent girls, dance in meticulously carved wooden masks as part of the rituals preparing them for adulthood. These masked performance help to make manifest the divinity represented by the mask, thus making the mysteries surrounding the gods more intelligible to the girls. These wooden masks cover the entire head and sometimes are ornamented with the actual horns of an animal, as the horns are believed to store the power of the dead animal.

References: Cornevin, Robert. *Le Theatre en Afrique Noire et a Madagascar.* Paris: Le Livre Africain, 1970; Richards, J. V. Olufemi. "The Sande Mask." *African Arts* 7, 2 (1974): 48–51.

Sandiwara

Java

Dramatic form from West Java. The name for this form has changed a few times since it was created by students of the Teacher's College and the School for Government Officials in the 1980s. It was first called *Komedie* and was concerned with contemporary topical issues, mostly domestic. Then it was called *Toneel*, the Dutch word for drama. That was rejected when sentiments turned against the Dutch. The current title, *Sandiwara*, simply means "drama." The form in Javanese areas is very much like **Wayang Wong,** a dance-drama styled after shadow puppet theater, without the dancing. **Wayang Kulit** shadow puppet theater plays, historical plays, and original scripts are used for the repertory of *Sandiwara.* There are many performance styles used. In Sundanese areas, in west Java, it is performed as a dance-drama.

> References: Brandon, James. *Theatre in Southeast Asia.* Cambridge, MA: Harvard University Press, 1974; Brandon, James R. *Brandon's Guide to Theatre in Asia.* Honolulu: University Press of Hawaii, 1976; Hood, Mantle. "The Enduring Tradition: Music and Theatre in Java and Bali." In *Indonesia,* ed. Ruth McVey. New Haven, CT: Yale University Press, 1963.

Sangyang

Bali

Trance-dances performed by boys or girls to contact spirits. The style of dancing is similar to the **Legong** dance-drama. Musical accompaniment is performed by a chorus of men and women singing songs. These performances occur at a variety of religious festivals. The purpose is to contact gods for advice and good fortune. **Ketjak,** a monkey dance, derived from *Sangyang.*

> References: Brandon, James R. *Brandon's Guide to Theatre in Asia.* Honolulu: University Press of Hawaii, 1976; Covarrubias, Miguel. *Bali.* New York: Oxford University Press, 1972.

Sanskrit Drama

India

Classical drama that flourished from 100 B.C. to A.D. 1200. True to its name, Sanskrit drama was performed only in Sanskrit, making it an entertainment exclusively for the upper class, since the lower classes did not know Sanskrit. Throughout its reign as a leading form of entertainment, actors enjoyed full subsidies from their patron, the king of the time. It is not known exactly how these dramas were staged, but there are many clues from existing forms of drama that evolved from Sanskrit drama and from scripts that survived. The subject matter of a play determined the time of day it would be performed. A play of virtue was performed before noon, a robust play with music in the afternoon, and a **Rasa,** or erotic play, in the later part of the night. The term "rasa" also refers to an aesthetic experience of spiritual joy, which is the goal of the Indian performing arts. Plays lasted about four to five hours. The **Sutradhara,** the narrator and stage manager, introduced all of the characters before they entered the stage. Major characters spoke prose dialogue, and recited poetic verse. Singers sitting to the side of the main acting area sang verses describing the emotions of the characters on the stage, usually while that character performed stylized dance moves. At other times characters would dance to instrumental music.

There were four types of characters in a Sanskrit drama; sublime epic heroes, impetuous fierce demons, happy lovers and kings, and subdued ministers and merchants. The repertory was drawn from the **Ramayana** and the **Mahabharata,** both Hindu epic tales, as well as other sources. The emotions of love were always the central theme of a drama. Of the thousands of Sanskrit plays likely written by court poets, only about twenty-three are extant. These beautiful dramas elevated their spectators to a refined state of existence. Base acts and death were forbidden on the stage.

> See also Kudiyattam; Vidushaka
>
> References: Brandon, James R. *Brandon's Guide to Theatre in Asia.* Honolulu: University Press of Hawaii, 1976; *Sanskrit Drama.* Dir. Mrinalini Sarabhai. New York: Institute for Advanced Studies in Theater Arts, 1980, videocassette; Scott, A. C. *The Theatre in Asia.* New York: Macmillan, 1972; Varadpande, Manohar Laxman. *History of Indian Theatre.* New Delhi: Abhinav, 1987; Wells, Henry Willis. *The Classical Drama of India: Studies in Its Values for the Literature and Theatre of the World.* New York: Asia Publishing House, 1963.

Sarugaku

Japan

A kind of variety show, with singing, dancing, acrobatics, and juggling from early thirteenth-century Japan. Groups of *Sarugaku* players would become the exclusive performers for large shrines and temples, where they provided entertainment and instruction for the crowds gathered at festivals. During the later period of military rule in the sixteenth and seventeenth centuries, shoguns and other nobility patronized troupes and invited their favorites to give private performances. In this way performers from low social origin came into contact with highly refined culture. *Sarugaku* gradually developed by adding stories with dialogue. **Kanami Kiyotsugu** and his son **Zeami Motokiyo** were famous *Sarugaku* players who developed **Noh,** the classic masked dance-drama.

References: Scott, A. C. *The Theatre in Asia.* New York: Macmillan, 1972.

Satura
Italy

A native Italian drama from ancient Rome featuring humorous scenes from daily life, short dramatic sketches with no continuity of context.

References: Bieber, Margarete. *The History of the Greek and Roman Theater.* Princeton, NJ: Princeton University Press, 1961.

Satyr Play
Greece

A play of comic relief, often with obscene elements, that ended a day's performance in the ancient Athenian festival called the **City Dionysia.** Satyr drama most likely developed from the choral singing, by men dressed as **satyrs** in honor of the Greek god **Dionysus,** of the kind of hymn known as the **dithyramb,** as introduced by Arion in the sixth century B.C. Through a burlesque treatment of mythology, satyr plays ridiculed the gods and heroes of the great Greek stories. Each member of the **Greek chorus** for satyr plays dressed as a satyr, half beast and half man, with a large phallus, performing comical slapstick antics. The structure for a satyr play resembled that employed in **Greek tragedy,** with the action divided into a series of episodes separated by choral odes. Unlike tragic characters, the characters in satyr plays were not fully developed. Playwrights did not seek to use satyr plays to improve society through their humor as they did **Greek comedy.**

In 501 B.C. the satyr play was included in the dramatic contest among the three dramatists chosen to perform their works at the City Dionysia. Thus, each dramatist presented three tragedies and one satyr play in one day. Only one script survives of this genre, *Cyclops* by **Euripides,** about Odysseus confronting the one-eyed, man-eating giant, with help from some local satyrs.

References: Arnott, Peter D. *The Ancient Greek and Roman Theatre.* New York: Random House, 1971; Bieber, Margarete. *The History of the Greek and Roman Theater.* Princeton, NJ: Princeton University Press, 1961; Ley, Graham. *A Short Introduction to the Ancient Greek Theater.* Chicago: University of Chicago Press, 1991; Walton, Michael. *Living Greek Theatre: A Handbook of Classical Performance and Modern Production.* New York: Greenwood, 1987.

Satyrs
Greece

Male worshipers of the Greek god **Dionysus,** who were portrayed in Greek art as half man and half beast. Worshipers of Dionysus, when exalted by wine and ecstatic dancing, believed themselves to be satyrs. Performers of the kind of hymn in honor of Dionysus known as the **dithyramb** began to wear the costume of the satyr in the beginning of the sixth century B.C. It is believed that in Greece the practice of dramatically representing someone other than oneself grew out of this tradition as well as the ecstasy of wine.

See also Satyr Play

References: Bell, Robert E. *Place-Names in Classical Mythology: Greece.* Santa Barbara, CA: ABC-CLIO, 1989; Bieber, Margarete. *The History of the Greek and Roman Theater.* Princeton, NJ: Princeton University Press, 1961; Cornford, F. M. *The Origins of Attic Comedy.* London: Edward Arnold, 1914; Else, G. F. *The Origin and Early Form of Greek Tragedy.* Cambridge, MA: Harvard University Press, 1965; Parada, Carlos. *Genealogical Guide to Greek Mythology.* Jonsered: P. Astroms Forlag, 1993.

Saudi Arabia

Theatrical traditions of storytelling and dance date back to a pre-Islamic Saudi Arabia, such as the *Ardha,* an athletic and dangerous sword dance in which a poet sings verses. Western-style theater was late in coming to Saudi Arabia because of strong Islamic sentiments. The first performance to be presented to a public audience was an adaptation of **Molière**'s *Le Médecin Malgré Lui* (*Doctor by Force,* as it was translated into Arabic; 1974).

Though many conservative Saudi Arabians oppose the theater, plays of moral worth are allowed and the government even created a the Saudi Society for Culture and Art to support the performing arts. Plays by Saudi authors include *Train of Luck* (1976) by al-Hamdan, *The Night of Nalfila* (1975) by Abdul-Rahman al-Mraikhi, and *The Locust* (1987) by Ali-Sad. Islamic religious feelings run so strong in Saudi Arabia that dramatic performances are very infrequent and only amateur.

>   **See also** Arab Theater
>   **References:** Landau, Jacob. *Studies in the Arab Theater and Cinema.* Philadelphia: University of Pennsylvania Press, 1958

Sbek Thom
See Nang Sbek

Scandinavian Cinema
Denmark, Finland, Iceland, Norway, Sweden

The Scandinavian countries—**Sweden, Norway, Denmark, Iceland,** and **Finland**—have a long rich history in cinema. Sweden has clearly been the Scandinavian leader in film production and artistic achievement, with Denmark in second place. Before the advent of sound, Scandinavian silent films were distributed domestically and throughout Europe. The language barrier has limited the popularity of sound films. Scandinavian films are characterized by strong human passions conveyed by use of the distinctive natural imagery of the Swedish landscape. **Ingmar Bergman** is not only the most well-known name associated with film in Scandinavia, but he was also arguably the most influential force in new cinema directions in the last half of the twentieth century.

Some of the first films in Sweden, appearing as early as 1898, were scenes from dramatic plays, comedies, and even news events. Sweden experienced a golden age of silent film from 1914 to–1921 with the directing talent of Charles Magnusson, who discovered and gave work to many talented technicians, performers, and directors, notable among them the former stage actor and Victor Sjostrom (1879–1960). Because of Sweden's neutral stance in World War I, 1914–1918, its film wartime production surpassed its European neighbors, resulting in worldwide attention to Swedish films.

During the 1920s and 1930s competition from Europe and, especially, the **United States** caused Swedish filmmakers to compromise their national identity in film by seeking more commercial appeal. Hollywood drew away some of Sweden's brightest film stars, such as Greta Garbo and Lars Hanson. The Swedish film *Intermezzo* (1936) gained international acclaim, rare for Swedish films of this decade, and made the Hollywood career of its star, Ingrid Bergman. Sweden was again neutral during World War II, 1939–1945, which gave its film industry another boost because of decreased competition. Ingmar Bergman began directing for the cinema in 1946 with the film *Crisis* and went on to become one of the most important creative forces in film worldwide. Film production in Sweden has been low since the early 1960s. The Swedish Film Institute was established in 1963 to award funding to projects with high artistic merit. Films of quality to emerge after this include Bo Widerberg's *Raven's End* (1963), Jan Troell's *The Emigrants* (1971), Bergman's *Fanny and Alexander* (1983), and Lasse Hallstrom's *My Life as a Dog* (1985). Erik Pauser and Johan Soderberg created the musical film *Lucky People Center International* (1998) by slicing and dicing innumerable clips shot over years of world touring. David Flamhole created a Swedish crime drama film, *Lithium* (1999).

Film production in Denmark began as early as 1898 and by 1910 exceeded a hundred films a year from the Nordisk Films company alone. Superstars of this early era included Asta Nielsen (1883–1972), Valdemar Psilander, and Olaf Fonss. By the 1920s competition from other European countries and Hollywood had dealt a crushing blow to the Danish film scene and caused many of its brightest film talents to search for opportunities in other lands. One comic duo, Harold Madsen and Carl Schenstrom, was able to achieve international success with its comedies, which resembled those of Laurel and Hardy.

Carl Dreyer stands out in the 1940s for his masterpiece *Day of Wrath* (1943), along with Lau Lauritzen, who created *The Red Earth* (1945). Throughout the 1950s and most of the 1960s the Danish film industry produced mostly light comedies for domestic audiences and pornographic films for an international market. The Danish government made an effort to fund films of quality in 1965 when it established the Danish Government Film Foundation. Recent talent in Danish film includes Jorgen Foos, Bille August, who directed *Pelle the Conqueror* (1988), Elizabeth Rygard, Susanne Bier, and Birger Larsen.

Film production developed late in Norway, with its first feature film, *The Perils of a Fisherman*, coming out in 1907. There was not much film activity again until the Norsk Film studio opened in 1935. The Norwegian government became more involved in the production of films in the 1950s and by the 1970s had taken control of Norsk Film. Government subsidies contributed to the making of Anja Mikkelsen's *Wives* (1974), and Lasse Glomm's *The Second Shift* (1977). Currently talented film directors in Norway include Oddvar Einarson, Svend Wam, Ola Solum, Nils Gaup, and Martin Asphaug.

Film production in Finland started late and has been sparse; it began with documentaries and short films for entertainment purposes. In 1919 two former stage actors, Erkki Karu and Teuvo Puro, started Suomi Film company, which made feature-length films usually starring Ruth Svellmann. Finish filmmaking peaked in the 1950s with the production of internationally acclaimed films such as *The White Reindeer* (1952), and *The Unknown Soldier* (1955). In 1967 the Finnish director Jorn Donner returned from a long stay in Sweden and made successful films such as *Black on White* (1968), and *Fuck Off!—Images from Finland* (1971). Currently active Finnish filmmakers include Aki and Mika Kaurismaki, Matti Kassila, and Renny Harlin, who now directs action films in Hollywood.

References: Bergman, Ingmar. *Images: My Life in Film.* Trans. Marianne Ruuth. New York: Arcade, 1994; Cowie, Peter. *Scandinavian Cinema: A Survey of the Films and Film-Makers of Denmark, Finland, Iceland, Norway and Sweden.* London: Tantivy, 1992; Katz, Ephraim. *The Film Encyclopedia.* New York: Harper Perennial, 1994.

Scandinavian Theater

Denmark, Finland, Iceland, Norway, Sweden

The countries of Scandinavia, including **Denmark, Norway, Sweden,** and **Iceland,** are considered a linguistic and cultural complex. **Finland** is sometimes included in Scandinavia because of its geological proximity and because Sweden controlled the territory from 1154 to 1809; however political and cultural independence have been a goal of Finland for centuries. The development of Scandinavian theater has been richly influenced by continual interactions with the rest of Europe, mainly through itinerant troupes that brought European traditions to Scandinavia. In the second half of the nineteenth century, Scandinavian theater rose in prominence because of the work of its two most famous playwrights, **Henrik Ibsen** and **August Strindberg** and through the works of individuals such as **Eugenio Barba.** Generous government subsidies have promoted a thriving theater scene.

The earliest extant Scandinavian play was a thirteenth-century Swedish Easter drama. Easter plays and Resurrection plays, popular in Scandinavia from the thirteenth century well into the sixteenth century, remained inside church walls and were performed largely to entertain and teach the congregation. The Reformation, a sixteenth-century movement that caused the separation of various Protestant sects from the Roman Catholic Church, contributed to the suppression of these performances, as well as of Epiphany plays, which enacted the three wise men approaching the manger where the Christ Child lay.

Miracle plays, which are dramatizations of the lives and deeds of Christian saints, were also popular in Scandinavia during the Middle Ages. The Swedish play *Tobie Comedie* (Tobie Comedy) (1550), and the Danish play *Ludus de Sancto Canuto Duce*, a play about a Danish saint murdered in 1131, are examples of this form. The latter was an outdoor spectacle performed on mansions, with over thirty speaking roles. Medieval audiences relished enactments of torture and executions. Dummies were hanged in some performances, so that the utmost torture could be enacted on the sinner. In another Danish miracle play, *Dorothea Komedie*, 1507, actors imitated torturing the male actor playing Saint Dorthea, brought him to the block, and only at the last minute was a dummy substituted so that it could be beheaded.

Beginning in the sixteenth century, humanistic theater was encouraged by the Protestant church during the Reformation to teach good manners and high morals. The plays produced were from Greek and Roman classical literature as well as new Latin and vernacular works by teachers at schools and universities. The schoolmasters were directors and sometimes playwrights, and the students were the actors. Imitating classical plays, humanistic playwrights often included musical and choreographic elements. These performances were free of admission charges, and a feast shared by the student performers and the audience sometimes followed. School dramas even entertained at court. The popularity of these humanist dramas began to fade around 1650.

The seventeenth and eighteenth centuries were rich theatrically, with the courtly **Ballets de Cour** and with traveling itinerant players, both of which traveled to Scandinavia from the rest of Europe, bringing with them the influence of theatrical traditions from **England, France, Italy,** and **Germany.** In the eighteenth century, control of the theater passed from royalty to the private sector, with amateur groups finding ample support from popular audiences.

In the beginning of the nineteenth century, the dominant force in Scandinavian theater was the public theaters, each producing plays in its own language. The nineteenth century was an exceptional era for the emergence of great actors, many of the best coming from the Danish Royal Theater. By the mid-1880s, **naturalism** became the dominant acting style of the Scandinavian theater, mainly inspired by Ibsen and by Strindberg's early work. Strindberg and Ibsen have continued to be performed often in Scandinavia and in the entire Western world, and they remain groundbreaking in their provocative considerations of difficult social issues.

Touring of productions to all regions of each Scandinavian country became widespread during the first half of the twentieth century and still is of high national value in bringing living theater to all citizens of Scandinavian countries. A new generation of playwrights who contributed to the modernist movement in the 1930s and 1940s included Kaj Munk (1898–1944), Kjeld Abell, and Nordahl Grieg (1902–1943). In the 1950s and 1960s the dominant style of acting was psychologically motivated naturalism of the kind needed for the plays of **Eugene O'Neill,** and so skilled were the actors in this style that, shortly before

his death, O'Neill sent a message of thanks to the Scandinavian theater for the excellent productions of his plays over the years. At the end of the 1960s theater throughout Scandinavia began to be used as a political tool opposing the oppression of the poor. Theater groups visited schools and factories to educate those who they believed were being oppressed. These theater groups became resident in towns that would subsidize their productions. They created their works in a democratic, nonauthoritarian, collective way, thus modeling the society they envisioned.

From the 1970s to the present the theater in all Scandinavian countries has been generously supported by government subsidy. Many outstanding directors continue the development of Scandinavian theater; **Ingmar Bergman,** for example, did remarkable experimental productions of the classics well into the 1980s. Other notable directors include Wilhelm Carlsson, Peter Langdal, and Lars Knutzon.

See also Latin Humanistic Comedy; Romanticism
References: Brunius, Niklas, Goran O. Eriksson and Rolf Rembe. *Swedish Theatre.* Trans. Keith Bradfield. Stockholm: Swedish Institute, 1967; Hillestrom, Gustaf. *Theatre and Ballet in Sweden.* Trans. Anne Bibby. Stockholm: Swedish Institute, 1953; Kvam, Kela. "Betty Nansen: A Unique Figure in Danish Theatre." In *Nordic Theatre Studies: Yearbook for Theatre Research in Scandinavia,* ed. Kela Kvam, 69–78. Denmark: Institute for Theatre Research, University of Copenhagen, 1988; Marker, Frederick. *A History of Scandinavian Theatre.* Cambridge: Cambridge University Press, 1996; Sprinchorn, Evert. *The Genius of the Scandinavian Theater.* New York: New American Library, 1964; Torch, Chris. "A Letter from Scandinavia about Theatre, Community, and the Future." *Drama Review* 27, 4 (Winter 1983): 87–91; Torppedersen, B. "Theater in Denmark." *Revue du Cinema* 353 (1980).

Schechner, Richard (1934–)
United States

Director, theater innovator, and, from 1962 on, editor of the prestigious *Tulane Drama Review,* which, when he moved to New York, became *The Drama Review.* Committed to expanding his audience in the American South to include deprived black communities, Schechner was one of the founders of the **Free Southern Theater** in New Orleans. After studying with **Jerzy Grotowski,** in 1967

Schechner formed the Performance Group in a converted garage on Wooster Street in New York to explore theatrical possibilities. In 1968 they performed Dionysus in 69, a ritual response to The Bacchae by **Euripides.** In it a line of nude actors enacted a rebirth by passing a man and woman through a birth canal created by their own spread legs. Their next work was Commune, which was more a demonstration of community than a story and relied heavily on audience participation. They also did Sam Shepard's The Tooth of Crime, 1972, Brecht's Mother Courage and Her Children, 1974, Marilyn Project, 1975, Oedipus, 1977, Cops, 1978, and The Balcony, 1979. Around 1975 the group began to change; some members, such as Spalding Gray, left to pursue their own work. In 1980 Schechner ceased work with The Group at the Garage. They became known as the Wooster Group and continued to creating experimental works, with Elizabeth LeCompte leading.

Schechner continues to be an important theoretical and creative force in American theater. He is an active theater scholar, writing on ritual and performance, as well as doing critical reviews of current work. As a theater artist, Schechner recently directed the East Coast Artists in a 1999 production of Hamlet in New York.

References: Bigsby, C. W. E. A Critical Introduction to Twentieth-Century American Drama. New York: Cambridge University Press, 1985; Dawson, Barbara. "A Letter to Richard Schechner." Drama Review 37, 2 (1993): 15; Schechner, Richard. Performance Theory. New York: Routledge, 1988; Schechner, Richard. "ARTNOW." Drama Review 40, 3 (Fall 1996): 7–8.

Schiller, Friedrich von (1759–1805)

Germany

German playwright and poet who created dramas for the theater that were charged with emotional intensity, lyrical beauty, and strong dramatic drive. Schiller wrote his first play, The Robbers, in 1781, at the age of twenty-two. His poetic language, well-crafted form, and elevated ideals made his plays extremely popular and often produced. In 1798 Schiller joined **Goethe** at his theater at Weimar. Schiller was the more flamboyant of the two, yet they worked well together, creating a style of acting based on their shared yearnings for simplicity, dignity and harmony in the theater. It was here Schiller wrote one of his most famous plays, Maria Stuart, 1799. After teaching at the University at Jena, he spent the last few years of his life at Weimar.

See also Romanticism

References: Goethe, Johann Wolfgang von. Correspondence between Goethe and Schiller. Trans. Liselotte Dieckmann. New York: P. Lang, 1994; Miller, Ronald. The Drama of Schiller. Harrogate, UK: J. Oade, 1966; Ueding, Gert. Friedrich Schiller. Munchen: C. H. Beck, 1990.

Scotland

An ancient kingdom now united with **England, Wales,** and Northern Ireland in the United Kingdom. **Morality play**s and festival pageants were popular there in the fourteenth, fifteenth and sixteenth centuries; an example is Ane Pleasant Satyre of the Thrie Estaitis by Sir David Lyndsay, from 1552. An early example of indigenous drama in Scotland is the tragedy Douglas, 1756, by John Home. Scotland also has a rich theater tradition in music halls.

A bright spot in Scottish theater history is the Glasgow Repertory Theatre, which contributed greatly to the repertory movement in Scotland. It operated from 1909 until 1914, when the outbreak of World War I forced it to close. Founder Alfred Wareing assembled an excellent group of actors to produce a wide range of works. Resources from this group were later developed into the Scottish National Players, 1921–1948, made up of predominantly amateur actors. Many alternative, left-wing theater groups with amateur actors formed between the two World Wars, such as the Worker's Theatre Group (1937–1940). In 1943 a playwright named James Bridie (1888–1951) started the Citizen's Theatre in Glasgow and went on to start the College of Drama in the Royal Scottish Academy of Music in 1950.

The Edinburgh Festival was first started in 1947 by Rudolph Bing and is now a major international festival. It takes place in late August and early September for three weeks and attracts internationally famous theater companies, such as the **Comédie Française** from France. In the 1950s the Edinburgh Fringe, featuring experimental performances, was introduced to the festival, which attracted many more experimental professional and amateur groups.

The Citizens', or Princess's Theater, which was founded in 1943 in Glasgow by the Scottish playwright James Bridie to prevent the city from depending on London for good drama. (Archive Photos)

The 1960s witnessed the continuation of alternative theater, with companies such as the Close Theatre (1965–1973) in Glasgow and the Traverse Theatre in Edinburgh, begun in 1963 by Jim Haynes to promote new Scottish plays. This tradition continues, as the play *The Juju Girl* by Aileen Ritchie was presented at the Traverse as part of the Edinburgh Fringe Festival in 1999.

References: Boswell, James. *A View of the Edinburgh Theatre during the Summer Season.* Los Angeles: William Andrew Clark Memorial Library, University of California, 1976; Lawson, Robb. *The Story of the Scots Stage.* New York: E. P. Dutton, 1917; Stevenson, Randall, and Gavin Wallace. *Scottish Theatre since the Seventies.* Edinburgh: Edinburgh University Press, 1996.

Semar
Bali, Java

God-clown character in **Wayang Kulit,** traditional shadow puppet theater. Semar is a god who came down from heaven to check out the state of affairs on the earth. He is disguised in a bulbous body that can elicit laughter on sight. He has a troupe of followers, which some claim are his brothers. The rawhide puppet has articulated arms. The face is white to signify a clown character, and the body is gold with a checkered sarong painted on. He interprets the dialogue of the high gods, who speak in ancient Jawa, which the village people do not understand.

See also *Pak Dogol*

References: Keeler, Ward. *Javanese Shadow Plays, Javanese Selves.* Princeton, NJ: Princeton University Press, 1987; Mulyono, Sri Ir. *Human Character in the Wayang.* Singapore: Gunung Agung, 1981; Ulbricht, H. *Wayang Purwa: Shadows of the Past.* Kuala Lumpur, Malaysia: Oxford University Press, 1970.

Sembene, Ousmane (1923–)
Senegal

The leading filmmaker of sub-Saharan Africa, born in Senegal. In 1948 he sailed as a stowaway to France, where he worked as a manual laborer and wrote. His first novel, *Le Docker Noir* (The Black Docker), was published in 1956. Upon returning to Senegal he changed from writing to filmmaking as a means of reaching the people of his home country. After studying at the Moscow Film School in 1962 he returned home to begin making shorts. His first feature film *La Noire de . . .* (Black Girl of . . .), 1966, brought him instant international recognition. One of his most complex films, *Xala* (Impotence), 1974, is a satire about the Senegalese upper crust and its long-standing imitation of European decorum. In the film the male actors all wear European clothing and speak French, while the female characters are all clothed in colorful native garb and speak the native language of Wuluf, showing how the women function as the keepers of Senegal's true identity.

> **References:** Katz, Ephraim. *The Film Encyclopedia.* New York: Harper Perennial, 1994; Mast, Gerald. *A Short History of the Movies.* 4th ed. New York: Macmillan, 1986.

Sendratari
Bali, Java

Dance-drama in a condensed format made for tourists. This form was developed in the 1960s and 1970s in response to the growing tourist interest. It is based on Javanese dance-drama styles. It is quite similar to **Wayang Wong,** the dance-drama based on shadow puppet theater (See **Wayang Kulit**), but with no narration or dialogue. All dramatic content is pantomimed. The performances use short, easy-to-follow episodes from the **Ramayana,** a Hindu epic tale. The costumes and music are both the same as other traditional Javanese dance forms such as **Ketoprak** and **Wayang Topeng.**

> **References:** Brandon, James R. *Brandon's Guide to Theatre in Asia.* Honolulu: University Press of Hawaii, 1976.

Seneca (5 B.C.–A.D. 65)
Italy

Roman philosopher and tragic playwright, widely read and greatly admired during his lifetime and long afterward for his rhetoric and philosophy. The nine plays by Seneca that survive are all adapted from works of **Greek tragedy** and are the only remaining Latin tragedies. His tragedies were not written for performance in Roman theaters because most aristocrats, including Seneca, despised the coarse theatrical practices of the day. Instead, his plays were read aloud to exclusive audiences in private readings. **Nero,** who was named emperor in A.D. 54, was Seneca's pupil.

Seneca had a profound influence on the dramatic literature around the time of the Renaissance. Renaissance writers adopted many of the characteristics of Seneca's work. One characteristic is that his plays were in five episodes divided by choral interludes. Other characteristics include elaborate speeches, an interest in morality, scenes of violence and horror, preoccupation with magic and death, and characters with a single obsessive passion.

Plays by Seneca include two plays about Hercules, *Trojan Women, Phoenician Women, Medea, Phaedra, Oedipus, Agamemnon,* and *Thyestes.*

> **References:** Bieber, Margarete. *The History of the Greek and Roman Theater.* Princeton, NJ: Princeton University Press, 1961; Dorey, Thomas Alan. *Roman Drama.* New York: Basic Books, 1965; Gentili, Bruno. *Theatrical Performance in the Ancient World: Hellenistic and Early Roman Theatre.* Amsterdam: Gieben, 1979; Taylor, David. *Acting and the Stage.* Boston: George Allen & Unwin, 1978.

Sepukku
Japan

Honorable method of committing suicide in Japan, with a knife thrust into the stomach, pulled across the stomach, and then across the throat.

See also Samurai

Serf Theater
Poland, Russia

By the second half of the eighteenth century in **Russia** and **Poland,** many noblemen who were impressed by court entertainments ventured to create their own private theaters on their estates. They forced their serfs to act, dance, and sing for their guests. As the opulence of this fad grew, some noblemen would fund performances that included hundreds of actors, and many built magnificent theaters in their homes. Many of the female serfs who were actresses and dancers were concubines for their masters. Serf actors of both sexes were trained with strict and brutal discipline. If any performance failed to please their master, they were sometimes beaten in front of the guests. Serf actors could be bought, sold, and traded.

One exception to this cruel treatment was the Count Peter Sheremetyev, who treated his serf actors very well. His company of over two hundred actors achieved a level of artistic excellence such that it was admired by many of the aristocracy and foreign dignitaries. In fact, Sheremetyev fell in love with his lead serf actress, Parasha Zhemchugova, and was granted special permission by the czar to marry her.

By the nineteenth century many of Russia's most talented actors were of this dismal origin; all the same, once freed, they owed their training to having once been serf actors.

References: Slonim, Marc. *Russian Theater, From the Empire to the Soviets.* Cleveland: World, 1961.

Serunai
Malaysia
Melodic reed instrument in a Malaysian **gamelan,** a traditional orchestra.

See also *Wayang Siam*
References: Matusky, Patricia. "Music in the Malay Shadow Puppet Theater (Volumes I and II)." Ph.D. diss. Ann Arbor, MI: Proquest, 1980.

Shadow Puppets
Cambodia, China, Egypt, Germany, India, Indonesia, Malaysia, Thailand, Turkey, United States
Shadow puppets are most often flat figures, made usually of rawhide, wood, or paper, created to represent a character; they are used in shadow play. Shadow play occurs in a performance setting in which the light source originates from behind a screen; between the light source and the screen there are moving objects, people, or puppets that block the light and create moving shadows. One of the most highly refined forms of shadow puppet theater is the Javanese **Wayang Kulit.** In it the intricately carved rawhide shadow figures cast moving shadow images of the heroes and demons from the great Hindu epic tales. Other forms of the Wayang Kulit developed in **Java,** such as the **Wayang Pantja Sila,**

Wayang Suluh, Wayang Tengul, Wayang Djawa, Wayang Madya, Wayang Gedog, and **Wayang Klitik**; the latter uses flat wooden puppets instead of rawhide. Closely related to the Javanese style is the Malaysian **Wayang Siam** and **Wayang Melayu** and the Thai **Nang Talung.** Other Thai forms of shadow play include **Nang Yai** and **Nang Sbek,** which were strongly influenced by the Cambodian **Nang Sbek Touch.**

In **China** there is an ancient form of human shadow play, **Qiao-Ying Xi,** and a form of shadow puppet theater, **Pi-ying Xi. India** hosts a rich variety of shadow puppet traditions, including **Tholu Pava Koothu, Tholu Bommalata, Mysore Shadow Puppet Theater,** and the ancient **Ravanachhaya.** Shadow puppet theater in the Middle East appears in the **Arabic Shadow Puppet Theater** of **Egypt** and the Turkish **Karagoz.**

Shadow puppet theater in the West is often thought of as a precursor of the cinema. Silhouette shadow shows of intricately cut-out figures were very popular in Germany and Italy in the latter part of the eighteenth century. This style also appeared in the **United States** in the **vaudeville** circuits, but was surpassed and replaced by cinema. **Lotte Reiniger** is a twentieth-century German shadow artist who makes films of shadow puppet plays and performs live. Other contemporary performance artists in the United States, such as Meredith Monk, Ping Chong, and **Robert Wilson**, have utilized shadow play in their performances.

See also Cambodia; Malaysia; Thailand
References: Ransome, Grace Greenleaf. *Puppets and Shadows: A Selective Bibliography to 1930.* Lewiston, NY: Edwin Mellen, 1997; Tillis, Steve. *Towards an Aesthetics of the Puppet: Puppetry as a Theatrical Art.* New York: Greenwood, 1992.

Shakespeare, William (1564–1616)
England
English playwright, actor, and poet, generally regarded as the finest playwright of the Western world. Shakespeare is renowned for infusing incredible depth of meaning in the most refreshing twists of language. Shakespeare was born in Stratford-on-Avon and in 1582 married Ann Hathaway, with whom he had three children. In 1592, he moved to London and by 1594 worked for the

A scene from Shakespeare's Antony and Cleopatra *at London's Drury Lane Theater in 1873 (Bettmann/Corbis)*

Chamberlain's Men, an Elizabethan theater company for which Shakespeare acted and wrote plays, and of which he became a shareholder. Here he is on the cast list for many productions of plays by other playwrights and of his own; he is on the cast list, for example, as the Ghost in *Hamlet*. By 1599 Shakespeare owned a tenth share of the Globe Theatre, and in 1610, when the Chamberlain's Men became the King's Men, he sold his share and retired comfortably in Stratford.

Although there is some controversy over the exact number of extant plays that were actually written by Shakespeare, his canon is generally accepted as consisting of the thirty-six plays from the First Folio, the great collection published by two of his actors after his death in 1623. He was a master of nearly every genre, such as comedy, with *A Midsummer Night's Dream*, to take just one example; the history play, with *Julius Caesar*; tragedy, with *King Lear*, *Macbeth*, *Hamlet*, and *Othello*; and fantasy, with above all *The Tempest*. Shakespeare created characters of such complexity and emotional depth that actors still measure their worth and accomplishments by their ability to interpret them, be it Hamlet, Lady Macbeth, King Lear, or Othello.

References: Baker, Henry Barton. *English Actors from Shakespeare to Macready*. New York: H. Holt, 1879; Chinoy, Helen Krich, and Toby Cole. *Actors on Acting*. New York: Crown, 1970; Edgecombe, David. *Theatrical Training during the Age of Shakespeare*. Lewiston, NY: Edwin Mellen, 1995; Thomson, Peter. *Shakespeare's Professional Career*. New York: Cambridge University Press, 1992.

Shantala
India

One of the earliest known dancers of **Bharata Natyam,** classical female solo temple dances, who lived in the twelfth century in the south of India. She was a queen, wife of King Vishnuvardhana of Karnataka. She danced in the Belur temple, erected A.D. 1117 after her husband's conversion to **Hinduism.**

References: Varadpande, Manohar Laxman. *Krishna Theatre in India*. New Delhi: Abhinav, 1982.

Shaw, George Bernard (1856–1950)
England, Ireland

English playwright and critic, born in Dublin. As a young man, Shaw saw **Henry Irving** perform in Dublin and was deeply impressed with his performance. Raised in poverty in Dublin, Shaw moved to London in 1876 to work as a writer. He was exposed to Marxist thought in 1882, which led to his development as a socialist and an enthusiast of the Fabian Society, an association of socialists founded in 1883 by a small group of middle-class intellectuals. He worked as a theater critic, and Shaw's critiques of many of the great actors of his time, such as **Sarah Bernhardt** and Irving, remain as the liveliest testimonies to their craft. Shaw championed the superior quality of **Henrik Ibsen**'s plays and the realism he achieved. Both Shaw's plays and his personal conversation were witty and provocative. His *Mrs. Warren's Profession*, 1898, was banned until 1925. His most notable plays include *Man and Superman*, 1904, *Major Barbara*, 1905, *Pygmalion*, 1914 (which was adapted into the musical *My Fair Lady* in 1955), and *Saint Joan*, 1924, which was first performed by Sybil Thorndike in the title role. Shaw's plays require a style of acting that is not just realistic but also able to transmit the ideas central to his plays. In 1925 Shaw received the Nobel Prize for literature.

References: Bentley, Eric. *Bernard Shaw*. Norfolk, CT: New Directions, 1957; Chinoy, Helen Krich, and Toby Cole. *Actors on Acting*. New York: Crown, 1970; Fromm, Harold. *Bernard Shaw and the Theatre in the Nineties: A Study of Shaw's Dramatic Criticism*. Lawrence: University of Kansas, 1967.

Sheng
China

Male character in **Peking Opera.** There are four categories of character roles in Peking Opera; Sheng, male; **Dan,** female; **Ching,** painted face; and **Chou,** comic roles. There are role divisions within Sheng, the male character type. The *Lao-sheng* is the old man with a white beard. The *Hsii-sheng* is the middle-aged male with the black beard. The *Hsias-sheng* is the young male with no beard. He is the romantic lover and usually carries a fan. The *Wu-sheng* is a warrior male who performs amazing acrobatic feats. The *Hung-sheng* is the red-faced male.

See also *Hualian*
References: Scott, A. C. *The Theatre in Asia*. New York: Macmillan, 1972.

Shepard, Sam (1943–)
United States

Playwright, movie actor, and musician, who varies so greatly in theme and style that he defies categorization. Shepard stands as one of the greatest writers of the late twentieth and early twenty-first centuries. His first plays, *Cowboys* and *The Rock Garden*, were produced at Theater Genesis in 1964. Both prolific and eclectic, he is said to have written the play *Chicago* in one day. *The Tooth of Crime*, 1972, is a rock drama. *Curse of the Starving Class*, 1976, more realistic than some of his other work, is in a rural setting and is about loss of hope and relationships. He won a Pulitzer Prize for *Buried Child* in 1979. Shepard and Joseph Chaikin, founder of the **Open Theater,** performed *Shepard's Tongues* at the Magic Theater in San Francisco in 1978.

He has performed in many of his own screen plays, including *Fool for Love*, 1985, and *Paris, Texas*, 1985, directed by Wim Wender.

References: Marranca, Bonnie, ed. *American Dreams: The Imagination of Sam Shepard*. New York: Performing Arts Journal Publications, 1981; Patraka, Vivian. *Sam Shepard*. Boise, ID: Boise State University, 1985; Wade, Leslie. *Sam Shepard and the American Theatre*. Westport, CT: Greenwood, 1997.

Sherpas
Nepal

Inhabiting the northeast section of Nepal along the south foothills of the Himalayan mountains, the Mahayana Buddhist Sherpas are one of the few existing remnants of Tibetan culture. Though they have been separate from Tibet for more than 300 years, the culture, religion, and language are very much the same. Little was known about these people until 1950, when mountaineering expeditions to the Himalayan peaks reported their rich culture. International awareness of these people and the plight of the Tibetan people came when Chinese armies invaded the country of Tibet in 1950 to claim it as Chinese territory. The Sherpas are devoutly Buddhist and mainly work the land and raise livestock. The **Mani-rimdu** is an outdoor three-day dance-drama performed by Buddhist monks twice a year for the Sherpa people.

References: Brandon, James. *The Cambridge Guide to Asian Theatre*. New York: Cambridge University Press, 1993; Fantin, M. *Mani Rimdu, Nepal, the Buddhist Dance Drama of Tengpoche*. Singapore: Toppan; New Delhi: distributed by the English Book Store, 1976; Jerstad, Luther G. *Mani-Rimdu: Sherpa Dance-Drama*. Seattle: University of Washington Press, 1969; Manandhar, J. K. *Nepal, Legend and Drama*. Banepa Wankhya: Sukha Veti Manandhar, 1982.

Shimpa
Japan

Literally, "New School"; melodramatic form of modern theater. This new form of performance was heavily influenced by **Kabuki** theatrical conventions, so much so that it is actually stylistically halfway between Kabuki and Western-style drama. Sentimental and not intellectually taxing, Shimpa is simply for the sake of pure entertainment and has no agenda to promote. This form dramatizes social customs of a certain period. Unfulfilled love and dramatic tragic endings are characteristic of Shimpa. Up to the 1960s the two most famous Shimpa performers were Hanayagi Shotaro, a man who was famous for playing female roles and young male lover roles, and Mizutani Yaeko, a much loved actress who portrayed the beautiful young girl role often. They often performed together as tragic lovers with no hope for a union in this world. Shimpa still has a following and great box office appeal, more so than **Shingeki,** pure modern drama.

References: Brandon, James R. *Brandon's Guide to Theatre in Asia*. Honolulu: University Press of Hawaii, 1976; Scott, A. C. *The Theatre in Asia*. New York: Macmillan, 1972.

Shingeki
Japan

Modern Japanese drama. Shingeki grew out of **Shimpa,** melodramatic modern Japanese drama. Shingeki became associated with left-wing proletarian causes. During the 1930s and 1940s modern drama was heavily censored and prohibited in some instances. During the American occupation, traditional Japanese theater was feared for its feudalistic spirit. However, when constraints of the occupation were over, there was an renewed interest in traditional forms of theater, mainly **Kabuki,** which greatly overshadowed modern drama. Throughout the 1950s Shingeki troupes performed translations of Western dramas. The first overwhelmingly popular Japanese play was Twilight Crane by Junji Kinoshita. Despite a rocky history, Shingeki drama continues to flourish and branch out into new creative modes of expression.

See also Shingkuk

References: Brandon, James R. *Brandon's Guide to Theatre in Asia*. Honolulu: University Press of Hawaii, 1976; Scott, A. C. *The Theatre in Asia*. New York: Macmillan, 1972.

Shingkuk
Korea

Modern Korean drama that started in 1908 when Korean students studying in Tokyo performed the first Korean translation of a Western play. In the beginning Shingkuk was melodramatic, like Japanese **Shimpa,** modern Japanese melodrama. By the 1920s the audience for modern drama grew, and more serious plays were presented. There was enough national interest that a National Theatre was built in 1950 in Seoul as a partially subsidized home for modern dance, drama, and music, with resident companies. There are also many private professional Shingkuk troupes.

References: Brandon, James R. *Brandon's Guide to Theatre in Asia*. Honolulu: University Press of Hawaii, 1976.

Shinto
Japan

Medieval indigenous cult of the sun goddess, and an institutional adaptation of the archaic religion of Japan. Shinto literally means "way of the gods" and is based on a form of nature worship. It is characterized by a simple reverence in the presence of natural phenomena, which were deified. In practice, Shinto and **Buddhism** maintain a close interrelationship since the tenth century A.D. The same priests often officiated at both altars, and the Shinto deities were considered to be in the service of the **Buddha.**

Shinto has deep nationalistic overtones, since it served to unite the many cults and shrines throughout Japan during medieval times. Many early traditional Japanese dance-dramas were performed at Shinto festivals, in or around Shinto shrines.

References: Aherne, Consuelo Maria, Paul Kevin Meagher, and Thomas C. O'Brien, eds. *Encyclopedic Dictionary of Religion.* 3 vols. Washington, DC: Corpus Publishers, 1979; Eliade, Mircea, ed. *The Encyclopedia of Religion.* 16 vols. New York: Macmillan, 1987.

Shite
Japan
Lead actor, protagonist of **Noh,** masked dance-drama from medieval Japan. The *Shite* always wears a mask. The *Shite* character may be either male or female, but since there are only male performers in Noh, a male portrays both sexes. The *Shite* always starts and ends a scene at the stage pillar designated to the *Shite,* the first pillar off the bridgeway, in back to the audience's left.

See also *Waki*

References: Scott, A. C. *The Theatre in Asia.* New York: Macmillan, 1972.

Shiva
India
One of the three major Hindu gods; known as the destroyer of the universe. Those who follow the cult of Shiva, known as Saivism, Sivaism, or Saiva Siddhanta, see him as the destructive power from which all creation and regeneration originates. He is characteristically portrayed as the **Nataraja,** the Lord of the Dance, and he is symbolized by the lingam, the sacred phallus.

See also Vishnu

References: Aherne, Consuelo Maria, Paul Kevin Meagher, and Thomas C. O'Brien, eds. *Encyclopedic Dictionary of Religion.* 3 vols. Washington, DC: Corpus Publishers, 1979; Eliade, Mircea, ed., *The Encyclopedia of Religion.* 16 vols. New York: Macmillan, 1987.

Shomin-geki
Japan
Middle-class comedy; type of Japanese film, a category of **Gendai-geki,** Japanese films based on modern life.

References: Mast, Gerald. *A Short History of the Movies.* 4th ed. New York: Macmillan, 1986.

Shootingway
United States
Ceremony of the Navajo (indigenous people of present-day New Mexico and Arizona, ranging also into Colorado and Utah) of the epic drama *Shootingway,* which lasts nine nights and eight days and includes nearly ninety hours of music, prayer, sand paintings, dramatic stagings, movement, and costumes. It is done to heal individuals who have suffered trauma, to recapitulate the first time it was done for humans by the Holy People, and as a symbolic enactment of the myth. It is centered around a Holy Young Man who seeks knowledge about sacred things and his encounters with Snake People, Thunder People, Buffalo People, the Sun, the Moon, and other deities.

Dramatic portions of the ceremony are largely symbolic and have a practical result as their end. For example, in the Shock rite, the protagonist is seated in the middle of an elaborate snake sand-painting that is on the ground. From the north and the south, two actors, one costumed and made up as a black bear and one as Holy Young Man, rush toward the protagonist and stand threateningly over him, screaming to drown out the singing. This shock is meant to dispel fear and instill confidence. Dramatic enactment is not a primary part of the *Shootingway* ceremony, which is mostly song and prayer, but it does serve to emphasize key moments and to enhance the focus on the forces at play.

References: McAllester, David. "Shootingway, an Epic Drama of the Navajos." In *Southwestern Indian Ritual Drama,* ed. Charlotte J. Frisbie, 199–237. Albuquerque: University of New Mexico Press, 1980.

Sierra Leone
The capital city, Freetown, founded in 1787 by the British Sierra Leone Company, began as a haven for freed slaves. This settlement became a melting pot for former African slaves from all over the world, as well as for British officers and the indigenous people. This combination led to the formation of the Krio language, a largely urban language that is the lingua franca in Sierra Leone. In the 1960s a popular urban theater tradi-

tion, **Krio theater,** developed out of an effort to promote the Krio language.

The traditional roots of drama in Sierra Leone reach back into many of the indigenous people's cultures, such as the Mende people with their **Sande Masks.** Initiates of the Mende female initiation organization performed masked dances as part of their initiation into adulthood as women.

References: Abraham, Arthur. *Cultural Policy in Sierra Leone.* Paris: UNESCO, 1978; Akar, John. "The Arts in Sierra Leone." *Africa Forum* (Fall 1965): 87–91; Banham, Martin. *African Theatre Today.* London: Pitman, 1976.

Singapore

Predominantly a Chinese city, Singapore has a cultural scene that gains much vitality from the influence of its minority populations, the Malays, Indians, and Westerners. Singapore was a part of the Federation of Malaya from 1959, when it gained independence from the British, to 1963. Known now for its incredibly efficient government, Singapore enjoys a flourishing economy and a very high standard of living, though without some of the civil freedoms expected by Westerners.

Chinese, Indian, and Malay folk dances are performed at various religious celebrations and cultural festivals. Amateur and experimental groups performing Western-style theater present plays and performances regularly, most often in "Singlish" (Singapore English). Chinese *Wayang* is an expression used in Singapore to indicate Chinese-style **Peking Opera.** A form of glove puppet theater for children, Pu-tai-hi, is performed in the streets and in the courtyards of temples.

References: Brandon, James R. *Brandon's Guide to Theatre in Asia.* Honolulu: University Press of Hawaii, 1976; Pong, Chau Soo. "Chinese Opera in the Park." *Performing Arts* 1, 1 (1984): 9–12; Yousof, Ghulam-Sarwar. "Traditional Theatre in South East Asia." *Performing Arts* 2 (July 1985): 37–49.

Siva

See Shiva

Skene

Greece

In ancient Athenian drama, the scene building located on the stage, with one or more doors open-

ing to the acting areas; used as a background from which actors could enter. It also had a practical function as a room in which actors could change their costumes. The front of the skene was no doubt decorated, but probably not more than once a year, rather than for each play. Painted scenery or architectural features could have been fixed along the front. There may have been a low wooden stage platform in front of the doors. **Aeschylus**'s *Oresteia*, produced in 458 B.C., was the first to require a *skene*.

References: Bieber, Margarete. *The History of the Greek and Roman Theater.* Princeton, NJ: Princeton University Press, 1961; Capps, Edward. "The Stage in the Greek Theatre According to the Extant Dramas." Ph.D. diss., Yale University, 1891; Halleran, M. R. *Stagecraft in Euripides.* London: Croom Helm, 1985; Seale, D. *Vision and Stagecraft in Sophocles.* London: Croom Helm, 1982; Taplin, Oliver. *The Stagecraft of Aeschylus.* Oxford: Clarendon, 1977.

Slave Actors

Italy, Mexico, Russia, United States

In many areas of the world and during different eras, the wealthy have forced their slaves to entertain them. In Roman ancient drama, almost all actors were slaves, who were trained rigorously and berated for poor performances. For Aztec festivals in **Mexico,** a slave was used to represent the god **Quetzalcóatl** and was actually sacrificed on the final day of the festival. In Russia during the eighteenth century, noblemen who wanted to emulate court entertainment forced their serfs to perform in elaborate displays, which required harsh training and strict rehearsals. Female performing serfs were often forced to be the concubines of the noblemen. During the nineteenth century in the **United States,** African American plantation slaves were often made to dance for their owners.

Forcing another human to entertain and bring merriment while enslaved seems a most ironic cruelty. In the Russian noble homes, slave performers were even beaten in front of the guests if their performance did not create the desired mirth. In some cases, freed slaves did go onto become professional actors and entertainers, having received their first training and experience from their former owners.

See also Actual Death in the Theater; Roman Theater, Ancient

Slovakia

Slovakia was originally settled in the ninth century and then became part of **Hungary** from the eleventh century until almost World War I (1914–1918). The Slovaks then joined the Czechs of Bohemia to form Czechoslovakia in 1918. In 1993 Czechoslovakia split to form two different states, the **Czech Republic** and Slovakia.

Religious folk drama in the vernacular flourished in the seventeenth and eighteenth centuries. There is some evidence of German biblical plays and Latin school dramas predating this. The Slovaks were suppressed by the Hungarians, who ruled over the area from the eleventh to the fourteenth centuries and then from 1526 until World War I (1914–1918). In 1830 the satire *Kocurkovo* by Jan Chalupka (1791–1871) was the first amateur production in Slovak. Amateur theater continued through the nineteenth century and encouraged national pride and the yearning for their own expression. The Slovaks did not completely develop their own theater until 1918 when they joined Czechoslovakia. The first Slovak theater school was the Music School for Slovakia, founded in Bratislava in 1919.

In 1920 the Slovak National Theater took over the Municipal Theater in Bratislava, where performances in German and Hungarian had formerly taken place. Jan Borodac led the Slovak performances (there were also Czech performances there in the early years). The SNT added a touring company to perform for outlying areas. A uniquely Slovakian acting style developed through the 1930s and 1940s. While Germany divided Slovakia, from 1939 to 1945, theater production was extremely difficult. After 1945 many new theaters opened, and much activity resumed. The playwright Petr Karvas (born 1910) was instrumental in improving dramatic literature in the Slovak language. Opera is popular in Slovakia and often performed at the National Opera in Bratislava, as was *La Sonnambula* by Vincenzo Bellini in 1998.

See also Hungary

References: Blaho, Jaroslav. "Slovak Republic." In *The World Encyclopedia of Contemporary Theatre*, ed. Don Rubin. New York: Routledge, 1994, 755–766; Cesnakov-Michalcov, Milena. "The Staging of a New Year's Play at Presov (Eperies) in Eastern Slovakia in 1651." *Theatre Research International* 18, 3 (1993): 161–172; Hartnoll, Phyllis. *The Oxford*

The Slovak National Opera stages Prince Igor at the Edinburgh International Festival, August 1990. (Robbie Jack/Corbis)

Companion to the Theatre. New York: Oxford University Press, 1967; Lindovsk, Nadezda. "'Feminism' Is an Insult in Slovakia." Theatre Journal 47, 3 (1995): 381–392; Norton-Welsh, Christopher. "Opera around the World: Wide-Awake Sonnambula, Bratislava." Opera 49, 7 (July 1998): 842–844; Simko, Jan. "Shakespeare in Slovakia." Shakespeare Survey 4 (1951): 109.

Slovenia

The area that is now Slovenia was under German domination in the ninth century and became part of Yugoslavia in 1918. In 1945 the Academy for Theater, Radio, Film and Television was founded as part of the University of Ljubljana. Slovenia declared its independence in 1991. Since independence, alternative spaces such as the Slovene Youth Theater and warehouses have been used for experimental productions. See **Yugoslavia** for a history of theater in this area.

References: Frantar, Vladimir. "Opera around the World: Slovenia—A National Opera, Ljubljana." Opera 50, 3 (March 1999): 342; Frantar, Vladimir. "Opera around the World: Slovenia, Lijublajana Standard Ballo." Opera 49, 6 (June 1998): 728–729; Menashe, Louis, and Jasminka Udovicki. "Art, History, and Politics in the Former Yugoslavia: An Interview with Michael Benson." Cineaste 22, 2 (June 1996): 30–33; Molka, Viktor. "Slovenia." In The World Encyclopedia of Contemporary Theatre, ed. Don Rubin, 767–781. New York: Routledge, 1994.

Socialist Realism

Russia

Officially supported artistic doctrine enforced by the Soviet Communist Party from 1932 to 1991 in the **Soviet Union,** which demanded a truthful and historically accurate depiction of reality in its revolutionary development that should educate the masses in the spirit of socialism. The purpose of plays of this style was to encourage and support the emerging Communist regime. These plays were expected to feature a Soviet hero as the protagonist, a man or woman of the people, who is active, healthy, and without hesitation when it comes to overcoming obstacles to realizing a Communist society. The villain of these plays was generally a member of the bourgeoisie or an enemy nation. This rigid formula stifled much

creativity and kept the number of good plays during this era to a minimum. These works are generally tools for propaganda rather than works of art. The Communist Party-led Soviet Union officially fell in 1991, but policy toward the arts had become less severe even before then.

References: Bown, Matthew Cullerne. Art under Stalin. New York: Holmes and Meier, 1991; Grois, Boris. The Total Art of Stalinism: Avant-Garde, Aesthetic Dictatorship and Beyond. Trans. Charles Rougle. Princeton, NJ: Princeton University Press, 1992; Slonim, Marc. Russian Theater, From the Empire to the Soviets. Cleveland: World, 1961.

Sokari

Sri Lanka

One of the oldest theatrical forms of Sri Lanka, which celebrates the Sinhalese New Year (around September) by making a votive offering to the chief deity, the goddess Pattini, in hopes of securing her blessing for the community's well being and success for the coming year. It is performed in remote rural regions of Sri Lanka by male peasants. Performers receive careful instruction regarding their performance from elders in each village who are experienced in Sokari and devotional etiquette. In an outdoor clearing, the masked performers dance to lively music and mime the story of Sokari, a North Indian immigrant to Sri Lanka who has an extramarital affair and conceives a child. Her pregnancy suggests that Sokari may have evolved from ancient fertility ceremonies. Many comic adventures are enacted in song and dance throughout the performance. The festivities begin after sundown and continue through the night.

References: Brandon, James. The Cambridge Guide to Asian Theatre. New York: Cambridge University Press, 1993; de Zoete, Beryl. Dance and Magic Drama in Ceylon. London: Faber & Faber, 1957; Gunawardana, A. J. Theatre in Sri Lanka. Colombo: Department of Cultural Affairs, Sri Lanka, 1976.

Sophocles (496–406 B.C.)

Greece

Great ancient Greek tragic playwright. Of all the great tragedians, Sophocles won the most dramatic competitions at the Athenian festival called the **City Dionysia.** He first produced tragedies in

471, and by 468 he had beaten the first of the three great creators of tragedy, **Aeschylus,** and thirty years later, in 438, his younger contemporary, **Euripides.** Though he had trained in acting, music, and gymnastics in his youth, he did not perform in his own plays, as was the custom, because his voice was not strong enough.

Sophocles was innovative; he added painted scenery and added a third actor. As a playwright, he is known for his masterful ability to structure a play so that the moment of recognition, or **anagnorisis,** for the protagonist happens at the moment of the peripeteia, the moment that the falling action begins. This careful construction is why Aristotle used his work as a model for tragedy in the **Poetics.** The primary theme for Sophocles is the relationship between the individual and society. He put more emphasis on the individual and less on the chorus than Aeschylus did, but he did not go as far in this direction as Euripides.

Sophocles is believed to have written more than a hundred plays, but only seven complete tragedies survive: *Philoctetes* (409 B.C.), *Ajax* (441 B.C.), *Women of Trachis* (produced in Athens 430–420 B.C.), *Electra* (409 B.C.), and three plays drawn from the story of the same family, *Antigone* (441 B.C.), *Oedipus Rex* (430 B.C.), and *Oedipus at Colonus* (401 B.C.). Probably the best-known play from the Greek classical age is *Oedipus Rex.*.

> **References:** Burton, R. W. B. *The Chorus in Sophocles' Tragedies.* Oxford: Clarendon, 1980; Letters, Francis Joseph Henry. *Life and Work of Sophocles.* New York: Sheed and Ward, 1953; O'Connor, Margaret Brown. *Religion in the Plays of Sophocles.* Menasha, WI: George Banta, 1923; Seale, D. *Vision and Stagecraft in Sophocles.* London: Croom Helm, 1982; Sheppard, John Tresidder. *Aeschylus & Sophocles: Their Work and Influence.* New York: Longmans, Green, 1927.

South Africa

An anomaly in the African continent, South Africa has had a history of extremes; extreme wealth, extreme racism, extreme political tension; all giving rise to an extremely vibrant cultural outflowing. In addition to indigenous African groups, the oldest of which were the San, formerly called Bushmen, and the largest of which are the Xhosa and Zulu, South Africa has a large settler minority made up of Afrikaans-speaking descendants of seventeenth-century Dutch setters and English-speaking descendants of British immigrants, largely from the nineteenth century. Policies of racial separation developed by both settler communities culminated in the rigid and oppressive system of apartheid imposed by the Afrikaner–dominated Nationalist government after 1948. It was not until 1994 that the black nationalist movement, led by the African National Congress, achieved majority rule in South Africa. Before colonization South Africa was populated by the San and Bantu-speaking peoples, including the Zulu and Xhosa. The Portuguese were the first Western explorers to visit the area in 1488. The Dutch established a settlement in 1652. Great Britain disputed Dutch control during the eighteenth century and finally established rule after many bloody wars with the Zulu kingdom and white settlers. The discovery of diamonds and gold in the late 1800s provoked an enormous influx of British miners and opportunists. The Union of South Africa under Britain was established in 1910, a government that completely disallowed black involvement in government, a strict policy of racial separateness that later became known as "apartheid."

Indigenous performances in the area now called South Africa involved a richly varied abundance of traditions and rites that included strong theatrical elements. In the Zulu Kingdom there was the **Imbongi,** a professional praisesinger who performed poems, usually in honor of a chief, using mime and broad gestures to dramatize the chief's abilities and accomplishments. The **UmGubho** was a Zulu hunting dance that prepared men for the act of hunting. An awesome display of Zulu military strength was enacted in the **UmKhosi.** The izangoma, the Zulu traditional healers, are trained as performers whose primary function is healing. They are believed by many Zulu people to communicate messages from spirits to people and to bring energy and health. The nomadic San communities also traveled throughout the region, and an integral part of their life was performing **Khoi,** a kind of enactment that included dance, mime, and narrative elements.

British rule over South Africa extended into cultural aspects as well as political. Theater in the early nineteenth centuries was produced by actor-managers from Europe who performed imported plays acted by imported actors. Plays for that theater began to be written in Afrikaans at the end of the nineteenth century.

The first professional black theater troupe was Mthethwa's Lucky Stars, founded in Natal in 1927. They performed plays based on Zulu legends and customs. In South Africa one can use the term black theater, since the policy of apartheid strictly supervised and nearly prohibited racially mixed casts and audiences. Black theater in the twentieth century is predominantly an urban phenomenon. Blacks received an education controlled by whites and were not exposed to their own traditional heritage but rather to Western traditions. Thus, these imposed models were adapted to express the black South African's commitment to social and political change through dramas that embraced such themes. Many of these plays were banned, and playwrights were harassed by white authorities. Most dramas were and still are in English since it is the common language among varying tribes in urban centers.

The musical *King Kong*, 1959, about the rise and fall of a heavyweight boxer, was the first commercial success with white audiences achieved by black theater. Profits from this play were used to start a drama school, theater workshops, and the African Music and Dance Association. In the early 1960s **Gibson Kente** developed a form of musical drama, which set a pattern for township musicals focused upon a strong musical element, light entertainment, and spectacular dancing.

The late 1960s brought a wave of black theater groups to the cities, aimed at challenging the political and economic discrimination against black South Africans. Important theater groups of the 1970s committed to promoting black consciousness were the People's Experimental Theatre outside Johannesburg and the Theatre Council of Natal in Durban. By the end of 1975 many of these black voices were banned by white authorities. Several theaters were formed to promote indigenous South African theater. The first was the Space Theatre in Cape Town, which bussed townspeople to performances to encourage more involvement in theater. The Company (later called the Market Theatre) in Johannesburg began a tradition of encouraging actors, playwrights, and directors of all races to work together to create works of a truly multiracial nature. **Athol Fugard** is the most internationally renowned South African playwright. Though he is a white playwright, his plays are concerned with the social realities for all disenfranchised South Africans, blacks and whites. Other important efforts include **South African Worker Plays**, improvised plays created by the workers led by the Junction Avenue Theatre, and Workshop '71, which integrated traditional African storytelling methods into contemporary performance.

Some racially integrated work appeared in commercial theaters in the 1990s as part of a partial breakdown of racial exclusivity. A new union, the Performing Artists Workers' Equity, was formed and dedicated to eradicating all vestiges of race and gender discrimination in South African theater. Since the dismantling of the former government and the election of Nelson Mandela in 1994, the first black leader of South Africa, a painful past of civil strife is tempered by hope for a future of multiracial vitality and new forms of cultural expression.

The Market Theater presented *The Zulu* (2000) by Mbongeni Ngema in Johannesburg. It is described as a complex but celebratory musical epic. Beginning in 1999 the South African New Theater Trust began providing after-school instruction in the practices of Caribbean Carnival as a means of self-expression. In healing communities after so many decades of strife, traditions from other cultures are being borrowed.

References: Banham, Martin. *African Theatre Today.* London: Pitman, 1976.; Coplan, David. *In Township Tonight! South Africa's Black City Music and Theatre.* New York: Longman, 1985; Fuchs, Anne. *Playing the Market: The Market Theatre, Johannesburg, 1976–1986.* New York: Harwood Academic Publishers, 1990; Kavanagh, Robert. *Theatre and Cultural Struggle in South Africa.* London: Zed, 1985; Larlham, Peter. *Black Theater, Dance, and Ritual in South Africa.* Ann Arbor, MI: Proquest, 1985; Racstern, Olga. *Curtain Up! The Story of Cape Theatre.* Cape Town, South Africa: Juta, 1951.

South African Worker Plays

A form of community theater since 1979, pioneered by some members of the Junction Avenue Theatre Company of **South Africa.** Performed in public places such as churches and open yards, these theater pieces are created by workers during improvisational sessions that are focused on issues pertinent to the workers in the working environment. Actual workers performed as the actors in these productions. These were highly successful in some communities. One such success was a piece named *Security* in 1979, and another named *Ilanga Lizaphumela Abasebenzi* (The Sun Rises for the Workers). Their last performance of note was *Asinamali* (1986).

References: Kavanagh, Robert. *Theatre and Cultural Struggle in South Africa.* London: Zed Books, 1985; Larlham, Peter. *Black Theater, Dance, and Ritual in South Africa.* Ann Arbor, MI: Proquest, 1985.

Soviet Cinema

Although there was some early experimentation in silent filmmaking in Russia before the Revolution of 1917, the majority of films in the area known as the **Soviet Union,** which consisted of Russia and fourteen republics, were made under Marxist control and reflect that ideology. The Soviet Union was dissolved in 1991.

The films that were made in Russia prior to 1917 were subject to czarist control and were strictly censored. In prerevolutionary times foreign films were popular, and locally made films were of nearly every type. There were history films, literary films, imitations of imported comedies, and even dramatic productions like *The Picture of Dorian Gray*, 1915, by **Vsevolod Meyerhold**. Popular Russian movie actors of that time included Natalia Lisenko, Ivan Mozhukhin (1889–1939), and Vera Kholodnaya. After 1917, many leading Russian filmmakers, technicians, and actors emigrated to Europe or the **United States.**

Lenin, Russian leader until 1922, was aware of the power of cinema as a propaganda tool and a means for enlightening of the masses. He put his wife, Nadezhda Krupskaya, in charge of the governmental branch overseeing film. Many difficulties faced filmmakers at this time, including a shortage of raw film stock. Imported films were banned because they did not adhere to party ideology. In 1924 there was a special governmental debate that resolved to allow nonnaturalistic and avant-garde expression in film. From this loosening of control was born an exceptional period in

Soviet film. The most talented and prolific of film directors at this time included Sergei Eisenstein, Vsevolod Pudovkin, and Pudovkin and Alexander Dovzhenko (1894–1956). Unfortunately this artistic freedom barely lasted until the advent of sound, and already by 1928 Eisenstein was being criticized by party officials for his film *October*. Stalin increasingly demanded that the party doctrine on the arts, **socialist realism,** be applied to film as well as other arts. By the 1930s Soviet film was mediocre in quality and artistic content. Musicals and escapist comedies, such as Igor Savchenko's *Accordion*, 1934, were popular.

Films glorifying Stalin and Lenin became the rage in the late 1930s, and there were specific actors who made successful careers out impersonating these leaders. Boris Schukin portrayed Lenin in *Lenin in October*, 1937. Maxim Strauch also portrayed Lenin in films. An actor from Georgia gained fame portraying Stalin in such movies as *The Great Dawn/They Wanted Peace*, 1938. These movies continued into the 1950s and 1960s. World War II (1939–1945) brought about a revival of the documentary film genre. The most influential film produced during the war was Eisenstein's *Ivan the Terrible, Part 1*, 1945, because of its ambitious scale and powerful imagery.

In the postwar period, creativity was at an all-time low, and the insistence on socialist realism was growing. It was not until Stalin's death in 1953 that the stranglehold on artistic freedom was loosened. Films such as *The Cranes are Flying*, 1957, and *Ballad of a Soldier*, 1959, with a fresh lyricism and emotional truth, resulted. By the mid-1960s control had begun to tighten slightly again, so much so that Andrei Tarkovsky's *Andrei Rublev*, a movie about a fourteenth-century religious icon painter who lost his faith, was finished in 1966 but not allowed in the Soviet Union until 1971. By the late 1970s the republics of the Soviet Union were creating as many films as Russia itself. All films were heavily censored, and Western films were barely allowed in at all and then only for elite audiences.

Some films of artistic worth emerged from Russia in the 1980s, such as Gregori Chukrai's *Life Is Wonderful*, 1980, Elem Klimov's *Come and See*, 1985, and Tarkovsky's *Nostalgia*, 1983. In 1985 Mikhail Gorbachev became leader of the Soviet Union and instituted his policy of perestroika, or restructuring, and glasnost, or openness, thus ushering in a period of artistic freedom for filmmakers. The Soviet Filmmakers Union instituted an awards event at which a Georgian director, Tengiz Abuladze, won with his movie *Repentance* (1987).

The Soviet Union disbanded in 1991. The former republics and Russia, now freed from censorship and state control, struggle to produce works in their respective countries where political instability is widespread. Foreign films, which had been banned for so long, are stiff competition for locally produced movies. Despite these hardships, films of quality are being produced in Russia, including Lidia Bobrova's *Hey, You Geese!* 1992, and Alexander Mitta's *Lost in Siberia*, 1991. A limited number of films have emerged from the former republics at a slow yet steady rate. The Baltic countries have been some of the most prolific. Many outstanding directors from Georgia, such as Tengiz Abuladze, Lana Gogoberidze, and Rezo Tchkeidze, have been greatly limited by civil war and political instability. Georgian director Kakhaber Kakabidze created the film *The Lake* as a study of post-Soviet existence. In Uzbekistan directors such as Samir Abbasov, Yuri Sabitov, and Mairam Yusupova have been producing films since the 1990s. Bakhtia Khudonazarov and Tolib Khamidov are active directors in Tajikistan. In Kazakhstan Amir Karakulov and Yermek Shinarbaev are creating films of merit. Sergey Dvortsevoy from Kazakhstan directed the film *Bread Day* (1998). In Russia the filmmaker Nikita Mikhalkov created *The Barber of Siberia* (1999) and director Alexey Uchitel made *His Wife's Diary* (2001). Kyrgyzstan's first independent film, *The Adopted Son* (1999) was directed by Aktan Abdykalykov and explores the significance of ritual and tradition in rural Kyrgyzstan.

See also Estonia; Latvia; Lithuania

References: Babitsky, Paul. *The Soviet Film Industry.* New York: Published for the Research Program on the U.S.S.R. by Praeger, 1955; Katz, Ephraim. *The Film Encyclopedia.* New York: Harper Perennial, 1994; Leyda, Jay. *Kino: A History of the Russian and Soviet Film.* Princeton, NJ: Princeton University Press, 1983; Mast, Gerald. *A Short History of the Movies.* 4th ed. New York: Macmillan, 1986; Taylor, Richard, ed., trans. *The Film Factory: Russian and Soviet Cinema in Documents.* Cambridge, MA: Harvard University Press, 1988; Taylor, Richard. *Film Propaganda: Soviet Russia and Nazi Germany.* New York: I. B. Tauris, 1998.

Soviet Union

Armenia, Azerbaijan, Belarus, Estonia, Georgia, Kazakhstan, Kyrgyzstan, Latvia, Lithuania, Moldova, Russia, Tajikistan, Turkmenistan, Ukraine, Uzbekistan

In 1917 the Bolsheviks took power over Russia and began expanding and absorbing non-Russian territory that had been conquered by the Russian czars preceding them. The Union of Soviet Socialist Republics, or USSR, was formed from an enormous territory in northern Eurasia and was divided into fifteen republics. Beginning in the 1930s there were sporadic acts of anti-Soviet dissent throughout most of the republics because of ruthless Soviet repression, but none of them asserted their independence until 1990. The Soviet Union officially dissolved in 1991. Each of the former Soviet republics is now an autonomous nation, and many of them are struggling with political instability and economic hardship. **Russia** remains the largest of all the areas. **Georgia,** Armenia, and Azerbaijan are all a part of the Caucasus, an area between the Black and Caspian seas divided by the Caucasus Mountains. The Baltic states, **Lithuania, Latvia,** and **Estonia,** are considered as one geographical area since they are contiguous and are culturally somewhat similar. The five central Asian Soviet republics, Kazakhstan, Kyrgyzstan, **Tajikistan,** Turkmenistan, and Uzbekistan, are close geographically and similar culturally; they are all predominantly Muslim nations. Belarus, formerly known as Byelorussia, is culturally distinct, as is the Ukraine. Moldova borders on Romania in the west and Ukraine in the east.

The first theater in what is now Armenia is believed to have occurred in 56 B.C. when the Armenian king Artavazd built a Hellenistic theater in the capital city, Artashat. There are also some historical references to some theatrical activity during the Middle Ages. Shakespearean plays were extremely popular in the nineteenth century. Armenia's first Shakespearean actor of great was Bedros Adamian who dominated the stage in the 1880s. Locally written plays were also popular, such as *For the Sake of Honor* (1904) by Alexander Shirvanzade (1858– 1935), which by 1911 had been performed over 300 times. The establishment of the Armenian Soviet Republic in 1920 meant that the theater of Armenia had to serve the ideology of the republic exclusively. In 1939 a theater company from Armenia was honored by being invited to perform in Moscow.

Indigenous theater in Azerbaijan is rich in the tradition of storytellers, known as *ashyks*, who sang and told dramatic tellings of legends. There are also believed to have been puppet performances, theater games, and religious celebrations utilizing theater. The first professional theater company was founded by Mirza Fatali Akhundov (1812–1878). Groups of actors, known as *tovarishestva* (friendship groups) began forming in the very early twentieth century. By 1920 the theaters of Azerbaijan were all nationalized, and the state oversaw all theatrical activity and made sure it agreed with the state ideology. At the Azerbaijan Academic Drama Theater, director A. A. Tuganov (1871–1952) unsuccessfully tried to use the Stanislavski method of acting. Soviet repression of expression began to be felt in Azerbaijan in the 1930s, and many famous theater people were arrested. The Azerbaijan Academic Drama Theater, known as GAT, continued to be a major force through the twentieth century, though it grew stagnant. Tofik Kazymov (1921–1980) became director of GAT in 1963 and tried to rejuvenate the theater but was unable to make major changes.

In Uzbekistan there is a long and rich tradition of many popular performing arts, such as puppet shows, circuses, and folk singers. Still performed are also many ancient rituals, such as the harvest celebration, that have theatrical elements. The Khamza Theater opened in 1920 in Tashkent, run by a group of actors trained in Moscow. Theater flourishes in the Yakutia region, which presently has almost twenty theaters. In 1920 a theater made up of Russian actors performed largely propaganda plays, struggling to make it in this vast, cold land. In 1922 this group adopted a system of bartering firewood and barley for the price of admission. Within just a decade, this group became the Yakut State National Theater. This theater continues to flourish, performing local plays in Yakut, as well as Russian and European plays.

Theater traditions such as storytelling, singing stories and rituals are believed to have existed in Turkmenistan for centuries. The first theater com-

pany was formed due to Soviet involvement in 1925, the Turkmen Theater Company. Women were not allowed to join the company until 1929. Mostly Soviet propaganda plays were presented during the 1930s. Many amateur theater companies formed in the 1940s. In 1948 the major city, Ashkabad, suffered a sever earthquake that killed more than half of the population, including many theater people. A typical play of the style of work in Turkmenistan is *The Decisive Step* (1957) by B. Kerbabayev. Also representative are *The Kushka Fortress* (1964) by A. Adzhanov and *The Emir's Ambassador* (1970) by K. Kuliyev. Fresh work was finally witnessed in *The Lizard* (1987) directed by Kakadjan Ashirov, which broke from the confines of socialist realism and explored more poetic aspects.

In Belarus there is also a long rich tradition of acting and adult puppet theater, known as *Battaleika*, which has existed since the sixteenth century. The first professional theater was formed in 1907. After the Russian Revolution in 1917 Belarus theater expanded even more under Soviet encouragement. By 1941 there were over twenty operating theaters. Nazi occupation halted theatrical activity, but it resumed once the hostility ceased. Currently Belarus theater is the focus for dissent against governmental oppression.

The first theater known in Uzbekistan was puppet theater and groups of minstrels known as maskharoboz, who improvised comic skits. The Muslim movement known as Jadadism, founded by Ismail Bey Gaspirali (1851–1914) started a school in 1901 and used theater in the form of *janli surat* (living picture) to teach those who could not read. This was the main inspiration behind the beginnings of theater in Uzbekistan. Plays were performed only by men and propagated good morals such as the evil effects of alcoholism and wife beating. Soviet control of the theater began in the 1920s. Many theaters were constructed by the Soviets in their goal to bring theater to the masses in Uzbekistan. The status of the actor, which was low in Islamic society, was raised significantly under Soviet control, so long as the actor conformed to Soviet ideology. Even since the fall of the Soviet Union, theater in Uzbekistan remains under state control.

The Ukrainians have long had a vivacious independent theater of their own. Puppet shows featuring the character **Petrushka** were extremely popular from the tenth to the sixteenth centuries and were enjoyed by popular audiences. Religious Christian theater was brought to the Ukraine from Poland around the seventeenth century. These performances were academic, complete with written scripts, and they were performed by a trained company of actors, who were most often students. These performances toured during summer vacations, and rich landowners fed the actors in exchange for a show. Under Soviet rule the Ukrainian theater enjoyed the same government support and encouragement that all the republics received. Ukrainian theater still thrives even under austere economic hardship. The Golden Lion International Theater Festival has been in Lviv since 1993 and attracts many theater groups, experimental and student groups. The 1996 festival was centered on presenting the classics through experimental interpretations.

References: Hartnoll, Phyllis. *The Oxford Companion to the Theatre*. New York: Oxford University Press, 1967; Mally, Lynn. "The Rise and Fall of the Soviet Youth Theater TRAM." *Slavic Review* 51 (Fall 1992): 411–430; Schuler, Catherine. *Women in Russian Theatre*. London: Routledge, 1996; Slodkowski, Andrew, director and producer. *Baltic States*. San Ramon, CA: International Video Network, 1992; Speake, Graham. *Cultural Atlas of Russia and the Former Soviet Union*. London: Andromeda Oxford, 1998.

Soyinka, Wole (1934–)

Nigeria

Nigerian playwright, widely recognized as the greatest African playwright of his time. He was raised in western **Nigeria** as an Anglican. After college he worked in England for a year starting in 1959 as a play reader at the Royal Court Theatre. Next he started a company of actors, with whom he developed several experimental pieces, including *The Swamp-Dwellers*, 1958, which was produced in Nigeria. Back in Nigeria he formed the theater company, 1960 Masks, whose actors he trained between 1962 and 1965. During the Nigerian civil war beginning in 1967, Soyinka was imprisoned for two years for his politically volatile power as a writer. After a period of exile, 1969 to 1976, he continued creating experimental works at the University of Ife with the Guerrilla Theatre Unit.

Soyinka writes politically charged plays that create a dialogue of views and options rather than promoting any one stance. He is committed to exposing hypocrisy and corruption in political leaders, society, and in the individual. In the play *Opera Wonyosi*, 1977, Soyinka openly satirizes the emperor of the Central African Empire and the petty bourgeoisie who grew rich from his corruption. He weds the modern African individual to his or her cultural past in many of his works, as in *The Strong Breed*, 1962, in which a man tries to divorce his lineage as one of the "strong breed" (one who drives away bad spirits), but cannot escape his destiny even when working in a modern capacity for a foreign village. Other important plays include *The Lion and the Jewel*, 1959, *A Dance of the Forests* (1960), *The Bacchae of Euripides* (1973), *A Play of Giants* (1984), and *From Zia with Love* (1992). He is also a poet, novelist, and theorist. He was awarded the Nobel Prize for literature in 1986.

References: Banham, Martin. *African Theatre Today*. London: Pitman, 1976; Barrett, Lindsay. "The Popular Arts in Nigeria in the 1980's." *Positive Review* 1, 4 (1981): 24–27; Ekwuema, Lazarus E. N. "Nigerian Performing Arts, Past, Present and Future, with Particular Reference to Igbo Practice." *Presence Africaine* 92, 2 (1975): 195–213; Sonuga, Gbenga. "Nigerian Cultural Centres: Government Sponsorship of the Arts." *New Culture* 1, 10 (1979): 39–52.

Spaghetti Western

Italy

Italian version of the American Western, made in the 1960s. The most renowned director of this genre is Sergio Leone (born in 1929), who often cast **Clint Eastwood** as a silent loner seeking his own private justice outside the law. A typical scenario of a spaghetti Western shows a drifter entering town, getting involved in some conflict that ends in bloodshed and death for some, and then drifting out of town again. These films used minimal dialogue and communicated the response of the actors with facial sneers and grunts. This deadpan style of acting influenced a whole generation of film actors. Two of the best-known films by Leone are *A Fistful of Dollars*, 1964, and *The Good, the Bad, and the Ugly*, 1966.

References: Leprohon, Pierre. *Italian Cinema*. New York: Praeger, 1972; Mast, Gerald. *A Short History of the Movies*. 4th ed. New York: Macmillan, 1986.

Spain

Theater in Spain has seemingly been influenced by the Catholic Church more than by any other element. Spain had the self-appointed role of defender of the Catholic faith for centuries, as seen from the time of the founding of the Spanish Inquisition in 1481 and subsequent efforts to expel Jews, Muslims, and intellectuals who spoke out against the church, up until the death of the Catholic General Francisco Franco. Theatrical activity reaches back to the early **Roman drama,** since the Roman Empire (27 B.C.–A.D. 476) had a province in Spain and Roman theaters and circuses were plentiful in Spain. The Christian church councils repeatedly attempted to ban pantomime (see **Ancient Pantomime**), acting, and pagan rites and festivals that contained dramatic elements. To remedy the situation, the church welcomed into its walls some of the former dances and dramas of its recent converts. This proved to be too popular an inclusion, and by the seventh century the church officials were hardpressed to suppress these performances, once the entertainment became too lewd and degenerate.

Much of the south of Spain remained under Moorish control from the ninth to the eleventh centuries, but in the rest of Spain during medieval times liturgical drama began. A particularly Spanish religious play centers on the bodily assumption of the Virgin Mary to heaven. It was usually performed on scaffolds erected inside a cathedral. The heavens were represented in the roof of the cathedral, from which descended platforms representing clouds with actors portraying angels and saints upon them.

Beginning in the fourteenth century, the procession on **Corpus Christi,** an annual church festival, allowed laypeople to indulge their desire for performing and dramatic entertainment, while also allowing the clergy to instruct the people through dramatic presentations. In the late fourteenth century scripted various kinds of secular drama developed, such as the **Egloga,** the **Entremés,** and the **Auto Sacramental.** In both religious and secular dramas the comic rustic character **Pastor-Bobo** was often present.

Many factors contributed to the establishment of a thriving commercial theater in Spain in the sixteenth through the eighteenth century. The spirit of the Renaissance, which was spreading throughout Europe, infused writers and artist with a new enthusiasm. Visits from Italian **commedia dell'arte** troupes inspired and influenced many Spanish theater troupes. One of the first theater managers in Spain, **Lope de Rueda,** wrote and acted in *pasos,* or short comedies. In 1580 two significant performing places were rebuilt, the Corral de la Pacheca and the Corral de la Cruz, an event that caused a great number of theater companies to emerge.

Philip II, however, closed all the theaters down from 1598 to 1600 in the name of public morality; after 1600 several licensed companies resumed production under strict censorship. In 1608 women were allowed to appear on the stage, but not in men's clothing. The Golden Age of Spanish drama occurred between 1621 and 1665 under Philip IV, himself a dramatist and an actor (see **Royalty and World Leaders as Actors**). The Golden Age coincided with a time of Spanish political supremacy throughout Europe. In 1635 it is recorded that there were more than 2,000 actors and 40 theater companies in Madrid and approximately 300 theater companies in Spain. The fall of the Golden Age was in part brought about by criticism from the church, and many Spanish theaters were closed.

Italian opera was popular in Madrid and Barcelona in the late seventeenth century. The early nineteenth century saw the advent of Romantic drama, which reached its fullest expression in Spain in *Don Juan Tenorio* by playwright José Zorrilla, 1844. By the end of the nineteenth century the system of traveling companies featuring star performers predominated. Innovators in the early twentieth century include Martínez Sierra, who managed the Teatro Eslava from 1917 to 1925, introducing new techniques in acting, lighting, and scenic settings, along with his leading actress, Catalina Bárcena. In the late 1920s Cipriano Rivas Cherif, artistic director of Teatro Español, and Margarita Xirgu, actress and director of the company, established an innovative acting study group.

Poetic folk drama was mastered by Federico García Lorca (1898–1936), a dramatist and a poet recognized and admired throughout the world for his literary achievements. In 1933 he was appointed director of the traveling theater La Barraca, for which he wrote some of his most powerful works, *Bodas de Sangre* (Blood Wedding), 1933, *Yerma*, 1934, and *La Casa de Bernarda Alba* (The House of Bernarda Alba), 1934. In 1936 Lorca was arrested and executed by the Falangists.

The Spanish Civil War, 1936–1939, brought an abrupt end to further theatrical developments, and the arts were slow to recover from the stultifying effect of the war. Francisco Franco (1892–1975) emerged as dictator and imposed severe censorship on the arts for religious reasons and to suppress political opposition. During the 1960s Spain's theater continued to be extremely conservative, despite the relaxation in censorship laws. The works of Ramón del Valle-Inclán (1866–1936) were produced again (see **Esperento**), and that brought innovations from the rest of Europe to the attention of the Spanish audiences. To encourage and control innovation in Spanish theater, the government established the National Experimental Theatre in 1965, in which new acting and staging techniques were developed.

In 1975 Franco died, after which stability and economic recovery slowly came to the Spanish people. Likewise, the theater became more vibrant, and theater practitioners, such as Alfonso Sastre (b. 1926), began working publicly in Spain again with renewed vigor.

References: Gies, David Thatcher. *The Theatre in Nineteenth-Century Spain*. New York: Cambridge University Press, 1994; Londré, Felicia Hardison. *Federico Garcia Lorca*. New York: Frederick, 1984; McKendrick, Melveena. *Theatre in Spain: 1490–1700*. New York: Cambridge University Press, 1989; Zugasti, M. "Actors and Techniques of the Spanish Classical Theatre," *Bulletin of Hispanic Studies* 70, 2 (April 1993): 271–272.

Spanish Cinema

Censorship has been one of the most deciding factors in the development of film in Spain. As early as 1913 films were being monitored for moral content and the extent to which they supported the government. **Luis Buñuel,** the Spanish-born Surrealist film maker, fell victim to censorship and chose more hospitable locations in **France**, **Mexico,** and the **United States.** During the Franco regime (1939–1975), censorship controlled political matters and the treatment of domestic life, mandating the portrayal of women as docile workers at home and respect for clerical characters, as well as covering various moral issues.

By the 1930s feature films were being produced in Spain. Performer and director Florián Rey stands out as a highly creative contributor to the era with the 1929 film *La Aldea Maldita* (The Accursed Village). After the Spanish Civil War (1936–1939), the Franco regime took complete control over film production in Spain and used it largely as a propaganda machine. One man, minister of culture Admiral Luis Carrero Blanco, controlled film production from 1944 to 1973. Some films of artistic worth, which were more than simple vehicles for glorifying Spain, emerged during the regime. *Marcelino, Pan y Vino* (Marcelino, Bread and Wine) in 1954 was touching example of both a popular religious drama and a child-star film, starring six-year-old Pablito Calvo.

In the 1950s three extremely talented Spanish directors came to the forefront, Juan Antonio Bardem, Carlos Saura, and Luis Berlanga. Influenced by **Italian neorealism,** Bardem and Berlanga together created the film *Esa Pareja Feliz* (The Happy Family) in 1951. Saura directed an adolescent gangster film, *Los Golfos*, in 1959, after being inspired by the French **nouvelle vague** movement.

During the 1960s the rigidity of the regime's censorship was tested by many innovative films that were metaphorically critical of social conditions under Franco, films such as *El Buen Amor* (The Good Love), 1963, and *La Busca* (The Search), 1966. On a lighter note, and more popular, action thrillers, spy movies, and the comedies of Manuel Summers throve throughout the 1960s and into the 1970s.

In an atmosphere of more relaxed censorship, José Luis Borau wrote and directed *Mi Querida Señorita* (My Dearest Lady) in 1971, which was nominated for an Academy Award. Under the new socialist government in the 1980s, the comic director Pedro Almodovar brought Spanish cinema to the attention of the world with films such as *Qué He Hecho Yo Para Merecer Esto?* (What Have I Done to Deserve This?) 1984, and *Tie Me Up, Tie Me Down* 1989, starring Antonio Banderas, who has risen to international fame.

References: Buñuel, Luis. *My Last Breath*. London: Cape, 1984; Katz, Ephraim. *The Film Encyclopedia*. New York: Harper Perennial, 1994.

Sri Lanka

An independent island nation located directly below the southern tip of India. **Buddhism** is the religion practiced by the Sinhalese-speaking majority on the island with **Hinduism** practiced by the Tamil-speaking minority. Catholicism was brought to the area by the Portuguese, who conquered the coastal regions in the sixteenth century. They were ousted by the Dutch in the seventeenth century, who were later replaced by the British in the eighteenth century. In 1833 Sri Lanka was renamed Ceylon and became a British colony. Full independence was proclaimed in 1972, and the island was renamed the Republic of Sri Lanka.

Much of the theater in Sri Lanka emerged from the many rituals and ceremonies performed in the various folk religions practiced on the island. Many forms seem to have evolved from fertility ceremonies. *Rata Yakuma* is a ceremony, involving much use of song and mime, that is performed to ensure the safe passage of an unborn child into the world or to help an infertile couple conceive a child. A masked folk theater form named **Kolam** may also have evolved from ancient fertility ceremonies; one of its plays tells the story of a queen who was having a child and demanded entertainment, resulting in *Kolam*. **Sokari** is yet another ceremony that may have evolved from fertility ceremonies, as suggested by the fact that this celebration of the Sinhalese New Year dramatizes the story of an unfaithful wife who conceives a child.

There are also several theatrical forms practiced in Sri Lanka inspired by Christianity. **Pasku** is a Passion play. Originally designed to spread Christianity, but later adapted to tell nonreligious stories, **Nadagama** is a form of folk theater that throve in Sri Lanka in the nineteenth century. **Rukada** is a marionette theater form that utilizes the stories and songs of *Nadagama*.

References: Brandon, James. *The Cambridge Guide to Asian Theatre.* New York: Cambridge University Press, 1993; de Zoete, Beryl. *Dance and Magic Drama in Ceylon.* London: Faber & Faber, 1957; Gunawardana, A. J. *Theatre in Sri Lanka.* Colombo: Department of Cultural Affairs, Sri Lanka, 1976; Sarachchandra, Ediriweera R. *The Folk Drama of Ceylon.* 2d ed. Colombo: Department of Cultural Affairs, 1966.

Stanislavsky, Konstantin (1863–1938)
Russia

Director, teacher, cofounder of the **Moscow Art Theater,** creator of the Stanislavsky System of acting; his contribution to the art of acting was immense. He was passionately driven throughout his life to discover a method or system for expressing inner truth in the theater. He was a tireless pioneer in the modern theater and, though often misunderstood, is nearly worshipped by his followers.

An affluent youth, he was exposed to much culture and trained in the arts from an early age. He inherited a business from his wealthy father but was drawn away by his passion for theater. By the end of the 1890s he was directing and acting in an eclectic series of endeavors, realistic, symbolic, fanciful, and hard-hitting. In 1898 Stanislavsky met **Vladimir Ivanovich Nemirovich-Danchenko,** immediately realizing that they shared a vision of a new theater free from artificiality. That year they formed the Moscow Popular Art Theater, later the Moscow Art Theater (MAT), in a barn thirty miles from Moscow. They assembled a dedicated group of actors and worked relentlessly amidst an atmosphere of excitement, youthful optimism, and rebellion. One of the most revolutionary innovations was the insistence on an artistic ensemble molded by the director, in which every detail was attended to and the star system was abolished, a necessity if they were to achieve this goal.

Stanislavsky's theater was always an educational one, in which the actors were always gaining discipline and training. Even the audiences were trained by Stanislavsky to have more respect for the theatrical experience. He did this by not seating latecomers once the show had begun and by having the actors only bow at the end of the show. Actors of the MAT were expected to abandon the stock gestures and rhythms of speech popularized during the nineteenth century in Russia and seek a more realistic and true physical expression of the internal experience of the character. In staging a production, Stanislavsky had his actors imagine there was a fourth wall between themselves and the audience, which meant they sometimes turned their back to the audience and faced their partners more realistically. In his quest for realism in all elements, sound effects, authentic costuming, makeup, and acting, Stanislavsky attended exhaustively to every detail. He even had the cast of his *Julius Caesar* wear togas and tunics in their everyday life for days before the show.

Stanislavsky later experienced what is referred to as his "symbolic interlude," a time when he turned away from his hyperrealistic mountings of plays. He began representing a more spiritual reality in his work with *Ghosts*, 1904, and *Peer Gynt*, 1912–1913, both by **Henrik Ibsen.** Stanislavsky eventually evolved toward theoretical rules for acting derived from his experience in working with actors. These became know as the System in Russia and as the Method in Europe and the **United States,** where Russian actors taught the Stanislavsky System. To convey his idea of the acting process, Stanislavsky wrote *An Actor Prepares* and *Building a Character.* His ways became frozen and idealized by his followers, who sought to contain and fix his method. Stanislavsky, on the other hand, was continually discarding his old theories in his quest for truth in the theater. It is often forgotten that Stanislavsky attached great importance to the imagination of the actor, to the ability to visualize the part one is playing. Stanislavsky believed actors had to train to be able to reach a state of creative concentration and then to apply that to the development of a role.

After the 1917 Revolution, Stanislavsky ceased experimenting at the MAT and worked on formulating his principles for the actor's inner work. He continued directing until his death. His last production, *Tartuffe*, by **Molière,** was finished by others and presented in 1939 after his death.

References: Slonim, Marc. *Russian Theater, From the Empire to the Soviets.* Cleveland: World, 1961; Stanislavsky, Konstantin. *Stanislavsky on the Art of the Stage.* New York: Hill and Wang, 1961; Stanislavsky, Konstantin. *An Actor Prepares.* London: G. Bles, 1967; Stenberg, Douglas. *From Stanislavsky to Gorbachev: The Theater-studios of Leningrad.* New York: P. Lang, 1995.

Stasimon

See Greek Chorus

Stewart, James (1908–1997)
United States

Leading American film actor. After graduating from Princeton in 1932 he befriended Henry Fonda, and together they pursued their acting careers, first on Broadway and a little later in Hollywood. Stewart's charm as a lanky young man with an unassuming manner was brought to light by Frank Capra's sentimental comedies, such as *You Can't Take It with You,* 1938, and *Mr. Smith Goes to Washington,* 1939. Stewart's fame was secured when he won an Academy Award for *The Philadelphia Story,* 1940.

During World War II (1939–1945) Stewart was a bomber pilot and rose high in the ranks of the military. In his personal life, Stewart was an extreme conservative and always unwaveringly patriotic. In 1947 Stewart made one of the most loved films of all time, *It's a Wonderful Life.* He developed greatly as an actor and was able to portray a wide variety of types, from masculine leads to comic roles. Other remarkable films include *Rear Window,* 1954, *Vertigo,* 1958, *Anatomy of a Murder,* 1959, and *How the West Was Won,* 1962. He continued to perform into the 1990s, doing voice-over work for films.

See also Hitchcock, Alfred

References: Coe, Jonathan. *Jimmy Stewart: A Wonderful Life.* New York: Arcade, 1994; Dewey, Donald. *James Stewart: A Biography.* Atlanta, GA: Turner Publishing, 1996.

Stranitzky, Joseph Anton (1676–1726)
Austria

Austrian actor who entered the theater as a puppeteer traveling around to villages performing wherever he could. He became a dentist, a practice he continued alongside his theatrical work his entire working life. In Vienna he started a theater group called the German Comedians. By 1711 he had built a theater, which was the first permanent theater for comedy in German in any of the German-speaking territories. It is here that the comic character **Hanswurst** appeared, with his songs, dances, and comic antics. The plays at Stranitzky's theater were very similar to the *Haupt und Staatsaktionen* performed by wandering troupes in the sixteenth century.

References: Hartnoll, Phyllis. *The Oxford Companion to the Theatre*. New York: Oxford University Press, 1967; Robertson, Ritchie, and Edward Timms, eds. *Theatre and Performance in Austria: From Mozart to Jelinek*. Edinburgh: Edinburgh University Press, 1993.

Strasberg, Lee

See Actors Studio; Group Theater

Stratford Festival
Canada

The outdoor **Shakespeare** festival in the town of Stratford in Canada begun by Tom Patterson in 1952 is now a thriving major festival with consistently high artistic achievement and an international reputation. Patterson, born in Stratford in 1920, dreamed of a way to save his dreary hometown. He began working on the formation of an open-air festival in 1951 and luckily inspired the interest of the accomplished director Tyrone Guthrie in **England.** In turn, Guthrie secured the English actor Alec Guiness to play the lead in *Hamlet* in 1952. Performances took place under a tent on a thrust stage with seating on three sides.

The enthusiasm of this new enterprise attracted some of the best talent from all over Canada. The first year provided high-quality jobs for sixty-eight Canadian actors who were largely not experienced with performing Shakespeare. Guthrie nurtured the natural talent of the actors and allowed it to blossom in its own way, to be distinctively Canadian. Their 1953 production of *Richard III* put the Stratford Festival on the international map. In 1956 Guthrie left for Minneapolis, succeeded by Michael Langham. Although the festival has consistently brought in big name talent from England and the **United States,** many Canadian actors, such as Christopher Plummer and **William Hutt,** have acted consistently for the festival.

References: Bell, Karen. "The Stratford Season." *Performing Arts & Entertainment in Canada* 32, 3 (August 1999): 22–23; Garebian, Keith. *William Hutt: A Theatre Portrait*. New York: Mosaic Press, 1988; Gould, Allan, Jill Levenson, and Tom Patterson. "First Stages: The Making of the Stratford Festival." *Theatre Research International* 18, 3 (1993): 236–237; Portman, Jamie. *Stratford: The First Thirty Years*. Toronto: McClelland & Stewart, 1989.

Strindberg, August (1849–1912)
Sweden

Playwright, theorist, and novelist, who influenced the development of modern drama throughout the Western world. He wrote predominantly romantic dramas in his youth, naturalistic plays in his middle age, and more dreamlike expressionistic subjective dramas in his late years. In his writing Strindberg strove to create a poetic beauty that transcended the realistic illusion of **naturalism** popular at the time. He advocated a simplified approach to creating theatrical illusion that relied on the play, the dialogue, and the plot.

He wrote *Miss Julie* as a naturalistic tragedy in which an aristocratic young woman seduces the valet in the kitchen and eventually commits suicide. His first wife, Siri von Essen, played the title role at the premiere, offered as a private showing since it was publicly banned due to the subject matter. He met the actress Harriet Bosse when she performed in his drama *To Damascus* I, 1900, and married her within a year. Lars Hanson was a Swedish actor best known for his superb dramatizations of Strindberg's characters.

From 1900 to 1910 Strindberg and a young actor, August Flack, led the Intima Teatern (Intimate Theater), a theater group with a company of actors that experimented with a variety of staging effects to attain a fuller expression of the written word. In 1908 they premiered Strindberg's *The Ghost Sonata*, followed by many other plays including chamber theater. Strindberg was always searching for innovative ways of staging his dramas, going from extreme naturalism to expressionistic suggestions of place and setting. He even tried a Shakespearean stage, where there is no scenery, but only an unlocalized platform.

Three failed marriages in his life, all to actresses, are said to have been at the roots of his notorious misogyny and some of the mental breakdowns he suffered.

See also Shakespeare, William
References: Lucas, F. L. *The Drama of Ibsen and Strindberg*. New York: Macmillan, 1962; Marker, Frederick. *A History of Scandinavian Theatre*. Cambridge: Cambridge University Press, 1996; Ollen, Gunnar. *August Strindberg*. New York: Ungar, 1972; Smedmark, Carl Reinhold. *Essays on Strindberg*. Stockholm: Strindberg Society, 1966; Sprigge, Elizabeth. *The Strange Life of August Strindberg*. London: H. Hamilton, 1949.

Strophe

See Greek Chorus

Sullivan, Arthur

See Gilbert and Sullivan

Sunrise Ceremony

United States

Native American ceremony done by the White Mountain Apache in east-central Arizona that prepares a young girl for adulthood. The summer after a young girl first menstruates, her family arranges a Sunrise Ceremony to call down the spirit of Changing Woman, who bestows strength, physical and spiritual, and long life on a young woman. The ceremony lasts four days and takes the family months to prepare. The girl is costumed in a yellow buckskin robe and pants with turquoise and other beads richly decorating it. She carries a cane symbolizing long life.

The action takes place at a campsite with a specified dance ground that is covered with blankets. At one end of this area stand the medicine man, the drummers, and the singers. The singing of sacred songs and the dancing of the young girl invoke Changing Woman's presence, by which the girl is made holy. She is then an agent of healing for the whole community. Later in the ceremony the girl must put her cane on the ground and run around her cane as it is set at a distance in each of four directions, symbolizing the different stages in her life. She is, in effect, enacting the long life she hopes to secure through the ceremony. Crown Dancing is performed on the second night of the Sunrise Ceremony and again the following day.

References: Ganteaume, Cecile. "White Mountain Apache Dance: Expressions of Spirituality." In *Native American Dance: Ceremonies and Social Traditions*, ed. Charlotte Heth, 65–81. Washington, DC: Starwood, 1992.

Surabhi

India

Musical drama from the nineteenth century found in small rural villages where traveling troupes perform in Andra Pradesh and Tamil Nadu, in the south of India. Men and women robustly belt out songs, and the general performance quality is low. Plays are performed on run-down temporary stages.

References: Brandon, James R. *Brandon's Guide to Theatre in Asia.* Honolulu: University Press of Hawaii, 1976; Gargi, Balawanta. *Theatre in India.* New York: Theatre Arts Books, 1962; Yajnik, Ramanial Kanaiyaial. *The Indian Theatre.* London: Allen and Unwin, 1933.

Surrealism

France

An artistic movement driven by the desire to access the supposedly subconscious impulses of the artist, uncensored by the rational conscious mind; also involving the mingling of the strange with the familiar; perhaps most widely known in the works of the surrealist painter Salvador Dali. The term surrealism was first applied to theater in 1917 by Guillaume Apollinaire (1880–1918) to describe his play *Les Mamelles de Tiresias* (The Breasts of Tiresias). The play is characterized by a subjective flow of events that proceed regardless of logical progression, such that the breasts of the female protagonist float away and she becomes a man, as her husband takes over her work in creating children to populate the city. Amid this illogical stream of action are disparate occurrences of gestures, sounds, cries, and actions.

The movement has profoundly influenced theater, writing, art, and film.

See also Cocteau, Jean

Sutradhara

India

Narrator and stage manager who is present in many forms of traditional Indian dramas; originally narrator for **Sanskrit drama,** classical Indian drama. He almost always wears white and sometimes has two assistants. As narrator he introduces characters, controls entrances and exits, and often comments on the action or tells the audience the inner thoughts of characters. The *Sutradhara* is present in **Tamasha,** a form of opera, in **Ankai Nat,** an operatic dance-drama, in **Gopal Kala** and **Gaulan Kala,** two forms of drama about **Krishna,** the eighth and most important incarnation of the

Polish actors perform a surrealistic play at the opening of Cairo's Experimental Theatre Festival at the Opera House in the Egyptian capital, late September 2000. (AFP/Corbis)

Hindu god **Vishnu,** in *Dashavatar Kala,* dance-drama about the ten incarnations of Vishnu-Krishna, and other forms as well.

See also *Kattiakaran*

References: Gargi, Balawanta. *Folk Theater of India.* Seattle: University of Washington Press, 1966; Menon, Narayana, and Saryu Doshi. *The Performing Arts.* Bombay: Marg, 1982.

Sweden

The early history of Swedish theater is inseparable from that of **Scandinavian theater** in general. The first extant play from Sweden was an Easter celebration from Linkoping in the thirteenth century. These first actors were costumed priests, who performed the scene of the three Marys meeting the angel at the tomb of Christ. Starting in the sixteenth century, the church encouraged the schools to produce comedies and tragedies as a way of teaching good manners and high morals.

Another popular theater form alive throughout Scandinavian courts was the **Ballet de Cour,** brought to its peak by the Swedish Queen Christina, who had a passion for artistic expression in its most opulent forms. For her coronation, in 1650, the lavish entertainment lasted a week. The queen so loved the theater that she often performed such roles as a peasant girl, an amazon, and even the muse of war. She reportedly amazed her audiences with her great agility and skill, although who would dare write less of the performance of a queen? These performances began to abandon the medieval staging techniques used in the typical **morality play** and utilized perspective scenery from the Italian Renaissance.

Throughout the seventeenth and eighteenth centuries bands of itinerant players from other European countries were brought by the courts and were sometimes offered extended stays. With them came the style and influence of the rest of Europe. A new era in Swedish theater was ushered in by **Gustav III,** who ruled Sweden from 1771 to 1792. He had an enormous enthusiasm for the arts and participated in many aspects of productions. Sweden's first stars emerged during this time: Carl Stenborg and Elisabeth Olin. Both the Royal Dramatic Theater and the Royal Opera were founded in the seventeenth century and were flourishing by the eighteenth century, in spite of a decline of court drama and foreign troupes.

At the end of the nineteenth century, **August Strindberg** put Sweden in the forefront of theatrical reform and innovation. Productions of Strindberg's plays continue to be popular and often performed. **Ingmar Bergman,** an extremely prolific theater and film director, has produced many of Strindberg's dramas in his experimental remounting of famous plays. From the 1940s until his death in 1980, Alf Sjoberg was a director fiercely dedicated to theatrical experimentation. He worked to simplify the technical aspects of production so that theater would depend more on ensemble acting. Experimental theater flourishes in Sweden with a group organized by Suzanne Osten in Stockholm in the 1980s that has fostered exceptional work for over two decades.

See also Royalty and World Leaders as Actors

References: Brunius, Niklas, Goran O Eriksson, and Rolf Rembe. *Swedish Theatre*. Trans. Keith Bradfield. Stockholm: Swedish Institute, 1967; Hillestrom, Gustaf. *Theatre and Ballet in Sweden*. Trans. Anne Bibby. Stockholm: Swedish Institute, 1953; Lindvag, Anita. "Elsa Olenius and Our Theatre (The Stockholm City Theatre for Children and Young People)." In *Nordic Theatre Studies: Yearbook for Theatre Research in Scandinavia*, ed. Kela Kvam, 79–90. Denmark: Institute for Theatre Research, University of Copenhagen, 1988; Marker, Frederick. "The Actor in the Nineteenth Century: Aspects of Rehearsal and Performance in the Prenaturalistic Theater in Scandinavia." *Quarterly Journal of Speech* 51 (1965): 177–189; Marker, Lise-Lone, and Frederick Marker. *Ingmar Bergman: A Life in the Theater*. New York: Cambridge University Press, 1992; Marker, Frederick, *A History of Scandinavian Theatre*. Cambridge: Cambridge University Press, 1996; Sauter, Willmar. "Sweden." In *Nordic Theatre Studies: Yearbook for Theatre Research in Scandinavia*, 9–22. Copenhagen: Munksgaard International, 1989.

Switzerland

The first known theater in Switzerland consisted of religious dramas, largely **mystery plays.** Competition between Catholics and Protestants after the Reformation of the early sixteenth century had a favorable effect on the development of Swiss theater, as both factions increased their theatrical output through the sixteenth and seventeenth centuries to encourage conversions and retain believers. Jesuit theater was prevalent as well; in fact, performances they initiated in the village of Einsiedeln in the seventeenth century are still performed. In the eighteenth century traveling troupes began touring Switzerland, bringing with them theatrical influences from around Europe.

A professional theater, the Zurich Schauspielhaus (Zurich Theater), reached its peak artistically in the first half of the twentieth century. The famous director, A Reucher, there from 1901 to 1921, made this theater one of the most important German-speaking theaters. During World War II (1939–1945), while Germany was under control of the Nazi Party, many star Jewish actors who could not work in Germany toured Switzerland. In the 1970s many theater artists started small Freie Gruppen (free groups) such as Norbert Klassen's experimental studio am Montag. Frank Baumbauer became director of the Basler Theater in 1988 and started an annual program entitled Berliner Theatertreffen der zehn besten deutschsprachigen Inszenerunger (Berlin Meeting of the Ten Best Productions in German). The Zurich Ensemble presented Christophe Marthaler and Anna Viebrock's *20th Century Blues* (2000) is Basel. In Lucerne Albert Hirche directed *Hochzeit* (Wedding) (2000) by Elias Canetti. *Palpitations* (2000) is a production created by the Theatre Compagnie Markus Zohner (Markus Zohner Theater Company) of Switzerland.

See also Nazi Germany's Jewish Theater

References: Hartnoll, Phyllis. *The Oxford Companion to the Theatre*. New York: Oxford University Press, 1967.

Symbolism
France, Germany, Ireland, Russia, United States

An artistic movement based on the evocative power of poetry and symbols to convey the inner state of the artist intuitively to an audience or reader. It began in French literary circles in 1880 as a departure from traditional ways of writing, a reaction against strict technique and a liberation of the flow of writing to make it more fluid and less constricted. Symbolism in the theater also got its start in France with **Lugné-Poe** at the Théâtre d'Art in 1890. In contrast to acting that reflects the influence of **naturalism,** symbolic acting styles are much more theatrical, drawn out, and enigmatic—like the plays themselves. The symbolist movement greatly influenced Russian theater from 1906 to 1925, through the work of the famous Russian actress and theater owner, **Vera Kommissarzhevskaya,** and **Vsevolod Meyerhold.**

References: Carlson, Marvin. *The French Stage in the Nineteenth Century.* Metuchen, NJ: Scarecrow, 1972; Green, Michael, ed. *The Russian Symbolist Theatre: An Anthology of Plays and Critical Texts.* Ann Arbor, MI: Ardis Publishers, 1986; McCormick, John. *Popular Theatres of Nineteenth-Century France.* New York: Routledge, 1993; Robichez, Jacques. *Lugne-Poe.* Paris: L'Arche, 1955.

Syria

Until the nineteenth century Syria consisted of present-day Syria, **Lebanon, Israel,** and **Jordan.** Many types of theater flourished in Syria prior to the nineteenth century, including shadow puppet theater that was an adaptation of the Turkish *Karagoz,* primitive farces similar to the *Fasl Mudhik* of Egypt, and storytelling similar to the *Hakawati* of Turkey and Iran.

The first Syrian Western-style play, an adaptation of a play by the French playwright **Molière,** was translated and presented by Marun al-Naq-qash (1817–1855), who introduced a strong musical element into theater, a characteristic that has prevailed in Arab theater until present day. During the late nineteenth century many of the most prominent Syrian actors and playwrights, such as the actor Yusuf al-Khayyat, emigrated to Egypt, where conditions were much more favorable for the performing arts. Playwrights Sa'dallah Wannus and Muhammad Maghut excelled at developing Syrian theater in the 1940s and 1950s.

Egyptian and French films have been extremely popular in Syria since the 1940s and 1950s, but Muslim extremists have been very much against allowing women to view movies because of their sometimes lewd content. Other than documentaries and newsreels, the one film studio founded in Syria after the end of World War II produced nothing worthy of note. The film industry of Syria does not compare in quality or quantity to the success of other Arab nations.

References: Cachia, P. "The Dramatic Monologues of Al-Ma'arri'." *Journal of Arabic Literature* 1 (1970): 129–136; Landau, Jacob. *Studies in the Arab Theater and Cinema.* Philadelphia: University of Pennsylvania Press, 1958; Moreh, S. "The Arabic Theatre in Egypt in the Eighteenth and Nineteenth Centuries." *Etudes Arabes et Islamiques* 3 (1975): 109–113; Mostyn, Trevor, and Albert Hourani, eds. *The Cambridge Encyclopedia of the Middle East and North Africa.* New York: Cambridge University Press, 1988; Rosenthal, Franz. *Humor in Early Islam.* Westport, CT: Greenwood, 1976.

T

Tahiti

See Polynesia

Taiwan

The island called Taiwan has been an independent kingdom, a colony of Japan, and a Chinese province. Taiwan was under the control of the Chinese from the late seventeenth century until 1895, when Japan gained control after the first Sino-Japanese War. When mainland China was having its Communist Revolution, the government of the Republic of China moved to Taiwan in 1949 and called itself the "true China." When the traditional theater arts were banned from Communist China, Taiwan became one of the last places these traditional arts were performed.

The predominant theater form is *Gozai Xi,* or Taiwanese opera, which is a regional form of Chinese opera, originally from southern Fujian Province. it is styled after **Peking Opera,** and so the singing element is most important in *Gozai Xi.* Though mainland Chinese are a minority in Taiwan, their theatrical tastes have affected the development of the Taiwanese theater scene. Many Peking Opera troupes perform regularly in the capital city, Taipei, and travel to other areas also.

Modern theater has been present in Taiwan since 1911, when a Japanese director rounded up local actors to stage several productions. **Langren**

Ju, literally "ruffian drama," became the name for this style, since the actors in it were rough and boisterous men. Producing modern theater in Taiwan has been a continual struggle for the many dedicated artists who have experimented with Western and Taiwanese scripts. The government of Taiwan increased support for the arts in the 1980s significantly by building permanent theaters in many cities.

A local Taiwanese theatrical performance is **Po-the-hi,** glove puppet dramas performed for children.

> **References:** Brandon, James R. *Brandon's Guide to Theatre in Asia.* Honolulu: University Press of Hawaii, 1976; Howard, Roger. *Contemporary Chinese Theatre.* Hong Kong: Heinemann, 1978; Mackerras, Colin. *Chinese Theatre in Modern Times, from 1840 to the Present Day.* Amherst: University of Massachusetts Press, 1975; Scott, A. C. *The Theatre in Asia.* New York: Macmillan, 1972.

Tajikistan

The country now called Tajikistan has been inhabited since 3000 B.C.; it has undergone many invasions, first by Iranians, who converted the people to Islam, then by Mongols, Afghans, and Russians. In 1929 the Soviet Union officially declared the area the Tadzhik Republic under the USSR. During Soviet rule, many Russian theater artists were sent to the area to work in theaters. Vladimir Barbotko was a Russian actor trained at the **Moscow Art**

Theater who became a leading actor in Tajikistan from after World War II (1939–1945) to the 1990s. He performed at the Mayakovsky Theater, which still maintains a talented troupe of actors schooled in Russia. Under Soviet rule, all plays were performed in Russian, but since independence, plays are often performed in Tajik.

Tajikistan has endured great conflict and internal war since the fall of the Soviet Union. Theater is predominantly for the educated elite. The Mayakovsky still actively produces both classics and local playwrights and offers a generous season of children's theater. Some popular young troupes of actors tour from Dushanbe to Khodzhent. The Institute of the Arts in Dushanbe is a training facility for actors and other arts. There are also many private studios in the major cities of Tajikistan.

References: Speake, Graham. *Cultural Atlas of Russia and the Former Soviet Union.* London: Andromeda Oxford, 1998.

Talma, François (1763–1826)
France

Revolutionary actor who completely broke with the false and affected declamatory style popular in his time. Although he died never feeling as though he had had a role to suit his acting abilities, he paved the way for the new styles of **Romanticism** and realism in the art of acting.

Early in his life Talma lived in **England,** and there he became acquainted with the robust and truthful plays of **William Shakespeare**, which influenced his desire for reform and his dissatisfaction with the French style of acting. His first great role was the title character in *Charles IX,* by Joseph Chénier. To create a truthful portrayal of the character, he studied portraits of the historic figure and researched his history in depth. Breaking away from the **Comédie Française,** Talma started a rival theater group, Le Théâtre Français de la Rue de Richelieu, in 1791; the two theaters were united in 1799. Talma was honored by Napoleon and taken by the emperor to perform before the royalty of Europe.

References: Chinoy, Helen Krich, and Toby Cole. *Actors on Acting.* New York: Crown, 1970; Collins, Herbert. *Talma: A Biography of an Actor.* New York: Hill and Wang, 1964.

Tamasha
India

Opera with enticing songs and dances that flourished from the sixteenth through the eighteenth century under Maratha court sponsorship in Maharashtra State. In the nineteenth century, when court sponsorship ceased, crude landowners without a highly refined cultural aesthetic took over, and *Tamasha* became and still is vulgar. Because of the strong erotic elements, Tamasha is spurned by the upper class. Performances are made up of improvised dialogue full of humor and eroticism, and songs with underlying erotic significance, all based on stories of **Krishna,** the eighth and most important incarnation of the Hindu god **Vishnu,** his naughty childhood pranks, his flirtations with the *Gopis* (young milkmaids), and his love affair with Radha, his most favored Gopi.

An evening performance begins with songs called *Gana,* invoking **Ganesha,** the elephant-headed Hindu god. A play about an episode in Krishna's life ensues, for which there is no written script. Actors are given the main points of a story, and then they improvise from one song to the next. Lastly there are dances by the *Gopis,* which are provocative and sensuous, but also quite devotional. The dance in *Tamasha* does not borrow from classical or folk Indian dance traditions, but rather is a wild and erotic mixture of movements in a style all its own. An elderly lady, known as *Mavashi,* and a jester, known as *Songadya,* add humor to various scenes. The **Sutradhara,** the main singer and narrator, carries the story between the acts of the play by commenting on the action and by setting the next scene. The most important part of a show is the *Lavani,* a narrative poem put to music that tells a story with vigor and lusty energy. The first line is sung, and all following lines are quickly spoken by the *Sutradhara* in a singsong manner. Important lines are repeated. The *Lavani* takes incredible stamina to perform, and there are usually about thirty *Lavani* in a performance.

The setting is a low square outdoors platform with the audience seated on three sides in an enclosed area. The dancers wear glittering saris with tinkling bells on their ankles. Along the back of the stage sits the drummer, who plays with impressive gusto, and musicians playing metal cymbals and one stringed wooden instrument.

Tamasha is a theater of release. The almost exclusively male audience can indulge their senses and appetites and forget about their problems. A female dancer is socially outcast, so she is a free spirit, with a life of sexual freedom. The government has passed laws forbidding vulgarity in Tamasha, but these laws are difficult to enforce.

Songs from this form were transformed and used in early **Hindi Movies,** and then were taken back again by Tamasha and used in their modernized form.

References: Brandon, James R. *Brandon's Guide to Theatre in Asia.* Honolulu: University Press of Hawaii, 1976; Gargi, Balawanta. *Folk Theater of India.* Seattle: University of Washington Press, 1966; Varadpande, Manohar Laxman. *Krishna Theatre in India.* New Delhi: Abhinav, 1982; Vatsyayan, Kapila. *Traditional Indian Theatre: Multiple Streams.* New Delhi: National Book Trust, 1980.

Tan
China

Female role in **Peking Opera.** This role was played by men until 1911, when the first actresses were allowed on stage. The teachings of Confucius did not allow men and women to mingle in society, and thus the need for female impersonators came about. In the 1920s the male actor **Mei Lan Fang** elevated the status of the actor playing this role above all others. Before that it was the *Laosheng,* a bearded male role, that was most respected. The vocal technique of the Dan is characterized by a high shrill falsetto that creates rippling cadences of sound. The physical techniques include graceful movements of the arm with the long **water sleeves** as a sign of refinement. Water sleeves are exaggerated cuffs at the end of the sleeves that hang down to almost knee level on the actor. These actors sought to imitate the walking style of women with bound feet (see **Foot Binding**). Within classical Chinese dramatic literature, each type of female character is rigidly prescribed. The role divisions for female characters are as follows. The *Ching-I* is the virtuous woman, who is obedient and shy. She sings and wears the long water sleeves. The *Hua-Tan* is the "flower female," or coquette, who uses expressive hand gestures. Her acting skill is most important. The *Wu-Tan* is the militant female or the

amazon. The *Lao-Tan* is the old female, who usually uses a cane. The *Tsai-Tan* is the female clown or matchmaker.

References: Scott, A. C. *The Theatre in Asia.* New York: Macmillan, 1972.

Tateyaku
Japan

A character type in Japanese cinema, the powerful male lead. The two types of leading male roles in Japanese films are *Tateyaku,* the strong virile man, and **Nimaime,** the sweet mild man. Tateyaku was made famous by the actors Sessue Hayakawa and **Toshiro Mifune.** This character is similar to the kind of American male character often portrayed by **John Wayne** and Clark Gable. Many film stories evolved from differences between these two male type characters. The Tateyaku corresponds to the **Shite** in Noh, classic Japanese masked dance-drama. Japan's cinema descended directly from the traditional theater forms, **Noh, Kabuki,** a seventeenth–century form of drama, and **Bunraku,** puppet drama. The early cinema used the stylizations of the theater rather than a style of its own.

References: Mast, Gerald. *A Short History of the Movies.* 4th ed. New York: Macmillan, 1986.

Tati, Jacques (1908–1982)
France

French actor and film director, known as the idiosyncratic comic star of his own movies. After being a professional rugby player in his youth, Tati turned to the cabaret, where he performed comic skits impersonating top athletes of the day. His popularity and success prompted him to begin making short films of his comic skits. His first feature-length film *Jour de Fête,* 1949, was an original contribution to French cinema because of its unique visual humor, created by juxtaposing the warmth of Tati's character with the mechanical modern world. In *Les Vacances de Monsieur Hulot* (Mr. Hulot's Holiday), 1953, Tati firmly developed the character he played in his next three films, an oddly simple man who at nearly every turn encounters obstacles and misadventures. In *Mon Oncle* (My Uncle), Tati's character is the only source of warmth and authenticity for the children in a cold and modern world. The settings are nearly

Jacques Tati in the hilarious French film Mon Oncle (My Uncle) *(1958). (Kobol Collection/Spectra/Gray/Alterdel/Centaure)*

characters as well: The mischievous fountain in an ultramodern lawn seems to purposely humiliate Tati, and numerous other modern gadgets malfunction when under his control. His silent, mostly physical comedy is comparable to that of **Charlie Chaplin**.

Financial difficulties continually plagued the production of his films. His final two films are *Playtime*, 1968, and *Parade*, 1974.

> **References:** Katz, Ephraim. *The Film Encyclopedia*. New York: Harper Perennial, 1994; Maddock, Brent. *The Films of Jacques Tati*. Metuchen, NJ: Scarecrow, 1977.

Taylor, Elizabeth (1932–)
United States

Leading American film actress, long considered the most beautiful woman in America. She was discovered by movie scouts when only ten while living in Los Angeles. She was a lovely self-confident girl in love with a horse in *National Velvet*, 1944. After adolescence she blossomed into a stunning woman and performed in more mature movies such as *Father of the Bride*, 1950. She matured into an accomplished actress with such sizzling roles as Maggie in *Cat on a Hot Tin Roof*, 1958. She made the epic flop *Cleopatra* in 1963 with **Richard Burton**, with whom she had a long and torrid relationship. She won an Academy Award for her outstanding performance as Martha in *Who's Afraid of Virginia Woolf*, 1966. Her numerous marriages and divorces have been widely noted. Since the 1980s she has dedicated herself more to charitable causes, largely AIDS research, than to performing. She did perform the voice for Baby Maggie for the television show *The Simpsons*.

> **References:** Kelley, Kitty. *Elizabeth Taylor, the Last Star*. New York: Simon and Schuster, 1981; Taylor, Elizabeth. *Elizabeth Taylor; An Informal Memoir*. New York: Harper & Row, 1965.

Taymor, Julie (1948–)
United States

Designer, director, and writer, whose ingenious use of puppets, costumes, and settings create richly fantastic productions on stage and in film; well known for her design and direction of Walt Disney's *Lion King* on Broadway. Her inspiration is cross-cultural, drawing from traditions of various countries to enrich her work. For example, when she directed Stravinsky's *Oedipus Rex* in 1992 in Japan, she had two images of the character of Oedipus, one the actor and the other a skeletal puppet that acted as his alter ego.

Taymor trained at L'Ecole de Mime Jacques Le Coq (The Jacques Le Coq School of Mime) in Paris directly after high school, after which she attended Oberlin College in Ohio, where she joined a professional theater group. She studied the tradition of puppetry called **Wayang Kulit** in performance in Indonesia, and in Japan she studied on the island of Awaji, where a pre-**Bunraku** style of puppetry was still performed. In the late 1970s she lived in Bali and created the theater piece *Tirai*. The sacredness of creating art in Bali is something Taymor has carried into her own work.

Performers in her pieces are often relegated to being an extension of their design, like living puppets. The performer, who is often masked, must seek to draw out the character through movement and vocal expression. Taymor stages serious dramas using imaginative and often haunting puppets, masked performers, and shadow play. In the **United States** she has tried to avoid being categorized as a creator of children's theater because of her use of puppets. In 1986 she directed and designed **Shakespeare**'s *Tempest*, in which she created a terra cotta clay pot mask to fit over the head of Caliban, who came on stage by literally emerging from the sand, dressed in only a loin cloth.

In the medium of film she created *Fool's Fire* in 1992, based on Edgar Allan Poe's story *Hop-Frog*, using stylized puppets and richly costumed midgets in a distorted setting. In 2000, she directed a boldly macabre version of Shakespeare's *Titus Andronicus* called simply *Titus*, with a star-studded cast, including **Anthony Hopkins** in the title role.

References: Blumenthal, Eileen, and Julie Taymore. *Julie Taymor, Playing with Fire: Theatre, Opera, Film.* New York: Harry N. Abrams, 1995; Boepple, Leanne. "Rites of Passage." *Lighting Dimensions* (March 1998): 48–53; Noh, David. "Re-Imagining Titus." *Film Journal International* 103 (February 2000): 12, 14, 16.

Ta'ziya
Iraq, Turkey

Persian passion play of the Shiite Muslims, which represents the suffering and death of the prophet's descendants; Islam's oldest and perhaps only indigenous drama. An account of a performance in the tenth century reports people with faces painted black and with disheveled hair, beating their chests and singing mournful songs for Hussein, a descendant of the Islamic prophet, who was martyred in 680. This Persian ritual play commemorates the slaughter of Hasan, Hussein, and other members of the prophet's family. Most *Ta'ziya* plays were written and performed in Persian, but a few were performed in Arabic and even Turkish.

Performances were packed full of gruesome and overdone stage effects. Dripping real blood, Hussein's gory head recited holy verses, and a warrior with no arms gripped a sword with his teeth and killed his opponent. During performances feelings ran so high that grief-stricken actors have been known to commit suicide, and spectators became so frenzied that they attacked foreigners in the streets. After World War II the government imposed some limits on performances, attempting to make them more restrained.

Actors were untrained and usually thought to be too declamatory but, because of their sincere enthusiasm, are said to have left a deep impression. Men played all female roles and all beasts, except horses, since real ones were used. Performances are now rare.

References: Landau, Jacob. *Studies in the Arab Theater and Cinema.* Philadelphia: University of Pennsylvania Press, 1958; Moreh, S. "The Arabic Theatre in Egypt in the Eighteenth and Nineteenth Centuries." *Etudes Arabes et Islamiques* 3 (1975): 109–113.

El Teatro Campesino
United States

Chicano political theater founded in 1965 by Luis Valdez, who left the **San Francisco Mime Troupe,** of which he was a member, for the fields of migrant workers in California, to help their cause when they went on strike. Valdez led workers to perform for other workers in improvised skits based on their real life experiences. Performances were meant to inspire the audience into action against their oppressive employers. *La Quinta Temporado* (The Fifth Season, 1966), was a production in which a farm contractor was satirized by worker-performers.

Chicano theater in general developed in several forms. An *acto* is a short dramatic piece. A *corrido* (ballad) is structured around songs that tell stories, and a *mito* is based on a story, but enacted more like a ritual that conveys the Chicano perspective on the world. Many of the pieces were written in "Spanglish," an often humorous mixture of Spanish and English that reflected in its language the situation of Mexican Americans. In these works Chicano theater artists attempted to find a manner of expression distinct from the dominant white culture.

In 1970 Valdez created El Centro Campesino Cultural in California as a collective on a large piece of land. Shows performed there include *Vietnam Campesino*, 1970, which likened the plight of migrant workers to that of Vietnam peasants, and *Mundo*, 1975.

Valdez was invited to write for the Mark Taper Forum in Los Angeles, which resulted in *Zoot Suit*, 1978, a celebratory play about life in the barrio that also illustrates the unfair treatment of Chicanos by the law. After *Zoot Suit* failed on Broadway in New York, Valdez returned to his roots and focused on the spiritual nature of Chicanos. Actors were no longer asked to explore the immediate political situation around them, but rather their own inner state, their spiritual and cultural development. El Teatro Campesino went a long way in replacing negative Mexican stereotypes through positive creations. In 1981 Valdez made a film version of *Zoot Suit*. Other films include *La Bamba* (1987) about the late 1950s pop idol, Ritchie Valens, and *The Cisco Kid* (1994), which he shot on location in Mexico.

References: Bigsby, C. W. E. *A Critical Introduction to Twentieth-Century American Drama*. New York: Cambridge University Press, 1985; Garza, Roberto J., ed. *Contemporary Chicano Theatre*. Notre Dame: University of Notre Dame Press, 1976; Kanolles, Nicolas, ed. *Mexican American Theatre, Then and Now*.

Houston, TX: Arte Publico, 1983; Valdez, Luis. *Actos*. Fresno, CA: Cucaracha, 1971.

Teatro del Angel
Chile, Costa Rica

Chilean theatrical troupe founded in Costa Rica in 1974 by Alejándro Sieveking, a leading playwright in **Chile** for over thirty years, and his wife, Bélgica Castro, a famous Chilean actress. The two were on tour in South and Central America when they learned that it was unadvisable for them to return to Chile, where their troupe was originally based, due to the political situation. Thus, they went into voluntary exile in Costa Rica, along with fellow actors Dionisio Echeverría and Lucho Barahona. During the initial period with the troupe in Costa Rica they performed in high schools and at universities until, in 1976, they obtained their own theater, subsidized in part by the Costa Rican Ministerio de Cultura (Ministry of Culture). Sieveking directed all the plays presented at the Teatro del Angel and acted in most as well.

In 1984 Seiveking and Castro returned to Santiago, Chile, and immediately began filming a television series that he wrote and she acted in entitled *Amigos del Alma* (Friends of the Spirit). Both are still active in Chilean theater and television.

References: Thomas, Charles Philip. "Chilean Theater in Exile: The Teatro del Angel in Costa Rica 1974–1984." *Latin American Theatre Review* 19, 2 (Spring 1986): 97–101.

Teatro Gaucho
Argentina, Uruguay

Theatrical form of the late nineteenth century that featured the popular **gaucho** character, the fiercely independent cowboy of South America. These dramas were most often melodramatic, full of extreme pathos and violent action. They had a romantic emotional appeal to the provincial audiences in Argentina and Uruguay, who strongly identified with these plays and recognized themselves in the language, attitudes and actions of the characters. So much was this true that in 1886 during a production of *Juan Moreira* a peasant girl jumped onto the stage to aid an actress fighting with the gaucho character, insisting she had conceived his child.

One of the first appearances of the gaucho character on the stage was in the Latin American Sainete (short farces), El Detalle de la Acción Maipú (Battle of Maipú Detail), 1818, of which the author is unknown. In 1884 José J. Podestà, who began as a circus clown and became an impresario, acted out one of the famous gaucho legends from the novel Juan Moreira for a country audience. This is considered to be the first indigenous source of Western-style drama in South America. Because Podestà was first a circus performer, he adapted his style of theater to be performed in a circus arena, with full capabilities for huge music and dance displays, galloping horses, and elaborate fight scenes with no amount of stage blood spared. All of these elements came to characterize Teatro Gaucho.

One of the most famous gaucho plays is by Orosmán Moratoria (1859–1898), entitled Juan Soldão(1894). The last gaucho piece of merit was Calandria, 1896, by Martiniano Leguizamón (1858–1935). Once gaucho dramas were performed in legitimate theaters and not the circus ring, the possibilities of staging outrageous fights and spectacle associated with gaucho dramas lessened, as did its appeal with its popular audience.

Some elements of Teatro Gaucho are utilized by **Latin American liberation theater,** since it shares a common goal, that of demanding justice and freedom from the oppression of colonization.

> **References:** Versènyi, Adam. Theatre in Latin America: Religion, Politics, and Culture from Cortés to the 1980's. New York: Cambridge University Press, 1993; Weiss, Judith A. Latin American Popular Theatre: The First Five Centuries. Albuquerque: University of New Mexico Press, 1993.

Temple, Shirley (1928–)
United States

Child film actress who danced and sang her way deep into the heart of the American people. Temple began her major film career with Baby Take a Bow in 1934, and within that same year she soared to fame as America's beloved child star. Her sunny disposition, interrupted only by exaggerated pouts or burst of precocity, was the perfect antidote for the Depression years of the 1930s. Her darling figure, bouncing curls, and sparkling personality made her a hit in such movies as Curly Top, 1935, Poor Little Rich Girl, 1936,

Heidi, 1937, Little Miss Broadway, 1938 and The Little Princess, 1939.

In order to get her to act all of the necessary emotions, directors sometimes resorted to dirty tricks with the child actress, such as telling her that her pet turtle had died to get her to cry. She performed with many top African American dancer-performers during a time when commingling of the races on film usually only occurred in a master-servant role. True, these black partners were often servants, but she and they shared a unique camaraderie and warmth that came through in their dances. Her role as an ambassador is one she continued into her adult life as U.S. ambassador to Ghana, 1974–1976, and later to Czechoslovakia.

She tried to continue her career past adolescence in the 1940s, but she lost her box office appeal. In 1998 she was recipient of the Kennedy Honors, through the Kennedy Center in Washington, D.C., for her lifetime achievement in the performing arts.

> **References:** Hammontree, Patsy. Shirley Temple Black: A Bio Bibliography. Westport, CT: Greenwood, 1998; Windeler, Robert. The Films of Shirley Temple. Secaucus, NJ: Citadel, 1978.

Teng-ying Xi
See Pi-ying Xi

Terence (185–160 B.C.)
Italy

Publius Terentius Afer, a comic playwright of ancient Rome. Originally from Africa, Terence arrived in Rome a slave but was later freed; he began writing at eighteen years of age. Terence was more serious and complex than **Plautus,** the other comic playwright of ancient Rome whose works survive, who died about the time Terence was born. A refined and morally eminent playwright, Terence believed comedy should be instructive to the audience. The Roman audiences of his day were made up of all classes of people and could be easily coaxed away by a more sensational performance occurring simultaneously at a festival at which he might have been performing. It was the custom of the time to use the prologue of a play to explain the plot but instead Terence used his prologues to plead with his audience to give him a fair hearing and not believe any negative criticism they might have heard.

Six plays by Terence survive, *The Woman from Andros*, 166, *The Mother-in-Law*, 166 and 165, *The Self-Torturer*, 163, *The Eunuch*, 161, *Phormio*, 161, and *The Brothers*, 160. Terence died in Greece, where he had gone in search of more original material for his plays.

See also Roman Comedy

References: Arnott, Peter D. *The Ancient Greek and Roman Theatre*. New York: Random House, 1971; Bieber, Margarete. *The History of the Greek and Roman Theater*. Princeton, NJ: Princeton University Press, 1961; Norwood, Gilbert. *The Art of Terence*. Oxford: B. Blackwell, 1923; Norwood, Gilbert. *Plautus and Terence*. New York: Cooper Square, 1963; Taylor, David. *Acting and the Stage*. Boston: George Allen & Unwin, 1978.

Terrukutta
India

Folk opera performed in the streets in Southeast India. An all-male cast enacts scenes from the **Mahabharata,** the great Hindu epic tale, mostly in song, with minimal speaking, and in great realistic detail. A performance opens with an invocation to **Ganesha,** the elephant-headed Hindu god. An actor wearing an elephant mask performs a dance to a song worshipping Ganesha. Other gods are praised and invoked through songs by the chorus. Then **Kattiakaran,** the stage manager and narrator, introduces himself and the drama from behind a curtain held up by two people. He is dressed lavishly in a flowing tunic and a gold headpiece. When characters enter, they introduce themselves in the third person in song and then they shift to prose. The **Komali,** a buffoon or clown character, always makes an unusually impressive entrance by jumping onto the stage from a tree or rolling down a stack of hay. He has much freedom in his performance style, as he may yell at the audience to be attentive and laugh at the folly of the king.

The acting style sometimes becomes so realistic during battle scenes that actors have committed physical violence. An example of graphic portrayal of violence is when Draupadi, the wife of the five Pandava brothers in the *Mahabharata*, is insulted by their enemy. She vows not to let her hair

fall loose again until she can dip it in the blood of her foe. The eldest Pandava smashes the thigh of a clay effigy of their enemy, which is filled with blood, and blood squirts forth.

The stage for performances is 14 feet square and at street level, with the audience sitting on three sides. Musicians sit along the back of the square. Costumes are unrealistically designed to exaggerate and embellish the human form. Actors wear high headpieces of gold with many small pieces of mirror attached to them and large shoulder decorations like three-dimensional curly wings. Every character wears ankle bells for dancing. The makeup involves symbolic coloring to signify character types. Musical accompaniment is performed by small flute, drums, and cymbals; more recently a harmonium has been added.

References: Brandon, James R. *Brandon's Guide to Theatre in Asia*. Honolulu: University Press of Hawaii, 1976; Gargi, Balawanta. *Folk Theater of India*. Seattle: University of Washington Press, 1966.

Terry, Ellen (1844–1928)
England

English actress from an acting family, who began acting as a child at the age of eight in Charles Kean's production of **Shakespeare**'s *Winter's Tale*. In 1861 she joined the Haymarket Company. In 1878 **Henry Irving** cast Terry as Ophelia in his production of *Hamlet*, and he kept on casting her in the leading female roles opposite himself in his shows until 1896. As an actress she stressed imagination, industry, and intelligence, but, she professed, the greatest of the three was imagination. In 1903 she managed the Imperial Theatre in Westminster, where she worked with her son, the stage designer **Gordon Craig**. She performed in **George Bernard Shaw**'s *Captain Brassbound's Conversion*, (1906) in a role created especially for her by Shaw. These two maintained a flirtatious epistolary relationship for many years. Terry last performed in 1925 and was also that year honored with the title of Dame Ellen Terry.

References: Auerbach, Nina. *Ellen Terry, Player in Her Time*. New York: W. W. Norton, 1987; Manvell, Roger. *Ellen Terry*. New York: Putnam, 1968; Terry, Ellen. *The Story of My Life*. New York: Schocken, 1982.

Tewa Ritual Performance
United States

The Tewa are Pueblo Indians who speak the Tewa language and reside in many villages of the Rio Grande region in New Mexico. Their ritual performances include dance, song, drumming, elaborate costuming, and dramatic skits. Performances are seasonal, such as the winter prayers for successful hunting and summer performances for fertile crops. Many aspects of these performances are held in great secrecy, since Spanish missionaries of the seventeenth century disapproved of these rituals and considered them to be devil worship. Even though many ritual performances are overtly Roman Catholic celebrations for saints or Christian holidays, there lies beneath the obvious content an ancient adherence to the Tewa's age-old connections to the earth and spirit worlds, connections they did not relinquish when they were converted to Christianity.

Performances take place in a variety of places, such as a village plaza or a kiva, a partially underground ceremonial chamber. Tewa clowns and comic characters are an important and popular element of these performances. Most commonly humor is found in parody that mock foreigners, local happenings, and people. The most obvious dramatic impersonation takes place in these humorous episodes, which are interludes interspersed throughout the more serious dance rituals. These parodies can be performed by a large group, such as the Comanche Dance, in which many Tewa dress in exaggerated and gaudy Comanche traditional dress and make fun of these Southern Plains Indians. One account of this dance says that it commemorates a time when the Tewa beat the Comanche in a battle.

Some of these parodies are performed as skits by several clowns or by just one solo performer, who is sometimes a member of a ceremonial clown society. While dressed in a loincloth with black and white paint on their bodies, they imitate Catholic priests and mock the rituals they perform. An easy target for mockery are the tourists with their tacky clothes; dressed in imitations of these clothes, performers mimic their insatiable desire to take pictures.

Mockery performs a vital service in a changing world for the Tewa people. It reasserts again

again the supremacy of the Tewa way as being the right way.

References: Sweet, Jill. "The Beauty, Humor, and Power of Tewa Pueblo Dance." In *Native American Dance: Ceremonies and Social Traditions*, ed. Charlotte Heth, 83–103. Washington, DC: Starwood, 1992.

Thailand

A strong monarchy has led the kingdom of Thailand, formerly Siam, through centuries of cultural prosperity. In the fourteenth century the Thai army invaded Angkor in Cambodia and captured Cambodian court musicians and dancers. Exchanges of performing traditions have occurred between Thailand and many of its neighbors, including Burma, Laos, China, and Malaysia. During the seventeenth and eighteenth centuries, Thailand was the only Southeast Asian country to avoid European colonization. Thailand is still led in part by a well-loved monarch, who governs with a parliament and prime minister. Though Hinduism has greatly influenced the Thai arts, the country is almost entirely Buddhist (see **Buddhism**), with a very small Muslim minority mainly in the south.

The oldest known form of Thai dance-drama is **Lakon Jatri,** performed only by men accomplished at singing, acting, pantomiming, and delivering dialogue. A similar form, **Manora** is performed in the northern part of Malaysia and southern Thailand. Both forms use the *Manora* story, from the **Jataka,** a collection of stories about the former incarnations of Gautama **Buddha**, enacting the love affair of the mythical bird princess Manora. **Lakon Nok,** popular drama from the south, evolved from *Lakon Jatri*. The action in *Lakon Nok* became much faster paced than in *Lakon Jatri*, and the long dance sequences were taken out. Extremely popular in the 1920s and 1930s, **Likay** is a popular opera performed in urban areas by unemployed court performers.

Inspired by original Cambodian forms, **Lakon Nai** is an all-female classical dance-drama adapted from the Cambodian court dances in the fourteenth century. **Khon** is a masked dance-drama by men in the Thai courts from the fourteenth century. Two narrators perform all of the narration, singing, and dialogue while other performers pantomime the action. The story often dramatized in these two forms is the **Ramukien,** the Thai version of the great Hindu epic, the **Ramayana. Pin Peat** (or *Pi Phat*) is the name of the traditional orchestra that accompanies live performances of dance and drama in Thailand. It is made up of an oboe, a set of tuned bronze bowls, a xylophone, drums, and cymbals.

Puppet theater and shadow play have enjoyed a rich history in Thailand alongside the human theater. Believed to be from the thirteenth century, **Nang Yai** is a form of shadow play using large flat carved shadow figures reaching 5 feet in height. Two narrators perform the dialogue, and other performers manipulate the figures from behind the screen so that only the shadows are visible to the audience. **Nang Ram** (or **Nang Rabam**) is a dance version of *Nang Yai*. A tradition of shadow play from the south is known as **Nang Talung,** in which small rawhide puppets with articulated arms are manipulated by a **Nai Nang,** a puppet master. **Hun Krabok** is a form of rod puppet theater from the twentieth century featuring puppets with carved wooden heads and cloth clothing.

References: Bachfield, August. "Theatre in Siam." *Erdball* 2 (1928): 335–377; Brandon, James. "Theatre in Thailand." In *The Performing Arts in Asia,* ed. James R. Brandon. Paris: UNESCO, 1971; Sariman, Chua. "Traditional Dance Drama in Thailand." In *Traditional Drama and Music of Southeast Asia,* ed. Mohd. Taib Osman, 165–171. Kuala Lumpur: Dewan Bahasa Dan Pustaka Kementerian Pelajaran Malaysia, 1974; Ginsburg, Henry D. "The Manohra Dance-Drama: An Introduction." *Journal of the Siam Society* 60 (1972): 169–181; Montri, Tramote. "Thai Puppeet Show." *Silpakorn* 4, 2 (1960): 48–54; Redwood, John Elkert. "The Siamese Classical Theatre." *Educational Theatre Journal* 5 (1952): 100–105; Rutnin, Mattani, ed. *The Siamese Theatre: Collections of Reprints from Journals of Siam Society.* Bangkok: Siam Society, 1975; Yupho, Dhanit. *Classical Siamese Theatre.* Trans. P. S. Sastri. Bangkok: Hatha Dhip, 1952; Yupho, Dhanit. *The Khon and Lakon.* Bangkok: Department of Fine Arts, 1963; Yupho, Dhanit. *Khon Masks.* Thai Culture, New Series. Bangkok: Fine Arts Department, 1968.

Théâtre du Soleil

See Mnouchkine, Ariane

Theodora
Constantinople

Famous **mime** performer of the sixth century A.D., first mistress and then wife of Byzantine emperor Justinian. As a performer she was known for her sharp wit and shamelessness.

References: Bieber, Margarete. *The History of the Greek and Roman Theater.* Princeton, NJ: Princeton University Press, 1961; Chinoy, Helen Krich, and Toby Cole. *Actors on Acting.* New York: Crown, 1970; Taylor, David. *Acting and the Stage.* Boston: George Allen & Unwin, 1978.

Theologicals
India

Popular genre of movies in India from the 1950s onward in which Hindu deities are portrayed by actors. These movies usually portray scenes from the **Ramayana** and the **Mahabharata,** both Hindu epic tales.

See also Hindi Movies
References: Chakravarty, Sumita. *National Identity in Indian Popular Cinema.* Austin: University of Texas Press, 1993.

Therukoothu
See Terrukutta

Thespis (sixth century B.C.)
Greece

Traditionally the first poet to create **Greek tragedy** and the first actor in Greek theater; in the middle of the sixth century he distinguished himself from the **Greek chorus,** portraying a god or hero and entering into dramatic confrontation with the chorus. When Thespis first brought his invention of theater into Athens in 560, his work was labeled dangerous deceptions by the Athenian lawgiver Solon. In 534, as an old man, Thespis, was the first to win the dramatic contest for tragedy at the Athenian festival in honor of Dionysus called the **City Dionysia.** Use of masks helped him portray a variety of different characters in one play.

References: Bieber, Margarete. *The History of the Greek and Roman Theater.* Princeton, NJ: Princeton University Press, 1961; Chinoy, Helen Krich, and Toby Cole. *Actors on Acting.* New York: Crown, 1970; Else,

G. F. *The Origin and Early Form of Greek Tragedy.* Cambridge, MA: Harvard University Press, 1965; Ley, Graham. *A Short Introduction to the Ancient Greek Theater.* Chicago: University of Chicago Press, 1991; O'-Connor, John Bartholomew. *Chapters in the History of Actors and Acting in Ancient Greece.* Chicago: University of Chicago Press, 1908.

Thimig, Helene (1889–1974)
Austria, Germany, United States

Austrian actress who came from a family of actors. She began training in Berlin and began acting at the Deutsches Theatre (German Theater) in 1919 under **Max Reinhardt**, where she played many leading roles. She fled Germany when the Nazis took control in 1933 and emigrated to Hollywood. She married Reinhardt in 1938 and lived with him in Hollywood until his death in 1943. She returned to Vienna to resume acting and in 1948 became the director of the Max Reinhardt Acting School in Vienna.

> **References:** Carter, Huntly. *The Theatre of Max Reinhardt.* New York: B. Blom, 1964; Chinoy, Helen Krich, and Toby Cole. *Actors on Acting.* New York: Crown, 1970.

Thoai Kich
Vietnam

Modern Vietnamese drama (also *Kich Noi*). These modern Western style performances originated from the kind of drama brought by the French during colonial times, beginning at the end of the nineteenth century. During the colonial period, performances of these plays were allowed when the plays were complimentary to France and restricted if any anti-French sentiments were espoused. The scripts are adaptations of Western plays or original Vietnamese stories. In order to pass government censorship under the Communist regime the stories usually do not have a serious theme. Vietnamese audiences tend to find these performances tiresome because the actors just sit around and talk. This form tends to appeal only to educated audiences. It is still performed today in Saigon and a few other large cities. Presenters often mix a play with entertainment that has more popular appeal such as music, dancing or even a jazz band to attract an audience.

> **References:** Brandon, James R. *Brandon's Guide to Theatre in Asia.* Honolulu: University Press of Hawaii, 1976.

Tholu Bommalata
India

Shadow puppet theater from Andhra Pradesh dating back to the third century B.C. that enjoyed a history of consistent royal patronage.

> **References:** Awasthi, Suresh. "Shadow Plays of India and Their Affinities with the Shadow Plays of Southeast Asia." In *Traditional Drama and Music of Southeast Asia*, ed. Mohd. Taib Osman, 112–119. Kuala Lumpur: Dewan Bahasa Dan Pustaka Kementerian Pelajaran Malaysia, 1974; Brandon, James R. *Brandon's Guide to Theatre in Asia.* Honolulu: University Press of Hawaii, 1976.

Tholu Pava Koothu
India

Shadow puppet play from Kerala State in south India. From behind a backlit white muslin screen many puppeteers manipulate rawhide shadow puppets, dramatizing the great Hindu epic tale, the **Ramayana.** Only the shadow images of the puppets are visible to the audience. It takes forty-one days to present the cycle, but it can be abridged to as few as seven days.

A performance begins with an invocation to **Ganesha,** the elephant-headed Hindu god. Then two Brahman puppets come on the screen to give a synopsis of the play to be presented for the evening. Throughout the dramatization of the story the two Brahman puppets reappear to comment on the action. A blessing song ends a performance each night. The performance style is similar to the Javanese **Wayang Kulit,** shadow puppet theater. However, the *Wayang Kulit* has only one puppeteer, and *Tholu Pava Koothu* has many.

The screen is 15 feet long, with a row of lights all along the bottom of the screen on the inside away from the audience. The puppets are carved from one piece of rawhide in either a sitting or a standing pose. Puppets have one articulated arm that can be manipulated. Perforated holes in the rawhide delineate ornamentation on costumes, head dresses, and jewelry. Puppets are painted with heavy paint to be so opaque that a strong black shadow appears on the screen. One wooden rod is sewn along the center of the puppet to support it, and another wooden rod controls the articulated arm. The average number of puppets used in a performance is forty-two.

The Tamil version of the *Ramayana*, the *Kamba Ramayana* of the eleventh century, is used for performances. It is supplemented by poetic prose pieces created by the puppeteers themselves, also in Tamil. Improvised dialogue can be in the local language, Malayalam.

Tholo Pava Koothu is still a living tradition today in Kerala State.

References: Awasthi, Suresh. "Shadow Plays of India and Their Affinities with the Shadow Plays of Southeast Asia." In *Traditional Drama and Music of Southeast Asia*, ed. Mohd. Taib Osman, 112–119. Kuala Lumpur: Dewan Bahasa Dan Pustaka Kementerian Pelajaran Malaysia, 1974; Brandon, James R. *Brandon's Guide to Theatre in Asia*. Honolulu: University Press of Hawaii, 1976.

Thompson, Emma (1959–)
England

English actress, born in London of a longtime theater family, who began acting as a child. After studying at Cambridge, she worked as a stand-up comic, for television, and in live theater on the West End. A radiant and intelligent actress, she exudes ease and confidence as a performer. She began collaborating with Kenneth Branagh, to whom she was married for many years, and starred opposite him in many Shakespearean productions on stage and film such as *Henry V*, 1989, and *Much Ado About Nothing*, 1993. Her other films include *Dead Again*, 1991, *Howards End*, 1992, for which she won an Academy Award for Best Actress, *In the Name of the Father*, 1993 and *Sense and Sensibility*, 1996. In 1998 Thompson costarred in the film *Winter Guest* with her mother, Phyllida Law. In 1998 Thompson starred as the wife of the president of the **United States** in the movie *Primary Colors* opposite John Travolta.

References: Branagh, Kenneth. *Beginning*. New York: Norton, 1990; Fuller, Graham. "Cautionary Tale–Sense and Sensibility." *Sight and Sound* 6, 3 (1996): 20–25; Hunter, Stephen. "Movies: *The Winter Guest: Fade to Gray*." *Washington Post* (16 January 1998): B6; Rynning, Ronald. "All the President's Women: Ronald Rynning Talks to the Stars of *Primary Colors* and Discovers It's a Red, White and Blue Movie." *Film Review* (October 1998): 40–45.

Kenneth Branagh and Emma Thompson in the film Much Ado about Nothing *(1993). (Kobol Collection/Coote, Clive/Sam Goldwyn/Renaissance Films/BBC)*

Thymele

Greece

The altar on an ancient Greek stage used for sacrificial offerings.

> **References:** Bieber, Margarete. *The History of the Greek and Roman Theater.* Princeton, NJ: Princeton University Press, 1961; Capps, Edward. "The Stage in the Greek Theatre According to the Extant Dramas." Ph.D. diss., Yale University, 1891.

Tomabo

Madagascar

A children's conversation game in Madagascar. By imitating adults, children learn a more sophisticated manner of speaking. They imitate the way adults speak, drawing out the subtlest aspects of speech, adult customs, and social mores. The object of this performance game is to learn the rules for adult polite conversation and thus to be gradually initiated into society. Adults who watch and listen often chuckle and are amused by the children behaving and speaking in a somewhat stilted manner. *Tomabo* is simultaneously amusement and training for children.

> **References:** Haring, Lee. *Verbal Arts in Madagascar: Performance in Historical Perspective.* Philadelphia: University of Pennsylvania Press, 1992; Kent, Raymond. *From Madagascar to the Malagasy Republic.* New York: Praeger, 1962; Ruud, Jorgen. *Taboo: A Study of Malagasy Customs and Beliefs.* New York: Humanities, 1960.

Tomo

Japan

Walk-on role in **Noh,** masked dance-drama of medieval Japan.

> **References:** Ernst, Earle. *The Kabuki Theatre.* New York: Oxford University Press, 1956. Reprint, Honolulu: University Press of Hawaii, 1974; Inoura, Yoshinobu, and Toshio Kawatake. *The Traditional Theater of Japan.* New York: Weatherhill in collaboration with Japan Foundation, 1981.

Tou

China

Master puppeteer in **Fu Tai Hsi.**

Township Musicals

See Kente, Gibson

Tragic Acting in Ancient Greece

Greece

When in the middle of the sixth century B.C. **Thespis,** costumed as a god or hero character, stepped away from the chorus to answer a question posed by its members, he simultaneously created the first tragedy and the first actor. The importance of the actor, as opposed to the chorus, steadily increased; the playwright **Aeschylus** introduced a second actor, and **Sophocles** introduced a third actor. When Aeschylus added a second actor, he also distinguished the profession of actor from the poet. Before the introduction of the second actor, the dramatist himself acted in his own work. In 449 B.C. a contest for best actor was introduced at the greatest of the Athenian festivals at which drama was performed, the **City Dionysia.** Throughout the fourth century B.C. the quality of acting increased, and the leading actors, such as **Polus,** became famous individuals esteemed by the state, just as the great tragic playwrights had been in the fifth century B.C. However, ordinary actors were still looked down upon and thought to be immoral.

On the basis of terracotta statuettes of actors from the classical period, it is assumed that actors of the time used free and expressive gestures and movements of the whole body. Because of the large size of the theaters, all movement must have been strong and simple for them to have communicated to the entire audience. The physical demands on actors were extreme, sometimes calling upon them to dance ecstatically or rave in madness, as in the *Bacchae* by **Euripides.** Actors not only had to be masterful speakers, but they also had to be able to declaim and sing to music. By the way the words are written, it is supposed that lines must have been delivered in a highly stylized grand manner, one reason the tragedies were so easily parodied by **Greek comedy.** Enunciation and clarity of voice were more important qualities than volume, since the Greek theaters had excellent acoustics. The spoken word could easily be heard even in the farthest rows of seating. All actors were male, but they were called upon to portray female characters as well as male.

The masks worn by actors represented the outstanding features of the personality of a given character. By donning the mask, an actor could submerge his personality and become the character he wished to portray. There are paintings from the classical period that feature an actor studying his mask to prepare himself for portraying a role.

Until the fourth century B.C., the Athenian magistrate in charge of the City Dionysia drew lots to decide which of the three selected competing poets would get which of the three leading actors to perform the *protagonist*, or leading role, in their dramas. Since each poet presented three tragedies and one **satyr play** on a single day, actors needed to have incredible stamina to be able to perform from dawn to dusk. After the fourth century B.C. each leading actor performed the lead role in one drama of each poet.

The state furnished and paid for three actors for each poet; thus, all but the lead actor had to play many parts in one drama. The second actor was called the *deuteragonist*, and the third actor, the *tritagonist*. If it was logistically impossible to cover all the parts with three actors, a fourth actor could be added at the expense of the **choregos,** a wealthy citizen who sponsored a drama. These were usually nonspeaking roles, such as servants, attendants, soldiers, or even children. When playing more than one role, the second and third actors not only had to change their masks and costumes but also their style of moving and voice to suit each role.

The great actors of the fourth century began to alter the dramatic literature from the fifth century (namely the works by Aeschylus, Sophocles, and Euripides, which continued to be performed) to create more dramatic role for themselves to suit their specific talents. Soon after this practice started, official copies of the classical tragedy scripts were deposited in the state archives. Any altering of scripts from their original form was outlawed and punishable by heavy penalties and fines

See also Greek Chorus

References: Bieber, Margarete. *The History of the Greek and Roman Theater.* Princeton, NJ: Princeton University Press, 1961; Chinoy, Helen Krich, and Toby Cole. *Actors on Acting.* New York: Crown, 1970; Hunninger, B. "Acoustics and Acting in the Theater of Dionysus Eleuthereus." *Mededelingen der Nederlandse Akademie van Wetenschappen* 9 (1956); O'Connor, John Bartholomew. *Chapters in the History of Actors and Acting in Ancient Greece.* Chicago: University of Chicago Press, 1908; Shister, Famic Lorine. "The Portrayal of Emotion in Tragedy." *American Journal of Philology* 66 (1945): 377–397; Walton, Michael. *Living Greek Theatre: A Handbook of Classical Performance and Modern Production.* New York: Greenwood, 1987.

Transylvania

See Romania

Las Tres Caídas de Jesucristo
Mexico

Passion play; literally, *Jesus Christ's Three Falls,* still presented on Holy Thursday (the Thursday of Holy Week) in many Mexican villages. Unlike other folk dramas, in which there is a scenario improvised upon by actors, this drama is fully scripted; it dramatizes the sufferings of Jesus between the Last Supper on Holy Thursday and his death on Good Friday, and then, three days after the initial performance, the resurrection of Christ. The first part of the play is generally performed at various sites around the village, and the resurrection is often presented in a church, using a suspended two-dimensional image of Christ among the clouds. In some villages the role of Jesus Christ is played by a priest, who gives sermons to the audience at key points in the story, rendering the performance quite didactic.

As it is performed in Ixtapalapa, Mexico, the actor portraying Jesus, a man from the community, is required to go into seclusion thirty days before the show to spiritually purify himself in preparation for the role. The actors who portray the two thieves who were crucified on either side of Jesus each go into seclusion for fifteen days, again in order to achieve the purified state necessary to portray these roles. This tradition of actors going into seclusion is reminiscent of the ritual purification of the actor portraying the role of **Quetzalcóatl** in the annual Aztec festival for Quetzalcóatl.

References: Usigli, Rodolfo. *Mexico in the Theater.* Trans. Wilder P. Scott. University, MS: Romance Monographs, 1976; Versènyi, Adam. *Theatre in Latin America: Religion, Politics, and Culture from Cortés to the 1980's.* New York: Cambridge University Press, 1993.

Trinidad Carnival

In grand style, this pre-Lenten annual festival has been the pinnacle of cultural expression in Trinidad for 200 years. Predominantly this event is a parade of original costumes worn by masked revelers who perform songs, dances, and dramatics of various spectacular forms. The French brought the carnival to Trinidad in the 1780s, and the British, who took control in 1802, continued the tradition until the slaves were freed in 1834. At that point the blacks took over this event and transformed it into a dynamic expression of their newfound freedom. The government at many points feared the rowdiness and volatile social criticism enacted in the dramatic skits, but attempts to suppress this activity have led to violence but never complete success. Among the first black carnival performances were the *Canboulay*, which dramatized horrific scenes from the days of slavery. Creatures from folktales and myths also played a role, depicted in costume-like sculptures that enacted their stories.

In the twentieth century the carnival grew in respectability and was tolerated more readily by the government. Calypsonians, local professional singers, performed music nightly and usually ended their programs with a dramatic skit centered on some local event. Music played an important role in the carnivals, both as accompaniment for dramatic enactments and as entertainment in its own right. Gourd rattles, bamboo bands, and steel bands made from discarded petrol drums were a creative response to a need for an indigenous musical expression that would be accessible and affordable.

References: Banham, Martin. *African Theatre Today*. London: Pitman, 1976; Gibbons, Rawle A. "Traditional Enactments of Trinidad—Towards a Third Theatre." Master's thesis, University of the West Indies, 1979; Hill, Errol. *The Jamaican Stage: 1655–1900*. Amherst: University of Massachusetts Press, 1992.

Trionfi

Scandinavia, Denmark, Sweden, Norway

Royal processions, popular during the sixteenth and seventeenth century in Scandinavia, that evolved during the Italian Renaissance. In coronation processions the ascending royalty would masquerade as gods of antiquity or historical heroes.

Amazed spectators lined the streets as the richly costumed and masked royalty passed, joined by elaborate pageant wagons hosting frozen scenes of costumed actors portraying some fantastical story, legend, historical event, or flight of the imagination. Actors in an allegorical pose depicting some vice or virtue were also popular on these pageant wagons. The events were not all solemn. One monarch humorously impersonated a pope and another appeared in an opulent woman's gown.

See also Royalty and World Leaders as Actors
References: Marker, Frederick. *A History of Scandinavian Theatre*. Cambridge: Cambridge University Press, 1996.

Trios

Ghana, Togo

Concert parties of coastal Ghana and, its neighbor, Togo. These touring theatrical troupes, made up of performers referred to as "Comedians," are the only professional theaters in the region. They perform improvised comic skits centered on immediate concerns of their audiences. Believed to have begun in 1918, concert parties grew popular with the creation of the Bob Johnson company in the 1930s. The local method of performing known as *Kasandwon*, a combination of speech and song, was utilized to create plays out of ordinary life stories. Trios flourished in the 1960s and 1970s, and many companies toured successfully. Each had a large repertory of many plays that, though improvised, remained loosely constant.

References: Antubam, Kofi. "Arts of Ghana." *United Asia* 9, 1 (1957): 61–70.; Banham, Martin. *African Theatre Today*. London: Pitman, 1976; McHardy, Cecile. "The Performing Arts in Ghana." *Africa Forum* 1, 1 (Summer 1965): 113–117.

Tritagonist

See Tragic Acting in Ancient Greece

Trott

Cambodia

Folk dance-drama, which enacts a deer hunt, that may have descended from prehistoric times. *Trott* has ritual elements. It was believed that animistic spirits would bring good fortune to the hunters if *Trott* was performed before a hunt. Performers wearing masks play such characters as a hunter, a deer, a girl, and a demon. Some performers sit outside the performance area chanting and drumming.

> References: Brandon, James. *Theatre in Southeast Asia.* Cambridge, MA: Harvard University Press, 1974; Meyer, Charles. "Cambodian Dances." *Nokor Khmer* 3 (1970): 2–27.

Tsure
Japan

Attendant character to either of the two leads, **Shite,** first lead, or **Waki,** second lead, in **Noh,** masked dance-drama of medieval Japan. The *Tsure* wears a mask and attends to the needs, such as costume adjustment or supplying a specific property, of the lead characters.

> References: Inoura, Yoshinobu, and Toshio Kawatake. *The Traditional Theater of Japan.* New York: Weatherhill in collaboration with Japan Foundation, 1981; Scott, A. C. *The Theatre in Asia.* New York: Macmillan, 1972.

Tukang Karut
Malaysia

Leader in **Dikir Barat,** choral chanting of Koranic verses.

> References: Brandon, James. *Theatre in Southeast Asia.* Cambridge, MA: Harvard University Press, 1974.

Tunisia

There is minimal theatrical activity in largely Muslim Tunisia, since the tenets of Islam do not allow dramatic representation. Turkish-style **Karagoz,** a form of shadow puppet theater, was performed with much lewdness and many indecent jokes to satisfy the culturally unsophisticated workers. Plays were about local interests, acted out by puppeteers using primitive rawhide puppets that were unicolored and hardly ever translucent.

A few scant Tunisian acting groups active in the nineteenth and twentieth centuries had and continue to have a difficult time attracting audiences. Some Egyptian acting troupes tour through Tunisia. An Egyptian theater practitioner, Zaki Tulaimat, came to Tunisia, assembled a troupe from native actors, and produced an Arabic version of *The Merchant of Venice* in 1954, but his involvement did not change the situation significantly. Progress was made in the 1940s and 1950s predominantly through the exceptional work of director Munsef Sweisi and the experiments of the New Theater Group.

Young filmmakers who have received European training have injected a new energy into the film industry. In recent years many quality films that explore pertinent social issues are being made by such filmmakers as Ridha Behi, Nasir Katari, Mahmud ibn Mahmud, and Lotfi Essid.

> References: Landau, Jacob. *Studies in the Arab Theater and Cinema.* Philadelphia: University of Pennsylvania Press, 1958; Moreh, S. "The Arabic Theatre in Egypt in the Eighteenth and Nineteenth Centuries." *Etudes Arabes et Islamiques* 3 (1975): 109–113; Mostyn, Trevor, and Albert Hourani, eds. *The Cambridge Encyclopedia of the Middle East and North Africa.* New York: Cambridge University Press, 1988.

Tuong Tao
Vietnam

Popular form of Chinese-style opera (see **Peking Opera**). This form was very popular in the early 1920s. *Tuong Tao* evolved from **Hat Boi,** classical Vietnamese opera, and differs in that it got rid of the stiff conventionalized acting style and the loud Chinese musical instruments. It used the ornate costumes and the style of makeup from *Hat Boi,* and added elaborate scenery. The language was changed to be more accessible to the lower class and the tunes were popularized. In the 1930s this form was absorbed into *Cai Luong,* and performances are now difficult to find.

> References: Brandon, James. *Theatre in Southeast Asia.* Cambridge, MA: Harvard University Press, 1974.

Turkey

The land that now constitutes Turkey was conquered by a surprising number of empires, including the Persian empire in the sixth century B.C., the Roman empire by the first century A.D., the Byzantine empire in the seventh century, and the Ottoman empire in the fourteenth century;

Turkey finally became an independent republic in 1923. Because Turkey lies between Asia and Europe, its performing arts have been influenced by both. **Karagoz,** a form of shadow puppet theater, is believed to have been influenced by **Pi-ying Xi,** Chinese shadow puppet theater. **Orta Oyunu,** improvised comedies, is believed to be heavily influenced by the **commedia dell'arte,** Italian sixteenth- and seventeenth-century improvised comedy. **Meddah** is a very old tradition of storytelling in Turkey whose origins are not known.

In the early nineteenth century, modern drama began in Turkey, based on Western forms of theater. Native playwrights began following the European model, but they experienced serious censorship problems until the early twentieth century. In 1936 the State Conservatory for Music and Drama was founded in Turkey. During the 1940s Turkey established regional theaters, set up state theaters and operas, and supported playwrights. Following World War II, theater was encouraged by the government, and it still thrives in both state-supported and private playhouses. Perhaps the reason this Islamic nation tolerates the performing arts is because their cultural tendency toward dramatic expression was securely woven into their national character before Islam was introduced.

Turkish cinema was dominated from the mid-1920s through the mid-1940s by one former theater person turned filmmaker, Muhsin Ertegrul. Young directors, such as Lutfi Akad, who returned from film studies overseas, changed the direction of cinema in Turkey with such films as *Death of a Whore* (1949), influenced by Italian neorealism. In 1948 the government put in place a tax break for filmmakers, paving the way for productions of all types, especially melodramas, musicals, and romances.

References: al-Khozai, Mohamed. *The Development of Early Arabic Drama.* London, New York: Longman, 1984; Landau, Jacob. *Studies in the Arab Theater and Cinema.* Philadelphia: University of Pennsylvania Press, 1958; Martinovitch, Nicholas. *Turkish Theatre.* New York: Theatre Arts, 1933; Moreh, Shmuel. *Live Theatre and Dramatic Literature in the Medieval Arab World.* New York: New York University Press, 1992; Mostyn, Trevor, and Albert Hourani, eds. *The Cambridge Encyclopedia of the Middle East and North Africa.* New York: Cambridge University Press, 1988.

Turkmenistan
See Soviet Cinema; Soviet Union

Tyi Wara
Mali

Dance that glorifies agriculture performed by the Bamana (indigenous term for Bambara) and the Maninka (or Makinke) people, all living in west central Mali. Historically for these people, farming has been a necessity for survival and is viewed as the noblest profession in life. The *Tyi Wara* is traditionally described as being a half-animal, half-man supernatural being who first taught the people how to farm the land.

The structure of a performance begins with the creating of an appropriately charged atmosphere, accomplished by having the women sing and clap their hands. Once the dance begins, the male masked figure emerges from the bush leaning in a bent position on a sort of cane called a *sunsun* stick. The performer wears a headdress that resembles the horns of an antelope, with the rest of his head and body covered with strips of dried fibers and cloth. He moves slowly around the perimeter of the area, ending in front of the drummers. The female figure, performed by a male, emerges and does the same, ending also in front of the drummers. Then both circle the area together. As the clapping and drumming intensifies, both race into the center of the circle and jump in the air, imitating the leaps of the antelope. The male figure makes high-pitched screeching sounds to evoke the cries of the wild animal. Dust flying, the male makes an impressive show, as his athletic dance evokes the wild animal. The *Tyi Wara* ends his dance by jumping high into the air and landing low on the ground in a squatting position. Usually the female figure then does a shorter, less impressive version of the same sequence, with less athletic ability. Usually a short man is best at mimicking the movements of the antelope. As a rule the men who perform this dance do not practice beforehand.

Whereas *Tyi Wara* was danced in the fields to invoke the supernatural being, it has moved into the village square, with greater emphasis on entertainment. The headdresses are either vertical, usually more abstract, or horizontal, usually more

Bambara men in Mali wear antelope masks to dance to Tyi Wara, the mythological half-man, half-antelope, who is believed to bring good luck to farmers. (Charles & Josette Lenars/Corbis)

realistic, both with horns on top to represent the antelope. The rest of the costume draws upon admirable attributes of a variety of animals, such as the horn bill and the anteater. A veil hangs in front of the face of the performer. Strips of dried fibers, burlap, and cotton cloth cover the rest of the body.

Certain aspects of this performance vary from village to village, but the core of the dance remains similar. *Tyi Wara* has undergone many devel-opments through its known history. Many people are now converting to Islam, resulting in this dance becoming obsolete as an expression of their beliefs.

References: Banham, Martin. *African Theatre Today.* London: Pitman, 1976; Imperato, Pascal James. "Contemporary Adapted Dances of the Dogon." *African Arts* 5, 1 (1971): 28–33, 68–71; Warren, Lee. *The Theater of Africa: An Introduction.* Englewood Cliffs, NJ: Prentice-Hall, 1975.

U

Ukraine
See Soviet Cinema; Soviet Union

UmGubho
South Africa
Hunting dance performed by Zulu tribesmen before going on a hunt. The men would enter a cattle enclosure making prideful claims of their strength and power while imitating the action of stabbing a deer. This activity created enthusiasm for the hunt. This traditional rite has disappeared, primarily due to Western influence.

> **References:** Larlham, Peter. *Black Theater, Dance, and Ritual in South Africa.* Ann Arbor, MI: Proquest, 1985.

UmKhosi
South Africa
A royal military celebration intended to strengthen the army and the king by magical means; also a way of giving thanks to ancestors for the abundance they granted the living. This ceremony, which usually took place in January, ceased in 1879 after the British troops crushed the Zululand rebellion. The king had the dominant role, but the entire nation gathered to be actors or spectators, as many as 20,000 at the peak of the Zulu nation, from the sixteenth to the eighteenth century. The event began as the king dressed in special costume rushed into the center of a large arena. He strutted about brandishing his war shield in his left hand and his scepter in his right. The crowd cheered as the king shouted and made strong gestures. There were two choruses placed at opposite sides of the arena, the "white" regiment made up of older men and the "black" regiment made up of younger men. The two choruses performed contrasting chants and songs and danced in nearly perfect synchronization until midday. This was all designed to strengthen the king and his warriors against their enemy.

On the evening of that same day, a black bull was stolen from some nearby king. The bull was meant to represent that enemy king and was ritually killed. As the bull was brought to the ground barehanded and slaughtered, chanting and songs accompanied. This activity was intended to give strength and cruelty to the warriors.

> **References:** Larlham, Peter. *Black Theater, Dance, and Ritual in South Africa.* Ann Arbor, MI: Proquest, 1985.

United Kingdom
See England; Ireland, Scotland; Wales

United Kingdom Cinema
One of the first film artists to emerge in **England** was Cecil Hepworth (1874–1953), who entered the business in 1896. He created *Alice in Wonderland*, 1903, and *Rescued by Rover*, 1905. In these early days

films were shown at fairgrounds and other temporary locations; toward the end of the first decade of the twentieth century, movie houses became prevalent. Stage actors and acting conventions of the stage were used in many films, such as *Henry VIII*, 1911, starring Herbert Tree. Beginning in the early 1920s, Britain had a difficult time competing with films from the **United States.** Popular films of the 1920s include George Pearson's *Nothing Else Matters*, 1920, and *Reveille*, 1924, which featured England's star of the silent era, Betty Balfour (1903–1979). During this time the career of **Alfred Hitchcock**, master of the suspense drama and the thriller, started. Hitchcock directed England's first talkie, *Blackmail*, 1929.

In the 1930s Alexander Korda arrived in England from his native **Hungary** and directed *The Private Life of Henry VIII*, 1933, which brought international attention to Britain. Numerous propaganda films were made during World War II (1939–1945), such as the documentary *London Can Take It*, 1940, and the fiction films *In Which We Serve*, 1942, and *Millions Like Us*, 1943. After World War II the British government hampered the development efforts of movie producers such as Arthur Rank by excessive taxation and regulations. In addition, competition from television became an issue for British film in the 1950s. The Free Cinema movement—led by Lindsay Anderson (1923–1994), Tony Richardson (1928–1991), and Karel Reisz—began in the 1950s as a revolt against traditional British values and created films with social relevance such as *Room at the Top*, 1958, and, in 1959, a film version of the play *Look Back in Anger*, by **John Osborne**.

Funding from the United States was behind most of the huge successes of the 1960s, such as *Lawrence of Arabia*, 1962, starring **Peter O'Toole**. Talent from the United States also made its way over to England, with Stanley Kubrick directing *Dr. Strangelove* in 1964. Exceptional films of the 1970s include *The Go-Between*, 1971, Kubrick's *A Clockwork Orange*, 1971, *The Ruling Class*, 1972, *Monty Python and the Holy Grail*, 1975, *The Pink Panther Strikes Again*, 1976, and *Midnight Express*, 1978.

International attention came to Britain in the 1980s with the two successes *Chariots of Fire*, 1981, and *Gandhi*, 1982. Producer Ismail Merchant and director James Ivory have successfully created many lavish literary adaptations such as *A Room*

with *a View*, 1985. Peter Greenaway created the visually lush *Prospero's Books*, an adaptation of **Shakespeare**'s *Tempest*, in 1988, with **John Gielgud** as Prospero. Greenaway's next film, *The Cook the Thief His Wife and Her Lover*, 1989, received a controversial X rating from the Motion Picture Association of America, raising questions about the distinction between pornography and the artful treatment of nudity and violence. The film *My Left Foot*, 1989, won an Academy Award for British actor Daniel Day Lewis. Successes of the 1990s include *The Crying Game*, 1992, and *Orlando*, 1993. A bright acting talent of the late 1990s is Anna Friel, who appeared in *Mad Cows*, 1999.

See also Monty Python

References: Aldgate, Anthony. *Best of British Cinema and Society from 1930 to the Present.* New York: I. B. Tauris, 1999; Curran, James, and Vincent Porter. *British Cinema History.* Totowa, NJ: Barnes and Noble, 1983; Murphy, Robert. *The British Cinema Book.* London: BFI Publishing, 1997.

United States

Theater in the United States of America is as varied and rich in traditions as the multifaceted population of its home. The first theater to occur in the area that is now the United States was **Native American theater.** The second known example of theater in the "New World" was that performed by the Spanish in the South and Southwest, such as two comedies performed at a mission in Florida in 1567. Theater on the East Coast began with settlers from **England** who imported English theater traditions, plays, and even actors. Performances started as early as 1665. Actor Lewis Hallam (1712–1758) formed a troupe in Williamsburg, Virginia, in 1752, called the American Company, but met with resistance from the Puritans and Quakers who had moral objections with the theater. The southern gentry of the United States were more hospitable to the theater, as they lived a leisurely life and sought out entertainment.

In 1774 the war for independence put a halt to the development of the theater. Once peace and independence were won, Lewis Hallam Jr. (1740–1808) restarted the American Company. It was still common at this point to recruit actors from England for the American stage. Also in the early nineteenth century it became common for English star actors to tour the states and perform their most famous roles, with locals performing the rest of the roles. Popular native actors who began in New York are James Henry Hackett (1800–1871) and Edwin Forrest (1806–1872), who had an oratorical delivery that became the style in early America. Perhaps the most famous of the first actresses in the United States was **Charlotte Cushman. Edwin Booth** introduced a more subtle approach to acting than was then the style.

Acting has long been a family affair in the United States, the most famous example being the **Barrymore Family.** In the nineteenth century, star actors were so much the center of the theater that plays were written specifically to highlight the talent of a given actor. Leading actors of the nineteenth and early twentieth centuries include Fanny Davenport (1850–1989), Adelaide Neilson (1846–1880), Otis Skinner (1858–1942), and Steele Mackaye (1844–1894).

Popular theater was largely expressed through **minstrel**s and later **vaudeville. Yiddish Theater** got an early start in America, as Jews emigrated from Europe. Prior to 1917, African American actors had only found acceptance in minstrels and musical comedies; in 1917, however, *Three Plays for a Negro Theatre*, by Ridgely Torrence (1875–1950), allowed African American actors to perform in a more realistic and dignified portrayal of themselves.

Before World War I (1914–1918), many small experimental theater groups started around the country, taking inspiration from the same trend in Europe. In 1919 the Theatre Guild was an art theater with an attached school that stressed ensemble playing. They produced the work of many American playwrights who became successful, such as **Eugene O'Neill.** During the Depression that started in 1929, social theater gained momentum, as a result of the oppression suffered by the working class. Theater became a tool for social change in the hands of groups such as the Group Theatre and the New Theater League, which produced such outstanding works as *Waiting for Lefty* and *Awake and Sing!*, both by Clifford Odets (1906–1963), and both produced in 1935. In the same year, the **Federal Theater Project** was begun by the national government

to provide jobs for theater people. The work of these theaters and such pioneers as **David Belasco** led the way toward a greater realism in acting and stage design.

After World War II (1939–1945) the Group Theater and their inner approach to acting ruled the American scene; it was known as the Method, based on the work of the Russian **Konstantin Stanislavsky.** The **Actors Studio** was formed in 1947, using the same approach and serving as a training ground for actors. **Tennessee Williams** was the playwright to provide the written vehicle for this new psychologically realistic acting. Another leading American playwright of the time was **Arthur Miller.** A leading actress, **Stella Adler,** was one of many who was instrumental in bringing the Stanislavsky system to the United States and teaching it to generations to follow.

The **American Negro Theater** began in 1940 and proved an important model for a serious African American theater in the states. **Alice Childress** gained prominence acting with them and went on to become an important American playwright. Numerous alternative theaters, such as the **Living Theater** in 1948, **San Francisco Mime Troupe** in 1949, **Bread and Puppet Theatre** in 1962, the **Open Theater** in 1963, **Free Southern Theater** in 1963, and **Richard Forman**'s Ontological Hysterical Theater, started all over the United States and challenged the normal theater status quo. During this time, the art of the actor often became a more collective endeavor, so many of these groups stand out more than do individuals. Hispanic American theater has expanded greatly since the initial work of **El Teatro Campesino** in 1965, with New York troupes such as the Puerto Rican Theater and Repertorio Espagnol (Spanish Repertory).

In the 1970s individual performers such as **Spalding Gray** led the way for many one-person shows to follow. **Lee Breuer, Robert Wilson,** and the new genre called the **happening** fused the visual arts with avant-garde theater. In the 1970s and 80s, gay theater artists began to assert themselves and to portray their own lifestyles to the general public in an often flamboyant and celebratory display. In theater this movement found its voice in 1972 in Doric Wilson's theater, The Other Side of Silence, and in 1982 with Harvey Fierstein's *Torch Song Trilogy*, which he performed on

Broadway. Leading American playwrights who got their starts in the 1960s and 1970s include **Sam Shepard** and **David Mamet.** In the world of puppetry as it was presented in film and on television, performer, designer, and director **Jim Henson** did more to vitalize the form in a popular arena than any other artist in America. **Julie Taymor** is an American theater artist who has created serious works using puppets and sculptural costuming and has reached wide recognition with her design and direction of *The Lion King* for Disney in the 1990s.

America has always lacked a national theater that could be a permanent training ground and a place of employment for outstanding American actors. Since the 1990s it has been common for actors from film and television to act on the stage, an interesting example being Calista Flockhart, the star of the television show *Ally McBeal*, performing in *Bash* off Broadway in New York and in the film version of **Shakespeare**'s *Midsummer Night's Dream* (1999). Alternative theater in the 1990s has taken some interesting turns, such as the **Burning Man** art/theater event in the Southwest desert, which creates a community that is its own entertainment.

> **See also** African American Theater; Schechner, Richard
>
> **References:** Demastes, William. *Beyond Naturalism: A New Realism in American Theatre.* New York: Greenwood, 1988; Garza, Roberto J., ed. *Contemporary Chicano Theatre.* Notre Dame: University of Notre Dame Press, 1976; Harris, Andrew. *Broadway Theatre.* New York: Routledge, 1994; Kanolles, Nicolas, ed. *Mexican American Theatre, Then and Now.* Houston, TX: Arte Publico, 1983; Mordden, Ethan. *The American Theatre.* New York: Oxford University Press, 1981; Pacheco, Patrick. "In the Company of Calista: She's Dreamed a 'Midsummer' Dream, and Taught Us All about Ally. But Deep Down Calista Flockhart Is an Off-Broadway Baby." *InTheatre* 93 (5 July 1999): 18–22; Taylor, Thomas. *American Theatre History: An Annotated Bibliography.* Pasadena, CA: Salem, 1992.

U.S. Cinema

The **United States** of America has made an enormous contribution to the art and industry of film and is responsible for the creation of mega-movie-stars now popular throughout the world, who can garner outrageous fees for each film, and who figure in the consciousness of young people as near-deities. This worship has fostered in actors an interesting and uniquely American mix of narcissism and self-expression that blurs the line between acting a part and becoming a part created by and for the media.

Film in this country had humble beginnings, often being shown by 1900 as part of a vaudeville program or by a traveling showman in any vacant hall available. By World War I (1914–1918) the film industry was really making strides. **Charlie Chaplin** began his career by 1914 and filmmaker D. W. Griffith gave a start to both **Lillian Gish** and **Mary Pickford.** The budding star system also included Douglas Fairbanks (1883–1939), Gloria Swanson (1897–1983), Rudolph Valentino (1895–1926), Buster Keaton (1895–1946), and John (1882–1942), Lionel (1878–1954), and Ethel Barrymore (1879–1959).

The technology for sound came in the late 1920s with the first full-length talkie being *The Jazz Singer* in 1927, starring Al Jolson (1887–1950). This new development dramatically changed the talents demanded of actors for films. Actors with speech problems or heavy accents had trouble getting work. Many Broadway actors already trained vocally made the move to Hollywood for more lucrative work in films. The musical movie *Singing in the Rain*, 1952, starring Gene Kelly (1912–1996), is a wonderful parody of the troubles and possibilities faced during this switch from silent to sound.

Between the two World Wars, popular film actors included Bing Crosby (1904–1977), **Bette Davis,** W. C. Fields (1879–1946), Clark Gable (1901–1960), Cary Grant (1904–1986), Myrna Loy (1905–1993), Mickey Rooney, and Mae West (1893–1980). When World War II (1939–1945) broke out, many of Hollywood's best actors went into active service, such as **James Stewart,** or on tour to entertain troops, such as Bob Hope. More abundant in enthusiasm than lasting artistic value, the many war films include *Yankee Doodle Dandy*, 1942 starring James Cagney (1899–1986). Two of America's most valued movies did emerge during this time, *Casablanca*, 1942, starring Humphrey Bogart (1899–1957) and Ingrid Bergman (1913–1982) and *Citizen Kane*, 1941, by **Orson Welles.**

After the war the advent of television and the baby boom, which kept young couples home at night, put a damper on film's popularity. Another negative influence on film actors resulted from the hearings of the House Un-American Activities Committee, which sought to flush out the Communist leanings of many Hollywood actors, directors, and writers. The unofficial blacklist that resulted from these efforts ended many careers and caused a lot of bad feelings in the industry.

The 1950s brought with them a new naturalism in American movies, which had previously tended to gloss over any negative aspects of life; social issues were looked at in a candid and even cynical way. The film *Streetcar Named Desire*, based on the play by **Tennessee Williams,** in 1951 ushered in the new Method style of acting, based on complete identification with the inner personality of the character being portrayed, brought to the screen by the shockingly raw and brutal performances of **Marlon Brando** and Vivien Leigh. *Rebel without a Cause,* 1955, starring **James Dean,** spoke about the alienation of youth and also featured Method acting, as formulated and disseminated by the **Actors Studio** in New York.

The movies produced in 1950s and 1960s fell into one of the standard categories to be discussed later. The Vietnam War served as a horrific setting for many brutally realistic films, including *The Deer Hunter,* 1978, and *Apocalypse Now,* 1979, starring Martin Sheen and Robert Duvall. Many films also attempted to expose some of the underbelly of society, beginning with *Easy Rider,* 1969, starring Peter Fonda and Dennis Hopper, *Midnight Cowboy,* 1969, starring Dustin Hoffman and Jon Voight and *Taxi Driver,* 1976, starring Robert De Niro and Jodie Foster as a young prostitute. George Lucas's *Star Wars* burst onto the scene in 1977 and was outrageously popular, even though the acting in the science fiction adventure was dull and two-dimensional, as is also true in all of the many sequels. Another fantasy movie to reach similar heights of popularity was Steven Spielberg's *E.T.* in 1982. *The Terminator,* 1984, and *Terminator 2,* 1991, both featuring Arnold Schwarzenegger, body-builder turned actor, took the fantasy thriller to the next level of intelligence and suspense.

Starting in the 1960s there was a noticeable shift of focus from star performers to directors. Directors who created either exceptional works with a style so distinctive that it had become

their signature became a draw for the public, directors such as Francis Ford Coppola, Woody Allen, and Spike Lee. Lee created many provocative works focused on race in America with, one of which was *Do the Right Thing,* in 1989, in which he also performed.

The United States has not only produced great movies, it has produced whole genres. The Western was an original American creation that dominated the screen beginning in the 1920s and was taken to a high level by the work of Howard Hawks, John Ford, and **John Wayne.** Some of the best American Westerns include *My Darling Clementine,* 1946, and *Red River,* 1948. The anti-Western questions the hypocrisy of the 'shoot-'em-up morality that supposedly won the West. Movies such as *Unforgiven,* 1992, directed by and starring **Clint Eastwood,** take a deeper look at the random killings often seen in Westerns.

Another genre that is an original American creation is the musical film, one of the first being *Broadway Melody,* in 1929. The quality of acting in these light romances was stressed less than the quality of dancing and singing. *42nd Street,* 1933, starred Ruby Keeler (1909–1993) and featured the sensational choreography of Busby Berkeley (1895–1976). Also popular during this era were the many movies made with the phenomenal dance duo Fred Astaire (1899–1987) and Ginger Rogers (1911–1995). One of the best-loved musical films ever made was *The Wizard of Oz,* 1939, starring Judy Garland (1922–1969), who began as a child vaudeville performer and became a world-famous star. The integration of outstanding dance in a musical was wonderfully achieved by Gene Kelly, who made *An American in Paris,* 1951, and *Singing in the Rain,* 1952. Outstanding musical films of the 1960s include *West Side Story,* 1961, *My Fair Lady,* 1964, *The Sound of Music,* 1965, and *Funny Girl,* 1968, starring Barbra Streisand portraying singer-comedienne Fanny Brice. In the 1970s the rage was John Travolta, starring in *Saturday Night Fever,* 1977, and *Grease,* 1978.

Comedy in American films has stretched in many directions, from the hilarious antics of the Marx Brother, to **Lucille Ball,** to the one-of-a-kind **Woody Allen,** to the comedy of **Whoopi Goldberg.** One of the most popular film teams in comedy was the partnership of Dean Martin (1917–1995) and Jerry Lewis, who got their start in *My Friend Irma* in 1949. In the 1970s Mel Brooks made several comedies, including *Blazing Saddles*, 1974. Top comedic actors of the 1970s and onward have mostly been actors who were former cast members of the television show *Saturday Night Live*, including Bill Murray, Gilda Radner (1946–1989), Chevy Chase, Dan Akroyd, John Belushi (1949–1982), Eddie Murphy, Chris Farley (1946–1989), and Mike Myers. Other popular comedic actors of this era include Goldie Hawn, Steve Martin, Robin Williams, and Michael J. Fox.

The gangster movie became a popular genre in the 1930s, beginning in 1931 with *Little Caesar* and *Public Enemy*, starring James Cagney (1899–1986), who went on to become a renowned screen-gangster. Humphrey Bogart began a like career in *The Petrified Forest* in 1936. The genre was revived with the influential film *Bonnie and Clyde*, in 1967, and raised to the level of high art with the films *The Godfather*, 1972, *The Godfather Part II*, 1974, and *Godfather III*, 1990, all directed by Francis Ford Coppola.

Extremely popular in America has been and is the horror genre, which began in 1931 with *Dracula*, starring Bela Lugosi (1882–1956), and *Frankenstein*, starring Boris Karloff (1887–1969). Both actors went on to make many more horror films. A satire of the horror genre in the form of a musical movie is *The Rocky Horror Picture Show*, 1975, which now enjoys a cult following and has come to involve audience participation. Through the 1980s the mediocre *Friday the Thirteenth*, 1980, and its many sequels packed in young audiences. *Scream*, 1996, was a product of the 1990s that kept the genre alive.

Cinema in the United States remains an arena for the discussion of important issues, such as the death penalty in *Dead Man Walking*, 1995, rape in *The Accused*, 1988, political corruption in *All the President's Men*, 1976, and matters of reality itself and how it is perceived in *The Matrix*, 1999. On the lighter side, American cinema has set trends in high fashion, created catch phrases, such as "I'll be back" from *The Terminator*, and provided delightful escapism accessible to the masses for over a century.

References: Belton, John. *American Cinema/American Culture*. New York: McGraw-Hill, 1994; Blum, Richard. *American Film Acting: The Stanislavsky Heritage*. Ann Arbor, MI: UMI Research Press, 1984; Cortes, Carlos. *Chicanas in Film: History of an Image*. Binghamton, NY: Bilingual Press, 1985; Diawara, Manthia, ed. *Black American Cinema*. New York: Routledge, 1993; Erens, Patricia. *The Jew in American Cinema*. Bloomington: Indiana University Press, 1984; McCaffrey, Donald. *Guide to the Silent Years of American Cinema*. Westport, CT: Greenwood, 1999; Slide, Anthony. *Early American Cinema*. Metuchen, NJ: Scarecrow, 1994.

Uzbekistan

See Soviet Cinema; Soviet Union

V

Vaudeville

United States

American vaudeville was a format for presenting a variety of entertaining acts to a popular audience; it began in the 1860s and lasted until the late 1920s. The term was also used in **France** to apply to musical comedies and comedic plays, such as those by Eugène Scribe, but this use is not related to the American form. American vaudeville evolved from **minstrels** and burlesque but was cleaned up for a family audience. Some performers were even fined by the management if they used offensive material in their acts. The first vaudeville theater to open was the Fourteenth Street Theater in 1881. After that, a quick proliferation occurred, until there were thousands of small vaudeville houses throughout the nation. Touring vaudeville acts became a big business by the turn of the century.

A wide variety of acts were included in a single night's billing: songs, acrobatic dances, comedy, dramatic scenes, ventriloquists, juggling, magic shows, **mime**, and animal tricks. True to the diversity of the American population, much of the comedy was based on stereotypical parody of various races such as Jews, African Americans performed in blackface, and Italians.

The life of a vaudeville performer was most often a nomadic one, performing one-night stands in small towns along the railroad. The advent of cinema struck a near fatal blow to vaude-

ville, and the Depression finished the job. The Palace Theater in New York, the most prominent vaudeville house, closed its doors in 1932. Many performers who literally grew up in vaudeville went on to be America's top movie stars, including Al Jolson, W. C. Fields, Will Rogers, the **Marx Brothers, Mary Pickford**, and George Burns.

> **References:** Slide, Anthony. *The Encyclopedia of Vaudeville.* Westport, CT: Greenwood, 1994; Staples, Shirley. *Male-Female Comedy Teams in American Vaudeville, 1865–1932.* Ann Arbor, MI: Proquest, 1984; Stein, Charles, ed. *American Vaudeville as Seen by Its Contemporaries.* New York: Knopf, 1984.

Vedas

India

Primary sacred scriptures of **Hinduism,** comprised of hymns, treatises, and other writing. Veda means knowledge in Vedic, the archaic form of the Sanskrit language in which the Vedas were composed. Believed to have existed since the beginning of time and to have been "heard," or cognized, by inspired Brahmans, the Vedas evolved into their present written form between 1400 and 400 B.C.

> **References:** Aherne, Consuelo Maria, Paul Kevin Meagher, and Thomas C. O'Brien, eds. *Encyclopedic Dictionary of Religion.* 3 vols. Washington, DC: Corpus Publishers, 1979; Eliade, Mircea, Eliade, ed. *The Encyclopedia of Religion.* 16 vols. New York: Macmillan, 1987; Scott, A. C. *The Theatre in Asia.* New York: Macmillan, 1972.

An advertisement for a vaudeville show. (Library of Congress)

Versus Fescennini

Italy

Primitive pre-dramatic exchanges in verse performed in Rome during the first few centuries of the Roman Republic (509–527 B.C.), named after the territory of Fescennium. These unrefined improvisations, comprised of jokes and satire, were popular at the harvest festivals and weddings. These plays eventually declined into such moral corruption that they had to be monitored by law.

> References: Bieber, Margarete. *The History of the Greek and Roman Theater*. Princeton, NJ: Princeton University Press, 1961.

Vidushaka

India

Jester or clown character in **Sanskrit drama,** classical Indian dramatic form from 100 B.C. to A.D. 1200. This character type originated in folk plays predating Sanskrit drama.

> References: Tilakasiri, J. *The Puppet Theatre of Asia*. Ceylon: Department of Cultural Affairs, 1968; Varadpande, Manohar Laxman. *Krishna Theatre in India*. New Delhi: Abhinav, 1982.

Vietnam

Theater in Vietnam is a cultural mix, partly a local creation, but influenced by Chinese and Western colonial styles. Inspired by contact with the Chinese, **Hat Boi** (or *Hat Cheo*) is classical opera, very similar to **Peking Opera. Tuong Tao,** a popular form of Chinese-style opera, evolved from Hat Boi, loosening the strict acting conventions of Peking Opera and dispensing with the loud Chinese-style music. Tuong Tao was absorbed into **Cai Luong,** which became the most popular Vietnamese entertainment in the 1920s. All classes of Vietnamese people have enjoyed and supported this form, best loved for its strongly emotional songs sung by famous actors.

In the nineteenth century, **Thoai Kich** (or *Kich Noi*) evolved based on French dramas brought by French colonists for elite audiences of the well-educated Vietnamese interested in Western culture.

> References: Addis, Stephen. "Theatre Music of Vietnam." *Southeast Asia: An International Quarterly* 1 (Winter/Spring 1971): 129–152; Fenn, Jeffery W. *Levitating the Pentagon: Evolutions in the American Theatre of the Vietnam War Era*. Newark: University of

Delaware Press, 1992; Huynh Khac Dung. *Hat Boi, Theatre Traditional du Viet Nam*. Siagon: Kim Lai an Quam, 1970; MacKerras, Colin. "Theatre in Vietnam." *Asian Theatre Journal* 4, 1 (1987): 1–28; Nguyen Phuoc Thien. "Cai Luong and the Vietnamese Theatre." *Viet-My* 8, 4 (December 1963): 2–10; Valdez, Luis. *Actos*. Fresno, CA: Cucaracha, 1971; Weiss, Peter. *Discourse on Vietnam*. London: Calder and Boyars, 1970.

Vilar, Jean (1912–1971)
France

Actor, director, writer, theater manager, who began acting minor roles at the Théâtre de l'Atelier under the direction of **Charles Dullin**. In 1947, after touring with a group of other young ambitious actors from 1941 to 1943, he coordinated the founding of the Avignon Festival, an international event presenting high-quality acting of classic dramatic literature from all over Europe. In 1951 Vilar was appointed director of the Théâtre National Populaire, a huge theater with inexpensive tickets, intended to be a theater for the common people. Here Vilar presented the classics in an arrestingly simple way, using nearly a bare stage with only essential scenic elements. He encouraged free movements and grand gestures from the actors and was innovative in the way he arranged group scenes in a play. He emphasized costuming to communicate the nature, status, and temperament of the character.

References: Roy, Claude. *Jean Vilar*. Paris: Calmann-Levy, 1987.

Vishnu
India

One of the three major gods of **Hinduism**; known as the preserver of the universe. Those who are especially devoted to him are called Vaishnavas, or Vishnuvites, and to them, Vishnu is supreme among all gods. Because of his continued devotion to the human race, Vishnu has incarnated himself in many forms, including a fish, a boar, and a dwarf. The two most popular incarnations are Rama, hero of the Hindu epic tale, the **Ramayana;** and **Krishna,** a famous seducer of women in his youth and a wise counselor in the other great Hindu epic tale, the **Mahabharata,** in his later years. Some Hindus believe that the **Buddha**

was also an incarnation of Vishnu, though Buddhists do not accept this claim.

See also Vishnu-Krishna; Shiva
References: Aherne, Consuelo Maria, Paul Kevin Meagher, and Thomas C. O'Brien, eds. *Encyclopedic Dictionary of Religion*. 3 vols. Washington, DC: Corpus Publishers, 1979; Eliade, Mircea, ed. *The Encyclopedia of Religion*. 16 vols. New York: Macmillan, 1987; Varadpande, Manohar Laxman. *Krishna Theatre in India*. New Delhi: Abhinav, 1982.

Vishnu-Krishna
India

Krishna devotees see Krishna, who is an incarnation of **Vishnu,** as being synonymous with Vishnu and refer to him as Vishnu-Krishna.

See also Hinduism; Shiva
References: Brandon, James R. *Brandon's Guide to Theatre in Asia*. Honolulu: University Press of Hawaii, 1976; Eliade, Mircea, ed., *The Encyclopedia of Religion*. 16 vols. New York: Macmillan, 1987; Varadpande, Manohar Laxman. *Krishna Theatre in India*. New Delhi: Abhinav, 1982.

Volkov, Fyodor (1729–1763)
Russia

Russian actor, director, and teacher. Though he had a humble upbringing, Volkov was passionately in love with the theater and went to Saint Petersburg to learn it. Upon returning home to his small town of Yaroslavl, he trained his brothers and friends to mount amateur theater productions in a fixed-up barn. In the early 1750s his local audience received his work so enthusiastically that they built him a 1000-seat theater. Word passed to the Czarina Yelisaveta, who invited Volkov and his company to Saint Petersburg. After witnessing their performance of *The Repentance of A Sinner*, she was so impressed that she sent many of his actors for more training at the Academy for the Nobility.

Volkov and his company then began performing at the new national theater in Saint Petersburg with a subsidy, performing mostly French comedies. As an actor he had many of the courtly mannerisms imported by the French troupes in Russia. He spoke his lines in a singsong manner. He acted in a highly emotional style, often shouting his lines at the climax of a scene. After 1762, Volkov and his brother were knighted and began work on an enormous outdoor festival in Moscow that was to last two weeks. It included classic Greek characters enacting scenes on chariots that were driven by oxen. During the rehearsal process for this spectacle, Volkov literally caught his death of cold and died at the age of thirty-four.

References: Gregor, Joseph. *The Russian Theatre: Its Character and History with Especial Reference to the Revolutionary Period*. Philadelphia: J. B. Lippincott, 1929; Slonim, Marc. *Russian Theater, From the Empire to the Soviets*. Cleveland: World, 1961.

W

Wagner, Richard (1813–1883)
Germany

German composer who called his grand operas "music dramas" and worked to rid them of the prevailing artificiality of operatic style. His most famous work, *The Ring Cycle*, took him over twenty-five years to complete and was finally performed in his own theater in Bayreuth in 1876. He wanted to create a unified work of art in which all elements worked to serve one overriding expression. This required new rehearsal methods. The norm was for each musical aspect of an opera—such as the strings, the winds, and the singers—to rehearse separately. He gathered his musicians together a year before the performance to rehearse. He wanted the physical setting of the theater space to plunge the audience's attention into the world of the stage. To this end, he sank the orchestra into a pit lower than the stage, hiding it completely from the audience's view. He also darkened the area in which the audience was seated. Other operas by Wagner include *The Flying Dutchman*, 1841, *Tristan and Iseult*, 1865, and his final work, *Parsifal*, 1882.

> **References:** Carlson, Marvin. *The French Stage in the Nineteenth Century.* Metuchen, NJ: Scarecrow, 1972; Fricke, Richard. *Wagner in Rehearsal, 1875–1876: The Diaries of Richard Fricke* (Bayreuth Vor Dreissig Jahren). Trans. George Fricke. Stuyvesant, NY: Pendragon, 1998; Wagner, Richard. *The Diary of Richard Wagner 1865–1882: The Brown Book.* Trans. George Bird. New York: Cambridge University Press, 1980.

Wajda, Andrzej (1926–)
Poland

Director of film and theater, known primarily for his filmmaking but also as a prolific and influential director of live theater. Wajda made his mark as a young director in the "new wave" in Polish cinema with such films as *Carnal*, 1956, and *Ashes and Diamonds*, 1958. In theater, Wajda directed an eclectic mix of classics and modern dramas. He never established his own company as did his contemporaries **Jerzy Grotowski** and **Tadeusz Kantor**, but instead moved from one company to another, freely crossing over between film and theater. He utilized many of the same actors on the screen and on stage. Other exceptional films by Wajda include *Birchwood*, 1970, and *Danton*, 1982. His most influential theater productions include *The Possessed*, 1971, *The Danton Affair*, 1975, *Antigone*, 1984, and *Crime and Punishment*, 1984. In 1999 Wajda released his film *Pan Tadeusz*.

> **References:** Karpinski, Maciej. *The Theatre of Andrzej Wajda.* Trans. Christina Paul. New York: Cambridge University Press, 1989.

Wak Long
Malaysia

Clown character in **Wayang Siam,** shadow puppet theater of northern Malaysia. As the loyal sidekick of **Pak Dogol,** the clown-god disguised as a servant, Wak Long is an accomplice in Pak Dogol's many capers, often involving some mighty Hindu god from the **Ramayana,** Hindu epic tale.

References: Sweeney, P. L. *The Ramayana and the Malay Shadow-Play.* Kuala Lumpur: National University of Malaysia Press, 1972.

Wakashù
China

Young boys who portrayed female roles. In China before the twentieth century, when there was complete segregation of women from ordinary society, having female impersonators was a practical solution for the theater. Attractive boys trained from an early age to simulate feminine mannerisms. They acted female roles in the play and sometimes waited tables in character during performances as added titillation for the male audience. Homosexuality was an acknowledged part of being a catamite, even though it was a harshly punishable offense. Actors as a general group were associated with sexual perversion and promiscuity. Male children at the age of seven began training to be catamites. It was a very hard life. They were separated from their families and their homes. Sometimes their families sold them to a troupe. Sometimes the young boys ran away from home to apprentice with a troupe. Apprenticing was the only way of training these boys. Training had to start young, and students had to work very hard since getting a position in a troupe was so highly competitive.

See also Tan

Waki
Japan

The second actor in **Noh,** masked dance-drama from medieval Japan. The *Waki* does not wear a mask as the lead actor, **Shite,** does. Each of the four pillars on a Noh stage is named after one of the character types in the form. The stage pillar designated as the Waki is the pillar farthest from the bridgeway, front and to the audience's right.

See also Nimaime

References: Scott, A. C. *The Theatre in Asia.* New York: Macmillan, 1972.

Wales

This principality in western Britain has its theatrical roots in the eisteddfods, ancient bardic festivals of music and poetic plays. Real Welsh theater, however, developed, like theater in **Ireland,** as a nationalistic reaction to British colonialism. Welsh-speaking theater was begun in part by the playwright Saunders Lewis (1893–1985). In the early twentieth century, many English-speaking theaters were started, such as the Sherman Theatre in Cardiff, the Theatre Clwyd in Mold, and the Torch Theatre in Dyfed. A popular actor of the time, Meredith Edwards (1918–1899), began his career on the stage in Wales and later moved to **England** to perform both in theater and in films such as *A Run for Your Money,* 1950.

The Welsh poet Dylan Thomas (1914–1953) wrote a radio script called *Under Milk Wood* about a Welsh seaside village, which contains a tender and humorous picture of Welsh thought and behavior; it was narrated by the well-known **Richard Burton** in 1954. Burton himself was born and raised in South Wales; he went on to be a celebrated Shakespearean actor in England and a Hollywood movie star, with such movies as *Who's Afraid of Virginia Woolf?* 1966. In 1962 government subsidies allowed the creation of a permanent Welsh Theatre company, with bases in Cardiff and Bangor, in order to provide quality plays in both English and Welsh. In Cardiff the play by Patrick Jones, *Everything Must Go,* was presented in 1999.

Welsh actress Catherine Zeta Jones has become a glamorous leading actress in Hollywood with *The Mask of Zorro,* 1998, and *Entrapment,* 1999. Also in *The Mask of Zorro* was **Anthony Hopkins**, an actor of Welsh descent who has achieved great success in Hollywood.

See also Shakespeare, William

References: Baker, Pam. "To Catch a Thief: She Buckled the Swash of Antonio Banderas in *The Mask of Zorro* and Now in *Entrapment* Catherine Zeta Jones Has Master Thief Sean Connery Shaken and Stirred . . . !" *Film Review* 583 (July 1999): 68–71; Baker, Pam. "Obituaries: Meredith Edwards, 81, February 8 1999." *Classic Images* 286 (April 1999): 51; Price, Cecil John Layton. *The English Theatre in Wales in the Eighteenth and Early Nineteenth Centuries.* Cardiff: University of Wales Press, 1948; Taylor, Anna-Maria. *Staging Wales: Welsh Theatre 1979–1997.* Cardiff: University of Wales Press, 1997.

Wasan Kwaikwayo
Niger, Nigeria

Popular improvised theater in **Niger** and **Nigeria**; also called *Teyatur,* derived from the

French word for theater. Primarily an urban form of entertainment, this popular theatrical form aims at attracting a mass audience. This is a new dramatic oral tradition that began forming around the 1970s and continues to evolve. Plays are performed in Hausa, the language most widely spoken in Niger and Nigeria. The original form for *Wasan Kwaikwayo* was derived from Western theater during the colonial period in Niger and northern Nigeria. However, there are many aspects of production that deviate from typical Western plays. There are no playwrights, no directors, and no scripts. Plays are created through a communal effort involving the actors' improvisation, drawing deeply upon their village traditions and cultural background. The subject matter for these plays is drawn from topical themes that immediately concern the community in which a performance is taking place.

Performances occur in the evening in conjunction with other events, such as musical performances and traditionally based dance-dramas known as ballets (see **African Ballets**). The audience is seated around a raised stage in an outdoor auditorium. Actors portray fictional characters in these plays, which progress from one scene to the next with breaks in between. There is considerable popular support and interest for this kind of theater, and performances are even broadcast on local television and radio stations.

References: Beik, Janet. *Hausa Theatre in Niger: A Contemporary Oral Art.* New York: Garland, 1987; Chaibou, Dan-Inna. "La Theatralite en Pays Hawsa." Université Nationale de Côte d'Ivoire, 1978–1979.

Water Sleeves
China

An extended part of the sleeve in a **Peking Opera** costume; about 14 inches long, made of white silk; manipulated by the actor to enhance his or her performance. As Peking Opera actors perform songs or dialogue they are constantly matching the rhythm of their speech or song with the movement of these flowing silk sleeves. The sleeves can be dropped down suddenly and then gracefully gathered around the wrist again. The actor never gathers the material on one arm with the other hand. The water sleeves are controlled only by careful flips of the wrist and movements

of the forearm. The water sleeve is an invaluable tool for the Peking Opera actor, the mastery over which requires years of practice and instruction. Water sleeves are often used for asides, moments when an actor hides him or herself from the other actors on stage to reveal inner thoughts to the audience.

References: Barba, Eugenio, and Nicola Savarese. *The Secret Art of the Performer: A Dictionary of Theatre Anthropology.* New York: Routledge, 1991; Scott, A. C. *The Theatre in Asia.* New York: Macmillan, 1972.

Wayang Beber
Java

Paper-scroll storytelling performance. This form probably dates back to the fourth or fifth century and is definitely older than the **Wayang Kulit.** A **dalang,** a puppet master, tells a story with musical accompaniment while unrolling a long picture scroll made of paper. He holds two poles, one in each hand, and unwinds with one hand while winding with the other to expose the portion of the scroll that corresponds to the story. *Wayang Kulit* largely replaced this form at court functions and religious celebrations as *Wayang Kulit* grew in sophistication. It is rarely performed now.

References: Brandon, James. *Theatre in Southeast Asia.* Cambridge, MA: Harvard University Press, 1974.

Wayang Djawa
Java

Shadow puppet theater developed to tell stories about Prince Diponegoro, famous for rebelling against the Dutch in the nineteenth century. The performance conventions, setting, manner of performing, and occasion for performances, are almost identical to those for the **Wayang Kulit.**

References: Brandon, James. *Theatre in Southeast Asia.* Cambridge, MA: Harvard University Press, 1974.

Wayang Gedog
Java

Shadow puppet theater portraying the **Panji tales.** This form was created in 1553 in order to dramatize the adventures of Prince Panji. The theatrical conventions, setting, manner of performing, and occasion for performances, are almost identical to those for the **Wayang Kulit.**

> **References:** Brandon, James. *Theatre in Southeast Asia.* Cambridge, MA: Harvard University Press, 1974.

Wayang Golek
Java

Rod puppet theater (*Golek* means "doll"). The Javanese form of *Wayang Golek* was created about 150 years ago by Javanese **Wayang Kulit** puppet masters residing in Sunda, west Java. It is believed to have evolved because people wanted to be able to watch the *Wayang Kulit* during the day and because the Sundanese people preferred the realism of three-dimensional wooden figures. One puppeteer, or **dalang,** controls all the puppets. The performance conventions, setting, manner of performing, and occasion for performances, are very much like the *Wayang Kulit*, except that there is no screen upon which shadows are cast. The puppets are viewed directly, and the *dalang* is entirely visible.

The puppets have a wooden carved head on a rod with a crossbar that serves as shoulders. There are wooden arms that are hinged at the elbow and shoulder. A thin rod is attached to the upturned palm of each puppet's hand. A *dalang* puts his hand under the skirt of the puppet and can turn the head and lift the shoulders from controls in the waist area of the puppet. He controls both of the arm rods with the other hand. Some warrior puppets are constructed to have heads that can be catapulted off their shoulders into the audience during a ferocious battle scene. Moans and cheers come from the audience when such special effects are done. During a performance the puppets are lined up along the screen extending farther to each side beyond the screen. They are either thrust into green banana logs or are hung on strings. They are an impressive sight, and are readily available for the *dalang*. The *dalang* performs all the narration, dialogue, and songs. He is respected in society as an essential link to the past, as he has mastery over Hindu and animistic forces.

The repertory is drawn from the same plays used for *Wayang Kulit* from the **Mahabharata** and the **Ramayana,** two Hindu epic tales. Originally the **Menak** cycle of stories were dramatized; they were about the adventures of Amir Hamzah, a famous Islamic hero. Musical accompaniment is performed by a Sundanese version of the traditional **gamelan** orchestra, more robust than the Javanese variety. Recently, performances have become lighter in theme and less philosophical. The same stories are used, but the comedy and action are emphasized. It is now common to have a female singer of popular songs. She is often more prominent than the *dalang* in performances.

> **References:** Brandon, James. *Theatre in Southeast Asia.* Cambridge, MA: Harvard University Press, 1974; Brandon, James R. *Brandon's Guide to Theatre in Asia.* Honolulu: University Press of Hawaii, 1976; Tilakasiri, J. *The Puppet Theatre of Asia.* Ceylon: Department of Cultural Affairs, 1968.

Wayang Jawa
See Wayang Melayu

Wayang Klitik
Java

Shadow puppet theater using flat wooden puppets instead of rawhide puppets. This tradition tells stories about Damar Wulan of Majapahit. The theatrical conventions, setting, manner of performing, and occasion for performances, are almost identical to those for the **Wayang Kulit.**

> **References:** Brandon, James. *Theatre in Southeast Asia.* Cambridge, MA: Harvard University Press, 1974.

Wayang Kulit
Bali, Java, Malaysia

Shadow-puppet theater of Southeast Asia. *Wayang Kulit*, literally "show of skins," is the general term for the shadow puppet theater found throughout most of Southeast Asia. It is a combination of intricately designed rawhide puppets casting shadows on a screen, the hypnotic music of the live **gamelan,** a traditional orchestra, and the puppet master dramatizing a tale from one of the great Hindu epics, the **Ramayana** or the **Mahabharata.** This form likely originated in Java around the tenth century A.D., though there are some scholars who claim it was brought to Java from either India or

Shadows cast by the intricately carved rawhide puppets of the Wayang Kulit *(shadow puppet theater) in Java. (Photo by Beth Osnes)*

China. Performances take place outdoors from sundown till the early morning hours. It often takes a few successive evenings to perform a specific episode.

Wayang Kulit functions as a form of entertainment, a means of celebrating life events, such as weddings or a successful harvest, a way to appease or feed the gods, a tool for restoring balance to the community, and a healing ceremony. There are many rituals integral to a performance, which serve to gain favor from the good gods and ensure protection from the evil spirits, both being manifest in the shadows caused by the puppets. The puppets are carved from rawhide in the image of the Hindu gods from the epic tales. They are almost always shown in profile, with one or two articulated arms. In Malaysia and Bali the clown characters also have a movable lower jaw. There is one supporting rod that the puppet is slid into; a thin rod of bamboo is cut down the middle and the raw hide puppet is inserted and secured. Thin rods are also attached to the movable arms. Out of respect for the gods they represent, puppets are painted with exquisite detail, even though the colors are generally not seen by the audience.

A puppet master, called a **dalang,** manipulates all the puppets from a seated position behind the screen. He also performs all the narration, dialogue, and songs. He uses no script. He improvises based on his thorough knowledge of the stories. A *dalang* must have great versatility in his voice to mimic the feminine refined voice of a princess and the rough gravely growl of a demon. He must also have a quick wit and good comic timing for the comic interludes, starring the clown character **Semar,** in Java and Bali, or **Pak Dogol,** in Malaysia. The setting for a performance works as a metaphor for the way villagers view their relationship with spiritual forces. The *dalang* is seen by the villagers as a symbol for God, giving life to all the rawhide puppets, which represent humanity. The light that hangs about a foot behind the screen in the center is seen by the villagers as being another symbol for God, the creative force. The banana log at the foot of the screen inside the hut, which is a stand for the puppets, represents the earth for the villagers. The rectangular screen upon which the shadows are cast represents for the villagers the sky and the heavens.

A puppet master usually brings over a hundred puppets to a performance, though the given episode may only require ten to twenty. There are very few properties used in performance. Small rawhide representations of scrolls or knives sized to fit into the hand of a puppet are secured to a thin rod and placed in the puppet's hand. There are a few cutout buildings, trees, or caves, but location is usually revealed by the narration. The stories are predominantly drawn from the **Mahabharata** and the **Ramayana.** The stories of many local folk characters have been woven into these Hindu epics, as these tales have become assimilated to different areas of Southeast Asia. For example, *Pak Dogol,* a Malaysian folk character, a divine clown, is cast in the *Ramayana* as servant to King Rama.

A puppet master has liberty to tell a given episode in whatever manner he wishes, so long as he doesn't offend his audience. A Southeast Asian audience knows the stories of the Hindu epic tales intimately, so a *dalang* must portray each character in a manner expected by the audience. For example, **Hanuman** must be performed with incredible energy and strength. Rama must be performed as being dignified and with the decorum fitting an honorable king. A puppet master may diverge into a comical chase scene that could last an hour before returning to the tale. He may also slow down an emotional moment to fully explore the depth of feeling.

The music is performed by a gamelan, a traditional orchestra of gongs, drums, cymbals, and sometimes a melodic reed instrument. The musical ensemble accompanies the songs, provide traveling, fighting, or marching music, and accents dramatic actions or statements. The puppet master cues them using a wooden clapper placed either under his knee or on the side of his puppet chest, which he can also hit with his knee or foot.

There have been some innovations and changes in the *Wayang Kulit.* An oil lamp has been replaced by an incandescent bulb in all areas of Southeast Asia except Bali. Almost every performance now uses an electronic amplification system, which can make the music sometimes painfully loud. In Malaysia puppets are often painted with translucent paint so that the colors will show through in the shadows. The color is added to help shadow theater compete with television and movies in its appeal to the younger generation. Popular puppet masters are broadcast on the radio in Java and on the east coast of Malaysia. A superstar *dalang* in Java can command a high salary and attract many people to his performance. For a description of schools and training for performers, see **Dalang.**

References: Brandon, James. *Theatre in Southeast Asia.* Cambridge, MA: Harvard University Press, 1974; Osnes, Mary Beth. "Malaysia's Evolving Shadow Puppet Theatre." *Asian Theatre Journal* 9 (Spring 1992): 112–116; Sweeney, P. L. Amin. *Malay Shadow Puppets: The Wayang Siam of Kelantan.* London: British Museum Publications, 1980; Ulbricht, H. *Wayang Purwa: Shadows of the Past.* Kuala Lumpur, Malaysia: Oxford University Press, 1970; Van Ness, Edward, and Shita Prawirohardjo. *Javanese Wayang Kulit.* New York: Oxford University Press, 1984; Yousof, Ghulam-Sarwar. *Southeast Asian Traditional Performing Arts: A Preliminary Bibliography.* Penang, Malaysia: Southeast Asian Studies Program, 1990.

Wayang Madya

Java

Shadow puppet theater enacting tales about the kings of East Java. Performance conventions, setting, manner of performing, and occasion for performances, are almost identical to those for the **Wayang Kulit.**

References: Brandon, James. *Theatre in Southeast Asia.* Cambridge, MA: Harvard University Press, 1974.

Wayang Melayu

Malaysia

A form of **Wayang Kulit,** shadow puppet theater, performed in northern Malaysia (also known as *Wayang Jawa*). This form has obvious Javanese roots but was modified a great deal by Malaysian practitioners. The courtly style of moving the puppets slowly and the design of the puppet's themselves is distinctively Javanese. It was primarily an entertainment for aristocrats and only throve under their patronage. There is only one surviving *Wayang Melayu* **dalang,** or puppet master, who is partially retired already. He has no students, so this form nears extinction. The puppets for this form resemble but are less ornate than the Javanese puppets. The performance style is refined and slow. The repertory borrows from the **Ramayana,** the **Mahabharata,** and the **Panji tales.**

References: Osnes, Mary Beth. "Malaysia's Evolving Shadow Puppet Theatre," *Asian Theatre Journal* 9 (Spring 1992): 112–116; Sweeney, P. L. *The Ra-*

Malasian puppet master Dalang Hussain with two puppets he uses to perform Wayang Melayu, the traditional shadow puppet theater of Malaysia. Dalang Hussain is the last practitioner of this form; with his passing, it will become extinct. (Photo by Beth Osnes)

mayana and the Malay Shadow-Play. Kuala Lumpur: National University of Malaysia Press, 1972.

Wayang Orang
See Wayang Kulit; Wayang Wong

Wayang Pantja Sila
Java

Nationalistic form of shadow puppet theater created in the 1950s. *Pantja Sila* is the doctrine put forth by former president Sukarno to serve as the spiritual foundation of the Indonesian Republic. *Wayang Pantja Sila* grew out of **Wayang Suluh,** a propagandistic form of shadow puppet theater performed during the Indonesian revolution against the Dutch, 1945–1949. The need for *Wayang Suluh* disappeared with the end of the revolution, and the form became extinct. A government information unit leader who was also a **dalang,** a puppet master, created *Wayang Pantja Sila.* The five main characters represent the five principles of the new republic: belief in God, nationalism, humanity, sovereignty of the people, and social justice. This form is completely supported and subsidized by the government. The main theatrical conventions, setting, manner of performing, and occasion for performances are similar to conventions for the **Wayang Kulit.**

> **References:** Brandon, James. *Theatre in Southeast Asia.* Cambridge, MA: Harvard University Press, 1974.

Wayang Siam
Malaysia

A form of **Wayang Kulit,** traditional shadow puppet theater, performed in northeast Malaysia. The *Wayang Siam* is the most prominent form of Malaysian shadow puppet theater. It shares many attributes with the Thai shadow-puppet theater, since the two forms developed together as performers crossed the border between the two countries. There are even some Thai words used in incantations within the performance. The puppets have tall crowns and are much more full-bodied than the elongated Javanese puppets. The performance style is strong and robust, yet it can be refined when necessary. There are many local Malaysian gods and demigods who have been woven into the Wayang Siam version of the **Ramayana. Pak Dogol,** a very high god who covered himself in mud to go unnoticed by the humans, and his sidekick, **Wak Long,** are the two most prominent local characters who provide much humor. Performances take place in a raised performance hut with the muslin screen leaning down toward the audience in the front. The **dalang,** puppet master, and the musicians sit in the hut with almost no room to spare. There is a opening ceremony performed by a student *dalang* called the *Dalang Muda* (Young Puppet Master). It has a fixed structure that includes singing, dialogue, narration and all kinds of puppet movement. The musical accompaniment is provided by a **gamelan,** a traditional orchestra, with musicians playing gongs, drums, cymbals, and one melodic reed instrument called a **Serunai.** To become a *dalang* of the *Wayang Siam,* a young person usually begins learning to play an instrument in the orchestra. Eventually he is taught the opening ceremony. After years of private lessons with the puppet master, he has his graduation performance and is bathed with limes by his teacher in ritual called **Pelimau.** There are a few instances of women training to be a puppet master, but there are no established female *dalang. Wayang Siam* is now only performed in Trengganu and Kelantan.

References: Matusky, Patricia. "Music in the Malay Shadow Puppet Theater (Volumes I and II)." Ph.D. diss., Ann Arbor, MI: Proquest, 1980; Osnes, Mary Beth. "A Survey of Shadow Play in the Malaysian Traditional Shadow Puppet Theatre." Ann Arbor, MI: Proquest, 1992; Osnes, Mary Beth, "Shadow Puppet Theatre in Malaysia: Many Traditions, One God," *Quest* (Spring 1994): 70–73, 89; Sweeney, P. L. *The Ramayana and the Malay Shadow-Play.* Kuala Lumpur: National University of Malaysia Press, 1972.

Wayang Suluh
Java

Revolutionary form of **Wayang Kulit,** shadow puppet theater. During the Indonesian revolution against Dutch rule, 1945–1949, the Indonesian Ministry of Information sent propaganda out into the villages through the medium of shadow puppet theater, a form very familiar to the Indonesian people. Short simple plays about peasants and soldiers working together to gain freedom for their country were dramatized using realistic rawhide cutout puppets of peasants, soldiers, and political figures. Puppet masters would travel with a portable screen, an oil light, and just enough puppets to perform. The Dutch confiscated and destroyed *Wayang Suluh* puppets whenever they could find them. Once the revolution ended, this form lost its reason for being and was replaced by **Wayang Pantja Sila.**

References: Brandon, James. *Theatre in Southeast Asia.* Cambridge, MA: Harvard University Press, 1974.

Wayang Tengul
Java

A form of **Wayang Kulit,** shadow puppet theater, that dramatizes stories about Amir Hamzah, a great Islamic hero who converted much of the Arab world to Islam (see **Menak**). The performance conventions, setting, manner of performing, and occasion for performances, are almost identical to the conventions for the *Wayang Kulit.*

References: Brandon, James. *Theatre in Southeast Asia.* Cambridge, MA: Harvard University Press, 1974; Van Ness, Edward, and Shita Prawirohardjo. *Javanese Wayang Kulit.* New York: Oxford University Press, 1984.

Wayang Topeng
Bali, Java, Sunda

Masked dance-drama. This form originated from ancient Javanese masked dances that were performed to honor the sprits of the dead. After the fourteenth century, Indian-style dance blended with the Javanese masked dance to dramatize episodes from the **Panji tales.** In this form, *Wayang Topeng* became very popular in Java, Sunda (west Java), and Bali. This form is unusual, in that it has been simultaneously performed for the courts by court performers and by villagers as a folk performance. Three to four performers portray a number of roles, dancing and performing scenes from the Panji tales. Performers simply change their mask to represent a different character. In Bali the main actors have attendants who speak their lines for them.

References: Brandon, James. *Theatre in Southeast Asia.* Cambridge, MA: Harvard University Press, 1974; Brandon, James R. *Brandon's Guide to Theatre in Asia.* Honolulu: University Press of Hawaii, 1976; Emigh, John. "Playing with the Past: Visitation and Illusion in the Mask Theatre of Bali." *Drama Review* 20, 2 (June 1979): 11–36; Hood, Mantle. "The Enduring Tradition: Music and Theatre in Java and Bali." In *Indonesia*, ed. Ruth McVey. New Haven, CT: Yale University Press, 1963; de Zoete, Beryl, and Walter Spies. *Dance and Drama in Bali.* London: Faber & Faber, 1938.

Wayang Wong
Bali, Java, Malaysia

Dance-drama styled after the **Wayang Kulit,** shadow puppet theater (also *Wayang Orang,* meaning "human puppet" or "human show"). *Wayang Wong* was started in the eighteenth century under the patronage of the courts of Yogjakarta and Surakarta in Java. Until the 1940s week-long performances in the royal courts were quite common. The first private troupe was formed by a wealthy Chinese businessman. *Wayang Wong* was extremely popular with the general public. The courts no longer support *Wayang Wong,* so it is only commercial.

This form has borrowed movement techniques from the movements of the shadow puppets in *Wayang Kulit.* Performers speak and sing as they move and dance as though they are two-dimensional puppets. In Bali the emphasis is on performers delivering long poetic speeches. In Java dance and action are more prominent. The role of the **dalang,** or puppet master, but is limited to singing narration between scenes. When *Wayang Wong* was first developed, normal court attire was worn as a costume. Then costumes were designed to resemble the shadow puppets. In Bali it is a folk art, not a court-sponsored event. Thus, the costumes in Bali are much more humble, and the performance style is looser. In Java masks are seldom ever used, but in Bali they are used for all but the refined hero characters. The repertory is also borrowed from the shadow puppet theater, as is the style of musical accompaniment. In Java the teaching of this form is done in palaces and at special schools in Yogjakarta and Surakarta, schools that are both private and sponsored by the government. There are presently over a dozen commercial troupes. To appeal to a modern audience they, like the *Wayang Kulit,* emphasize the comic scenes with the clown characters performing physical stunts and pranks.

References: Brandon, James. *Theatre in Southeast Asia.* Cambridge, MA: Harvard University Press, 1974; Brandon, James R. *Brandon's Guide to Theatre in Asia.* Honolulu: University Press of Hawaii, 1976; Kam, Garret. "Wayang Wong in the Court of Yogyakarta: The Enduring Significance of Javanese Dance Drama." *Asia Theatre Journal* 4, 1 (1987): 29–51; Ludwig, Ruby Ornstein. "Wayang Wong, the Javanese Classical Theatre." *World Music* 18, 1 (1976): 15–22; Soedarsono. *Wayang Wong: The State Ritual Dance Drama in the Court of Yogyakarta.* Yogyakarta, Java: Gajah Mada University Press, 1984.

Wayne, John (1907–1979)
United States

Legendary film actor in American Westerns, who came to embody the American spirit through the rugged character he created in his films. Born

John Wayne in the film True Grit *(1969) (Kobol Collection/ Paramount)*

Marion Michael Morrison, Wayne worked at the Fox studio on vacations from college and there was noticed and befriended by director John Ford. Wayne started with bit parts in 1928, getting his first leading role with *The Big Trail*, 1930. After this, he played the strong silent Western hero in many low-budget films. His break came in 1939, when Ford cast him in *Stagecoach*.

In his career, which lasted into the 1970s, Wayne appeared in nearly 250 films, often portraying a cowboy, sheriff, or army officer fighting for a just cause. His range of expression as an actor was never wide vocally or physically, but there was a strength and depth to his character that made him an archetypal embodiment of the American spirit, especially as seen in the legends of the West. He portrayed the harsh and driven leader of a cattle drive in *Red River*, 1938, and played another dark role as an Indian hunter in *The Searchers*, 1956. He took his screen persona to heart and in his life championed a conservative patriotism. He directed and starred in a pro-Vietnam film, *The Green Berets*, in 1968. Wayne won an Oscar for best actor with his portrayal of a western marshal in *True Grit*, 1969.

References: Davis, Ronald. *Duke: The Life and Image of John Wayne*. Norman: University of Oklahoma Press, 1998; McGhee, Richard. *John Wayne: Actor, Artist, Hero*. Jefferson, NC: McFarland, 1990.

Webber, Andrew Lloyd (1948–)
England

Composer of musicals and operas, who began collaborating with librettist Tim Rice (b. 1944), when both were in their twenties, with *Joseph and His Amazing Technicolour Dreamcoat*, 1968, at the Young Vic in London. Their next hit, *Jesus Christ Superstar*, 1970, a religious rock musical, brought the rise to prominence of the British musical above the Broadway product that had previously reigned supreme. Their next collaboration was *Evita*, 1976, featuring the popular song "Don't Cry for Me Argentina." Webber is a master at writing memorable emotionally charged songs that allow the dramatic content of his musicals to take flight. Webber went on to write *Cats*, 1981, *Phantom of the Opera*, 1985, and *Aspects of Love*, 1989, all of which transferred to New York's Broadway from London and toured widely. A movie version of *Evita* was made in 1996 starring Madonna and Antonio Banderas.

References: Ganzl, Kurt. *British Musical Theatre*. New York: Oxford University Press, 1986.

Weigel, Helene (1900–1971)
Germany

German actress, wife of **Bertolt Brecht**. She is said to have best exemplified the acting theories of Brecht. She began as an actress at the age of eighteen when she portrayed Marie in *Woyzeck*, by Georg Buchner (1813–1873). She was a greatly celebrated actress in her own right in Frankfurt and Berlin before marrying Brecht in 1928. She left Germany with Brecht in 1933 because of the rise of the Nazis and performed occasionally while in exile. Returning from the **United States** in 1948, she and Brecht founded the Berliner Ensemble in 1949 as a group of actors within the Deutsches Theater (German Theater). She exemplified the acting appropriate to **epic theater,** performing the leading female roles in Brecht's *Mother Courage* (1941), *The Caucasian Chalk Circle* (1948) and many others. She remained detached from the character she was portraying so that the audience did not fall into the emotionality of the scene, but, rather remained actively considering the relevance politically and socially, thus creating the **alienation effect** Brecht desired. As an actress she is described as having had an unemotional yet penetrating voice. Weigel took control of the ensemble after Brecht's death in 1956 and continued producing plays in the Brechtian style.

References: Chinoy, Helen Krich, and Toby Cole. *Actors on Acting*. New York: Crown, 1970; Speirs, Ronald. *Bertolt Brecht*. New York: St. Martin's, 1987.

Weiss, Peter (1916–)
Germany

German playwright, film director, painter, and writer, who became widely known for his play *The Persecution and Assassination of Marat As Performed by the Inmates of the Asylum of Charenton under the Direction of the Marquis de Sade*, or, as it is often called, *Marat/Sade*. Exiled by Nazis from Germany in 1934, Weiss began writing dramas in Sweden in the 1940s. *Marat/Sade* was first produced in Berlin in 1963 at the Schiller Theater and later that same year by the **Royal Shakespeare Company** under the direction of **Peter Brook**. This acclaimed production is one of the finest know examples of the theater of cruelty conceptualized by **Antonin Artaud**, and it included in its cast Ian Richardson, Glenda Jackson, and Patrick Magee. This seminal work was created relying heavily upon improvisations during the rehearsal process and tight ensemble playing during the performance. The emphasis was not on the "star" performers but on the interplay between all of the performers.

One for long titles, Weiss also wrote a documentary drama, *Discourse on the Historical Background and the Course of the Continuing Struggle for Liberation in Vietnam as an Example of the Necessity of Armed Warfare by the Oppressed against their Oppressors and Furthermore on the Attempts of the United States of America to Annihilate the Basic Principles of the Revolution*, in 1968. His plays stand as excellent examples of **documentary theater.**

References: Chinoy, Helen Krich, and Toby Cole. *Actors on Acting*. New York: Crown, 1970; Holderness, Graham, ed. *The Politics of Theatre and Drama*. New York: St. Martin's, 1992; Welch, David. *Propaganda and the German Cinema 1933–1945*. Oxford: Clarendon, 1983.

Welles, Orson (1915–1985)

United States

Actor for the stage and film and famous film director, best known for his masterpiece, *Citizen Kane*, 1941, in which he starred as the newspaper tycoon Kane (based on William Randolph Hearst), which he co-wrote and directed at the young age of twenty-five. Many hail this movie as the finest American movie ever made.

Welles came from a privileged background and excelled artistically at a young age. An orphan by age twelve, Welles snuck into the theater scene in **Ireland** at the Gate Theatre and eventually landed on Broadway in 1934. With John Houseman, Welles formed the Mercury Theatre in 1937, where they produced both innovative drama and radio broadcasting. After Welles's spectacular entrance into film with *Citizen Kane*, he next directed *The Magnificent Ambersons*, 1942. The next year he married one of Hollywood's most glamorous leading actresses, Rita Hayworth (1918–1987). As an actor, Welles gave an overpowering performance as Rochester in the film *Jane Eyre*, 1944. He worked for two years on the bizarre thriller *The Lady from Shanghai*, 1948, in which he costarred with Hayworth.

After several failures, Welles renounced Hollywood and went into a self- proclaimed exile to Europe, where he continued to act in other's movies directed by others, such as *The Third Man*, 1949, in order to finance his own movies, such as *Othello* in 1952, in which he played the title role. In 1956 he returned to the **United States** to perform in his own production of *King Lear* on Broadway and direct the film *Touch of Evil*, 1958. Welles never recaptured the artistic mastery he showed in *Citizen Kane*, yet he remained active in film, theater, and television until his death in 1985.

References: Brady, Frank. *Citizen Welles, A Biography of Orson Welles*. New York: Scribner, 1989; Cowie, Peter. *The Cinema of Orson Welles*. New York: Barnes, 1965; France, Richard. *The Theatre of Orson Welles*. Lewisburg, PA: Bucknell University Press, 1977.

Well-Made Play

France

Phrase referring to a model of playwriting made popular in France during the nineteenth century by Eugène Scribe (1791–1861), which emphasized the play of manners, suspense, and reversals or unexpected twists in the action. This plot formula allowed Scribe to be extremely prolific and yet maintain a base level of quality in his writing, a combination that led to his extreme success. For example, he was under contract with the Théâtre du Gymnase (Theater of the Gymnasium) to annually write twelve full-length plays, but he sometimes exceeded expectations, producing up to eighteen plays during the course of some years. Another French writer, Victorien Sardou (1831–1908), also popularized and utilized this formula, continuing Scribe's tradition.

References: Matthews, Brander. *French Dramatists of the 19th Century*. New York: C. Scribner's Sons, 1881.

Wen-Ching

China

Civil painted-face role in **Peking Opera,** a category of **Ching,** superhero characters from historical legends who wear fierce makeup in Peking Opera.

References: Scott, A. C. *The Classical Theatre of China*. London: Allen & Unwin, 1957; Scott, A. C. *The Theatre in Asia*. New York: Macmillan, 1972.

Wen-Chou

China

Civil or scholar type of **Chou,** clown role in **Peking Opera.**

> See also *Wu-Chou*
>
> References: Scott, A. C. *The Classical Theatre of China.* London: Allen & Unwin, 1957; Scott, A. C. *The Theatre in Asia.* New York: Macmillan, 1972.

Wilde, Oscar (1854–1900)

England, Ireland

English playwright. Wilde was born in Ireland, studied at Oxford, and then moved permanently to **England.** Always an extravagant dresser, Wilde was a celebrated wit and conversationalist in London society. He was a proponent of "art for art's sake," believing art did not need to promote morality, that art was its own end, not a means to an end. He was especially successful with drawing room comedies such as *Lady Windermere's Fan,* 1892, *A Woman of No Importance,* 1893, *An Ideal Husband,* 1895 (made into a film in 1999), and his most successful play of all, *The Importance of Being Earnest,* 1895. In 1892 he wrote *Salomé* in French for the great **Sarah Bernhardt**.

Wilde was careless with his many homosexual affairs, which he mostly had with beautiful young men, and even flaunted his gay lifestyle, which was illegal at the time. In 1895 Wilde sued the Marquess of Queensberry for slander, but during that trial it was learned that Wilde was having a homosexual affair with Queensberry's son, Lord Alfred Douglas, which caused Wilde to be charged with offenses to minors. The first trial against Wilde ended in a hung jury, the second trial with a guilty verdict. After his famous trial, he was sentenced to two years of hard labor. After his release he left for France, poor in health and wealth, and resided there until his death just three years later.

Wilde's trials are a fascinating topic, primarily because of his sparkling intellect and his free thought, so in conflict with the values of his time. Peter Finch created the film *The Trials of Oscar Wilde,*

A scene from the film version of Wilde's celebrated play The Importance of Being Earnest *(1952). (Kobol Collection/British Film Makers)*

1960. The recent play, *Gross Indecencies*, 1997, by Moises Kaufman is a provocative examination of the three trials of Oscar Wilde.

References: Mason, Stuart. *Bibliography of Oscar Wilde.* London: T. W. Laurie, 1914; San Juan, E. *The Art of Oscar Wilde.* Princeton, NJ: Princeton University Press, 1967.

Williams, Tennessee (1911–1983)
United States

One of America's greatest playwrights, who brought sexual frankness and complex psychology to the American stage and screen. Born Thomas Lanier Williams, he grew up poor in the South in a repressed household where his being homosexual was not accepted. Williams created powerful and succinct metaphors of the human condition, more specifically, of the climate and attitudes of the South. Indeed, his plays seem to sweat with the heat and humidity caused by both the temperature and human tension.

The Glass Menagerie, 1945, is a tender and pathetic portrayal of a damaged girl. *A Streetcar Named Desire*, 1947, is a disturbing story of sexual repression and delusion. Other plays include *Summer and Smoke*, 1948, *Cat on a Hot Tin Roof*, 1955, *Orpheus Descending*, 1957, and *Suddenly Last Summer*, 1958. Williams provided many outstanding roles suitable for the new Method style of acting emerging from the **Actors Studio.** His later work did not have the appeal of the earlier plays. In his personal life he struggled with drug and alcohol addiction.

References: Jackson, Esther. *The Broken World of Tennessee Williams.* Madison: University of Wisconsin Press, 1965; Roudane, Matthew, ed. *The Cambridge Companion to Tennessee Williams.* New York: Cambridge University Press, 1997; Smith, Bruce. *Costly Performances: Tennessee Williams: The Last Stage.* New York: Paragon House, 1990; Williams, Tennessee. *Conversations with Tennessee Williams.* ed. Albert Devlin. Jackson: University Press of Mississippi, 1986.

Wilson, Robert (1941–)
United States

Creator of the Theater of Images in the 1970s, which sought to redefine time and space in a theatrical setting. Wilson uses mostly untrained performers as elements in a visual theater often void of plot, character, or conflict, his performance verging on being classified as **happenings.** Wilson was born in Texas, with a speech impediment that he overcame through dance therapy. This impediment led to his lack of reliance on speech in his theater. He worked with children suffering from brain damage, using repeated movement as a method of breaking through blocks in the brain. He later utilized this same technique in creating operatic-scale theater events.

In *Deafman Glance*, 1971, gestures from a deaf boy Wilson worked with became raw material. In *Overture for Ka Mountain and Gardinia Terrace, a story about a family and some people changing*, 1972, members of Wilson's family performed. When performed in Iran, the show lasted 168 hours, in Paris, 24 hours. *Einstein on the Beach*, 1976, with music by Philip Glass, is one of his best-known works. Wilson did much of his work in Europe, where he found greater support for his large scale, interdisciplinary productions. In 1993 Wilson's home base became the Alley Theater in Houston, Texas.

References: Fairbrother, Trevor. *Robert Wilson's Vision.* Boston: Museum of Fine Arts, 1991; Marranca, Bonnie. *Robert Wilson: The Theatre of Images.* New York: Harper, 1984; Shyer, Laurence. *Robert Wilson and His Collaborators.* New York: Theatre Communication Group, 1989.

Wu
China

Warrior male role in **Peking Opera,** a subcategory of **Sheng,** the category of male characters in the Peking Opera.

References: Scott, A. C. *The Theatre in Asia.* New York: Macmillan, 1972.

Wu-Ching
China

Militant painted-face role in **Peking Opera,** a category of **Ching,** superhero characters from historic legends who wear fierce makeup.

References: Scott, A. C. *The Theatre in Asia.* New York: Macmillan, 1972.

Wu-Chou
China

Militant or thief clown, a category of **Chou,** clown character in **Peking Opera.**

See also *Wen-Chou*

References: Yang, Daniel Shih-P'eng. *An Annotated Bibliography of Materials for the Study of the Peking Opera.* 2d ed. Wisconsin China Series. Madison: University of Wisconsin, 1967.

Y

Yakshagana

India

Folk opera honoring **Krishna,** the eighth and most important incarnation of the Hindu god **Vishnu**; from Mysore State, believed to have evolved from the sixteenth century. Sanskrit is used in the opening invocation, but otherwise the songs and dialogue are performed in the vernacular language, Kannada, so that a rural audience can understand. This colorful and vigorous folk opera includes acting, singing, and great acrobatic feats, all in honor of Krishna. Men portray all the male roles, and young men all female roles.

A performance opens with two performers representing Krishna and Balarama, another incarnation of Vishnu (the audience finds no problem with two incarnations of the same god performing on stage simultaneously). These two dance and sing in praise of Krishna. Then two other dancers perform a duet and sing of the glory of Krishna and about his flirtations and naughty pranks in his childhood. Then from behind a curtain held up by two people, a majestic version of the character Krishna makes a dramatic entrance and dances majestically to a song sung by the chorus. A play enacting a part of Krishna's life follows. The narrator is the most important performer. He introduces scenes by painting the place and situation in poetic language. In the battle scenes performers show great athletic skill, as they spin and leap into mighty crashes with each other. The dancing that occurs throughout the evening features complicated steps and codified hand gestures. The evening concludes with a song that invokes the ten incarnations of **Vishnu-Krishna.**

Performances usually occur in the open air in an enclosed area. Krishna's costume is yellow, and he wears a gold glittering turban. On his face he wears blue makeup, with deep red on his lips. Other male characters wear rich golden costumes, with bells on their ankles and high headpieces that fan out to the sides and reach a point at the top. They wear white face makeup with darkly outlined eyes. The female characters generally wear ornate saris. All characters perform barefoot. Occasionally topics other than the life of Krishna are dramatized. The musical accompaniment for *Yakshagana* includes vigorous drumming and singing by a chorus of singers seated off to the side.

References: Brandon, James R. *Brandon's Guide to Theatre in Asia.* Honolulu: University Press of Hawaii, 1976; Gargi, Balawanta. *Folk Theater of India.* Seattle: University of Washington Press, 1966; Varadpande, Manohar Laxman. *Krishna Theatre in India.* New Delhi: Abhinav, 1982; Vatsyayan, Kapila. *Traditional Indian Theatre: Multiple Streams.* New Delhi: National Book Trust, 1980.

Yangju Sandae

See Sandae

Yemen

Though there probably was some theatrical activity associated with religious worship earlier on, the first evidence of theater in Yemen occurred when a student group at the Government School formed in 1910. In early Yemen theater, foreign plays such as Shaw's *Pygmalion* were performed in translation. Later, plays by native writer were used, such as Ash-Sharifi's *In the Land of Two Edens* (1963), which focuses on the tragic reign of Imam Ahmad in Yemen in the 1940s and 1950s. The National Theater Company was established in 1971 in Aden, and two years later another National Theater Company was started in Sana'a.

See also Arab Theater
References: Landau, Jacob. *Studies in the Arab Theater and Cinema.* Philadelphia: University of Pennsylvania Press, 1958

Yiddish Theater

Argentina, Poland, Romania, Russia, United States
Jewish theater was slow to develop and indeed even forbidden on religious grounds for centuries. It was not until the nineteenth century that religious restrictions loosened enough to allow a Jewish theater to emerge. The Yiddish language is derived from German, Hebrew, and some Slavic languages and is associated with the Jewish people. The father of Yiddish theater is Avraham Goldenfudim, who presented the first public performance of a Yiddish play in Romania in 1876, a musical comedy called *The Recruits.* The popularity of this production threw open the floodgates and the dramatic expression that had been repressed came pouring out.

Trouble for the Jewish people escalated with the banning of all Jewish theater in Russia in 1883 and the increased persecution of Jews throughout Europe. This situation caused a major exodus to **England** and the Americas, mostly the **United States**. Theater became a tool for retaining cultural richness and solidarity in this new land, and many Yiddish theaters began in most of the larger cities in the United States After World War I (1914–1918) in America the Yiddish Art Theater, led by Maurice Schwartz, produced high-quality ensemble playing by outstanding actors. Other Yiddish theaters flourished around the world,

such as the Polish State Yiddish Theater, the Romanian State Theater and the Moscow State Jewish Theater.

By the 1930s the Yiddish language declined in popular use, so much so that use of the Yiddish language in theater made no sense. Also, in contrast to past centuries, there is now a strong Jewish presence in the arts, and the contribution to theater and film by Jews has been immeasurable.

See also Argentinean Jewish Theater
References: Kadison, Luba. *On Stage, off Stage: Memories of a Lifetime in the Yiddish Theatre.* Cambridge, MA: Harvard University Press, 1992; Lifson, David. *The Yiddish Theatre in America.* New York: T. Yoseloff, 1965; Rosenfeld, Lulla. *Bright Star of Exile: Jacob Adler and the Yiddish Theatre.* New York: Crowell, 1977.

Yokthe Pwe

Myanmar
Marionette theater, originating in the fourteenth century, when it was customarily performed at temple festivals. At first it comprised simple animal plays performed to amuse children. Later complete puppet plays were produced, in the likeness of **Zat Gyi,** Burmese court drama. Puppets were preferred to live actors by the minister of theater because his regulations regarding theater were easier to enforce with one puppeteer than with a whole troupe of actors. The technique for moving these puppets is extremely complicated, since some puppets have up to sixty strings. One of the most complicated puppet characters is **Apuodaw,** who appears in the **Jataka,** the stories of the former births of Gautama Buddha. The puppets appear to wear masks like the Thai **Khon** dancers.

References: Brandon, James. *Theatre in Southeast Asia.* Cambridge, MA: Harvard University Press, 1974; Brandon, James R. *Brandon's Guide to Theatre in Asia.* Honolulu: University Press of Hawaii, 1976.

Yuan Chu

China
Northern drama. The Yuan dynasty (1279–1368) was established by Ogutan Khan, son of Genghis Khan. In 1280 Kublai Khan, a Mongol, overthrew the southern part of the country and united all of

U Than Nyunt *performs* Yokthe Pwe *at the Mandalay Marionettes Theater in Mandalay, Myanmar.* (Photo by Beth Osnes)

China under his control. During this time of foreign rule, Chinese scholars, denied any other employment, took an interest in writing drama in order to make a living, thereby creating Yuan drama. Yuan dramas are comprised of four acts and a wedge (prologue or epilogue). The two major roles are Mo, male, and **Tan,** female. All the song passages are given to the major roles. All other characters speak their dialogue without singing. All songs must belong to the same musical scale and have the same pattern. The lute is the key accompanying instrument. There are "set the scene" poems consisting of four rhyming lines followed by a self-introduction. The various types of drama focus on love and intrigue, religion and the supernatural, history, domestic life, murder and lawsuits, and bandits and heroes. Of these plays, 160 have survived.

References: Chia-Chien, Chu. *The Chinese Theatre.* Trans. James A. Graham. London: John Lane, 1922; Kalvodova, Sis, and Vanis Kalvodova. *Chinese Theatre.* Trans. Iris Urwin. London: Spring House, 1957;. Scott, A. C. *The Classical Theatre of China.* London: Allen & Unwin, 1957; Scott, A. C. *The Theatre in Asia.* New York: Macmillan, 1972.

Yuan Drama

See Yuan Chu

Yueju

See Kwangtung Hsi

Yugen

Japan

Originally, used only to refer to the dark or obscure hidden meaning of the Buddhist Sutras. To evoke the subtle quality associated with *Yugen* came to be the aesthetic goal of **Noh,** masked dance-drama of medieval Japan. Yugen came to refer to a courtly and dignified form of beauty characterized by gentleness and aristocratic refinement. The symbol for Yugen is a swan with a flower in its bill.

References: Scott, A. C. *The Theatre in Asia.* New York: Macmillan, 1972.

Yugoslavia

Yugoslavia was formed in 1918 when the Austro-Hungarian empire collapsed after World War I. The Kingdom of the Serbs, Croats, and Slovenes was formed from the former provinces of **Croatia,** Dalmatia, **Bosnia and Herzegovina, Slovenia,** Voyvodina, and the independent state of Montenegro. The name was later changed to Yugoslavia. In 1945 Josip Broz, known as Marshal Tito, became head of the Yugoslavian government until his death in 1980. He was a Communist but rejected the Stalinist policy of Stalin dictating

policy to all Communist countries, and thus Yugoslavia remained free from Soviet control. By 1991, Slovenia, Bosnia and Herzegovina, and Croatia had declared independence. Extreme conflict between the various ethnic groups of these areas both plagues the development of culture and increases the desperate need for the healing power of the arts.

Theater in the area of Yugoslavia developed much the same as the rest of Europe from the Middle Ages through the eighteenth century with liturgical dramas, Jesuit Theater, and touring companies from France and German-speaking areas. In the sixteenth century secular theater, including masquerades and citizen's comedy, grew. Many ethnic groups, the most important being the Serbs, the Croats, the Slovenians and the Macedonians, each had their own languages and contributed various accomplishments to the development of theater in the region.

Serbian theater owes much of its development to Joakim Vujic (1772–1847), who is considered the father of Serbian theater. He formed an amateur acting company in 1838, organized a school for theater, and formed amateur dramatic societies. Vujic created the first professional theater company in the area later known as Yugoslavia, the Novi Sad, which performed in Belgrade. They performed many of the comedies of Serbian playwright Jovan Sterija (1806–1856). There was a Serbian traveling acting company from 1839–1841 in Zagreb. The Serbian National Theater in Belgrade opened in 1869 and had to be repaired after both the first and second world wars. Nusic Branislav (1864–1938), a Serbian theater manager and playwright, wrote and produced many popular comedies with biting satire on society. The Belgrade International Theater Festival began in 1967 and is still in existence.

In the sixteenth century Croatian theater began, with secular farces and pastorals performed in Dubrovnik. During the seventeenth century in Dubrovnik, public performances of secular dramas performed by amateur troupes were presented in city squares. Throughout the eighteenth century German and Italian acting companies performed in local palaces and the homes of nobility. In 1797 in Zagreb the first permanent theater hall was created in the palace of

Count Amade, and for thirty-seven years public performances were given there. In 1861 the theater in Zagreb became a state-subsidized national theater under the direction of Dmitrije Demetar (1811–1872). Andrija Fijan (1851–1911), an actor at the Zagreb Theater, portrayed many of the great roles from **Shakespeare,** including Hamlet, Othello, and King Lear. With a noble figure and a beautiful voice with near-perfect diction, he ruled the stage for over forty years. The actress Marija Ruzicka Strozzi (1850–1937), a celebrated tragedienne, was known as the Slavic **Sarah Bernhardt**. She was the leading lady at the Zagreb Theater for sixty-nine years. In Zagreb the Croat National Theater mounts many works with large casts and enormous settings. The Zagreb Dramatic Theater is an offshoot of the National Theater that began in 1953. Young actors from this theater, led by Mladen Skiljan, produce plays by Yugoslavian authors and other European classics. Comedy and light operettas are often performed at The Comedy Theater in Zagreb. The Theatre 2000 in Pula was formed in 1997 by leading Croatian actors to break away from the country's officially sanctioned theater. Political unrest since the breakup of Yugoslavia in 1991 forms the background for many new theatrical works, including *Snake Skin,* 1998, by Croatian playwright Slobodan Snajder.

Slovene theater had a similar beginning as other regions in the area, with religious dramas in the native language by the seventeenth century. There is an extant Slovene **Passion Play** dating from 1721. Throughout the eighteenth century German and Italian acting troupes performed in local palaces and in the homes of nobility. A Slovene playwright known simply as Linhart (1756–1795) wrote local comedies about peasant life. In 1850 the first worker's theater was formed in Idrija for mining communities. In 1861 Slovenes founded a National Reading Room, located in Ljubljana, which organized amateur performances. Soon after, in 1867, the Dramatic Society was founded, and in 1869 a permanent school for dramatic art was formed. A Slovene theater company in Ljubljana opened with a new theater building in 1892. Outstanding actors include Sofija Borstnik Zvonarjeva (1868–1949) and Anton Cerar-Danilo (1858–1947). A cultural center in Trbovlje opened in 1957, hous-

ing a theater space that has encouraged more live theater in the area. The Ljubljana Opera is active, with a production of *Ballo* in 1998 and *Equinox*, by Marjan Kozina, a Slovenian composer, in 1999.

Between the two world wars (1919–1941), the people of Yugoslavia found themselves united politically for the first time. Theaters were under the control of the central government. The most noteworthy director during this time was Branko Gavella (1885–1962), who directed many works of classical world literature throughout Yugoslavia. He also produced many plays by native playwrights. When the Germans invaded in 1941, theater came to a standstill, but by the end of World War II in 1945, theater in Yugoslavia experienced a growth spurt. Companies of young actors formed even in remote regions. In Macedonia there were six active theaters by the 1940s. D. Kjostarov, a prolific producer in Skopje, created many important theater works. The Dubrovnik Festival for the Arts began in 1950, making it a great central activity for theater. Theater since the breakup of Yugoslavia in 1991 has been largely political. Questions of ethnicity in war-torn Bosnia and Herzegovina have been addressed by a variety of community-based theater creations including *Where Are You From?* in 1997 and *Podrum*, a play performed by youth, between 1996 and 1998. The play *Euroalien* (1998) by Macedonian playwright Goran Stefanovski explores the clash between an emerging post–Cold War European identity and national or regional identities.

References: Badalic, Josip. *Bibliografija Hrvatske Dramske I Kazalisne Knjizevnosti*. Zagreb: Jugoslavenska Akademija Znanosti I Umjetnostil, 1948; Dobrowolsky, Ferdinand. *The Theatre in Yugoslavia*. Belgrade: Museum of Theatre Art, 1955; Dolan, Jill. "Linking Art and Politics: KPGT, The Zagreb Theatre Company (Yugoslavia)." *Carleton Drama Review* 27 (Spring 1983): 82; Hartnoll, Phyllis. *The Oxford Companion to the Theatre*. New York: Oxford University Press, 1967; Kuftinec, Sonja. "'Odakle Ste?' (Where Are You From?): Active Learning and Community-Based Theatre in Former Yugoslavia and the U.S." *Theatre Topics* 7, 2 (September 1997): 170–186; Kuftinec, Sonja. "Playing with Borders: Dramaturging Ethnicity in Bosnia." *Journal of Dramatic Theory and Criticism* 13, 1 (Fall 1998): 143–156; Laurie, Edith. "The Theatre Expands in Yugoslavia." *Theatre Arts* 36 (April 1952): 24; Legyel-Bosiljevac, Aranka. "Yugoslavia." In *The World Encyclopedia of Contemporary Theatre*, ed. Don Rubin, 948–956. New York: Routledge, 1994; Menashe, Louis, and Jasminka Udovicki. "Art, History, and Politics in the Former Yugoslavia: An Interview with Michael Benson." *Cineaste* 22, 2 (June 1996): 30–33; Nicholson, Anne Gregory. "The Stage in Yugoslavia." *Drama* 12 (1933/1934): 22; Predan, Alija. "Theatre in Yugoslavia." *Drama* 3 (1984): 30; Seton, Marie. "Theatre in Yugoslavia." *Drama* 3 (Autumn 1947): 19; Welsh, James. "Two from Yugoslavia: The Theme of War." *Literature/Film Quarterly* 3 (Summer 1975): 286.

Yugoslavian Cinema
Bosnia-Herzegovina, Croatia, Serbia, Slovenia

Yugoslavia was created in 1918 to unify the Serbs, Croats, and Slovenes. The first feature film in the area that was to be Yugoslavia was *Karageorge*,

A scene from Emir Kusturica's film Black Cat White Cat *(1998) (Kobol Collection/Pandora Films)*

1910, directed by Jules Barry, which was a dramatization of the life of a Serbian hero. Film production after World War I (1914–1918) was sparse. Prior to World War II (1939–1945), the best filmmaker was Mihailo-Mika Popovic who directed *With Faith in God* (1934). In 1945 the State Film Enterprise was created; it subsidized filmmaking in all areas of Yugoslavia. The creation of feature films was slow to develop in maturity and quality, but the creation of animated films throve. By the 1960s the film industry increased production and quality with films such as *Alphabet of Fear* (1961), *Bitter Grass* (1965), *When I'm Dead and White* (1968) and *It Rains in My Village* (1969). In the 1970s many leading filmmakers worked abroad because of censorship at home. In the late 1970s and 1980s many filmmakers returned, because of a more relaxed artistic climate, and started a movement, known as the Prague School because many of them had trained in Czechoslovakia. Included in this movement was director Rajko Grlic, who created *The Melody Haunts My Memory* (1981), and Variola Vera, who created *Tito and Me* (1991).

The breakup of Yugoslavia in 1991 was nearly fatal for the film industry. Filmmakers who had once cooperated and worked on each other's films were now divided by political conflicts and racial wars. The Belgrade International Film Festival began again in 1996 after being cancelled for two years due to the war. Filmmaker Emir Kusturica directed *Underground* (1995), which explores the history of his country, Serbia. Other filmmakers sometimes depart from the dismal subject of politics with comedic films such as *Black Cat White Cat* (1999), directed by Emir Kusturica.

References: Horton, Andrew. "Festivals: The Belgrade International Film Festival." *Cineaste* 22, 2 (June 1996): 56–57; Katz, Ephraim. *The Film Encyclopedia.* New York: Harper Perennial, 1994; Menashe, Louis, and Jasminka Udovicki. "Art, History, and Politics in the Former Yugoslavia: An Interview with Michael Benson." *Cineaste* 22, 2 (June 1996): 30–33; Milgrom, Al. "Communiques: The Sarajevo Film Festival." *Cineaste* 24, 1 (December 1998): 89; Wrathall, John. "Reviews: 'Black Cat White Cat.'" *Sight and Sound* 9, 5 (May 1999): 41–42; Yarovskaya, Marianna. "Reviews: 'Underground.'" *Film Quarterly* 51, 2 (Winter 1997–1998): 50–54.

Z

Zamfirescu, George Mihail (1898–1939)
Romania

Romanian playwright, director, and novelist of the early twentieth century. As a young man Zamfirescu organized an amateur theater group in 1918 in Transylvania called the Society for Theater and Romanian Culture, which toured the provinces. His first big success as a playwright occurred in 1927, when the Bulandra Theater performed his play *Miss Natasia,* a tragicomedy. His next play *Orders Come from Suceava,* 1927, was a history play. In the following year his play *Sam* caused a great controversy and was deemed politically subversive.

In 1931 he created his own theater troupe, The Mask, to perform for the workers in the area and to encourage young native playwrights and actors. After that group disbanded, he started another group in 1932 called Thirteen and One. In 1933 he was appointed adjunct director of the National Theater in Jassy, but he lost that appointment because of his political views. Poor health caused by near poverty brought on his early death in 1939, still a young man.

> **References:** Lamb, Ruth Stanton. *The World of Romanian Theatre.* Claremont, CA: Ocelot, 1976.

Zanni
Italy

Comic male servant stock character type in **commedia dell'arte,** improvised Italian sixteenth- and seventeenth-century comedy. These characters were most celebrated for their impressive acrobatic stunts and comic tricks. Historically this type of character has appeared in two roles. The first was the servant role **Brighella,** the sly instigator of intrigues and schemes, and the second was **Arlecchino,** the simpleminded clown servant in patched attire, who interrupted the action with comic gags known as **lazzi.** Actors throughout the centuries created many variations on the *Zanni* character, often devising new proper names for their creations, such as Pedrolino, Truffaldino, and Pulcinella.

In Venice, *Zanni* is a shortened form of the name Giovanni and was given to migrants to Italian cities. Thus, as migrant workers, the *Zanni* characters spoke loudly, like those who make their living in the outdoor market. Their movements were often urgent, exaggerated, and comical. A half mask covering only the forehead, cheeks, and nose was worn. The longer the nose on the mask, the more stupid the *Zanni* character.

The English word "zany" has its origin in the *Zanni* character.

> **References:** Chinoy, Helen Krich, and Toby Cole. *Actors on Acting.* New York: Crown, 1970; Craig, Edward Gordon. "The Characters of the Commedia Dell'Arte." *The Mask* (January 1912); Rudlin, John. *Commedia Dell'Arte: An Actor's Handbook.* London and New York: Routledge, 1994.

Zarzuela

Spain

A short opera, usually based on a mythological theme, named after the palace of La Zarzuela, where the first of its kind, by Pedro Calderón de la Barca (1600–1681), was performed in 1657. This form of elaborate court play featured light dramatic action, frequently interrupted by musical numbers. Lavish production qualities were the primary focus of these productions, with innovative use of perspective in scenic design. The means of production for scenic effects were concealed to create pure spectacle for the audience. Acting seems to have been secondary to the visual spectacle. The popularity of these and other court dramas caused the decline in the commercial theater, such as the **Auto Sacramental,** because the public theaters could not afford to compete with the sophisticated spectacle created in the generously financed court dramas.

An abbreviated version of the *zarzuela*, known as *Género Chico*, evolved in the Caribbean in the late eighteenth century.

References: McKendrick, Melveena. *Theatre in Spain: 1490–1700.* New York: Cambridge University Press, 1989; Polito, Antonio. *Spanish Theatre: A Survey from the Middle Ages to the Twentieth-Century.* Salt Lake City: Department of Languages, University of Utah, 1967.

Zat Gyi

Myanmar

Masked dance-drama performed for the Burmese court. Zat Gyi was sponsored by Burmese kings during the period from 1750–1850, but when the British took control in 1885, the kings lost their power. Since then performances of this form have been rare. When this genre was first performed, the plays were almost exact copies of Thai court drama. As Burmese poets began to write their own plays, Zat Gyi was adjusted to suit Burmese tastes. The main story that inspired plays was the **Ramayana,** a Hindu epic tale, which was changed slightly to suit Burmese Buddhist beliefs. In India, Rama was believed to be an incarnation of **Vishnu,** the Hindu god, but the Burmese told the story as though Rama were an incarnation of the **Buddha.** As well as court performers, professional troupes took up the genre and traveled about the countryside performing their own versions of the repertory used in court. These traveling troupes were largely responsible for disseminating the *Ramayana* story throughout Myanmar.

References: Brandon, James R. *Brandon's Guide to Theatre in Asia.* Honolulu: University Press of Hawaii, 1976.

Zat Pwe

Myanmar

Dance-drama based on Burmese legends. *Zat Pwe* movement is a combination of classical Thai dance, Burmese dance, and the Western ballet brought by the British when they colonized Burma in the eighteenth century. Performances consist of men and women singing, dancing, and performing dialogue. A show lasts about nine hours, but the high point is after midnight, when the lead actors exhibit their virtuosity. The lead actor takes the stage, singing a bit, and then he or she breaks into a rigorous and impressive dance that lasts less than a minute. Other actors and actresses follow suit, eventually joined by the clowns. Performers wear slippers as in ballet and do leaps and turns that are based on standard Western ballet moves. They also incorporate turned out elbows and bent legs with a low torso posture, as in most Asian dancing. Actors improvise much of their dialogue during a performance. The scripts are comic romance stories. Instead of conflict, humor is the main theme. The hero princes do a great deal of laughing. There are up to ten highly skilled clown performers. Musical accompaniment is performed by a **Saing** orchestra composed of drums, gongs, bells, cymbals, a reed instrument, and a xylophone. There is an instrument consisting of 21 tuned drums in a circular frame that is unique in all of Asia. In society the star performers of Zat Pwe are idolized. Zat Pwe performances are the last remains of Burmese court drama and can be found in central and southern Myanmar.

See also Pya Zat; Zat Gyi

References: Brandon, James R. *Brandon's Guide to Theatre in Asia.* Honolulu: University Press of Hawaii, 1976; Brandon, James. *Theatre in Southeast Asia.* Cambridge, MA: Harvard University Press, 1974.

Zen Buddhism

China, Japan

A school of Mahayana **Buddhism** from the sixth century A.D. When Buddhism first entered China from India in the first century A.D., Taoist priests welcomed it. The combination of Taoist quietism and Buddhist meditation produced Zen. In the seventh century, Zen was introduced to Japan from China.

Zen stresses single-mindedness and intuitive insight cultivated through both mental and physical disciplines. Through austerity, Zen promoted strength and mental alertness. From the thirteenth to the sixteenth century, Zen helped to shape the ethical code of the **samurai** class. Zen influences on the Japanese arts is profound, and it is clearly seen in **Noh,** the classic masked dance-drama. Artistic creations influenced by Zen are characterized by simplicity, serenity, composure, and spontaneity.

References: Aherne, Consuelo Maria, Paul Kevin Meagher, and Thomas C. O'Brien, eds. *Encyclopedic Dictionary of Religion.* 3 vols. Washington, DC: Corpus Publishers, 1979; Eliade, Mircea, ed. *The Encyclopedia of Religion.* 16 vols. New York: Macmillan, 1987.

Zhang Kui

See **Zhang Mu**

Zhang Mu

China

Chinese rod puppet theater (also called *Zhang-tou Kui-iei*, the term used in the Sung dynasty). The smallest type of rod puppet is 12–18 inches tall and comes from Northern China. One puppeteer can manipulate two puppets. The medium-sized puppet is 3 feet tall and was popular in Szechuan, Hunan, Hai-nan, Yang-chou, and Shanghai. Near Hai-nan Island there is an interesting performance style in which both the puppet and puppeteer are visible and active in the drama. The puppeteer performs songs as he controls the puppets. The largest type of rod puppet in China, called *Da Mu Nao-ke* (literally "large wooden skull"), almost 5 feet high, is from the northern part of Szechuan. Fine carving and sophisticated mechanics allow many features on the puppet's face to move. Yilong County in Szechuan is famous for a troupe named Yin-yang. They combine these large rod puppets with small child performers riding on the backs of adult performers. Children play major roles and mimic the movements of the puppets as they interact with them. Most of the puppets are supported by a long rod, sometimes with a coiled spring between the head and shoulders. Others have eyes and mouths movable by wires running down and through the puppet. The hands of the puppets are operated by two thin rods, which are as long as the puppet's costume. Chinese rod puppets have no legs.

Bibliography

Abaya, Consuelo. "The Fiesta." *Philippines Quarterly* 1, 4 (March 1952): 29–35.

Abbott, George Fredrick. *Macedonian Folklore*. Cambridge: University Press, 1903.

Abdel-Wahab, Farouk. *Modern Egyptian Drama: An Anthology*. Minneapolis: Bibliotheca Islamica, 1974.

Abimbola, Wande, ed. *Yoruba Oral Tradition: Poetry in Music, Dance and Drama*. Ile-Ife, Nigeria: Department of African Languages and Literature, University of Ife, 1975.

Abraham, Arthur. *Cultural Policy in Sierra Leone*. Paris: UNESCO, 1978.

Abrams, Steve. "Cirque du Soleil." *Puppetry Journal* 49 (Summer 1998): 19.

Abramson, Glenda. *Modern Hebrew Drama*. New York: St. Martin's, 1979.

Adamson, Joe. *Grocho, Harpo, Chico, and Sometimes Zeppo; A History of the Marx Brothers and a Satire on the Rest of the World*. New York: Simon and Schuster, 1973.

Addis, Stephen. "Theatre Music of Vietnam." *Southeast Asia: An International Quarterly* 1 (Winter/Spring 1971): 129–152.

Adler, Stella. *Stella Adler on Ibsen, Strindberg, and Chekhov*. New York: Knopf, 1999.

Aerts, Theo. "Christian Art from Melanesia." *Bikmaus: A Journal of Papua New Guinea Affairs, Ideas and the Arts* 5 (1984): 47–83.

Aherne, Consuelo Maria, Paul Kevin Meagher, and Thomas C. O'Brien, eds. *Encyclopedic Dictionary of Religion*. 3 vols. Washington, DC: Corpus, 1979.

Aithnard, K. M. *Some Aspects of Cultural Policy in Togo*. Paris: UNESCO, 1976.

Akar, John. "The Arts in Sierra Leone." *Africa Forum* (Fall 1965): 87–91.

Albuquerque, Severino J. *Violent Acts: A Study of Contemporary Latin American Theatre*. Detroit: Wayne State University Press, 1991.

Alcide, Marie-Jose. "Theatrical and Dramatic Elements of Haitian Voodoo." Ph.D. diss., City University of New York, 1988.

Aldgate, Anthony. *Best of British Cinema and Society from 1930 to the Present*. New York: I. B. Tauris, 1999.

Aleksiev, Aleksandar. *Founders of Macedonian Drama*. Skopje: Misla, 1972.

Alexander, Edward. "Shakespeare's Plays in Armenia." *Shakespeare Quarterly* 9 (1958): 387.

Ali, Z. S. "Centre for Black and African Arts and Civilization." *Nigeria Magazine*, 128–129 (1979): 51–61.

Allen, Elphine. "Australian Aboriginal Dance." In *The Australian Aboriginal Heritage: An Introduction through the Arts*, ed. R. M. Berndt and E. S. Phillips. Sydney: Australian Society for Education through the Arts in Association with Ure Smith, 1973.

Allen, James Turney. "Greek Acting in the Fifth Century." *University of California Publications in Classical Philology* 15 (1916): 279–289.

Alpert, Hollis. *The Barrymores*. New York: Dial Press, 1964.

Alterescu, Simion. *An Abridged History of Romanian Theatre*. Bucharest: Academiei Republicii Socialiste Romania, 1983.

Anand, Mulk Raj. *The Indian Theatre*. London: D. Dobson, 1950.

And, Metin. *Culture, Performance and Communication in Turkey*. Tokyo: Institute for the Study of Languages and Cultures of Asia and Africa, 1987.

———. *A History of Theatre and Popular Entertainment in Turkey*. Ankara: Forum Yayinlari, 1963–1964.

Anderson, Joseph L., and Donald Richie. *The Japanese Film: Art and Industry.* Princeton, NJ: Princeton University Press, 1982.

Andre, Frank, *Jean-Louis Barrault.* Hamburg: Johannes Maria Hoeppner, 1957.

Anger, Cedric. "Cahier Critique: Balade Funéraire: 'Trafico' Critical Notebook." *Cahiers du Cinema* (March 1999): 66–67.

Ansorge, Peter. *Disrupting the Spectacle: Five Years of Experimental and Fringe Theatre in Britain.* London: Pitman, 1975.

Antoine, Andre. *Memories of the la Théâtre-Libre.* Trans. Marvin Carlson. Florida: University of Miami Press, 1964.

Antola, Livia, and Everett Rogers. "Television Flows in Latin America." *Communication Research* 11, 2 (1984): 183–202.

Antubam, Kofi. "Arts of Ghana." *United Asia* 9, 1 (1957): 61–70.

———. *Ghana's Heritage of Culture.* Leipzig: Koehler & Amelang, 1963.

D'Aponte, Mimi Gisolfi. *Seventh Generation: An Anthology of Native American Plays.* New York: Communications Group, 1999.

Appleton, William Worthen. *Charles Macklin: An Actor's Life.* Cambridge, MA: Harvard University Press, 1960.

Aquino, Francisca Reyes, and Leonor Orasa. *Philippine Folk Dances.* 5 vols. Manila: Kayamanggi Press, 1953–1966.

Archey, Gilbert. "Polynesia, Polynesian Cultures." *EWA* 11 (1966): 438–466.

Arden, Harvey. *Dreamkeepers: A Spirit-Journey into Aboriginal Australia.* New York: Harper Collins, 1994.

Armes, Roy. *French Film.* New York: Dutton, 1970.

———. *Third World Film Making and the West.* Berkeley: University of California Press, 1987.

Armstrong, Alan. *Maori Action Songs.* Wellington, NZ: A. H. & A. W. Reed, 1960.

Arnaud, Lucien. *Charles Dullin.* Paris: L'Arche, 1952.

Arnott, Peter D. *The Ancient Greek and Roman Theatre.* New York: Random House, 1971.

———. *Greek Scenic Conventions in the Fifth Century* B.C. Westport, CT: Greenwood, 1978.

———. *Public and Performance in the Greek Theatre.* New York: Routledge, 1989.

Arnott, W. G. *Menander, Plautus, Terence.* Oxford: Clarendon Press, 1975.

Arntzen, Knut. "New Theatre in Norway: From Group Theatre to Project Theatre." *Scandinavia* 31, 2 (November 1992): 187–202.

Arquilles, P. F. "The Duplo and Karagatan: Two Basic Types of Drama in the Philippines during the Spanish Regime." *F. J.* 1, 4 (November 1964): 48–52.

Artaud, Antonin. *The Theatre and Its Double.* Trans. Mary Caroline Richard. New York: Grove, 1958.

———. *Le Theatre et Son Double.* Paris: Gallimard, 1938.

Asante, Molefi K. *African Culture: The Rhythms of Unity.* Westport, CT: Greenwood, 1985.

———. *The Afrocentric Idea.* Philadelphia: Temple University Press, 1987.

Asian Traditional Performing Arts (Conference). *Dance and Music in South Asian Drama.* Tokyo: Academia Music, 1983.

Askin, Leon. *Quietude and Quest: Protagonists and Antagonists in the Theatre, on and off Stage.* Riverside, CA: Ariadne, 1989.

Aston, Elaine. *Sarah Bernhardt: A French Actress on the English Stage.* New York: St. Martin's, 1989.

Atigbi, I. A. *Nigeria Traditional Festivals: A Guide to Nigeria Cultural Safari.* Lagos: Nigerian Tourist Association, 1972.

Auerbach, Nina. *Ellen Terry, Player in Her Time.* New York: W. W. Norton, 1987.

Australian Institute of Aboriginal Studies. *A Wlbiri Fire Ceremony.* Berkeley: University of California Extension Media, 1977.

Aveilana, Dassy H. "The Native Theatre." *Philippine Quarterly* 1, 4 (March 1952): 60–62.

Awad, Ramsis. *Shakespeare in Egypt.* al-Qahirah, Egypt: al-Hayah al-Misriyah all-Ammah lil-Kitab, 1986.

Awasthi, Suresh. "Shadow Plays of India and Their Affinities with the Shadow Plays of Southeast Asia." In *Traditional Drama and Music of Southeast Asia,* ed. Mohd. Taib Osman, 112–119. Kuala Lumpur: Dewan Bahasa Dan Pustaka Kementerian Pelajaran Malaysia, 1974.

Axton, Richard. *European Drama of the Early Middle Age.* London: Hutchinson, 1974.

Ba Han. "The Evolution of Burmese Dramatic Performance and Festival Occasions." *Guardian* 13, 9 (September 1966): 18–24.

Babitsky, Pual. *The Soviet Film Industry.* New York: Published for the Research Program on the U.S.S.R. by Praeger, 1955.

Bablet, Denis. *Edward Gordon Craig.* Paris: L'Arche, 1962.

Bachfield, August. "Theatre in Siam." *Erdball* 2 (1928): 335–377.

"Backstage: Vaclav Havel on the Town: Dinner and a Play." *Washington Post,* 15 September 1998, E.

Badalic, Josip. *Bibliografija Hrvatske Dramske I Kazalisne Knjizevnosti.* Zagreb: Jugoslavenska Akademija Znanosti I Umjetnostil, 1948.

Badawi, M. *Early Arabic Drama.* Cambridge: Cambridge University Press, 1988.

———. "Medieval Arabic Drama: Ibn Daniyal." *Journal of Arabic Literature* 13 (1982): 83–107.

Bahoken, J. C., and Engelbert Atangana. *Cultural Policy in the United Republic of Cameroon.* Paris: UNESCO, 1976.

Bain, D. *Actors and Audience.* Oxford: Oxford University Press, 1977.

Bains, Y. S. *English Canadian Theatre 1765–1826.* New York: Peter Lang, 1998.

Baker, Henry Barton. *English Actors from Shakespeare to Macready*. New York: H. Holt, 1879.

Baker, Kit. "Performance Review: *Macbeth* by William Shakespeare." *Theatre Journal* 50, 2 (May 1998): 242–246.

Baker, Pam. "To Catch a Thief: She Buckled the Swash of Antonio Banderas in *The Mask of Zorro* and Now in *Entrapment* Catherine Zeta Jones Has Master Thief Sean Connery Shaken and Stirred . . . !" *Film Review* 583 (July 1999): 68–71.

Balasaraswati, T. "On Bharata Natyam." *Sangeet Natak Journal* (April 1984): 8–13.

Balk, Wesley H. *The Dramatization of 365 Days*. Minneapolis: University of Minnesota Press, 1972.

Ball, John. *A Bibliography of Canadian Theatre History, 1583–1975*. Toronto: Playwrights Co-op, 1976.

Ball, John, and Richard Plant. *Bibliography of Theatre History in Canada: The Beginnings through 1984*. Toronto: ECW Press, 1993.

Ball, Lucille. *Love, Lucy*. New York: G. P. Putnam's Sons, 1996.

Banas, Raymundo C. *Philipino Music and Theater*. Quezon City: Manlapaz Publishing, 1969.

Bandem, I Made. "Notes on the Development of the Arja Dance Drama." *Indonesia Circle* 3 (March 1983): 28–32.

Bandler, V. "The Cry From An Island in the Cliffs (The Theater Scene in Finland and Sweden)." *Theater Heute* 21, 10 (1980).

Bandy, Mary Lea. *Rediscovering French Film*. Boston: Little Brown, 1983.

Banerjee, Projesh. *Art of Indian Dancing*. New Delhi: Sterling, 1985.

Banham, Martin. *African Theatre Today*. London: Pitman, 1976.

Banham, Martin, Errol Hill, George Woodyard, and Olu Obafemi, eds. *The Cambridge Guide to African and Caribbean Theatre*. New York: Cambridge University Press, 1994.

Bannerman, Eugen, and Adrian Pecknold. "Carte Blanche: The Canadian Mime Theatre: A Thirty-Year Retrospective." *Canadian Theatre Review* 96 (Fall 1998): 83–86.

Baram, Amatzia. *Culture, History, and Ideology in the Formation of Bathist Iraq, 1968–89*. New York: St. Martin's, 1991.

Baraza: A Journal of the Arts in Malawi. Zomba, Malawi: Department of Fine and Performing Arts, Chancellor College, 1983–.

Barba, Eugenio. *Beyond the Floating Islands*. New York: PAJ Publishers, 1986.

Barba, Eugenio, and Nicola Savarese. *The Secret Art of the Performer: A Dictionary of Theatre Anthropology*. New York: Routledge, 1991.

Barber, Laurie. *New Zealand: A Short History*. Auckland: Century Hutchinson, 1989.

Barbour, Sheena, ed. *Irish Performing Arts Yearbook*. London: Rhinegold, 1992.

Barlow, Cleve. *Tikanga Whakaaro: Key Concepts in Maori Culture*. New York: Oxford University Press, 1991.

Barnard, Tim. *Argentine Cinema*. Toronto: Nightwood Editions, 1986.

Barnett, Dennis. "Performance Review: 'The 1997 BITEF Festival.'" *Theatre Journal* 50, 3 (October 1998): 389–394.

Barnouw, Erik, and S. Krishnaswamy. *Indian Film*. New York: Columbia University Press, 1963.

Barrault, Jean-Louis. *The Theatre of Jean-Louis Barrault*. New York: Hill and Wang, 1961.

Barrett, Lindsay. "The Popular Arts in Nigeria in the 1980s." *Positive Review* 1, 4 (1981): 24–27.

Barrow, Terence. *Art and Life in Polynesia*. Wellington: Reed, 1972.

Barton, John. *Playing Shakespeare*. New York: Methuen in Association with Channel Four Television Co., 1984.

Barton, Ruth. "Contemporary Irish Cinema: Feisty Colleens and Faithful Sons: Gender in Irish Cinema." *Cineaste* 24, 2–3 (March 1999): 40–45.

Bartsch, Shadi. *Actors in the Audience: Theatricality and Doublespeak From Nero to Hadrian*. Cambridge, MA: Harvard University Press, 1994.

Basch, Kenneth. "Cinema Venezuela." *New Orleans Review* 7, 2 (1980): 185–189.

Bates, William Nickerson. *Euripides: A Student of Human Nature*. Philadelphia: University of Pennsylvania Press, 1930.

Batusic, Nikola. "Croatia." In *The World Encyclopedia of Contemporary Theatre*, ed. Don Rubin. New York: Routledge, 1994: 170–184.

Baxter, J. *The Australian Cinema*. Sydney: Pacific Books, 1970.

Bazin, Andre. *French Cinema of the Occupation and Resistance*. New York: Fredrick Ungar, 1981.

———. *What Is Cinema?* 2 vols. Berkeley and Los Angeles: University of California Press, 1971.

Beacham, Richard. *The Roman Theatre and Its Audience*. Cambridge, MA: Harvard University Press, 1992.

Beadle, Richard. *The Cambridge Companion to Medieval English Theatre*. New York: Cambridge University Press, 1994.

Beardsley, Monroe C. *Aesthetics from Classical Greece to the Present: A Short History*. New York: Macmillan, 1966.

Beare, W. "Masks on the Roman Stage." *Classical Quarterly* 33 (1939): 139–146.

Beauman, Sally. *The Royal Shakespeare Company: A History of Ten Decades*. New York: Oxford University Press, 1982.

Becher, Alton. "The Journey through the Night: Some Reflections on Burmese Traditional Theatre." *Drama Review*, 15 (Winter 1970): 83–87.

Beckwith, Martha W. *The Kumulipo: A Hawaiian Creation Chant*. Honolulu: University Press of Hawaii, 1972.

Beik, Janet. *Hausa Theatre in Niger: A Contemporary Oral Art.* New York: Garland, 1987.

Bell, Robert E. *Place-Names in Classical Mythology: Greece.* Santa Barbara, CA: ABC-CLIO, 1989.

Belo, J. *Bali: Rangda and Barang.* 2d ed. Seattle: Monographs of the American Ethnological Society, 1966.

Belton, John. *American Cinema/American Culture.* New York: McGraw-Hill, 1994.

Beltran, Luis Ramiro. "TV Etching in the Minds of Latin America: Conservatism, Materialism and Conformism." *Gazette* 24, 1 (1978): 61–65.

Benedetti, Jean. *Stanislavski and the Actor.* New York: Routledge/Theatre Arts Books, 1998.

Benedetti, S. "The Origins of Improvisational Comedy or Commedia-dell'Arte." *Rassegna Della Letteratura Italiana* 102, 1 (January–June 1998): 240–242.

Bennett, Wycliffe. "The Jamaican Theatre: A Preliminary Overview." *Jamaica Journal* 8 2–3 (Summer 1974): 3–9.

Bentley, Eric. *Bernard Shaw.* Norfolk, CT: New Directions, 1957.

Bergman, Ingmar. *Images: My Life in Film.* Trans. Marianne Ruuth. New York: Arcade Publishing, 1994.

Berlogea, Ileana. "Shakespeare in Romania." *Shakespeare Quarterly* 31 (1980): 405.

Bermel, Albert. *Farce: A History from Aristophanes to Woody Allen.* New York: Simon and Schuster, 1982.

Berndt, R. M., and E. S. Phillips. *The Australian Aboriginal Heritage: An Introduction through the Arts.* Sydney: Ure Smith, 1973.

Best, Kenneth Y. *Cultural Policy in Liberia.* Paris: UNESCO, 1974.

Bettelheim, Judith. "Jonkonnu and Other Christmas Masquerades." In *Caribbean Festival Arts,* 39–71. Seattle: University of Washington Press, 1988.

Betti, Liliana. *Fellini: An Intimate Portrait.* Boston: Little, Brown, 1979.

Bevington, David. *Medieval Drama.* Boston: Houghton, 1975.

Bibliowicz, Azriel. "Be Happy Because Your Father Isn't Your Father: An Analysis of Colombian Telenovelas." *Journal of Popular Culture* (Winter 1980): 476–485.

Bieber, Margarete. *The History of the Greek and Roman Theater.* Princeton, NJ: Princeton University Press, 1961.

———. "The Statuette of an Actor of New Comedy." *Bulletin of the Art Museum, Princeton University* (1951): 4–12.

Bigsby, C. W. E. *A Critical Introduction to Twentieth-Century American Drama.* New York: Cambridge University Press, 1985.

———. *David Mamet.* New York: Methuen, 1985.

Biner, Pierre. *Living Theatre.* New York: Horizon Press, 1972.

Binyon, Helen. *Puppetry Today.* New York: Watson-Guptil Grove, 1966.

Bjurstrom, Per. *Feast and Theatre in Queen Christina's Rome.* Stockholm: 1966.

Black, Lendley. *Mikhail Chekhov as Actor, Director, and Teacher.* Ann Arbor, MI: UMI Research Press, 1987.

Blackham, Olive. *Shadow Puppets.* New York: Harper, 1960.

Blacking, John. "Songs, Dances, Mimes and Symbolism of Venda Girls' Initiation Schools." *African Studies* 28, 3 (1969): 149–191.

Blackmun, Barbara, and Matthew Schoffeleers. "Masks of Malawi." *African Arts* 4 (1972): 36–41, 69, 88.

Blaho, Jaroslav. "Slovak Republic." In *The World Encyclopedia of Contemporary Theatre,* ed. Don Rubin. New York: Routledge, 1994, 755–766.

Blaicklock, E. M. *The Male Characters of Euripides: A Study in Realism.* Wellington: New Zealand Press, 1952.

Bleasdale, Alan. *Are You Lonesome Tonight?* Boston: Faber & Faber, 1985.

Bloch, Maurice. *Ritual, History, and Power: Selected Papers in Anthropology.* Atlantic Highlands, NJ: Athlone, 1989.

Blum, Richard. *American Film Acting: The Stanislavsky Heritage.* Ann Arbor, MI: UMI Research Press, 1984.

Blumenthal, Eileen, and Julie Taymore. *Julie Taymor, Playing with Fire: Theatre, Opera, Film.* New York: Harry N. Abrams, 1995.

Boal, Augusto. *Theater of Oppression.* Paris: La Decouverte, 1985.

Bock, Audie. *Japanese Film Directors.* New York: Kodansha International, 1978.

Boepple, Leanne. "Rites of Passage." *Lighting Dimensions* (March 1998): 48–53.

Bohlin, P. "Between Dance and Theater (The Current Dance Scene in Sweden)." *Ballet International* 14, 6 (1991): 38–39.

Bohmer, Gunter. *Puppets.* London: Macdonald, 1969.

Bondan, Molly, Teguh S. Dhamal, Haryono Guritno, and Pandam Guritno. *Lordly Shades: Wayang Purwa Indonesia.* Jakarta: Bapak Probosoetedjo, 1984.

Bondanella, Peter, ed. *Federico Fellini: Essays in Criticism.* New York: Oxford University Press, 1978.

Booth, Edwin. *Between Actor and Critic: Selected Letters of Edwin Booth and William Winter.* Princeton, NJ: Princeton University Press, 1971.

Boothby, Richard. *A Brief Discovery Or Description of the Most Famous Island of Madagascar Or St. Laurence in Asia Near unto East-India.* 2d ed. London: Printed for John Hardesty, 1647.

Borgal, Clement. *Jacques Copeau.* Paris: L'Arche, 1960.

Boswell, Fred, and Jeanetta Boswell. *What Men or Gods Are These? A Genealogical Approach to Classical Mythology.* Metuchen, NJ: Scarecrow Press, 1980.

Boswell, James. *A View of the Edinburgh Theatre during the Summer Season.* Los Angeles: William Andrew Clark Memorial Library, University of California, 1976.

Botombele, Bokonga Ekanga, director. *Cultural Policy in the Republic of Zaire: A Study.* Paris: UNESCO, 1976.

Bovin, Mette. "Provocation Anthropology: Bartering Performance in Africa." *The Drama Review: A Journal of Performance Studies* 32, 1 (Spring 1988): 21–41.

Bowers, Faubion. *The Dance of India.* New York: Columbia University Press, 1953.

———. *Japanese Theatre.* New York: Hill and Wang, 1964.

———. *Theatre in the East.* New York: T. Nelson, 1956.

Bown, Matthew Cullerne. *Art under Stalin.* New York: Holmes and Meier, 1991.

Boyle, Catherine M. *Chilean Theater, 1973–1985: Marginality, Power, Selfhood.* Cranbury, NJ: Associated University Presses, 1992.

———. "Images of Women in Contemporary Chilean Theater." *Bulletin of Latin American Research* 5, 2 (1986): 81–96.

Boyle, Richard, and Oliver Stone. *Oliver Stone's Platoon & Salvador: The Original Screenplays.* New York: Vintage Books, 1987.

Bradley, David. *From Text to Performance in the Elizabethan Theatre.* New York: Cambridge University Press, 1992.

Brady, Frank. *Citizen Welles, A Biography of Orson Welles.* New York: Scribner, 1989.

Branagh, Kenneth. *Beginning.* New York: Norton, 1990.

Brandon, James. *The Cambridge Guide to Asian Theatre.* New York: Cambridge University Press, 1993.

———. *On Thrones of Gold.* Cambridge, MA: Harvard University Press, 1970.

———. *Brandon's Guide to Theatre in Asia.* Honolulu: University Press of Hawaii, 1976.

———. *Theatre in Southeast Asia.* Cambridge, MA: Harvard University Press, 1974.

———, ed. "Theatre in Thailand." In *The Performing Arts in Asia.* Paris: UNESCO, 1971.

Brandt, George, ed. *German and Dutch Theatre, 1600–1848.* New York: Cambridge University Press, 1993.

Brask, Per, and William Morgan, eds. *Aboriginal Voices.* Baltimore: John Hopkins University Press, 1992.

Brathwaite, Edward. *Folk Culture of the Slaves in Jamaica.* London: New Beacon Books, 1974.

Brauerhoch, Annette. "VIPER: The Twelfth International Film and Video Convention, Lucerne." *Screen* 33 (Autumn 1992): 321–333.

Braun, Edward. *Meyerhold: A Revolution in Theatre.* Iowa City: University of Iowa Press, 1995.

Braun, Kazimierz. *A History of Polish Theater, 1939–1989.* Westport, CT: Greenwood, 1996.

———. "Performance Review: The Golden Lion International Theatre Festival." *Theatre Journal* 49, 3 (October 1997): 346–348.

Brecht, Stefan. *Peter Schumann's Bread and Puppet Theatre.* New York: Routledge, 1988.

Brelsford, William Vernon. *African Dances of Northern Rhodesia.* Livingstone: Rhodes-Livingstone Museum, 1959.

Brewer, Gay. *David Mamet and Film: Illusion / Disillusion in a Wounded Land.* Jefferson, NC: McFarland, 1993.

Brisbane, Katherine, ed. *Australia Plays.* London: Nick Hern Books, 1989.

Brockett, Oscar. *Century of Innovation: A History of European and American Theatre and Drama since 1870.* Englewood Cliffs, NJ: Prentice-Hall, 1973.

Brook, Peter. *The Shifting Point.* New York: Harper & Row, 1987.

Brooke, I. *Costume in Greek Classic Drama.* London: Methuen, 1962.

Broom, Leonard, and Frank Speck. *Cherokee Dance and Drama.* Norman: University of Oklahoma Press, 1983.

Broom, Leonard, and Frank Gouldsmith Speck. *Cherokee Dance and Drama.* Berkeley: University of California Press, 1951.

Brotherton, John. *The Pastor-Bobo in the Spanish Theatre before the time of Lope de Vega.* London: Tamesis, 1975.

Brown, Bruce Alan. *Gluck and the French Theatre in Vienna.* New York: Oxford University, 1991.

Brown, Kenneth. *The Brig: A Concept for Theatre or Film.* New York: Hill and Wang, 1965.

Brownell-Levine, Virginia A. "Religious Syncretism in Contemporary Brazilian Theatre." *Latin American Theatre Review* 13, 2 (Summer 1980): 111–117.

Browning, M. "Micronesian Heritage." *Dance Perspectives* 43 (Autumn 1970): 7–49.

Brunet, Jacques. "The Cambodian Nang Sbek and Its Audience." In *The Performing Arts in Asia,* ed. J. R. Brandon. Paris: UNESCO, 1971.

———. "The Comic Element in the Khmer Shadow Theatre." In *Traditional Drama and Music of Southeast Asia,* ed. Mohd. Taib Osman, 27–29. Kuala Lumpur, Malaysia: Dewan Bahasa Dan Pustaka Kementerian Pelajaran Malaysia, 1974.

———. "The Shadow Theatre of Cambodia." In *Traditional Drama and Music of Southeast Asia,* ed. Mohd. Taib Osman, 52–57. Kuala Lumpur, Malaysia: Dewan Bahasa Dan Pustaka Kementerian Pelajaran Malaysia, 1974.

Brunius, Niklas, Goran O. Eriksson, and Rolf Rembe. *Swedish Theatre.* Trans. Keith Bradfield. Stockholm: The Swedish Institute for Cultural Relations with Foreign Countries, 1967.

Bruno, Thomas. "Performance Reviews: Eclipsed by Patricia Burke Brogan." *Theatre Journal* 51, 2 (May 1999): 219–221.

Bryan, T. Avril. *Censorship and Social Conflict in the Spanish Theatre: The Case of Alfonso Sastre.* Washington, DC: University Press of America, 1982.

Buckle, Richard. *Katherine Dunham: Her Dancers, Singers, Musicians.* London: Ballet Publications, 1949.

Buenaventura, Enrique. *El Arte Nuevo de Hacer Comedias y el Nuevo Teatro.* 5. Cali, Colombia: TEC Publications, n.d.

Bulgarian Centre of the ITI. *The Bulgarian Dramatic Art.* Sofia: National Centre of Propaganda and Information, 1979.

Buller, Edward. *Indigenous Performing and Ceremonial Arts in Canada: An Annotated Bibliography of Canadian Indian Rituals and Ceremonies.* Toronto: Association for Native Development in the Performing and Visual Arts, 1981.

Bunnag, Tej. "Hun Krabook: Thai Classical Puppets." *Impact Magazine,* October 16, 1971.

Buñuel, Luis. *My Last Sigh.* New York: Vintage Books, 1984.

Burns, Bradford E. *Latin American Cinema: Film and History.* Los Angeles: UCLA Latin American Center, 1975.

Burton, Hal. *Great Acting.* New York: Bonanza Books, 1967.

Burton, Julianne. *Cinema and Social Change in Latin America: Conversations with Filmmakers.* Austin: University of Texas Press, 1986.

————. *New Latin American Cinema: An Annotated Bibliography of English Language Sources.* New York: Cineaste, 1976.

Burton, R. W. B. *The Chorus in Sophocles' Tragedies.* Oxford: Clarendon Press, 1980.

Butcher, Maryvonne. "Franc's Film Renascence." *Commonweal* (January 8, 1960): 414–416.

Butler, James. *The Theatre and Drama of Greece and Rome.* San Francisco: Chandler, 1972.

Byrski, Maria Christopher. *Concepts of Ancient Indian Theatre.* New Delhi: Munshiram Manoharlal, 1974.

Cachia, P. "The Dramatic Monologues of Al-Ma'arri'." *Journal of Arabic Literature* 1 (1970): 129–136.

————. "The Theatrical Movement of the Arabs." *Middle Eastern Studies Association Bulletin* 16, 1 (July 1982): 9–23.

Callan, Michael. *Anthony Hopkins: The Unauthorized Biography.* New York: Scribner, 1994.

Cameron-Wilson, James. "Film Reviews: *Love Is the Devil.*" *Film Review* (October 1998): 25.

Campschreur, Willem, and Joost Divendal, eds. *Culture in Another South Africa.* New York: Olive Branch Press, 1989.

Capps, Edward. "The Stage in the Greek Theatre According to the Extant Dramas." Ph.D. diss., Yale University, 1891.

Carlson, Marvin. *The French Stage in the Nineteenth Century.* Metuchen, NJ: Scarecrow Press, 1972.

————. *The German Stage in the Nineteenth Century.* Metuchen, NJ: Scarecrow Press, 1972.

Carnival '78. Produced and directed by Regge Life. 10 min. New York: Black Filmmaker Foundation, n.d. 16mm. Color.

Carpenter, Frederic. *Eugene O'Neill.* New York: Twayne, 1964.

Carter, Alan. *John Osborne.* Edinburgh: Oliver & Boyd, 1969.

Carter, Huntly. *The Theatre of Max Reinhardt.* New York: B. Blom, 1964.

Carver, Benedict. "Fine Line OKs First Picture in Two Years." *Variety* 374 (26 April 1999–May 1999): 10.

Casson, Lionel. *Masters of Ancient Comedy.* New York: Minerva Press, 1967.

Ceballos, Patricia R. "The Fiesta Plays of Bohol." *Philippine Studies* 23 (1975): 190–222.

Cerny, Jindrich. "Czech Republic." In *The World Encyclopedia of Contemporary Theatre,* ed. Don Rubin. New York: Routledge, 1994, 196–200.

Cesnakov-Michalcov, Milena. "The Staging of a New Year's Play at Presov (Eperies) in Eastern Slovakia in 1651." *Theatre Research International* 18, 3 (1993): 161–172.

Chaibou, Dan-Inna. "La Theatralite en Pays Hawsa." Université Nationale de Côte d'Ivoire, 1978–1979.

Chaikin, Joseph. "The Open Theatre." *Carleton Drama Review* 9, 2 (Winter 1964): 191.

Chakravarty, Sumita. *National Identity in Indian Popular Cinema.* Austin: University of Texas Press, 1993.

Chambers, Colin. *Other Spaces: New Theatre and RSC.* London: Eyre Methuen, 1980.

Champagne, Lenora. *French Theatre Experiment Since 1968.* Ann Arbor, MI: UMI Research Press, 1984.

Chanan, Michael. *Chilean Film.* London: British Film Institute, 1976.

Chanan, Michael, ed. *Twenty-five Years of the New Latin American Cinema.* London: British Film Institute/Channel Four Television, 1983.

Chapman, Graham. *The Complete Monty Python's Flying Circus.* New York: Pantheon Books, 1989.

Charles Lyons, ed. *Critical Essays on Henrik Ibsen.* Boston: G. K. Hall, 1987.

Charlot, John. *Chanting the Universe: Hawaiian Religious Culture.* Honolulu: Emphasis International, 1983.

Cheianu, Constantin. "Moldova." In *The World Encyclopedia of Contemporary Theatre,* ed. Don Rubin. New York: Routledge, 1994, 593–595.

Chekhov, Anton, *Dear Writer, Dear Actress: The Love Letters of Anton Chekov and Olga Knipper,* Hopewell, NJ: Ecco Press, 1997.

Chia-Chien, Chu. *The Chinese Theatre.* Trans. James A. Graham. London: John Lane, 1922.

Chifunyise, Stephen J. "The Development of Theatre in Zimbabwe." Pp. 103–106 in *Art from the Frontline: Contemporary Art from South Africa, Angola, Botswana, Mozambique, Tanzania, Zambia, Zimbabwe,* by Peter Sinclair and Emma Wallace. London: Frontline States/Karia Press, 1990.

"Chilean Theater, 1973–1993: The Playwrights Speak." Trans. Alfred Mac Adam. *Review* 49 (Fall 1994): 84–89.

Chinoy, Helen Krich, and Toby Cole. *Actors on Acting.* New York: Crown, 1970.

Chisholm, A. H. "Aborigines: Dancing." In *The Australian Encyclopedia,* ed. Ronald M. Berndt and Catherine H. Berndt. East Lansing: Michigan State University Press, 1958.

————, ed. *The Australian Encyclopaedia*. Sydney: Angus & Robertson, 1958.

Choondal, C. *Contemporary Indian Theatre: Interviews with Playwrights and Directors*. New Delhi, 1989.

Chothia, Jean. *Andre Antoine*. New York: Cambridge University Press, 1991.

Christoffersen, Erik Exe. "The Presence Radiated by the Actor-Dancer: On ISTA (International School of Theatre Anthropology)." *Nordic Theatre Studies: Yearbook For Theatre Research in Scandinavia*, 47–52. Copenhagen: Munksgaard, 1989.

Chua Sariman. "Traditional Dance Drama in Thailand." In *Traditional Drama and Music of Southeast Asia*, ed. Mohd. Taib Osman, 165–171. Kuala Lumpur, Malaysia: Dewan Bahasa dan Pustaka, 1974.

Cibber, Colley. *An Apology for the Life of Colley Cibber*. Ann Arbor: University of Michigan Press, 1968.

————. *Careless Husband: An Appreciation of Colley Cibber, Actor and Dramatist*. New York: Haskell House, 1967.

Cioffi, Kathleen. *Alternative Theatre in Poland 1954–89*. Canada: Harwood Academic, 1996.

Clark, Paul. *Chinese Cinema: Culture and Politics Since 1949*. New York: Cambridge University Press, 1987.

Clark, Veve A. "Contemporary Forms of Popular Theatre in Haiti." *Ufahamu* 12, 2 (1983): 93–100.

Coe, Jonathan. *Jimmy Stewart: A Wonderful Life*. New York: Arcade, 1994.

Coe, Richard. *The Vision of Jean Genet*. New York: Grove, 1968.

Cohen, Deborah. "Honduras Celebrates the 'IV Festival de Teatro por la Paz.'" *Latin American Theatre Review* 26, 1 (Fall 1992): 149–151.

Cole, Herbert M., ed. *I Am Not Myself: The Art of African Masquerade*. Los Angeles: Museum of Cultural History, UCLA, 1985.

Collins, Charles William. *Great Love Stories of the Theatre: A Record of Theatrical Romance*. New York: Duffield, 1911.

Collins, Herbert. *Talma: A Biography of an Actor*. New York: Hill and Wang, 1964.

Le Congo au Festival de Lagos, 1977 (World Black and African Festival of Arts and Culture, 1977). Brazzaville: Republique Populaire du Congo, Ministere de l'Enseignement Superieur, Charge de la Culture et des Arts, 1977.

Conlin, D. A. "The World of Roman Costume." *American Journal of Archaeology* 102, 4 (October 1998): 842–843.

Conolly, L. W. *Canadian Drama and the Critics*. Vancouver: Talonbooks, 1987.

Constanlino, Josefino. "Early Drama Forms in the Philippines." *Philippines Quarterly* 1 (1961): 34–36.

Conteh-Morgan, John. *Theatre and Drama in Francophone Africa: A Critical Introduction*. New York: Cambridge University Press, 1994.

Cooke, William. *Memoirs of Charles Macklin*. London: J. Asperne, 1806.

Coomaraswamy, Ananda K. *The Dance of Shiva: Fourteen Indian Essays*. New York: Noonday Press, 1957.

Copeau, Jacques. *Copeau: Texts on Theatre*. Ed. and trans. John Rudlin and Norman H. Paul. New York: Routledge, 1990.

Coplan, David. *In Township Tonight! South Africa's Black City Music and Theatre*. New York: Longman, 1985.

Corliss, Richard. "Show Business: Dazzling Decalogue: Krzsztof Kieslowski's 10-Part Masterpiece Finally Comes to the U.S. Thou Shalt Not Miss It." *Time* 152, 4 (July 27, 1998): 61.

Cornevin, Robert. *Le Theatre en Afrique Noire et a Madagascar*. Paris: Le Livre Africain, 1970.

Cornford, F. M. *The Origins of Attic Comedy*. London: Edward Arnold, 1914.

Cortes, Carlos. *Chicanas in Film: History of an Image*. Binghamton, NY: Bilingual Press, 1985.

Costantino, Roselyn. "Theatre in Mexico: New Challenges, New Visions." *Latin American Theatre Review* 28, 2 (Spring 1995): 132–140.

Costanzo, Susan. "Reclaimed the Stage: Amateur Theater-Studio Audiences in the Late Soviet Era." *Slavic Review* 57, 2 (Summer 1998): 398–424.

Covarrubias, Miguel. *Bali*. New York: Oxford University Press, 1972.

Cowie, Peter. *The Cinema of Orson Welles*. New York: Barnes, 1965.

————. *Scandinavian Cinema: A Survey of the Films and Film-Makers of Denmark, Finland, Iceland, Norway and Sweden*. London: Tantivy, 1992.

Craig, Edward Gordon. "The Characters of the Commedia Dell'Arte." *The Mask* (January 1912).

————. *Henry Irving*. New York: Longmans, Green, 1930.

Crothers, J. Frances. *The Puppeteer's Library Guide: The Bibliographic Index to the Literature of the World Puppet Theatre*. Metuchen, NJ: Scarecrow, 1971–1983.

Crowley, F. K. ed. *A New History of Australia*. Melbourne: William Heinemann, 1974.

Cruz, Duarte Ivo. *Introducao Ao Teatro Portuguesa Do Século XX* (*An Introduction to the Portuguese Theatre of the Twentieth Century*). Lisbon: Espiral, 1969.

Csato, Edward. *The Polish Theatre*. Warsaw: Polonia Publishing House, 1963.

Cuisiner, Jeanne. *Le Theatre d'Ombres a Kelantan*. Paris: Gallimard, 1957.

Curran, James, and Vincent Porter. *British Cinema History*. Totowa, NJ: Barnes and Noble, 1983.

Curry, Renee, ed. *Perspectives on Woody Allen*. New York: G. K. Hall, 1966.

Czerwinski, E. J. *Contemporary Polish Theater and Drama* (*1956–1984*). Westport, CT: Greenwood, 1988.

Dail-Jones, Megan. "A Culture in Motion: A Study of the Interrelationship of Dancing, Sorrowing, Hunting, and Fighting as Performed by the Women of Central Australia." Master's thesis, University of Hawaii, 1984.

Daniel, Curt. "The Freeest Theater in the Reich: In the German Concentration Camps." *Theatre Arts* 25 (November 1941): 801–807.

Daniel, Lee A. "The Loa: One Aspect of the Sorjuanian Mask." *Latin American Theatre Review* 16, 2 (Spring 1983): 43–49.

Dansey, Harry. *The Maori in Colour.* London: Reed, 1973.

Darlington, William Aubrey. *Laurence Olivier.* London: Morgan-Grampian, 1968.

David, Richard. *Shakespeare in the Theatre.* New York: Cambridge University Press, 1978.

Davidson, Michael. "Opera Around the World: Netherlands—A Human 'Ring,' Amsterdam." *Opera* 50, 10 (October 1999): 1214–1216.

Davis, Merry Anne. "News: International: Vassili Sulich Stages Oedipus in Dubrovnik Festival." *Dance Magazine* 72, 8 (August 1998): 32.

Davis, R. G. *The San Francisco Mime Troupe: The First Ten Years.* Palo Alto, CA: Ramparts, 1975.

Davis, Ronald. *Duke: The Life and Image of John Wayne.* Norman: University of Oklahoma Press, 1998.

Dawson, Barbara. "A Letter to Richard Schechner." *Drama Review* 37, 2 (1993): 15.

Dean, Beth. *South Pacific Dance.* Sydney: Pacific Publications, 1978.

Decharme, Paul. *Euripides and the Spirit of His Dramas.* New York: Macmillan, 1906.

Demastes, William. *Beyond Naturalism: A New Realism in American Theatre.* New York: Greenwood, 1988.

Derkeke, U Ba Cho. "The Burmese Marionette Stage." *Asian Horizon* 1 (1948): 51–56.

Devrient, Eduard. *Geschichte Der Deutschen Schauspielkunst.* Munich: Langen Muller, 1970.

Dewey, Donald. *James Stewart: A Biography.* Atlanta, GA: Turner Publishing, 1996.

Dhani Nivat, Prince. "The Dalang." *Journal of the Siam Society* 43, 2 (1955): 113–135.

———. *The Khon.* Bangkok: Sivaporn, 1962.

———. "The Masked Play." *Standard* 310 (1952): 12–13, 18.

———. "Nang Talung." *Journal of the Siam Society* 47 (1959): 181.

———. "Pageantry of the Siamese Stage." *National Geographic Magazine* 91 (February 1947): 209–212.

———. "The Shadow Play as a Possible Origin for the Masked Play." *Journal of the Siam Society* 37 (1948): 26–32.

Diawara, Manthia, ed. *Black American Cinema.* New York: Routledge, 1993.

Diderot, Denis. "The Paradox of Acting." In *Masks Or Faces,* ed. William Archer. New York: Hill and Wang, 1957.

DiFusco, John, and written by the original cast. *Tracers: A Play.* New York: Hill and Wang, 1986.

Dissanayake, Wimal. *Melodrama and Asian Cinema.* New York: Cambridge University Press, 1993.

Dixon Library (University of New England). *Australian Plays in Manuscript: A Checklist of the Campbell Howard Collection Held in the Dixon Library, University of New England.* Armidale, Australia: Dixon Library, University of New England, 1984.

Dobrowolsky, Ferdinand. *The Theatre in Yugoslavia.* Belgrade: Museum of Theatre Art, 1955.

Doelwijt, Thea. "Towards a Surinamese Theatre." *Black Arts* 5, 1 (1981): 38–43.

Dolan, Jill. "Linking Art and Politics: KPGT, The Zagreb Theatre Company (Yugoslavia)." *Carleton Drama Review* 27 (Spring 1983): 82.

Doll, Susan. *Understanding Elvis: Southern Roots vs. Star Image.* New York: Garland, 1998.

Donahue, Francis. "Toward a Mexican National Theater." *Revista/Review Interamericana* 19, 3–4 (1989): 29–40.

Donohoe, Joseph, and Jonathan Weiss, eds. *Essays on Modern Quebec Theatre.* East Lansing: Michigan State University Press, 1995.

D'Ooge, Martin Luther. *The Acropolis of Athens.* New York: Macmillan, 1908.

Dorcy, Jean. *A la Recontre de la Mime et des Mimes: Decroux, Barrault, Marceau.* Neuilly-sur-Seine: Cahiers de Danse et Culture, 1958.

Dorey, Thomas Alan. *Roman Drama.* New York: Basic Books, 1965.

Dorsinville, Roger. "Rediscovering Our Cultural Values." Pp. 130–137 in *Black People and Their Culture,* ed. Linn Shapiro. Washington, DC: Smithsonian Institution, 1976.

Dreier, Martin. "The Swiss Theatre Collection: The Challenge of Four Languages and Cultures." *Museum International* 49 (April 1997): 13–18.

Drewal, Henry John. "Efe: Voiced Power and Pageantry." *African Arts* 7, 2 (1974): 26–29, 58–66, 82–83.

———. "Gelede Masquerade: Imagery and Motif." *African Arts* 7, 4 (1974): 8–19, 62–63, 95–96.

Drewal, Margaret Thompson, and Henry John Drewal. "Gelede Dance of the Western Yoruba." *African Arts* 8, 2 (1975): 36–45, 78–79.

Drucker, Philip. *Kwakiutl Dancing Societies.* Berkeley: University of California Press, 1940.

Ducan, M. H. *Harvest Festival Dramas of Tibet.* Hong Kong: Orient, 1955.

Duchartre, Pierre-Louis. *The Italian Comedy (Comedie Italienne).* Trans. Randolph Weaver. New York: Dover Grove, 1966.

Duckworth, G. E. *The Nature of Roman Comedy.* Princeton, NJ: Princeton University Press, 1952.

Dukore, Bernard F. *Dramatic Theory and Criticism.* Chicago: Holt, Rinehart and Winston, 1974.

Dulac, Germaine. *Ecrits sur le Cinema: 1919–1937.* Paris: Editions Paris Experimental, 1994.

Dunham, Katherine. *Dances of Haiti.* Los Angeles: Center for Afro-American Studies, 1983.

Dussane, Beatrix. *An Actor Named Moliere* (Comedier Nomme Moliere). Trans. Lewis Galantiere. New York: C. Scribner's Sons, 1937.

Dutt, U. *Towards a Revolutionary Theatre*. Calcutta: Sarkar, 1982.

Dutu, Alexandru. "Recent Shakespeare Performances in Romania." *Shakespeare Survey* 20 (1967): 125.

Early Minstrel Show. (Sound recording.) New York: New World Records, 1985.

East, N. B. *African Theatre: A Checklist of Critical Materials*. New York: Africana, 1970.

Edgecombe, David. *Theatrical Training during the Age of Shakespeare*. Lewiston, NY: Edwin Mellen, 1995.

Edwards, Flora Mancuso. "The Theater of the Black Diaspora: A Comparative Study of Black Drama in Brazil, Cuba and the United States." Ph.D. diss., New York University, 1975.

Edwards, Gwynne, *Dramatists in Perspective: Spanish Theatre in the Twentieth Century*, Wales: St. Martin's, 1985.

Ehrenberg, Victor. *The People of Aristophanes: A Sociology of Old Attic Comedy*. New York: Barnes & Noble, 1974.

Eichberg, Henning. "The Nazi Thingspiel: Theatre For the Masses in Fascism and Proletarian Culture." *New German Critique* 11 (Spring 1977): 133–150.

Einarsson, Sveinn. "Iceland." In *Nordic Theatre Studies: Yearbook for Theatre Research in Scandinavia, 46*. Copenhagen: Munksgaard International, 1989.

———. "Frú Stefania: The First Icelandic Actress." In *Nordic Theatre Studies: Yearbook for Theatre Research in Scandinavia*, ed. Kela Kvam, 41–48. Denmark: Institute for Theatre Research, University of Copenhagen, 1988.

———. "Icelandic Theatre History: Some Questions." In *Nordic Theatre Studies: Yearbook For Theatre Research in Scandinavia*, 91–94. Copenhagen: Munksgaard International, 1989.

Eiseman, Fred B. *Bali Sekala & Niskala: Essays on Religion, Ritual, and Art*. Berkeley, CA: Periplus Editions, 1989.

Eisner, Lotte. *The Haunted Screen: Expressionism in German Cinema*. Berkeley: University of California Press, 1969.

Ekwuema, Lazarus E. N. "Nigerian Performing Arts, Past, Present and Future, with Particular Reference to Igbo Practice." *Presence Africaine* 92, 2 (1975): 195–213.

Eliade, Mircea, ed. *The Encyclopedia of Religion*. 16 vols. New York: Macmillan, 1987.

Ellis, Catherine. "Functions and Features of Central and South Australian Aboriginal Music." In *Australian Aboriginal Music*, ed. Jennifer Isaacs, 23–26. Aboriginal Artists Agency, 1979.

Else, G. F. *The Origin and Early Form of Greek Tragedy*. Cambridge, MA: Harvard University Press, 1965.

Emerson, Nathaniel B. *Unwritten Literature of Hawaii: The Sacred Songs of the Hula*. Washington, DC: Government Printing Office, 1909.

Emigh, John. *Masked Performance*. Philadelphia: University of Pennsylvania Press, 1996.

———. "Playing with the Past: Visitation and Illusion in the Mask Theatre of Bali." *Drama Review* 20, 2 (June 1979): 11–36.

Enohoro, Ife. "Second World Black and African Festival of Arts and Culture: Lagos, Nigeria." *Black Scholar* (September 1977): 26–33.

Erens, Patricia. *The Jew in American Cinema*. Bloomington: Indiana University Press, 1984.

Ernst, Earle. *The Kabuki Theatre*. New York: Oxford University Press, 1956. Reprint, Honolulu: University Press of Hawaii, 1974.

Eshete, Aleme. *The Cultural Situation in Socialist Ethiopia*. Paris: UNESCO, 1982.

Espino, F. L. "A Literal Imitation of Christ." In *Filipino Heritage: The Making of a Nation*, ed. Alfredo R. Roces, pp. 1230–1232. Manila: Lahing Pilipino Publishing, 1977.

———. *The Encyclopedia of World Theater*. New York: Charles Scribner's Sons, 1977.

Etherton, Michael. *The Development of African Drama*. New York: Africana, 1982.

Ettinghausen, R. "The Dance with Zoomorphic Masks and Other Forms of Entertainment Seen in Islamic Art." *Arabic and Islamic Studies in Honor of Hamilton A. R. Gibb* (1965): 211–224.

Eyman, Scott. *Mary Pickford: America's Sweetheart*. New York: D. I. Fine, 1990.

Eynat-Confino, Irene. *Beyond the Mask: Gordon Craig, Movement, and the Actor*. Carbondale: Southern Illinois University Press, 1987.

Eyo, Ekpo. "Abua Masquerades." *African Arts* 7, 2 (Winter 1974): 52–55.

Fabian, Johannes. "Popular Culture in Africa: Findings and Conjectures." *Africa* 48, 4 (1978): 315–334.

Fairbrother, Trevor. *Robert Wilson's Vision*. Boston: Museum of Fine Arts, 1991.

Fairman, Richard. "People: 249-Maria Guleghina." *Opera* 50, 2 (February 1999): 145–150.

Fantin, M. *Mani Rimdu, Nepal, the Buddhist Dance Drama of Tengpoche*. Singapore: Toppan; New Delhi: distributed by the English Book Store, 1976.

Farrier, Francis Quamina, chairperson. *Theatre 2*. Guyana Ministry of Education, Social Development and Culture. Georgetown: Department of Drama, 1979.

Farwell, Byron. *Burton: A Biography of Sir Richard Francis Burton*. New York: Holt, Rinehart and Winston, 1963.

Fasuyi, T. A. *Cultural Policy in Nigeria*. Paris: UNESCO, 1973.

Faulder, Dominic. "Thailand's Puppet Theatre." *Sawasdee* 18 (August 1989): 14–20.

Feldman, S. "The Spanish Stage." *Latin American Theatre Review* 28, 1 (Fall 1994): 179–180.

Fellini, Federico. *Fellini on Fellini*. New York: Delacorte, 1976.

Felner, Mira. *Apostles of Silence: The Modern French Mimes*. Rutherford, NJ: Fairleigh Dickinson University Press, 1985.

Fencl, Otakar. *The Czechoslovak Theatre Today*. Prague: Artia, 1963.

Fenn, Jeffery W. *Levitating the Pentagon: Evolutions in the American Theatre of the Vietnam War Era*. Newark: University of Delaware Press, 1992.

Fenollosa, Ernest, and Ezra Pound. *Noh: The Classical Noh Theatre of Japan*. Originally published as *Noh*. New York: New Directions, 1916. Reprint, Westport, CT: Greenwood, 1977.

Fenton, William. *The Falce Faces of the Iroquois*. Norman: University of Oklahoma Press, 1987.

Ferguson, John. *A Companion to Greek Tragedy*. Austin: University of Texas Press, 1972.

Fernandez, Oscar. "Black Theater in Brazil." *Educational Theater Journal* 29, 1 (March 1977): 5–17.

———. "Black Theatre: United States and Brazil." Pp. 275–284 in *Homenaje a Lydia Cabrera*, ed. Reinaldo Sánchez and José Antonio Madrigal. Miami, FL: Universal, 1978.

———. "The Contemporary Theatre in Rio de Janeiro and in Sao Paulo, 1953–1955." *Hispania* (December 1956): 423–432.

Ferner, Susan M. "Drama, Action and Change: Sistren, A Woman's Theatre Collective in Jamaica." Master's thesis, Carleton University, 1986.

Ferreiro, C. "Spanish Theatre." *Estreno-Cuadernos Del Teatro Espanol Contemporaneo* 20, 1 (Spring 1994): 54.

Ferris, Lesley. *Crossing the Stage: Controversies on Cross-Dressing*. New York: Routledge, 1993.

Figueiredo, Vera de, Director, and Members of Beija Flor Samba School. *Creation of the World: A Samba-Opera*. New York: Cinema Guild, n. d.

Filewod, Alan. *Collective Encounters: Documentary Theatre in English Canada*. Toronto: University of Toronto Press, 1987.

Finch, Christopher. *Jim Henson, The Art, The Magic, The Imagination*. New York: Random House, 1993.

Finelli, P. M. "Commedia dell'Arte." *Theatre Journal* 51, 4 (December 1999): 480.

Fitzhugh, William. *Inua: Spirit World of the Bering Sea Eskimo*. Washington, DC: Published for the National Museum of Natural History by the Smithsonian Institution Press, 1982.

Fitz-Simon, Christopher. *The Irish Theatre*. Thames & Hudson: London, 1982.

Flaherty, Gloria. "Empathy and Distance: Romantic Theories of Acting Reconsidered." *Theatre Research International* 15 (Summer 1990): 125–141.

Flanagan, Hallie. *Arena: The History of the Federal Theatre*. New York: B. Bloom, 1940.

Fleming, John. "Forging a Honduran Identity: The People's Theatre of Teatro la Fragua." *Latin American Theatre Review* 28, 1 (Fall 1994): 139–152.

Fletcher, Tom. *100 Years of the Negro in Show Business*. New York: Burdge, 1954.

Flueckiger, Joyce Burkhalter, and Laurie J. Sears, eds. *Boundaries of the Text: Epic Performances in South and Southeast Asia*. Ann Arbor: Center for South and Southeast Asian Studies, University of Michigan, 1991.

Fodeba, Keita. "African Dance and the Stage." *World Theatre* 7, 3 (1958): 164–178.

Fontane, Theodor. *Shakespeare in the London Theatre 1855–58*. London: The Society for Theatre Research, 1999.

Ford-Smith, Honor. "Sistren—Jamaican Women's Theatre." In *Cultures in Contention*, ed. Douglas Kahn and Dianne Neumaier, 84–91. Seattle, WA: Real Comet Press, 1985.

Ford-Smith, Honor, and Harclyde Walcott, directors. *Sweet Sugar Rage: A Documentary*. Kingston, Jamaica: Sistren Theatre Collective, n.d.

Fotheringham, Richard. *Sport in Australian Drama*. Cambridge: Cambridge University Press, 1992.

Fowler, Henry. "A History of Theatre in Jamaica." *Jamaica Journal* 2, 1 (March 1968): 53–59.

Fowler, J. Beresford. *Stars in My Backyard: A Survey of the Australian Stage*. Ilfracombe, UK: A. H. Stockwell, 1962.

Fraden, Rena. *Blueprints For a Black Federal Theatre, 1935–1939*. New York: Cambridge University Press, 1994.

Fraizier, Adrian. *Behind the Scenes at the Abbey*. Berkeley: University of Californial Press, 1990.

France, Richard. *The Theatre of Orson Welles*. Lewisburg, PA: Bucknell University Press, 1977.

Franco, Jean. *On Edge: The Crisis of Contemporary Latin American Culture*. Minneapolis: University of Minnesota Press, 1992.

Franklin, Lillian Cleamons. "The Image of the Black in the Cuban Theater: 1913–1965." Ph.D. diss., Ohio State University, 1982.

Franses, Philip Hans. "Theatre-Going in Rotterdam, 1802–1853: A Statistical Analysis of Ticket Sales." *Theatre Survey—The Journal of the American Society for Theatre Research* 39, 2 (November 1998): 73–97.

Frantar, Vladimir. "Opera around the World: Slovenia—A National Opera, Ljubljana." *Opera* 50, 3 (March 1999): 342.

———. "Opera around the World: Slovenia, Lijublajana Standard Ballo." *Opera* 49, 6 (June 1998): 728–729.

Frasca, R. A. *The Theater of the Mahabharata*. Honolulu: University of Hawaii Press, 1990.

Fraser, Peter. *Punch and Judy*. New York: Van Nostrand Reinhold, 1970.

Frazer, James George. *Anthologia Anthropologica. The Native Races of Africa and Madagascar*. Ed. Robert Angus Downie. London: P. Lund, Humphries 1938.

Frazier, Adrian. *Behind the Scenes:Yeats, Horniman and the Struggle for the Abbey Theatre.* Berkeley: University of California Press, 1990.

Frewin, Leslie. *Blond Venus: A Life of Marlene Dietrich.* London: MacGibbon and Kee, 1955.

Frey, Martin. *Kreatieve Marge: Die Entwincklung des Niederlandischen Off-Theatres (The Creative Fringe: The Development of Dutch Off-Theatre).* Vienna: Bohlau, 1991.

Fricke, Richard. *Wagner in Rehearsal, 1875–1876: The Diaries of Richard Fricke (Bayreuth Vor Dreissig Jahren).* Trans. George Fricke. Stuyyesant, NY: Pendragon, 1998.

Fricker, Karen. "Legit: Dublin, N.Y. Prep for Friel Deal." *Variety* 374, 9 (19 April 1999–25 April 1999): 51, 56.

———. "Legit Reviews: *Love in the Title.*" *Variety* 374, 5 (22 March 1999–28 March 1999): 47–48.

———. "Legit Reviews: Abroad: *The Whisperers.*" *Variety* 374, 12 (10 May 1999–16 May 1999): 148.

———. "Postmark Belfast: A World Apart." *American Theatre* 16, 6 (July–August 1999): 54–57.

Fromm, Harold. *Bernard Shaw and the Theatre in the Nineties: A Study of Shaw's Dramatic Criticism.* Lawrence: University of Kansas, 1967.

Fuchs, Anne. *Playing the Market: The Market Theatre, Johannesburg, 1976–1986.* New York: Harwood Academic, 1990.

Fuller, Graham. "Cautionary Tale–Sense and Sensibility." *Sight and Sound* 6, 3 (1996): 20–25.

Furness, John. *Kathakali: The Dance-Drama of Kerala.* London: British Broadcasting Company, 1967.

Fusco, Coco, ed. *Reviewing Histories: Selections from New Latin American Cinema.* Buffalo, NY: Hallwalls Contemporary Art Center, 1987.

Gadberry, Glen. "Nazi Germany's Jewish Theatre." *Theatre Survey* 21, 1 (May 1980): 15–32.

Gaensbauer, Deborah, *The French Theater of the Absurd,* Boston: Twayne, 1991.

Gagen D. "The Spanish Theater from 1960–1975." *Bulletin of Hispanic Studies* 71, 2 (April 1994): 289–290.

Gallafent, Edward. *Clint Eastwood: Filmmaker and Star.* New York: Continuum, 1994.

Galloway, Doug. "Obituaries: Frantisek Vlacil." *Variety* 373, 13 (15 February 1999–21 February 1999): 74.

Ganelin, Charles. *Rewriting Theatre: The Comedia and the Nineteenth-Century Refundicion.* Lewisburg, PA: Bucknell University Press, 1994.

Ganteaume, Cecile. "White Mountain Apache Dance: Expressions of Spirituality." In *Native American Dance: Ceremonies and Social Traditions,* ed. Charlotte Heth, 65–81. Washington, DC: Starwood, 1992.

Ganzl, Kurt. *British Musical Theatre.* New York: Oxford University Press, 1986.

Garebian, Keith. *William Hutt: A Theatre Portrait.* New York: Mosaic Press, 1988.

Garfield, David. *The Actors Studio: A Player's Place.* New York: Collier, 1984.

Gargi, Balawanta. *Theatre in India.* New York: Theatre Arts, 1962.

———. *Folk Theater of India.* Seattle: University of Washington Press, 1966.

Garza, Roberto J., ed. *Contemporary Chicano Theatre.* Notre Dame, IN: University of Notre Dame Press, 1976.

Gasparovic, Darko. "Contemporary Croatian Drama." *Bridge* 55 (1978): 120.

Gassner, John. "The Group Theatre, in Its Tenth Year: A Critical Estimate." *Theatre Arts* 24 (1940): 729.

Gauss, Rebecca, *Studio of the Moscow Art Theatre from 1905–1927.* Ph.D. diss., University of Colorado. Ann Arbor, MI: UMI, 1997, 37888530.

Gautier, Jean Jacques. *Le Comedie Francaise.* Paris: Wesmael-Charlier, 1964.

Genet, Jean, *The Selected Writing of Jean Genet,* Hopewell, NJ: Ecco Press, 1993.

Gentili, Bruno. *Theatrical Performance in the Ancient World: Hellenistic and Early Roman Theatre.* Amsterdam: Gieben, 1979.

Ghitulescu, Mircea. "Romania." In *The World Encyclopedia of Contemporary Theatre,* ed. Don Rubin, 682–703. New York: Routledge, 1994.

Gibbons, Rawle A. "Traditional Enactments of Trinidad—Towards a Third Theatre." Master's thesis, University of the West Indies, 1979.

Gielgud, John. *Gielgud: An Actor and His Time.* New York: C. N. Potter, 1980.

Gieling, Lia. "Netherlands." In *The World Encyclopedia of Contemporary Theatre,* ed. Don Rubin, 596–613. New York: Routledge, 1994.

Gies, David Thatcher. *The Theatre in Nineteenth-Century Spain.* New York: Cambridge University Press, 1994.

Gilbert, W. S. *Book and Lyrics of the Best-Known Gilbert & Sullivan Operas and the Bab Ballads.* New York: Three Sirens, 1932.

Ginsburg, Henry D. "The Manohra Dance-Drama: An Introduction." *Journal of the Siam Society* 60 (1972): 169–181.

Gladkov, Aleksandr Konstantinovich. *Meyerhold Speaks, Meyerhold Rehearses.* Trans. Alma Law. Amsterdam: Harwood Academic, 1997.

Gladso, Svein. "Norway." In *Nordic Theatre Studies: Yearbook for Theatre Research in Scandinavia,* 34–40. Copenhagen: Munksgaard, 1989.

Glenny, Misha. "If You Are Not for Us—Wilder Than *MASH:* That's the Verdict on a Major Now Film out of the Former Yugoslavia." *Sight and Sound* 6 (1996): 10–13.

Glickman, Nora, and Gloria F. Waldman. *Argentine Jewish Theatre: A Critical Anthology.* Cranbury, NJ: Associated University Presses, 1996.

Goethe, Johann Wolfgang von. *The Autobiography of Johann Wolfgang Von Goethe.* Trans. John Oxenford. New York: Horizon, 1969.

————. *Correspondence between Goethe and Schiller.* Trans. Liselotte Dieckmann. New York: P. Lang, 1994.

————. "Rules For Actors (1803)." *Quarterly Journal of Speech Education* 13, 3 (June 1927): 247–256, 259–264.

Goetz-Stankiewicz, Marketa. *The Silenced Theatre: Czech Playwrights without a Stage.* Toronto: University of Toronto Press, 1979.

Gogol, Nikolai. *The Theater of Nikolay Gogol: Plays and Selected Writings.* Trans. Milton Ehre and Fruma Gottschalk. Chicago: University of Chicago Press, 1980.

Goldberg, Rose Lee. *Performance Art.* New York: Harry N. Abrams, 1988.

Gonzalez, Alexander, ed. *Assessing the Achievement of J. M. Synge.* Westport, CT: Greenwood, 1996.

Goodale, Jane. "The TIWI Dance for the Dead." *Expedition: The Bulletin of the University Museum of the University of Pennsylvania* 2, 1 (1959): 3–13.

Goodale, Katherine. *Behind the Scenes with Edwin Booth.* New York: Houghton Mifflin Company, 1931.

Goonatilleka, M. H. *Nadagama: The First Sri Lankan Theatre.* Delhi: Sri Satguru, 1984.

Goorney, Howard, and Ewan MacColl. *Agit-Prop to Theatre Workshop: Political Playscripts 1930–50.* Dover, NH: Manchester University Press, 1986.

Gopinath. *"Kathakali," Sangeet Natak Akademi, Dance Seminar Papers.* New Delhi: Sangeet Natak Akademi, 1958.

Gordon, Lois. *The World of Samuel Beckett.* New Haven, CT: Yale University Press, 1996.

Gordon, Mel. "Lazzi: The Comic Routines of the Commedia Dell'arte." Performing Arts Journal Publications, 1983.

Gottschild, Brenda Dixon. *Digging the Africanist Presence in American Performance.* Westport, CT: Greenwood, 1996.

Gould, Allan, Jill Levenson, and Tom Patterson. "First Stages: The Making of the Stratford Festival." *Theatre Research International* 18, 3 (1993): 236–237.

Gradev, Dimiter. *Bulgarian Puppet Theatre.* Sofia: Information Centre, 1979.

Graham, Peter. *The New Wave.* Garden City, NY: Doubleday, 1968.

Graham, Ronnie. *The World of African Music.* London: Pluto, 1992.

Graham-White, Anthony. *The Drama of Black Africa.* New York: Samuel French, 1974.

Gray, Spalding. *Impossible Vacation.* New York: Knopf, 1992.

————. *Swimming to Cambodia.* New York: Theatre Communication Group, 1985.

Green, Michael, ed. *The Russian Symbolist Thetre: An Anthology of Plays and Critical Texts.* Ann Arbor, MI: Ardis, 1986.

Greenwood, Leonard Hugh Graham. *Aspects of Euripidean Tragedy.* New York: Russell & Russell, 1972.

Gregg, Karl. *An Index to the Spanish Theatre Collection in the London Library.* Charlottesville, VA: Biblioteca Siglo de Oro, 1984.

Gregor, Joseph. *The Russian Theatre: Its Character and History with Especial Reference to the Revolutionary Period.* Philadelphia: J. B. Lippincott, 1929.

Grey, Sir George. *Polynesian Mythology and Ancient Traditional History of the Maori As Told by Their Priests and Chiefs,* ed. W. W. Bird. New York: Taplinger, 1970.

Grey, John. *Black Theatre and Performance: A Pan-African Bibliography.* New York: Greenwood, 1990.

Griaule, M. *Masques Dogons.* Paris: Institut d'Ethnologie, 1938.

Griffin, Robert. *High Baroque Culture and Theatre in Vienna.* New York: Humanities Press, 1972.

Grimard, Luc. "Historical Existence of the Haitian Theatre." *World Theatre* 16, 5–6 (1967): 534–535.

Grobel, Lawrence. *Converstions with Marlon Brando.* London: Bloomsbury, 1991.

Grois, Boris. *The Total Art of Stalinism: Avant-Garde, Aesthetic Dictatorship and Beyond.* Trans. Charles Rougle. Princeton, NJ: Princeton University Press, 1992.

Groslier, George. "Royal Dancers of Cambodia." *Asia* 22, 1 (1922): 47–53, 74.

Grossvogel, David. *The Blasphemers: The Theater of Brecht, Ionesco, Beckett, Genet.* Ithaca, NY: Cornell University Press, 1962.

Groves, William McDonald. "The Commedia Dell'Arte and the Shakespearean Theatre: A Study of the Relevance of Applying Commedia Dell'Arte Techniques to Shakespearean Production." Ph.D. diss. Ann Arbor, MI: Proquest, 1983.

Gudehus, Lesley. "A Half-Hour with Derek Jacobi: An Interview." *Dramatics* 60, 1 (September 1988): 16.

Guinea. Ministere du Domaine de L'Education et de la Culture. *Cultural Policy in the Revolutionary People's Republic of Guinea.* Paris: UNESCO, 1979.

Gullberg, Elsa. *The Thread of Ariadne: A Study of Ancient Greek Dress.* Goteborg: P. Astrom, 1970.

Gunawardana, A. J. *Theatre in Sri Lanka.* Colombo: Department of Cultural Affairs, Sri Lanka, 1976.

Guritno, Pandam. *Wayang Kebudayaan Indonesia Dan Pancasila.* Jakarta: Penerbit Universitas Indonesia, 1988.

Gutiérrez, Gustavo. *A Theology of Liberation.* Maryknoll, NY: Orbis, 1973.

Gutierrez, Lazardo. "Television in Latin America." *Journal of Telecommunications* 28 (November 1961).

Hackett, Jean. *The Actor's Chekhov.* Newbury, VT: SK, 1993.

Hadethy, Waleed H. "Educational Theatre in Iraq: Elementary and Secondary Levels." Ph.D. diss. Ann Arbor, MI: University Microfilms, 1986.

Hall, H. Gaston. *Comedy in Context: Essays on Moliere.* Jackson: University Press of Mississippi, 1984.

Halleran, M. R. *Stagecraft in Euripides.* London: Croom Helm, 1985.

Hamilton, Edith. *Mythology.* New York: New American Library, 1969.

————. *The Roman Way.* New York: W. W. Norton, 1932.

Hammerschmidt, U. "A Report on Summer Theater in Tampere, Finland." *Theater Heute*, 10 (1991): 49–50.

Hammond, Albert. "The Moving Drama of the Arts in Ghana." *Sankofa Magazine* 1, 2–3 (1977): 7–10, 13–14.

Hammontree, Patsy. *Shirley Temple Black: A Bio Bibliography.* Westport, CT: Greenwood, 1998.

Hansen, H. Harald. *Mongol Costumes.* New York: Thames and Hudson, 1994.

Hansen, Kathryn. *Grounds for Play: The Nautanki Theatre of North India.* Berkeley: University of California Press, 1992.

Haring, Lee. *Verbal Arts in Madagascar: Performance in Historical Perspective.* Philadelphia: University of Pennsylvania Press, 1992.

Harper, Peggy. "Dance in Nigeria." In *Dance in Africa, Asia and the Pacific: Selected Readings*, ed. Judy Van Zile, 148–163. Manoa: University of Hawaii at Manoa, 1976.

Harris, Andrew. *Broadway Theatre.* New York: Routledge, 1994.

Hartnoll, Phyllis. *The Oxford Companion to the Theatre.* New York: Oxford University Press, 1967.

Harwood, Ronald. *The Ages of Gielgud: An Actor at Eighty.* New York: Limelight Editions, 1984.

Hassiotis, Natasha. "On Stage: Euripides in Albania: 'The Women of Troy' in Athens." *Ballet International-Tanz Aktuell* (January 1999): 58.

Hatch, James, ed. *Black Theatre U.S.A.: Plays by African Americans, 1847–Today.* New York: Free Press, 1996.

Hathaway, Robert. *Love in the Early Spanish Theatre.* Madrid: Plaza Mayor, 1975.

Hatley, Barbara. "Ketoprak: Performance and Social Meaning in a Javanese Popular Theatre Form." Ph.D. diss., University of Sydney, 1985.

———. "Wayang and Ludruk: Polarities in Java." *Drama Review* 15, 3 (1971): 88–101.

Hattaway, Michael. *Elizabethan Popular Theatre: Plays in Performance.* London: Routledge and Kegan Paul, 1982.

Hautzinger, Sarah. "Chile: Street Theater Takes Risks." *NACLA Report on the Americas* 21, 4 (July–August 1987): 10–11.

Hawley, J. S. *At Play with Krishna.* Princeton, NJ: Princeton University Press, 1981.

Hay, Samuel. *African American Theatre: An Historical and Critical Analysis.* New York: Cambridge University Press, 1994.

Hayman, Ronald. *Arthur Miller.* New York: Ungar, 1972.

———. *Eugene Ionesco.* New York: Ungar, 1976.

———. *Samuel Beckett.* New York: Ungar, 1973.

Haynes, Lorien. "The Brit at the Back: Flying the Flag for Homegrown Talent: Anna Friel." *Film Review* 587 (November 1999): 98.

Hays, Michael. *The Public and Performance: Essays in the History of French and German Theater, 1871–1900.* Ann Arbor, MI: UMI Press, 1982.

Heath, Sally. "The Development of Native American Theatre Companies in the Continental U.S." Ph.D. diss. Ann Arbor, MI: UMI, 1995.

Heck, Thomas. *Commedia Dell'Arte: A Guide to the Primary and Secondary Literature.* New York: Garland, 1988.

Heiberg, Hans. *Ibsen: A Portrait of the Artist.* Trans. Joan Tate. London: Allen and Unwin, 1969.

Heiberg, Johanne Luise. *Et Liv Gjenoplevet I Erindringen.* 5th ed. 4 vols. Copenhagen: Niels Birger Warmberg, 1973–1974.

Heidrun, Adler. "Julio Ortega's Peruvian Inferno." *Latin American Theatre Review* 15, 1 (Fall 1981): 53–58.

Heilpern, John. *How Good Is David Mamet, Anyway?: Writings on Theatre—and Why It Matters.* New York: Routledge, 2000.

Hein, Norvin. *The Miracle Plays of Mathura.* New Haven, CT: Yale University Press, 1972.

Helavuori, Hanna-Leena, and Irmeli Niemi. "Finland." In *Nordic Theatre Studies: Yearbook For Theatre Research in Scandinavia*, 41–45. Copenhagen: Munksgaard, 1989.

Heras, G. "Contemporary Spanish Theatre Scene." *Anales de la Literatura Espanola Contemporanea* 18, 3 (1993): 625–637.

Herbert, Ian. "Out of Europe." *Theatre Record* 18, 14 (July 1998): 876, 943.

Herbstein, Denis. "Reporter's Notebook: The Hazards of Cultural Deprivation." *Africa Report* (July–August 1987): 33–35.

Herrick, Marvin T. *Italian Comedy in the Renaissance.* Urbana: University of Illinois Press, 1960.

———. *Italian Tragedy in the Renaissance.* Urbana: University of Illinois Press, 1965.

Herst, Beth. "Quiet Apocalypses: The Textual Theatre of Clare Coulter." *PAJ—A Journal of Performance and Art* 22, 1 (January 2000): 65–71.

Hewitt-Myring, Philip. "The Open-Air Theatre in Barbados." *Bim* 7, 25 (July–December 1957): 56–57.

Higham, Charles. *Bette: The Life of Bette Davis.* New York: Macmillan, 1981.

Hill, Errol. *The Jamaican Stage: 1655–1900.* Amherst: University of Massachusetts Press, 1992.

———. "Traditional Figures in Carnival: Their Preservation, Development and Interpretation." *Caribbean Quarterly* 31, 2 (June 1985): 14–34.

———. *The Trinidad Carnival: A Mandate for a National Theater.* Austin: University of Texas Press, 1972.

Hill, John. "Contemporary Irish Cinema: Filming in the North." *Cineaste* 24, 2–3 (March 1999): 26–27.

Hillebrand, Harold Newcomb. *Edmund Kean.* New York: AMS Press, 1966.

Hillestrom, Gustaf. *Theatre and Ballet in Sweden.* Trans. Anne Bibby. Stockholm: Swedish Institute, 1953.

Hironaga, Shuzaburo. *Bunraku: Japan's Unique Puppet Theatre.* Tokyo: Tokyo News Service, 1973.

Hirsch, Foster. *A Method to Their Madness:The History of the Actors Studio.* New York: W. W. Norton, 1984.

Hobbs, Gloria L. "Human Rights through Cultural Expression." Crisis (August–September 1977): 376–377.

Hofstede, David. *James Dean:A Bio-Bibliography.* Westport, CT: Greenwood, 1996.

Holderness, Graham, ed. *The Politics of Theatre and Drama.* New York: St. Martin's, 1992.

Holloway, Ron. "Communiques:The Karlovyvary Film Festival." *Cineaste* 24, 1 (December 1998): 86–87.

Holmes, Martin Rivington. *Shakespeare and Burbage:The Sound of Shakespeare as Devised to Suit theVoice and Talents of His Principal Player.* London: Phillimore, 1978.

Holt, M., "Twentieth Century Spanish Theatre and the Canon," *Anales de la Literatura Espanola Contemporanea* 17, 1–3 (1992): 47–54.

Hontineros-Avellana. "Philippine Drama: A Social Protest." In *Brown Heritage: Essays on Philippines Cultural Tradition and Literature,* ed. Antorio G. Manuud. Quezon City: Ateneo de Manila University Press, 1967.

Hood, Mantle. "The Enduring Tradition: Music and Theatre in Java and Bali." In *Indonesia,* ed. Ruth McVey. New Haven, CT:Yale University Press, 1963.

Hope,Thomas. *Costumes of the Greeks and Romans.* New York: Dover Grove, 1962.

Horne, Donald. *The Australian People.* London: Angus & Robertson, 1972.

Horowitz, Susan. *Queens of Comedy: Lucille Ball, Phyllis Diller, Carol Burnett, Joan Rivers, and the New Generation of Funny Women.* Amsterdam: Gordon and Breach, 1997.

Horton, Andrew. "Festivals: The Belgrade International Film Festival." *Cineaste* 22, 2 (June 1996): 56–57.

Horwitz, Simi. "Face to Face: Joseph Chaikin Directs Arthur Miller: 'Making Ordinary Moments Extraordinary.'" *Back Stage* 39, 3 (16 January 1998–22 January 1998): 5, 33.

Houston, Mary Galway. *Ancient Greek, Roman and Byzantine Costume and Decoration.* London: A. & C. Black, 1947.

Howard, Roger. *Contemporary Chinese Theatre.* Hong Kong: Heinemann, 1978.

Howitt, Alfred. "On Some Australian Ceremonies of Initiation." *Royal Anthropological Institute Journal* 13 (1884): 432–459.

Hsu,Tao-Ching. *The Chinese Conception of the Theatre.* Seattle: University of Washington Press, 1985.

Htin Aung, U. *Burmese Drama:A Study with Translations of Burmese Plays.* Calcutta: Oxford University Press, 1937.

Hubbard,Thomas K. *The Mask of Comedy:Aristophanes and the Intertextual Parabasis.* Ithaca, NY: Cornell University Press, 1991.

Huettich, H. G. *Theater in the Planned Society: Contemporary Drama in the German Democratic Republic in Its Historical, Political, and Cultural Context.* Chapel Hill: University of North Carolina Press, 1978.

Hunningher, B. "Acoustics and Acting in the Theater of Dionysus Eleuthereus." *Mededelingen der Nederlandse Akademie vanWetenschappen* 9 (1956).

Hunt, Albert, and Geoffrey Reeves. *Peter Brook.* New York: Cambridge University Press, 1995.

Hunt, Hugh. *The Abbey: Ireland's National Theatre, 1904–1978.* Dublin: Gill & Macmillan, 1979.

Hunter, Stephen. "Movies: TheWinter Guest: Fade to Gray." *Washington Post* (16 January 1998): B6.

Hur, Soon-Ja. "The Development of Professional Resident Theatre Companies in South Korea from the Conclusion of the Korean War." Ph.D. diss. Ann Arbor, MI: Proquest, 1991.

Huynh Khac Dung. *Hat Boi,Theatre Traditional duViet Nam.* Siagon: Kim Lai an Quam, 1970.

Hyder, A. R. Z. "'A Small House beside a Highway': A Play for Television with an Essay, Development of Drama and Theatre in East Pakistan." Master's thesis, University of Hawaii, 1968.

Hymes, Jo Ann. *Asia through Film:An Annotated Guide to Films in the University of Michigan Audio-Visual Education Center.* Ann Arbor: Center for Japanese Studies, University of Michigan, 1976.

Hyppolite, Michelson Paul. *A Study of Haitian Folklore.* Trans. Edgar LaForest. Port-au-Prince: Imprimerie de l'Etat, 1954.

Ibn al-Nadim, M. *The Fihrist of al-Nadim:A Tenth-Century Survey of Muslim Culture.* Trans. and ed. Bayard Dodge. New York: Columbia University Press, 1970.

Ibsen, Henrik. *The Correspondence of Henrik Ibsen.* Trans. Mary Morison. London: Hodder and Stoughton, 1905.

Igbo Traditional Life, Culture, and Literature. Trans. M. J. C. Echeruo and Emmanuel N. Obiechina. Owerri, Nigeria: Conch Magazine, 1971.

Immoos,Thomas. *Japanese Theatre.* Trans. Hugh Young. Originally published as *Japanisches Theater.* New York: Rizzoli, 1977.

Imperato, Pascal James. "Contemporary Adapted Dances of the Dogon." *African Arts* 5, 1 (1971): 28–33, 68–71.

———. "The Dance of the Tyi Wara." *African Arts* 4, 1 (1970): 8–13.

Index of Arts and Cultural Organizations in Zimbabwe as at June 1985. Harare: National Arts Foundation of Zimbabwe, 1985.

Inoura,Yoshinobu, and Toshio Kawatake. *The Traditional Theater of Japan.* New York: Weatherhill in collaboration with Japan Foundation, 1981.

"Iraq,Traditional Rhythmic Structures (Sound Recording)." Program notes in English and French by Habib Hassan Touma. France: Auvidis, for the Conseil International de la Musique, 1992.

Ireland, S. *Aeschylus.* Oxford: Oxford University Press, 1986.

Irving, Laurnece. *Henry Irving: An Actor and His World.* London: Faber and Faber, 1951.

Iyer, K. Bharatha. *Dance Drama of India and the East.* Bombay: Taraporevala, 1980.

Jackson, Esther. *The Broken World of Tennessee Williams.* Madison: University of Wisconsin Press, 1965.

Jacobi, Derek. "Derek Jacobi on Shakespearean Acting." *Shakespeare Quarterly* 36 (1985): 134.

Jacobs, Diane. *But We Need the Eggs: The Magic of Woody Allen.* New York: St. Martin's, 1982.

Jarratt, Vernon. *The Italian Cinema.* New York: Macmillan, 1951.

Jasper, Gertrude Rathbone. *Adventures in the Theatre: Lugne-Poe and the Theatre de L'Oeuvre to 1899.* New Brunswick, NJ: Rutgers University Press, 1947.

Javillonar, Elna V. "The First Vernacular Zarzuela." *Philippine Studies* 12 (April 1964): 323–325.

Jenkins, Linda. "The Performances of the Native Americans as American Theatre." Ph.D. diss., University of Minnesota, 1975.

Jenkins, Ron. "Becoming a Clown in Bali." *Drama Review* 2 (June 1979): 49–56.

Jennings, La Vinia Delois. *Alice Childress.* New York: Twayne Grove, 1995.

Jerstad, Luther G. *Mani-Rimdu: Sherpa Dance-Drama.* Seattle: University of Washington Press, 1969.

Jeyifo, Biodun. *The Truthful Lie: Essays in a Sociology of African Drama.* London: New Beacon Books, 1985.

Johansson, M. "Spanish Theatre of the Mid-Twentieth-Century." *Moderna Sprak* 88, 1 (1994): 83–90.

Johns, Eric. "Jamaican Renaissance." *Theatre* (Spring 1947): 35–37.

Johnson, Ellen, ed. *American Artists on Art From 1940 to 1980.* New York: Harper & Row, 1982.

Johnson, Marie. *Ancient Greek Dress.* Chicago: Argonaut, 1964.

Johnson, Randal. *Cinema Novo X 5: Masters of Contemporary Brazilian Film.* Austin: University of Texas Press, 1984.

Johnston, Kaarin. "Native American Theatre: A Study of the American Southwest Indian." Thesis, University of South Dakota, 1975.

Johnston, Lolo Bob. *The Theater of Belize: An Illustrated Study of the Emergence and Growth of a Young Nation's Theatrical Impulse.* North Quincy, MA: Christopher Publishing, 1973.

Johnston, Mary. *Exits and Entrances in Roman Comedy.* Geneva, NY: W. F. Humphrey, 1933.

Jones, Clifford Reis. "The Temple Theatre of Kerala: Its History and Description." Master's thesis, University of Pennsylvania, 1968.

Jones, Clifford Reis, and Betty True Jones. *Kathakali: An Introduction to the Dance-Drama of Kerala.* New York: Theatre Arts, 1970.

Jones, James Earl. *James Earl Jones: Voices and Silences.* New York: Scribner, 1993.

Jones, Kent. "Body and Soul: The Cinema of Atom Egoyan." *Film Comment* 34 (January–February 1998): 32–39.

Jorgensen, Aage. "Touring the 1970s with Solvognen in Denmark." *Drama Review* 26, 3 (Fall 1982): 15–28.

Jose, Arthur Wilberforce, and Herbert James Carter, eds. *The Australian Encyclopaedia.* Sydney: Angus & Robertson, 1926–1927.

Joseph, Herbert S., ed. *Modern Israeli Drama: An Anthology.* Rutherford, NJ: Fairleigh Dickinson University Press, 1983.

Kabikowski, Tomasz. "Performance Review: *November Night,* by Stanislaw Wyspianski." *Theatre Journal* 50, 4 (December 1998): 518–521.

Kaeppler, A. "Movement in the Performing Arts of the Pacific Islands." In *Theatrical Movement: A Bibliographic Anthology,* ed. Robert Fleshman. Metuchen, NJ: Scarecrow Press, 1986.

Kahansky, Mendel. *The Hebrew Theatre: Its First Fifty Years.* New York: Ktav Publishing, 1969.

Kahle, P. "The Arabic Shadow Play in Egypt." *Journal of the Royal Asiatic Society of Great Britain and Ireland* (1940): 21–34.

———. "The Arabic Shadow Play in Medieval Egypt (Old Texts and Old Figures)." *Journal of the Pakistan Historical Society* (April 1954): 85–115.

Kalvodova, Sis, and Vanis Kalvodova. *Chinese Theatre.* Trans. Iris Urwin. London: Spring House, 1957.

Kam, Garret. "Wayang Wong in the Court of Yogyakarta: The Enduring Significance of Javanese Dance Drama." *Asia Theatre Journal* 4, 1 (1987): 29–51.

Kamalish, K. C. *Vision of Sacred Dance.* Madras: Karpakam Achakam, 1987.

Kanolles, Nicolas, ed. *Mexican American Theatre, Then and Now.* Houston, TX: Arte Publico, 1983.

Kanski, Josef. "Opera around the World: Poland-Warsaw: *Boccanegra* Sails In." *Opera* 49, 5 (May 1998): 580–581.

Karan, Pradyumna Prasad. *Bhutan: A Physical and Cultural Geography.* Lexington: University of Kentucky Press, 1967.

———. *The Himalayan Kingdoms: Bhutan, Sikkim, and Nepal.* Princeton, NJ: Van Nostrand, 1963.

Karpinski, Maciej. *The Theatre of Andrzej Wajda.* Trans. Christina Paul. New York: Cambridge University Press, 1989.

Katz, Ephraim. *The Film Encyclopedia.* New York: Harper Perennial, 1994.

Katzer, Julius, *A. P. Chekhov,* Moscow: Foreign Language Publishing, 1960.

Kavanagh, Robert. *Theatre and Cultural Struggle in South Africa.* London: Zed, 1985.

Kawatake, Toshio. *Japan on Stage: Japanese Concepts of Beauty As Shown in the Traditional Theatre (Butai no oku no*

Nihon). Trans. P. G. O'Neill. Originally published as *Butai No Oku No Nihon.* Tokyo: 3A, 1990.

Kay, Iris. "FESTAC 1977." *African Arts* 11, 1 (October 1977): 50–51.

Kazacoff, George. *Dangerous Theatre: The Federal Theatre Project as a Forum for New Plays.* New York: P. Lang, 1989.

Kedjanyi, John. "Observations on Spectator-Performance Arrangements of Some Traditional Ghanaian Performances." *Research Review* (Legon) 2, 3 (1966): 61–66.

Keeler, Ward. *Javanese Shadow Plays, Javanese Selves.* Princeton, NJ: Princeton University Press, 1987.

Keene, Donald. *Bunraku: The Art of the Japanese Puppet Theatre.* Tokyo: Kodansha International; New York: Harper & Row, 1973.

Kehr, Dave. "The Discreet Charm of Rotterdam." *Film Comment* 32, 2 (March–April 1999): 68–69.

———. "Kieslowski's Trilogy: Blue, White, Red." *Film Comment* 30, 6 (1994): 10–21.

Kelley, Kitty. *Elizabeth Taylor, the Last Star.* New York: Simon and Schuster, 1981.

Kelly, Catriona. *Petrushka: The Russian Carnival Puppet Theatre.* New York: Cambridge University Press, 1990.

Kelly, Emmet. *Clown.* New York: Prentice-Hall, 1954.

Keller, Ward. *Javanese Shadow Puppets.* Singapore: Oxford University Press, 1992.

Kemp, Gerard. "Mervyn Blake Actor Extraordinaire." *Plays and Players Applausee* 519 (February 1998): 34.

Kendall, William. "Shakespeare in Yugoslavia." *Drama* 3 (Winter 1951): 33.

Kennedy, Scott. *In Search of African Theatre.* New York: Scribner, 1973.

Kent, Raymond. *From Madagascar to the Malagasy Republic.* New York: Praeger, 1962.

Kerbs, Stephanie Laird. "Non-Verbal Communication in Khon Dance-Drama: Thai Society on Stage." Ph.D. diss., Harvard University, 1975.

Kermina, F. "Gustave III of Sweden, The King of Theater." *Historia*, 528 (1990): 60–68.

Kernan, Margot. "Cuban Cinema Today." *Film Quarterly* 39, 2 (1975–1976): 45–51.

Khan, Mohamed. *An Introduction to the Egyptian Cinema.* London: Informatics, 1969.

al-Khozai, Mohamed. *The Development of Early Arabic Drama.* London and New York: Longman, 1984.

Kidd, Ross. "A Testimony from Nicaragua: An Interview with Nidia Bustos, the Coordinator of Mecate, the Nicaraguan Farm Workers' Theatre Movement." *Studies in Latin American Popular Culture* 2 (1983): 190–201.

Kiernander, Adrian. *Ariane Mnouchkine and the Theatre du Soleil.* New York: Cambridge University Press, 1993.

Kilroy, Tom. "A Generation of Irish Playwrights." *Irish University Review* 22, 1 (Spring/Summer 1992): 135–141.

Kimbell, David. *Italian Opera.* New York: Cambridge University Press, 1991.

Kimber, Robert. "Performance Space as Sacred Space in Aranda Corroboree: An Interpretation of the Organization and Use of Space as a Dramatic Element in the Performance of Selected Aboriginal Rituals in Central Australia." Ph.D. diss., University of Colorado, 1988.

King, Bruce, ed. *Contemporary American Theatre.* New York: St. Martin's, 1991.

King, John. *Magical Reels: A History of Cinema in Latin America.* London: Verso, 1990.

Kingston, Beverley. *The Oxford History of Australia.* Vol. 3. New York: Oxford University Press, 1988.

Kipkorir, B. E. *Towards a Cultural Policy for Kenya: Some Views.* Nairobi: Institute of African Studies, University of Nairobi, 1980.

Kirby, Michael. *Futurist Performance.* Trans. Victoria Nes Kirby. New York: E. P. Dutton, 1971.

Kirihara, Donald. *Patterns of Time: Mizoguchi and 1930s.* Madison: University of Wisconsin Press, 1992.

Kitto, H. D. F. "The Dance in Greek Tragedy." *Journal of Hellenic Studies* 75 (1955): 36–41.

Klajn, Hugo. "Shakespeare in Yugoslavia." *Shakespeare Quarterly* 5 (1954): 41.

Klein, Holgar, and Peter Davidhazi, eds. *Shakespeare and Hungary.* Lewiston, NY: Edwin Mellen, 1996.

Kneubuhl, V. "Traditional Performance in Samoan Culture." *Asian Theatre Journal* 4, 2 (1987): 166–176.

Koanantakool, P. C. "Relevance of the Textual and Contextual Analyses in Understanding Folk Performance in Modern Society: A Case of Southern Thai Shadow-Puppet Theater." *Asian Folklore Studies* 48, 1 (1989): 31–57.

Kobler, John. *Damned in Paradise: The Life of John Barrymore.* New York: Atheneum, 1977.

Kofoworola, Ziky, and Yusef Lateef. *Hausa Performing Arts and Music.* Lagos: Department of Culture, Federal Ministry of Information and Culture, 1987.

Korenhof, Paul. "In Review: From around the World—Amsterdam." *Opera News* 63, 10 (April 1999): 86–87.

Kotsilibas-Davis, James. *The Barrymores: The Royal Family in Hollywood.* New York: Crown, 1981.

Kracauer, Siegfried. *From Caligari to Hitler: A Psychological History of the German Film.* New York: Noonday, 1959.

Kraus, Gottfried. *The Salzburg Marionette Theatre.* Salzburg: Residenz Verlag, 1966.

Krol, John Cardinal. *Pope John Paul II.* New York: Catholic Book Publishing, 1979.

Kubrick, Stanley. *Full Metal Jacket: The Screenplay.* New York: Knopf, 1987.

Kuftinec, Sonja. "'Odakle Ste?' (Where Are You From?): Active Learning and Community-Based Theatre in Former Yugoslavia and the U.S." *Theatre Topics* 7, 2 (September 1997): 170–186.

————. "Playing with Borders: Dramaturging Ethnicity in Bosnia." *Journal of Dramatic Theory and Criticism* 13, 1 (Fall 1998): 143–156.

Kuhns, David. "Wedekind, the Actor: Aesthetics, Morality, and Monstrosity." *Theatre Survey* 31 (November 1990): 144–164.

Kullman, Colby, and William C. Young. *Theatre Companies of the World*. Westport, CT: Greenwood, 1986.

Kun, Kuo Pao. *The Coffin Is Too Big for the Hole . . . And Other Plays*. Singapore: Times Books International, 1990.

Kvam, Kela, ed. "Betty Nansen: A Unique Figure in Danish Theatre." In *Nordic Theatre Studies: Yearbook for Theatre Research in Scandinavia*, 69–78. Denmark: Institute for Theatre Research, University of Copenhagen, 1988.

————. *Women in Scandinavian Theatre*. Copenhagen: Munksgaard, 1988.

Kvam, Kela, and Janet Szatkowski. "Denmark." In *Nordic Theatre Studies: Yearbook for Theatre Research in Scandinavia*, 23–33. Copenhagen: Munksgaard International, 1989.

Kvam, Wayne. "On Stage in the Third Reich: An Unrecorded Letter." *Theatre Survey* 28 (November 1987): 102–105.

Laclere, Adhemard. "Le Theatre Cambodgien." *Revue d'Ethnographie et de Sociologie* 1, 11–12 (1910): 257–282.

Lacy, Suzanne. "Finland: The Road of Poems and Borders." *Journal of Dramatic Theory and Criticism* 5, 1 (Fall 1990): 211–222.

Lamb, Ruth Stanton. *The World of Romanian Theatre*. Claremont, CA: Ocelot, 1976.

Lamont, Rosette. *Ionesco: A Collection of Critical Essays*. Englewood Cliffs, NJ: Prentice-Hall, 1973.

Lampert-Greaux, Ellen. "Underwater Delights: Luc Lafortune Gives the Cirque du Soleil an Aquatic Glow at Bellagio." *Lighting Dimensions* 23, 1 (January 1999): 46–51, 72, 74.

Lancaster, Henry Carrington. *The Comedie Francaise, 1701–1774: Plays, Actors, Spectators, Finances*. Philadelphia: American Philosophical Society, 1951.

Landau, J. M. "Popular Arabic Plays, 1909." *Journal of Arabic Literature* 17 (1986): 120–125.

Landau, Jacob. *Studies in the Arab Theater and Cinema*. Philadelphia: University of Pennsylvania Press, 1958.

Langbacka, Ralf. "Brecht in Finland." *The Brecht Yearbook* 20 (1995): 128–133.

Larlham, Peter. *Black Theater, Dance, and Ritual in South Africa*. Ann Arbor, MI: Proquest, 1985.

Laurie, Edith. "The Theatre Expands in Yugoslavia." *Theatre Arts* 36 (April 1952): 24.

Lawler, Lillian Beatrice. *Dance of the Ancient Greek Theatre*. Iowa City: University of Iowa Press, 1964.

Lawson, Robb. *The Story of the Scots Stage*. New York: E. P. Dutton, 1917.

Leabhart, Thomas. "Cirque du Soleil." *Mime Journal* (1986): 1–7.

————, ed. *Canadian Post-Modern Performance*. Claremont, CA: Ponoma College Theatre Department, 1986.

Lecouvreur, Adrienne. *Lettres de Adrienne Le Couvreur*. Paris: Librairie Plon, 1892.

Lee, Duhyun. *Pongsan Mask Dance-Drama: Korean Pongsan Mask Dance: Drama Troupe*. Seoul: Korean Culture and Arts Foundation, 1983.

Legyel-Bosiljevac, Aranka. "Yugoslavia." In *The World Encyclopedia of Contemporary Theatre*, ed. Don Rubin, 948–956. New York: Routledge, 1994.

Leiter, Samuel. *From Stanislavsky to Barrault: Representative Directors of the European Stage*. New York: Greenwood, 1991.

Lekis, Lisa. "The Dance as an Expression of Caribbean Folklore." In *Caribbean: Its Culture*, ed. A. Curtis Wilgus, 43–73. Gainesville: University of Florida Press, 1955.

Lemon, Alaina. "Hot Blood and Black Pearls: Socialism, Society, and Authenticity at the Moscow Teatr Romen." *Theatre Journal* 48 (December 1996): 479–494.

Lent, John A. *Asian Film Industry*. Austin: University of Texas Press, 1990.

Lentz, Harris. "Obituaries: Frantisek Vlacil, 74, January 28, 1999." *Classic Images* 286 (April 1999): 57.

————. "Obituaries: Meredith Edwards, 81, February 8 1999." *Classic Images* 286 (April 1999): 51.

Leon, Walfrido De. "The Passion and the Passion Play in the Philippines." *College Folio* (December 1910): 55–64.

Léon-Portilla, Miguel. *Aztec Thought and Culture: A Study of the Ancient Nahuatl Mind*. Trans. Jack Emory Davis. Norman: University of Oklahoma Press, 1963.

Leonard, C. "Contemporary Realist Theatre." *Estreno-Cuadernos Del Teatro Espanol Contemporaneo* 21, 2 (Fall 1995): 57.

Leonard, Dorothy. "Ladies of Ludruk." *Orientations* 5, 4 (April 1974): 3–4.

Leprohon, Pierre. *Italian Cinema*. New York: Praeger, 1972.

Letters, Francis Joseph Henry. *Life and Work of Sophocles*. New York: Sheed and Ward, 1953.

Levenson, Deborah. "Guatemala: The Murder of an Actor and a Theater." *NACLA Report on the Americas* 23, 3 (September 1989): 4–5.

Levine, D. N. *Wax and Gold: Tradition and Innovation in Ethiopian Culture*. Chicago: University of Chicago Press, 1965.

Ley, G. "The Orchestra as Acting Area in Greek Tragedy." *Ramus—Critical Studies in Greek and Roman Literature* 14, 2 (1985): 75–84.

Ley, Graham. *A Short Introduction to the Ancient Greek Theater*. Chicago: University of Chicago Press, 1991.

Ley-Piscator, Maria. *The Piscator Experiment: The Political Theatre*. New York: J. H. Heineman, 1967.

Leyda, Jay. *Dianying: An Account of Films and the Film Audience in China*. Cambridge, MA: MIT Press, 1972.

———. *Kino: A History of the Russian and Soviet Film*. Princeton, NJ: Princeton University Press, 1983.

Liebrecht, Henri. *Histoire du Théâtre Français Bruxelles*. Geneva: Slatkine Reprints, 1977.

Lifson, David. *The Yiddish Theatre in America*. New York: T. Yoseloff, 1965.

Lim, Dennis. "Film: *The Wall; The First Night of My Life*." *Village Voice* 44, 10 (16 March 1999): 134.

Lindfors, Bernth, ed. *Forms of Folklore in Africa: Narrative, Poetic, Gnomic, Dramatic*. Austin: University of Texas Press, 1977.

Lindovsk, Nadezda. "'Feminism' Is an Insult in Slovakia." *Theatre Journal* 47, 3 (1995): 381–392.

Lindvag, Anita. "Elsa Olenius and Our Theatre (The Stockholm City Theatre For Children and Young People)." In *Nordic Theatre Studies: Yearbook for Theatre Research in Scandinavia*, ed. Kela Kvam, 79–90. Denmark: Institute for Theatre Research, University of Copenhagen, 1988.

Little, A. M. G. *Myth and Society in Attic Drama*. New York: Columbia University Press, 1942.

Litto, Frederick M. "Some Notes on Brazil's Black Theatre." In *Black Writer in Africa and the Americas*, ed. Lloyd W. Brown, 195–221. Los Angeles: Hennessey and Ingalls, 1973.

Liu, Charles A. *A Study-Manual for the Sorrows and Joys of Middle Age (Ai Loh Chung Nien)*. Princeton, NJ: Princeton University Press, 1978.

London, John, ed. *Theatre under the Nazis*. New York: Manchester University Press, 2000.

Londré, Felicia Hardison. *Federico Garcia Lorca*. New York: Frederick Ungar., 1984.

Long, Roger. "Friend or Foe? Technology and Its Impact on Javanese Wayang Kulit." *Performing Arts* 2 (July 1985): 28–32.

Loomis, George. "Opera around the World: Lithuania—Vilnius: *Tosca* in Tradition." *Opera* 49 (May 1998): 577–578.

López, Ana. "Our Unwelcomed Guests: Telenovelas in Latin America." In *To Be Continued . . . Soap Operas around the World*, ed. Robert C. Allen, 256–275. London: Routledge, 1995.

Lord, L. E. *Aristophanes: His Plays and His Influence*. London: Harrap, 1925.

Lucas, Frank L. *Drama of Chekhov, Synge, Yeats, and Pirandello*. London: Cassell, 1963.

Lucas, F. L. *The Drama of Ibsen and Strindberg*. New York: Macmillan, 1962.

Lucini, Lyonel, director. *Carnival: Force of Love and Kindness*. University Park, PA: Pennsylvania State University, n.d.

Ludwig, Ruby Ornstein. "Wayang Wong, the Javanese Classical Theatre." *World Music* 18, 1 (1976): 15–22.

Luzuriaga, Gerardo. *Popular Theater for Social Change in Latin America: Essays in Spanish and English*. Los Angeles: UCLA Latin American Center Publications, 1978.

Ly Singko. "Lakon and the Chinese Theatre." *Eastern Horizon* 4 (1965): 25–28.

M'Bengue, Mamadou Seyni. *Cultural Policy in Senegal*. Paris: UNESCO, 1973.

MacClintock, Lander. *Contemporary Drama of Italy*. Boston: Little, Brown, 1920.

MacDougall, Jill. *Performing Identities on the Stages of Quebec*. New York: Peter Lang, 1997.

Mackenzie, C. G. "Questions of Identity in Contemporary Hong-Kong Theater." *Comparative Drama* 29, 2 (Summer 1995): 203–215.

MacKerras, Colin. *Amateur Theatre in China 1949–1966*. Canberra: Australian National University Press, 1973.

———. *Chinese Theatre in Modern Times, from 1840 to the Present Day*. Amherst: University of Massachusetts Press, 1975.

———. *Rise of the Peking Opera, 1770–1870: Social Aspects of the Theatre in Manchu China*. Oxford: Clarendon Press, 1972.

———. "Theatre in Vietnam." *Asian Theatre Journal* 4, 1 (1987): 1–28.

Macleod, Joseph. *Actors Cross the Volga: A Study of the 19th Century Russian Theatre and the Soviet Theatres in War*. London: G. Unwin, 1946.

Macleod, Joseph Todd Gordon. *A Theatre Sketch Book*. London: Allen & Unwin, 1951.

Macotela, Fernando. "Mexican Popular Cinema of the 1970s: How Popular Was It?" *Studies in Latin American Popular Culture* 1 (1982): 27–34.

Madden, David. *Harlequin's Stick, Charlie's Cane: A Comparative Study of Commedia Dell'Arte and Silent Slapstick Comedy*. Bowling Green, OH: Popular Press, 1975.

Maddock, Brent. *The Films of Jacques Tati*. Metuchen, NJ: Scarecrow, 1977.

Magee, Bryan. *Aspects of Wagner*. New York: Stein and Day, 1969.

Mahar, William. *Behind the Burnt Cork Mask: Early Blackface Minstrels and Antebellum American Popular Culture*. Urbana: University of Illinois Press, 1999.

Mahores, Resil B. "Folk Drama and Social Organisation." *Philippine Studies* 29 (1981): 230.

Mair, Lucy. "A Yao Girl's Initiation." *Man*, 50 (1951): 60–63.

Major, Wade. "AFM Reviews: 'Prague Duet.'" *Box Office* 135, 1 (January 1999): 51.

Maland, Charles. *Chaplin and American Culture: The Evolution of a Star Image*. Princeton, NJ: Princeton University Press, 1989.

Malloy, James. *Black Theatre: The Making of a Movement*. San Francisco: California Newsreel, 1992.

Mally, Lynn. "Performing the New Woman: The Komsomolka as Actress and Image in Soviet Youth

Theater." *Journal of Social History* 30 (Fall 1996): 79–95.

———. "The Rise and Fall of the Soviet Youth Theater TRAM." *Slavic Review* 51 (Fall 1992): 411–430.

Malyusz, Edith Csaszar, ed. *The Theater and National Awakening.* Atlanta: Hungarian Cultural Foundation, 1980.

Mama, Amina. "Arts: Songs of the People (On the Nngaali Ensemble, a Cultural Group From Uganda)." *West Africa* (May 11, 1987): 917–919.

Manandhar, J. K. *Nepal, Legend and Drama.* Banepa Wankhya: Sukha Veti Manandhar, 1982.

Mander, Gertrud. *Jean Baptiste Moliere.* Velbert: Friedrich, 1967.

Manheim, Michael, ed. *The Cambridge Companion to Eugene O'Neill.* New York: Cambridge University Press, 1998.

Manvell, Roger. *Chaplin.* Boston: Little Brown, 1974.

———. *Ellen Terry.* New York: Putnam, 1968.

———. *New Cinema in Europe.* New York: Dutton, 1966.

———, ed. *International Encyclopedia of Film.* New York: Crown, 1972.

Manvell, Roger, and Heinrich Fraenkel. *The German Cinema.* New York: Praeger, 1971.

Manzalaoui, Mahmoud. *Arabic Writing Today: Drama.* Cairo: American Research Center in Egypt, 1968–1977.

Marayan, R. K. *Mahabharata.* London: Mandarin Paperbacks, 1991.

Marceau, Marcel. *Meet Marcel Marceau.* (Videocassette.) Sandy Hook, CT: Video Yesteryear, 1999 (original 1965).

Marglin, Frederique Apffel. *Wives of the God-King: Rituals of the Devadasis of Puri.* New York: Oxford University Press, 1989.

Marinetti, Filippo Tommaso, Emilio Settimelli, and Bruno Corra. "The Synthetic Futurist Theatre." In *Art and the Stage in the Twentieth Century,* ed. Henning Rischbieter. Greenwich, CT: New York Graphic Society, 1968.

Marker, Frederick. "The Actor in the Nineteenth Century: Aspects of Rehearsal and Performance in the Prenaturalistic Theater in Scandinavia." *Quarterly Journal of Speech* 51 (1965): 177–189.

———. *A History of Scandinavian Theatre.* Cambridge: Cambridge University Press, 1996.

Marker, Lise-Lone. *David Belasco: Naturalism in the American Theatre.* Princeton, NJ: Princeton University Press, 1975.

Marker, Lise-Lone, and Frederick Marker. *A History of Scandinavian Theatre.* New York: Cambridge University Press, 1996.

———. *Ingmar Bergman: A Life in the Theater.* New York: Cambridge University Press, 1992.

Markham, Sir Clements. *Incas of Peru.* London: Smith, Elder, 1910.

Marlowe, Christopher. *The Life of Marlowe and the Tragedy of Dido, Queen of Carthage.* New York: Gordian, 1966.

Marranca, Bonnie, ed. *American Dreams: The Imagination of Sam Shepard.* New York: Performing Arts Journal Publications, 1981.

———. *Robert Wilson: The Theatre of Images.* New York: Harper, 1984.

Marre, Jeremy. *There'll Always Be Stars in the Sky: Indian Film Music Phenomenon.* Newton, NJ: Shanachie Records, 1992.

Marsh, Dave. *Elvis.* New York: Rolling Stone, Times Book, 1982.

Marshall, Paule. "Carnival in Rio." *Our World* (July 1955): 36–46.

Martin, Ben. *Marcel Marceau, Master of Mime.* New York: Paddington, 1978.

Martin, John W. *The Golden Age of French Cinema, 1929–1959.* Boston: Twayne, 1983.

Martinovitch, Nicholas. *Turkish Theatre.* New York: Theatre Arts, 1933.

Masekela, Barbara. "The ANC and the Cultural Boycott." *Africa Report* (July–August 1987): 19–21.

Mason, Stuart. *Bibliography of Oscar Wilde.* London: T. W. Laurie, 1914.

Massey, Reginald, and Jamie Massey. *Dances of India.* London: Tricolour, 1989.

Mast, Gerald. *A Short History of the Movies.* 4th ed. New York: Macmillan, 1986.

Mathur, Jagdish C. *Drama in Rural India.* New York: Asia Publishing House, 1964.

Matta, Roberto da. "Carnival in Multiple Planes." In *Rite, Drama, Festival, Spectacle: Rehearsals toward a Theory of Cultural Performance,* ed. John J. MacAloon, 230–246. Washington, DC: American Ethnological Society, 1984.

———. "On Carnival, Informality, and Magic: A Point of View from Brazil." In *Text, Play and Story: Construction and Reconstruction of Self and Society,* ed. Edward Bruner, 230–246. Washington, DC: American Ethnological Society, 1984.

Matthews, Brander. *Actors and Actresses of Great Britain and the United States from the Days of David Garrick to the Present Time.* New York: Cassell, 1886.

———. *French Dramatists of the 19th Century.* New York: C. Scribner's Sons, 1881.

Mattsson, Inger, ed. *Gustavian Opera: An Interdisciplinary Reader in Swedish Opera, Dance, and Theatre 1771–1809.* Stockholm: Royal Swedish Academy, 1991.

Matusky, Patricia. "Music in the Malay Shadow Puppet Theater (Volumes I and II)." Ph.D. diss. Ann Arbor, MI: Proquest, 1980.

———. "Musical Instruments and Their Function in the *Wayang Siam* of Malaysia." *Performing Arts* 3 (August 1986): 18–25.

Maugd-Soep, Carolina. *Chekhov and Women: Women in the Life and Works of Chekhov.* Columbus, OH: Slavica, 1987.

Mbughuni, L. A. *Cultural Policy of the United Republic of Tanzania*. Paris: UNESCO, 1974.

McAllester, David. "Shootingway, an Epic Drama of the Navajos." In *Southwestern Indian Ritual Drama*, ed. Charlotte J. Frisbie, 199–237. Albuquerque: University of New Mexico Press, 1980.

McBride, Murdoch. "For Actors Studio's 50th Year, A Group Theatre Retrospective." *Back Stage* 39, 17 (24 April 1998–30 April 1998): 3, 49.

McCaffrey, Donald. *Guide to the Silent Years of American Cinema*. Westport, CT: Greenwood, 1999.

McCann, Graham. *Rebel Males: Clift, Brando and Dean*. New Brunswick, NJ: Rutgers University Press, 1993.

McCann, John. "Opera around the World: Belgium: Antwerp." *Opera* 49, 11 (November 1998): 1355.

McCormick, John. *Popular Theatres of Nineteenth-Century France*. New York: Routledge, 1993.

McDivitt, Jane M. "Afro-Brazilian Theatre." Master's thesis, Harvard University, 1971.

McGuire, Paul. *Australian Theatre: An Abstact and Brief Chronicle in Twelve Parts*. London: Oxford University Press, 1948.

McHardy, Cecile. "The Performing Arts in Ghana." *Africa Forum* 1, 1 (Summer 1965): 113–117.

McKean, Philip F. "From Purity to Pollution? The Balinese Ketjak (Monkey Dance) as Symbolic Form in Transition." In *Imagination of Reality: Essays in Southeast Asian Coherence Systems*, ed. A. L. Becker and Aram A. Yengoyan, 293–302. Norwood, NJ: Ablex, 1979.

McKendrick, Melveena. *Theatre in Spain: 1490–1700*. New York: Cambridge University Press, 1989.

McPharlin, Paul. *Puppet Theatre in America: A History, 1524–1948*. Boston: Plays, 1969.

Mda, Zakes. *When People Play People: Development Communication through Theatre*. London: Zed, 1993.

Medrano, Hugo. "Argentine 'Theater of the Grotesque.'" *Americas* 37, 2 (March–April 1985): 56–57.

———. "A Long Run in Uruguay." *Americas* 38, 2 (March–April 1986): 62–63.

———. "The New Bloom of Peruvian Theater." *Americas* 36, 5 (September–October 1984): 58–59.

Mei-shu, Huang. "Taiwan Huaju De Huigu Yu Zhanwang (The Past and Future of Spoken Drama in Taiwan)." In *Muqien Muhou, Taishang Taixia*. Taipei, 1980.

Meihy, Jose Carlos Sebe. *Carnaval, Carnavais*. Sao Paulo: Editora Atica, 1986.

Meils, Cathy. "Film: International: 'Fire' Lights Way for Polish Film's Future." *Variety* 372, 13 (Nov. 1998): 17–18.

Menashe, Louis. "Communiues: Lisbon's International Encounters in Documentary Cinema." *Cineaste* 23 (April 1998): 55.

Menashe, Louis, and Jasminka Udovicki. "Art, History, and Politics in the Former Yugoslavia: An Interview with Michael Benson." *Cineaste* 22, 2 (June 1996): 30–33.

Mendoza, Liwaway. "Lenten Rites and Practices." *Drama Review* 21, 3 (September 1977): 21–32.

———. "Postmark Poland: Seven Years after the Revolutions." *American Theatre* 14 (October 1997): 90–92.

Menon, Narayana, and Saryu Doshi. *The Performing Arts*. Bombay: Marg Grove, 1982.

Mensah, Atta Annan. "Performing Arts in Zambia." *Bulletin of the International Committee on Urgent Anthropological and Ethnological Research* 13 (1971): 67–82.

Merkin, Daphne. "The Current Cinema: Going Abroad." *New Yorker* 74, 11 (May 11, 1998): 107–108.

Merriam, Alan, ed. "Arts, Human Behavior and Africa." *African Studies Bulletin* 5, 2 (May 1962): 2–70.

Merrill, Lisa. *When Romeo Was a Woman: Charlotte Cushman and Her Circle of Female Spectators*. Ann Arbor: University of Michigan Press, 1999.

Meserve, Mollie Ann, and Walter J. Meserve. *A Chronological Outline of World Theatre*. New York: Feedback Theatre & Prospero Press, 1992.

Metge, Joan. *The Maoris of New Zealand Rautahi*. Boston: Routledge & Kegan Paul, 1976.

Metraux, Alfred. *Black Peasants and Voodoo*. New York: Universe, 1960.

Meyer, Charles. "Cambodian Dances." *Nokor Khmer* 3 (1970): 2–27.

Meyer, Michael. *Henrik Ibsen*. Garden City, NY: Doubleday, 1971.

Michaelis de Vasconcellos, Carolina. "Shakespeare in Portugal." *Jahrbuch Der Deutschen Shakespeare—Gesellschaft* 15 (1880): 266.

Michel, Manuel. "Mexican Cinema: A Panoramic View." *Film Quarterly* 18, 4 (Summer 1965): 46–55.

Mikhail, E. H. *The Abbey Theatre: Interviews and Recollections*. Totowa, NJ: Barnes & Noble, 1988.

Milgrom, Al. "Communiques: The Sarajevo Film Festival." *Cineaste* 24, 1 (December 1998): 89.

Miller, John. *Judi Dench: With a Crack in Her Voice*. New York: Welcome Rain, 2000.

Miller, Ronald. *The Drama of Schiller*. Harrogate, UK: J. Oade, 1966.

Milleret, Margo. "Acting into Action: Teatro Arena's Zumbi." *Latin American Theatre Review* 21, 1 (Fall 1987): 19–27.

Miocinovic, Mirjana. "The Other Serbia." *Performing Arts Journal* 53 (1996): 27–31.

Mitchell, Loften. *Black Drama: The Story of the American Negro in the Theatre*. New York: Hawthorn Books, 1967.

Mitchell, J. Clyde. *The Kalela Dance: Aspects of Social Relationships among Urban Africans in Northern Rhodesia*. Manchester, UK: Manchester University Press, 1956.

Mlama, Penina Muhando. *Culture and Development:The Popular Theatre Approach in Africa*. Uppsala: Scandinavian Institute of African Studies, 1991.

Mlama, Penina O. "Tanzania's Cultural Policy and Its Implications for the Contribution of the Arts to Socialist Development." *Utafiti* 7, 1 (1985): 9–19.

Modiano, Marko. "An Early Swedish Stage Production of D. H. Lawrence's *The Daughter-in-Law*." *D. H. Lawrence Review* 17, 1 (Spring 1984): 49–59.

Moe Kyaw Aung. "Burmese Marionettes for Modern Audiences." *Forward* 6 (1967): 17–20.

Moebirman. *Wayang Purwa*. Jakarta: Yayasan Pelita Wisata, 1973.

Mohamed Abdel Hai. *Cultural Policy in the Sudan*. Paris: UNESCO, 1982.

Molka, Viktor. "Slovenia." In *The World Encyclopedia of Contemporary Theatre*, ed. Don Rubin, 767–781. New York: Routledge, 1994.

Monaco, James. *The New Wave:Truffaut, Godard, Chabrol, Rohmer, Rivette*. New York: Oxford University Press, 1976.

Montanaro, Tony. *Mime Spoken Here:The Performer's Portable Workshop*. Gardiner, ME: Tilbury House, 1995.

Montes, Carmen Marquez. "X Festival Del Sur— Encuentro Teatral Tres Continentes (10th Festival of the South—Theatrical Meeting of Three Continents)." *Latin American Theatre Review* 31 (Spring 1998): 201–204.

Montet, E. *La Religion et le Theatre en Perse*. Paris: Leroux, 1887.

Montri, Tramote. "Thai Puppet Show." *Silpakorn* 4, 2 (1960): 48–54.

Moore, Gerald. "The Arts in the New Africa." *African Affairs* 66, 263 (April 1967): 140–148.

Morash, Christopher. "Ireland." In *The World Encyclopedia of Contemporary Theatre*, ed. Don Rubin, 467–495. New York: Routledge, 1994.

Morckhoven, Paul Van. *The Contemporary Theatre in Belgium*. Brussels: Information and Documentation Institute, 1970.

Mordden, Ethan. *The American Theatre*. New York: Oxford University Press, 1981.

Moreh, S. "The Arabic Theatre in Egypt in the Eighteenth and Nineteenth Centuries." *Etudes Arabes et Islamiques* 3 (1975): 109–113.

———. "The Jewish Theatre in Iraq in the First Half of the Twentieth Century." *Pe'amim Studies in the Cultural Heritage of Oriental Jewy* 23 (1985): 64–98.

———. *Live Theatre and Dramatic Literature in the Medieval Arab World*. New York: New York University Press, 1992.

———. "Live Theatre in Medieval Islam." *Studies in Islamic History and Civilization in Honour of Professor David Aylalon* (1986): 565–611.

———. "The Shadow Play (*Khayal Al-Zill*) in the Light of Arabic Literature." *Journal of Arabic Literature* 18 (1987): 46–61.

———. "Ya'qub Sanu, His Religious Identity and Work in the Theatre and Journalism, According to the Family Archive." In *The Jews of Egypt*, ed. S. Shamir, 111–129, 244–264. Boulder, CO: Westview, 1987.

Morgan, Clyde. "International Exchange: The 2nd World Festival of Black Art and Culture: Lagos." *Dance Magazine* (July 1977): 90.

Morphy, Howard. *Ancestral Connections:Art and an Aboriginal System of Knowledge*. Chicago: University of Chicago Press, 1991.

Morris, Robert J. "The Theater of Julio Ortega since His Peruvian Hell." *Latin American Theatre Review* 19, 2 (Spring 1986): 31–37.

Morrison, Miriam. "The Expression of Emotion in Court Dances of Yogyakarta." *Asian Music* 7, 1 (1975): 33–38.

Morton, Carlos. "The Nicaraguan Drama: Theatre of Testimony." *Latin American Theatre Review* 17, 2 (Spring 1984): 89–92.

Mosier, John. "Film." In *Handbook of Latin American Popular Culture*, ed. Harold E. Hinds and Charles M. Tatum, 173–189. Westport, CT: Greenwood, 1985.

———. "The Importance of Popular Cinema in Latin America." *Studies in Latin American Popular Culture* 1 (1982): 179–186.

Moss, Leonard. *Arthur Miller*. Boston: G. K. Hall, 1980.

Mosse, George. *Nazi Culture*. New York: Grosset & Dunlap, 1966.

Mostyn, Trevor, and Albert Hourani, eds. *The Cambridge Encyclopedia of the Middle East and North Africa*. New York: Cambridge University Press, 1988.

Mubin, Sheppard. "The Khmer Shadow Play and Its Links with Ancient India." *Journal of the Malayan Branch, Royal Asiatic Society* 41, 213 (July 1968): 199–204.

Mueller, Roswitha. *Valie Export: Fragments of the Imagination*. Bloomington: Indiana University Press, 1994.

Mujica, Barbara. "Encore for a National Treasure." *Americas* 43, 2 (1991): 50–53.

Mukhopadhyay, Durgadas, ed. *Lesser Known Forms of Performing Arts of India*. New Delhi: Sterling, 1978.

Mulyono, Sri Ir. *Human Character in the Wayang*. Singapore: Gunung Agung, 1981.

———. *Simbolisme dan Mistikisme Dalam Wayang*. Jakarta: CV Haki Masagung, 1989.

Mumford, Meg. "Brecht Studies Stanislavski: Just a Tactical Move?" *New Theatre Quarterly* 11 (Aug. 1995): 241–258.

Murdock, George. *Africa: Its Peoples and Their Culture History*. New York: McGraw-Hill, 1959.

Murphy, Joseph M. *Working the Spirit: Ceremonies of the African Diaspora*. Boston: Beacon, 1994.

Murphy, Robert. *The British Cinema Book*. London: BFI Publishing, 1997.

Murray, G. G. A. *Aeschylus:The Creator of Tragedy*. Westport, CT: Greenwood, 1978.

Murray, Gilbert. *Aristophanes: A Study*. New York: Russell & Russell, 1964.

———. *Euripides and His Age*. New York: Oxford University Press, 1946.

Murray, Jocelyn, ed. *Cultural Atlas of Africa*. New York: Facts on File, 1981.

Musafija, Mair. "Bosnia-Herzegovina." In *The World Encyclopedia of Contemporary Theatre*, ed. Don Rubin, 143–154. New York: Routledge, 1994.

Mydans, Shelley. "The Ancient Dance of Burma Comes to Dazzle American Audiences." *Smithsonian* (1975): 70–79.

Myers, D. H. *The Last Days of Mr. Punch*. New York: McCall, 1971.

Myerson, Michael. *Memories of Underdevelopment: The Revolutionary Films of Cuba*. New York: Grossman, 1973.

Myrsiades, Linda S. *Karagiozis: Culture and Comedy in Greek Puppet Theater*. Lexington: University Press of Kentucky, 1992.

———. *The Karagiozis: Heroic Performance in Greek Shadow Theater*. Hanover, NH: University Press of New England, 1988.

Nagy, Peter. "Hungary." In *The World Encyclopedia of Contemporary Theatre*, ed. Don Rubin, 427–450. New York: Routledge, 1994.

Narayana, Birendra. *Hindi Drama and Stage*. Delhi: Bansal, 1981.

Nardocchio, Elaine. *Theatre and Politics in Modern Quebec*. Edmonton, AB: University of Alberta Press, 1986.

Narwekar, Sanjit. *Directory of Indian Film-Makers and Films*. Westport, CT: Greenwood, 1994.

Nascimento, Abdias do. "Afro-Brazilian Culture." *Black Images* 1, 3–4 (Autumn/Winter 1972): 41–46.

———. "Mission of the Brazilian Experimental Theatre." *Crisis* 56 (1949): 274–275, 283.

———. "The Negro Theater in Brazil." *African Forum* 2 (1967): 20–34.

Ndakivangi Mantumba Nimambu. *Heritage Culturel Zairois*. Kinshasa: Centre Protestant d'Éditions et de Diffusion, 1978.

Ndeti, Kivuto. *Cultural Policy in Kenya*. Paris: UNESCO, 1975.

Nelson, Benjamin. *Arthur Miller: Portrait of a Playwright*. New York: McKay, 1970.

Nemirovich-Danchenko, Vladimir. *My Life in the Russian Theatre*. New York: Theatre Arts, 1968.

Neog, Maheswar. *Sankaradeva and His Times*. Gauhati, India: Gauhati University, 1965.

Neuhaus, Hans. "Barong." *Djawa* 18 (1937): 203–239.

Neves, David. "In Search of the Aesthetics of the Brazilian Cinema." *New Orleans Review* (1982): 63–68.

Newberry, Wilma. *The Pirandellian Mode in Spanish Literature From Cervantes to Sastre*. Albany: State University of New York Press, 1973.

Nguyen Phuoc Thien. "Cai Luong and the Vietnamese Theatre." *Viet-My* 8, 4 (December 1963): 2–10.

———. "Vietnamese Theatre: The Show Must Go On." *Vietnam Magazine* 7, 5 (1974): 12–15.

Nicholson, Anne Gregory. "The Stage in Yugoslavia." *Drama* 12 (1933/1934): 22.

Nicolaisen, Jay. *Italian Opera in Transition, 1871–1893*. Ann Arbor, MI: Proquest, 1980.

Nicoll, Allardyce. *The English Theatre: A Short History*. London: Nelson, 1936.

———. "Masks, Mimes and Miracles: Studies in the Popular Theatre." London: G. C. Harrap, 1931.

Niebuhr, Carsten. *Travels through Arabia and Other Countries in the East*. Trans. Robert Heron. Edinburgh: R. Morison and Son, 1792.

Niedzialkowski, Stefan. *Beyond the Word: The World of Mime*. Troy, MI: Momentum Books, 1993.

Nketia, J. H. Kwabena. "The Creative Arts and the Community." *Proceedings of the Ghana Academy of Arts and Sciences (Accra)* 8 (1970): 71–76.

Nkwoh, Marius. *Igbo Cultural Heritage*. Onitsha, Nigeria: University Publishing, 1984.

Noble, Peter. *British Theatre*. London: British Yearbooks, 1946.

Noccioli, Guido. *Duse on Tour: Guido Noccioli's Diaries, 1906–1907*. Trans. Giovanni Pontiero. Amherst: University of Massachusetts Press, 1982.

Noh, David. "Re-Imagining Titus." *Film Journal International* 103 (February 2000): 12, 14, 16.

———. *Performative Circumstances from the Avant Garde to Ramlila*. Calcutta: Seagull Books, 1983.

Nolin, Bertil. "A Successful Realization of Group Theater in Sweden." *Scandinavian Studies* 43 (1971): 22–34.

Norton-Welsh, Christopher. "Opera around the World: Wide-Awake *Sonnambula*, Bratislava." *Opera* 49, 7 (July 1998): 842–844.

Norwood, Gilbert. *The Art of Terence*. Oxford: B. Blackwell, 1923.

———. *Essays on Euripidean Drama*. Berkeley and Los Angeles: University of California Press, 1954.

———. *Plautus and Terence*. New York: Cooper Square, 1963.

Novicki, Margaret. "Burkina Faso: A Revolutionary Culture." *Africa Report* (July–August 1987): 57–60.

Nunley, John, and Judith Bettelheim, eds. *Caribbean Festival Arts*. Seattle: University of Washington Press, 1988.

Nwoko, Demas. "The Aesthetics of African Art and Culture." *New Culture* 1, 1 (1978): 3–6.

Obraztsov, Sergei Vladimirovich. *The Chinese Puppet Theatre*. Trans. J. T. MacDermott. London: Faber and Faber, 1961.

Obrebski, Jozef. *Ritual and Social Structure in a Macedonian Village*. Amherst: International Area Studies

Programs, University of Massachusetts at Amherst, 1977.

O'Connor, John Bartholomew. *Chapters in the History of Actors and Acting in Ancient Greece.* Chicago: University of Chicago Press, 1908.

O'Connor, Margaret Brown. *Religion in the Plays of Sophocles.* Menasha, WI: George Banta, 1923.

O'Connor, Patrick. *Dietrich: Style and Substance.* New York: Dutton, 1992.

Oderman, Stuart. *Lillian Gish: A Life on Stage and Screen.* Jefferson, NC: McFarland, 2000.

Offen, Ron. *Brando.* Chicago: Regnery, 1973.

Ogden, Dunbar H. *Performance Dynamics and the Amsterdam Werkteater.* Berkeley: University of California Press, 1984.

O'Grady, Deirdre. *The Last Troubadours: Poetic Drama in Italian Opera 1597–1887.* New York: Routledge, 1991.

Ogunba, Oyin, and Abiola Irele, eds. *Theatre in Africa.* Ibadan, Nigeria: Ibadan University Press, 1978.

Ojo, G. J. Afolabi. *Yoruba Culture: A Geographical Analysis.* Ife, Nigeria: University of Ife Press, 1967.

Okpewho, Isidore. *The Epic in Africa: Towards a Poetics of the Oral Performance.* New York: Columbia University Press, 1979.

Olaerts, Ann. "Flemish Playwrights." *Articles 7* (Summer 1991).

Olinger, Marc. "Luxembourg." In *The World Encyclopedia of Contemporary Theatre,* ed. Don Rubin, 569–570. New York: Routledge, 1994.

Oliver, D. *A Solomon Island Society.* Cambridge, MA: Harvard University Press, 1955.

Olivier, Laurence. *On Acting.* New York: Simon and Schuster, 1986.

Ollen, Gunnar. *August Strindberg.* New York: Ungar, 1972.

O'Malley, Conor. *A Poet's Theatre.* Dublin: Elo Press, 1988.

Oman, Carola. *David Garrick.* London: Hodder and Stoughton, 1958.

Omotoso, Kole. *The Theatrical into Theatre: A Study of the Drama and Theatre of the English-Speaking Caribbean.* London: New Beacon Books, 1982.

D'Ooge, Martin Luther. *The Acropolis of Athens.* New York: Macmillan, 1908.

Opoku, A. A. *Festivals of Ghana.* Accra: Ghana Publishing, 1970.

Oreglia, Giacomo. *The Commedia dell'Arte* (Commedia dell'Arte). Trans. Lovett Edwards. New York: Hill and Wang, 1968.

Orenstein, Claudia. *Festive Revolutions: The Politics of Popular Theatre and The San Francisco Mime Troupe.* Jackson: University Press of Mississippi, 1998.

Orloff, Alexander. *Carnival: Myth and Cult.* Worgl, Austria: Perlinger, 1981.

Orosa, Rosalind. "The Guerilla Theatre in the Philippines." *Asian Pacific Quarterly* 3, 2 (1971): 43–50.

Ortolani, Benito. *The Japanese Theatre: From Shamanistic Ritual to Contemporary Pluralism.* New York: E. J. Brill, 1990.

Osman, Mohd. Taib, ed. *Traditional Drama and Music of Southeast Asia.* Kuala Lumpur: Dewan Bahasa Dan Pustaka Kementerian Pelajaran Malaysia, 1974.

Osnes, Mary Beth. "Malaysia's Evolving Shadow Puppet Theatre." *Asian Theatre Journal* 9 (Spring 1992): 112–116.

———. "A Survey of Shadow Play in the Malaysian Traditional Shadow Puppet Theatre." Ann Arbor, MI: Proquest, 1992.

———. "Shadow Puppet Theatre in Malaysia: Many Traditions, One God." *Quest* (Spring 1994): 70–73, 89.

Ottenberg, Simon. "Afikpo Masquerades: Audience and Performers." *African Arts* 6, 4 (1973): 32–36.

———. *Anthropology and African Aesthetics.* Accra: Ghana Universities Press, 1971.

p'Bitek, Okot. *Africa's Cultural Revolution.* Nairobi: Macmillan, 1973.

Pacheco, Patrick. "In the Company of Calista: She's Dreamed a 'Midsummer' Dream, and Taught Us All about Ally. But Deep Down Calista Flockhart Is an Off-Broadway Baby." *InTheatre* 93 (5 July 1999): 18–22.

Paine, Albert. *Life and Lillian Gish.* New York: Macmillan, 1932.

Palls, Terry Lee. "The Theatre in Revolutionary Cuba: 1959–1969." Ph.D. diss., University of Kansas, 1974.

Panchal, Goverdhan. *Bhavai and Its Typical Aharya.* Ahmedabad: Darpana Academy of the Performing Arts, 1983.

Pandeya, A. C. *The Art of Kathakali.* Allahabad: Lotabostam, 1961.

Panizo, Alfredo P. O. Z., and Rodolfo V. Cortez. "Introduction to the Pampango Theatre." *Unitas* 41, 1 (March 1968): 124–137.

Pankhurst, E. Sylvia. *Ethiopia: A Cultural History.* Essex, UK: Lalibela House, 1955.

Panovski, Naum. "Art and Performance Notes: Landscape for New Millennium: Slobodan Snajder, Croatian Playwright." *PAJ—A Journal of Performance and Art* 20, 3 (September 1998): 76–78.

Parada, Carlos. *Genealogical Guide to Greek Mythology.* Jonsered: P. Astroms Forlag, 1993.

Parry, David. "The Burmese Theatre." *Eastern World* 3 (December 1949): 29–31.

Parsons, Philip, and Victoria Chance, eds. *Companion to Theatre in Australia.* Sydney: Currency Press, 1995.

Pasquariello, Anthony M. "The Evolution of the *Saintete* in the River Plate Area." *Latin American Theatre Review* 17, 1 (Fall 1983): 15–23.

———. "Theatre in Colonial Spanish America: Religious and Cultural Impact." *Hispanic Journal* 10, 1 (Fall 1988): 27–38.

Patraka, Vivian. *Sam Shepard*. Boise, ID: Boise State University, 1985.

Patterson, Michael. *German Theatre Today: Post-War Theatre in West and East Germany, Austria and Northern Switzerland*. New York: Pitman, 1976.

———. *The Revolution in German Theatre: 1900–1933*. London: Routledge and Kegan Paul, 1981.

Pausanias. *The Acropolis of Athens: As Described by Pausanias, Other Writers, Inscriptions and Archaeological Evidence*. Chicago: Ares, 1976.

Paxman, Andrew. "Mipcom '98: Telenovelas: Novela Craze Hits Auds across Global Spectrum." *Variety* 372, 7 (28 September 1998–4 October 1998): M38–M40.

Peacock, James. "Comedy and Centralisation in Java: The Lubruk Plays." *Journal of American Folklore* 80, 318 (October–December 1967): 345–356.

———. "Javanese Folkdrama and Social Change." Ph.D. diss., Harvard University, 1965.

Peking Opera Troupe of Shanghai. *Taking Tiger Mountain by Strategy*. Peking: Foreign Language Press, 1971.

Percival, John. *Theatre in My Blood: A Biography of John Cranko*. New York: F. Watts, 1983.

Pereira, Joseph R. "The Black Presence in Cuban Theatre." *Afro-Hispanic Review* 2, 1 (January 1983): 13–18.

Perkins, Don. "From Megaworlds to Mini-Magic: Catalyst Theatre's Process for Small-Scale Spectacle." *Canadian Theatre Review* 97 (Winter 1998): 12–17.

Perrier, Paulette. "The Yard Theatre: Jamaica." *Black Theatre* 5 (1971): 9–10.

Perrone, Charles A. "Dissonance and Dissent: The Musical Dramatics of Chico Buarque." *Latin American Theatre Review* 22, 2 (Spring 1989): 81–94.

Peterson, Bernard. *The African American Theatre Directory, 1816–1960: A Comprehensive Guide to Early Black Theatre Organizations*. Westport, CT.: Greenwood, 1997.

Petropoulos, Constantina. "Byrne, Gabriel." *Current Biography* 60, 5 (May 1999): 5–7.

Phelan, John Leddy. *The Millennial Kingdom of the Franciscans in the New World: A Study of the Writings of Gerónimo De Mendieta (1525–1604)*. Berkeley: University of California Press, 1956.

Phillips, Gene. *Alfred Hitchcock*. Boston: Twayne, 1984.

Pick, Zuzana M. *Latin American Filmmakers and the Third Cinema*. Ottowa: Carleton University, 1978.

———. *The New Latin American Cinema: A Continental Project*. Austin: University of Texas Press, 1993.

Pickard-Cambridge, Sir Arthur Wallace. *Dramatic Festivals of Athens*. 2d ed. Oxford: Clarendon, 1962.

———. *The Theatre of Dionysus in Athens*. Oxford: Clarendon, 1946.

Pickford, Mary. *Sunshine and Shadow*. Garden City, NY: Doubleday, 1955.

Pierson, Colin M. "Portugal's Geraao De 70: Drama Influenced by a Changing World." *Theatre Research International* 20 (1995): 1–6.

Piette, Alain. "Crommelynck and Meyerhold: Two Geniuses Meet on the Stage." *Modern Drama* 39 (Fall 1996): 436–447.

Pilgrim, Frank. *The National Cultural Centre: Souvenir Programme, First Performance, May 1976*. Georgetown: National History and Arts Council, 1976.

Pine, Richard. *Brian Friel and Ireland's Drama*. London: Routledge, 1991.

Pintzka, Wolfgang. *Helene Weigel, Actress: A Book of Photographs*. Leipzig: VEB Offizin Andersen Nexo, 1961.

Pitcher, Harvey. *Chekhov's Leading Lady: A Portrait of the Actress Olga Knipper*. New York: F. Watts, 1980.

Planchon, Roger. *Les Libertins*. Villeurbanne: Theatre National Populaire, 1996.

Playfair, Giles. *Kean*. New York: E. P. Dutton, 1939.

Podlecki, A. J. *The Political Background of Aeschylean Tragedy*. Ann Arbor: University of Michigan Press, 1966.

Polansky, Susan. "Provocation to Audience Response: Narrators in the Plays of Antonio Buero Vallejo." *Letras Peninsulares* 1, 2 (1988): 200–223.

Polito, Antonio. *Spanish Theatre: A Survey from the Middle Ages to the Twentieth-Century*. Salt Lake City: Department of Languages, University of Utah, 1967.

Pompilus, Pradel. "Tendencies of the Haitian Theatre." *World Theatre* 16, 5–6 (1967): 534–536.

Pong, Chau Soo. "Chinese Opera in the Park." *Performing Arts* 1, 1 (1984): 9–12.

Popkin, Cathy. *The Pragmatics of Insignificance: Checkov, Zoshchenko, Gogol*. Stanford, CA: Stanford University Press, 1993.

Popovic, Vladeta. "Shakespeare in Post-War Yugoslavia." *Shakespeare Survey* 4 (1951): 117.

Portman, Jamie. *Stratford: The First Thirty Years*. Toronto: McClelland & Stewart, 1989.

Porton, Richard. "Film Reviews: Felicia's Journey." *Cineaste* 25 (December 1999): 42–43.

———. "Lisbon's International Encounters in Documentary Cinema." *Cineaste* 24 (September 1999): 46–47.

Power, Paul. "Contemporary Irish Cinema: The Irish Are Rising Again: Profiles of New Filmmaking Talent." *Cineaste* 24, 2–3 (March 1999): 74–75.

———. "Irish Films Seeing More Green." *Variety* 374, 11 (3 May 1999–9 May 1999): 26.

Prampolini, Enrico. "The Futurist Pantomime." In *Art and the Stage in The Twentieth Century*, ed. Henning Rischbieter. Greenwich, CT: New York Graphic Society, 1968.

———. "Futurist Scenography." In *Total Theatre*, ed. E. T. Kirby. New York: E. P. Dutton, 1969.

Predan, Alija. "Theatre in Yugoslavia." *Drama* 3 (1984): 30.

Price, Cecil John Layton. *The English Theatre in Wales in the Eighteenth and Early Nineteenth Centuries*. Cardiff: University of Wales Press, 1948.

Pronko, Leonard Cabell. *Guide to Japanese Drama*. Boston: G. K. Hall, 1984.

Prudhoe, John. *The Theatre of Goethe and Schiller*. Totowa, NJ: Rowman and Littlefield, 1973.

Quaghebeur, Marc. "The Current Situation of the French-Language Theatre of Belgium." In *An Anthology of Contemporary Belgian Plays*, ed. David Willinger, 291–295. New York: Whitston, 1984.

———. "Introduction to Belgian Theatre." *Gambit* 11, 42–3 (1986): 9–24.

Quiles, Edgar. "The Theatre of Augusto Boal." Ph.D. diss. Ann Arbor, MI: University Microfilms, 1981.

Qureshi, M. Aslam. *Wajid Ali Shah's Theatrical Genius*. Lahore, Pakistan: Vanguard, 1987.

Rabe, David. *The Vietnam Plays*. New York: Grove, 1993.

Racstern, Olga. *Curtain Up! The Story of Cape Theatre*. Cape Town, South Africa: Juta, 1951.

Rahul, Ram. *Modern Bhutan*. New York: Barnes & Noble, 1972.

Ramasubramaniam, V. "The Mediaeval and the Pre-Modern Burmese Theatres." *Bulletin of the Institute of Traditional Cultures* (January–June 1974): 106–117.

Ransome, Grace Greenleaf. *Puppets and Shadows: A Selective Bibliography to 1930*. Lewiston, NY: Edwin Mellen, 1997.

Rebello, Luiz Francisco. *History of Theatre: Synthesis of Portuguese Culture*. Trans. Candida Cadavez. Lisbon: Imprensa Nacional-Casa da Moeda, 1991.

Redmond, James. *Farce*. New York: Cambridge University Press, 1988.

Redwood, John Elkert. "The Siamese Classical Theatre." *Educational Theatre Journal* 5 (1952): 100–105.

Reed, C. L. "Bina Suarga: A Balinese Shadow Play as Performed by Ida Bagus Ngurah." *Asian Theatre Journal* 3, 1 (1986): 1–33.

Reed, Terence. *The Classical Centre: Goethe and Weimar*. New York: Barnes & Noble, 1980.

Rees, K. "The Three-Actor Rule in Menander." *Classical Philology* 5 (1910): 291–302.

Rehm, Rush. *Greek Tragic Theatre*. New York: Routledge, 1992.

Reiniger, Lotte. *Shadow Theatres and Shadow Films*. New York: Watson-Guptil Grove, 1970.

Renner, Pamela. "The Zone of Fantastic Reality: Cirque du Soleil Takes Clowning in a New Direction." *American Theatre* 16 (December 1999): 28–30.

Rentse, Anker. "The Kelantan Shadow-Play." *Journal Malayan Branch* 14 (1936): 284–301.

———. "The Origin of the Wayang Theatre (Shadow Play)." *Journal Malayan Branch* 20 (1947): 12–15.

Reston, James Jr. *Coming to Terms: American Plays & the Vietnam War*. New York: Theatre Communications Group, 1985.

Reyes Navares, Beatriz. *The Mexican Cinema: Interviews with Thirteen Directors*. Trans. Carl Mora and Elizabeth Gard.

Albuquerque: University of New Mexico Press, 1976.

Richards, J. V. Olufemi. "The Sande Mask." *African Arts* 7, 2 (1974): 48–51.

Richards, Terry. "Film Reviews: *Buttoners*." *Film Reviews* 563 (February 1999): 37.

Richards, Thomas. *At Work with Grotowski on Physical Actions*. New York: Routledge, 1995.

Richardson, Helen Elizabeth. "The Theatre du Soleil and the Quest for Popular Theatre in the Twentieth Century." Ph.D. diss. Ann Arbor, MI: University Microfilms International, 1991.

Richardson, Joanna. *Sarah Bernhardt*. London: M. Reinhardt, 1959.

Richmond, Farley P., Darius L. Swann, and Phillip B. Zarrilli, eds. *Indian Theatre: Traditions of Performance*. Honolulu: University of Hawaii Press, 1990.

Richtarik, Marilynn J. *Acting between the Lines: The Field Day Theatre Company and Irish Culture Politics, 1980–1984*. New York: Oxford University Press, 1994.

Richtman, Jack. *Adrienne Lecouvreur: The Actress and the Age*. Englewood Cliffs, NJ: Prentice-Hall, 1971.

Ridgeway, W. *The Dramas and Dramatic Dances of Non-European Races*. Cambridge: Cambridge University Press, 1915.

Riggs, Arthur S. "The Drama of the Filipinos." *Journal of American Folklore* 17, 67 (December 1904): 279–285.

Rimer, Thomas J. *Toward a Modern Japanese Theatre: Kishida Kunio*. Princeton, NJ: Princeton University Press, 1974.

Risum, Janne. "Towards Transparency: Soren Kierkegaard on Danish Actresses." In *Nordic Theatre Studies: Yearbook for Theatre Research in Scandinavia*, ed. Kela Kvam, 19–30. Copenhagen: Institute for Theatre Research, University of Copenhagen, 1988.

Robert, Lucie. "The New Quebec Theatre." In *Canadian Canons: Essays in Literary Value*, ed. Robert Lecker, 112–123. Toronto: ECW Press, 1982.

Robertson, Ritchie, and Edward Timms, eds. *Theatre and Performance in Austria: From Mozart to Jelinek*. Edinburgh: Edinburgh University Press, 1993.

Robichez, Jacques. *Lugne-Poe*. Paris: L'Arche, 1955.

Robinson, David. *Chaplin, His Life and Art*. New York: McGraw-Hill, 1985.

Robinson, Horace. "A Brief Visit to Theater in Finland." *Players Magazine* 40 (1964): 176–177.

Robinson, Jeffery. *Bette Davis, Her Film and Stage Career*. New York: Scribner, 1982.

Rolfe, Bari. *Commedia Dell'Arte: A Scene Study Book*. San Francisco : Persona, 1977.

Rollyson, Carl. *Marilyn Monroe: A Life of the Actress*. Ann Arbor, MI: UMI Research Press, 1986.

Rondi, Gian. *Italian Cinema Today*. New York: Hill and Wang, 1965.

Roosman, R. S. "Cross-Cultural Aspects of Thai Drama." *Journal of Oriental Literature* 8 (January 1967): 43–51.

Rosenfeld, Lulla. *Bright Star of Exile: Jacob Adler and the Yiddish Theatre.* New York: Crowell, 1977.

Rosenthal, Franz. *Humor in Early Islam.* Westport, CT: Greenwood, 1976.

Roth, Beulah. *James Dean.* Corte Madera, CA: Pomegranate Artbooks, 1983.

Roudane, Matthew, ed. *The Cambridge Companion to Tennessee Williams.* New York: Cambridge University Press, 1997.

Rouse, John. *Brecht and the West German Theatre: The Practice and Politics of Interpretation.* Ann Arbor: University of Michigan Press, 1989.

Rowland, Benjamin. *The Art and Architecture of India.* New York: Penguin, 1981.

Roy, Claude. *Jean Vilar.* Paris: Calmann-Levy, 1987.

Royal University of Fine Arts, Cambodia. "Shadow Plays in Cambodia." In *Traditional Drama and Music of Southeast Asia,* ed. Mohd. Taib Osman, 47–51. Kuala Lumpur: Dewan Bahasa Dan Pustaka Kementerian Pelajaran Malaysia, 1974.

Rudlin, John. *Commedia Dell'Arte: An Actor's Handbook.* London and New York: Routledge, 1994.

Rudlin, John, and Antonio Fava. *Masks of the Commedia Dell'Arte.* Arts Documentation Unit, n.d. Videocassette.

Rudolph, Lloyd. *Cultural Policy in India.* Delhi: Chanakya Grove, 1984.

Rustom, Bharucha. *Theatre and the World: Essays on Performance and Politics of Culture.* Columbia, MO: South Asia Publications, 1990.

Rutnin, Mattani. "Nang Talung and Thai Life." *East Asian Cultural Studies* 15 (March 1976): 45–52.

———. "Nang Yai: The Thai Classical Shadow Play and the Wat Kanon Troupe of Rajburi." *East Asian Cultural Studies* 15 (March 1976): 53–59.

———, ed. *The Siamese Theatre: Collections of Reprints from Journals of Siam Society.* Bangkok: Siam Society, 1975.

———. "The Role of Shadow Play in Modern Thai Society." *Bangkok Post Sunday Magazine* (November 17, 1974): 13–14.

Ruud, Jorgen. *Taboo: A Study of Malagasy Customs and Beliefs.* New York: Humanities, 1960.

Ryall, Tom. *Alfred Hitchcock and the British Cinema.* Atlantic Highlands, NJ: Athlone, 1996.

Ryan, Peter, ed. *Encyclopaedia of Papua and New Guinea.* Melbourne: Melbourne University Press, 1972.

Rynning, Ronald. "All the President's Women: Ronald Rynning Talks to the Stars of Primary Colors and Discovers It's a Red, White and Blue Movie." *Film Review* (October 1998): 40–45.

Sachs, Albie. "Mozambican Culture: A Crowded Canvas." *Southern Africa Report* (Toronto) 4, 1 (July 1988): 21–24.

Sadoul, Georges. *French Film.* London: Falcon, 1953.

Salerno, Henry F. *Flaminio Scala's Scenarios of the Commedia Dell'Arte.* New York: New York University, 1967.

Salmane, Hala, Simon Hartog, and David Wilson, eds. *Algerian Cinema.* London: British Film Institute, 1976.

Salmon, Eric, ed. *Bernhardt and the Theatre of Her Time.* Westport, CT.: Greenwood, 1984.

Salomon, Roberto. "Theatre in El Salvador during the Eighties." *Latin American Theatre Review* 25, 2 (Spring 1992): 173–180.

Salvini, Tommaso. *Leaves from the Autobiography of Tommaso Salvini.* New York: Century, 1893.

Salz, Melissa. "Theatre of Testimony: The Work of Emily Mann, Anna Deavere Smith and Spalding Gray." Ph.D. diss., University of Colorado, 1996.

Samson, Leela. *Rhythm in Joy.* New Delhi: Lustre Press, 1987.

San Juan, E. *The Art of Oscar Wilde.* Princeton, NJ: Princeton University Press, 1967.

Sandbach, F. *The Comic Theatre of Greece and Rome.* New York: Norton, 1977.

Sanskrit Drama. Dir. Mrinalini Sarabhai. New York: Institute for Advanced Studies in Theater Arts, 1980. Videocassette.

Sarachchandra, Ediriweera R. *The Folk Drama of Ceylon.* 2d ed. Colombo: Department of Cultural Affairs, 1966.

Sariman, Chua. "Traditional Dance Drama in Thailand." In *Traditional Drama and Music of Southeast Asia,* ed. Mohd. Taib Osman, 165–171. Kuala Lumpur: Dewan Bahasa Dan Pustaka Kementerian Pelajaran Malaysia, 1974.

Sartre, Jean Paul. *Being and Nothingness: An Essay on Phenomenological Ontology.* New York: Washington Square Press, 1966.

Saunders, C. *Costume in Roman Comedy.* New York: Columbia University Press, 1909.

Sauter, Willmar. "Sweden." In *Nordic Theatre Studies: Yearbook for Theatre Research in Scandinavia,* 9–22. Copenhagen: Munksgaard International, 1989.

Sayler, Oliver Martin. *Max Reinhardt and His Theatre.* New York: Brentano's, 1924.

———. *Performance Theory.* New York: Methuen Drama, 1988.

Schechner, Richard. "ARTNOW." *Drama Review* 40, 3 (Fall 1996): 7–8.

———. *Performance Theory.* New York: Routledge, 1988.

Scheit, Gerhard. *Hanswurst und der Staat.* Vienna: Deuticke, 1995.

Schickel, Richard. *Brando: A Life in Our Times.* New York: Atheneum, 1991.

———. *Clint Eastwood: A Biography.* New York: Knopf, 1996.

Schieffelin, Edward. *The Sorrow of the Lonely and the Burning of the Dancers.* New York: St. Martin's, 1976.

Schipper, Mineke. *Theatre and Society in Africa.* Trans. Ampie Coetzee. Athens: Ohio University Press, 1982.

Schmidt, Paul. *Meyerhold At Work.* Trans. Paul Schmidt. Austin: University of Texas Press, 1980.

Schoenberg, Claude-Michel. *Miss Saigon*. Milwaukee, WI: Hal Leonard Corporation, 1990.

Scholes, Percy Alfred. *A Miniature History of Opera for the General Reader and the Student*. New York: Oxford University Press, 1931.

Schopf, Davor. "Opera around the World: Croatia—Split." *Opera* 49, 4 (April 1998): 418.

Schuler, Catherine. *Women in Russian Theatre*. London: Routledge, 1996.

Schwartz, Isidore Adolphe. *The Commedia Dell'Arte and Its Influence on French Comedy in the Seventeenth Century*. Paris: H. Samuel, 1933.

Schwartzman, Karen. "A Descriptive Chronology of Films by Women in Venezuela 1952–92." *Journal of Film and Video* 44, 3–4 (Fall 1992 and Winter 1993): 33–50.

Schwoch, J. "Latin American Television: A Global View." *Historical Journal of Film, Radio and Television* 19, 4 (October 1999): 555–556.

Scofield, John. "Life Slowly Changes in a Remote Himalayan Kingdom." *National Geographic* 150 (November 1976): 658–683.

Scott, A. C. *The Classical Theatre of China*. London: Allen & Unwin, 1957.

———. *The Kabuki Theatre of Japan*. 1955. Reprint, London: Allen & Unwin, 1956.

———. *Literature and the Arts in Twentieth Century China*. Garden City, NY: Doubleday, 1963.

———. *The Theatre in Asia*. New York: Macmillan, 1972.

Scott, John Adams. *Homer and His Influence*. Boston: Marshall Jones, 1925.

Scott, William Clyde. *Musical Design in Aeschylean Theater*. Hanover, NH: Published for Dartmouth College by University Press of New England, 1984.

Seale, D. *Vision and Stagecraft in Sophocles*. London: Croom Helm, 1982.

Searle, Townley. *A Bibliography of Sir William Schwench Gilbert with Bibliographical Adventures in the Gilbert & Sullivan Operas*. London: John McQueen, 1931.

Segal, Arthur. *Theatres in Roman Palestine and Provincia Arabia*. New York: E. J. Brill, 1995.

Sein, Kenneth, and J. H. Withey. *The Great Po Sein: A Chronicle of the Burmese Theatre*. Bloomington: Indiana University Press, 1965.

Sellin, Eric, *Dramatic Concepts of Antonin Artaud*, Chicago: University of Chicago Press, 1968.

Semsel, George S., and Xia Hong, eds. *Chinese Film Theory: A Guide to the New Era*. Trans. Li Xiaohong Hou Jianping and Fan Yuan. New York: Praeger, 1990.

Senelick, Laurence. *The Changing Room: Sex, Drag, and Theatre*. New York: Routledge, 2000.

———. *Wandering Stars: Russian Emigre Theatre*. Iowa City: University of Iowa Press, 1992.

Seton, Marie. "Theatre in Yugoslavia." *Drama* 3 (Autumn 1947): 19.

———. "The Theatre in Yugoslavia." *Theatre Arts* 31 (October 1947): 68.

Severn, Bill. *Shadow Magic: The Story of Shadow Play*. New York: David McKay, 1959.

Shah, Panna. *The Indian Film*. Bombay: Motion Picture Society of India, 1950.

Shen Hua. "Viet Nam's Brilliant Hat Cheo Opera." *Chinese Literature* 12 (1960): 195–197.

Sheppard, John Tresidder. *Aeschylus & Sophocles: Their Work and Influence*. New York: Longmans, Green, 1927.

Shim, Jung Soon. "Trends in Contemporary Culture: In Search of Diversity—Korean Theatre in the 1980s." *Korean Culture (Hanguk Munhwa)* 12, 3 (Fall 1991): 4.

Shipley, Joseph. *The Art of Eugene O'Neill*. Seattle: University of Washington Book Store, 1928.

Shister, Famic Lorine. "The Portrayal of Emotion in Tragedy." *American Journal of Philology* 66 (1945): 377–397.

———. "The Portrayal of Emotion in Tragedy." *American Journal of Philology* 69 (1948): 229–231.

Shoulov, Iosif. *The Bulgarian Theatre*. Trans. Elena Mladenova. Sofia: Foreign Language Press, 1964.

Shvydkoi, Mikhail. "Nostalgia for Soviet Theatre—Is There Hope for the Future?" *Performing Arts Journal* 15 (January 1993): 111–119.

Shyer, Laurence. *Robert Wilson and His Collaborators*. New York: Theatre Communication Group, 1989.

Siclier, Jacques. "New Wave and French Cinema." *Sight & Sound* 30, 3 (Summer 1961): 116–120.

Sieber, Roy. "The Arts and Their Changing Social Function." *Annals of the New York Academy of Sciences* 96, 2 (January 1962): 653–658.

Sieg, Katrin Sieg. *Exiles, Eccentrics, Activists: Women in Contemporary German Theater*. Ann Arbor: University of Michigan Press, 1994.

Sifakis, G. M. *Studies in the History of Hellenistic Drama*. London: Athlone, 1967.

Silberman, Marc. "The Actor's Medium: On Stage and in Film." *Modern Drama* 39 (Winter 1996): 558–565.

Siljan, Rade. *Macedonian Drama: The Nineteenth and Twentieth Centuries*. Skopje: Makedonska Kniga, 1990.

Simko, Jan. "Shakespeare in Slovakia." *Shakespeare Survey* 4 (1951): 109.

Simmonds, E. H. S. "New Evidence on Thai Shadow Play Invocation." *Bulletin, School of Oriental and African Studies* 24, 3 (1961).

Simmons, Ernest Joseph. *Chekhov: A Biography*. Boston: Little, Brown, 1962.

Simon, Erika. *Antike Theater* (The Ancient Theatre). Trans. C. E. Vafopoulou. New York: Methuen, 1982.

Simpson, Alan. *Beckett and Behan, and a Theatre in Dublin*. London: Routledge and Paul, 1962.

Sinclair, Keith, ed. *The Oxford Illustrated History of New Zealand*. New York: Oxford University Press, 1990.

Skuncke, Marie-Christine. *Sweden and European Drama: 1772–1796: A Study of Translations and Adaptations.* Uppsala: Almquist & Wiksell, 1981.

Slide, Anthony. *Early American Cinema.* Metuchen, NJ: Scarecrow, 1994.

———. *The Encyclopedia of Vaudeville.* Westport, CT: Greenwood, 1994.

———. *The International Film Industry: A Historical Dictionary.* New York: Greenwood, 1989.

Sloat, Susanna. "Cirque du Soleil Quidam." *Attitude—The Dancer's Magazine* 13 (Fall 1998): 78–79.

Slodkowski, Andrew, director and producer. *Baltic States.* San Ramon, CA: International Video Network, 1992.

Slonim, Marc, *Russian Theater, From the Empire to the Soviets,* Cleveland: World, 1961.

Smedmark, Carl Reinhold. *Essays on Strindberg.* Stockholm: Strindberg Society, 1966.

Smith, Bruce. *Costly Performances: Tennessee Williams: The Last Stage.* New York: Paragon House, 1990.

Smith, D. "Actors and Theatrical Techniques in Spanish Classical Theatre." *Modern Language Review* 88, 1 (Jan. 1993): 232–234.

Smith, Ed. "Special Reports: The Performing Arts in Jamaica: Theater." *Black World* 23 (July 1974): 47–48, 73–77.

Smith, Geri. "Rio de Janeiro: A Spectacle of Fantasy and Rhythm." *Americas* 38 (November–December 1986): 20–25.

Smith, K. K. "The Use of the High-Heeled Shoe or Buskin in Greek Tragedy." *Harvard Studies in Classical Philology* 16 (1905): 123.

Smith, Myron J. *Air War Southeast Asia, 1961–1973: An Annotated Bibliography and 16mm Film Guide.* Metuchen, NJ: Scarecrow, 1979.

Smith, Paul Christopher. "Tradition and Experimentation: Mexico City Theatre, Summer 1989." *Latin American Theatre Review* 24, 1 (Fall 1990): 137–147.

Smith, William Charles. *The Italian Opera and Contemporary Ballet in London, 1789–1820.* London: Society for Theatre Research, 1955.

Smith, Winifred. *Italian Actors of the Renaissance.* New York: Coward-McCann, 1930.

Smithies, Michael. "The Giant Shadow Play of Thailand." *Orientations* 4, 8 (August 1973): 47–50.

———. "Likay: A Note on the Origin, Form and Future of Siamese Folk Opera." *Journal of the Siam Society* 60 (1971): 159–181.

———. "Thai Shadow Play Figures." *Arts of Asia* 3, 5 (September–October 1973): 38–42.

Smithies, Michael, and Eauyporn Kerdchouay. "Nang Talung: The Shadow Theatre of Southern Thailand." *Journal of the Siam Society* 60, 1 (1972): 379–390.

Snow, Lois Wheeler. *China on Stage: An American Actress in the People's Republic.* New York: Random House, 1972.

Soedarsono. *Wayang Wong: The State Ritual Dance Drama in the Court of Yogyakarta.* Yogyakarta, Java: Gajah Mada University Press, 1984.

Sofola, J. A. *African Culture and the African Personality: What Makes an African Person African.* Ibadan, Nigeria: African Resources, 1973.

Solomos, A. *The Living Aristophanes.* Ann Arbor: University of Michigan Press, 1974.

Song Ban. *The Vietnamese Theatre.* Hanoi: Languages Publishing House, 1960.

Sonuga, Gbenga. "Nigerian Cultural Centres: Government Sponsorship of the Arts." *New Culture* 1, 10 (1979): 39–52.

———. "The Performing Arts in Contemporary Nigeria." *New Culture* 1, 1 (November 1978): 37–42.

South Africa Department of Information. *South African Tradition: A Brief Survey of the Arts and Cultures of the Diverse People of South Africa.* Pretoria: Department of Information, 1974.

Sowlie, Wallace. *Age of Surrealism.* Bloomington: University of Indiana Press, 1960.

Spaight, George. *The History of the English Puppet Theatre.* London: George Harrap & Co., 1990.

Speake, Graham. *Cultural Atlas of Russia and the Former Soviet Union.* London: Andomeda Oxford, 1998.

Speirs, Ronald. *Bertolt Brecht.* New York: St. Martin's, 1987.

Sperdakos, Paula. "Acting in Canada in 1965: Frances Hyland, Kate Reid, Martha Henry and John Hirsh's *The Cherry Orchard* at Stratford." *Theatre Research in Canada* 19, 1 (Spring 1998): 35–62.

Spoto, Donald. *Blue Angel: The Life of Marlene Dietrich.* New York: Doubleday, 1992.

Sprigge, Elizabeth. *The Strange Life of August Strindberg.* London: H. Hamilton, 1949.

Sprinchorn, Evert. *The Genius of the Scandinavian Theater.* New York: New American Library, 1964.

Stalberg, Roberta Helmer. *China's Puppets.* San Francisco: China Books, 1984.

Stanislavsky, Konstantin. *An Actor Prepares.* London: G. Bles, 1967.

———. *Building a Character.* Trans. Elizabeth Reynolds Hapgood. New York: Theatre Arts Books, R. M. MacGregor, 1967.

———. *Stanislavsky on the Art of the Stage* New York: Hill and Wang, 1961.

Staples, Shirley. *Male-Female Comedy Teams in American Vaudeville, 1865–1932.* Ann Arbor, MI: UMI Research Press, 1984.

Staub, Nancy. "Reviews: 'Golem.'" *The Puppetry Journal* 50, 3 (Spring 1999): 20–21.

Steene, Brigitta. *August Strindberg: An Introduction to His Major Works.* Atlantic Highlands, NJ: Humanities, 1982.

Stefanova-Peteva, Kalina. "Bulgaria." In *The World Encyclopedia of Contemporary Theatre,* ed. Don Rubin,

155–168. New York: Routledge, 1994.

Stefanovski, Risto. "Macedonia." In *The World Encyclopedia of Contemporary Theatre*, ed. Don Rubin, 571–572. New York: Routledge, 1994.

———. *The Theatre in Macedonia*. Skopje: Misla, 1990.

Stein, Charles, ed. *American Vaudeville as Seen by Its Contemporaries*. New York: Knopf, 1984.

Stein, Louise. *Songs of Mortals, Dialogues of the Gods: Music and Theatre in Seventeenth-Century Spain*. Oxford: Clarendon Press, 1993.

Steinem, Gloria. *Marilyn*. New York: New American Library, 1987.

Stenberg, Douglas. *From Stanislavsky to Gorbachev: The Theater-studios of Leningrad*. New York: P. Lang, 1995.

Sterling, Adeline. "Drama and Music in Siam." *Inter-Ocean* 13 (1932): 139–144.

———. "The Shadow Play in Siam." *Inter-Ocean* 13 (1932): 57–60.

Sterne, Richard. *John Gielgud Directs Richard Burton in Hamlet: A Journal of Rehearsals*. New York: Random House, 1963.

Sternfeld, Fredrick William. *The Birth of Opera*. New York: Oxford University Press, 1993.

Stevenson, Randall, and Gavin Wallace. *Scottish Theatre since the Seventies*. Edinburgh: Edinburgh University Press, 1996.

Stewart, John. *Italian Film: A Who's Who*. London: McFarland, 1994.

Stewart, John A. "The Burmese Stage." *Journal of the Royal Society of Arts* 87, 4516 (June 1939): 761–775.

Stoll, Anita, and Dawn Smith. *The Perception of Women in Spanish Theater of the Golden Age*. Cranbury, NJ: Associated University Presses, 1991.

Stopes, C. C. *Burbage and Shakespeare's Stage*. London: A. Morning, 1913.

Straubhaar, Joseph. "Television." In *Handbook of Latin American Popular Culture*, ed. Harold E. Hinds and Charles M. Tatum, 109–129. Westport, CT: Greenwood, 1985.

Straumanis, Alfreds. *Confrontation with Tyranny: Six Baltic Plays with Introductory Essays*. Prospect Heights, IL: Waveland, 1977.

———. *Fire and Night, Five Baltic Plays*. Prospect Heights, IL: Waveland, 1986.

Strauss, Leo. *Socrates and Aristophanes*. New York: Basic, 1966.

Stuart, Andrea. "Making Whoopi: Andrea Stuart Explores the Extraordinary, and Unlikely, Success of Whoopi Goldberg." *Sight and Sound* 3 (1993): 12–13.

Styan, J. L. *Chekhov in Performance: A Commentary on the Major Plays*. New York: Cambridge University Press, 1971.

———. *Max Reinhardt*. New York: Cambridge University Press, 1982.

Su-shang, Lu. *Taiwan dienyin xiju shi* (A history of cinema and drama in Taiwan). Taipei: Yin hua chu ban bu, 1961.

Suzuki, Tadishi. *The Way of Acting: The Theatre Writings of Tadashi Suzuki*. Trans. Thomas Rimer. Originally published as *Ekkyo Suru Chikara*. New York: Theatre Communications Group, 1986.

Swart, Sharon. "Benelux: Flanders Fest Marks 25th Anniverary." *Variety* 372, 8 (5 October 1998): 55.

Sweeney, P. L. Amin. *Malay Shadow Puppets: The Wayang Siam of Kelantan*. London: British Museum Publications, 1980.

———. *The Ramayana and the Malay Shadow-Play*. Kuala Lumpur: National University of Malaysia Press, 1972.

Sweet, Jill. "The Beauty, Humor, and Power of Tewa Pueblo Dance." In *Native American Dance: Ceremonies and Social Traditions*, ed. Charlotte Heth, 83–103. Washington, DC: Starwood, 1992.

Szekely, Csilla. "American Dramas on the Hungarian Stage, 1918–1965." *Hungarian Studies in English* 3 (1967).

Szekely, Gyorgy. "A Theatrical Guide to Hungary." *Theatre Research, Recherches Théâtrales* 9, 1 (1967): 5–14.

Tabucchi, Antonio. *Il Teatro Portoghese Del Dopoguerra (Portuguese Theatre since World War II)*. Rome: Abete, 1976.

Tanzania. Ministry of Arts and Culture. Dar es Salaam: Sub-Committee on Publications, Committee for the Preparations for Black and African Festival of Arts and Culture. Dar es Salaam: Ministry of National Culture and Youth, 1977.

Taplin, Oliver. *Greek Tragedy in Action*. Berkeley: University of California Press, 1978.

———. *The Stagecraft of Aeschylus*. Oxford: Clarendon Press, 1977.

Tatlow, Anthony. *The Mask of Evil: Brecht's Response to the Poetry, Theatre and Thought of China and Japan: A Comparative and Critical Evaluation*. European University Papers. Las Vegas, NV: P. Lang, 1977.

Taub, Michael, ed. *Modern Israeli Drama in Translation*. Portsmouth, NH: Heinemann, 1993.

Tausie, Vilsoni. *Art in the New Pacific*. Suva: Institute of Pacific Studies in collaboration with the South Pacific Commission, 1980.

Taylor, Anna-Maria. *Staging Wales: Welsh Theatre 1979–1997*. Cardiff: University of Wales Press, 1997.

Taylor, David. *Acting and the Stage*. Boston: George Allen & Unwin, 1978.

Taylor, Diana. *Negotiating Performance: Gender, Sexuality, and Theatricality in Latin America*. Durham, NC: Duke University Press, 1994.

———. *Theatre of Crisis: Drama and Politics in Latin America*. Lexington: University Press of Kentucky, 1991.

Taylor, Elizabeth. *Elizabeth Taylor; An Informal Memoir*. New York: Harper & Row, 1965.

Taylor, John Russell. *Anger and After: The Angry Theatre: New British Drama*. New York: Hill and Wang, 1969.

Taylor, Julie. "The Politics of Aesthetic Debate: The Case of Brazilian Carnival." *Ethnology* 21 (1982): 301–311.

Taylor, Richard, ed., trans. *The Film Factory: Russian and Soviet Cinema in Documents.* Cambridge, MA: Harvard University Press, 1988.

———. *Film Propaganda: Soviet Russia and Nazi Germany.* New York: I. B. Tauris, 1998.

Taylor, Thomas. *American Theatre History: An Annotated Bibliography.* Pasadena, CA: Salem, 1992.

Terry, Ellen. *The Story of My Life.* New York: Schocken Books, 1982.

Tha Myat. "The Burmese Marionette Show." *Sawaddi* (July–August 1974): 26–28.

Thiher, Allen. *The Cinematic Muse: Critical Studies in the History of French Cinema.* Columbia: University of Missouri Press, 1979.

Thomas, Charles Philip. "Chilean Theater in Exile: The Teatro del Angel in Costa Rica 1974–1984." *Latin American Theatre Review* 19, 2 (Spring 1986): 97–101.

Thomas, Ernst. *Contemporary Music Theater* (Zeitgenossisches Musiktheater). Hamburg: Deutscher Musikrat, 1966.

Thompson, John. *Monty Python: Complete and Utter Theory of the Grotesque.* London: BFI Publishing, 1982.

Thomson, George Derwent. *Aeschylus and Athens: A Study in the Social Origins of Drama.* London: Lawrence and Wishart, 1946.

Thomson, Peter. *Shakespeare's Professional Career.* New York: Cambridge University Press, 1992.

Tiersma, Peter. *Language-Based Humor in the Marx Brothers Films.* Bloomington: Indiana University Linguistics Club, 1985.

Tilakasiri, J. *The Puppet Theatre of Asia.* Ceylon: Department of Cultural Affairs, 1968.

———. *Puppetry in Ceylon.* Colombo: Department of Cultural Affairs, 1961.

Tillis, Steve. *Towards an Aesthetics of the Puppet: Puppetry as a Theatrical Art.* New York: Greenwood, 1992.

Tomlinson, Richard Allan. *Epidauros.* Austin: University of Texas Press, 1983.

Torch, Chris. "A Letter from Scandinavia about Theatre, Community, and the Future." *Drama Review* 27, 4 (Winter 1983): 87–91.

Tornqvist, Egil. *Between Stage and Screen: Ingmar Bergman Directs.* Amsterdam: Amsterdam University Press, 1995.

Torppedersen, B. "Theater in Denmark." *Revue du Cinema* 353 (1980).

Traditional Festivals. Enugu, Nigeria: Cultural Branch, Information Unit, 1979.

Tran Van Khe. *Traditional Theatre in Vietnam.* ed. James R. Brandon. Paris: UNESCO, 1971.

Traore, Bakary. *The Black African Theatre and Its Social Functions.* Trans. Dapo Adelugba. Ibadan, Nigeria: Ibadan University Press, 1972.

Trelles Plazola, Luis. *South American Cinema: Dictionary of Film Makers.* Rio Piedras: Editorial de la Universidad de Puerto Rico, 1989.

Trensky, Paul. *Czech Drama since World War II.* White Plains, NY: Sharpe, 1978.

Turnbaugh, Douglas Blair. *Notating Asian Dance.* New York: Asia Society Performing Arts Programme, 1975.

Turner, Victor. "Carnival, Ritual, and Play in Rio de Janeiro." In *Time Out of Time: Essays on the Festival,* ed. Alessandro Falassi, 74–90. Albuquerque: University of New Mexico Press, 1987.

Tyler, Parker. *Chaplin, Last of the Clowns.* New York: Vanguard Press, 1948.

Tynan, Kenneth. *A View of the English Stage 1944–63.* London: Davis-Poynter, 1975.

Ueding, Gert. *Friedrich Schiller.* Munich: C. H. Beck, 1990.

Ukadike, Nwachukwu Frank. *Black African Cinema.* Berkeley: University of California Press, 1994.

Ulbricht, H. *Wayang Purwa: Shadows of the Past.* Kuala Lumpur, Malaysia: Oxford University Press, 1970.

Unrah, Vicky Wolff. "Cultural Enactments: Recent Books on Latin American Theatre." *Latin American Research Review* 28, 1 (1993): 141–149.

de Usabel, Gaizka S. *The High Noon of American Films in Latin America.* Ann Arbor, MI: Proquest, 1982.

Usigli, Rodolfo. *Mexico in the Theater.* Trans. Wilder P. Scott. University, MS: Romance Monographs, 1976.

Usmiani, Renate. *Second Stage: The Alternative Theatre Movement in Canada.* Vancouver: University of British Columbia Press, 1983.

Valdez, Luis. *Actos.* Fresno, CA: Cucaracha Press, 1971.

———. *Selections.* Houston, TX: Arte Publico, 1971.

Van Abbe, Derek Maurice. *Drama in Renaissance Germany and Switzerland.* Parkville: Melbourne University Press, 1961.

van Boer, Bertil, ed. *Gustav III and the Swedish Stage.* Lewiston, NY: E. Mellen, 1993.

van der Kroef, Jusuts M. "The Roots of Javanese Drama." *Journal of Aesthetics and Art Criticism* 12 (March 1954): 318–327.

van Hoof, Paul. "25th Flanders International Film Festival-Ghent: Elmer Bernstein & Michael Kamen at the Flemish Opera." *Soundtrack* 17, 68 (Winter 1998–1999): 48–50.

Van Leest, Hyung-a-Kim. "Political Satire in Yangja Pyolsandae Mask Drama." *Korea Journal* 31, 1 (Spring 1991): 87.

Van Ness, Edward, and Shita Prawirohardjo. *Javanese Wayang Kulit.* New York: Oxford University Press, 1984.

van Schoor, Jaak. "The Contemporary Flemish Scene." In *An Anthology of Contemporary Belgian Plays, 1970–1982,* ed. David Willinger, 6–10. New York: Whitston, 1984.

————. "Belgium." In *The World Encyclopedia of Contemporary Theatre*, ed. Don Rubin, 109–113. New York: Routledge, 1994.

Van Zile, Judy. *Dance in Africa, Asia and the Pacific: Selected Readings*. Manoa: University of Hawaii at Manoa, 1976.

Varadpande, Manohar Laxman. *Ancient India and Indo-Greek Theatre*. Atlantic Highlands, NJ: Humanities, 1981.

————. *History of Indian Theatre*. New Delhi: Abhinav Grove, 1987.

————. *Krishna Theatre in India*. New Delhi: Abhinav Grove, 1982.

————. *Religion and Theatre*. Atlantic Highlands, NJ: Humanities, 1983.

————. *Traditions of Indian Theatre*. New Delhi: Abhinav Grove, 1979.

Varadpande, Manohar Laxman, and Sunil Subhedar, eds. *The Critique of Indian Theatre*. Atlantic Highlands, NJ: Humanities, 1982.

Varneke, Boris. *History of the Russian Theatre, Seventeenth through Nineteenth Century*. New York: Hafner, 1971.

Vatsyayan, Kapila. *Traditional Indian Theatre: Multiple Streams*. New Delhi: National Book Trust, 1980.

Veidlinger, Jeffrey. "Let's Perform a Miracle: The Soviet Yiddish State Theater in the 1920s." *Slavic Review* 57, 2 (Summer 1998): 372–397.

Versényi, Adam. *Theatre in Latin America: Religion, Politics, and Culture from Cortés to the 1980s*. New York: Cambridge University Press, 1993.

Vesilind, Priit. "The Baltic Nations." *National Geographic* 178, 5 (November 1990): 2–36.

Vial, Veronique. *"Wings": Backstage with Cirque du Soleil!!* Santa Fe, NM: Tondo Books, 1999.

Videbaek, Bente. *The Stage Clown in Shakespeare's Theatre*. Westport, CT: Greenwood, 1996.

Vince, Ronald W. *Ancient and Medieval Theatre: A Historiographical Handbook*. Westport, CT: Greenwood, 1984.

Virulrak, Surapone. "Likay: A Popular Theatre in Thailand." Ph.D. diss., University of Hawaii, 1980.

Vittorini, Domenico. *The Drama of Luigi Pirandello*. 2d ed. New York: Russell & Russell, 1969.

Wace, Alan John Bayard. *A Companion to Homer*. New York: St. Martin's, 1962.

Wachter, Hans-Christof. *Theater Im Exil: Sozialgeschichte des Deutschen Exiltheaters 1933–1945*. Munich: Hanser, 1973.

Wade, Leslie. *Sam Shepard and the American Theatre*. Westport, CT: Greenwood, 1997.

Wadely, Donald Ray. *Lope de Vega and the Elizabethans*. Diss. 1977. Ann Arbor, MI: University Microfilms, 1977, 29645107.

Wagenknecht, Edward. *Lillian Gish: An Interpretation*. Seattle: University of Washington, 1927.

Wagner, Anton. *Contemporary Canadian Theatre: New World Visions*. Toronto: Simon & Pierre, 1986.

Wagner, Richard. *The Diary of Richard Wagner 1865–1882: The Brown Book*. Trans. George Bird. New York: Cambridge University Press, 1980.

Walcot, P. *Greek Drama in Its Theatrical and Social Context*. Cardiff: University of Wales Press, 1976.

Waley, Arthur. *The No Plays of Japan*. London: Allen & Unwin, 1921. Reprint, London: Unwin Hyman, 1988.

Walton, Michael. *The Greek Sense of Theatre: Tragedy Reviewed*. New York: Methuen, 1984.

————. *Greek Theatre Practice*. Westport, CT: Greenwood, 1980.

————. *Living Greek Theatre: A Handbook of Classical Performance and Modern Production*. New York: Greenwood, 1987.

Wan-wa, Li. "Man-Tan Xianggang Huaju Fazhan" (Random Talks on the Development of Spoken Drama in Hong Kong). *Hong Kong Literature Monthly* 3 (March 1985).

Warner, Elizabeth. *The Russian Folk Theatre*. The Hague: Mouton, 1977.

Warren, Lee. *The Theater of Africa: An Introduction*. Englewood Cliffs, NJ: Prentice-Hall, 1975.

Waxman, Samuel Montefiore. *Antoine and the Theatre-libre*. Cambridge, MA: Harvard University Press, 1926.

Weaver, William. *Duse: A Biography*. San Diego, CA: Harcourt Brace Jovanovich, 1984.

————. *The Golden Century of Italian Opera from Rossini to Puccini*. London: Thames and Hudson, 1980.

Webster, Thomas Bertram Lonsdale. "The Costume of the Actors in Aristophanic Comedy." *Classical Quarterly* 5 (1955): 94.

————. *The Greek Chorus*. London: Methuen, 1970.

————. *Greek Theatre Production*. London: Methuen, 1970.

————. *An Introduction to Menander*. Manchester: Manchester University Press; New York: Barnes & Noble, 1974.

Weideli, Walter. *The Art of Bertolt Brecht*. New York: New York University Press, 1963.

Weightman, J. G. "New Wave in French Culture." *Commentary* (September 1960): 230–240.

Weiss, Judith A. *Latin American Popular Theatre: The First Five Centuries*. Albuquerque: University of New Mexico Press, 1993.

Weiss, Peter. *Discourse on Vietnam*. London: Calder and Boyars, 1970.

Welch, David. *Propaganda and the German Cinema 1933–1945*. Oxford: Clarendon, 1983.

Wells, Henry Willis. *The Classical Drama of India: Studies in Its Values for the Literature and Theatre of the World*. New York: Asia Publishing House, 1963.

Welsh, James. "Two from Yugoslavia: The Theme of War." *Literature/Film Quarterly* 3 (Summer 1975): 286.

Wembah-Rashid, J. A. R. "Isinyago and Midimu: Masked Dancers of Tanzania and Mozambique." *African Arts* 4, 2 (1971): 38–44.

Wernblad, Annette. *Brooklyn Is Not Expanding:Woody Allen's Comic Universe*. Rutherford, NJ: Fairleigh Dickinson University Press, 1992.

Whitfield, Eileen. *Pickford:The Woman Who Made Hollywood*. Lexington: University Press of Kentucky, 1997.

Widmer, Ellen, and David Der-wei Wang, eds. *From May Fourth to June Fourth: Fiction and Film in Twentieth-Century China*. Cambridge, MA: Harvard University Press, 1993.

Wieners, Brad. *Burning Man*. San Francisco: Hardwired, 1997.

Wild, S. "A Juggler's Programme in Medieval Islam." In *La Signification du Bas Moyen Age dans l'Histoire et la Culture du Monde Arabe*, ed. R. Matran. Aix-en-Provence: Actes du 8me Congres de l'Union Europeenne des Arabisants et Islamisants, 1976.

Wild, Stephen. "Men as Women: Female Dance Symbolism in Walbiri Men's Rituals." *Dance Research Journal* 10, 1 (1977–1978): 14–22.

Willett, John. *The Theatre of Erwin Piscator: Half a Century of Politics in the Theatre*. London: Eyre Methuen, 1978.

Williams, A. R. "Eighty Years of Elegance and Excellence." *Americas* 39, 5 (September–October 1987): 14–19.

Williams, Drid. "The Dance of the Bedu Moon." *African Arts* 2, 1 (1968): 18–21.

Williams, Hugh Noel. *Queens of the French Stage*. New York: Charles Scribner's Sons, 1905.

Williams, Simon. *German Actors of the Eighteenth and Nineteenth Centuries: Idealism, Romanticism, and Realism*. Westport, CT: Greenwood, 1985.

Williams, Tennessee. *Conversations with Tennessee Williams*. ed. Albert Devlin. Jackson: University Press of Mississippi, 1986.

Wilmer, Steve. "Women's Theatre in Ireland." *New Theatre Quarterly* 7, 28 (November 1991): 353–360.

Windeler, Robert. *The Films of Shirley Temple*. Secaucus, NJ: Citadel, 1978.

Winkler, Elizabeth. *The Clown in Modern Anglo-Irish Drama*. Frankfurt: P. Lang, 1977.

Winstedt, Richard O. *The Malays: A Cultural History*. Singapore: Graham Brash, 1981.

Winter, William. *The Life of David Belasco*. New York: Moffat, Yard, 1918.

Wolford, Lisa. *Grotowski's Objective Drama Research*. Jackson: University Press of Mississippi, 1996.

Wollenberg, Hans. *Fifty Years of German Film*. New York: Arno, 1972.

Woods, Leigh. "Theater in Iceland: The Quest for National Identity." *Scandinavian Review* 73, 3 (Autumn 1985): 55–63.

Woods, Leigh, and Agusta Gunnarsdottir. *Public Selves, Political Stages: Interviews with Icelandic Women in Government and Theatre*. Amsterdam: Harwood Academic, 1997.

Woodward, Ian. *Glenda Jackson: A Study in Fire and Ice*. New York: St. Martin's, 1985.

Woodyard, George W., and Vicky Wolff Unruh. "Latin American Theatre Today: A 1992 Conference in Kansas." *Latin American Theatre Review* 26, 2 (Spring 1993): 6–8.

Worden, Robert, and Andrea Matles Savada. *Mongolia: A Country Study*. Washington, DC: Federal Research Division, 1991.

Worrall, Nick. *The Moscow Art Theatre*. New York: Routledge, 1996.

Worth, Katharine. *The Irish Drama of Europe from Yeats to Beckett*. Atlantic Highlands, NJ: Humanities, 1978.

Wrathall, John. "Reviews: 'Black Cat White Cat.'" *Sight and Sound* 9, 5 (May 1999): 41–42.

———. "Reviews: 'Savior.'" *Sight and Sound* 8 (July 1998): 51–52.

Wright, Barbara Ann Stein. "Wayang Siam: An Ethnographic Study of the Malay Shadow Play of Kelantan." Ph.D. diss. Ann Arbor, MI: Proquest, 1980.

Xavier, Sister Francis. "Dancing and Singing in the Gilbert Islands." *Mana* 1 (December 1976).

Yajnik, Ramanial Kanaiyaial. *The Indian Theatre*. London: Allen and Unwin, 1933.

Yang, Daniel Shih-P'eng. *An Annotated Bibliography of Materials for the Study of the Peking Opera*. 2d ed. Wisconsin China Series. Madison: University of Wisconsin, 1967.

———. "The Traditional Theatre of China in Its Contemporary Setting: An Examination of the Patterns of Change within the Peking Theatre since 1949." Ph.D. diss., University of Wisconsin, 1968.

Yarovskaya, Marianna. "Reviews: 'Underground.'" *Film Quarterly* 51, 2 (Winter 1997–1998): 50–54.

Yates, W. E., and John McKenzie, eds. *Viennese Popular Theatre: A Symposium*. Exeter: University of Exeter, 1985.

Ye Dway. "Dramatic Conventions of the Burmese Puppet Theatre." *Guardian* 22, 2 (February 1975): 10–11, 17.

Young, Deborah. "Film: Reviews: *Rehearsal For War*." *Variety* 371 (18 May 1998—24 May 1998): 75.

———. "Film Reviews: *The Wall*." *Variety* 371, 12 (3 August 1998—9 August 1998): 40.

Young, E. P. "Theatre in the Democratic Republic of Viet Nam." *New Orient* 1, 6 (1960): 1–4.

Young, Jordan. *The Beckett Actor: Jack MacGowran, Beginning to End*. Beverly Hills, CA: Moonstone Press, 1987.

Yousof, Ghulam-Sarwar. *The Kelantan "Mak Yong" Dance Theatre: A Study of Performance Structure*. Ann Arbor, MI: Proquest, 1976.

———. "Feasting of the Spirits: The Berjamu Ritual Performance in the Kelantanese *Wayang Siam* Shadow Play." *Journal of Malaysian Studies* 1 (June 1983): 95–115.

———. *Southeast Asian Traditional Performing Arts: A Preliminary Bibliography*. Penang, Malaysia: Southeast Asian Studies Program, 1990.

————. "Traditional Theatre in South East Asia." *Performing Arts* 2 (July 1985): 37–49.

Yung, Bell. *Cantonese Opera: Performance as a Creative Process.* Cambridge and New York: Cambridge University Press, 1989.

Yupho, Dhanit. *Classical Siamese Theatre.* Trans. P. S. Sastri. Bangkok: Hatha Dhip, 1952.

————. *The Khon and Lakon.* Bangkok: Department of Fine Arts, 1963.

————. *Khon Masks.* Thai Culture, New Series. Bangkok: Fine Arts Department, 1968.

————. *The Preliminary Course of Training in Thai Theatrical Art.* Thai Cultural Series, 15. Bangkok: National Culture Institute, 1954.

Zagagi, Netta. *The Comedy of Menander: Conventions, Variations, and Originality.* Bloomington: Indiana University Press, 1995.

Zarrilli, Phillip. *The Kathakali Complex: Actor, Performance & Structure.* New Delhi: Abhinav Grove, 1984.

Zatlin, Phillis. *Cross-Cultural Approaches to Theatre: The Spanish-French Connection.* Metuchen, NJ: Scarecrow, 1994.

————. "Metatheatre and the Twentieth-Century Spanish Stage." *Anales de la Literatura Espanola Contemporanea* 17, 1–3 (1992): 55–74.

de Zoete, Beryl. *Dance and Magic Drama in Ceylon.* London: Faber & Faber, 1957.

de Zoete, Beryl, and Walter Spies. *Dance and Drama in Bali.* London: Faber & Faber, 1938.

Zola, Emile. *Le Naturalisme au Théatre.* Paris: E. Fasquelle, 1912.

Zucker, Carole. *In the Company of Actors: Reflections on the Craft of Acting.* New York: Theatre Arts/Routledge, 1999.

Zugasti, M. "Actors and Techniques of the Spanish Classical Theatre." *Bulletin of Hispanic Studies* 70, 2 (April 1993): 271–272.

Zuntz, G. *The Political Plays of Euripides.* Manchester: Manchester University Press, 1955.

Index

About the Author

Beth Osnes, who holds a Ph.D. in theater from the University of Colorado at Boulder, was a 1991 Fulbright scholar in Malaysia, where she conducted field research on the traditional shadow puppet theater. She has continued to lecture at universities here and abroad on the Asian performing arts and has published numerous articles on the subject. Currently, she is creating an educational video on the performing arts of Cambodia and Myanmar from her recent travels there. In addition to performing in many of her own original one-woman shows, Beth Osnes teaches theater at the University of Colorado in Boulder.